WOMEN'S health & WELLNESS 2003

Real Life Solutions from the Editors of *Health* magazine

Oxmoor House.

©2002 by Oxmoor House, Inc.
Book Division of Southern Progress Corporation
P.O. Box 2463, Birmingham, Alabama 35201

Published by Oxmoor House, Inc.

Hardcover ISBN: 0-8487-2573-5
Softcover ISBN: 0-8487-2581-6
ISSN: 1537-4394
Printed in the United States of America
First Printing 2002

The articles in this book were printed in *Health* magazine and prepared in accordance with the highest standards of journalistic accuracy. Unless otherwise noted, these articles have not been updated since their original publication in 2002. Readers are cautioned not to use information from this book as a substitute for professional health care and advice.

....

To order additional publications,
call 800-633-4910

For more books to enrich your life,
visit **oxmoorhouse.com**

Cover: Photography by Richard Hume

Health

Editor and Vice President: Doug Crichton
Executive Editor: Lisa Delaney
Design Director: Paul Carstensen
Managing Editor: Candace H. Schlosser
Articles Editor: Elena Rover
Senior Editors: Nichole Hoskins (Fitness), Warner McGowin, Susie Quick (Food and Nutrition)
Beauty and Fashion Editor: Colleen Sullivan
Associate Editors: Abigail M. Walch, Laurie Herr
Editorial Coordinator: Christine O'Connell
Assistant Editors: Su Reid, Leah Wyar (Beauty)
Art Director: Amy Heise
Concept Director: Lori Bianchi Nichols
Graphic Designers: Christen Colvert, Soo Yeon Hong
Photo Coordinator: Angie Wilson Kelly
Assistant Photo Coordinator: Jeanne Dozier Clayton
Copy Chief: John R. Halphen
Production Manager: Faustina S. Williams
Research Editors: Martha Yielding Scribner, Eric Steinmehl
Production Editor: Julie Fricke Collins
Assistant Copy Editor: Julie H. Bosché
Office Manager: Stephanie Wolford
Editorial Assistants: Emily S. Delzell, Amanda Storey, Sara Jane Weeks
Health.com Editor: Jerry Gulley II
Health.com Managing Editor: Vanessa Rush

OXMOOR HOUSE, INC.

Editor-in-Chief: Nancy Fitzpatrick Wyatt
Senior Health Editor: Sandy McDowell
Art Director: Cynthia R. Cooper
Copy Chief: Catherine R. Scholl

Editors: Suzanne Powell, Patricia Wilens
Copy Editor: L. Amanda Owens
Editorial Assistant: McCharen Pratt
Designer: Melissa Jones Clark
Publishing Systems Administrator: Rick Tucker
Director, Production and Distribution: Phillip Lee
Books Production Manager: Theresa L. Beste
Associate Production Manager: Larry Hunter
Production Assistant: Faye Porter Bonner

Contributors
Copy Editor: Chris Mohney
Designer: Amy Bickell
Indexer: Denise Getz
Editorial Consultant: Bill Gottlieb
Editorial Intern: Sarah Jackson

CONTENTS AT A GLANCE

CONTENTS

VII. Mind and Spirit: Relax, Revitalize, Renew

VIII. Relationships and Sex: Secrets of Happiness

EDITORS' PICKS

Here's a look at some of our favorite stories appearing in this year's edition of *Women's Health and Wellness.*

Herbs: The New Cure for Menopause?

Can herbs fill the void left by HRT?

Natural remedies successfully ease menopause symptoms for many women. But are they safe?. . . page 93

Five Women, One Weight—See How the Same Weight—140 Pounds—Looks on These Women

Can your health be summed up in a number?

Your scale can't tell you if you eat enough veggies or do enough cardio. Five women weigh in on why the numbers aren't so important when it comes to being healthy and feeling good.. . . page 104

page
104

page 242

The Last Ab Workout You'll Ever Need

Crunching till the cows come home won't get you the flat abs you want.

Rotate our three routines to keep your muscles guessing and your tummy slim and trim.. . . page 242

Diet Foods You'll Love

Stop starving yourself. You may be derailing your weight loss efforts.

Seven delicious foods go from off-limits to must-have when it comes to staving off binges and keeping your appetite satisfied longer. And your taste buds will thank you.. . . page 180

page 258

Can You Be Fat and Fit?

Being healthy does not always equal being thin.

Find out why changing your weight may be just as difficult as changing your height—and why, when it comes to fitness, being overweight doesn't necessarily mean poor health.. . . page 258

EDITOR'S NOTE

Sure, you want to be healthy— to look great and feel your best. Who doesn't? But time and reality have a nasty habit of wrecking dream worlds, often making it too tough to make the right choices for living a healthier life. That's why we created *Women's Health and Wellness 2003*. The second in a series, it's packed with smart advice and informative updates on everything from medicine and fitness to stress-relief, relationships, sex, and more. In other words, this book makes healthy living easy.

For more than 15 years, *Health* magazine has been the premier provider of power for living well. We've written literally billions of words on the subject, in fact. This book, though, distills a year's worth of that wisdom into one special volume, making it simple to find whatever it is you need.

Whether it's improving your diet, bringing peace to your schedule, or learning more about your body's needs, this book delivers all you need to achieve your health goals.

You'll find practical solutions to real-life issues in our eight comprehensive chapters: Breakthroughs in Women's Health, The Female Body, Everyday Wellness, Food and Nutrition, Fitness, Healthy Looks, Mind and Spirit, Relationships and Sex. For example, discover how to boost your mood in "9 Easy Ways to Shake the Blahs" (page 312). And see how a fitness excursion with your partner can show you his true colors in "Sweat Together, Stay Together?" (page 358).

Good health is more than just eating well and looking good. Truly healthy women radiate that news from the inside out, which is why this book covers all aspects of a healthy lifestyle, from a workout for your hips (page 239) to an achievable guide to happiness (page 306), or finding and maintaining female friendships (page 374).

I hope you enjoy this year's edition of *Women's Health and Wellness*, and that it becomes a trusted resource for living life on your own terms—both healthfully and well.

Warm regards,

Doug Crichton
Editor-in-Chief, *Health*

chapter 1

breakthroughs
in women's
health

the year's top discoveries in
medical and alternative care

the year's most exciting
BREAKTHROUGHS
in MEDICINE
and what they can mean for you

Exciting new drugs and treatments are helping women live longer, healthier lives—today and tomorrow.

BY JOHN F. WASIK

Medicine in 2001 was full of contrasts—from headline-grabbing high-tech devices that seemed straight from the pages of science fiction to less-heralded breakthroughs in life-saving drug therapies. With the help of medical experts across many specialties, *Health* reviewed the research and developed our annual roundup of the top advances for the year. There were many worthy discoveries to consider, but we honed the list down to the breakthroughs that signaled a new direction or a significant step forward in the standard treatment of major diseases. Some of the achievements are ready to benefit patients today, while others will take years to prove their promise—but all mark major progress toward better health for women and their families.

HIGH-TECH TICKER
a potential cure for thousands who die waiting for new hearts

The first achievement on our list made big news and captured our imaginations. The new mechanical AbioCor heart was successfully implanted into five patients by late 2001. The device could help more than 100,000 heart patients per year, about half of them women, estimates Tim Gardner, M.D., chief of cardiac surgery at the University of Pennsylvania Medical Center and one of the country's top transplant surgeons.

Heart disease is the leading killer of both women and men in the United States, with about 700,000 fatalities per year. Approximately 4,000 people who need new hearts are currently on the National Transplant Waiting List. Each year, about 2,000 receive hearts, according to the United Network for Organ Sharing, which maintains the list. Since 1988, 9,126 patients have died waiting for a transplant.

The AbioCor heart could save people in similar straits. The self-sufficient heart is a quantum leap from its noisy predecessor, the Jarvik 7, which required that compressed air be forcefully pumped through a huge hose directly into a recipient's chest. This meant patients could not leave their beds and were at high risk for infections. Blood clots caused strokes in some; the man who lived the longest (620 days) suffered four strokes, the first just 18 days after surgery.

This new heart pumps without the aid of external tubes and regulates blood flow automatically, allowing the recipient to move around freely. Also, patients don't need to take toxic antirejection medications since the mechanical heart is made of metal and plastic, materials the body likely won't reject. At press time, doctors were monitoring the progress of the five heart recipients and planned to seek U.S. Food and Drug Administration (FDA) approval for a larger trial.

Patients waiting for transplants often die before suitable donor hearts become available. The new artificial heart could keep them ticking.

BETTER BIRTH CONTROL
if you've ever forgotten to take your pill, try one of these methods instead

The birth control pill marked its 50th anniversary in 2001, a major year for new nonoral contraceptive options. Mirena, the next generation of intrauterine devices (IUDs) and the most effective reversible contraceptive, became available. And NuvaRing, a vaginal ring that releases hormones, gained FDA approval. These new contraceptive methods should help reduce the more than 3 million unintended pregnancies in the United States each year; more than half occur with women using birth control.

Since the pill's introduction in 1951, there have been very few advances in reversible contraception—and none of them has challenged the pill's popularity. But while it boasts a 99.9 percent effectiveness rate when taken as directed, the reality is that women sometimes forget a dose or neglect to take it at the same time each day. As a result, the true effectiveness rate is actually 94 percent.

With Mirena, there's virtually no chance to slip up. It offers double protection: Like the old IUDs, its presence in the uterus physically disrupts the environment so fertilized embryos cannot attach. It also releases very small amounts of levonorgestrel, a hormone similar to the body's natural progestin, which causes cervical mucus to become so thick that sperm are unable to reach the egg. Priced at about $500, Mirena must be inserted by a specially trained doctor, but it works for up to five years. Women continue to have monthly ovulation cycles with Mirena, but many experience a dramatic decrease in menstrual bleeding. Fertility returns rapidly once the IUD is removed, with 80 percent of women conceiving within one year.

The NuvaRing is a completely new concept in contraception. This flexible vaginal ring is about 2 inches in diameter and provides low time-released doses of progestin and estrogen, the same hormones that are in the pill. A woman can insert the ring herself—no need for a doctor's visit—and keep it in place for three weeks. It's removed for a week each month to allow for menstruation (most women start their periods two to three days after removing the ring). The ring is 98 to 99 percent effective when used properly. While the NuvaRing has similar side effects to the pill, it requires no daily upkeep—so there's less room for error. It costs from $30 to $40 a month.

STEM CELLS TURN TO BLOOD
the first step in actual stem-cell use could lead to more breakthroughs

You couldn't turn on the news in early 2001 without hearing something about stem cells, the "seeds" for more than 200 different cell types. It's hoped that stem cells can be programmed to repair any kind of human tissue and lead to cures for ailments from heart disease to diabetes to Parkinson's. But first, scientists must discover how to prompt stem cells to transform themselves into specific types of tissue. In fall 2001, researchers at the University of Wisconsin-Madison announced the first success in getting embryonic cells to pick an identity: they had coaxed stem cells into becoming blood cells.

In addition to progressing stem-cell research in general, this breakthrough could lead to the elimination of future blood shortages. It also heralds a potential boon to the thousands of patients who need blood transfusions and bone marrow to treat cancers and leukemias. Today, about 75 percent of such patients can't get transplants because a perfect match cannot be found, says Dan Kaufman, M.D., Ph.D., a hematology fellow at the University of Wisconsin-Madison Medical School and lead author of their study. But he warns that it could take years before such applications will become available.

Progress was also made on the policy front. Despite the controversy surrounding the use of stem cells taken from

Stem-cell research could lead to the end of blood shortages and save the lives of patients who need blood transplants and bone marrow to treat cancers and leukemias.

fetuses, which must be destroyed to harvest the cells, President George W. Bush publicly gave his support for continuing research with existing supplies of embryonic stem cells. Researchers say this supply is not sufficient, but the president's move allowed the National Institutes of Health to commit government funds to numerous stem-cell research projects.

CURING CANCER
this drug cured study patients
without devastating side effects

Cancer treatment is irreverently called "slash, burn, and poison" because of trauma caused by surgery, radiation, and chemotherapy. A recently approved drug, Gleevec, represents a new approach to treatment that doesn't destroy the patient's quality of life along with the disease.

Gleevec got "fast-tracked" by the FDA for the treatment of chronic myeloid leukemia (CML), one of the four major types of the blood cancer leukemia. CML affects some 30,000 people; between 20 and 30 percent of patients die within two years of diagnosis.

The traditional way of treating leukemia is to use chemotherapy to destroy cancer cells, with one unfortunate side effect: it severely suppresses the body's immune system. This, in turn, can cause nausea, debilitating lethargy, and even life-threatening infections. Instead of attacking the entire immune system, Gleevec works by targeting the specific chemicals that are believed to prompt the production of cancer cells.

In clinical trials, Gleevec produced complete remission in 51 of 54 patients. "This is virtually unheard of in cancer treatment," explains Alan Kinniburgh, Ph.D., vice president of research for the Leukemia and Lymphoma Society. Moreover, the drug achieved these results without any of the side effects of traditional cancer drugs.

In October 2001, the manufacturer, Novartis, submitted an approval request to the FDA to use the drug to treat inoperable or metastatic gastrointestinal tumors called gists, a type of soft-tissue sarcoma. Gleevec may also be effective in treating other forms of leukemia, and there is hope that it will work for all soft-tissue sarcomas.

CAMERA IN A PILL
a pain-free way to diagnose digestive
disorders that works better than surgery

The M2A is a minimiracle for anyone who has ever had her small intestine "scoped" by endoscopy, a painful procedure that involves snaking a long tube down the throat and requires deep sedation. Right out of the 1960s movie *Fantastic Voyage*, the M2A is a tiny video camera enclosed in a pill-sized capsule that begins to transmit images after it's swallowed, taking 50,000 color pictures that it transmits to a recorder worn on a belt. Patients can go about their normal activities, and the camera-capsule is painlessly excreted 24 to 72 hours later. (Thankfully, the patient is not required to return it.)

About 10 million Americans are hospitalized each year for gastrointestinal illnesses, everything from gastrointestinal bleeding to Crohn's disease to ulcerative colitis. Problems of the small intestine—bleeding, inflammation, or ulcers—are particularly hard to diagnose. Unlike the somewhat large U-shaped colon, which is fairly easy to evaluate, the small intestine is a coiled mass of tissue some 20 feet long that has not previously been easy to inspect without surgery or endoscopy.

Although not designed to totally replace endoscopy, the M2A will be a vast improvement over that technique alone. In one trial, the camera system detected 86 percent of small-intestine lesions, compared with a 50 percent discovery rate with the endoscope. "For what I do, this is a phenomenal tool, because determining the cause of gastrointestinal bleeding is so frustrating," says Blair Lewis, M.D., a gastroenterologist at Mount Sinai Hospital and

A new drug produced **complete remission** in 51 of 54 trial patients, with none of the side effects caused by traditional treatments.

the study's lead researcher. "Large amounts of the small intestine usually can't be evaluated without cutting people open."

TREATING BROKEN SPINES

two medications will help prevent paralysis after a spinal-cord injury

About 11,000 Americans damage their spinal cords each year, 20 percent of them women. Because the spinal cord is the main pathway for messages from the brain to reach all the nerves in the body, damage to it has severe effects: after an injury, more than half of patients are left with upper- and lower-body paralysis, and less than 1 percent recover before they leave the hospital.

In 2001, two separate research teams developed drugs that promise to improve the odds. The medications may prevent damage to nerve cells after trauma to the spinal cord. Cytrx, a pharmaceutical company based in Atlanta, plans to begin clinical testing soon of CRL-1550, a medication that protects and restores nerve cells if it is administered within six hours of an accident. The early studies show an 80 percent recovery of nerve-cell function when the drug is injected following spinal trauma. A team at the Weizmann Institute of Science in Israel is working on a vaccine that will have similar restorative effects if used within seven days of injury. The researchers planned to begin human testing in 2002.

Both research teams say their drugs will not help those who are currently paralyzed. However, they do hope that the new medications could be administered in ambulances or in emergency rooms to people whose spinal cords have been damaged, so that one day they will be able to walk home.

FEWER FINGER PRICKS

better blood-sugar control helps prevent deaths from heart disease, blindness, and amputations

The 8 million women in this country who suffer from diabetes are more likely than their 8 million male counterparts to develop serious diabetes-related complications, from kidney failure, heart disease, and circulatory

problems to blindness and amputation. Close monitoring of blood-sugar levels can help delay or prevent these types of complications. In 2001, the FDA approved a new, painless way for adult diabetics to keep tabs on their blood-sugar levels.

People with diabetes generally check their glucose levels one to three times a day by pricking a finger to extract a drop of blood to analyze it. The result: sore fingertips and few data points. A device called the GlucoWatch Biographer straps on like a watch and provides readings every 20 minutes for 12 hours, after being calibrated with one measurement taken with a finger prick. In addition to providing 36 readings, the watch sounds an alarm if blood-sugar levels reach dangerously high or low levels, or if they drop too rapidly—day or night.

Researchers hope the medication can be administered in ambulances or in emergency rooms to people with spinal cord injuries, so that **one day they will be able to walk home.**

How it works: The GlucoWatch sends a weak electrical current into the arm that extracts fluid from the skin; the fluid is then evaluated for glucose levels by a thin plastic sensor. In clinical trials, the watch was very effective most of the time; it was ineffective when a person was sweating and was less effective at detecting low blood-sugar levels. The watch should be on the market soon at a cost of about $500.

OPERATIONS OVERHEARD

a tool that will catch medical mistakes before it's too late

The ubiquitous "black box" found on airplanes may soon be coming to a hospital near you. Surgeons in England and Scotland are testing "clinical data recorders" in operating rooms in an attempt to catch and prevent medical errors. In this country, an estimated 44,000 to 98,000 people die each year due to medical mistakes, according to an Institute of Medicine study. Many of those tragic mishaps could be prevented through monitoring of procedures and medications. For those that can't be prevented, a record of the cause might help hospitals develop methods to prevent similar mistakes from happening.

Ara Darzi, M.D., a surgeon at the Imperial College in London, says the device will link audio-video recording of surgeries with real-time information on the patient's vital signs and any medical equipment being used. "We will for the first time have a comprehensive and objective record of the entire procedure," he says.

Although no U.S. hospitals have immediate plans to install the data recorders, Darzi reports that several leading institutions have expressed an interest in academic and development collaborations. ✳

John F. Wasik is an award-winning health and finance writer. His latest book is **The Bear-Proof Investor.**

HPV Doesn't Have to Spell Cancer

A recent study brings good news to the more than 20 million Americans infected with the human papilloma virus (HPV), which is America's most common sexually transmitted disease (STD). Scientists recently discovered that even though HPV causes 93 percent of cervical cancer cases, a cancer sentence isn't inevitable—and the virus itself, which is untreatable, often vanishes on its own.

In a 10-year study at the University of California at San Francisco, researchers tracked approximately 600 sexually active women between ages 13 to 21 and found that more than half of them became infected with HPV. And each new sexual partner caused a woman's risk of infection to increase tenfold. But HPV did not necessarily lead to the benign lesions that can develop into cervical cancer. "People had assumed that if you were infected with HPV, then you developed lesions right away," says lead researcher Anna-Barbara Moscicki, M.D. Yet during the study, 70 percent of the women with HPV did not develop lesions at all. Only about 5 to 10 percent of women who have lesions develop cervical cancer. And women who get the lesions treated before they can progress have a survival rate of almost 100 percent.

Here's another positive finding: 90 percent of the women who became infected cleared the virus within three years. "It's like having the sniffles," Moscicki says. "It's an infection that your body can usually handle; your immune system recognizes the virus and gets rid of it."

All this good news is no reason to adopt a free-loving attitude when it comes to your sexual health. Currently, no treatment exists for HPV, and preventing the virus means abstaining from any kind of skin-to-skin contact. "Unfortunately, condoms don't seem to protect you," Moscicki explains (although they are still very valuable for preventing other STDs).

It's also very easy to become reinfected with HPV. Some women get persistent HPV infections, and those with recurring infections are more likely to develop precancerous cells. Cigarette smoking was another factor that significantly increased the risk of women developing lesions. Discuss your risk factors with your gynecologist to see how often you need Pap smears and tests to detect HPV. And be sure you don't skip exams for fear of a bad result. "An irregular Pap smear does not mean that you're going to get cancer," Moscicki says.

The end of the HRT era?

BY EVA MARER

The recent shutdown of a government-run hormone-replacement therapy (HRT) study may signal a major shift in the way women cope with menopause. While hormones may be safe for short-term relief of hot flashes and other symptoms, researchers have found that prolonged use of the popular combined estrogen/progestin pill Prempro could increase your risks of heart attack, cancer, and stroke. While the findings do not necessarily rule out such HRT options as lower doses, other forms of estrogen such as estradiol and estrone, and different routes of delivery like the estrogen or combination patch, women are steamed over the news (and it's not just a hot flash).

But one boon is that more research is looking into alternative menopause treatments. For the all-in-one approach, Menopause Relief and Promensil are two popular natural remedies that some women swear knock out menopause symptoms. However, rigorous studies like the one on Prempro have not been conducted on alternative remedies, so questions remain on their effectiveness and long-term safety. If you go beyond the basics of diet and exercise, see a health professional—an M.D. or a menopause counselor—to develop the best plan for your overall well-being.

Here's a look at some natural fixes that may be able to calm specific menopausal woes.

Hot Flashes
Natural fix: Savor soy; cut out caffeine, hot drinks, alcohol, and spicy foods. Buzz: A study in the journal *Obstetrics and Gynecology* found that women who consumed about 80 milligrams of isoflavones a day—roughly 2 cups of soy milk or 1 cup of edamame—had fewer hot flashes than non-soy eaters. Avoiding spicy foods, which raise body temperatures, should put out the internal fires, too. Caveat: Your body may not absorb the isoflavones in supplements as well as those in foods—so, try tofu.

Night Sweats
Natural fix: Black cohosh (found in products such as Remifemin). Buzz: This traditional Native American remedy—taken in a 20-milligram tablet twice daily—has long been used in Germany to treat woes from hot flashes to mood swings and irritability. Clinical data shows only

that it mops up excessive sweating, but a major National Institutes of Health study currently underway should provide more conclusive information in the next few years. Caveat: Rare side effects include nausea, vomiting, dizziness, and visual disturbances. The German Federal Institute for Drugs and Medical Devices (which approved the supplement in 1989) recommends using black cohosh for no longer than six months.

Sleepless Nights
Natural fix: Valerian. Buzz: Hailed as "the 19th-century Valium," this herb has been approved in Germany as a mild tranquilizer for restlessness and sleep troubles—and it won't leave you bleary-eyed the next morning (tablets contain the recommended 1-gram dose). Caveat: Talk to your doctor if you suffer from chronic insomnia to determine the underlying cause and the appropriate treatment, and stop taking valerian if you feel restless or headachy.

Irregular Bleeding
Natural fix: Chaste berry, also known as vitex. Buzz: Naturalists believe this herb balances hormone levels and recommend it to ease the heavy bleeding common in perimenopause. Clinical trials have shown that it may have a progesterone-like effect, normalizing the lengths of each phase of the menstrual cycle. The typical dose is one 175-milligram capsule per day of standardized extract (check the label to make sure this is what you're getting). Caveat: This remedy may reduce your libido.

Vaginal Dryness
Natural fix: Sex, lubricants such as Astroglide, and moisturizers such as Replens. Buzz: Doctors say that regular intercourse is nature's prescription for plentiful vaginal moisture—just smooth your moves with a water-based lubricant such as Astroglide to reduce the chance of irritation. For longer-lasting benefits, check out Replens, an over-the-counter vaginal moisturizer that has been shown to restore moisture and elasticity on par with a prescription estrogen cream. Caveat: With the exception of vitamin E oil, avoid oil-based lubricants such as Vaseline, which can lead to infection. ✳

THE NEW
Medical
Professionals

They look like real doctors, and they're quickly becoming
one of the hottest trends in health care. You may know them as
physician assistants, nurse practioners, or nursing assistants.
Here's how you can get the best care from them.

BY RICK CHILLOT

No wonder everyone's trying to take charge of her own health: Even when you manage to find a doctor who's in sync with your personality and preferences, chances are you won't spend more than a couple of minutes with her during your appointment. More likely, you'll be baring and sharing all with one of the various people in her entourage of medical professionals. Ever since the rise of physician assistants (P.A.s) and nurse practitioners (N.P.s)—nondoctor clinicians who can prescribe drugs, give injections, offer advice, and administer tests—doctors have started behaving more like rock stars or corporate CEOs, making cameos to a grateful few. And it's unlikely that things will change anytime soon: The number of these pseudo-docs is expected to grow as much as 60 percent by 2005, while the number of medical doctors will expand by just 10 percent. Also, nursing assistants, whom you see mainly in hospitals, are picking up the slack as the number of R.N.s declines.

There is good news, though, despite this shift in medical care: In some cases, these pseudo-docs can give you physician-level health care. Studies show that people treated by P.A.s and N.P.s do just as well as those seen by physicians, at least for routine health problems. These clinicians may have more time to listen to what you're telling them or had training that was more oriented toward direct patient care.

But don't dismiss your doctor just yet: There's still no substitute for the experience and training that comes with medical school. "Physicians usually spend twice as long in the education process as N.P.s or P.A.s," says. James Rohack, M.D., a trustee of the American Medical Association who practices in Temple, Texas. You may not need that kind of expertise for your cold sore or sprained ankle, but, as Rohack points out, "the more training you have, the better suited you are to separate the life-threatening health problem from the common illness that will get better by itself."

The ideal situation may be one that involves the best of both worlds: doctors who have P.A.s or N.P.s in their practices, or private-practice N.P.s who have stable links to a network of M.D.s. Still, it raises questions about who is qualified to do what—which becomes especially important when someone (not your doctor) comes at you with an injection or whips out a prescription pad to get you something for your hay fever. Here's how to tell what you're getting when you encounter a pseudo-doc in your quest for good health care.

Physician Assistants: Almost a doctor

Who they are: These clinicians extend the reach of the physician, standing in for him or her in the more mundane cases (like doing lab tests or diagnosing stomach bugs), which allows the doctor to attend to serious conditions. The first P.A. program was created in the 1960s to address a doctor shortage and allow army medics to apply their skills to civilian life. Today, P.A.s typically go through a two-year program affiliated with a medical school or university. Some P.A. schools confer a master's degree on their graduates; others offer a bachelor's or associate's degree or a certificate. All P.A. programs in the United States must be accredited, and all P.A.s must pass national board exams.

What they can do: P.A.s have a lot of autonomy, depending on how comfortable the doctor is with their level of experience. They can give exams, make diagnoses, prescribe medicine, and assist in surgery. For common ailments and basic procedures, such as wrapping a sprained ankle or prescribing something for your sinus infection, a physician assistant should be fine. But the physician is ultimately responsible for your care, and a P.A. should turn things over to the doctor if, for example, a test turns up something out of the ordinary.

What they can't do: As you might guess from the title, physician assistants must operate under the supervision of a licensed physician. State law sets general boundaries (for example, Indiana, Louisiana, and Ohio don't allow P.A.s to write prescriptions), but for the most part it's the supervising physician who determines the P.A.'s day-to-day responsibilities.

photo by Jason Todd

*Best of both worlds:
a doctor who has a
physician assistant or nurse
practioner on staff.
But you still need to know
who can do what.*

What you should know: Although P.A.s work under a doctor's supervision, that M.D. does not have to be on the premises. That means that if you have an unusual or complicated case, you may have to make another appointment to see a physician. And while P.A.s do receive extensive training in basic primary care, you should always feel comfortable asking for an M.D.

Nurse Practitioners: Super R.N.s

Who they are: Now about 80,000 strong in the United States, nurse practitioners are the medical experts of the nursing world, providing health care as well as traditional nursing care. They are practicing R.N.s (typically with four years of undergraduate nursing education) who've gone on to earn a master's-level degree in nursing (usually a two- to three-year program).

What they can do: Like P.A.s, nurse practitioners can do many tasks your doctor used to, from giving physicals to coming up with treatment plans. N.P.s primarily focus on preventive care and basic treatment. In certain states, they can set up their own practices, although only 10 percent of them operate independently. In every state except Georgia they are licensed to prescribe medicine.

What they can't do: Limits on what a nurse practitioner can do are set by each state's Nurse Practice Act. Any major differences among state regulations involve how autonomous N.P.s can be and what kinds of prescriptions they can write. In some states, N.P.s must practice in collaboration with a physician.

What you should know: Because nurse practitioners can work independently, it's easy to confuse them with M.D.s or think they are equivalent. Be sure you ask what degree your care provider has and ask the N.P. who he or she will consult with if there's a problem or an emergency. Even independently practicing N.P.s should have access to a physician in case the need arises.

when the doctor's not in

Who's that guy with the syringe—and is he qualified to use it? Here's how to know at a glance.

	PHYSICIAN ASSISTANT	NURSE PRACTITIONER	NURSING ASSISTANT
training	typically, a two-year program after earning an undergraduate degree	usually, must first obtain R.N. certification and have nursing experience, then earn master's-level degree	no universal guidelines; many nursing assistants have taken N.A. courses at community colleges or in college, and some hospitals offer on-the-job training
administer injections?	yes	yes	no
diagnose illnesses?	yes	yes	no
write prescriptions?	in most states	in most states	no
national certification?	mandatory	optional	not available
independent practice?	no, always under supervision of an M.D.	can practice independently in some states; most require association with a physician	no; must be under supervision of a registered nurse
more information	www.apa.org	www.aanp.org	www.cna-network.org

Nursing Assistants: Just the basics

Who they are: Also known as nurse's aides, care assistants, and by other titles, nursing assistants work with the elderly, disabled, people recovering from surgery, and anyone else who needs help with daily living. This, too, is a growing field: There are about 2.5 million nurse assistants in the United States today, and it's expected that there will be a need for 750,000 more in the next two years. With the exception of nursing-home staff, there are no national requirements for training and certification of nursing assistants. That means anyone can call herself a nursing assistant—and that may be why some patients have made claims of abuse or inept care.

What they can do: Nursing assistants can practice basic skills to help a patient get through his or her day. They work in hospitals, nursing homes, and private homes. Daily tasks could include anything from brushing a patient's teeth to shifting a patient to prevent bedsores.

What they can't do: Nursing assistants are there to provide care, not therapy or treatment. That means they can't give shots or administer medicine—but they can test blood pressure, pulse, or temperature, for example. Although they will observe and report changes in a patient's health status, it's up to the supervising nurse or doctor to decide what those changes mean. If you're being treated by a nursing assistant, make sure they call in an N.P., P.A., or a doctor if you have any concerns.

Nursing assistants are some of the least-regulated health-care workers. That's why you need to check references and ask hard questions.

What you should know: Nursing assistants are among the least-regulated people in medicine. When hiring an N.A. for in-home help with a disabled loved one, be sure to check references and ask hard questions about training and experience. Each state maintains an abuse registry that lists censured N.A.s. To see that list, contact your state's human-services office. And be sure the N.A. works under close supervision of a nurse or physician. ✱

Pennsylvania-based freelance writer Rick Chillot covers health and other topics.

New Kind of Leeches May be Used in Hospitals

Did you know doctors are still using leeches in hospitals? The blood-sucking parasites help re-establish blood supply and nourish tissue after surgery. But if the idea of being suctioned by a slimy pond-dweller makes you squirm, we've got good news. Scientists are developing a mechanical leech to ease the stress squeamish patients feel when confronted by the live variety, says developer Nadine Connor, Ph.D., an associate scientist at the University of Wisconsin-Madison.

Leech farmers remain nonplussed about the man-made competition. "We've been hearing about this mechanical leech for years," says Rudy Rosenberg, vice president of Leeches USA, which supplies hospitals with the creatures. But "the simplicity of the real thing can't be replicated," he says. The leeches don't bother most patients, he claims, and "children even give their leeches pet names." As long as Spot, Rover, and Fido continue to do their work, Rosenberg isn't planning a going-out-of-business sale anytime soon.

BLOOD SUBSTITUTES:
Better Than the Real Thing?

A NEW ADDITION TO THE LIST of medical marvels could be appearing at an operating table near you. So-called blood substitutes—manufactured from synthetic products or from human red blood cells and cow's blood—hold several advantages over the real thing: They can be used in people of any blood type, can be stored longer than donor blood, and are not likely to transmit disease. "These products could have several important roles in medicine, including stabilizing trauma patients before they get to the hospital," says Peter L. Page, M.D., senior medical officer for the American Red Cross Biomedical Services. And for operations that require a lot of blood, the subs will help ease the strain on the donor supply.

But the imitation can't replace the real deal in every case. Donor blood can sustain the body for weeks, while the body uses up the substitutes in a day. "The products are not good for people with anemia or certain cancers because the frequency of transfusions would make them impractical," Page says. "Also, they don't supply plasma or platelets, which are essential for patients undergoing heart surgery or chemotherapy for some cancers and to prevent bleeding."

The blood subs could be available by the end of 2002, pending government approval. This doesn't mean you should skip the local blood drive, however. Donor transfusions will still be required to treat longer-lasting conditions. You can call a local blood bank or the Red Cross hot line (800-448-3543) to see if you'd make a good donor.

healthBUZZ

thumbs UP

Peer-pressure diets: Team up to beat fat. In a University of Florida study, dieters on all sorts of weight-loss plans who gathered for weekly support meetings lost an average of 24.2 pounds in six months, versus the 20 pounds lost by the solo dieters.

Brain candy: Watch a movie, read a book, hang out with some friends—and save your mind. Taking part in leisure activities reduces your risk of developing dementia (and possibly Alzheimer's) by 38 percent, according to a study published in *Neurology.*

thumbs DOWN

Sheep: Next time you're caught wide-eyed at night, forget counting these woolly creatures. Oxford psychologists found that slumber-seekers had better luck imagining soothing waterfalls or tranquil riverside picnics.

A nation of users: More than 80 percent of American adults take at least one type of medication—from over-the-counter remedies to prescription drugs to dietary supplements—in any given week, according to a study in *The Journal of the American Medical Association.* Talk to your doctor about potentially dangerous combinations.

a breath of Fresh Medicine

Inhalers aren't just for asthma anymore.
Soon everything from pain medication to menopause
drugs might be just a breath away.

BY LAURA FLYNN McCARTHY

Adrienne Perutelli was just 21 years old when she was diagnosed with Type I diabetes. Because Type I diabetics can't treat their condition with diet and exercise alone, this Richardson, Texas, resident spent 20 years giving herself injections of insulin four to five times every day. "Keeping my blood sugar at a normal level meant having a very rigid schedule," she recalls. "I always had to eat breakfast, lunch, and dinner at the right time. And I always had to know that I'd be eating in a place where I could have a clean surface on which to set up my injection and give myself a shot."

All of that changed about 18 months ago, when Perutelli, now 45, enrolled in a study on inhaled insulin at Baylor University Medical Center in Dallas. She started inhaling her insulin three times a day and injecting it only once, first thing in the morning. For someone who had spent nearly half of her life encumbered with the traditional treatments for diabetes, the difference proved to be remarkable. "I have much more flexibility now," Perutelli says. "I still try to eat a meal within 15 minutes of inhaling my insulin, but I know that I can inhale it easily anywhere in just a few seconds. And if more than 15 minutes elapses after I take it and before I eat, it's not a disaster."

That kind of convenience may soon be a reality not just for diabetics like Perutelli, but also for people with a host of other conditions, from menopause to multiple sclerosis. Although inhalable medicines have been talked about for years, researchers are finally discovering ways to make them work. If these new drugs make it to the market, it will mark a giant step in the evolution of modern medicine—one that will make many people's lives healthier and easier.

Getting this far hasn't been a simple feat. Inhalable medications have been around since the 1950s, when they were administered by inhalers that used chlorofluorocarbons, or CFCs. But in 1996, the U.S. Food and Drug Administration (FDA) banned the use of these ozone-damaging CFCs in most products. Researchers frantically started working on new ways to deliver asthma medication directly to the lungs. What resulted in the late 1990s was the introduction of much better asthma treatments—and new curiosity about what other drugs could be inhalable. Once scientists figured out a way to make drug particles small enough to be absorbed through the lungs and into the bloodstream, they knew expansion into other, more mainstream drugs might be possible.

It's easy to see why researchers believe inhalables are so promising. For starters, they offer an alternative to needles, which, although effective, have a number of drawbacks. Needle shots are painful and inconvenient, and skipping treatments is a major temptation, especially for people like Perutelli, who need injections several times a day.

And unlike drugs that are delivered through needles and pills, inhalables go straight to the lungs, the most absorptive organ in the body. They hold a further advantage over pills: Inhalables don't have to be broken down by the digestive system, the reason for nausea among some pill-takers.

But supporters claim these aren't the only reasons inhalables are better than injections and pills. They also start to work faster than traditional meds. "The peak concentration of medication in the blood occurs about one hour after an injection, but as soon as 10 to 30 minutes if the drug is inhaled," says Andy Clark, Ph.D., president of the International Society for Aerosols in Medicine. "For drugs that provide pain relief, improved breathing, blood-sugar control, or other treatments that are needed quickly, inhaled medication may be better."

Still, drug manufacturers face some substantial obstacles. "The biggest challenge in making these new inhalable medications available will be how to deliver the proper dose consistently and reliably," says Robert Temple, M.D., associate director for medical policy for the FDA's Center for Drug Evaluation and Research. "Inhaling things is tricky. If you got twice as much asthma medicine as you needed, it might not make a difference. But if you inhaled twice as much morphine as you needed, that could be a big problem."

Researchers believe that improved technology holds the answer. They say the new inhalers will be dose-specific, releasing only a certain amount of drug per inhalation. That way, patients won't face the risk of over-medicating. And because the new inhalers aim to deliver the drug in the beginning of a breath, users won't have to worry about taking in less than a dose, either.

But regulating dosage is only one of the challenges drug researchers face, says Alan Goldhammer, Ph.D., associate vice president for regulatory affairs for the Pharmaceutical Research and Manufacturers of America. With each new inhalable drug they come up with, scientists will have to figure out how to keep the proteins from breaking down at room temperature, put them into aerosol form, and then make sure the proteins are absorbed by the lungs and the bloodstream, Goldhammer says.

Researchers claim they are solving these problems. New foil packaging, they say, keeps proteins in medicines stable at room temperature. And most significantly, they have discovered how to make proteins into much smaller

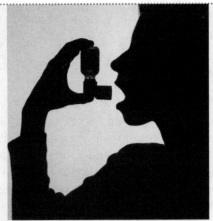

medical milestones

Inhalable medications mark another step in the amazing evolution of drug development and delivery. Here are a few other highlights of medical progress through the ages.

2600 B.C.

Bet you didn't know that suppositories were among the first important developments in drug delivery. Their use dates back more than four millennia.

1st century A.D.

Although they were first used by the Mesopotamians, the Egyptians, and the Greeks, pills were first named by the Romans. They dubbed them *pilula*.

1657

Technically, the first injections were poisoned arrows used as weapons. But in 1657, Sir Christopher Wren injected a drug intravenously, ushering in a new method of drug delivery.

1979

The U.S. Food and Drug Administration approved the first skin-patch drug. Used for motion sickness, it paved the way for more uses, such as decreasing menopausal symptoms and controlling blood pressure.

2002

The future is almost here. Drug companies are testing inhalable medications for everything from cystic fibrosis to menopause. Approval of these drugs will mark a new milestone.

If these new drugs make it to the market, it will mark
a giant step in the evolution of modern medicine—*one that*
will make many people's lives healthier and easier.

particles than ever before, which means the proteins can be made into an aerosol form that can move through the lungs and into the blood. That's why it now may be possible to use inhalables for all kinds of drugs that were not an option before, and it's the main reason scientists like Clark are so excited. "These advances will mean new kinds of inhalable medications in the future," Clark explains.

Questions remain: When will that future arrive? And will it really translate into an abundance of inhalable medicines for all kinds of common ailments? Getting FDA approval for the new form of insulin is the first step. Pfizer plans to apply for approval after final studies are complete, which means that its product, Exubera, could be on the market in 18 months or so. At least three other U.S. companies are working on their own inhaled form of insulin. Meanwhile, drug companies are now testing medications for cystic fibrosis, emphysema, and multiple sclerosis, among other conditions. Researchers say that if insulin proves successful, it will mark the beginning of a new era in medicine.

This kind of medical evolution has happened before. Lawrence Block, Ph.D., professor of pharmaceutics at Duquesne University in Pittsburgh, says medicinal patches took a similar route from the lab to the pharmacy shelf. "In the early 1980s, the FDA approved the first transdermal patch, for a motion-sickness drug," Block says. "Once that technology was seen as viable, more and more companies started investigating the potential of patches, and now we have at least 10 different drugs—from blood-pressure medication to estrogen and even a once-a-week form of birth control—delivered through the skin by a patch. And more are in the pipeline. We could see a similar pattern with new inhalable medications once the insulin-based product is approved."

The implications of that development will be huge, and not simply because inhalables are more convenient than other drugs. According to Clark, ease of use translates into healthier living. "People are more likely to take their medications if they're easy to take," Clark says. "And that means better health for people using these drugs." ✳

Laura Flynn McCarthy is a New Hampshire–based writer.
Her work has appeared in Self, Fitness, *and* Vogue,
among others.

Alternative—or Mainstream?

By age 33, 30% of pre–baby boomers, 50% of baby boomers, and 70% of post–baby boomers have used some form of complementary or alternative medicine.

—*Annals of Internal Medicine*

Snooze-Free Allergy Aid

Now you can be rid of sneezing without snoozing: A study published in the *British Medical Journal* found that tablets containing extracts of the herb butterbur are as effective as antihistamines in treating hay-fever symptoms—with fewer side effects such as drowsiness. As with any herbal remedy, get your doctor's OK first.

take-home medical tests: do they make the grade?

With all the hype about home-based medical tests, it's starting to sound like you can get an entire checkup without leaving home. But before you turn your bathroom into a lab, know that we found that most tests failed to make the grade. We had two testers try each brand and also asked registered pharmacist Leo McStroul, owner of Plaza West Pharmacy in Northridge, California, to rate each one. The take-home lesson? "If you're concerned, you should contact a health-care provider," McStroul says. "Don't plan your life on the results of these tests."

	COLON CANCER TEST	CHOLESTEROL TEST	BREATH ALCOHOL LEVEL TEST	HOME DRUG TEST
test question	What's going on with my movements (we're not talking spatial)?	Is my double-cheeseburger fetish catching up with me?	Do I need to call a cab to get home?	Is my kid on grass?
who it's for	Folks who are scared of the doctor or grossed out by stool samples, which most lab tests require	People too cheap to spring for a real test	Revelers sober enough to follow directions such as "do not inhale"	Suspicious parents or curious spouses
brand	First Check Home Screening Test for Early Warning Signs of Colorectal Disease	CholesTrak Home Cholesterol Test	First Check Breath Alcohol Tester	First Check THC
price	$9.99 for a 3-day test	$16.95 for 2 tests	$5.99 for 3 tests	$9.99 for 1 test
how it works	Just do number two and toss the test pad into the toilet. If the pad turns blue, there's blood in the sample.	Prick your own finger and let it bleed onto the handy test device.	Exhale into the tube for 12 seconds. If the little yellow crystals turn blue, your alcohol level is at or above 0.08 percent, the legal intoxication level in most states.	The test looks for traces of marijuana in urine. Just make sure your kid isn't hoarding switcheroo samples in his room, à la *American Beauty*.
user comments	"I just turned 52 and haven't had a colonoscopy yet. Now that this test was negative, I feel I can put it off for another year."	"The box didn't really explain what the results mean."	"A great party favor—I tested all my friends!"	"Don't let your kid do this test unsupervised—he may be too stoned to follow the rather complicated directions!"
pharmacist's take	"A negative result only means that the test did not detect blood in this stool at this time. You need to check with your physician."	"The test may be accurate, but it only provides total cholesterol reading—not HDL ("good"), LDL ("bad"), and triglycerides—so it's not all that helpful."	"This test might give you a false sense of security. If you think you may be too drunk to drive, you probably are."	"The test is accurate, but you may have to work on repairing trust."
we say	Skip the home test and see your doctor instead.	Do you really want to prick your own finger for an incomplete result? You need all the numbers, so get the complete workup at your annual physical.	This could be useful in figuring out how many drinks is too many—but it won't stand up in court. Save your money for a cab home.	Try good, old-fashioned communication. If that fails, put your money into family counseling instead.
total score	C	B	C	C+

A Landmark Case Challenges Medical Treatment of Pain

The doctors had the means to relieve the suffering of her dying father. So why did he spend his last days in such pain? Beverly Bergman went to court to ensure that no one would have to endure what her family went through, and we all won.

BY NANCY STEDMAN

PHOTOGRAPHY BY BROWN CANNON

Bill Bergman was a man of few words and many scruples—the sort who didn't like to draw attention to himself. And so he probably would have been mortified to hear that, after his intensely painful death, he starred in a landmark lawsuit that would eventually help protect other aging patients from suffering a similar fate. A gun-toting detective for 37 years at Western Pacific Railroad, the handsome Scandinavian-American worked close by his much-adored wife, Barbara, a payroll employee and union vice president for the same company. Together, in the Northern California town of Hayward, they raised three children: Beverly, now 46, the peacemaker of the family; Robert, 41, the clown with a melancholy streak; and Alice, 51, the iconoclast who always maintained a measure of independence from her family.

Bill was often eclipsed by his funny and vivacious wife. "My mother was like the biggest thing in the room," recalls Bev, an advocate for mentally ill people who now lives in the same home where she and her siblings grew up. "My father was very quiet. He would just sit in the background and let my mom be right out there." Away from the job, Bill tended to pursue solitary pleasures. "He loved to putter around the house," Bev adds. "He would paint anything that stayed still."

It was only after their mother's death from lung cancer in 1995, though, that Bev, Robert, and Alice really got to know their father: that he had only gone to baseball games to please their mother, that he was an opera fan. The more the kids learned about their father, the closer they grew to him during the three years before his death. "He was always good about telling us he loved us," Bev says, "but he got a lot more huggy in the last few years."

So it was especially sad for the siblings when their dad passed away in 1998. But what made Bill's death more than a tragic family loss was the fact that he had spent his final week in excruciating pain. Bill's suffering—by almost all accounts unnecessary—led Bev and her siblings to bring and win an elder-abuse lawsuit against his physician for inadequate pain management, the first suit of its kind in the United States.

Equally important, the case helped spark legislative remedies for families who believe that their loved one's pain is being undertreated—a disturbingly common problem. According to one recent report, half of all terminally ill patients in the United States experience moderate to severe pain. The Bergman case also sent a message to doctors across the nation, one they clearly got: Anecdotal reports suggest that in the wake of the case, physicians are signing up for pain-management courses in increasing numbers. The distress of one quiet man was heard 'round the medical world.

By her own reckoning, Bev Bergman inherited her social activism from her mother and her bulldog persistence from her father. She spent much of the 1980s protesting the building of nuclear power plants in her native California. A naturally reserved woman whose face can light up unexpectedly with a smile—or with outrage at a social or personal injustice—she was a peer drug counselor in high school and made her career in social services. "She's always been a very shirt-off-your-back kind of person," says her brother, Robert. And he should know. A heavy drinker for years, he turned to her in 1988 when his problem got out of control. "I probably wouldn't be alive today if she had not been there," he says. "She drove me to the detox center. She was with me the whole time and helped me get sober."

Bev, the only sibling without children, also took over the care of her mother after she was diagnosed with terminal lung cancer. Bev set up a hospital bed in her own apartment and arranged for hospice nurses and home health aides during the workday. After two months, her mother died at Bev's home. "She had a very peaceful death," Bev says.

> What made Bill's death more than a tragic family loss was the fact that he had spent his final week in **excruciating pain.**

Not so for her dad. The longest nine days in Bev's life began in mid-February 1998, when she discovered her father crumpled over in a chair, unable to move. "I'm in terrible pain," whispered Bill, who was not inclined to show weakness. He was rushed to the emergency room of nearby Eden Medical Center, a 275-bed hospital in Castro Valley. The next day, an E.R. physician gave Bill two small doses of morphine, the drug of choice for severe pain, according to guidelines issued by the U.S. Agency for Health Care Policy and Research. It was the last morphine, the last shred of relief, Bill Bergman would receive until just before he died.

The internist who took over his case, Wing Chin, M.D., a former chief of staff at the medical center, admitted Bill to the hospital and ordered low doses of Demerol, a much weaker painkiller. And since it was prescribed on an

27

Bev could hear her father moaning in pain, unable to sleep.
"I'd play music to distract him," she recalls. "And it would
work for a while. But then the pain would just come back."

as-needed basis, Bill had to wait until he was extremely uncomfortable before getting relief. His medical charts tell the horrific tale: His discomfort ranged mostly between 7 and 10 (the most excruciating level of pain).

Doctors diagnosed Bill with compressed vertebrae, but the family suspected lung cancer was the real cause of pain for their father, a longtime smoker. Bill's initial tests for lung cancer were inconclusive, and he declined to undergo invasive tests for a definitive diagnosis. Nevertheless, he became convinced he was going to die, and wanted to be at home when it happened. He was released from the hospital on Saturday, and Bev moved back into the family's home to take care of him. She was shocked to learn that Chin had only prescribed Vicodin, a moderate pain reliever. It wasn't powerful enough: Bev could hear her father moaning in pain, unable to sleep. "I'd play music to distract him," she recalls. "And it would work for a while. But then the pain would just come back."

By Monday, Bill's pain was the most intense he had ever experienced. "He was clutching on to the trapeze bars above the bed, saying how awful it was," Bev says. A sympathetic and persistent hospice nurse managed to get a prescription for liquid morphine from Bill's former family practitioner. It was not until that afternoon that he finally received a dose. "In about an hour he went to sleep," Bev says. "The next day his breathing got shallower, and he died." It was February 24, 1998, nine days after Bill first collapsed.

More than four years later, Bev still cries at the memory of those dark days. "When something happens like this, it makes you think of all the things you could have done differently," she says. "I think I was depending too much on the nurses. The first nurse who came to the house

didn't call the doctor about pain medication. We're taught not to question authority, and because nurses and doctors are the ones who went to school, they know best. But that's not really true."

None of us would ever want our parents to go through what Bill Bergman did. However, the chances that they could are frighteningly high. The pain-medication needs of elderly patients, who often feel reluctant about complaining to or questioning their doctors, are especially likely to be overlooked. Some 40 percent of nursing-home patients with chronic or acute pain are not receiving treatment that relieves it, according to a study published in October 2001 in *The Journal of the American Medical Association.* "There's no type of health-care institution other than the hospice that's doing a good job of pain management," says the study's lead investigator, Joan Teno, M.D., of Brown University's Center for Gerontology and Health Care Research.

Considering that there is a small armament of pain-relief medication available to the informed physician, why do so many patients seem to be losing the battle against pain? "Doctors are usually so worried about over-prescribing for pain that we often underprescribe," says Robert Brody, M.D., chief of the Pain Consultation Clinic at San Francisco General Hospital. Part of the problem is rooted in old-fashioned American values. "Our culture tends to admire stoicism," says Linda Emanuel, M.D., Ph.D., the director of the Buehler Center on Aging at Northwestern University. Another issue is the chance of addiction. But even with morphine and other opiates, the most effective painkillers, there is only a slight risk. The American legal system has generally stressed the importance of preventing addiction over the need to

We're taught not to question authority, and because
nurses and doctors are the ones who went to school, they
know best. But that's not really true.
—*Beverly Bergman*

relieve pain—even among terminally ill patients. In fact, some states place almost insurmountable barriers in the way of doctors who want to prescribe narcotic painkillers.

Despite the legal hurdles, the medical establishment has acknowledged the problem of insufficient pain relief—and is slowly addressing it. In 1998, the Federation of State Medical Boards, which regulates physicians, adopted a set of model guidelines for pain management. California was actually ahead of the curve. In 1994, the Medical Board of California mailed a guidebook to all state doctors, encouraging them to aggressively treat their patients' pain. And in 1997, California's legislature passed a Pain Patient's Bill of Rights, guaranteeing that all citizens had the right to be informed of, and to choose among, their pain-relief options—including narcotics. Neither of these initiatives, though, helped Bill Bergman.

A few weeks after Bill died, Bev contacted a malpractice lawyer. She was so disturbed by watching her father suffer that she was in therapy for post-traumatic stress disorder. She told the lawyer what had happened and passed along a comment from a hospice nurse who cared for her dad that suggested Chin had a pattern of ignoring his patients' discomfort. "I wanted Dr. Chin to change his ways so other people wouldn't have to go through this," Bev explains. "I didn't want any harm to come to him. I just wanted him to become educated."

As it turned out, an ordinary malpractice case would not work in California: State law doesn't allow people to collect damages for pain and suffering after someone's death. A lawyer pointed Bev to Compassion in Dying Federation (CIDF), a nonprofit advocacy group in Portland, Oregon, concerned with improved end-of-life care. First, they tried to get the Medical Board of California, the regulatory agency for physicians, to discipline Chin for his failure to treat Bill Bergman prior to his death. But the board refused to take corrective action.

The next step—taking Chin to court—was much riskier, but Bev and her siblings were in lockstep on this issue. "We talked about it, and we all agreed we had to do something," Robert says. Bev, as usual, was the logical point person. Says Robert, "My sister had the fortitude to fight—she has the heart of a lion, and she has the knowledge to deal with the legal system."

Kathryn Tucker, legal director for CIDF, opted for a novel approach: Sue Chin and the Eden Medical Center in civil court for elder abuse, which requires a higher level

how you can help someone you love

Which patients have the most trouble getting compassionate pain relief? Children, the elderly, women, and minorities—the least powerful people in society, says Barbara Coombs Lee, president of the Compassion in Dying Federation. Here are some effective ways to ensure that your loved one is receiving the relief he or she needs.

• Make sure you can get a prescription written night or day, weekday or weekend: Write down the name and phone number of the doctor who covers for the patient's regular physician.

• Keep a pain record. Note the location, time of day, severity, and what relieved the pain. Share this information with the doctor or nurse.

• Don't let your loved one wait until pain is excruciating to treat it. "Pain is easier to control when it's mild than when it's severe," says Joan Teno, M.D., of Brown University's Center for Gerontology and Health Care Research.

• Insist that the doctor provide the patient with enough pain medication for nights, weekends, and holidays.

• Ask about the patient's orders for pain medication. See that they cover frequency, dosage, and type of medication. If you have questions, be assertive and ask the doctor.

• If your loved one is in a hospital or nursing home, make sure that his or her pain levels are communicated to the nursing staff and, equally important, that the staff is responding appropriately. "You may have to ask again and again," says Robert Brody, M.D., chief of the Pain Consultation Clinic at San Francisco General Hospital. Still not getting any satisfaction? Speak to the medical director or nursing supervisor.

of proof than malpractice. The chances of winning were so slim that Tucker spent weeks looking for a lawyer who was willing to take the job of co-counsel. She finally enlisted attorney Jim Geagan. The stakes were high for the entire Bergman family. If they lost the case, the Bergmans—all modest earners—would be liable for Chin's legal costs, which could be $40,000 to $50,000. "I would have been responsible if things turned out badly," Bev says. "I would have ruined the family." So she gave her siblings several chances to back down. They adamantly declined.

On May 17, 2001, after two years of legal wrangling, the trial began. Medical lawsuits are a nasty business. The plaintiffs need to prove, in effect, that a highly trained professional acted incompetently. The doctor, in turn, wants to save his reputation by blaming bad outcomes on someone—or something—else. The ugly stuff started right away. During his opening statement, Chin's defense attorney, Robert M. Slattery, insinuated that Bev had killed Bill Bergman when she gave him the final dose of morphine secured by the hospice nurse. The Bergman side gasped at this type of accusation.

As days turned into weeks, tensions in the courtroom grew. Says Bev, "I didn't like being on the stand. It felt like you were going through it all over again. And the attorney kept hammering on the same thing, trying to make you contradict yourself, trying to discredit you." Her sister, Alice, left the courtroom four or five times when Chin and the medical-center nurses seemed to display callousness about her father's pain. "We weren't supposed to get emotional," Alice says, "but at some points we wanted to wring their necks."

The stress took its toll. Robert lost 15 to 20 pounds during the three-week trial; Bev lost 5. All of them—Geagan included—had trouble sleeping. "I had never had a case with more of an effect on public health," he says. "I thought, 'What if I try it and we lose? The message would be that you can undertreat the elderly for pain and it doesn't matter.'"

In their case, the Bergmans' lawyers charged that Chin was woefully underinformed about pain-management strategies. In fact, he admitted to no education on this subject beyond a pharmacology class in medical school 30 years ago and a lunchtime seminar more recently. The Bergmans also cast doubt on Chin's assertion that Bill Bergman had reacted negatively to the morphine given him in the emergency room: Chin had not noted this reaction on Bergman's chart or relayed it to the nurses. Further, expert witnesses said it was unlikely that Bev had hastened her dad's death. (Chin's lawyers were

repeatedly contacted to comment on the story, but they did not return phone calls.)

Both sides rested their case and the jury adjourned. After four very long days of deliberation, they returned to the courtroom. Bev, Robert, Alice, and Alice's 26-year-old daughter, Jennifer, sat holding hands, waiting for the verdict. Although they were all terrified about the jury's decision, the three siblings had never felt closer. Says Bev, "I felt like my family had united to do the right thing." The jury agreed, finding for the Bergmans and awarding them $1.5 million, a sum that vastly exceeded their expectations. "It was kind of a sad victory because we really weren't trying to harm Dr. Chin," Bev says. "We didn't jump up and down, but we were glad."

Even though the award was reduced to $250,000 (to comply with the elder-abuse statute limit), the decision was widely hailed as precedent-setting. "It demonstrated that the court considers adequate pain management a part of good medical practice," says David E. Joranson, director of the Pain and Policy Studies Group at the University of Wisconsin Medical School. The verdict has also encouraged doctors, perhaps nervous about their own pain-management practices, to sign up for pain-relief seminars. A few months after the trial's conclusion, California Governor Gray Davis signed a law that might ease the need for related lawsuits. Bev testified on behalf of this statute, which requires state doctors to undergo continuing education and calls on the Medical Board of California to track complaints about the mishandling of pain care by physicians—the first such law in the country.

After the trial, many people who had never met Bill Bergman told his kids that their father would have been proud of them. Their immediate reaction was to disagree. Says Bev, "At first I thought he would think I'm making too much of this, because he was so stoic." But after further reflection she changed her mind. "I think he would be happy for us, that we've done something to help other people. I think he would like that." ✳

> We've done something to **help other people.** I think he would like that.
> —*Beverly Bergman*

Nancy Stedman is a New York–based freelance writer who contributes to The New York Times, Good Housekeeping, *and* People.

junk food goes to court

Is it another case of Americans jumping on the litigation bandwagon, or should restaurants be held responsible for neglecting the health of their customers?

BY NANCY STEDMAN

We had to laugh when we first heard that a guy in New York City had filed suit against fast-food manufacturers for the oversizing of his waistline. It seemed like just another example of the "See you in court!" culture gone amok. Then we looked around at the onslaught of high-fat, high-sugar foods in schools, restaurants, supermarkets, and TV ads—and we stopped short. Some $117 billion a year is spent on treating the 61 percent of overweight Americans for diet-related conditions like adult-onset diabetes and cholesterol-clogged arteries—money that comes out of your taxes and health insurance premiums. Clearly, this is no laughing matter.

The obesity epidemic is of such serious dimensions that it may be time to start thinking outside the sugar-coated-cereal box. The medical costs of overeating are significantly higher than those of smoking or alcohol abuse, according to a recent analysis by Roland Sturm, Ph.D., and RAND, a nonprofit research institution. "If you're in an environment where food is offered all the time, like cigarettes were 45 years ago, it has an impact on how much you eat," Sturm says. Perhaps, as with tobacco and alcohol, producers and consumers share in the culpability for overindulgence.

Fast food, soda companies, and the like have played a major role in creating America's fat crisis, say critics like Marion Nestle, Ph.D., chair of New York University's department of nutrition and food studies. "Food companies will make and market any product that sells, regardless of its nutritional value or its effect on health. In this regard, food companies hardly differ from cigarette companies," she charges in her controversial new book *Food Politics: How the Food Industry Influences Nutrition and Health.* Because processed foods create a much higher profit margin than fruits and vegetables, the food industry funnels the majority of its annual $11 billion advertising budget to promote not-so-healthy foods such as potato chips.

Legal expert John Banzhaf, a George Washington University Law School professor who was an original architect of the lawsuits against the tobacco industry, thinks the answer may lie in bringing the food industry to court. (Coincidentally, cigarette companies own many of the biggest processed-food firms.) However, the

The obesity epidemic has reached critical dimensions. The medical costs of overeating are now actually significantly higher than those of smoking or alcohol abuse.

prospects of a successful class-action lawsuit look slim. One hurdle is this: Whereas any exposure to cigarettes is harmful, foods like Krispy Kreme doughnuts can be easily integrated into a healthy diet—so long as they are eaten in moderation. And while tobacco is physiologically addictive, junk food is not. Plus, it's difficult enough to link heart disease to a diet—much less pin it on Taco Bell. "If someone dies from diseases brought on by obesity, it would be hard to say what percentage of the damage was caused by inactivity and what percentage by each of the hundreds of thousands of foods available," Banzhaf says.

Nonetheless, the talk about lawsuits has broadened the tactics of concerned folks determined to fight fat. One approach, which was included in a bill introduced into the California Senate in 2002 (and later abandoned), is to levy a small tax on soft drinks and use the money to fund programs that promote healthy eating. Such initiatives can be successful, as was shown in a campaign that encouraged Wheeling, West Virginia, residents to switch from whole or 2 percent milk to 1 percent or skim. In one month, one-third of the high-fat-milk drinkers switched to low-fat.

> ## Government intrusion has crossed a line.
> The vast majority of Americans don't like being told what to eat and what to feed their kids.
>
> *-John Doyle, Center for Consumer Freedom co-founder*

manufacturers are "found" money, funds that may, for instance, pay for sports programs that might otherwise be abandoned.

Yet numerous school districts across the country have turned back the tide of commercialism. Earlier this year, Oakland, California, banned the sale of soft drinks, candy, and similar foods in its schools; in Texas, new laws prohibit the sale of such items in the vicinity of school cafeterias.

Not surprisingly, the food industry opposes any interference with the free market. The Center for Consumer Freedom (CCF), a group that represents restaurant and tavern owners, is running radio ads attacking so-called "junk science"—such as the government's contention that 300,000 people each year die from obesity-related illnesses. "Government intrusion has crossed a line," says John Doyle, CCF co-founder. "The vast majority of Americans don't like being told what to eat and what to feed their kids."

> ## Even the IRS is weighing in on the **battle of the bulge,** allowing overweight people to deduct the costs of certain weight-loss programs.

The biggest battles are now being waged on behalf of school kids. One target is television food commercials geared toward children, more than 90 percent of which promote fast food, sugary cereals, soda, cookies, and candy. Inside schools, recent efforts have focused on stopping the proliferation of vending machines. A study of the 25 largest school districts in California by the Public Health Institute in Berkeley found that at least one school in each district has signed up for some sort of soft-drink distribution. "The more soda the school sells, the more money it makes," says lead study author Amanda Purcell. The schools in the study got one-time signing bonuses ranging from $25,000 to $1,000,000. For cash-strapped schools, the payments from soda

Yet even in the most conservative corners, panic about the obesity epidemic is leading to intervention. For instance, the Internal Revenue Service recently announced that overweight people can deduct the costs of certain weight-loss programs. Other options include subsidizing healthy foods in vending machines so they are cheaper than junk food, a tactic that has been shown to improve eating habits. And life insurance companies already have the legal right to impose higher premiums on obese people, as with smokers. It's clear that the social acceptability of obesity is on the decline.

Lawsuits? Please, spare us. But until Americans are able to make more intelligent food choices on their own, people will need some creative nudges in the right direction from government and others concerned about public health. ✳

Nancy Stedman is a New York City–based freelance writer who also contributes to The New York Times *and* People.

Good Question
about Women's Health

by Nancy Snyderman

Ibuprofen: The Latest Defense Against Alzheimers

I have a family history of Alzheimer's, and I recently heard that ibuprofen could help prevent it. How much do I need to take to get the benefits?

Many studies have tried to figure out what causes Alzheimer's and how to avoid getting it. Until now, nobody has found any answers. A recent study published in *The New England Journal of Medicine* provides evidence that nonsteroidal anti-inflammatory drugs (NSAIDs) like ibuprofen might prevent the disease.

The researchers followed 7,000 people in the Netherlands for about seven years. All of the participants were age 55 or older and free of dementia at the beginning of the study. The results showed that the people who used NSAIDs, such as ibuprofen (Advil or Motrin) and naproxen (Aleve), for two or more years were 80 percent less likely to develop Alzheimer's compared with the non-NSAID users.

However, researchers have yet to explain how NSAIDs actually work to decrease the risk for Alzheimer's. One of the many theories is that NSAIDs might reduce levels of amyloid-beta, a protein that accumulates in the brains of people with the disease. Only with further research will doctors figure out the link.

Until then, based on the study findings and the fact that ibuprofen is a pretty safe drug (assuming you don't have kidney problems), it's certainly worth talking to your doctor about taking NSAIDs, especially if you have a family risk of Alzheimer's. Be aware that NSAIDs can have side effects, such as gastrointestinal bleeding, and can interact with other medications. So don't start popping pills unless you're under the supervision of your doctor.

The Link Between Low Bone Density and Asthma

I've been using a steroid inhaler to control asthma for years. Will it increase my risk for osteoporosis later in life?

Researchers have long known that oral and injected steroid drugs commonly prescribed to treat asthma accelerate bone loss, but doctors assumed that inhaled drugs would be less harmful because they are delivered directly to the lungs. However, many physicians have started to question whether the steroids in sprays could spread through your bloodstream and into your bones, causing them to thin. In a recent study published in *The New England Journal of Medicine,* researchers measured the bone density of 109 asthmatic women between the ages of 18 and 45 who regularly used steroid inhalers. Over the course of three years, the researchers found that the women's average bone density had dropped—and that the more frequently they used their inhalers, the greater their bone loss.

This doesn't mean you should toss your inhaler. Do, however, ask your doctor if you can safely lower your steroid dose. Make sure to take precautions to reduce the risk of bone loss: Do such weight-bearing exercises as walking or running, don't smoke, make sure to get 1,200 milligrams of calcium daily, and talk to your doctor about whether you should be on bone-building medications such as alendronate. If you take more than eight puffs a day from your inhaler, consider getting a bone-density test every few years to monitor your bone mass.

Nancy Snyderman, M.D. is a medical correspondent for ABC News and author of **Girl in the Mirror: Mothers and Daughters in the Years of Adolescence.**

ECSTASY: the "Party" drug Goes from Club to Doctor's Couch

A new study puts a killer drug on trial. Should ecstasy be legalized to treat psychological trauma?

BY CHRISTIE ASCHWANDEN

On the street, rave-goers have labeled it "the love drug." Newspaper reports have dubbed it a killer. But for Marcela Ot'alora, ecstasy was a lifesaver.

Repeatedly raped when she was a teenager, Ot'alora spent years locked in the grip of post-traumatic stress disorder (PTSD). "My whole body would go into a panic," says Ot'alora, now 42 and a therapist in Lafayette, Colorado.

Desperate, Ot'alora took ecstasy—the drug scientists call MDMA—during a supervised therapy session. That was 17 years ago, when therapists were legally giving it to their clients in small doses to help emotional healing. Those therapy sessions changed Ot'alora's life. For the first time, she says, she felt safe to confront details she'd suppressed for years.

Now, Ot'alora is part of a growing movement to make ecstasy legal again as a controlled medication. Working with the Multidisciplinary Association for Psychedelic

Studies (MAPS), a Florida-based nonprofit group that funds research into therapeutic uses for psychedelic drugs, Ot'alora and others are arguing that the drug has powerful healing potential, particularly for PTSD. And their cause is gaining steam: In November 2001, the U.S. Food and Drug Administration approved a clinical trial of laboratory-made, purified ecstasy for PTSD—the first such trial in almost two decades.

The federal government banned ecstasy in 1985, after it showed up on the club scene. A group of psychiatrists sued to keep the drug legal for research and medical use, but their suit failed. MAPS has revived the debate: The group hopes to reverse the government's decision by funding the controlled studies they say are necessary to give the drug a fair hearing.

The first step toward that goal is a study by South Carolina psychiatrist Michael Mithoefer, M.D., and his wife, Annie, a licensed psychiatric nurse,. They will give 12 patients a single dose of ecstasy in a supervised setting.

A second group will receive a placebo; both groups will undergo conventional therapy afterward. Ot'alora is consulting with the Mithoefers during their trial and working as a therapist for a similar MAPS-funded study under way in Spain. Both studies are part of the association's five-year, $5 million plan to gain approval for ecstasy as a prescription drug.

"I call it Prozac-plus," says MAPS president Rick Doblin, Ph.D. "Prozac gives people a greater comfort level in their own skin. MDMA takes this to the next level." Like Prozac, the drug boosts levels of serotonin, a brain chemical that regulates mood, sleep, and appetite. But while Prozac nudges serotonin levels up just a notch, ecstasy sends them soaring. It also hikes levels of another brain chemical called dopamine. The resulting euphoria lasts about five hours.

"In the same way a glass of wine can loosen you up, a dose of MDMA can help people loosen up to explore their inner selves," says Julie Holland, M.D., a psychiatrist at Bellevue Hospital in New York and editor of *Ecstasy, the Complete Guide: A Comprehensive Look at the Risks and Benefits of MDMA*.

Michael Mithoefer says the drug facilitates therapy by allowing patients to face their traumatic experiences with less fear and shame. "MDMA increases empathy for oneself," he says. "Many people with PTSD erroneously blame themselves, and that guilt is a barrier to healing." If studies like Mithoefer's result in ecstasy being available as a medicine, its uses may not be limited to PTSD. Before it was outlawed, ecstasy had been used in couples therapy; psychologists believed it helped couples discuss their hot-button issues without becoming defensive. Some experts also believe the drug helps with depression. Doblin says MAPS would also like to study the potential of MDMA therapy to help terminally ill patients face death without anxiety and fear.

There are several problems with the push to take ecstasy from the clubs to the therapist's couch, though. For starters, growing evidence suggests that the drug might cause damage to the cells that release serotonin in the brain. "The data in animals are quite compelling," explains George Ricaurte, M.D., a pharmacologist at Johns Hopkins Medical Institution in Baltimore. Ricaurte says that human studies imply the drug causes similar damage in people, though scientists aren't exactly

black market to supermarket?

If ecstasy is approved as a medicine, it may not be the only drug to go from the street to the pharmacy. Here are some others that may one day make the switch.

lysergic acid diethylamide (LSD)
Street name: Acid
The buzz: Hallucinogen made famous by Timothy Leary's motto Turn On, Tune In, Drop Out.
The studies: Studies in the '60s hinted that LSD might lessen anxiety and depression in the terminally ill. Now the Orenda Institute, a psychedelic-studies organization in Baltimore, is hoping for U.S. Food and Drug Administration (FDA) permission to test whether LSD can abate depression and anxiety in cancer patients.

marijuana
Street name: Pot, weed, grass
The buzz: A mellow, euphoric high
The studies: A White House-commissioned report issued in 1999 concluded that marijuana has the potential to ease anxiety, stimulate appetite, calm nausea, and relieve pain. At least nine states have passed medical-marijuana laws, though federal officials are reluctant to legalize it.

psilocybin
Street name: Magic mushrooms or 'shrooms
The buzz: Hallucinogenic effects much like LSD
The studies: At the University of Arizona, an FDA-approved trial is under way to test the effect of psilocybin on obsessive-compulsive disorder. Swiss researchers are planning to test psilocybin's power to treat depression.

Despite ecstasy's potentially **lethal side effects,** proponents say small doses are safe.

sure what the repercussions are yet. A few studies have found moderately impaired memory in frequent ecstasy users, but researchers can't conclusively blame the drug since most heavy ecstasy users tend to also take other illicit drugs.

I don't want MDMA to be a street drug. **I want it to be a medication.** I've personally seen how it can help people.

—Marcela Ot'alora

Still, brain damage is only one potential problem. MDMA decreases the body's ability to regulate temperature. "There are people taking ecstasy at raves and ending up with heat stroke," Holland says. Ecstasy also elevates a hormone that spurs water retention, so when users take in more fluid than normal they can experience cramps, seizures, and potentially fatal brain swelling. And even when ecstasy is taken in a controlled environment, the day after can be tough: The initial serotonin rush seems to temporarily deplete the brain's supply of this neurochemical, leading to a post-ecstasy funk rave-goers call "the terrible Tuesdays."

Despite these potential side effects, Mithoefer contends that ecstasy is safe as long as it's given in small doses under medical supervision. "We already have a lot of evidence showing that there's no toxicity with this dose level administered in a clinical setting," he says. And Holland points out that taking a small dose of ecstasy once or twice in a lifetime in a doctor's office is hardly the same thing as taking it every weekend at a rave. "Like any potent medication," she explains, "there's a dose that's safe and a dose that's not."

But Glen Hanson, Ph.D., the acting director of the National Institute on Drug Abuse, says labeling any dose safe sends a perilous message. "Taking it once a month isn't likely to do permanent damage," he says. "But it's difficult and dangerous to generalize and say that one dose is never harmful." Hanson worries that any endorsement of ecstasy by the government would be interpreted to apply to street ecstasy. And because it's not regulated, there's no way of knowing what's in the ecstasy pills passed around at raves: Some contain amphetamines, for instance.

But these concerns don't soften the resolve of ecstasy's advocates. "I don't want MDMA to be a street drug. I want it to be a medication," Ot'alora says. "I've personally seen how it can help people." For Mithoefer, the movement to test ecstasy is an ethical issue. "I see people every day whose lives are severely disrupted, and they're suffering because of PTSD. Many of these people aren't helped enough by existing treatments," he says. "If you don't allow investigation into something that might help ease people's suffering, you're taking away their rights." ✳

Christie Aschwanden is a Contributing Editor.

Natural Dental Products: They Don't Always Measure Up

Americans' latest natural-is-better bias is now turning up in the dental market. Between 1999 and 2000, spending on toothpastes, rinses, and dental flosses with ingredients like essential oils and herbs tripled to $304 million. As with other back-to-nature trends, "people want things with natural ingredients because they perceive them as healthier," says Peter Jacobsen, Ph.D., D.D.S., professor in the department of pathology and medicine at the University of the Pacific School of Dentistry in San Francisco.

So what are you getting for your money? Au naturel offerings claim to give the same results as traditional counterparts. That's true in most rinses and flosses, like Desert Essence's Tea Tree Oil Dental Floss, which uses the antiseptic properties of tea tree oil to kill germs, and Kiss My Face's Fresh Breath Mouthwash, which is alcohol-free and has a peppermint taste.

But toothpaste is a different story. Ingredients like menthol, eucalyptol, thymol, and mint oil can freshen breath, and chemical-free abrasives like baking soda, silica, clay, or chalk can whiten teeth. But many natural pastes are missing fluoride. (One exception is Tom's of Maine's Natural Fluoride Toothpaste.) "Research has shown that fluoride is the most effective way to stop tooth decay, so it's an important ingredient," Jacobsen says. If you're set on using a paste that doesn't have the element, it's smart to drink fluoridated water. (Beware: Many bottled waters don't have fluoride.)

New Relief for Dentist-Phobes

When Claire Zukerman raves to her friends about a "soothing experience," they might think she's describing a day with Deepak Chopra—but she's actually talking about a trip to the dentist. Massage and reflexology before, during, and after her dentist visits have replaced Novocain and Valium, once staples of Zukerman's regular checkups. "For the first time in my life, I'm not petrified and uncomfortable at the dentist," she says.

According to dental associations nationwide, an increasing number of dentists are adopting alternative techniques to prove that drilling and pampering can indeed mix. Hypnosis, acupuncture, and yogic breathing are increasingly popular and can help some people, says Matthew Messina, D.D.S., the consumer adviser for the American Dental Association. Patients can even find anxiety relief with gimmicks, such as virtual-reality glasses and headphones to distract the open-jawed from the drill.

So will Novocain be needled out? "Not at all," Messina says. "If Novocain and other dental anesthetics work for you, stick with them. Alternative treatments are good for those who don't want chemical solutions for pain or for dentist-phobes who need an added dose of distraction to quell anxiety." Call your local dental association for information on practitioners in your area.

KAVA CAUTION

The herbal supplement kava has been touted as a natural antidote to stress and insomnia. But users may be better off unwinding in a hot bath instead. After German scientists reported the supplement may cause liver damage, the Swiss government pulled it off the market, and British officials asked herbal-food stores to voluntarily pull the supplement from their aisles. On this side of the pond, the U.S. Food and Drug Administration is investigating kava complaints.

Link Found Between Depression and Low Bone Density

WOMEN SUFFERING from depression often say that they can feel it in their bones—and they may be right. Low bone-mineral density (BMD), the hallmark of osteoporosis, is more common in depressed people than in the general population.

To better understand a possible link, the National Institute of Mental Health (NIMH) has launched a study to monitor stress hormones and bone loss in 160 depressed women ages 21 to 45. "We know that depression is a disease not just of the soul and mind but also of the body," explains lead researcher Giovanni Cizza, M.D., Ph.D. "The question is if there is something intrinsic to depression

that might affect bones." One hypothesis is that cortisol, the "fight or flight" hormone known to be elevated in depressed people, may contribute to bone loss. Depression is also associated with decreased estrogen and human growth hormone levels, which can possibly weaken bones.

These findings do not necessarily mean depression is an osteoporosis sentence—it's only one risk factor. But women who suffer from depression should be aware of the extra risk and take a few preventive steps. For those under the age of 50, making sure to get 1,000 milligrams of calcium a day and cutting out other risk

factors, such as smoking, can help. So can starting to exercise, especially since depressed women tend to be less active, says Suzette Evans, Ph.D., associate professor of clinical neuroscience in psychiatry at Columbia University.

If you suffer from depression and have other osteoporosis risk factors, such as menopause or maternal history of the disease, ask your doctor for a bone-density test, the most reliable predictor of osteoporosis. The good news is that depression and osteoporosis are very treatable, especially when caught early. "The key is to be aware of the connections and make the diagnosis," Cizza says.

the Medicine of Music

Can music heal you? Many doctors think so.
That's why they're prescribing it for everything from
breast cancer to labor pains. Listen in on the trend.

BY ELLEN MAZO

PHOTOGRAPHY BY MONICA BUCK

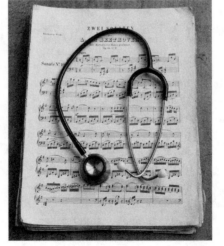

Gary Wieczorek stares blankly from his wheelchair at the two women standing in his 11th floor hospital room. "How are you?" one of them asks. He barely nods in response. Just minutes later, however, as music therapist Aimee Kaufman strums her guitar and Pittsburgh Symphony violist Penny Anderson plays her viola, Wieczorek is singing, *"Doe, a deer, a female deer, re, a drop of golden sun ..."*

A recent victim of a devastating stroke, the 42-year-old lawyer is struggling to relearn how to speak the words in his head. The process is a tough one, except when he sings. In speech, his consonants may be slurred, but when set to music—*"mi, a name I call myself"*—they are clear enough to be understood. Wieczorek becomes visibly more relaxed. The three move on to more lyrics from

The Sound of Music, then they end the 30-minute session with "Zippity Do-Dah, Zippity Day!"

"Be sure to tell your speech therapist how much better you're doing on your sounds," Kaufman says to Wieczorek as she and Anderson pack up their instruments and sheet music to move on to the next patient, a gunshot victim in the rehab unit at the University of Pittsburgh Medical Center's Montefiore Hospital.

Not long ago, guitars and violas would have seemed completely out of place in a hospital, where scalpels and syringes are the typical instruments of choice. But that's all changing. In medical settings throughout the country, music therapy is gaining ground as a legitimate and powerful way to treat patients with conditions ranging from breast cancer to labor pains. The American Music Therapy Association (AMTA) boasts around 4,000 members in North America, and about 200 music therapists are on staff in U.S. hospitals. More than 70 colleges and universities offer undergraduate and/or master's degrees in music therapy; others, such as Temple University in Philadelphia, New York University, and Lesley University in Cambridge, Massachusetts, offer Ph.D.s.

For Penny Anderson, music therapy has a personal side: The 52-year-old used music in her own experience with breast cancer before she started performing for patients at area hospitals. Now she plays her viola regularly for women recovering from ovarian- and breast-cancer surgeries, and for their families and friends in the waiting rooms.

One afternoon after her diagnosis in the summer of 1999, Anderson, who has been with the Pittsburgh Symphony since 1980, turned on Pink Floyd's *Dark Side of the Moon* and searched for the song "Money." The music made her laugh when she thought she had little to laugh about. Not only was she dealing with a life-threatening disease, she had to miss the symphony's European tour that fall. So Anderson tried comforting herself by listening to jigs and reels by the Chieftains and other Celtic musicians—the same pieces she would have performed on tour in Ireland. It worked.

"The music was powerful. It calmed and supported me and helped me deal with my roller-coaster emotions," Anderson says. Following her mastectomy, she endured four rounds of chemotherapy by listening to music—from Gregorian chants and Bobby McFerrin tunes to the a cappella strains of Chanticleer—before and during her treatments. "I found this impressive resource inside me," Anderson says. "Music was building my confidence in my ability to heal."

The effects weren't just emotional. After the mastectomy, Anderson didn't require any post-op pain medicine. And in May 2001, while undergoing six hours of breast-reconstruction surgery, she surprised William Swartz, M.D., her surgeon at Shadyside Hospital in Pittsburgh, when she required smaller doses of anesthesia than expected. "I can't say for sure that the music was the only reason," he says, "but I do think it helped reduce Penny's anxiety. She was very relaxed and very calm."

While no one has absolutely proven that music therapy heals, there is compelling evidence that it helps.

get in tune

Do you know someone who might benefit from music therapy? To find out more about the treatment, contact the American Music Therapy Association (AMTA) at 301-589-3300, visit www.musictherapy.org, or send an e-mail to info@musictherapy.org. You can also get information from www.nccam.nih.gov, the National Center for Complementary and Alternative Medicine's Web site.

To find a music therapist in your area, contact your local hospital, rehabilitation center, or the AMTA.

Rates for individual sessions vary by region, from $40 to $58 an hour. Music therapy performed in a hospital or rehabilitation setting is often covered by insurance when prescribed by a physician. There is rarely outpatient reimbursement from federal or private insurers.

To find out who's qualified, get in touch with the AMTA, which sets standards for music therapists. Although there are different certification levels, the important thing is that a therapist is board certified. Ask if she is before using her.

*Advocates say that **music therapy works** because it helps people relax and reduces the brain's perception of stress.*

In one study at the Center for Biomedical Research in Music Therapy at Colorado State University, stroke and Parkinson's patients were offered music therapy as part of their recovery. Those who used the treatment increased their stride length by 100 percent compared with those who didn't listen to music during recovery. The rhythmic beat of music seems to help patients develop their physical stability and movement. Doctors are also using music for children with learning disabilities who are trying to build their language skills.

Music-therapy advocates believe the main benefit is that it helps people relax, which in turn triggers the release of endorphins, the body's natural painkillers. "Music reduces the perception of pain and reduces the way the brain responds to stress," explains Bruce S. Rabin, M.D., medical director of the Health Enhancement Program for the University of Pittsburgh Medical Center, which offers stress-reduction sessions. "It helps block out or redirect stress hormones, lowering your blood pressure and easing your anxiety."

Rabin is such a believer in music therapy that he is leading an effort to use the treatment in all hospitals in the University of Pittsburgh Medical Center system. He says that music doesn't just help patients, but employees too. "The employees are entranced," Rabin says. "When they hear the music in the hallways, they feel better as well."

But of course, it's the patients who matter most. On this day at Montefiore in Pittsburgh, Kaufman and Anderson move to the room of the 21-year-old gunshot victim, whom doctors believe will have to spend the rest of his life in a nursing home receiving 24-hour care. Like

Wieczorek, the stroke victim, this patient is working to get his speech back.

Kaufman taps lightly on a drum while Anderson strums the strings of her viola. The young man then accompanies them in a faint, melodic voice, singing along in lyrics of his own:

Having trouble taking care of myself.
Having trouble with my eyes,
Having trouble with my arms,
Having trouble with my legs.
But I'm still wise,
And I'll beat this thing,
'Cause I'm gonna laugh,
And I'm gonna sing. ✳

Ellen Mazo has been a health writer for 15 years. Her book, **The Immune Advantage,** *was published in January 2002.*

Be Your Own Alternative Healer

You don't need to find a healer from the Far East—or even Deepak Chopra—to benefit from alternative remedies. "Alternative medicine emphasizes self-awareness and self-care and is well-suited for home," says James S. Gordon, M.D., chair of the White House commission on complementary- and alternative-medicine policy. Try your hand at one of these four practices in the privacy of your home:

1 Hypnosis: If your idea of hypnosis is to be lulled into a stupor, you'd be better off reading *War and Peace.* With Nike-inspired messages like "I'm a winner," the meditative mantras of self-hypnosis are empowering. Studies show it's effective in

reducing stress or managing pain. You can try entrancing yourself with the book *Effective Self-Hypnosis* by C. Alexander Simpkins.

2 Reflexology: Discover the pleasure spots on your hands and feet that, when touched, act like stress switches: Touch one spot and turn off the tension in another body part. For more information, check out www.reflexology-research.com, read *My Reflexologist Says Feet Don't Lie* by Kevin and Barbara Kunz, or pick up a pair of Season's reflexology socks that mark the key spots to rub (call 800-776-9677 for details).

3 Reiki: It sounds hokey, but this Japanese healing technique claims

that the hands possess energy that can reduce anxiety. A Reiki follower might simply hold her hands an inch away from your head for several minutes to cure a headache. For more healing tips, visit www.reiki.org or call 800-332-8112.

4 Acupressure: Like acupuncture minus the needles, acupressure can help press away your aches and pains. Simply apply gentle but firm pressure with your hands several times a day to acupressure points, holding for one to three minutes. If you would like to gain a better understanding, read *Instant Emotional Healing: Acupressure for the Emotions* by George J. Pratt and Peter T. Lambrou or you can visit www.acupressure.com.

COMING SOON:
A New Way to Relieve Asthma Suffering

ASTHMATICS may soon breathe a lot easier: A breakthrough treatment could be available within a year.

Current asthma medications work by reducing the inflammation that makes breathing a chore, but the new drug Xolair (omalizumab) operates at a more basic level. It short-circuits the allergic reactions that often can trigger asthma attacks.

"In clinical trials, Xolair markedly reduced the number of attacks in people with allergic asthma," says Jonathan Corren, M.D., associate clinical professor of medicine at the University of California at Los Angeles. "And 40 percent of adults studied were able to stop using inhaled steroids."

Allergies are the most common cause of asthma, responsible for some 60 to 70 percent of cases. Xolair releases mouse-derived antibodies, which wipe out the chemicals that jump-start symptoms such as sneezing and wheezing.

But Xolair will not be the first-line treatment for these sufferers, Corren says. The medication is inconvenient (users must receive injections every two to four weeks depending on their weight and antibody count) and will likely be pricey. Still, Xolair will be a good alternative for sufferers who just can't shake their asthma symptoms with existing meds.

Stick It to Me

In a recent German study of more than 40,000 patients suffering from ailments ranging from headaches to back pain, 90 percent found relief through acupuncture treatments.

Popular Attractions

Eleven percent of households own magnetic-therapy products, such as bracelets, wraps, shoe insoles, or mattress toppers.

—*International Housewares Association*

ginger: the supplement that can combat arthritis pain

Ginger isn't just for ale. It may also be one of the best ways to treat osteoarthritis pain. University of Miami Medical School scientists found that a dietary supplement made of ginger extract offered as much relief as conventional painkillers, without the side effects—old news to practitioners of Chinese and Indian medicine, who have been using the root for more than 2,500 years.

the foot bone's connected to the...shoulder bone?

Got a stiff shoulder? Rub circles just below the outside edge of your little toe. According to the ancient technique of reflexology, gentle pressure applied to points on the feet can stimulate healing in other body parts. For more, pick up Denise Whichello Brown's new book, *Reflexology Basics.*

The Truth Behind the New Quick-Fix Therapy

EMDR is a new controversial treatment for stress and emotional traumas. It's gaining widespread popularity. But does it work?

BY TIMOTHY GOWER

Anita Anderson tried all sorts of ways to relieve her fear of flying. She listened to soft music before takeoff, made herself think soothing thoughts—nothing worked. Then, the 52-year-old from Brewster, Massachusetts, learned that a psychotherapist friend of hers had been trained to perform EMDR, a new treatment that allegedly relieves anxiety quickly. She promptly made an appointment.

The first portion of the 30-minute session was standard psychotherapy—some talk and relaxation exercises, mostly. Then the appointment took an unconventional turn. The therapist asked Anderson to stare at a board studded with a horizontal row of tiny lightbulbs and follow the lights as they blinked on and off, creating a left-to-right effect. After a few minutes, the therapist turned off the light board, the two talked some more, and the session was over.

About two months later, Anderson flew to Italy with her husband and, for the most part, kept her cool. She thinks EMDR did the trick. "I don't know how it works," she says, "but it did."

> After talking, patients are asked to stare at a board studded with a horizontal row of tiny lightbulbs and **follow the lights** as they blink on and off, creating a left-to-right effect.

More and more psychotherapy patients agree with Anderson. Developed in the late 1980s by California psychologist Francine Shapiro, Ph.D., EMDR—which stands for "eye-movement desensitization and reprocessing"—is rapidly gaining popularity. Shapiro estimates that over 2 million patients have received the treatment, and the number of therapists trained to use it has more than doubled since 1995, to about 40,000 worldwide. EMDR is now regularly offered to patients in some Veterans Administration hospitals. Although created to treat emotional trauma such as post-traumatic stress disorder (PTSD), it's also being applied to a range of conditions, including depression, phobias, and eating disorders. Some athletes even undergo the treatment to improve physical performance.

But despite this new popularity, EMDR has many outspoken critics. They say that the eye movements and the other similar, alternating-sensory stimulation used by the EMDR therapists—such as electronic tones or hand taps—are nothing but hocus-pocus. And that's just the beginning. The ongoing squabble between these two factions gets ugly—fast.

Observers on both sides of the EMDR controversy disagree passionately about how the therapy works.

Proponents speculate that moving the eyes back and forth may trigger a mental process similar to REM sleep and that the brain rewires itself in this state in order to store long-term memories. Shapiro theorizes that alternately stimulating the left and right hemispheres of a person's brain while he or she concentrates on the traumatic event may speed up the ability to "process," or lay to rest a disturbing memory. She feels that these memories, which are rooted deep in the brain, may be the cause of many kinds of psychological distress.

Other psychologists believe EMDR works for reasons that have nothing to do with its signature eye movements. Matthew Friedman, M.D., director of the National Center for PTSD in White River Junction, Vermont, and one of the nation's foremost experts on traumatic stress, says EMDR is appealing because patients don't have to find the words to describe their inner pain. "I think there's clear evidence that the rhythmic movements don't make a difference," Friedman says, "but I think EMDR does work." The therapy's strength, he says, may lie in what it lacks: a lot of talking. "It may be a gentler form of therapy because the patient doesn't have to make the traumatic material explicit, doesn't have to recite it. He or she just has to think about it."

But skeptics maintain that the treatment is nothing more than a mixed bag of established psychotherapeutic approaches with some worthless distractions added to make it seem new and special. One outspoken doubter, University of Arkansas psychologist Jeffrey M. Lohr, Ph.D., sums up Shapiro's claims in this way: "Nonsense. There's no neurological evidence that anything changes in the brain due to EMDR."

Lohr and several of his colleagues have published a series of papers in psychology journals arguing, among other things, that the eye movements used in EMDR don't play any role in the treatment of psychological problems. In one study, for instance, a group of combat veterans who were suffering from emotional trauma underwent classic EMDR. Meanwhile, researchers gave a similar group of veterans a nearly identical program of therapy, only these participants were told to keep their eyes still. In the end, both of the treatments worked equally well. Lohr says his group also analyzed several similar studies and "uniformly found that there is nothing special about the eye movements."

The skeptics' criticisms of EMDR don't stop there. Emory University psychologist Scott Lilienfeld, Ph.D., for instance, suggests that Shapiro exaggerates the benefits of EMDR. He notes that many of the glowing studies she cites compared patients who were receiving EMDR with patients waiting to receive treatment, for example. "In other words, EMDR is better than nothing," Lilienfeld says, adding that these patients may have felt better simply because they received treatment—any treatment—period.

Lingering doubts about EMDR's effectiveness infuriate Shapiro. "It's extremely frustrating to hear these same statements over and over again," she said during one of several phone interviews in which she defended EMDR against its critics. She insists that researchers who have found no benefit to EMDR either performed it wrong, studied too few people, or allowed personal bias to skew their results.

Lohr suggests that Shapiro is so vehement about EMDR because of the money that's at stake. She has a tremendous business interest to protect, he says. For one thing, if it becomes clear that eye movements have no therapeutic worth, therapists might be less inclined to sign up for the $450 weekend-long certification seminars offered by Shapiro's EMDR Institute. (Therapists must attend two seminars to achieve "full therapeutic utilization and understanding of the myriad applications of EMDR," according to the Institute's Web site.)

Despite the questions about EMDR, many therapists—and their clients—are convinced it works. For Anita Anderson, it doesn't matter whether she had to lie back on a couch and talk about her childhood or simply stare at some flashing lights, as long as she was able to fly to Italy without sweaty palms and runaway anxiety. "If it took bells and whistles, that's OK with me," she says. "If the end result was the same, who cares what I had to do?" ✳

> One patient who underwent EMDR therapy is unfazed by the contoversy. "If the end result was the same," she says, **"who cares what I had to do?"**

Contributing editor Timothy Gower authored A Doctor's Guide to Herbs and Supplements.

Q+A
Check with Your Doc Before Taking this Herb

I'm thinking about taking Saint-John's-wort to get me out of a funk I can't shake. Is it worth a try?

NOT WITHOUT seeing a doctor first. Before taking anything to lift a dark mood, you need to figure out if you're depressed, and only a health professional can tell you that for sure. Your doctor can then help you determine if Saint-John's-wort may help.

The herb has gotten a bad rap lately. A study in the *Journal of the American Medical Association* said it was only as effective as a placebo in people with moderately severe depression. But people who tend to find the most benefit from it—those with mild to moderate depression—weren't looked at in these recent studies. If your doctor thinks you fall into these categories and you don't want to take prescription meds, you may want to give the herb a try. Some people prefer the supplement to drugs because it's inexpensive, doesn't require a prescription, and may have fewer side effects. Look for the words "standardized extract" on the label. This means the product is likely to have an effective amount of active ingredient.

Read Labels to Find Real Aromatherapy

Since your nose doesn't always know, check the labels of aromatherapy products to tell the real thing from synthetic poseurs. If you see the following info, you've got good scents:

- the country of origin
- how the plant was grown (wild or farmed)
- the plant parts and method of extraction
- the common and botanical names for the source of the essential oil

ALOE ALERT:
For Skin Only, Not the Stomach!

Some alternative-healing Web sites may claim that drinking aloe juice will cure your woes, but they lack one important factor: evidence that it works. In fact, aloe contains laxative compounds that can cause cramping or diarrhea. Aloe's healing power is strictly external—it's still great for soothing cuts and burns.

BEYOND BONES:
the calcium health kick

New research suggests the bone-building mineral calcium also protects against heart disease and colon cancer. In a study published in *The American Journal of Medicine*, scientists found that women who took 1,000 milligrams of calcium daily had four times higher levels of high-density lipoprotein (HDL, good cholesterol) after 12 months than the placebo group.

In a separate study, Harvard University researchers found that people who consumed at least 1,250 milligrams of calcium a day over a decade (most used supplements to reach that amount) were less likely to develop certain types of colon cancer. For a calcium boost, try eating some of these foods: yogurt, broccoli, bok choy, dried figs, kale, sardines, and almonds.

The average woman gets about 625 milligrams of calcium a day. The recommended amount for adults under 50 is 1,000 milligrams; 1,200 for those over 50.

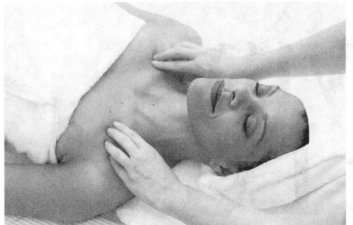

A Guide to Massage Techniques:
choose one that's right for you

Because spa massage menus offer more options than the beverage list at Starbucks, we asked Brenda L. Griffith, president-elect of the American Massage Therapy Association, and Margaret Avery Moon, director of the Desert Institute of the Healing Arts in Tucson, Arizona, to make sense of all this kneading—to make sure you get rubbed the right way.

TYPE	PREPARE FOR	WHAT IT CAN DO	PRIME CANDIDATES
Swedish massage	A rhythmic rubdown with long, gliding, soothing movements from head to toe	• Relax your body and mind •Soothe aches and pains • Enhance blood flow to tissue	Kink-necked cubicle slaves and migraine-prone managers
Sports massage	Serious kneading; deep, targeted movements to really work sore spots and tight muscle groups	• Help prevent injury and soothe muscle aches after an overambitious workout (moves lactic-acid buildup)	Sore weekend warriors and the slightly masochistic (this is an intense rub)
Shiatsu (or Zen Shiatsu)	Careful probing (with thumbs, knuckles, elbows, and even feet) of pressure points all over the body (*shi* means "finger"; *atsu* means "pressure")	• Ease aches and pains • Claims to free internal "blockages" of all kinds (this is the laxative on the massage roster)	Weary world-travelers and angst-ridden writers who need to work through creative blocks
Thai massage	A two-hour mix of stretching, reflexology-like palm massage, and partner yoga (sometimes your masseuse is almost pretzeled around your body)	Help increase joint flexibility, stretch taut muscles, and work out stubborn knots; realign the whole body	The most uptight types and the more modest minded (you keep your clothes on)
Hot stone massage	Warm basalt stones placed on pressure points, on tense muscles, and between your toes	Rub you into deep relaxation; the warmth and weight loosen tight muscles and joints	Presidents of start-up dot-coms and java junkies seeking "profound calm"
Chi Nei Tsang (or Tsung)	Gentle massaging of the entire abdominal area, starting at the belly button and working the energy of the internal organs (translation: outer body relaxation)	"Reduces built-up internal congestion"—massage lingo that means it helps you let out any pent-up tension that might be tying your body in knots	Holistic health nuts in search of detoxification and emotional cleansing
Pregnancy massage	Gentle, soothing kneading of ballooning bellies, overburdened backs, and sore shoulders while reclined on a special table with a hole for expanded tummies	Help reduce stress, relieve strain on back and shoulders, increase mom-to-be's body awareness; claims to keep stretch marks at bay	Pregnant women and their partners (who can learn some take-home tips)

Living Out Loud

A year ago, Sarah, Todd, and Samantha McBride were deaf to the world around them. Now, thanks to a medical miracle, they're discovering the sound of family.

BY NELL BERNSTEIN

PHOTOGRAPHY BY ROBERT HOLMGREN

Two-year-old Samantha McBride sits on the floor of her Menlo Park, California, living room, scribbling with a crayon as she waits for her father to take her to preschool. When the loud blare of sirens from a fire engine racing down the street fills the room, Samantha's eyes widen with excitement. She taps her earlobe and looks up at her father to see if he heard what she did. Todd McBride nods, and she returns a mischievous grin, as if they've got a secret.

In a sense, they do. While watching a child discover the world is enough to fascinate any parent, the sensation is particularly strong for Todd and his wife, Sarah. Until summer 2001, Samantha wouldn't have been aware of the sirens outside, nor would her parents. All three of them were deaf.

Now, the entire McBride family is making its way—tentatively but avidly—into a brand new world filled with sound, thanks to a device called a cochlear implant. Samantha is finding out there is nothing funnier than a barking dog, that the Rolling Stones records her grandparents still listen to are better than any Barney sing-along CD. Now 28-year-old Sarah knows that her husband speaks more softly than she does, that the heating vent in her living room makes an irritating rattle, and that dinner-table conversation is punctuated by the clatter of silverware on plates. Todd, 38, has discovered that a car makes a clicking sound when you signal a turn, and that a tiny cricket—multiplied by thousands—can create a powerful racket. He's also learned that there's no sound more gorgeous than his daughter's laugh.

And although Samantha is only 2 years old, she is, in a sense, responsible for bringing the McBride family into this noisy new world. Without her, it's likely that Todd and Sarah would never have made the decision that has drastically changed all of their lives.

Before Samantha's birth in September 1999, Sarah and Todd had little reason to consider making any radical changes in their lives. "Todd and I never even talked about cochlear implants until Sammy came into our life," recalls Sarah, who met Todd at a friend's birthday party seven years earlier. Both had learned to speak and read lips as children, and to sign as teenagers. They were able to communicate with each other and their many deaf friends, and—to a lesser but sufficient extent—the larger world.

That's not to say that life was easy for the couple. Sarah and Todd both struggled in school, from elementary through college. It was hard for them to understand teachers' lectures when they were still learning to read lips, and school districts at that time weren't required to provide for students with disabilities. Sarah, who now works as a job-placement specialist for the deaf, has still not finished college. Dressed in jeans and a white V-neck T-shirt, she has shoulder-length blond hair and an animated face. "I told a high-school teacher I wanted a sign-language interpreter, and she told me they couldn't afford it," she says. "It still makes me mad. All my life I missed so much in school."

It took Todd, who was recently laid off from his job as a computer-company accountant, 10 years to get his college degree. Although he speaks more slowly than his wife, Todd is a determined communicator: He enunciates each word with focus, pausing frequently to make sure he is understood. He says he and Sarah wanted to spare Samantha the struggles they faced as deaf people in a culture tuned to the hearing.

"Your world is the hearing world," he says over the patter of his daughter's feet on the hardwood floor. "Mine is the deaf world. I want Samantha to be successful in your world."

Spending time in the McBride household is a little like visiting Zurich or Montreal, a multilingual city where the residents shift easily from one language to another. Todd and Sarah communicate privately in a combination of staccato speech and extravagant gestures—a marital

Todd has discovered that a car makes a clicking sound when you signal a turn, and that insects can create a powerful racket.

He's also learned that there's no sound more gorgeous than his daughter's laugh.

Doctors showed the McBrides the pictures: The line was flat.

Samantha's birth brought her parents' deafness into sharp focus. Instead of waking up at night to the sound of their baby crying, they were roused by a light flashing in their bedroom—a strobe-like signal that their child needed them, activated by cries they could not hear. As Samantha became old enough to begin trying to talk, they saw her grow increasingly frustrated when she was unable to communicate what she wanted. They also worried about her safety; she would not hear them if, for example, they called out a warning as she ran into a street.

Still, Sarah hated the idea of putting her daughter through the procedure of getting a cochlear implant: Surgeons would administer general anesthesia, make an incision from her ear to her hairline, and then insert a quarter-sized receiver under her skin. After waiting a month or so for her to heal, doctors would hook a microphone over Samantha's ear and turn on the implant. Sound would travel from the microphone to a speech processor, which converts the sound into a digital signal that the implanted receiver can read. This coded signal travels into the fluid-filled cochlea in the inner ear, then to the brain, which processes it as

Spending time in the McBride household

is a little like visiting Zurich or Montreal, a multilingual city where the residents shift easily from one language to another.

dialect incomprehensible to outsiders. "Todd never yells," Sarah says, smiling. "We always sign when we fight." With their daughter and hearing friends, they speak slowly and carefully, their speech still carrying the exaggerated cadences of the deaf. When Sarah finds it difficult to make herself understood, stumbling over a name or a proper noun, she picks up one of the crayons her daughter has left scattered on the coffee table and spells out the words. As for Samantha, she is fluent in the simple words and phrases that comprise a 2-year-old's basic vocabulary, but also lets loose long streams of baby jargon that only her parents can decipher.

Sarah says that the decision to get a cochlear implant for Samantha wasn't easy. For starters, Todd and Sarah had to accept the fact that their daughter was deaf. Doctors had never known the cause of either parent's deafness, and the condition did not run in their families. So when audiologists tested Samantha just two days after her birth and told the McBrides she had failed the test, "I said 'No, no, no,'" Sarah remembers. "I thought they were just assuming she was deaf because her parents were."

But the baby failed a second test, then a third. Finally, at only three weeks old, Samantha underwent a procedure that measures brain-wave response to sound.

comprehensible sound. The results, doctors told the McBrides, would be remarkable. If everything went according to plan, Samantha would be able to hear the same range of sounds as anyone else, from the tiny trill of a sparrow to the large boom of a bass drum.

After one more brain-wave hearing test confirmed that Samantha was deaf, Sarah called Becky Highlander, an audiologist at the California Ear Institute at Stanford University. "We want the whole family to get implants," she told Highlander. "We want to be the same, for Samantha."

On the morning of June 16, 2001, Sarah and Todd both entered Stanford Hospital for surgery. They would have it first, with Samantha following one month later. This way, Todd and Sarah would have time to adjust to the implants and help their daughter with the transition. As nurses prepped her for the 8 a.m. procedure, Sarah was terrified, but not for herself. All she could think about was the knowledge that her daughter would be next.

Todd came out of surgery with a mild headache, but although her surgery went well, Sarah woke up in excruciating pain, "like a gunshot to my head." Again, she thought of Samantha. How could she subject her to this?

Highlander assured the McBrides that babies respond better than adults. "She promised me Sammy wouldn't be in pain," Sarah says, her voice rising with anxiety even at the memory.

As the weeks passed, Sarah grew increasingly nervous. The night before Samantha's surgery on July 16, Sarah told Todd she just couldn't go through with it. "We have

to get it over with," he answered. Samantha, who was not allowed to eat or drink before the surgery, was crying for milk and could not sleep. The whole family stayed awake until 6 a.m., when it was time to leave for the hospital.

Despite Sarah's fears, the baby's surgery went smoothly. It took only 45 minutes, and Samantha woke up confused but comfortable. It wasn't long before she was playing with her toys, paging through a book, and reveling in the attention from her grandparents, aunt, teacher, speech therapist, and doctor—all of whom gathered around her hospital bed to welcome her into a new world.

On July 25, Sarah and Todd turned on their implants for the first time while Samantha continued to recover from surgery. Sarah jumped back and ripped off the microphone when the first rush of sound hit her. "It was awful," she recalls. "I heard water running, cars driving by, Samantha yelling—it was too much information at the same time."

As the days passed, though, the chaos began to sort itself out, one sound emerging after another—the audible world growing comprehensible as it became familiar. In a speech-therapy class, Todd and Sarah learned how to recognize words and sentences by listening, rather than by reading lips. A month after activating her implant, Sarah attended a bridal shower and sat down at a table with 40 other women. "Each one introduced herself and said how she knew the bride," Sarah recalls, "and I understood everyone. Before, I would have understood only three or four people."

Simple, direct communication
is something Todd and Sarah never had as children. They don't want Sammy to experience the same struggles of growing up deaf.

"Everyone has a different voice," she says. "My mom, my sister, and aunt sound the same. My manager at work—her voice is smooth and gentle. Samantha's voice is so soft and beautiful—a girl's voice."

When Todd lost his keys, Sarah was thrilled to find them while doing the laundry—**she heard them jingling** in a pants pocket.

Todd found the transition more difficult. The aural barrage made him dizzy, and he struggled to make sense of it. But Sarah helped, reminding him of why he'd gone through the surgery; they were doing this for their daughter as much as for themselves, and Samantha's implant would be activated soon. The first time Sarah used a telephone, she turned around and told Todd, "You need to work hard because you need to be able to do this, too." As the weeks progressed, with the support from his speech therapists, Todd's comprehension steadily improved.

Still, the only assurance that they'd made the right decision would be knowing that Samantha's surgery had worked. Exactly four weeks after her parents turned on their implants, Samantha sat in Becky Highlander's office, waiting for hers to be activated. At first, Highlander set the implant to a low volume, and Samantha barely reacted. Highlander turned up the volume. Startled, Samantha burst into tears and leapt into her father's arms.

But it wasn't long before Samantha was "looking around, starting to talk more, listening to other people," Sarah says. Soon, she was running to the kitchen windowsill—where the three devices sit in a tangle of wires, batteries, and chargers when they aren't in use—the moment she got out of bed in the morning. At a school for deaf children in Redwood City, which she has been attending since infancy, Samantha

gets therapy aimed specifically at helping implant users learn to hear and understand speech. Her comprehension is growing each day, and her personality is evolving, too. "Before, I'd make her something for breakfast, and she'd get mad," Sarah says. "She would try to tell me what she wanted, but I didn't understand. Now if she asks for eggs and oatmeal, she gets eggs and oatmeal."

That kind of simple, direct communication is something Todd and Sarah never had as children, and Sarah has not forgotten the struggles of growing up deaf. "At Thanksgiving or Christmas with my family, everyone would be talking and I would feel left out," she says. "Or people would be discussing issues at a party and I never understood them. But Sammy won't miss anything."

In the months after their implants were turned on, the McBrides began to explore the audible world together. They went to the Mexican coast, where all three heard the sound of the surf for the first time. When Todd lost his keys, Sarah was thrilled to find them while doing the laundry—she heard them jingling in a pants pocket. They turned the volume up on their television (they still use closed captioning, too, out of habit). And, like those born with hearing intact, they quickly discovered that not all sounds are welcome: They had to install soundproof windows to block the noise of traffic on the busy thoroughfare outside. And whenever the family is trying to watch its

budget, Sarah knows to avoid stores with soothing New Age background music; "it makes me want to stay in the store longer and tempts me to shop more!"

In the midst of all this thrilling cacophony, a single sound stands out: Samantha's voice. "I love to hear her talking, saying 'Mommy' and 'Daddy,'" Sarah says. "That's my favorite."

A little after noon, Samantha comes home from school. The day that started with the wail of fire engines outside is now filled with a different sound: the noise of Samantha's shrieks as she bursts through the door. They are the piercing wails of a child who is ready for her nap. Todd trails behind his daughter into the room, and Sarah gives her a hug while lowering the volume on her transmitter; when Samantha is tired, the sound of life can be overwhelming.

Samantha snuggles beside her father in an overstuffed chair. "I feel so proud," he says, "knowing she will be fine when she grows up."

Sarah picks up Samantha from the chair and carries her into her bedroom to play before her nap. Laughter emanates from the back of the house. "Can you hear her? I'm so happy," Todd says, cradling his hands across his heart in a gesture that means love. Even now, there are times when signs and silence say the most. ✳

> For Sarah and Todd, the sweetest sound is their child's voice, saying "Mommy" and "Daddy."

Based in Berkeley, California, Nell Bernstein has also written for magazines such as O *and* Marie Claire.

New Study Reveals That Talking with Your Hands is Actually a Good Thing

SCIENCE is rewriting social etiquette. Talking with your hands, once ranked right up there with playing with your food or talking back to elders on the list of things to avoid, is actually beneficial: It makes thinking easier, according to a new study. Researchers at the University of Chicago found that people who moved their hands while talking were able to remember more than people who kept their hands still.

Gesturing seems to make speech less of an effort, which in this case probably left more mental resources available for memory, say the researchers. If you want to tap into this phenomenon, don't make a conscious effort to gesture. Just tell yourself it's OK to use your hands and let nature take its course. "These are just spontaneous, natural movements," says lead study author and psychologist Susan Goldin-Meadow, Ph.D. "I tell people, don't worry about what you look like, just gesture up a storm."

VitalStats

89 | Percent of Americans who believe genetics to be one of the top three causes of cancer

5 to 10 | Percent of cancers attributable to genetics

72 | Percent of Americans who believe pesticide residues cause cancer

47 | Percent who believe breast implants cause cancer

35 | Percent who believe power lines cause cancer

0 | Types of cancers proven to be caused by pesticides, breast implants, or power lines

22 | Percent annual increase in Americans who use elliptical fitness machines

1 | Rank of elliptical machines among the 10 fastest-growing gym activities

540 | Approximate calories burned per hour by a 125-pound person on an elliptical machine

360 | Approximate calories burned on a step machine

660 | Approximate calories burned swimming freestyle

$400 billion | Amount Americans charge annually

$50 billion | Amount charged annually for related finance fees

$8,123 | Average credit-card balance carried each month by each American household with a card

60 | Percent of Americans ages 18 to 29 with a preference for spending over saving money

37 | Percent of Americans over 65 with a preference for spending money

32 | Percent of Americans who worry about paying household monthly bills

Sources: American Institute for Cancer Research, SGMA Motley Fool, RAM Research Group, Gallup Poll

How E-Mail Can Help You Get the Medical Answers You Need

Don't feel like explaining over the phone to your physician—and your eavesdropping co-workers—about the complications of your Prozac dose? Try communicating by e-mail. About 25 percent of doctors who log on to the Internet regularly use e-mail to communicate with patients, according to the American Medical Association. "E-mail is more spontaneous than letter writing and more permanent than speaking on the phone," says Daniel Sands, M.D., of Beth Israel Deaconess Medical Center in Boston, who co-authored guidelines on e-mail communication with patients. Sands offers these tips on making e-doctoring more effective for everyone.

When to log on: E-mail is ideal for follow-up medical questions, medication and treatment instructions, and interpretations of lab-test results.

In the subject header: Don't write, "Am I pregnant?" Instead write, "Question from your patient." You should avoid sending highly sensitive materials through e-mail, since they can be intercepted or accidentally sent to the wrong person.

In the message: Write a clear and concise message that explains your medical condition, any unusual symptoms you're experiencing, and drug reactions. If you find yourself writing a long message, a telephone call or appointment might be a better way to get in touch with your doctor.

Before you hit "send": Include your full name—your doctor may not be able to figure it out from your e-mail address. Also include your phone number.

Getting the most: When you reply to e-mails, include the text of the preceding messages so you and your doctor are on the same page.

When to log off: Of course, in an emergency, forgo the keyboard and call your doctor immediately.

chapter 2

the female body

finding the treatments that are right for you

Doctors Learn to Stop Treating a Woman Like a Man

Research is proving what we've known all along: Women and men are *not* the same. Understanding these key medical differences could save your life.

BY JENNIFER PIRTLE

We're all for equal pay at work, equal opportunities in the world, and equal prices at the dry cleaner. But one place where women shouldn't be treated the same as men is on the examining table. Until very recently, everything about the world of medicine—from the doctor's office to the research lab—reflected a male-minded bias: that aside from reproductive health, it's OK to view men and women as identical. Thankfully, scientists are beginning to realize that women are more than the sum of their Fallopian tubes, ovaries, and mammary glands. "We are finding that in every system of the body, from the hairs of our heads to the way our hearts beat, there are significant, unique, sex-based differences in human physiology," says Marianne Legato, M.D., author of the book *Eve's Rib: The New Science of Gender-Specific Medicine and How It Can Save Your Life.* "Those distinctions are transforming the way doctors prevent and treat disease."

In the past, the so-called bikini view of women's health meant that doctors and health-care policy makers relied on research performed on men to draw conclusions for both sexes. "There's a growing awareness that the medical thinking wasn't telling the whole story," says Sherry Marts, Ph.D., scientific director for the Washington, D.C.-based Society for Women's Health Research.

Women are playing a greater research role, partly because in 1993 Congress began requiring the National Institutes of Health (NIH) to include women in scientific studies. Changes are also afoot in major hospitals and even in medical manufacturing plants, where companies are now exploring ways to make artificial heart valves smaller for women's hearts. "Tailoring both therapy and approaches to sex-specific treatments is resulting in improved care for both genders," Marts says—and that is translating into differences in the doctor's office. As a result, the future of medicine looks brighter for men as well as women.

From muscle mass to migraines, here's a heads-up on seven key differences between men and women and how they could affect your health.

Drugs

A growing number of studies shows that the safety and effectiveness of some drugs, including antihistimines, antibiotics, and pain relievers, vary depending on your sex. While there are several theories to explain these differences, one reason may lie in the female belly. Women's stomachs produce less acid and empty slower than men's, giving the body more time for drugs to absorb—and increasing the time they're effective.

Female hormonal surges, though, can make some drugs wear off more quickly. Progesterone, for example, is thought to change the way the stomach, lungs, and bladder work, so drugs are metabolized faster—especially before menstruation. "Women prone to seizures or asthmatic attacks right before their periods benefit significantly when their medication is temporarily increased," Legato says.

What you should do: If you take prescription drugs for epilepsy, asthma, arthritis, migraines, diabetes, or depression, ask your doctor about adjusting your dose or prescribing another drug to use just before your period.

Weight

When it comes to the scale, women face an uphill battle. Not only do they begin life with higher levels of body fat than men, they lose more muscle with age. And muscle is key to fending off excess weight: A pound of muscle at rest burns 35 calories a day; a pound of body fat burns just two calories.

Gender bender: Women's bodies contain relatively less water than men's, so it's crucial to get your eight glasses a day to avoid dehydration.

"Between the ages of 30 and 50, women lose 5 to 10 pounds of muscle because of disuse," says Pamela Peeke, M.D., assistant professor of medicine at the University of Maryland in Baltimore and author of *Fight Fat After Forty*. "A man will also lose mass, but at a much lower rate because of testosterone in his body." And while women are losing muscle, they're also gaining fat. "Women can literally double their body-fat levels after age 30," Peeke says.

What you should do: Weight training is the key to muscling out fat. Although any type of exercise will temporarily raise your metabolism, building muscle mass through strength training will permanently elevate it.

Heart

Ask a woman to describe the symptoms of a heart attack and she'll probably clutch her chest or point to pain or numbness in her left arm. But while men will

If a woman calls 911 with heart attack symptoms, she may be told she has indigestion or is experiencing an anxiety attack.

exhibit these classic signs, one in five women will not, Legato says. "Some women are more likely to have pain in their upper abdomen, shortness of breath, profuse sweating, and jaw pain," she says. The fact that many health professionals are not clued in to these differences raises the risk of misdiagnosis: Call 911 and you may be told you have indigestion or are experiencing an anxiety attack.

Currently, cardiovascular disease kills more women each year than all types of cancer combined. Even so, aggressive treatment in women lags behind that of men. "Doctors are less likely to give life-prolonging treatments, such as angioplasty, to women due to fears that women's arteries are too small to withstand certain procedures," Legato says. (Recent research suggests that age could be a factor in the differences in treatment since female heart patients tend to be older than male heart patients.) The reality is that while women's hearts may be relatively smaller than men's, their arteries often are not.

What you should do: No matter what your sex, high cholesterol, high blood pressure, poor diet, smoking, and lack of exercise increase your risk of heart disease. Women in particular need to watch their HDL cholesterol: Low levels of this "good" cholesterol are more risky for women than men. Research also suggests that women need to pay closer attention to their triglycerides. For those considering birth-control options, the Pill is now a heart-safe choice: Today's low-dose pills carry a much lower risk of heart disease than early versions.

Stress

A frazzled female is likely to pick up the phone and unwind by chatting with a girlfriend, says Shelley Taylor, Ph.D., a psychology professor at the University of California at Los Angeles and the author of *The Tending Instinct: How Nurturing Is Essential to Who We Are and How We Live*. "It's part of the 'tend and befriend' pattern: Females often respond to stressful situations by protecting and nurturing their young and by seeking social contact

the female perspective

For more information about gender-based medicine, check out the following sites:

Society for Women's Health Research
www.womens-health.org

The Partnership for Gender-Specific Medicine at Columbia University
cpmcnet.columbia.edu/dept/partnership/publications.html

National Women's Health Information Center
www.4woman.gov

National Women's Health Resource Center
www.healthywomen.org

and support from other people, especially other females," she explains. Men, on the other hand, tend to react to stress with the classic "fight or flight" response—either by becoming verbally aggressive or by withdrawing altogether.

The root of these differences may be the hormone oxytocin, which helps drive the urge to nurture. People with high levels of oxytocin are calmer, more relaxed, and more social. The hormone, which is released in times of stress, may make women less vulnerable to stress-related conditions, such as high blood pressure. "In women, estrogen enhances the effect of oxytocin," Taylor says. Men aren't so lucky: "The effects of the hormone seem to be reduced by testosterone. Men are more likely than women to develop certain stress-related disorders, including hypertension and alcohol and drug addiction," she says.

What you should do: Even when your week is on overload and you don't think you have time to bond with friends, pick up the phone. Touch can also help increase oxytocin levels, so squeeze a massage into your schedule.

Pain

Research suggests that women experience more pain than men in situations of equal injury or illness, says Jon D. Levine, M.D., Ph.D., director of the NIH Pain Research Center. But women's pain is routinely dismissed as psychological. "Because they are female, there is a higher chance that doctors will label their pain as 'not real,' " Levine says.

Levine suspects the difference in pain sensitivity is in part hormonal, but he's currently researching other explanations as well. Some evidence suggests that progesterone may heighten a woman's sensitivity to pain, while testosterone mutes a man's.

What you should do: Demand pain relief, whether you're a man or a woman. The stress from pain could slow your healing time. If your cries for relief go unheard, find another doctor who is more sensitive to your pain.

Migraines

Women are three times more likely than men to get these debilitating headaches, according to the National Headache Foundation. Drops in estrogen levels may trigger the attacks, since 70 percent of the most severe migraines experienced by women are premenstrual. Women ages 25 to 45 are most likely to suffer from hormone-triggered migraines. "The majority of these women get relief from their headaches during pregnancy," says Stephen Silberstein, M.D., professor of neurology at the Jefferson Medical College of Thomas Jefferson University in Philadelphia. But females don't have a monopoly on migraines: Men are more likely than women to start getting them in their 50s; doctors suspect the culprit is falling testosterone levels.

Women are **three times more likely** to suffer from migraines than men.

What you should do: Lifestyle changes are probably the best way to make peace with your migraines. "Before your periods, skip alcohol—especially red wine—sharp cheeses, and some artificial sweeteners, which contain migraine-causing nitrates," says Michael Welch, M.D., vice-chancellor of research at the University of Kansas Medical Center in Kansas City. Birth control–pill users can try taking them continuously (rather than having a week off each month) to break the cycle of estrogen-triggered migraines. Making sure you get the recommended daily allowance of magnesium (400 milligrams) may also ease the ache.

Wrinkles

Thanks to differences that are more than skin-deep, women are more prone to furrowed brows and crow's-feet. "We see the most change after menopause," says David Leffell, M.D., chief of dermatological surgery at Yale University School of Medicine and author of *Total Skin: The Definitive Guide to Whole Skin Care for Life.* "Estrogen levels drop, causing oil glands to slow production of emollients and skin to become much drier." With fewer fat cells beneath the skin and lower amounts of collagen and elastin, women's skin is generally thinner than men's. Thin skin is more likely to wrinkle and reveal other signs of aging, such as spider veins. Women who smoke fare even worse: Female smokers have triple the risk for wrinkling than nonsmokers (that risk is just over two times higher for men).

What you should do: Relax a bit about your diet as you get older: A few extra pounds could plump up your skin and help keep estrogen—and moisture—levels up. As you lose weight, your skin sags because there's less fat underneath it (think of a raisin versus a grape). And the extra fat may act as a factory for the moisture-enhancing hormone estrogen. ✳

Jennifer Pirtle also writes about health for **Self, Shape, Fitness,** *and* **Good Housekeeping** *magazines.*

How Medical Studies Are Shortchanging Women

MEN AND WOMEN are obviously different—and it's not just a matter of his and hers razors. Recognizing the importance of sex-based biological differences, the National Institutes of Health (NIH) started requiring that women be included in clinical trials in 1993. Yet a 2001 study conducted by the Institute of Medicine, a division of the National Academy of Sciences, suggests that more needs to be done.

While both the NIH and the U.S. Food and Drug Administration mandate that women be included in clinical trials, analyzing the findings by sex is still not routinely done, says Phyllis Greenberger, executive director of the Society for Women's Health Research, a nonprofit group that helped sponsor the study.

"Without sex-based analysis, we have no way of knowing whether the same interventions, therapies, or drugs are equally effective in women and men," Greenberger says. Researchers never would have known, for example, that women respond better to a type of painkiller called kappa-opioids—drugs that had previously been all but abandoned because clinical trials on men showed them to be ineffective.

"Understanding biological differences will help both sexes and also help us understand more about the mechanisms of disease," Greenberger says. To find out how to make your voice heard on Capitol Hill, visit the Society for Women's Health Research (www.womens-health.org).

Hear no evil
Why women avoid the gynecologist

28 percent of American women don't get yearly gynecological exams.

14 percent avoid the gynecologist because they're worried about a diagnosis.

why young women's hearts stop

Sudden cardiac death claims six times as many lives as car accidents. Here's what's behind this mysterious killer, and how you might save a life.

BY MARY DUFFY

It was the eve of her wedding, and 28-year-old Melissa Spencer was exasperated. After months of planning for the big event, she wanted everything to be perfect. But on that Friday night, prewedding stress was putting a damper on the rehearsal dinner, recalls Melissa's sister Sue (we've changed the family members' names for this story). Then something went very wrong: "My sister was about to sit down, when suddenly her whole body arched back, like she was having a seizure," Sue says.

In the seconds it took their father, a doctor, to reach her, Melissa's heart had stopped. Dr. Spencer began CPR as friends and family looked on. He resuscitated his daughter, and she was rushed to the hospital. In the emergency room, physicians ordered blood work and an electrocardiogram, but neither test showed anything abnormal. Though she was quite thin, Melissa, a marathon runner, seemed healthy. After a few hours of tests and observation, the episode was chalked up to dehydration and stress. On her

insistence—and with a warning to keep her fluid intake up—Melissa was released. The wedding went on as planned the next day. On Sunday morning, the newly married couple boarded a plane in Boston for their honeymoon in Hawaii. A few hours into the flight, Melissa had another seizure. The plane made an emergency landing in Colorado, but it was too late. Melissa Spencer was dead.

Some 250,000 people in the United States succumbed to sudden cardiac death (SCD) in 1999—that's more than six times the number of people who die in traffic accidents during the average year. The victims of SCD are generally older people, but more and more young folks are falling prey—Boston Celtic Reggie Lewis and ice skater Sergei Grinkov among them. According to a

Anything that creates significant changes in electrolyte balance—blood levels of potassium, calcium, and magnesium—can lead to life-threatening arrhythmias and cardiac arrest.

recent report from the Centers for Disease Control and Prevention (CDC), deaths among 15- to 34-year-olds increased by 10 percent between 1989 and 1996. Even more shocking, the rate of SCD in young women jumped by 30 percent over the same period. "While explaining the increase will take further investigation, we can speculate that it's caused by an increase in obesity, smoking, and other risk factors for cardiovascular disease," says the CDC's Zhi-Jie Zheng, M.D., Ph.D., the lead researcher for the study. But like Melissa Spencer, many of its victims have no known heart disease or health problems. Thankfully, researchers are making progress in identifying risk factors, which could help prevent deaths.

While the underlying causes of SCD vary, in most cases it unfolds the same way: Something triggers the electrical impulses in the heart to misfire, causing an abnormal heartbeat (arrhythmia). The beat can become rapid or chaotic or both, making it impossible for the organ to pump blood to the rest of the body. Without immediate medical intervention, the cardiovascular system rapidly collapses. SCD, by definition, occurs within one hour of initial symptoms. However, the heart's rhythm can almost always be restored to normal if treated promptly with an electrical charge to the heart from a defibrillator (think *ER*, when Dr. Green yells "clear" and uses paddles to shock the patient). As at Melissa's rehearsal dinner, CPR might work if a defibrillator is not available.

Not all arrhythmias are harmful. The term refers to any change in the regular heartbeat, and it can be fleeting and innocuous. Stimulants, including caffeine, chocolate, alcohol, herbal medications, tobacco, decongestants, and illicit drugs, can trigger an arrhythmia, as can stress and certain medical conditions, such as overactive thyroid. And according to Nieca Goldberg, M.D., chief of the Women's Heart Program at Lenox Hill Hospital in New York City, "These arrhythmias are resolved when the trigger is removed. So stop drinking the caffeine, for example, and you'll stop the arrhythmia."

Although a heart attack can lead to SCD, it's not the same thing. A heart attack is a type of plumbing problem: An artery blockage interrupts the heart's own blood supply, causing damage to the heart muscle and increasing the likelihood that the body's electrical system will malfunction, bringing on an arrhythmia and, possibly, SCD.

SCD victims may not show symptoms of it, but they almost always turn out to have heart-disease risk factors:

ready to rescue—learn CPR

Only the pros should pull out the paddles and zap a person whose heart has stopped, right? Not so, say experts. When you call 911 for an ambulance, ask for instructions, too—you can save a life.

While researchers still grapple with what causes sudden cardiac death (SCD), they do know that an unexpected element—namely, you—may be critical in saving a life. Bystanders who intervene immediately with defibrillation or CPR can vastly improve someone's chances of survival, whether they have medical training or not.

Studies have shown that having automated external defibrillators (AEDS)—a scaled-down version of the hospital device—available in public places can significantly reduce the number of SCDS. An AED will only activate defibrillation in cases of cardiac arrest, so it is virtually impossible to accidentally hurt someone with it. And it is easy to operate. In fact, researchers from the University of Seattle found that after just one minute of instruction, sixth graders successfully administered defibrillation within 90 seconds (paramedics did it in 67 seconds).

In the hope of avoiding deaths like Melissa Spencer's, the Federal Aviation Administration recently ruled that U.S. airlines must carry AEDS on board. The devices are also available in other public places, such as shopping malls and golf courses. In fact, Los Angeles announced in January 2002 the largest scale program in the U.S. to put these devices where people can access them. Proximity is key, says Douglas P. Zipes, M.D., president of the American College of Cardiology. For every minute lost in the resuscitation process, the risk of death increases by 10 percent, he says.

In a recent article in the American Heart Association journal *Circulation*, Zipes calls for development of a program called Save a Victim Everywhere (SAVE), which would train teams of neighbors to use an AED and administer CPR while waiting for emergency medical personnel to arrive.

But why wait for training? A study in the same issue of *Circulation* showed that when an untrained Good Samaritan administered CPR while being instructed over the phone by a 911 operator, the victim had a 45 percent better chance of survival than did victims who received no CPR before emergency technicians arrived.

Heart disease is perceived as a problem of older people. Danger signs in young women are often dismissed.

In 90 percent of the cases, people who've died have had narrowing in two or more major coronary arteries. Two-thirds of victims show scarring from a prior heart attack that, in many cases, went undetected. It's not surprising, then, that the same factors that make you susceptible to heart disease—high cholesterol, diabetes, and so on—also increase your risk of SCD. According to the American Heart Association, for example, smokers have two to four times the SCD risk of nonsmokers.

But what really confuses the issue and makes it scarier is that SCD can hit people like Melissa Spencer, who don't have those risk factors. Although her family will never know exactly what caused Melissa's death, Sue believes it may have been a history of anorexia that, in effect, short-circuited her sister's electrical system. "My father surmised that Melissa had depleted her potassium, which may have triggered previously undetected arrhythmia," she says.

In fact, Zheng says, some studies do suggest a link between eating disorders and SCD. Anything that creates significant changes in electrolyte balance—blood levels of potassium, calcium, and magnesium—can lead to life-threatening arrhythmias and cardiac arrest, Goldberg says. To help maintain the right balance of electrolytes, it's important that you stay well-hydrated, avoid diuretic

Sisters: Sue (right) and Lisa gathered for Melissa's wedding—a few days later for her funeral. The former marathon runner had no known risk factors, but died when her heart stopped on the way to her honeymoon.

and laxative abuse, and eat a balanced diet.

In some cases of SCD, the cause may be an underlying physical disorder, such as an enlargement of the heart muscle—a problem you're born with and may not know you have—that sets the stage for a fatal arrhythmia. Tragically, for many young victims, the first sign of trouble is also the last: sudden cardiac death.

When Italian researchers discovered that young competitive athletes (ages 12 to 35) were more than twice as likely to be victims of sudden death as their non-athletic counterparts, they found that congenital abnormalities in the heart were strongly associated with the event. U.S. studies further the idea of heart abnormalities being at the root of the problem, finding the major cause of sudden death in young athletes to be an excessive thickening of the heart muscle (hypertrophic cardiomyopathy).

With such predisposing conditions, adrenaline released in intense physical activity can trigger SCD. This doesn't warrant avoiding sports, scientists say. Rather, it points to the need for more extensive screening methods for underlying heart disease among athletes.

Researchers at the University of California-San Diego are also uncovering a possible genetic link to the problem. The gene they discovered regulates critical electrical currents in the heart that are vital to normal, rhythmic

ENEMY NUMBER ONE
With 503,927 deaths each year, heart disease kills more American women than the next 14 causes of death combined (breast cancer included).

—American Heart Association

beating. Without it, as animal studies have hinted, some people may be susceptible to arrhythmia and sudden death. These findings hold promise for the development of therapies to prevent SCD.

While this research is promising, both Goldberg and Zheng point out the need for further studies. They hope to find out why there's been an increase in SCD among young women despite an overall national drop in deaths from heart disease. In the meantime, the best way to protect against this sometimes-symptomless killer is to live a heart-healthy lifestyle. "Eating a low-fat diet, getting regular exercise, keeping your weight at a healthy level, and not smoking are all ways to reduce the risk of SCD," Zheng explains. He advises people with a family history of early heart disease to ask their doctors about screening for cardiac conditions.

"Be aware that symptoms of heart disease are under-recognized in young women," Goldberg says. "Heart disease is still perceived as a disease of older men and women." Some signs of heart problems—feeling faint or having a racing heart or palpitations—mimic those of a panic attack, and women or their doctors may dismiss them as such.

In fact, several years ago, Sue, now 36, began having those symptoms. "I'd feel my heart racing and feel faint, and I would frighten myself wondering if this is what my sister felt," she says. Sue was acutely aware that a family history of early SCD greatly increased her risk for it, and she and her physician took the symptoms very seriously. The doctor ordered a battery of tests, including an echocardiogram, a stress test, and a Holter monitor to track her heart rhythms. It was only after those tests came back negative, and heart disease was ruled out, that a diagnosis was made: She was suffering from panic attacks. The tests put everyone's minds at ease that Sue's symptoms were not a sign of impending SCD.

Fortunately, Sue's panic attacks have since ceased. But her vigilance in practicing a heart-healthy lifestyle has not—nor should yours. After all, while SCD doesn't happen every day, heart disease—the leading killer of both men and women in America—does. That means that a few healthy changes can quite literally help save your life. ✳

Freelance writer Mary Duffy contributes frequently to The New York Times *and* Self.

Why You Can't Always Trust a Home Pregnancy Test

A RECENT STUDY finds new reason not to believe everything you read—particularly if it's the label of a home pregnancy kit. Commercial urine tests may not live up to their 99 percent accuracy claim, according to a report in *The Journal of the American Medical Association.*

The study found that at least 10 percent of all pregnancies are undetectable on the first day of a missed period—the day on which home kits claim to identify a new mom-in-waiting. The reason: variations in the time it takes for embryo implantation. "Pregnancy tests identify the presence of human chorionic gonadotropin (HCG), a hormone produced by placental cells. Before the embryo attaches itself to the uterine wall, there's no HCG present, so you'll always get a negative result," says lead researcher Allen Wilcox, M.D., Ph.D., senior investigator at the National Institute of Environmental Sciences. Commercial home pregnancy kits are even less sensitive than the tests used in the study, so Wilcox estimates the number of inaccurate results on the first day of a missed period could be as high as 25 percent.

Such unreliable results could have many harmful effects. "Some women who get false-negative results continue to smoke, drink alcohol, or take medications they'd avoid if they knew they were pregnant," says Margaret Plumbo, a certified midwife who teaches at the University of Minnesota.

For Sarena Olson, a 30-year-old mother of three, false-negative results caused an emotional, rather than physical, fallout. "I started testing the day I missed my period and got six negatives before finally testing positive eight days later," Olson says. "I felt like crying or yelling at someone."

Like Olson, many women want answers as early as possible. Home tests are still reliable tools when used wisely. One week after a missed period, 97 percent of women will get accurate results, Plumbo estimates. If you get a negative result and still have reason to think you're pregnant, wait one week and test again. Check out specific home-test profiles at www.fertilityplus.org/faq/hpt.html.

A CONTRACEPTIVE RENAISSANCE

The IUD makes a comeback. Should you rethink your birth-control method?

BY BETH HOWARD   PHOTOGRAPHY BY HOWARD L. PUCKETT

Julie Coleman (not her real name) never messes with her birth control. Well, almost never. In the past 18 years, the 49-year-old writer from New York City has dealt with it exactly three times: when she had her intrauterine device (IUD) replaced.

Less than 1 percent of women use the hassle-free IUD, compared with the 25 percent who use the Pill. "With a failure rate of well under 1 percent, the IUD is the single most effective reversible method of birth control—but highly underused," says James Trussell, Ph.D., director of population research at Princeton University.

Obviously, not everyone is as high as Trussell on the contraceptive. In fact, a recent study published in the journal *Obstetrics and Gynecology* shows that OB-GYNs rarely recommend IUDs, even though most say they consider the device to be safe and effective. Twenty percent of OB-GYNs had not inserted an IUD in the previous year, says lead study author Nancy Stanwood, M.D., an assistant professor of obstetrics and gynecology at the University of Rochester Medical Center. Despite the fact that the new devices now on the market have undergone—and passed—rigorous testing, the IUD's image still bears the scars of its litigious history, Stanwood says.

Neither doctors nor women seeking birth-control options can seem to forget when, in 1974, manufacturer A.H. Robins pulled the infamous Dalkon Shield IUD from the market in the wake of numerous lawsuits. The unique crab-shaped device caused severe pelvic infections, rendering some women infertile and even

Today's version is not your mother's IUD. We're light-years ahead of what we had a generation ago.
—David Grimes, M.D.

resulting in some deaths. "Today's version is not your mother's IUD," says David Grimes, M.D., a contraceptive researcher and vice president of biomedical affairs at Family Health International in Research Triangle Park, North Carolina. "We're light-years ahead of what we had a generation ago."

There are two IUDs available in the United States. Both are T-shaped and, unlike previous designs, are medicated with substances to enhance their effectiveness. The ParaGard Copper T 380A, introduced in 1988, releases copper over the course of 10 years into the uterus, thwarting fertilization by killing sperm. The Mirena IUD, recently approved in the United States but boasting a 10-year track record in other countries, works by releasing progestin over its five-year life span, causing the cervical mucus to thicken, stopping sperm. "You put an IUD in a woman and she has the same possibility of getting pregnant as a woman who has her tubes tied, yet an IUD is completely reversible," Stanwood says. That was the final selling point for Coleman, who was pretty sure she didn't want children but didn't want to close the door on the prospect in case she changed her mind. Plus, she admits, she was never very good at remembering to take a pill every day.

> ## did you know?
>
> Like birth-control pills, IUDs can be used as emergency contraception. The Copper T IUD can be inserted up to five days after sex to prevent pregnancy, then kept in place if a woman decides to stick with the IUD for her contraceptive method. (So far, the Mirena has not been studied for this use.) For information on this morning-after option, visit www.not-2-late.com or ask your doctor.

The IUD isn't free of side effects. Some women who use the Copper T report increased menstrual pain and bleeding. And although the chance of pregnancy is slim, women who do get pregnant have an increased risk of miscarriage or an ectopic pregnancy. On the plus side, studies suggest that users may experience a lower risk of endometrial cancer. And the progestin in Mirena helps reduce period pain and bleeding. In fact, some practitioners prescribe it as an alternative to hysterectomy in women with heavy bleeding.

Despite these advantages, IUDs aren't for everyone. They cost upwards of $400 (including insertion) although, over its life span, the IUD is cheaper than other types of contraception. (Some insurers cover the cost.) Most practitioners limit IUD use to women in monogamous relationships since it does not protect against STDs.

Researchers agree that more women could enjoy the freedom of IUDs without hormonal side effects or the bother of other forms of birth control. "They are completely different from the Dalkon Shield device of 30 years ago," Stanwood says. "Now is an exciting time for an IUD renaissance." ✳

Beth Howard is the author of **Mind Your Body: A Sexual Health and Wellness Guide for Women.**

Block Sperm *and* Germs

Contraception and protection against sexually transmitted diseases (STDS) may soon come in packages other than condom wrappers. Johns Hopkins University researchers and the private firm ReProtect have developed a contraceptive gel called BufferGel, which can kill sperm and many of the germs that cause STDS, researchers say. "Semen eliminates the protective acidity that naturally occurs in the vagina," says developer Richard Cone, Ph.D., professor of biophysics in Hopkins' Krieger School of Arts and Sciences. "BufferGel returns the acidity levels back to normal so sperm and germs will be killed." Because uterine contractions move not only sperm but also harmful bacteria through the uterus, researchers believe a barrier method used in combination with the gel will help prevent bacterial vaginosis and STDS such as chlamydia, gonorrhea, and perhaps even HIV and genital herpes.

In addition to its germ-killing benefits, BufferGel holds another advantage over conventional spermicides: It doesn't contain soaps or detergents, which can irritate the vagina and cause infection. Although still in clinical trials, it may one day be sold with a disposable, one-size-fits-all contraceptive device.

Give your Beauty Routine a Prenatal Check-up

Most women know that they should give up their nightly cocktail and overhaul their eating habits when they find out they're pregnant (or are trying to get that way). But beauty routines need a prenatal checkup as well, says Lisa Masterson, M.D., an OB-GYN at Cedars-Sinai Medical Center in Los Angeles. "The safest thing to do is to skip anything questionable during the first trimester, when most of the baby's important body parts are forming," she says. So keep the following in mind if your regimen includes:

Retin-A and other retinol products. Doctors believe using these vitamin A derivatives topically could have a negative effect because evidence has shown that taking high doses of vitamin A orally can cause birth defects.

Hair dye. Although the results of studies are mixed, there's a chance that harsh chemicals in permanent dyes could be absorbed through your scalp. Rather than risk harm to your baby, stick with vegetable dyes, clear glosses, and other gentle color options.

Bleaching toothpastes with the active ingredient carbomide peroxide. You'd have to ingest a lot to cause a problem, but doing so could restrict the flow of oxygen to the fetus.

Self-tanners. Go for the pale look since many self-tanners contain aminopheline, a caffeine derivative. "Again, we can't be sure how much is going to get into the bloodstream, but we know high amounts of caffeine aren't recommended during pregnancy," Masterson says.

Glycolic acid. During the first trimester, your skin can become very sensitive, and this ingredient may cause burning. Make sure to check with your doctor before resuming use during your second trimester.

All that said, you don't have to abandon your beauty routine altogether. The cosmetics industry has issued birth announcements for a growing family of product lines created for moms-to-be. Skin-care products such as those from Selph, Belly Basics, Mustela, Bella Mama, and Avon's BeComing Mom line feature only ingredients that are safe during pregnancy.

Q+A
Taking the Pill in a Different Time Zone

I'm going to France this summer, and I don't want to wake up at 4 a.m. just to stay on schedule with my birth-control pill. What should I do?

CHANGING TIME ZONES will probably mess more with your sleep patterns than it will with your pill's effectiveness. Most OB-GYNS will, if pressed, say that you should be covered if you take your pill within 24 hours of the last pill—the exact hour doesn't much matter. So it's OK to stick to your normal time when you get there: If you take your pill at 10 p.m. at home, for instance, take it at 10 p.m. France time. You have to be careful, though, when you head back west; you'll add hours to your day and run the risk of missing that 24-hour window. The best advice is to take one just when you arrive stateside (even if it's before 10 p.m. U.S. time). The following day, go back to your normal routine.

If you're on a Sunday-start pill, the time difference may mean you'll finish your pack a day early. Don't delay starting a new pack, though. For instance, if you take your last active pill on a Friday, take only one of the placebos (skip the usual week of placebos) and start the active pack on Sunday. The one exception: If you're on the low-dose or the progestin-only "minipill," timing is more critical. Work out a safe schedule with your gynecologist.

a week-by-week guide to your hormones

You know hormones can turn you into a raging tyrant or a lovable teddy bear. But do you know how to make the most out of hormonal ebbs and flows? Our guide tells you how to know when it's best to go out on the town, ask for a promotion, or stay at home and hibernate. The length of everyone's cycle is slightly different—anywhere from 21 to 35 days—so listen to your body first and then adapt these guidelines accordingly.

	WEEK 1 *week after period*	WEEK 2 *ovulation*	WEEK 3 *PMS*	WEEK 4 *period*
hormonal action	Estrogen builds up	Estrogen peaks. Progesterone starts to increase. LH (luteinizing hormone) surges just prior to ovulation.	Estrogen plummets. Progesterone surges.	Hormone levels decline sharply.
you feel	Energized and confident	Sexy and unstoppable	Irritable, angry, bloated, depressed	Bloated, dowdy, and home-bound
you should	Conquer the world, or at least a project at work. Ask someone for a date—or a raise.	Flirt, but also remember to watch out—you're attracted to brawn over brains now. You're at your most fertile, so plan ahead.	See a feel-good movie to boost your mood. Gain perspective by chatting with the gals.	Work out, avoid the scale, and get plenty of rest to let your body recharge.
Rx	Splurge on a steak—or extra spinach—to replenish the 13 milligrams of iron you lost the week before.	Go easy at the gym; you're more prone to injury than at other times of the month.	Calcium has been shown to relieve all major symptoms of PMS: Take 300 milligrams four times a day.	Drink lots of water and avoid caffeine in order to relieve bloating. For pain, take over-the-counter anti-inflammatories such as ibuprofen or naproxen.
extra tip	Quit smoking (or any other bad habits) this week; you're less likely to experience depression and other withdrawal symptoms.	Buy that strapless dress you've been eyeing—and strut your stuff.	Try gingko biloba to relieve breast tenderness and irritability. Magnesium may help alleviate bloating.	Stock up on nutrients. Vitamins B_{12}, B_6, and E have been shown to relieve cramps.
you identify with	Condoleezza Rice, Serena Williams, Debra Messing	Jennifer Lopez, Cher, Angelina Jolie, Madonna	Alanis Morissette, Tonya Harding, Courtney Love	Roseanne Barr, Delta Burke, Martha Stewart

Coping with the Pain of Infertility

What should you expect once you stop making love and start trying to make a baby?

BY SHERYL ALTMAN

We already had the names picked out: Benjamin for a boy; Carrie for a girl. And the first time we made love with the goal of creating a life, I cried.

"What's wrong?" my husband, Paul, asked. "It's the most beautiful thing we've ever done," I gushed. After a year of debating whether or not we were ready to start a family, this was it: I was certain that we had conceived.

When I got my period that month, I was shocked. I was 32 and healthy, so why hadn't it worked? I immediately called my girlfriends for their input. "Maybe your timing was off," suggested Stacy, a mother of two. "You're supposed to do it every other day—no more, no less."

"Did you stand on your head afterward?" asked Amy, who has three boys. "I used to do that. It works, but it gives you a headache." You've got to be kidding, I thought glumly.

Though well-meaning, my friends made me feel clueless. I made an appointment with my gynecologist to find out what was wrong. He assured me there was no problem—it just takes time. "Be patient," he told me. "It will happen."

I was patient yet determined. To be successful at conceiving, I decided, all I had to do was gather the facts. I scoured medical journals for articles, bought dozens of fertility books, charted my basal temperature, and watched closely for subtle changes in my cervical fluid. Every morning, like clockwork, I checked my ClearPlan Easy stick and waited for a double blue line to appear—a signal that said, "Hooray! I'm ovulating!"

When the stick said "Go for it!" we did—no matter where or when, or how little either of us was in the mood. Paul always tried to keep it fun: "I'm getting sooo turned on," he'd tease, watching me do the dishes. Although we never admitted it to each other, we both knew that somewhere along the way love-making becomes baby-making. Passion takes a back seat when the fertility clock is ticking.

My doctor had cautioned us that infertility often causes a strain on a marriage. There's a tendency to point fingers of blame or lash out in anger, fear, and pain. Despite our vow never to let this happen to us, the pressure was too great, the stakes too high. But I wasn't prepared for just how tough it got over the year and a half that we've been "trying." I had no

> *When you're trying to get pregnant, it feels like everyone is a mother but you.*

idea how furious I could get because my "procedures" were more painful than his. I didn't realize how alone I would feel. And I certainly didn't anticipate how Paul would react—or that I could be oblivious to his pain. More surprising, though, was realizing that it takes a strong marriage to survive this challenge—and rediscovering that we have one.

But I wasn't feeling so loving when my doctor suggested we go for a full fertility work-up, with tests for both of us. I used to faint at the sight of blood, but now I was giving vials of it several times a week to check my hormone levels. I was cultured, scanned, and sonogrammed. I had my Fallopian tubes flooded with dye. Paul, on the other hand, had to supply a sperm sample at a hospital lab. He called that morning from his cell phone. "It's a bathroom with a leather recliner," he whispered. "And you wouldn't believe this—they even have a TV in here with dirty videos!" I lost it. "That's it?" I demanded. "How can you complain about that after all I've gone through?"

Then came the day of the big blow-up in the middle of New York City's Fifth Avenue: "Well, it doesn't look like it's me, so it must be you," Paul remarked as we left the urologist's office. I ranted for several minutes, stopping traffic in the process, until he apologized.

Even more tense times followed—times when I was certain that Paul had no idea how I felt. How could he understand that every phone call from another girlfriend with "good news" was agonizing? Every baby shower I attended was unbearable? He seemed to be taking it all in stride, confident that this was just a temporary setback. ("We're not infertile; we're reproductively challenged!" he quipped.) Sometimes, his calmness soothed me; other times, it infuriated me. I wanted him to share the pain I was experiencing, both physically and emotionally.

We saw more doctors and had even more tests, yet no one could tell us why we weren't capable of getting pregnant. I was supposed to take heart in the fact that our case wasn't so unusual: After all, nearly 15 percent of infertility cases are never explained. But I didn't care how many other couples were going through this—*we* were going through this.

After a full year of trying, we were officially deemed "infertile"—joining the 6 million American women and men who have trouble conceiving—and we were bombarded with an alphabet of options: IUI, IVF, GIFT, and ICSI. We decided to try IUI (intrauterine insemination), the least invasive procedure on the list. When my doctor explained that he would be placing Paul's sperm into my uterus through a catheter, it sounded simple. But the procedure was excruciating: My uterus spasmed, and I felt waves of contractions. Paul, on the other hand, was out in the waiting room eating a bagel with cream cheese when the nurse called him in to comfort me. I lay there in the stirrups, sobbing and shaking uncontrollably. "It's OK," Paul said, draping himself over me like a blanket. "I hate this," I said. "I just don't think I can do all this."

But somehow I did—five more times—with no success. I couldn't help grieving month after month, feeling an enormous emptiness. One weekend, I found myself

how to be a friend to a friend who is infertile

Infertile couples often withdraw from family or friends, especially those with small children. "Because they tend to isolate themselves, what they need is good support from people who love them," says Alice D. Domar, Ph.D., director of the Mind/Body Center for Women's Health at Harvard University, which offers workshops for women dealing with infertility. "But often, people with the best intentions wind up saying or doing the wrong thing. And instead of helping the infertile couple, they make matters worse." How can you help a friend who's going through infertility treatment? Domar suggests the following:

Ask what you can do. Say, "I've never gone through what you're going through, and I don't know how you feel, so, please, tell me what you need."

Be a good listener. If your friend wants to vent, don't interrupt or change the subject. Let her talk out her emotions without your judgment or comments.

Be careful with advice. Ask if it's OK to pass on information or put her in touch with another friend who went through it. But don't tell her what to do.

Limit the baby talk. If you have a young child, resist the urge to share cute anecdotes or photographs. Understand that even being around an infant can be overwhelmingly painful.

Always honor her wishes. If your friend asks you to back off, then do it. Understand that if you are pregnant or have a new baby, your friend might not be able to have you in her life right now. One of the kindest things you can say is, "I promise I won't ask questions or intrude. Just know that whatever you need, I'm always available."

Infertility can isolate you from friends, family, and even your husband.

counting the number of baby strollers I passed on the street. Why was everyone a mother but me? I sat down on a curb and cried.

Under the circumstances, it became increasingly difficult to keep our problem from our families. At first, we thought it would be better that way—no questions, no unwanted advice. But then came my niece Emily's third birthday party.

We were surrounded with inquiring minds wanting to know: "So, when are you going to finally have a kid of your own?" "What are you waiting for?" "Isn't it time you two started a family?" I missed Emily blowing out her candles because I was hiding in the bathroom.

The next day, Paul called his mom and explained what was going on. He also asked that everyone back off. This was hard enough for us to deal with without the probing, however well-intended. Paul was my hero that day: I felt like he would protect me, no matter what. And I realized, for the first time, that this struggle wasn't just about me. We were on this journey together, a team.

Paul became my cheerleader, and reminded me of one of my great-grandmother's favorite motto: "Life is like a Ferris wheel. Sometimes you're at the top; sometimes you're at the bottom." For Hanukkah, he gave me a silver Ferris wheel charm on a chain. "Now when you're feeling blue, you can turn the wheel up again," he told me.

Our friends were really helpful, too. Lynne, a devout churchgoer, reassured us, "There is great comfort in knowing that some things are not in our hands. Maybe you need to slow down and let go." I thought about that—the idea that no matter how much research I did or how hard Paul and I tried, we just couldn't force it to happen.

So I took Lynne's advice and bought a yoga video. I mastered the deep, rhythmic breathing that's central to this ancient practice. The tension drained from my body, and I felt relaxed and at peace.

As I learned to slow down, Paul was trying to rev things up, at least in the bedroom. It was his idea to rekindle the romance in our relationship with a second "honeymoon getaway" in the Poconos, complete with a massage table, a heart-shaped tub, and a 7-foot-tall champagne-glass Jacuzzi. We laughed the whole weekend, especially when we turned off the lights and discovered that above our king-sized bed was a mirrored ceiling dotted with glow-in-the-dark stars. "Wouldn't it be so hilarious if we actually conceived our child here?" I pondered out loud. "How embarrassing!"

Even so, I made a wish on one of those stars and snuggled into my husband's arms. I'm still not sure if there's a baby in our future, but I do know one thing for certain: No matter what happens, we'll always have each other. ✳

Sheryl Altman is a New York City–based writer and editor who is keeping a journal of her infertility experiences for a book.

update: We are happy to inform you that Sheryl Altman and her husband were expecting their first child shortly after our press date.

good news: No Cancer Link
Found in Fertility Drugs

Along with the hope of fertility drugs came the fear that they could increase the risk of ovarian cancer. But a study published in the *American Journal of Epidemiology* found no link between the drugs and the disease. However, the researchers did find that women with fertility problems are at slightly increased risk for ovarian cancer.

"It is underlying biology, not fertility drugs, that elevate the risk of ovarian cancer," says lead researcher Roberta Ness, M.D., an associate professor at the University of Pittsburgh School of Public Health. Two specific groups, women with endometriosis and those with unexplained infertility, were most at risk of the disease. Ness suspects that inflammatory conditions of the pelvis could increase the risk of cancer. Future studies will look into the connection between cancer and conception. But for now, many women can rest easier when it comes to fertility drugs.

Eat to Take Your Period Off Pause

Stop blaming irregular periods on long workouts and start snacking. While researchers have long linked period pauses with too much activity, a preliminary study at Penn State suggests that too few calories is the real culprit behind athletic amenorrhea, a condition that can lead to bone loss. More research is needed, but consider adding a little more pasta to your plate if you train like a demon.

New Test Could Solve Miscarriage Mysteries

For women who have suffered through recurrent miscarriages—with no idea why—a simple, inexpensive blood test could provide answers. A study published in the *American Journal of Obstetrics and Gynecology* showed that a faulty X chromosome in women was the culprit in 15 percent of cases of multiple miscarriages. Until now, up to half of women who have had miscarriages remained in the dark about their loss, which adds extra—and often damaging—anxiety to the stress of trying to conceive again. "Women who have repeated miscarriages often feel like their bodies have failed them," explains Susan G. Mikesell, Ph.D., a psychologist who specializes in fertility and couples therapy. The test should offer women answers and ease some fears.

The genetic flaw is the largest known cause of miscarriages to date, and the blood test makes early detection easy, says W. Allen Hogge, M.D., one of the study's authors and professor of obstetrics, gynecology, and reproductive sciences at the University of Pittsburgh. For women who do get a positive test result, carrying a baby to term is still possible. "Women who have this anomaly should feel reassured because it gives them a reason and shows that they can still have a successful pregnancy," Hogge says.

Although there is still no known cure for the genetic flaw, about 60 percent of the women with this abnormality will have a successful pregnancy, and the women themselves are not at risk for any health problems. Finding the cause behind multiple miscarriages could prevent many women from undergoing expensive and often painful fertility tests and procedures. If you've had more than one miscarriage, ask your doctor whether the test is right for you.

What Age for Motherhood?

About 20 percent of American women have their first child after they turn 35.

—*www.InteliHealth.com*

BACK SAVERS FOR NEW MOMS

WITH A WEIGHTY bulge challenging their centers of gravity, it's no wonder that half of pregnant women battle back pain. Although most of the aches go away within six weeks of childbirth, about 15 percent of new moms still experience some lingering pain, says Alan M. Levine, M.D., a Baltimore-based orthopedic spine surgeon and editor in chief of the *Journal of the American Academy of Orthopaedic Surgeons*. Protect your back with Levine's strain-saving strategies:

Tone your muscles. During your pregnancy, keep exercising for as long as your doctor allows. After giving birth, start doing abdominal crunches and back extensions as soon as possible. (For most women having vaginal births, this means about a week; for C-sections, six weeks. Check with your doctor to be sure.)

Keep moving. Regular aerobic activity and stretching (as simple as bending over and reaching for your toes) will loosen and warm up muscles, making them less vulnerable to getting twisted and pulled out of whack. Lift correctly. Holding weight at arm's length will strain muscles more than carrying items close to your chest. Avoid reaching over obstacles: Lower the side of the crib; remove the high-chair tray. (Even nonmoms can benefit from lifting the right way.)

Carry with care. Do not prop a child on your hip; this overloads the back muscles. To even out the weight, try a backpack or a Snugli.

Just like extra pounds, back pain should eventually be part of a new mom's past. If you're using these strategies and pain persists longer than six weeks or gets worse, see a

doctor. Also, if the pain radiates from your back down into your legs, it could be a sign of something more serious, such as a disk herniation, which will need a doctor's attention.

Cesareans

DO YOU DESERVE A CHOICE?

More and more women are asking for C-sections. But the medical community isn't sure they should have the option.

BY MELBA NEWSOME

When Beth Gehring, a dentist from Blue Springs, Missouri, went into labor with her first child eight years ago, she never thought she'd have complications. Her sister had delivered seven kids—four born at home—with no problems. Surely those childbearing hips were genetic. Since Gehring would be delivering in a hospital with all the technology and expertise medicine has to offer, the birth would be a breeze, she reasoned. Twenty-one hours later, she wasn't so sure. After pushing for two straight hours, the baby remained stuck in the birth canal. "I felt like I was being ripped apart," she says. "I screamed for the doctor to cut me just to get it over with."

When baby Kylie finally entered the world at a robust 8 pounds, 3 ounces, Gehring was so thrilled that her pain immediately became a distant memory. Soon, however, she realized something was terribly wrong with her baby. Kylie's left arm lay motionless at her side, paralyzed. Even after surgery and rehabilitation, the child's limb still doesn't move with the freedom of her other arm.

Two years later, when Gehring got pregnant with her second child, her doctor insisted she try to deliver vaginally again. Fortunately, her son, Jordan, was born without incident. But Jordan was just a few months old when Gehring learned that Kylie's condition, known as brachial plexis palsy, resulted from nerve damage suffered during the delivery. Delving further, Gehring discovered that she was 16 times more likely to have the same problem with a subsequent birth, yet her doctor had been willing for her to risk another vaginal delivery. She was outraged. "If anybody had said to me there was a chance that Kylie could get stuck, get injured, or could die, I would have had a cesarean," Gehring says. "Whether or not there's a foreseeable problem, I think women should be offered the choice—especially when there's been a problem with a previous birth. A woman should be able to say 'I want a cesarean section.'"

Like Gehring, more women are demanding a say in how they deliver their babies. Some want to avoid the

A pregnant woman does not have the authority to demand that her baby be delivered surgically. Guidelines from hospitals and insurance companies dictate when surgery is appropriate.

rare-but-possible complications children can suffer in a vaginal delivery—from paralyzed limbs to cerebral palsy to skull fractures. Others fear for themselves the loss of urinary function or sexual sensation that may be side effects of labor. But officially, the decision of how a woman will give birth lies with the physician. Today, a pregnant woman does not have the authority to demand that her baby be delivered surgically. Guidelines from hospitals and insurance companies dictate when surgery is appropriate. Often, C-sections are emergencies, performed when labor is not progressing. But some women are requesting the surgery well before they head to the hospital, even if they do not have a high risk for complications. Some doctors agree that women should have the choice and they find ways to give patients what they want, although there is no way to measure how often that happens.

What is clear is that cesarean deliveries are on the rise: In 2000, they accounted for 23 percent of all births, and some experts are now predicting that this rate will exceed 30 percent within the next two years. But the current trend is due as much to the escalating legal risks that obstetricians face as to women's increasing clout in the doctor's office.

Seesawing C-Section Rates

C-sections were relatively rare until the 1980s, when rates skyrocketed, due in large part to the advent of fetal monitoring, which picks up more potential problems. By 1988, one in four babies was delivered by cesarean.

But the C-section rate then came under scrutiny from critics who claimed the procedure had evolved into a convenience for doctors to avoid midnight deliveries. Public-health officials launched a campaign to bring the rate down to no more than 15 percent of births, pointing to maternal risks like infection, hemorrhage, complications from anesthesia, and even death—plus premature birth and respiratory problems for the baby. C-sections were nearly twice as expensive as vaginal births, they added. The message took hold, and the C-section rate declined for nearly a decade.

But today, C-sections are hot again. One reason is the growing number of women for whom they are medically

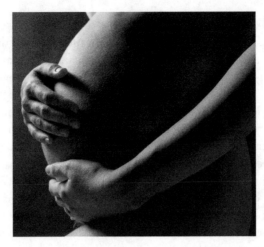

Even if a C-section is planned, there's no debating that a surgical delivery carries **more personal risks** than those that come with a vaginal birth.

necessary: More women in their late 30s and 40s are having babies, and older women generally make poorer candidates for vaginal birth. On average, they gain more weight, have bigger babies, and suffer higher rates of complication, such as high blood pressure and gestational diabetes. Each of these factors can make cesarean birth necessary. In 1999, a third of women over 40 and almost as many between ages 35 and 39 gave birth by cesarean, compared with just 17 percent of women ages 20 to 24.

Older women are also more likely to undergo infertility treatment, which is associated with a higher rate of cesareans. Doctors may be more willing to operate because it allows them to control the baby's birth, an important factor since it may be the woman's only chance at motherhood. Infertility treatment also can result in multiple pregnancies, a well-known risk factor for C-section.

Still, the medical professionals tend to frown on the surgical procedure as invasive and risky, at least when compared with a vaginal birth. That's why planned C-sections are officially allowed only in certain cases, such as when the fetus is in the breech position, when the mother has had a prior cesarean, or when she has a gynecological condition, such as a herpes outbreak, at the time of delivery.

Cesarean vs. Vaginal Delivery

It may not be fair to compare the success of an emergency C-section done when both mother and child are in distress with an uncomplicated vaginal birth. But even if a C-section is planned, there's no debating that the surgery carries more personal risks than a vaginal birth.

So why would a woman want a C-section if she doesn't need one? For starters, proponents of choice say vaginal birth is not risk-free, especially for the infant. Though extremely rare, skull fractures, paralyzed limbs, and brain damage can occur when a baby gets stuck on its way through the birth canal and must be extracted with forceps or a vacuum device. There's also the risk of death or permanent problems such as cerebral palsy, which may happen if a fetus is deprived of oxygen for too long during labor. Unfortunately, these events can rarely be predicted.

Mothers, too, may experience unpleasant and even debilitating consequences with vaginal births. One study found that natural delivery is associated with a higher incidence of urinary incontinence compared with cesareans. The risk is even higher when forceps are used. Some women opt for a small abdominal scar over the prospect of urine leakage for the rest of their lives.

The loss of sexual sensation is another common complaint among women who have given birth vaginally, says Frederic Frigoletto, M.D., chief of obstetrics at Massachusetts General Hospital in Boston. And the risk of this may increase if the mother is given an episiotomy—an incision in the tissue between the vagina and the perineum that widens the vaginal opening. In fact, data from the University of Ottawa shows that women who have episiotomies experience the lowest levels of sexual satisfaction up to three months after giving birth, compared with those who don't get them.

Women often report having sexual troubles for much longer. After giving birth to twins, for instance, Laurie Pressman (her name has been changed for this story), a 33-year-old writer from Long Island, New York, noticed a change. "It used to be that you could just look at me and I would have an orgasm," she says with a laugh. "After I had the kids, all that changed." Initially, Pressman thought she was just exhausted from the rigors of caring for two infants and believed that things would get better. By the time the children were 2 years old, however, her sex life had not improved. It wasn't until a friend complained of the same thing that she made the connection.

The site of the episiotomy can develop scar tissue that may interfere with sensory perception—just like incisions anywhere on the body, Frigoletto explains. Episiotomies are performed in nearly half of all vaginal births, triggering pain, the chance of infection, and occasionally permanent problems, such as fecal incontinence. Studies show that women are more likely to suffer such consequences if they have an episiotomy than if they tear spontaneously during delivery. (Because these episiotomy wounds tend to be more severe than tears, many doctors and midwives promote the idea of letting women tear naturally. This is

having your say today

You're not alone if you want a C-section even if it's not medically necessary. Nearly a third of female obstetricians in England would opt for a surgical birth without a medical reason, according to a 1996 survey (data is not available in the United States).

Still, experts suggest examining your reasons before pressing your doctor for surgery. Have you had a previous delivery that increases your chances for an adverse outcome? Or are you simply afraid of the pain of labor? Do a little research on the nonsurgical options and then, if you still want a cesarean, talk to your obstetrician. She may be able to put some of your fears to rest, says Men-Jean Lee, M.D., assistant professor of obstetrics and gynecology at the New York University Medical Center. And your physician can highlight any individual considerations; if you have a bleeding disorder or a heart condition, for example, the surgery may carry more than the usual risks.

Since you can't demand to give birth surgically—the decision ultimately lies with your obstetrician—it's vital to find a doctor whose philosophy about when to operate matches your own. Before you decide on a delivery doctor, be sure to ask for examples of when she would choose to perform a C-section and when she would not. Also find out the percentage of deliveries that are planned and emergency C-sections in her practice. And be sure to raise any worries you might have about a vaginal birth.

You may find a valuable ally: Some doctors will go out on a limb to honor your wishes, which could ease your dealings with your hospital or insurance company. Look for a doctor who will help you feel confident about the method of delivery selected. And do keep in mind that babies are delivered vaginally nearly 80 percent of the time, and the vast majority of births are safe for both mother and child.

one procedure that may fall to patient choice if a woman discusses it with her obstetrician.)

The VBAC Controversy

Patient choice is a particularly tricky subject when a woman has already had one C-section. "Once a cesarean, always a cesarean," was the motto, and a woman asking for a vaginal birth faced the same lack of choice that a woman wanting a C-section faces today.

But in the drive to lower C-section rates in the late 1980s, some hospitals and insurance companies established mandates that women try labor before resorting to surgery—a practice called VBAC (vaginal birth after C-section). A decade of mandated VBACs, however, resulted in a rise in the incidence of uterine rupture, when the uterus splits apart and requires emergency surgery, which can sometimes kill the child or the mother. A recent study in *The New England Journal of Medicine* shows that women undergoing VBACs have three times the risk of experiencing uterine rupture than women who have a repeat C-section.

Not surprisingly, mandated VBACs have fallen out of favor. The current thinking is that women who have had previous C-sections should, with their doctors, carefully weigh the risks before attempting a vaginal birth—one instance in which they are usually given a choice. And despite the alarming statistics, two-thirds who try VBAC will succeed, according to the American College of Obstetrics and Gynecology (ACOG).

Cesarean on Demand?

For women like Beth Gehring who have had a vaginal birth with serious complications, there is no mandate for choice in subsequent pregnancies. Frigoletto recalls a patient whose first child sustained severe brain damage during birth. When she became pregnant again, she was unwilling to risk another vaginal delivery. "She was shopping around for a doctor who would guarantee her a C-section," Frigoletto recalls. "If she couldn't find that, she was going to seek a pregnancy termination. To me, it wasn't a deal-buster to comply with her wishes." Apparently, the three other doctors who had turned her down felt differently.

In recent years, women like Frigoletto's patient and Gehring have gained some powerful allies—obstetricians who say that choosing a cesarean should be a mother's

the effects of C-sections

Vaginal birth carries more risks for both mom and child than many women realize. Still, C-sections might not always be the answer. Before you argue for one, be aware of the risks.

A cesarean is, of course, major surgery. Women who have them lose nearly twice as much blood as those who deliver vaginally, and there's a risk of adverse reactions to the anesthesia as well as infections that can jeopardize future pregnancies. Having any kind of surgery confers a greater risk for developing a potentially deadly blood clot, one of the major causes of death to women undergoing C-sections.

Women who get cesareans also have a longer and more painful recovery period. Post-operative nausea often waylays new mothers during the first precious days of their infants' lives. And, of course, the women will always carry a scar, although these days it is usually just 3 or 4 inches and located below the pubic hairline.

C-sections pose risks for the baby, too. The incidence of pulmonary hypertension—when a newborn's lungs can't pump enough oxygen into the blood—is almost five times higher than it is for babies delivered vaginally; passing through the birth canal helps squeeze fluid out of the lungs. While the total numbers are still low, at 4 per 1,000 births, 15 percent of babies with the problem do not survive. Also, planned C-sections carry the chance that the baby may be delivered before the lungs are fully developed. While such infants can be put on ventilators and are often successfully treated, this condition also can be fatal.

right and that keeping the mother out of the decision-making process denies her a voice in her own care. They include W. Benson Harer Jr., M.D., a former ACOG president. "Perhaps the time has come when the risks, benefits, and costs are so balanced between cesarean and vaginal delivery that the deciding factor should simply be the mother's preference for how her baby is delivered," he wrote three years ago in an editorial advocating patient choice in the ACOG *Clinical Review.* "Some people think they know what's best for the average woman and that they should make the decision for her," he adds today. "It goes to the historic tradition of denying women control over their bodies. I'm not promoting C-section. I'm promoting choice—that the decision should be made by the patient in consultation with her physician."

David Campbell Walters, M.D., an obstetrician and author of *Just Take It Out!: The Ethics and Economics of Cesarean Section and Hysterectomy,* is even more outspoken. "We live in a society where reproductive choice means whether or not to have an abortion," he says. "It's more controversial to ask for something you believe is safer for you and your baby than it is to kill your baby."

These voices are a minority, however. The medical establishment continues to have a strong bias against the procedure unless it's medically indicated, and many doctors won't perform what they consider unnecessary surgery. "Doctors are trained to do no harm, and by performing an invasive procedure against what was naturally intended, they may be doing that," says Men-Jean Lee, M.D., assistant professor of obstetrics and gynecology at New York University Medical Center. "Why put a patient through that if you don't need to?"

Because a cesarean is still more expensive than a vaginal birth, women can also expect some resistance from insurers. In 1997, an uncomplicated vaginal delivery cost about $4,720; an uncomplicated C-section cost $7,826. "If a health plan covers maternal benefits, it has to cover all medically necessary procedures that relate to it," says Molly Doll, a spokeswoman for the North Carolina Department of Insurance. "But if a C-section is not medically necessary, there's no requirement for the plan to cover it."

Even if a woman wanted to pay the medical bills and found a willing obstetrician, that won't guarantee she will get her way in the delivery room: Doctors have to answer to hospital administrative boards. "All C-sections are reviewed," Walters says. "The committee at my hospital will want to know why I'm doing elective C-sections with no medical indications. If I persist, they'll take my privileges away at that hospital."

Gaining the Right to Choose

The bottom line is that women don't get to choose how they will give birth, yet there are signs that the tide is shifting. A growing number of OB-GYNS don't object to planned cesareans if they feel the woman truly understands the risks. Some doctors even are willing to fudge the facts at a patient's request to get past hospital or

insurer guidelines. They may state that the baby is in the breech position, for instance, or that the mother isn't dilating, Harer says. Even the International Cesarean Awareness Network, formerly known as the Cesarean Prevention Movement, now focuses on providing women with access to accurate information about pregnancy and birth.

Ironically, one factor that may force greater acceptance of patient choice is obstetricians' exorbitant liability risks, Walters says. Obstetricians have some of the highest malpractice-insurance rates and are sued more frequently than most other medical professionals—an average of 2.53 times during their careers. One reason for such lawsuits: birth injuries caused by failure to perform a timely C-section. By this logic, more cesareans could mean fewer lawsuits. "I will tell you almost with a certainty that in five years, it will be 50 percent cesareans, and in 20 years, there will be no more vaginal births," Walters says. "If nothing else, the economics won't sustain the risk. There won't be anyone willing to take that risk."

But even if doctors are open to taking the chance, one thing seems clear: More women will be demanding a say in how they deliver their children—just as they have in so many other aspects of their health. ✳

Melba Newsome is a freelance writer in Matthews, North Carolina.

New Report Finds Breast-Feeding Protects Babies from Asthma

Breast-feeding nourishes more than bones and bonds—it can help protect children from developing asthma or wheezing later in life, Canadian researchers report. While children breast-fed for more than nine months were least at risk, four to six months of breast-feeding may also provide some protection.

New Nasal Spray Could Relieve PMS

Take a deep breath, hold it—now exhale your PMS. No, this is not some New Age scam to enlightened menstruation: It's a nasal spray that is under development by University of Michigan researchers to snuff out the mood swings that send many women into hiding the week before their periods start. The spray sends calming impulses to the area of the brain that regulates emotions and moods. If all goes as planned in the next phase of the trials, you could be sniffing out irritability in the next year.

The Vaginal Infection You Probably Don't Know Enough About

BY NOW, most women are hip to the risks of STDs and can probably reel off their latest Pap results from memory. But a far more common and potentially serious enemy is lurking—and may go undetected. Bacterial vaginosis (BV) is the most common vaginal infection to affect women of reproductive age. Once considered benign, BV is now associated with serious complications, including increased risk of HIV and other sexually transmitted viruses, pelvic inflammatory disease, and preterm labor.

The exact cause of BV is unknown, but the prevalence is striking, ranging from 10 percent among low-risk populations to 64 percent among women at high risk. Women at high risk are those who have had sex with multiple partners,

practiced unprotected sex, or had an STD in the past—or have mates with similar sexual histories.

To understand how BV works, you first need to understand the healthy vagina, says David Soper, M.D., vice chairman of the department of obstetrics and gynecology at the Medical University of South Carolina Charleston. *Lactobacilli,* a bacteria similar to the kind in yogurt, normally regulates the acid level in the vagina, making it an undesirable place for harmful germs. BV alters this healthy vaginal flora, inviting disease.

BV is easy to detect and treat, but many women don't report their symptoms. The primary symptom of BV is a "fishy smell to the vagina," Soper says. "Women with vaginas smelling like fish aren't eager to share that information with anyone."

Yet with mounting evidence about the harmful effects of BV, it pays to open up. Plus, treatment is painless. Once your doctor has tested for and verified the presence of BV, he or she will prescribe a five- or seven-day course of antibiotic pills or gel.

The most important weapon against BV may be women's attitudes about themselves. "Many women think their vaginas are dirty, so they ignore them or they practice douching, which does more harm than good," Soper says.

Many doctors now recommend BV screening once a year as part of a routine checkup, especially if you fall into a high-risk category. In addition, pregnant women, particularly those with a history of preterm labor, and those about to undergo gynecological surgery should get tested.

MORE MEDICAL ASSISTANCE FOR MENOPAUSE

MENOPAUSE HERALDS not merely a new phase of life but a host of new health issues. As baby boomers hit the life transition in droves, a new specialty has emerged: menopause providers. They're schooled in physical symptoms and treatment options of menopausal women, and they provide emotional support often needed in this life-changing time. We quizzed Jennifer Prouty, a woman's-health and psychiatric nurse practitioner and past chairwoman of the consumer-education committee for the North American Menopause Society (NAMS), about the evolving health care for women in transition.

Q: What is a menopause provider?
A: There are two groups: menopause clinicians, who have prescriptive authority (such as physicians), and menopause educators, who are licensed to provide health care (such as nurses). Almost 600 have been certified by NAMS.

Q: What are the main issues of women in transition?
A: Many women are experiencing the illness and death of a parent or a friend for the first time. They may experience these losses on an even deeper level because their bodies are changing. And relationships are shifting. Grown children may be leaving the house. Divorces are not uncommon. Many women feel a need to re-examine their lives at this stage. Some choose to switch careers, stay home, or go to work for the first time. For some, this is an intensely spiritual time. Whatever her experience, it's important for a woman to get support for her inner voice.

Q: Why would women need a menopause provider in addition to an OB-GYN?
A: For most women, hot flashes are not the whole issue. Menopause is more about experiencing and expressing a new take on life. Some women feel their doctor's practice has not aged with them. If a woman feels as though her doctor is less tuned in to her emotional and physical needs, she might consider seeking out the expertise of a health-care provider more responsive to the concerns of menopause.

Q: How can women find a menopause provider in their area?
A: Women can click on the consumer section of the NAMS Web site (www.menopause.org) to find menopause clinicians and discussion groups by state. Many doctors now have menopause counselors in their offices who can talk about the emotional as well as the medical aspects of menopause. I also encourage women to join or start a menopause-support group.

A New Way to Ease Menstrual Pain

A tiny magnet that clips to your underwear—a James Bond-style device to attract a lover? Not exactly. Women in England are attaching the discreet pear-shaped magnets called LadyCare to their bikini briefs to soothe period cramps or to the inside of bra cups to ease menstrual breast soreness.

People have been using magnets for years as alternative pain relievers for common injuries and conditions, such as tennis elbow or arthritis. But the idea that magnets could help quell menstrual pains is new. Derek Price, owner of MagnoPulse, the British company that makes LadyCare, says he stumbled on this application for magnets while researching their ability to boost sex drives (they proved less effective as aphrodisiacs). Proponents say that a magnet in the pelvic area could increase the flow of oxygen and nutrients to target and calm cramps. Anecdotal reports indicate that the majority of women who start wearing the magnet the day before their periods begin and stay magnetized throughout menstruation zap cramps without pills or side effects. But there are no large-scale studies to confirm these claims.

"It's an idea worth trying," says Marla Ahlgrimm, founder of Women's Health America, a national resource for information about premenstrual syndrome. "It's not harmful, and it's less invasive than medication—without the side effects." She cautions that women and their doctors must first rule out more serious causes for cramps before reaching for medication or magnets. LadyCare retails for about $40 and can be ordered online at www.ladycarehealth.com.

Good Question
about Women's Health
by Nancy Snyderman

Looking for the Safest Season to Be Pregnant

I read that women who give birth in winter are the most likely to suffer potentially dangerous complications like pre-eclampsia. Is there a "best time" to get pregnant?

Having suffered through my third trimester in the wilting heat of a Southern summer, I can tell you that there are certainly more comfortable times to be pregnant. But medically speaking, there's no one best time.

A recent study, though, did indicate a seasonal risk for pre-eclampsia, a life-threatening, high-blood-pressure complication that occurs in about 5 percent of pregnancies. The Norwegian study examined nearly 2 million deliveries between 1967 and 1998 and found that the risk of pre-eclampsia was 20 to 30 percent higher in December than in August.

But here's the rub: Doctors still don't know what causes pre-eclampsia, and the investigators couldn't pinpoint a direct seasonal cause and effect. Past studies have shown that pre-eclampsia occurs most commonly in first-time moms, teens, women over age 40, those with a multiple pregnancy (such as twins or triplets), African-American women, and women with diabetes.

Until science is able to provide a better understanding of the reasons behind the pre-eclampsia spike in December, I would say that the study is still inconclusive. Know your risks for pre-eclampsia, but try to enjoy your pregnancy as best you can—whenever it is.

Another Benefit of the Pill

Is it OK for me to skip the placebo week of my birth-control pills so that I don't get my period?

Besides the obvious appeal to many women who are tired of hassling with their periods, stopping menstruation can lower your risk of menstrual migraines, anemia, and endometriosis, which is believed to be linked to the number of menstrual cycles a woman goes through. For most women, skipping the placebo week seems to be fine. Studies have shown that there really is no reason for women to get their periods every month. The purpose of menstruation is to prepare the uterus for the embryo, and if you're using the pill to avoid pregnancy, menstruating regularly is like cooking for a dinner party you're not planning to have: It's unnecessary. In fact, clinical trials are currently under way for a new kind of birth-control pill that would require women to take a placebo week—and, therefore, have a period—only four times a year.

Even so, you need to be careful any time you manipulate your hormones. Check with your doctor before you totally abandon the placebo. If estrogen-dependent cancers (breast, uterine, or ovarian) or strokes run in your family, you might want to think twice before giving yourself an extra 12 weeks of estrogen yearly. And there's a cost issue, as well: Since the pill is not packaged for this type of use, you'd have to buy 17 packs to cover a year.

Nancy Snyderman, M.D. is a medical correspondent for ABC News and author of **Girl in the Mirror: Mothers and Daughters in the Years of Adolescence.**

Rape
The Road to Recovery

Rape survivors must cope not only with the physical wounds inflicted by their attackers, but also with health effects that can last a lifetime—in ways that the medical community is only now beginning to understand.

BY MELISSA CHESSHER

PHOTOGRAPHY BY ANN ELLIOTT CUTTING

For two hours, he owned my body. On a queen-sized mattress in a patch of forest near Fort Worth, Texas, the man who abducted me from a parking lot touched, penetrated, did to me whatever he wanted. He asked me questions and made demands: "What are your hot spots?" "Why don't you have kids?" "How much money do you make?" "Kiss me with your tongue." Moving his hands over my body, he paused to finger the stab wound from the knife he'd used to force me into my car. He asked if it hurt. I remember its sting and the rotten smell of his breath.

I looked into his face only once. "I know what you're doing," he said. "You're trying to remember my face. To tell the police. I could kill you right here and now, and they wouldn't find your body for weeks, maybe. The police will never find me. Remember that: I could kill you any time I want. Don't look at me." I believed him. I believed I would die that night, on that dirty mattress, in those pathetic woods.

After two hours, he ordered me to put my clothes back on. I scrambled into my skirt, my shirt, my jacket. He took all my jewelry, then climbed with me into my car again.

He told me to drive to the end of the road, then told me to stop. He grabbed my purse and got out of the car, stopping with the door ajar to speak to me for the final time.

"What's your horoscope?" he asked.

"Pisces," I answered.

"You have the bluest eyes I've ever seen," he said. And then he ran.

With the slam of the car door, my body and brain snapped in unison, decimating the steely distance I'd created to sustain me in those long hours. I unraveled. Screaming and sobbing, I drove as fast as I could, with one goal in mind—to get home.

That March night, I became one of the millions of women in the United States who have been raped. It's the most under-reported crime in America, but the government estimates that 17.7 million women in this country are survivors of rape or attempted rape. That's about 20 percent of the female population—one in five women. "Sexual-assault survivors are in our elementary schools, on our campuses, in our social circles, in our workplaces," says Dolores Card, a rape-victim counselor for 20 years and director of the Syracuse University R.A.P.E. Center in New York. "There are probably survivors in every aspect of your life, whether you're a teacher, counselor, or gas-station attendant."

Unlike me, the majority of rape victims (Card estimates 80 percent) know their attackers. But whether the perpetrator is the stranger who leaps out of the hedge or the friend-of-a-friend who takes her to dinner, raped women share a legacy of physical, emotional, and social problems. And I'm not talking about a few bad dreams and a case of the jitters. Sexual-assault survivors suffer long-term health consequences ranging in severity and specificity from chronic pain and headaches to irritable bowel syndrome and pelvic inflammatory disease. While awareness about the health ramifications of sexual assault grows, health professionals are just beginning to explore, research, and understand this medical knot woven by the interplay of body and mind—and to guide survivors to healing.

Popular images of rape survivors—from soaps and police dramas to true-life magazine articles—usually stem from the crime's immediate physical trauma and the emotional aftermath. We see the victim in a hospital, weeping and grateful to be alive. But the effects of rape go far beyond teary outbursts, lingering for years, even decades. "Many women let 20 or 30 years go by before they ever start to get help," says Kathleen Basile, Ph.D., a behavioral scientist in the Centers for Disease Control and Prevention's violence-prevention division. "Rape is not just a psychological problem; it's a social and public-health problem. It affects the physical and psychological health and well-being of half the population, and it is preventable."

Basile concedes the idea that women who have been raped are more susceptible to health problems than other women is relatively new, but she points to a growing number of studies connecting sexual violence and long-term wellness. Groundbreaking research on a group of 558 female military veterans compared the health of women who were victimized (physically assaulted, raped, or both) with those who weren't. The study, published in September 2000 in the *Journal of Obstetrics and Gynecology,*

Untying the knot woven by body and mind is crucial to guiding survivors to healing.

didn't measure specific conditions, such as ovarian cancer or high blood pressure, but it did examine health-related quality of life: general and mental health, pain, vitality, and physical and social functioning.

It found that victims of violence were far more likely to score poorly across the board on health issues. Women who were both raped and physically assaulted fared worst of all—on a par, in fact, with people suffering from major chronic illnesses like Parkinson's disease or diabetes. "More than a decade after rape or physical assault, women reported severely decreased health-related quality of life, with limitations of physical and emotional health," says Anne G. Sadler, R.N., Ph.D., the study's principal investigator and the coordinator of the Post-Traumatic Stress Disorder Clinical Team at the Iowa City Veterans' Administration Medical Center.

A Survivor's Tale: Racing Toward Recovery

Tricia Bland is living proof that what doesn't kill you makes you stronger. While growing up in Northern California's Portola Valley, Tricia was raped by a 45-year-old stranger during a visit to a nearby beach. She was 12. "My family didn't talk much about the attack," says Tricia, now 40. "They felt that if I talked about it, I would remember it, which wouldn't help me. It was just understood that in time we would heal and have that terrible day behind us."

So Tricia was left to recover on her own. Overweight as a child, she spent afternoons talking to God. She ran and learned to play softball and soccer, losing 37 pounds along the way. "I wanted to be fast and strong so I could ward off a future attacker," she says.

And she did: In 1982, as a sophomore at the University of California at Davis, Tricia was attacked by a serial rapist. She was his sixth victim—the only one to escape sexual assault. "I swore I would never go through rape again, so I fought back," she says. "I figured either he would die or I would." By the time a neighbor found her, Tricia was unconscious. Her eyes were swollen shut, her face and neck covered with hand-shaped bruises. "I just kept thinking, 'I keep coming out ahead; I keep coming out alive,'" she says. "That must mean something."

But her trials weren't over. Married, with a degree in nutrition, she became pregnant with quadruplets. One son and one daughter were dead at birth, yet Tricia put her loss in perspective: "I was blessed with more than most from a single pregnancy."

Then at age 31, after five surgeries over 12 years to clear her breasts of benign but suspicious masses, Tricia found another lump. On her doctor's advice, she had a double bilateral radical mastectomy. "Only then did I start feeling sorry for myself," she admits. "I quit exercising. I quit taking care of myself, which wasn't like me."

But then Tricia gave herself a year to regain her strength and get certified as a personal trainer—and she did it. Newly divorced, she joined a running group, where she met Glenn Bland. The two hit it off, and in September 2000 he proposed to her atop California's Mount Whitney in the Sierra Nevada Mountains.

With Glenn, she discovered adventure racing, multiday events that typically require competitors to navigate on foot, mountain bikes, and rafts on a course marked only by sparse

---

A 1998 study, meanwhile, found that 13 to 40 percent of women with three main common gynecological complaints—painful periods, heavy bleeding, and sexual dysfunction—had a history of sexual assault. "Even at the lowest percentage, which we know is a gross underestimate, that means that more than 1 in 10 of all women who come in with these symptoms has been sexually assaulted," explains researcher Jacqueline Golding, Ph.D., principal investigator for a five-year National Institute of Mental Health project exploring the link between health and sexual-assault history. And that's just the tip of the symptom iceberg: A Centers for Disease Control and Prevention (CDC) fact sheet lists these symptoms among rape's long-term by-products: chronic headaches, fatigue, sleep disturbance, recurrent nausea, eating disorders, and menstrual pain.

Amy Rohde's health problems included even more variations. A 38-year-old mosaic artist living in Syracuse, Rohde was abducted from a parking lot as she walked to her car after a late-night bartending shift. Her assailant forced her into the passenger seat, held her head down, and drove around the city for hours, repeatedly pulling off the road to rape her. Initially, Rohde earned praise from the crisis center for her positive attitude and quick recovery from the 1988 attack. But she continued to suffer physical complications that she felt stemmed from the assault. First she developed boils. Then over the years, Rohde also suffered from migraines, pelvic inflammation, painful intercourse, ovarian cysts, and chronic pain in her groin. "I've had so many health problems," she says, "and I remember wondering why it couldn't be a disease that could be diagnosed, so I could at least get some sort of treatment."

The physical reverberations of my experience were less dramatic, but no less significant. In the days following the rape, I told my story to the police, the rape counselor who met me at my home, the doctor who sewed up my cut, and a police secretary with an enormous beehive hairdo

checkpoints (think Eco Challenge). After competing in several races, the couple was invited to join a team for the Discovery Channel's World Championship Adventure Race, held in August 2001 in Switzerland. That meant rising at 3:45 a.m. every weekday to train for about four hours. On weekends, Tricia and Glenn would head for the nearby Sierra Nevada for biking, kayaking, and running. After eight months of training, the Blands' four-member Team Nextel lined up with 40 other teams on the Corvatsch Glacier in the Swiss Alps.

The race didn't start well. Sprinting down the glacial ice, Tricia slipped, sliding over snow-covered rock and "slicing both butt cheeks," she says. It took three hours for the bleeding to stop. "I just tied my jacket around my waist and kept going." But a series of missteps and diversions, from a rescue to a blizzard, cost the team precious time, making it impossible to reach the first checkpoint. They dropped out after about 30 hours.

As Tricia and Glenn greeted the nine exhausted teams that made it across the finish line, she said that the race was as hard as she expected it to be—and that she absolutely loved the experience. Tricia would probably say the same thing about her life. "I'm just trying to be the healthiest I can be in this life I've been given," she says. "Plus, I'm just getting started."

Indeed, many rape survivors' coping skills compromise their future, setting them up for a host of conditions that are either caused or made worse by lifestyle. "If you look at the possible long-term effects, you also have to explore how unresolved issues of victimization affect some of the choices survivors make, such as alcohol and other drug addictions and becoming involved in abusive relationships, even suicide attempts," Card says.

Terri Messman-Moore, Ph.D., an assistant professor of psychology at Miami University in Ohio, remembers one survivor she treated who, like me, refused to see her gynecologist for annual checkups. It's understandable that a woman who has been sexually violated would be hesitant—even fearful—to have a Pap smear. Yet a Pap smear is the best way to detect problems, such as early stages of uterine cancer and sexually transmitted diseases that, left untreated, could cause sexual dysfunction, infertility, or death. But the idea of preventive health care can get lost in a survivor's drive to manage her life and deny this history and its accompanying pain.

Basile, though, cautions against analyzing a victim's behavior in the aftermath of the attack. "You have to be careful when you talk about women making bad choices, because some people end up blaming the victim," she says. "They may not always be healthy choices for the victim, but they're ways of dealing with what has happened."

Some experts call survivors' tendency toward risky behavior "revictimization." In the strictest sense, it refers to childhood-sex-abuse survivors who experience sexual assaults as adults. But the term's definition is expanding. "There are researchers who define revictimization as any sort of repeated victimization," says Messman-Moore, one of the first academics to study this concept.

who recorded my statement. She sat stone-faced and completely silent as she typed the details of where my attacker had touched me and the threats he made. I felt ashamed, removed, alone, and I carried that isolation with me for years. At the end of each day, I retreated to my bedroom—often with ice cream or cookies to fill and numb me. Walking to and from my car made my palms sweat, anxiety dancing across me in waves. In social situations, I often drank to lift the veil of fear, and many times I couldn't remember how I arrived home. I jumped at the slightest noise and struggled in vain to claim one good night's sleep, ceaselessly replaying the memory in search of a missed moment when I might have run or punched my way to freedom. In the end, I gained about 20 pounds, spent a year or two as a binge drinker, and avoided doctors—particularly gynecologists.

When **memory of the trauma** is not addressed, the physical symptoms can linger.

Another factor that may contribute to survivors' continuing health problems is post-traumatic stress disorder, or PTSD. "Often, when the memory of the trauma and the patient's mental well-being are not addressed, the physical symptoms don't get a chance to remit and can consequently have a long-term impact on the body," says Pallavi Nishith, Ph.D., an associate research professor in the University of Missouri-St. Louis' psychology department.

Nishith documented the case study of a 34-year-old patient whose irritable-bowel symptoms—one of the conditions associated with sexual trauma—diminished after treatment for PTSD.

When Jane (as she was called in the case study) was 14 years old, she was raped by a neighbor's son. Later, she suffered panic attacks and depression, and developed an inflammatory bowel condition known as Crohn's disease. Jane was taken off solid food for a year, lost 60 pounds, and underwent two surgeries before joining a study of two standard treatments for rape-related PTSD:

- Prolonged exposure, which encourages survivors to talk about and re-experience emotions related to the event
- In-vivo exposure, where the victim physically confronts the source of her fear.

"The rapist in this case was an athlete, and the client generalized her fear to sporting goods stores," Nishith says. "In-vivo exposure involved her having to go shopping at sports stores for extended periods of time until her anxiety dissipated." After three months, Jane no longer exhibited signs of PTSD, major depression, or panic disorder, and her bowel disorder had significantly improved.

Survivor Kellie Greene believes PTSD was also behind her health complications and credits psychotherapy and antidepressants with helping her overcome them. In 1994, Greene's attacker ambushed her in her apartment, split her head open with a teakettle, and raped her. She says she hit rock bottom several months later when she cried uncontrollably in the shower for so long her body hurt. Her boyfriend and mother urged her to seek counseling and made sure she went. "PTSD can have different effects on you—not sleeping, not eating well, not getting the exercise you need," Greene says.

"I gained 50 pounds after the rape, for many reasons. I didn't want to be pretty anymore. I didn't want to stand out. But also because I wasn't able to get outside and enjoy going for a walk." It took five or six tries to find a therapist who would diagnose her symptoms accurately and prescribe anti-PTSD medication. "I remember the frustration of trying to find help," recalls Greene, now a survivors' advocate who co-wrote a Florida law mandating consecutive sentences for repeat sexual offenders. She also founded SOAR (Speaking Out About Rape), a nonprofit organization dedicated to protecting rights of sexual-assault victims. "Surviving the rape was the easy part," she remembers. "Going through everything else was really difficult."

Unfortunately, a person who experiences sexual assault today encounters many of the same obstacles that Greene, Rohde, and I faced. The American Medical Association (AMA), the CDC, and the American College of Obstetricians and Gynecologists (ACOG) have identified violence, and

Women rarely volunteer to their doctors that they're victims of rape, and doctors rarely ask.

sexual assault in particular, as one of the principal health concerns that women face in the 21st century. Both the AMA and the CDC have comprehensive diagnostic and treatment guidelines for violence and sexual abuse, and the ACOG has developed screening tools and training programs for the prevention and treatment of sexual assault. But women rarely volunteer to their doctors that they are rape victims. "It becomes something in the past that they try not to remember," Basile says.

And few physicians routinely ask. "When you're already trying to cram as much as you can into a brief office visit with a woman who is not professing sexual assault, to use a screening tool to look for it may be

Surviving rape was the easy part. **Going through everything else was really difficult.**

—rape survivor Kellie Greene

something that comes second in a physician's mind," according to ACOG spokesman Peter A. Schwartz, M.D. But many survivors—particularly those who did not initially seek support—spend their lives in and out of crises directly linked to victimization. It's critical, Sadler says, that nursing and medical schools train their students to recognize the long-term effects of rape, that screening for violence become routine, and that awareness campaigns, like those for breast and cervical cancers, educate the public about the health consequences of violence and how to prevent it.

Researchers only began exploring the physical aftermath of sexual assault about 10 years ago, and until that time, examples of physical-health ailments remained "clinical folklore." And at the moment, there are still many more questions than answers: Does the attack itself cause the health problems? Or is it the psychological response to the attack that's to blame? Questions like those deserve answers, because they will help hundreds of women like Greene, Rohde, and Jane (and me) in their quest to find help—the right kind of help—and, at last, to begin the real process of healing.

When I tell my story, it's the stab wound that captures most listeners' imaginations. It sent me to the hospital for stitches and signaled to all who heard it that my story was real, undeniable, horrifying. For me, though, the days and years that followed caused more pain than that swift cut. I felt as if the rapist took more than my confidence, self-esteem, and sense of the world as a safe place. He stole the Technicolor out of my life. The lowest point came when I measured my tailpipe and the distance from it to my car window as part of a plan to end my life. It wasn't until I volunteered at my local rape-crisis center that I began to understand my symptoms and the aftermath of my experience.

At the training sessions, I learned words such as "hyper-startle": The jumpiness I couldn't shake had a clinical definition and was a sign of PTSD. None of the doctors—the three therapists, the emergency-room physician who sewed me up after the attack, my primary-care physician, my gynecologist, or the doctor who put me on antidepressants—spoke those words or made that prognosis. Looking back, I believe I suffered a mixed bag of PTSD and depression, and that those issues compromised my ability to make healthy choices about my relationships, my health, my life. I wonder how different my life would have been if someone in a white lab jacket had sat down, listened to my story, and seen the health issues lurking in my tomorrows.

Luckily, thankfully, blessedly, I surrendered the tailpipe plan and dug myself out of the gray hole. I bungled a marriage and several other relationships, frequently returned to the comfort of social withdrawal, and swatted away depression. But I did a few things right. I continued my quest for the right therapist, and I continued volunteering at the rape-crisis center for three years. The stories I heard from other courageous women gave me the opportunity to say the things I always needed to hear: You are strong, you did everything exactly right because you're here, and you can make it.

I also hired a personal trainer who taught me how to reclaim my sense of power and strength. What began as cardio work and strength training evolved to include a few rounds with a punching bag. I relished the sound and feel of my fist thwacking the bag. Although I rarely punch today, I still lift weights several times a week and pound out my frustrations on a treadmill. Besides making me feel like Xena the Warrior Princess, it offers amazing endorphins. And that is the health legacy I cherish. I don't know if the old me would have boxed, driven to a hospital at 3 a.m. to comfort a pregnant woman who had been beaten and raped by a neighbor, or told the story of the most personal, frightening night of her life to an audience of strangers. But the new and improved me knows what she almost lost and refuses to surrender it without a fight.

My 9-year-old daughter also played a key role in helping me find my life's Crayola box of colors. And carrying her for nine months also performed a little revisionist history on my body. One strategically located stretch mark erased the scar left by my rapist's knife. ✳

Melissa Chessher lives in Lockerbie, Scotland, where she is working on a travel book about the area.

Bloating May Signal Ovarian Cancer

OVARIAN CANCER: No clinical guideline recommends screening for it, and yet it is the deadliest gynecological cancer and fifth most common cancer among American women. A new study offers hope for the early detection of what health experts call a silent killer because its symptoms—particularly in the earlier, more treatable stages—are generally thought of as nonspecific and are often missed.

While there is no simple way to diagnose ovarian cancer, like mammography for breast cancer and Pap smears for cervical cancer, a study led by Sara H. Olson, Ph.D., of Memorial Sloan-Kettering Cancer Center in New York suggests that there are some common symptoms. Olson has found that women with ovarian cancer are more likely than healthy women to experience bloating, fullness, and pressure in the abdomen and pelvis. These symptoms are constant in women with ovarian cancer, in contrast to the periodic complaints of healthy women.

Olson urges women who are experiencing these symptoms to see a doctor since early detection dramatically boosts survival rates. During the late stage, when most women are diagnosed with the disease, the five-year survival rate drops to 10 percent (compared with 80 percent if it is caught during the early stages). Women ages 35 or older should have a manual exam once a year to check for abnormal ovarian swelling or tenderness; starting at age 25, women with a family history of cancer (especially ovarian, breast, or colon) should have a sonogram twice a year. For more information about ovarian cancer, visit the National Ovarian Cancer Coalition's Web site at www.ovarian.org or call 888-682-7426.

Mammograms Without the Ouch

Most women over 40 who should be getting their yearly mammograms skip them, according to a recent study. A common reason: the pain. Fortunately, mammography may get a lot more comfortable: The U.S. Food and Drug Administration has approved a foam cushion that reduced discomfort in 74 percent of women in one study without affecting accuracy. The Woman's Touch MammoPad is available at a growing number of hospitals and breast-imaging centers across the country. Before you schedule your next screening, find out if the pad is available. If it's not, ask your doctor to check out www.mammopad.com for ordering information.

this little pill can prevent cancer

The progestin in oral contraceptives does more than keep the stork away; it may also provide the best protection against ovarian cancer. Duke University researchers found that the risk for the often-deadly cancer was cut by nearly half in all women taking oral contraceptives containing the hormones estrogen and progestin. And for women taking pills that had high levels of progestin, the risk was cut by an additional 50 percent. The findings could lead to new drugs that fight ovarian cancer.

milk:
the latest weapon in the battle against breast cancer

Women who drank milk as children and continue to drink at least three glasses a day as adults had half the rate of breast cancer compared with nonmilk drinkers, according to a new report in the *International Journal of Cancer*. The connection between milk and cancer remains unclear.

COMING SOON:
A Better Breast Test

You know the mantra: Regular mammograms could save your life. But when scientists at the National Cancer Institute (NCI) expressed doubts about mammography's worth in early 2002, you had to wonder if you should abandon the test and depend on a hand in the shower or at the doctor's office to detect a lump. In the end, the NCI, along with the American Cancer Society and the American Medical Association, reaffirmed its faith in mammograms. In fact, the feds updated their guidelines, recommending mammography for women 40 and older every one to two years (previous guidelines applied to women age 50 and older). But researchers are at work on alternative screening methods that could address some of mammography's limitations.

"For now, the mammogram is the best screening tool for women over 50," says Susan Love, M.D., an adjunct professor of surgery at University of California at Los Angeles and Medical Director of the Susan Love M.D. Breast Cancer Foundation. "But we desperately need something better for younger women and women at higher risk—those who have a family history of the disease, the breast-cancer gene, or who have already had cancer in one breast."

That need could be met with another test that's now being developed—a "breast Pap" that analyzes breast fluid. A University of California at San Francisco study of more than 7,000 women found that the fluid, when extracted from the milk ducts (where breast cancer starts) and analyzed, could help predict who would and wouldn't get the disease. Women who produced breast fluid with abnormal cells were 60 percent more likely to develop breast cancer than women with normal cells.

The key to understanding breast cancer could be in getting to where the disease starts—the milk duct.

The notion of suctioning breast fluid may sound intimidating, but the technique is noninvasive and generally painless, exerting no more pressure than that of a nursing infant, explains Margaret Wrensch, Ph.D., the study author and a professor of epidemiology and biostatistics.

Several methods of collecting breast fluid have been developed in recent years, but the most widely used is ductal lavage, a technique pioneered by Love. "There's no question in my mind that being able to get to where breast cancer starts—the milk duct—will be the key to figuring out and eradicating breast cancer," Love says.

The U.S. Food and Drug Administration has approved the ductal lavage technique and, in January 2002, a group of the nation's leading surgical oncologists issued the first clinical guidelines to help women and their doctors understand how to use it. It's currently recommended only for women at high risk. Love says that it's a great tool for women who need to make decisions such as whether to undergo further tests, have a preventive mastectomy, or start treatment with estrogen-blocking tamoxifen. "Until we have more data, we don't want to do this on everyone and risk overtreating people," Love cautions. Many insurance companies cover the procedure, which costs about $500 to $800 and is currently offered at about 135 centers nationwide. To find out more about it or to search by state for doctors offering ductal lavage, visit www.ductallavage.com.

Eventually, scientists hope to use breast fluid to chart the progress of abnormal cells, as well as identify potential markers for the disease and even carcinogens, such as PCBs, that may play a role in the disease. It's a long way off, but researchers hope the new techniques will become as commonplace as the routine Pap smear.

Breaking News on Breast Cancer

The latest research promises better detection, easier treatment, and healthier, longer lives for patients.

Breast cancer gets more attention than almost any other disease—including several that kill far more American women. Yet in spite of the billions spent on research, it's still tough to find, complex to treat, and impossible to cure. Today, though, hope is growing: Recent breakthroughs can predict whether the cancer is likely to spread, and can slash radiation treatment from six weeks to one. Still to come are new screening methods that are undergoing lab tests as we go to press.

The Latest from the Laboratory

BY MICHAEL CASTLEMAN

Every woman's wish list (short of a cure): better ways to find out exactly who has breast cancer and who doesn't, and treatments that don't diminish quality of life in the effort to add years to it. While scientists haven't yet been able to give us everything we want, they have managed to get us closer than ever. Here's a look at the year's most exciting advances.

Mammogram double check

Even for the most expert radiologist, finding tiny tumors on a mammogram is like searching for a brown sock in a dark closet—when you don't know if the sock is in there. When two radiologists read the same mammogram ("double reading" in medical parlance), detection rates improve about 15 percent. Replace that second radiologist with a computer, and detection rates jump 20 percent over a single read, according to recent research.

A computer-aided detection (CAD) system programmed to look for breast abnormalities is "like spell check in a word-processing program," says radiologist Peter Shile, M.D.,

medical director of the Susan G. Komen Breast Center in Peoria, Illinois, a facility that performs 3,000 mammograms monthly. "It highlights areas that deserve a second look." The radiologist then decides whether to follow up with a second mammogram or a biopsy.

The U.S. Food and Drug Administration was initially skeptical, suspecting that computer readings would lead to unnecessary biopsies by casting suspicion on healthy breast tissue. But after three good studies proved the accuracy of CAD readings, the FDA gave its final approval. In late 2001, health insurers began covering CAD-based double reads.

You won't find a CAD system at all hospitals, partly because the equipment costs about $200,000. The most common brand, the ImageChecker system from R2 Technologies, has been installed at about 300 facilities so far. CAD systems should become standard within the next five years, but you can spur the process by getting mammograms only at facilities that have one. "After a long day of reading mammograms, any radiologist's eyes will get tired," Shile says, "but the CAD system doesn't."

Heat-seeking scans

All cells create heat; cancer cells create slightly more than normal ones, which makes tumors somewhat warmer than the surrounding healthy tissue. Researchers have finally found a way to use thermal imaging—a method for mapping this temperature difference—to detect tumors. "Unlike older versions of thermal imaging, we don't just take a single infrared picture of the breast anymore," says Yuri Parisky, M.D., Chief of Breast Imaging Services at the University of Southern California Norris Comprehensive Cancer Center. "Today, we couple many pictures with a sophisticated computer analysis that calculates the probability that any portion of the breast is either normal or cancerous."

The new procedure, called computerized thermal imaging (CTI), could lead to fewer biopsies when used with mammography. In a pilot study four years ago at Howard University, radiologists analyzed CTI scans and mammograms in 100 women before they underwent biopsies. The physicians predicted cancer with about 97 percent accuracy—a huge improvement over the 85 percent rate for mammograms alone. "CTI scans also accurately determined that many of the suspicious spots on the mammograms were actually normal," Parisky says. In 2001, he led a follow-up of 2,000 women that showed results almost identical to those in the original study. (Results from some more-recent trials are not yet available.)

The test is painless, takes about 10 minutes, and provides immediate results. To have a CTI scan, you lie facedown on a special table, with one breast hanging through an opening into an imaging chamber. An air-conditioning system cools breast tissue to about 15 degrees below room temperature. "Normal blood vessels contract when cooled, but vessels feeding tumors don't," Parisky says. Infrared cameras then take thermal photographs that are computer-analyzed for abnormalities.

If CTI, which is awaiting FDA approval, were standard, doctors probably would still biopsy some sites the computer indicated were OK. But "it looks like we could safely reduce the number of breast biopsies by around 20 percent," Parisky says.

The Pap test for breasts

A group of top cancer surgeons is pushing a new test called ductal lavage as an addition to mammography for women at high risk. "Ductal lavage is similar to a Pap test in that it samples cells that can turn cancerous," says William Dooley, M.D., medical director of the Institute for Breast Health at the University of Oklahoma Medical Center. "But instead of swabbing the cervix, we extract cells from the milk ducts."

Since *Health* first reported on the FDA-approved technique in our May 2002 issue, the medical community has expressed even more interest in the test, particularly because of ongoing questions about mammography (see "Real-life Decisions About Mammograms," page 89). During the test, a physician uses a breast pump (similar to those used by nursing mothers) to stimulate the milk ducts so she can see where to insert a catheter that's about as thin as a human hair. A small amount of saline is pumped into and then drained out of the catheter, carrying some duct cells with it. Those cells are then analyzed; if they're precancerous, the woman can take tamoxifen, which has been shown to reduce the incidence of breast cancer in high-risk women by 49 percent.

Most women report that the procedure feels like tugging or pinching, making it less painful than mammography, says Henry Kuerer, M.D., Ph.D., director of the breast surgical-oncology training program at the University of Texas M. D. Anderson Cancer Center in Houston. "Ductal lavage in no way replaces mammography," he says. But when used together, the two tests can help a woman make tough decisions about treatment.

An ouchless early warning

In the future, a quick, painless, and inexpensive saliva test may identify breast cancer while sparing you the discomfort of mammography, says Charles F. Streckfus, D.D.S., assistant dean for research at the University of Mississippi School of Dentistry. The test, developed by Streckfus and his team over the past five years, spots unusually high levels of a protein that is a marker for the disease.

Breast tumors increase levels of a protein known as HER2/NEU in blood and saliva. Levels drop when treatment is successful and rise if the cancer returns, so it may help determine if a course of treatment is working, and whether there's a recurrence. For this test, you chew gum to trigger saliva secretion, then spit into a cup.

"You don't need to draw blood. You don't have to worry about needle accidents and bloodborne diseases," Streckfus says. "And a saliva test can be easily administered at health fairs and work sites. Women might even take it at home."

The downside: The test failed to find breast cancer in around 13 percent of cases, and it detected cancer where there was none in 35 percent. "No test is perfect," Streckfus says. "We hope the combined results of our test and mammography will be more accurate than either by itself." Because almost 40 percent of American women over age 40 haven't had a recent mammogram, this test may well be a boon for early detection.

Streckfus and his colleagues are wrapping up a study of 1,100 women that examines cancer-detection rates for mammography by itself, the saliva test alone, and the two tests together. Results should be available by the end of 2002; if they're favorable and the test wins FDA approval, it could be on the market by the end of 2003.

A sign that cancer will spread

A test for another protein in breast tumors could for the first time allow doctors to distinguish dangerously fast-spreading cancers from less-threatening ones. The RhoC protein, identified recently by University of Michigan researchers, enables tumor cells to invade new tissues and enter the bloodstream, which is how cancer spreads (or metastasizes). The protein is abundant in metastatic breast tumors but scant in normal breast tissue, benign lumps, and slow-growing breast tumors that are less likely to spread.

A team led by University of Michigan breast-cancer specialist Celina Kleer, M.D., tested for RhoC protein in 182 biopsy samples of malignant tissue and correctly identified 88 percent of tumors that had metastasized. The ability to identify potentially metastatic tumors has major implications for treatment: Women with cancers that are less likely to spread may be spared postsurgery chemotherapy and its side effects. It could also mean more aggressive treatment when high levels of RhoC are found.

As Kleer and her colleagues lay plans for a larger follow-up study to test for RhoC, it's too soon to tell when such a test might be available for general use. But Kleer estimates that it's at least two years away.

Radiation in just five days or less

Women who undergo lumpectomies typically must also undergo radiation every weekday for six weeks—a physically taxing treatment that can be inconvenient, particularly for patients who live in remote areas. "Women who can't get to the facility every day have to forgo radiotherapy, which leaves them at increased risk of recurrence. Or they have to have mastectomies," says Douglas Arthur, M.D., an associate professor of radiation oncology at Virginia Commonwealth University's Massey Cancer Center.

But a different way of administering radiation may cut the treatment down to two sessions a day for a total of five days. Instead of external radiation (think X-ray machines), radioactive seeds are planted in the breast to zap tissue surrounding where a lump was removed. The procedure, called brachytherapy, was first tried in breast-cancer patients more than a decade ago. But several new long-term studies prove brachytherapy is as effective as traditional radiation.

Breast-brachytherapy pioneer Robert Kuske, M.D., an oncology professor at the University of Wisconsin Hospital in Madison, uses a process that involves implanting 16 to 19 catheters into the breast in an operation that takes an hour or two. At each of the 10 follow-up treatment sessions, radioactive pellets the size of grains of rice are run through the catheters on a wire. The painless process takes about 15 minutes. After five days, the catheters are removed.

Brachytherapy is currently used in women whose early-stage breast cancer hasn't spread. The FDA recently approved a new device, called MammoSite, that delivers radiation through a balloon temporarily implanted in the breast, instead of multiple catheters. MammoSite simplifies the procedure for both the patient and the physician, and it should make brachytherapy more popular, Arthur predicts.

British researchers, meanwhile, recently announced that one-time radiation during lumpectomy may be just as effective as external radiation. In intraoperative radiotherapy, or IOR, the surgeon inserts a radiation-emitting probe where the tumor was removed, delivering the whole dose of radiation in just 25 minutes. Although all the patients in the study remained cancer-free for one year, follow-up studies are needed because the risk of recurrence remains high for five years, says researcher Jayant Vaidya, a breast surgeon at the University College London Medical School. Those studies are under way in Italy, Germany, Australia, and the United States. ✳

San Francisco writer Michael Castleman is the author of 10 health books, including **Blended Medicine,** *a home guide that combines mainstream and alternative therapies.*

Real-life Decisions about Mammograms

BY CHRISTIE ASCHWANDEN

When Danish researchers concluded in October 2001 that mammograms don't save lives, the news sparked heated debate that left women wondering what to do. Press coverage died down after several national associations reaffirmed their support for screenings of women 40 and older. "Mammograms can find breast cancers when they're very small," says Robert Smith, Ph.D., director of cancer screening at the American Cancer Society. "And the smaller the tumor, the greater the chances for successful treatment."

But while public debate has waned, confusion hasn't. After all, national guidelines don't—and can't—reflect the personal risks and reactions of each woman. So we interviewed four women who made very different decisions about mammography—for very different reasons. Their stories show just how complicated the right choice can be.

"I'm afraid of doing nothing."

Carol Milano, 55, got her first mammogram at age 30 because she has a family history of breast cancer and a set of fibrocystic breasts. "My gynecologist says it's really tough to tell what all my different lumps and bumps are," the New York–based author says. "Self-exams are useless for me."

For the last 25 years, Milano has gotten annual mammograms and clinical breast exams, plus sonograms for the past 15 years, to monitor her assorted lumps. And when a mammogram detected a suspicious mass about three years ago, her doctor ordered a biopsy. "It was negative," Milano says. Six months later, the doctor recommended another biopsy to make sure no tumor was lurking behind the scar tissue. "I screamed and yelled but really trusted him, so I finally agreed," Milano says. The second biopsy was negative, too.

The two biopsies only intensified Milano's fears about breast cancer—and left her with a scar about an inch and a half long. She was also frustrated by her doctor's order that she stay inactive while the incisions healed. "I've been running for 21 years, and I bike pretty regularly," Milano says.

Dense breasts run in Milano's family, so her sister and aunt get regular mammograms as well. And each has recently had suspicious results, prompting biopsies that turned up negative for cancer. Their experience is not uncommon: "Most women are not going to get breast cancer in their lifetimes,"

the ACS's Smith says. "But we need to test the many to find the few."

The threat of breast cancer feels real to Milano, and the stress of having so many tests compounds her fears. While she's done enough research to satisfy herself that mammograms are the right thing to do, she wishes there were a better alternative. "I hate mammograms—they're painful," she says. "And the debate about them makes me like them even less. But I don't know what else to do, and I'm afraid of doing nothing."

"I had no reason to think I would get cancer."

"I take this very personally, because a mammogram saved my life," 37-year-old Gina Vita says of the debate over testing. Although the Hingham, Massachusetts, office manager had no family history and no known risk factors, she decided to go along with her doctor's request that she have a baseline mammogram at age 35. The test showed evidence of microcalcification—calcium clusters in the breast that can have a number of causes, including cancer. "Everyone was telling me that it was nothing, but my gut instinct said, 'No, prove it.'" Vita insisted on a needle biopsy, which showed that she had invasive cancer.

As terrifying as the diagnosis was, Vita felt lucky. "I was relieved because it was caught so early," she says. Breast cancer in young women is often aggressive, and she's convinced that without the mammogram, her cancer would have spread further before it was found, significantly lowering her chance of survival. Vita first opted for three lumpectomies but eventually underwent a mastectomy. Follow-up tests have shown that none of her lymph nodes were affected, so her prognosis is excellent.

Because 70 percent of women diagnosed with breast cancer have no known risk factors, Vita believes that mammograms are important for all women. "I had no reason to think I would ever get breast cancer," she says.

As a former X-ray technologist, Vita realizes that the procedure isn't foolproof. "I have an 8-year-old daughter, and I hope and pray that there will be some major breakthroughs before she's an adult," she says.

"My doctor knows how I feel."

Liza Gross' 75-year-old mother is dying from breast cancer, but the 42-year-old science writer from Novato, California, is in no rush to get a mammogram. She worries that heavy promotion of a test scientists admit is flawed gives women a false sense of security. "What about women who have negative mammograms and think they're OK? Ten years ago, my mother had gotten her annual mammogram, and they said it was negative," she says. "Then, three months later, she found a lump in her right breast. It was cancer that had metastasized to her lymph nodes." False negatives are so common, in fact, that lawsuits against radiologists who read mammograms are among the leading types of medical-malpractice litigation in the United States, says Leonard Berlin, M.D., chairman of radiology at Rush North Shore Medical Center and the author of a report on delayed diagnosis.

Even when a tumor is found on the film, it may be too late. "What the experts are calling early detection is really only slightly earlier detection," says breast-cancer expert Susan Love, M.D. Gross is concerned about the risk with mammography itself. "Radiation is the only thing we definitely know causes breast cancer, and we're using it to detect it," she says. "Premenopausal women have breasts that are more sensitive to radiation." Love agrees that the radiation risk should not be ignored. "My concern is for women with a family history who start getting mammograms at 30. Even at this low dose, the radiation adds up," she says.

Gross believes the benefits don't outweigh the risks. "The clincher was a Canadian study showing that women who got mammograms and breast exams were no less likely to die than those who just got breast exams," she says. She relies on monthly self-exams, plus yearly exams from a trained physician. "My doctor knows how I feel about mammograms, and she hasn't suggested that I get one," Gross says.

"I'm not saying 'never.'"

Leslie Laufman, M.D., an oncologist at Hematology Oncology Consultants in Columbus, Ohio, doesn't get annual mammograms even though at age 55, she's solidly in the age range when the test is supposed to be most valuable. "I'm not saying I never would," she says. "But I'm not getting them now, and I don't have any plans to."

Within the last six years, Laufman has been on two panels that reviewed evidence about mammography for the National Cancer Institute. After poring over hundreds of pages of research, she concluded that mammograms had been greatly oversold. "We are informing a lot of women of cancer diagnoses, but many of them never needed to know they had cancer," she says. "Sometimes a mammogram will find a very fast-growing tumor, but for the most part, mammograms pick up very slow-growing cancers and noninvasive cancers," she says. For example, mammograms have increased the number of women diagnosed with ductal carcinoma in situ (DCIS), a lesion in the milk ducts. With 30 years of follow-up, only about one in three DCIS lesions ever develops into invasive cancer. But because doctors can't tell which ones those are, Laufman says, nearly all women diagnosed are advised to have surgery, often followed by radiation and tamoxifen. Yet two-thirds of these women would have been fine without any treatment at all. "We say mammograms are helping us cure lots of cancers, but they're mostly the ones that didn't need to be cured," she says.

"I believe that for postmenopausal women who do not have dense breasts, having a mammogram every two to three years would be reasonable," Laufman says. "Having them more frequently hasn't been proven to be useful. It's difficult to prove they are useful at all for women in their 40s.

"Some of my colleagues think I'm crazy to make public statements about this issue," she says. But the amount of testing and treatment concerns her because it leads to radiation exposure, unnecessary surgeries, and other negative outcomes. To find life-threatening tumors, Laufman advocates breast exams performed by professionals as an alternative to mammograms. "There's no downside to a physical exam," she says.

Another of Laufman's concerns is that, even in the best facilities, mammograms miss one out of five invasive cancers, especially in younger women. "A woman with an abnormality on a physical examination should not be reassured if her mammogram is normal. She needs a definite diagnosis. We doctors need to be better at reminding ourselves and informing women about the limitations of this test."

Laufman is also insulted by the medical community's attempt to distill the issue to a single message: Don't worry about the controversy, just get a mammogram. "As a woman, it frustrates me," she says. "The attitude is that women are too stupid to sort it out, so they need a simple answer. I have a lot more faith in women than that." ✳

Contributing Editor Christie Aschwanden is a member of the National Association of Science Writers.

Does Your Race Put You at Risk?

BY LINDA VILLAROSA

Is there a black breast cancer? That question is debated in hushed tones in church basements, at family reunions, across kitchen tables, and wherever African-American women gather.

Karen Eubanks Jackson of Houston isn't sure where she stands on the issue, but she knows that something strange is going on in her family. Eight years ago, Jackson, a wife and mother in Los Angeles, discovered a lump in her right breast and shortly afterward was diagnosed with cancer. "I didn't know anything about breast cancer," she says. "I thought it was something only white women got."

After surgery, chemotherapy, and radiation, she is now symptom-free. But through her experience, she discovered that two of her aunts suffered from the disease, and that it killed one of them. A third aunt had a double mastectomy, kept secret until after her death. Now, Jackson's mother is battling the disease. While Jackson's family isn't the first to experience a rash of diagnoses, her story adds to the perception held by some that breast cancer is more aggressive and more deadly for black women than it is for white women.

A surprising number of statistics back up that belief. On one hand, overall death rates from the disease are decreasing, and the incidence is lower among African-American women compared to white women. But black women who do get breast cancer are 50 percent more likely both to contract it before age 35 and die from it before age 50. In addition, they are more susceptible to an aggressive form of the disease that doesn't respond to some of the most common and successful treatments.

Scientists aren't positive why the disease affects blacks and whites differently. Most reject the idea of a specific cancer exclusive to blacks. A more plausible explanation is that a combination of factors, from genetics and biology to environment and diet, is setting African-American women up for a more virulent form of the deadly disease. It's a complex problem. And while the question "Is there a black breast cancer?" is simple, the answer is anything but.

Predisposition: nature or nurture?

Lovell Jones, Ph.D., director of the Center for Research on Minority Health at the University of Texas M. D. Anderson Cancer Center in Houston, has spent more than 20 years studying disparities in how some diseases play out between blacks and whites. He says the people who believe in a specific cancer that strikes only black women are confusing the issue. "This is not a different disease, but a different rate of a certain variation of a disease," he says. "There are white females who have the same premenopausal breast cancer that grows rapidly and resists treatment, but the frequency is different. It may be that the factors causing breast cancer are confronting black women more often than white."

One of those factors might be genetics. Although the research is still murky, scientists are trying to explain why African-American women are more frequently diagnosed with estrogen-receptor-negative tumors. These tumors don't feed off estrogen and grow more aggressively than other tumors; they also don't respond to tamoxifen, one of the most effective treatments for breast cancer. Researchers theorize that women with high estrogen levels are more likely to contract breast cancer early, and this early cancer more often takes the form of estrogen-receptor-negative tumors. Because black women are more likely to have high levels of estrogen, the result is that they may be more susceptible to this aggressive cancer.

But Lisa Newman, M.D., associate director of the Alexander J. Walt Comprehensive Breast Center at the Barbara Ann Karmanos Cancer Institute, says genes alone don't explain why breast cancer is more deadly for African-American women. "Nobody understands the whole picture. There are genetic influences to explain the unequal cancer burden, but it's much more complex than that. You have to look at nutrition, obesity, and the environment."

Researchers know that high-fat diets and lack of physical activity can increase estrogen levels. And African-American women typically consume more fatty foods and exercise less than their white counterparts. They are about 20 percent more likely to be overweight than white women; two out of every three African-American women are overweight. Where they live may also play a role. According to numerous national studies, blacks are much more likely than whites to live in areas polluted with dioxins, PCBs, and other cancer-causing chemicals. These lifestyle and environmental factors, combined with the genetic picture, pack a one-two punch for black women. And that combination often tips the balance.

Jones puts it simply: "If you have a white woman and a black woman with the same genetic predisposition but add in dietary, cultural, and environmental factors more common to blacks, the risk of early breast cancer is no longer the same."

The treatment gap

Predisposition isn't the only reason breast cancer is so dangerous for black women. According to several national studies and leading cancer experts, not only are blacks more apt to postpone medical treatment, but they tend to receive substandard medical care when they go to the doctor.

Distrust in American medicine has driven some black women away from their doctors, contributing to late diagnosis and early death. "I see that distrust all the time, and it can result in women being diagnosed at a later stage," says Otis W. Brawley, M.D., professor of medicine, oncology, and epidemiology at Emory University and associate director for cancer control at Winship Cancer Institute. "Three hours ago, I saw a young lady who watched a mass grow in her breast for well over a year. She didn't want to go to the doctor because she was afraid that she'd be lied to or used as a guinea pig."

One reason for that mistrust is racism—often subtle and inadvertent—in the medical community. In March 2002, the Institute of Medicine released a 562-page report that shows how deep the problem is. The findings, drawn from more than 100 documented studies, were indisputable: Even when African-Americans and other minorities have the same incomes, insurance coverage, and medical conditions as whites, they receive notably poorer care. Racial prejudices, the panel found, may be tainting physicians and other health professionals.

"If black women are not receiving the same level of care and treatment, that explains why they are diagnosed disproportionately at a stage when the disease is not curable," says Harold Freeman, M.D., one of the pre-eminent experts on cancer in minorities and director of the Center to Reduce Cancer Health Disparities at the National

Cancer Institute. "This report concludes that race, in and of itself, is a factor in determining how people are treated even when they are of the same status and economic class."

Poverty exacerbates the problem. U.S. Census figures show that more than 20 percent of African-Americans live below the poverty level; further, Henry J. Kaiser Family Foundation statistics released in February 2002 show that black women are three times as likely to be on Medicaid as white women. Studies show that poor people get worse care in all areas: A report that appeared in April 2002's *Journal of the National Cancer Institute* found that women on Medicaid were 41 percent more likely to be diagnosed with breast cancer at a late stage than non-Medicaid patients, and were 44 percent less likely to receive radiation. Not surprisingly, their risk of dying from the disease was three times higher than women of other races.

Moving forward

As scientists continue to try to solve the puzzle, African-American women are taking action, spreading news, support, and education to their peers. Karen Jackson, for example, founded a survivors' group, Sisters Network Inc.

Wanda Williams, a South Bend, Indiana, radio-show host and breast-cancer survivor, says this kind of self-initiated care is vital for black women. "It is up to us to be empowered about our health and encourage other black women to do the same. I was given a chance at life, so that is what I try to do every day."

For women everywhere, eliminating breast cancer altogether is the larger goal. But until then, women like Williams, along with doctors and researchers, are pushing to close the gap between blacks and whites. That requires grassroots activism, genetic research, education, and more. But for Harold Freeman, the answer is deceptively simple: Black women just need a level playing field. "When women are diagnosed at the same stage and receive the same treatment," he says, "there's no disparity in terms of race and status."

That, in itself, would be a remarkable start. ✳

Linda Villarosa, author of several books on health care for African-Americans, is a New York Times *contributing writer.*

HERBS:
the new cure for menopause?

More and more women are turning to natural remedies to treat menopausal symptoms. But are they effective?

BY TIMOTHY GOWER

Last winter, Veronica Windley opened windows and turned on fans while other New Yorkers bundled up against the cold. Every half-hour or so, she felt a wave of heat consume her body. At night, she often awoke with sweat-soaked sheets. By day, the sleep-deprived 45-year-old struggled to concentrate at her job as an office manager for a video production company while constantly searching for ways to cool down. "I'd be sitting at my desk, and, all of a sudden, it was like, 'Woo, what's going on?'" she recalls.

Windley's doctor explained that such hot flashes are a classic symptom of menopause. Restoring Windley's diminished estrogen levels with hormone-replacement therapy, or HRT, could easily douse the flames, the doctor said. But she wasn't interested. Her mother had died of cancer, and she had read somewhere that HRT might increase a woman's risk for the disease. "It was just really scary to me," Windley says. "I thought something herbal would be safer."

So Windley tried RemiFemin, over-the-counter pills containing an extract of a plant called black cohosh. In a couple of weeks, the hot flashes stopped completely.

About 75 percent of American women experience disconcerting symptoms as estrogen levels plummet. The most common complaint—the one that most often drives women to their doctors—is hot flashes, sudden increases in body temperature that usually last about four minutes and can be accompanied by sweating, heart palpitations, and dizziness. For 10 to 15 percent of menopausal women, hot flashes are more than just a nuisance—they're downright debilitating, disrupting sleep, work, and home life. For most women, this lasts for more than a year; for 25 percent of midlife women, it lasts for more than five years. Needless to say, lots of women are looking for solutions.

Increasingly, they're turning to natural remedies: According to a federally funded study of women ages

*Advocates claim that **natural remedies** ease the symptoms of hot flashes because they are rich in phytoestrogens. Some experts believe that black cohosh mimics a brain chemical that may **diminish symptoms of menopause**.*

93

*Supplement makers are not required by law to **prove the safety and effectiveness** of their products.*

45 and older, more than 20 percent used only alternative approaches to deal with menopausal symptoms, and 25 percent used both conventional and alternative treatments. Sales of products containing black cohosh have increased more than threefold since 1998. Even Bayer has added a "menopause health" product to its venerable line of One-A-Day multivitamins. But can supplements such as black cohosh and red clover really douse hot-flash flames for good?

Despite the success stories they hear from women like Veronica Windley, many doctors remain cautious about recommending alternatives to HRT. For one thing, HRT has been proven to provide complete relief for most hot-flash sufferers, and most experts say there's not enough strong evidence supporting herbal and natural remedies.

Recent studies, however, have cast doubt on some of the most compelling benefits attributed to the drug. The American Heart Association announced in July 2001 that it did not recommend HRT as an intervention to prevent heart attacks, saying there simply isn't enough evidence that restoring a woman's hormone levels protects her heart. In 2002, the American Heart Association, based on findings in the Women's Health Initiative, said HRT should not be used to prevent heart disease, even in healthy women. The Women's Health Initiative was not set up to study HRT use for treatment of menopause symptoms nor to test all forms of estrogen, so more research needs to be done in these areas.

The research on bone density has flip-flopped: A study published in *The Journal of the American Medical Association* in summer 2001 suggests that HRT isn't as effective at strengthening women's bones after age 60; a month later, the same journal reported that HRT does improve bone health in elderly women.

In HRT's favor, though, another recent study found that one long-standing deterrent—the fear that HRT increases breast-cancer risk—might be largely unfounded. But that probably won't be enough to sway the 60 to 65 percent of American women who could benefit from HRT but are currently not taking it, especially without the lure of healthier hearts and stronger bones. In addition, says gynecologist Lila Nachtigall, M.D., of the New York University School of Medicine, some of those women simply can't take estrogen—for example, women who have had breast cancer, endometrial cancer, or chronic liver disease. For these women, natural remedies such as black cohosh, soy, red clover, and dong quai seem particularly attractive.

Some remedies may have value, says San Francisco gynecologist Maida Taylor, M.D., who reviewed the science on herbs and menopause for the American College of Obstetricians and Gynecologists. But she stops shy of a ringing endorsement of the natural approach, saying further studies are necessary. "There is a huge body of literature showing that black cohosh isn't toxic, and there's some suggestion that it may work," she says of the herb, which was originally used for medicinal purposes by Native Americans. "I have no strong reason to tell people not to take it, but at the same time there is a need for caution in some high-risk cases."

Nachtigall is perhaps slightly more enthusiastic about red clover (sold as Promensil in the United States). She and several of her colleagues conducted a preliminary study of 23 women who took 40 milligrams of red-clover extract per day. After three months, most participants had half as many hot flashes as they had before taking red clover. "It's not as good as estrogen," Nachtigall says, "but it certainly did help."

Red clover—like the majority of plant-based menopause remedies—is a rich source of hormonelike chemicals called phytoestrogens. Although they aren't true estrogens, the molecules act like female hormones in a significant way: They attach themselves to the same receptors on human cells, the way a skeleton key fits into a lock. In this respect, proponents say, they

*Despite the success stories **many doctors remain cautious** about recommending alternatives to HRT.*

work much like HRT, providing a woman's body with enough estrogenlike activity to keep such menopausal symptoms as hot flashes at bay.

"In general, phytoestrogens are much, much weaker than estrogens," says family physician Marjorie Bowman, M.D., of the University of Pennsylvania School of Medicine, who wrote an extensive review on the scientific literature on herbs and menopause in *Archives of Internal Medicine* in 2001. In fact, she says, a phytoestrogen molecule has between .01 and .001 the potency of an estrogen molecule. Bowman says many women come to her saying they had tried herbs to relieve menopausal symptoms but were disappointed by the results. Phytoestrogen, Bowman explains, "just doesn't do the same things as estrogen; it doesn't cure the problem as well."

Other skeptics remind women that supplement makers are not required by law to prove to the U.S. Food and Drug Administration the safety and effectiveness of their products. And because herbs cannot be patented, the same companies are reluctant to invest in the kinds of studies that pharmaceutical companies are required to conduct on prescription and over-the-counter drugs. To fill the gap, the National Institutes of Health is sponsoring several studies. In one experiment, scientists at the University of Illinois have randomly assigned 112 menopausal women to receive daily doses of either red clover, black cohosh, HRT, or placebo pills. The participants will keep diaries for a year, recording how often they experience hot flashes and other menopausal symptoms. The study should be completed in 2003.

As clinical investigator Stacie Geller, Ph.D., explains, this study might determine that herbal remedies are not as effective as HRT, "but that they may work well enough." And for menopausal women who can't or won't use hormone-replacement therapy, that just might mean being able to get through the day—without losing their cool. ✳

Contributing editor Timothy Gower is the co-author (with Robert S. DiPaola, M.D.) of A Doctor's Guide to Herbs and Supplements.

remedies to try

The package of one herbal remedy says the concoction "supports hormonal balance so important for smooth menopausal transition." That assertion might sneak in under the U.S. Food and Drug Administration guidelines since it falls short of a medical claim—thanks to the word "supports." But are these kinds of pills worth the money?

Some of the ingredients might be helpful, and research is being conducted to find out. But if you want to try a natural remedy, here's a look at what is known so far. Talk to your physician before taking anything—herbal or otherwise.

Remedy	Theory	Supporting Evidence
Black Cohosh	Some scientists believe this remedy may mimic the brain chemical serotonin, which perhaps weakens menopausal symptoms.	Several studies have found that this herb relieves hot flashes. But in a 2001 study at Columbia University, black cohosh was no better than placebos at reducing the number of hot flashes in breast-cancer survivors, though it may have made them less intense.
Dong Quai	This Chinese herb is recommended for a variety of women's health problems. It was once believed to act like estrogen, but a 1997 study suggests otherwise.	In that same 1997 study, women given a daily 4.5-gram dose of dong quai had 25 percent fewer hot flashes—the same effect as in women given placebos. While traditional healers prescribe dong quai in tandem with other herbs, products on the U.S. market do not.
Evening-Primrose Oil	It's not clear how evening-primrose oil stops hot flashes, though its potential anti-inflammatory qualities might help with other menopausal problems.	In a 1994 study, women who took 4 grams of evening-primrose oil each day for six months experienced a slight reduction in nighttime hot flashes, though the supplements appeared to offer no other benefits.
Red Clover	Red clover is said to be one of nature's richest sources of isoflavones.	In one study, women who took 40 milligrams of red clover per day reduced hot flashes by 56 percent; however, researchers didn't compare the results with the effect in women receiving no therapy, so it's not clear how much benefit the herb actually offered.
Soy	Contains isoflavones, which may mimic missing hormones enough to reduce hot flashes.	Italian researchers found that women who consumed 76 milligrams of isoflavones per day had 45 percent fewer hot flashes after three months; however, women given placebos had a 30 percent reduction, suggesting that the soy had only a modest effect.

FEMALE TROUBLE:
when happy hour goes sour

A new portrait of a problem-drinker
is emerging, and its face is a woman's. Why the gender
gap in alcohol use is shrinking, and what that means
for women today—and in the future.

BY DEVON JERSILD

PHOTO ILLUSTRATIONS BY WILLIAM DUKE

The second season of *Sex and the City* is out on DVD, and a group of 20- and 30-something co-workers decide to organize a girls'-night-in marathon viewing. The bonus: Every time Carrie and crew down a Cosmopolitan, each woman in the group has to as well. It doesn't work out that way, actually (over the six hours of 30-minute episodes, that's a lot of booze), but suffice it to say the "girls" have a few that night, enough to make a couple of them feel pretty rough the next day.

So what's wrong with that? Who but the most buttoned-up teetotaler would deny a hard-working, responsible woman a happy-hour martini (or even a few too many) every once in a while? As long as she's not underage, pregnant, driving under the influence, or getting rip-roaring drunk each time she drinks, that is.

Alcohol in moderation can certainly enhance the enjoyment of food, friends, and life in general. But startling new evidence suggests that women may be taking their relationship with alcohol too lightly. Indeed, there are powerful indicators that soon there may be as many female alcoholics as male alcoholics. The implications are more than serious; they're deadly: There is a growing body of research linking as few as two drinks a day (sometimes even less) to health problems and showing that alcoholic women are much more vulnerable than men to alcohol-related disease, physical violence, and even death.

Women and Alcohol: By the Numbers

Statistics on women and alcohol paint a varied but troubling picture. On one hand, the number of adult women considered to be heavy drinkers (two or more drinks a day) has declined over the past 15 years. But societal changes and increases in drinking among certain groups of women in the population suggest that this trend will reverse in the future.

For instance, in 1993, the National Household Survey on Drug Abuse found that women who work outside the home are 67 percent more likely to drink heavily than homemakers. A more recent study by the National Center on Addiction and Substance Abuse puts that number even higher, at 89 percent. And, of course, more American women are working than ever before: In 1960, less than 20 percent of married women with children under age 6 were working outside the home; in 2000, 65 percent were.

There are some indications that the rate of heavy-drinking working women is due to an effort to fit into the male-dominated business world. An ongoing study by psychologist Sharon Wilsnack, Ph.D., and sociologist Richard Wilsnack, Ph.D., at the University of North Dakota School of Medicine and Health Sciences in Grand Forks, surveyed a nationally representative sample of 1,100 U.S. women, 696 of whom have been observed since 1981. They have found that women in male-dominated occupations (any occupation that the U.S. Census measures as more than 50 percent male, including law and engineering) drink more than women in traditionally female professions, such as teaching and nursing. Sharon Wilsnack suspects that the link between these types of jobs and drinking may not be coincidental. "In a male-dominated

Even when a man and a woman weigh the same, the **woman will get drunk on less alcohol**—and stay drunk longer. She's also more likely to suffer damage to her health.

environment," she says, "drinking may be symbolic of gender equality."

Neither the numbers nor the researchers suggest women should abandon the boardroom for the classroom or swap their careers altogether for life as stay-at-home moms in an effort to protect themselves from problem-drinking. But they are saying that working women should watch their level and frequency of consumption and fine-tune their radar for signs of growing dependence. "Drinking every night to relax is a major sign of trouble, even if you aren't drinking that much," Wilsnack says.

The increased rates of heavy drinking among working women, though, are nothing compared with what may happen in the next 20 years: Teenage and preteen girls are drinking in record numbers. Today, girls are four times more likely to start drinking before age 16 than their mothers were. This is particularly disturbing, because getting drunk at an early age is the best predictor of future alcoholism. In a 1998 analysis of 43,000 interviews by the National Institute on Alcohol Abuse and Alcoholism (NIAAA), researchers found that more than 40 percent of respondents who began drinking by age 15 eventually became alcoholic. The later in life the respondents started drinking, the less likely they were to become alcoholic: 25 percent of those who began drinking at age 17 became dependent on alcohol, compared with only 10 percent of those who began at age 21 or 22.

Working women, especially those in male-dominated fields, must watch out for dependence. **Drinking every night to relax is a major sign of trouble,** even if you aren't drinking that much.

"As many secondary-school girls are now drinking as boys, at just as young an age—which means they may be just as likely to get into trouble with alcohol down the road," says Mary Dufour, M.D., deputy director of the NIAAA, which should release results of a new national survey on drinking in America in fall 2002. While it's not possible to say with certainty what the NIAAA study will show, the statistics on working women and teenage girls point toward alcoholism—once considered predominantly a male problem—becoming increasingly gender-neutral. If the trends continue in the same direction, the percentage of alcoholic women may one day equal that of men—something that has never happened in America.

Alcohol and the Female Body

Men and women will never be equal, though, in their physical responses to alcohol. Alcohol is much more dangerous to a woman's health than a man's. "This is an area where there are true physiological differences, and women need to be aware of them," Dufour says.

Much has been written about alcohol's ability to lower heart-disease risk. But in women, this benefit applies mainly after menopause, and the effect peaks at one drink a day. Higher levels of consumption may be harmful to both post- and premenopausal women, according to studies by the American Heart Association.

Women's bodies process alcohol differently from men's. Even when a woman and a man weigh the same, the woman will get drunk on less alcohol—and stay drunk longer. That's partly because women absorb more of the alcohol they drink, perhaps because they have less of an enzyme (alcohol dehydrogenase) that breaks down

alcohol in the stomach lining. Fluctuations in hormonal levels during the menstrual cycle, as well as oral contraceptives, can slow the rate of alcohol metabolism.

Alcohol is also more likely to affect her health. A drinking woman's blood will contain alcohol at a higher concentration than a man's blood, even if they drink the same amount. That puts a woman's risk of liver cirrhosis at only two drinks a day; a man's is at four to six drinks a day. Heavy-drinking women also develop such physical complications as anemia, peptic ulcers, and alcohol-related hepatitis more quickly even than men who drink more than they do. The Harvard University Nurses' Health Study, which tracked 58,000 women for four years, found that the risk of developing high blood pressure begins at two to three drinks per day and increases with each additional drink. Dufour puts it this way: "For every organ we have studied so far, women seem more vulnerable to alcohol damage than men."

Women who drink are also more vulnerable to female-oriented diseases and conditions than women who don't drink at all or women whose consumption falls into the "light" (up to three weekly drinks) or "moderate" (four to 13 drinks a week) categories. Some studies suggest that at four drinks per day, a woman is up to 40 percent more likely to get breast cancer than women who drink less. For some women, even small amounts of alcohol can impair fertility, and, of course, alcohol can do devastating damage to a fetus.

African-American women may be at even greater risk of alcohol-related health problems than Caucasian women. For instance, African-American women who drink heavily are about seven times more likely to have a child with fetal alcohol syndrome than heavy-drinking white women. And the much-touted health benefits of one drink a day, while primarily limited to women who've been through menopause, don't apply to African-American women of *any* age.

For all women, when heavy drinking turns into alcoholism, their health suffers even more. An alcoholic woman's liquor of choice will damage all her major organs, and once she is sober, these organs will take longer

sobering stats

3 drinks a week = "light" consumption

what's one drink? **5** oz. of wine   **12** oz. of beer   **1.5** oz. of liquor (80 proof)

72 percent of alcoholic women under age 30 who also have an eating disorder

3 or more drinks a day = "heavy drinking"

A woman's risk of liver cirrhosis begins at only **2 drinks** a day.

A man's risk of liver cirrhosis begins at **4 to 6 drinks** a day.

Women who work outside the home are **67** percent more likely to drink heavily than homemakers.

Drinking at an early age is the best predictor of alcoholism.
The trend is evident in a recent national survey:

40 percent of respondents who began drinking by age 15 and became alcoholics
25 percent of those who began drinking at age 17 and became alcoholics
10 percent of respondents who started drinking at age 21 or 22 and became alcoholics

4 to 13 drinks a week = "moderate" consumption

Today's girls are four times more likely to start drinking before age **16** than their mothers were.

A woman's risk of developing high blood pressure begins at **2 to 3 drinks per day,** and increases with each additional drink.

Some studies suggest that at **4 drinks per day,** a woman is up to 40 percent more likely to get breast cancer than women who drink less.

49 percent of alcoholic women in relationships with heavy-drinking partners

6 percent of alcoholic men in relationships with heavy-drinking partners

There is a growing body of research linking **as few as two drinks a day** to health problems.

2X Female alcoholics are twice as likely to die as male alcoholics in the same age group.

Alcoholic women are at high risk for spousal abuse.
They are **nine times** more likely to be slapped by their husbands, **five times** more likely to be kicked or hit, **five times** more likely to be beaten, and **four times** more likely to have their lives threatened.

than a man's to repair. Female alcoholics are also at higher risk for other dangers, including physical and sexual assault. A study of spousal abuse among alcoholic and non-alcoholic women found that alcoholic women were nine times more likely to be slapped by their husbands, five times more likely to be beaten, five times more likely to be kicked or hit, and four times more likely to have their lives threatened.

Indeed, female alcoholics are twice as likely to die as male alcoholics in the same age group—even though male alcoholics die at three times the rate of men in the general population. The increased mortality is due partly to higher accident rates and victimization, but suicide also plays a role. In the general population, women attempt suicide more often than men, but men more frequently succeed in killing themselves. Among alcoholics, women have the higher suicide rate.

The Gender Gap in Recovery

Of course, women don't just experience different physical effects and risks from alcohol abuse. They also often have different types of recovery needs. Although more and more women are seeking treatment—for example, women make up one-third of the membership of Alcoholics Anonymous (AA) compared with one-fourth in 1968—there still remains a disconnect between the particular needs of many women in recovery and what mainstream treatment programs offer them. And the majority of programs, including AA, were originally designed for men.

"There's an 'add women and stir' approach that fails to recognize that women have distinct needs," says Donna Campbell, executive director of the Connecticut Women's Consortium, one of the country's only advocacy groups for women with addiction and mental-health problems. For example, Campbell says, women do not do well with the confrontational approaches that have been developed for men. "The traditional treatment model tries to reduce the so-called 'false pride' that is believed to cause addiction. But the relational approach says the opposite—that women's psychology depends on healthy relationships and connections, and that confrontation can lead to more self-harming behavior."

Often, women alcoholics have self-esteem issues that are likely compounded by the stereotypical view of an alcoholic woman as unnatural, unfeminine, and sexually promiscuous. When a woman's alcohol problem becomes conspicuous, Wilsnack says, "you see the attitude of society shift from indifference to outrage and an attempt to punish rather than treat the woman's drinking problems."

Women who internalize these attitudes typically seek isolation—not help. In a 2001 survey of 400 women in recovery, 79 percent said shame was the primary barrier to treatment. This may cause women to enter treatment "generally in a significantly more chronic phase of their illness," says Sharon Hartman, program director of Adult Extended Care Services for the Caron Foundation, one of the nation's largest treatment facilities.

Women may bring to treatment other issues that complicate recovery. According to a 1997 report from the American Medical Association, women more often than men have a history of depression that preceded their drinking. Women are more likely to have been sexually abused. An analysis of studies on drinking and eating disorders found that 72 percent of alcoholic women under 30 also have an eating disorder. "These needs are often not addressed," Campbell says, "and they can be the cause of relapses or a woman's failure to complete her treatment."

Teenage and preteen girls are drinking in record numbers. And getting drunk at an early age is a predictor of future alcoholism.

In addition, many clinicians say that families are much less likely to support a woman's recovery than a man's. "Women are still most often the caretakers," Campbell says. "There's an extra burden on them." Sometimes, husbands don't particularly want their wives to get sober—not surprising when you consider that 49 percent of alcoholic women are in relationships with heavy-drinking partners, as opposed to only 6 percent of alcoholic men. In a Georgia Tech School of Management study of 6,400 full-time employees from 84 work sites, wives often had a hand in referring husbands to alcohol treatment, whereas husbands rarely referred wives.

Female-focused recovery programs can provide women with solutions. Women-only AA meetings allow participants to focus on issues they might not address in mixed groups. Women for Sobriety (WFS), a self-help group founded in 1976 as an alternative to AA, urges positive thinking and reinforcement rather than the powerlessness and character defects that figure prominently in AA. And women who feel shame about their drinking may find that liberating. Unfortunately, WFS groups are rare, and many women still must cobble together a recovery program from a mix of male-oriented treatments and individual counseling.

That, in fact, is how Lizzie is dealing with her alcoholism. The athletic 27-year-old began drinking when she was 12. She felt invigorated by the sense of freedom and independence that drinking gave her. It made her feel

Women-only AA meetings allow them to focus on issues they might not address in mixed groups.

sexier, more a part of the crowd, more insulated from the pain she felt inside. "When I drank," Lizzie says, "it was a misguided attempt to make a connection with the world."

Ultimately, though, she had to face her alcohol problem. After a narrow escape from a car accident, Lizzie joined AA and began seeing a therapist—hopefully in time to avoid the physical damage so many women alcoholics suffer. "Before I got into recovery, alcohol was my substitute best friend," she says. "Now I'm learning what it means to have friends I can depend on." ✳

Devon Jersild is the author of Happy Hours: Alcohol in a Woman's Life.

Your Hormones Could Make You a Candidate for Addiction

Women have long held their hormones accountable for irrational emotional outbursts, cranky spells, and chocolate cravings. But a recent study funded by the National Institute on Drug Abuse warns that estrogen surges aren't just annoying—they could be harmful. They may make the brain more vulnerable to addiction.

University of Michigan researchers found that female rats that were given estrogen and cocaine over a period of three weeks learned to self-administer the drug much faster than either female or male rats that did not receive the hormone. The researchers explained that estrogen boosts levels of the neurotransmitter dopamine,

which fuels drug cravings—and, in this case, turned the rats into junkies. Addictive drugs such as nicotine and cocaine also pump up dopamine production, leading to a double whammy when estrogen and drugs are combined.

Those most at risk for estrogen-abetted addiction include teen girls and women on hormone replacement therapy (HRT). Estrogen levels naturally peak in adolescence, which makes teenagers who might try drugs even more at risk for drug abuse. "Just making women aware that estrogen can cause them to crave drugs may help more women say no to drugs," says the study's lead researcher Jill B. Becker, Ph.D., a professor of

psychology at the University of Michigan. Becker, who advocates early drug education and intervention, also recommends that women on HRT watch for increases in consumption of tobacco, alcohol, or other drugs and work with their doctors to find the lowest estrogen dose possible.

The estrogen-dopamine connection may also help explain why women experience cravings at various points in their menstrual cycles. Rather than reaching for a candy bar or a painkiller the next time you are hit by a hormonal tidal wave, try changing your environment: Dim the lights, take a hot bath, or just try to remove yourself from that stressful situation.

Research Discovers New Hope for Fibroid Sufferers

You don't need an M.D. to conclude that if your mom and sisters all suffer from uterine fibroids, the cause could be lurking in your genes. Now science has confirmed your suspicion. A team of international researchers has discovered a genetic mutation that may explain some cases of the benign but painful tumors, and lead to less-invasive treatments to stunt fibroid growth.

"This is the first gene that has been identified as a risk factor for developing fibroids," says Cynthia Morton, Ph.D., a professor of pathology at Brigham and Women's Hospital in Boston and the associate director of Harvard-Partners Center for Genetics and Genomics. The discovery could eventually lead to a blood test for early diagnosis.

That's good news for the estimated 25 percent of women—usually between the ages of 20 and 35—who suffer from fibroid symptoms. The condition isn't life-threatening, but it can cause severe symptoms, including pelvic pain, bleeding, fertility problems, and bowel trouble. A genetic link could answer riddles such as why African-American women are more prone to the disorder, and why they're two to five times as likely to suffer severe symptoms.

Given that fibroids are the most common reason for hysterectomy, doctors are seeking less-drastic treatment options. "Hysterectomy has so far proved the only definitive way of getting rid of the problem," says Elizabeth A. Stewart, M.D., a gynecologist and clinical director of the Center for Uterine Fibroids at Brigham and Women's Hospital. In addition to combing the genome, doctors are exploring new therapies, from hormone blockers to no-incision surgery that melts fibroids through focused ultrasound.

You can help advance the scientific cause: If you and a sister have both suffered from uterine fibroids, call 800-722-5520, ext. 80081 to participate in a genetics study at Brigham and Women's Hospital. Visit www.fibroids.net for more information.

> Given that fibroids are the most common reason for hysterectomy, doctors are seeking less-drastic treatment options.

Endometriosis:
Be Sure You Know the Signs

FOR A DISEASE that affects one in 10 women of childbearing age, it's troubling that endometriosis often falls below the public-health radar. Doctors have yet to determine the cause or cure for the chronic condition, which can cause debilitating pain and infertility. In part, a woman's reluctance to openly discuss symptoms has slowed diagnosis (which typically takes nine years), treatment, and research advancements. "Many of the symptoms of this disease tread on traditional taboos—problems with menstruation, pelvic pain, painful intercourse, bowel trouble, and infertility," says Mary Lou Ballweg, president and executive director of the Endometriosis Association, a nonprofit educational and research organization.

Pelvic pain, especially during menstruation and intercourse, is the signature of endometriosis. For unknown reasons, the tissue that lines the uterus (or endometrium), finds its way to other parts of the abdomen, including the ovaries, Fallopian tubes, outer lining of the uterus, and even the bowels. One study recently found similarities between endometriosis and autoimmune diseases, such as lupus or rheumatoid arthritis. This could push progress forward, as "female troubles" have not always drawn big government research grants in the past.

Although there is no cure for endometriosis, a variety of treatment options, from over-the-counter painkillers to hormone therapy and surgery, can help alleviate pain and slow the progress of the disease. You can find out more by visiting www.endometriosisassn.org or calling 800-992-3636.

that irritating itch could be yeast—or Something Else

Let your doctor decide.

Summer brings sun, sea, sand—and yeast infections. Finding cool relief in a pool or at the beach can mean spending the day in a wet bathing suit, a breeding ground for yeast. If you're like most women, you probably toss an over-the-counter remedy into your shopping basket whenever you feel that familiar vaginal itch-and-burn. But according to a new study, as many as 50 percent of women think they have yeast infections when they don't. As a result, they're wasting money on unnecessary medications and potentially missing more dangerous infections.

The study followed 95 women who had purchased over-the-counter remedies for vulvovaginal candidiasis (the technical term for yeast). Of these women, only one-third had correctly diagnosed a yeast infection. More than half had a mixed bag of problems, while 13 had no infections at all. "'Yeast infection' has become the layman's term for every kind of vaginal irritation in the same way that people say they have the flu whenever they feel stuffy," says lead study author Daron G. Ferris, M.D., a professor at the Medical College of Georgia.

Does that mean you have to endure a cold exam table every time you suspect a yeast infection? Not necessarily. But get a confirmation at least once before playing doctor, and don't be too quick to self-diagnose, Ferris says. If you're not sure what you have or if you experience fever, pelvic or abdominal pain, or vaginal bleeding, see your doctor. Your best bet is to prevent infections: Wash with a fragrance-free cleanser and pat dry, wear cotton underwear and panty hose that have a cotton crotch. And, if you're prone to infections, change into shorts instead of lounging around in your wet swimsuit all day.

healthBUZZ

thumbs UP

Sweating the small stuff: Researchers in Germany have discovered a protein called dermcidin that is secreted in sweat and may be a good defense against bacterial infections.

Beans: Researchers at Tulane University found that enthusiastic legume eaters—people who eat beans or peas at least four times a week—cut their risk of heart disease by 22 percent compared with legume dabblers.

thumbs DOWN

Working 9 to 5: The typical workday is out of sync with the body's natural clock, according to England's Sleep Council. Researchers found that most of the worldwide study participants were not fully alert in the middle of their days and would benefit from siestas.

Women's health: The National Women's Law Center doled out a grade of unsatisfactory to the United States on women's health issues. The center found that federal and state governments have done little to improve women's access to health coverage. Contact your local representative to voice your concerns.

Five Women, One Weight

SEE HOW THE SAME WEIGHT—

140 pounds

—LOOKS ON THESE WOMEN.

It's no surprise that the number on the scale isn't the key to how healthy these women are. So how can you assess your own health? We weigh in on the numbers that really matter when it comes to your body.

BY MELISSA SPERL

PHOTOGRAPHY BY MARILI FORASTIERI

Just about every woman has her "dream weight": what the scale read in high school or prebaby; what her sister weighs; what a certain actress weighs. She fixates on this number, devising exercise regimens and diets in order to reach it. What, though, does this number really mean? That when she gets there she'll be healthy and fit? Or simply that she'll look good in a pair of pleather pants?

The fact is that the same number can look very different on different women—and can mean a variety of things. Take the five women in this story. Each weighs 140 pounds, a full 12 notches below the weight of the average American woman. But would you know by looking at her that Ellen Wilson sweats it out on a bike five days a week and has done so for 20 years? The numbers on the scale don't say that Kim Clark gets her five servings of vegetables per day, or that Tracy Ducar can bench-press 150 pounds. Even the charts that consider both weight and height aren't very helpful. If you're 5 feet

5 inches tall, for instance, these charts say you should weigh between 111 and 150 pounds. That's a huge range, the difference between a size 2 and a size 12.

Body mass index, or BMI, is a better gauge than the weight charts because it correlates closely to body-fat percentage—often mentioned as the "gold standard" of determining physical health and fitness. Still, though, you can have low body fat and not be in good shape. So what if a skin-fold test says you have 18 percent body fat (a number most women dream of) if you can't go for a bike ride with your kids without feeling winded?

"Fitness is a combination of cardiovascular health, muscle health, strength, endurance, and a mental or spiritual state of being," emphasizes Carol L. Otis, M.D., the head of the Women's Sports Medicine Clinic at the Kerlan-Jobe Orthopaedic Clinic in Los Angeles and also the co-author of *The Athletic Woman's Survival Guide.*

Can you tell who is the healthiest?
Who eats the most or who exercises regularly?
You may be surprised at the answers.

crunching the numbers

Although most methods of judging your weight are just estimates, sometimes that's all you need for a quick health assessment. According to the American Dietetic Association, one of the best ways to find your target weight is to calculate your body mass index (BMI).

Your BMI is your weight in kilograms divided by your height in meters squared. But you can avoid the metric system by using the following shortcut.

Multiply weight in pounds by 704.5.
Divide that by height in inches squared.
So if you are 5 feet 4 inches tall (64 inches) and weigh 140 pounds, the numbers look like this:
140 pounds x 704.5 = 98,630
64 x 64 = 4,096 (height in inches squared)
98,630 ÷ 4,096 = 24.08

To skirt the math, use an online calculator, such as the one from the National Institutes of Health (NIH) (www.niddk.nih.gov/health/nutrit/pubs/unders.htm). Or go to www.health.com and get your number off our easy

table, "Are You Overweight?" in the "Weight" section of the site, under "The Basics."

According to the NIH, you are considered overweight if you have a BMI between 25 and 29.9. A BMI of 30 or higher is in the obese range. If your result is above the limit, take your ideal BMI and run the numbers in reverse to find your target weight. (One caveat: A very muscular person may have a higher BMI because muscle is so heavy, not because his or her weight is unhealthy.)

For a fast way to determine if your body-fat percentage is healthy, pinch the skin on the back of your upper arm. (Tense the muscle so you're just grabbing fat.) If you can pinch more than an inch, you're carrying around too much fat.

Where you carry fat is also important. Fat stored around your waist indicates a higher risk for heart disease and other conditions than that on your hips. The test: Measure your waist at its smallest point; measure your hips at their largest point. Divide the waist number by the hip number. Women should have a waist-to-hip ratio below 0.8; men should be below 1.0.

Throw away your scale, the experts advise, because weight doesn't really matter. But we say, get real: We love knowing what we weigh. Because even if the scale doesn't tell you everything you need to know, it's an easy way of keeping check on where you are now relative to where you were last month. You know if the needle is swinging to the right because you've added muscle (which does weigh more than fat) or you've just been eating too much junk.

Of course, if each added pound drives you to a drastic diet, you probably should wean yourself from the scale. But if you can maintain perspective about the numbers or just judge by how you feel—or the fit of those pleather pants—that's great. A healthy weight is about both body and mind. And your fitness is about determining your target weight and how to get there. These five women know when they are on track, and they treat their bodies right. What could be more beautiful than that?

Ellen Wilson

ELLEN WILSON
overcoming illness

HEIGHT: 5'1"
AGE: 40
OCCUPATION: STAY-AT-HOME MOM
HOME: SEARSPORT, MAINE

What she eats: Wilson revamped her diet after the birth of her daughter five years ago. She was diagnosed with a thyroid condition, which made it tough for her to return to her prebaby weight. She still struggles with the disease, but the new eating habits are part of what keeps her feeling healthy. Her main diet focus is getting at least four cups of veggies per day.

How she works out: Wilson has a self-made program she calls "Tour de Pants." She does four to five indoor and outdoor cycling sessions per week, working toward a new pair of pants she picked out in a catalog.

How she feels about 140: "When I look in the mirror, I see a normal American woman. Sure, I wish I were thinner—I would like to be between 120 and 125—but I'm thankful, since I have this problem with my thyroid, that my weight has been pretty stable."

Philosophy: "Before the baby, I weighed 117 pounds; I know that's not realistic now. You really can't go by weight. And for exercise, you have to do what you love. My husband swears that running works. For me, cycling works."

TRACY DUCAR
staying strong to perform

HEIGHT: 5'7"
AGE: 28
OCCUPATION: PROFESSIONAL SOCCER PLAYER
FOR THE BOSTON BREAKERS
HOME: WELLESLEY, MASSACHUSETTS

What she eats: Ducar tries to get protein at every meal—that's the key to her strength. It helps her develop more muscle and stay lean. Other than that, she just tries to eat healthfully, without obsessing about fat or calories.

How she works out: During the soccer season, she trains on the field two hours a day and lifts weights two or three times a week. Ducar also likes to run two or three times a week, because as a goalkeeper she doesn't get

Tracy Ducar

She runs outdoors in the summer, and in winter, she spends some time on the treadmill and some in a hip-hop funk dance class.

How she feels about 140: "It's the weight I feel best at. One summer I ran a lot and got down to 130, but it made me so thin that people asked if there was something wrong with me. That wasn't a good feeling. Anything more than 140 makes me feel sloppy, and anything less makes me feel undernourished. Clearly, this is the right weight for me."

Philosophy: "I've been a size 8 or 10 my entire life. I'll never be a 4; And I'll never be a 6. It's just not ever going to happen. I'm lucky that the weight I feel good at also looks pretty good on me. I'll continue to watch what I eat and exercise, but I know my limits. I've never had the hang-ups with food that I think a lot of other women have."

as much cardiovascular exercise from field training as she thinks she needs.

How she feels about 140: "I feel fit, lean, and strong at 140. If I drop far below that weight, I know I have lost critical muscle mass. As a professional athlete, having a good muscle base is paramount. When I am at 140, I feel confident and play better."

Philosophy: "I don't feel like a fanatic when it comes to food and nutrition. I'm definitely conscious, but I'm not counting every calorie. What I'm doing is easy for me. And when I take care of my training on and off the field, I feel like I do better on the field. The two go hand in hand."

PAULINE MILLARD
maintaining a healthy approach

HEIGHT: 5'7"
AGE: 24
OCCUPATION: WRITER, GRAD STUDENT
HOME: NEW YORK CITY

What she eats: Lots of fruit. "It gives me energy," says Millard. At lunch, she heads for sushi ("I'm totally addicted"), and for dinner, just about anything goes. Her hectic schedule means a lot of dinners out, which is easy and generally quick in New York City.

How she works out: Millard exercises four or five times a week because it relieves stress and lifts her mood.

Pauline Millard

Kim Clark

KIM CLARK
being her best inside and out

HEIGHT: 6'0"
AGE: 32
OCCUPATION: FITNESS MODEL
HOME: COATESVILLE, PENNSYLVANIA

What she eats: Her regimen is low-fat (less than 18 grams a day) and low-carb. On the days that she works out, though, Clark allows herself to go a little heavier on her self-proclaimed weaknesses: breads and pastas.

How she works out: A second-degree black belt in Tae Kwon Do, Clark is working toward master status (fifth-degree black belt). She trains in Tae Kwon Do three to four times a week for two hours a session. She also plays a weekly game of pick-up basketball.

How she feels about 140: "In my industry, 140 sounds like a lot, but for me it's an ideal weight. I'm in the best shape of my life: I feel healthy; my clothes fit well. I used to set my target at 135, but when I try to get down to that weight, I just don't feel as good."

Philosophy: "My main motivation for working out is to look and feel good. My grand master, Chae T. Goh, has

instilled in us a motto: 'When your body is fatigued, your mind takes over, and when you're mentally fatigued, your spirit takes over.' I carry this into my everyday life, and it helps me on auditions. I know I'm going to give the best of my ability, no matter whether I get the job or not."

Joyce Hundley

JOYCE HUNDLEY
focusing on the right goals

HEIGHT: 5'7"
AGE: 53
OCCUPATION: ANTITRUST ATTORNEY FOR THE U.S. DEPARTMENT OF JUSTICE
HOME: WASHINGTON, D.C.

What she eats: Hundley thinks her diet has always been reasonably nutritious, but she recently decided that it was time to become a little more knowledgeable about how to eat healthfully. So now she chooses skim milk

I **believe** that as long as I'm exercising, eating healthy, and feeling good, **140 is a good weight.**

—*Joyce Hundley*

and whole grains, cuts out red meats, and fills up her plate with more fresh vegetables.

How she works out: Hundley fits exercise into her busy schedule less than she'd like—but still manages to work out three times a week most of the time. Walking or jogging along the trails of a nearby city park is one of her favorite pastimes.

How she feels about 140: "I believe that as long as I'm exercising, eating healthfully, and feeling good, 140 is a good weight. At one time I thought I'd like to get down to 135, but that's just not realistic for me. Now I understand that it's more important that I feel like I'm living a full life."

Philosophy: "I've come to realize that my goal isn't to lose 10 pounds, although that would be OK. I want to be able to be active with my son and daughter. My main goal is to focus on nutrition and exercise so I can participate in the activities I enjoy with my friends and family." ✳

Freelance writer Melissa Sperl lives in Boston and also contributes to Women's Day, Travel Holiday, *and* WeightWatchers.com.

Frame Your Figure with These Cover-up Tips

Women spend painful afternoons searching for the perfect swimsuit. So why cover it up with a super-sized T-shirt? Invest in a fashionable cover-up style that will let you lounge poolside "without looking like you're trying to hide something," says Diane Irons, beauty/fashion expert and author of *14-Day Beauty Boot Camp*. Here are her tips for fitting your figure.

1 to shorten a long waist.
A pair of capri pants, such as L.L. Bean's Sport Capri Pants, makes legs look long and lean and visually breaks up a long-waisted body (they're also perfect if chubby knees are your nemesis).

2 to highlight great legs (and hide wide hips).
Draw attention to your legs and downplay your hips with a mid-thigh or shorter skirt, like Jantzen's Sorbet Stripe Skirt.

3 to minimize large breasts.
Slip on a tank-style dress, such as Speedo's Bamboo Tank Dress. A wrap skirt or a sarong is another good way for you to divert interest to your bottom half.

4 to trim your tummy.
Try a sarong or wrap skirt, such as this Mossimo at Target Matte Sarong, tied just above your hip bone on one side.

5 to slim down thighs.
Drawstring pants, like Jantzen's Wallflower Rayon Pant, can help thighs look trim. Or go for a longer sarong.

6 to add curves.
Tie a pareo in a lively print—like the Speedo Stripe Floral Pareo or Jantzen Leaf It Alone Pareo—right under your arms. This tactic is perfect for boy-shaped bodies.

7 for overall streamlining.
Opt for a cover-up made from light matte fabric, like a flowing chiffon (linen or heavy cotton is too clingy). "If you have too much fabric it'll simply add bulk," Irons says. Solids in black and navy are still the best flaw-hiders, but fabrics with a small print on a dark background work for most people.

Are Eating Disorders a Family Trait?

Anorexia and bulimia aren't just relics of pop culture and peer pressure. New research shows how a woman's genes may be a serious factor.

BY JENNIFER PIRTLE

Unlike many women who develop an eating disorder, Shannon Hurd did not grow up preoccupied with food. As a 16-year-old, she'd lunch on a cheeseburger and fries while her fellow high school cheerleaders picked over their minuscule salads. But when the young man whom Hurd, now 24, remembers as her first love, abruptly ended their relationship, everything changed for her. She soon plummeted into a deep depression and became anorexic. Over the course of the next several months, Hurd lost more than 50 pounds from her athletic 6-foot frame, dropping from 165 to 113.

Yet despite her ghostly pallor and the tendons that protruded, ropelike, through her skin, it wasn't until Hurd suffered a heart attack in 1994 that she realized the degree to which her eating habits had ravaged her body. Although she has now made it back to 165 pounds and has kept her weight stable for nearly five years, Hurd still gingerly navigates the road to psychological well-being. Currently a graduate student at the University of Colorado at Boulder, she says she has developed a lifesaving—but rigid—eating plan. She has dumped boyfriends and quit jobs just to avoid missing breakfast or lunch, nutritional lapses she fears might unravel the progress she's made. "Maintaining my weight is a full-time job," she says. "I didn't understand how complex recovery would be."

One reason women like Hurd have such difficulty overcoming eating disorders is that experts have never been able to nail down a specific cause. Of course, many people blame social pressures—the media's obsession with stick-thin models, for instance, or a mother's overbearing control of her daughter's diet. But biology, not society, may be the root of eating disorders. Some groundbreaking new research suggests that such factors as brain chemistry and genetics may set a woman up to develop a disorder later in life. This research could lay the groundwork for more effective treatments for eating disorders, including drug and gene therapy. Better yet, it might allow doctors to predict who is predisposed to developing them, allowing those women to get treatment before suffering emotionally and physically damaging illnesses.

> Some **groundbreaking new research** suggests that such factors as brain chemistry and genetics may set a woman up to develop a disorder later in life.

That's big news because, according to conservative estimates, eating disorders affect between 5 million and 10 million young women in the United States. In 2002, at least 50,000 individuals were predicted to die as a direct result of an eating disorder. "Currently, these disorders have the highest rates of death of any psychiatric illness, but we have not understood why women get them," says

Walter Kaye, M.D., professor of psychiatry at the University of Pittsburgh Medical Center. "If we can identify a population that is at risk, we are more likely to be successful in preventing the disorders."

Kaye is spearheading an international research project on the genetics of women with anorexia and bulimia. He first became interested in tracking the biology of these illnesses when he noticed particular patterns in eating-disorder patients: The disorders occur mainly in women, they begin at an early age, they seem to run in families, and they produce similar symptoms in patients. "To my mind, this suggests that there is some biological contributing factor," Kaye says.

Under Kaye's leadership, teams of researchers have been working with about 4,000 female participants for the past five years at centers in Germany, Italy, Canada, and five locations throughout the United States to unlock both the biological and genetic

stick-thin to healthy again

6' AND 113
After losing nearly a third of her body weight, Shannon Hurd suffered a heart attack at the age of 16.

7 YEARS LATER, 165
Hurd has kept her weight stable at 165 pounds for almost five years. But recovery hasn't been easy.

causes of eating disorders. Studies at the University of Pittsburgh are using brain-imaging scans to help identify regions of the brain that may make people more susceptible to developing eating disorders, particularly those regions that are affected by the serotonin system. The brain compound serotonin, derived from tryptophan—an amino acid found only in food—is involved in the transmission of nerve impulses and helps regulate mood, impulse control, and appetite levels. When people eat, their serotonin levels rise, contributing to satiety.

But in women with anorexia, some component of the serotonin system seems to be out of whack. Hurd and other women who have had eating disorders often speak

of the calmness and the intense pleasure that comes from not eating. "Anorexics would not do this unless it felt good," she says. Bulimics, as well, often report feelings of satisfaction after binge eating and purging.

To try to understand the pattern, Kaye's researchers compared levels of serotonin in women who were recovered from anorexia or bulimia for at least a year with healthy volunteers who had never had an eating disorder. They found that young women who have suffered from eating disorders have unusually high levels of serotonin. Researchers don't yet know if these differences in serotonin levels are the cause of anorexia and bulimia—or the result—but this discovery might be able to explain why

It's easy to blame social pressures for eating disorders—the media's obsession with stick-thin models, or a mother's overbearing control of her daughter's diet. But **biology, not society,** may be the root of the problem.

women with eating disorders feel full even when they haven't had food for days.

Kaye's research into some genetic component to eating disorders is highly preliminary, but it is just as provocative as the serotonin studies. At Kaye's study site at the University of California at Los Angeles, researchers discovered that women who had a family history of anorexia nervosa were 12 times more likely to develop the disorder. Women with bulimia in their families were four times more likely to become bulimic themselves. Studies done at Kaye's other collaborative sites—including the Neuropsychiatric Research Institute in North Dakota and sites in Virginia, Minnesota, and Australia—have shown similar results, both within families and in studies of twins.

These studies are merely the first steps toward isolating the specific genes that cause eating disorders. Kaye and his researchers say that may not happen for years, in part because they suspect many genes play a role. "In addition to the numerous genes, there are many cultural and psychosocial issues that are involved, too, which makes isolating the direct causes difficult," explains James Mitchell, M.D., president of the Neuropsychiatric Research Institute and one of Kaye's colleagues.

Kaye and his team of scientists are hopeful that their work will eventually lead to more successful treatments. Targeted medications could revolutionize the recovery from eating disorders, much as drugs have helped people with clinical depression, a disorder that also has a brain-chemistry component. And Mitchell says that with

how to reach out

When you suspect that someone you care about has an eating disorder, finding the right way to approach her can be difficult.

Suzanne Johnson, Ph.D., a clinical psychologist at the Adult Weight and Eating Disorders Center at Massachusetts General Hospital in Boston, offers these five tips for dealing with the situation.

Assess the possible causes of your friend's eating disorder before you approach her. An eating disorder might begin because of a person's desire to control the way she looks but continue for a totally different reason. "Typically, disorders are sustained because they're used to cope with some sort of stress or pain," Johnson says.

Don't approach her when you're feeling frustrated or highly emotional. Instead, wait for a time when you are more able to speak calmly with her, so you can project your caring and concern for her well-being.

Convey your concern in a nonjudgmental way. "Don't blame them or lay guilt trips," Johnson says. "Encourage them to talk about their conflicts and the problems they're experiencing."

Let her know why you think she has a problem. "Give evidence that focuses on the person's health rather than on her weight or appearance," Johnson suggests. Statements such as "You think about food so much you don't concentrate on your work" shift the attention to the fact that the person has a medical problem.

Be prepared for her reaction. "If you catch her when she's not ready to acknowledge she has a problem yet, she'll probably be defensive," Johnson says. "But if she clearly realizes it's a problem and she's struggling, she may be more open to hearing what you have to say." In any case, you should expect that it will take time and persistence to help her.

some recent advances in genetics research, gene therapy could be a possibility sometime in the future. "Some things that appear to be genetically preordained can be modified," he says.

But still, the most promising implications are in the area of prevention. Once the genetic research is complete, it is possible that doctors could identify high-risk women by their genotypes and offer preventive treatment before their disorders surface. Suzanne Johnson, Ph.D., a psychologist in the Adult Weight and Eating Disorders Program at Massachusetts General Hospital in Boston, says that the potential impact of this kind of prevention is tremendous. "Kaye's work could certainly be extremely helpful on a predictive level," she says. "If we could further narrow the age range of women who are susceptible to eating disorders, for instance, that would be very important."

> Women with eating disorders deal with **so much shame.** If we had a biological or genetic basis for these disorders, it may help alleviate that shame.
>
> —*Suzanne Johnson, Ph.D.*

Johnson also believes the research into the genetic and biological causes of eating disorders might help therapists who are working with eating-disorder patients. "Women with eating disorders are dealing with so much shame," Johnson says. "If we had a biological or genetic basis for these disorders, it may help them understand why they are predisposed to this set of symptoms and may help alleviate that shame."

As for Shannon Hurd, she hopes that at the very least, this new research might change public perception of the illness and silence the whispered refrain of, "Why don't they just eat?" After all, Hurd says, overcoming her anorexia wasn't simply about putting fork to food. "It's definitely not a disease about dieting," she says. "I never wanted to ruin my life." ✳

London-based writer Jennifer Pirtle has contributed to Fitness, Cosmopolitan, *and* Self, *among others.*

Eating Disorders Linked to Birth Dates

Your birth date may determine more than your astrological sign—it may signal an increased risk for eating disorders. In a study of roughly 6,200 women between the ages of 20 and 50, researchers from the Royal Cornhill Hospital in Aberdeen, United Kingdom, found that women born between March and June are 55 percent more likely to suffer from anorexia nervosa than women born at other times of the year. It seems that common winter infections could affect a fetus and cause brain damage that may lead to anorexia later in life. Previous studies have uncovered brain abnormalities in anorexics, reports lead investigator John M. Eagles, M.D., though their significance has been unclear.

Treating eating disorders has long been approached from a psychological standpoint, but this study highlights the importance of biology. Previous research has made similar biological connections between prenatal or infant exposure to season-specific viruses and psychiatric diseases, such as schizophrenia, Alzheimer's disease, and depression. Additional studies may help pinpoint the exact origin of these life-threatening conditions—and help expectant mothers better protect themselves and their babies.

ANOREXIA ALERT

It's hard enough to track adolescent mood swings. But try telling the difference between a fussy eater and a teen suffering from anorexia. *The Parent's Guide to Childhood Eating Disorders* by Marcia Herrin, R.D., and Nancy Matsumoto, offers some body clues that can tell you what your teen won't:

• lanugo hair (like that found on the bodies of newborns) on her face or body
• tearless crying
• hands and feet that are bluish and cold to the touch
• yellowish skin (caused by an excess of carotene, from eating too many veggies or poor liver function)

If you notice any of these signs, try to get your teen talking—to you or a professional.

VitalStats

3,500 Number of women who enter menopause each day

99.5 Temperature to which the body's surface can rise during a hot flash

3.5 Hours of weekly exercise found to reduce hot flashes

90 Percent survival rate of women with cervical cancer, detected at earliest stage

24 Percent survival rate of women with cervical cancer, detected at latest stage

13,000 Predicted number of newly diagnosed cervical cancer cases in 2002

28 Percent of women who don't get a gynecological exam each year

79 Percent of women who would rather be seen with messy hair than naked

61 Percent of women who would rather have great hair than great breasts

1.2 Bust-waist ratio of Julia Roberts

1.6 Average bust-waist ratio of a woman in a Rubens painting

78 Percent of families that eat fried foods at least four times each week

54 Percent of families that eat salads at least four times each week

4.4 Servings of fruits and vegetables the average American eats per day

5 Recommended number of servings

10 Percent of women who have ended a relationship online

40 Percent of women who have sent an e-card to show their affection

28 Percent of men who have

Sources: National Center for Policy Analysis, Census Bureau, USDA, 5 a Day, Transitions for Health Women's Institute, Kaiser Family Foundation, U.S. Department of Education, RealVision, Harper's Index, *Sex: A Natural History*, West Soy, Hallmark, ACS, Pantene, American Academy of Dermatology

Pay for My Pills!

Chances are good that your husband's insurance would cover Viagra but that you have to pay for your birth-control pills. Women have not missed the irony—and they're fighting back.

In a landmark federal case in 2001, 27-year-old pharmacist Jennifer Erickson sued her employer for sexual discrimination because birth control was not included in the company's comprehensive health plan—and won. In the wake of the decision, some employers across the country rushed to cover the pill, hoping to avoid similar lawsuits. An insurance commissioner in Washington state mandated equitable coverage for women, and at least 15 other states have adopted similar laws.

According to a University of Washington study on statewide coverage, 75 percent of women with private health insurance were not covered for contraception, even in programs that offer protection against sexually transmitted diseases. Similarly, nationwide, about 70 percent of women currently rely on private health insurance and may have to pay out of pocket for contraception. Even if a state mandates that employers cover the cost of the pill, compliance is low and hard to enforce.

If you believe in equity in prescription coverage, make your voice heard. Visit Planned Parenthood's Cover My Pills campaign site (www.covermypills.org) and click on "Send a Letter to Congress" to express your support.

pre-op pill precaution

IF YOU'RE SCHEDULED for surgery, add oral contraceptives to your list of things to avoid before going under the knife. Major operations increase your chance of experiencing a blood clot, and that risk is even greater if you're taking birth control pills.

To be on the safe side, stop taking your oral contraceptives about a month before the procedure and don't start again until you're fully healed. (Same rules apply should one of your limbs land in a cast.)

chapter 3

everyday wellness

smart help for common conditions

17 medical mysteries solved

Top docs talk straight about when a random health quirk is *really* a problem and when it's no big deal.

BY LINDA RAO

A mysterious pain ripples through your stomach. You suspect it's that second slice of cake coming back to haunt you. But your inner doctor starts making diagnoses: What if it's the deadly disease you read about in this morning's paper? To help you distinguish between a harmless ache and a serious problem, we asked a team of medical experts about the complaints they hear most often from female patients. Then we drilled down to the information you need to decide whether to relax in a bubble bath or seek professional help. Of course, if a symptom lasts longer than a week or you feel that something's really wrong, skip the soak and see your doc.

1 You're sporting a middle-aged man's hairstyle—more skin than hair.

So your hairline doesn't look like George Costanza's, but you'd feel better if you had a bit more coverage up top.
Relax in a bubble bath if:
• Thinning hair runs in your family. Although hormones, stress, and autoimmune diseases can make you lose hair, the most common cause is heredity. It's not life-threatening, but if the look isn't your style, ask your doctor for a minoxidil (Rogaine) prescription—it could spur new growth.

See your dermatologist if:
• You can't blame your bald patches on your parents, or if your scalp also itches or hurts. A fungal infection, such as ringworm, could be the culprit; antifungal shampoos and medications are the cure.

2 Your head throbs.

The kids, the job, the daily grind—it's no wonder that you have a killer headache.
Relax in a bubble bath if:
• You're hot, overtired, or stressed out, or it's 8 p.m. and you haven't eaten anything since breakfast. Take some Tylenol, unwind, and get something in your stomach (preferably something more substantial than the scraps left over from your family's dinner).
See your internist or optometrist if:
• Your pain keeps you up at night, or the throbbing interferes with your daily routine even after you've popped pain relievers.

the strain of stress
Approximately 90 percent of all headaches are related to tension, and more women suffer from these than men.

• You feel nauseated, see auras or flashing lights, or experience sensitivity to light along with your headache—you might have a migraine.
• You're tethered to the computer and think eyestrain is making your head ache; schedule an eye exam.
Call 911 if:
• You also feel weak or numb, have blurred vision, or experience swallowing difficulties—all of which are signs of a stroke.
• You're age 50 or older, and you have suddenly started getting persistent and recurring headaches. This could signal a ministroke or a brain tumor.
• Of the headaches you've suffered, you'd classify this one as the worst ever. Sharp, stabbing pains could indicate a brain hemorrhage or a ruptured blood vessel. If you have a stiff neck and fever, the diagnosis could be meningitis.

3 **You feel woozy when you stand up.**
You haven't had the bed spins this bad since college, and this time you haven't even been out until dawn. Low blood pressure, an inner ear problem, dehydration, anemia, or even a heart problem could rock your world, says ear, nose, and throat specialist James M. Chow, M.D., a professor at Loyola University Medical Center in Maywood, Illinois. Check with your doctor to figure out the best treatment.

4 **You're seeing the world through foggy glasses.**
It's hard to turn a blind eye on murky vision, but this isn't always cause for alarm.
Relax in a bubble bath if:
• Your arms just aren't long enough to read a menu anymore. It's probably time to admit you need reading glasses or adjust your prescription.
See your ophthalmologist if:
• Your distant vision has also worsened, which may mean something more serious, says Robert Maloney, M.D., a spokesman for the American Academy of Ophthalmology and associate clinical professor of ophthalmology at UCLA.
• Your vision suddenly turns blurry or blocked, which could signal anything from a clot or clogged blood vessel to an optic nerve problem or detached retina.

key cabinet members

It's always a good idea to stock your medicine cabinet with supplies for the inevitable bumps, bruises, and health problems that crop up when you least expect them. Here's a checklist of must-haves for at-home doctoring.

• Acetaminophen (Tylenol) for pain
• Adhesive bandages
• Antacids to quell heartburn
• Anti-inflammatory pain relievers (aspirin, ibuprofen, or naproxen sodium) for pain with inflammation
• Diphenhydramine (Benadryl) to treat allergies, hives, and random skin irritations
• Cortisone cream to stop itch
• Hydrogen peroxide to disinfect cuts and scrapes
• Ipecac for poisoning, if you have kids (always check with your local poison-control center first)
• Pepto-Bismol to ease stomach upsets
• Reusable hot/cold compresses for headaches and sore, strained muscles

Remember:
If a symptom lasts longer than a week or you feel something's really wrong, go straight to the doctor.

• It's as if someone pulled a dark shade down over just one of your eyes—you may have glaucoma, a cataract, or another condition. Treatments range from eyedrops to surgery.

5 **Your eyes are as red as cranberries.**
Allergies and unidentified flying objects aren't the only things that can make your eyes look a little bloodshot.
Relax in a bubble bath if:
• The redness clears up in a day. It's probably a passing irritation.
See your ophthalmologist if:
• Your eye is red and achy; it could be glaucoma.
• You've just had a cold or have eye discharge, which could mean conjunctivitis.

• Your vision is also affected. It's likely that you have conjunctivitis, but it could also be a blood clot or a weakened blood vessel.

• You wear contacts. You may have scratched your cornea; this could lead to permanent vision loss.

6 Your hearing is muffled.

What's that, you say? It's the same disorienting feeling you get when there's water in your ears.

Relax in a bubble bath if:

• Your ears pop when you wake up, and your hearing comes and goes. Wax could be blocking your ear canal. When you yawn or pull on your earlobe, the wax may move, returning your hearing to normal. Try an over-the-counter earwax softener. (Never clean with a cotton swab, which can push wax farther in.) Next time you see your doctor, ask for a thorough ear exam.

See your internist if:

• You suddenly can't hear, and neither earwax softeners nor yawning helps. It could be a ministroke or a viral infection, which might be remedied with steroids.

• You have hearing loss with ear pain. You could have fluid in your ear that needs to be drained, or you may have an infection.

7 You can't shrug off shoulder pains.

Sure, you're carrying a lot of responsibility, but your shoulders shouldn't feel the burden.

Relax in a bubble bath if:

• You feel better after resting and icing the joint. That dull ache could be a sign you've overworked your rotator cuff, which can get injured by repetitive actions, such as practicing your tennis serve all afternoon or throwing the ball to your dog. Rest and recover fully before perfecting your Serena serve to prevent a "frozen shoulder," which can result in a total loss of mobility.

See your orthopedist if:

• You feel a stabbing, severe, or persistent pain that doesn't respond to pain relievers and ice within a week. You might have torn cartilage and may need surgery.

8 Your heart is pounding to a new beat.

It's not first love making your heart go pitter-patter.

Relax in a bubble bath if:

• You notice a skipped beat, which is typically an out-of-sync heart rhythm. While it's usually nothing to worry

about, you should mention the irregularity at your next doctor's visit.

• You suspect your racing heart is related to the closing of your biggest account ever at work.

See your internist or cardiologist if:

• Your heart randomly kicks into overdrive but then quickly returns to normal. A problem in one of your heart's chambers could be throwing off the rhythm. This may be caused by changes in the natural electrical impulses that regulate your heartbeat. You should see your doctor promptly.

Call 911 if:

• Skipped beats cause chest discomfort or make you feel dizzy, lightheaded, or short of breath; your heart's blood-pumping ability could be affected.

• Your heart races for longer than a few minutes.

9 Your breasts are leaking fluid.

They may catch you off guard, but leaky breasts usually are not life-threatening.

Relax in a bubble bath if:

• You've had a baby in the last year—ah, the joys of motherhood.

See your ob-gyn if:

• There's no baby in sight. You may have a pituitary tumor, although an underactive thyroid gland or anything that stimulates the nerve supply to your nipple can trigger discharge. Medication or surgery generally fixes the leak.

• With or without a baby in tow, the color is funky. A milky or greenish discharge or one that contains pus could indicate an infection.

• The discharge is bloody. This may indicate abnormal breast tissue, cancer, or a tumor on the milk ducts.

10 You feel as gassy as a balloon in the Macy's Thanksgiving Day parade.

A buzz kill to a romantic night, maybe, but a medical emergency, usually not.

Relax in a bubble bath if:

• Over-the-counter meds, such as Gas-X or Phazyme, take the wind out of you—or if it passes on its own.

See your internist if:

• You don't feel better within a few weeks of cutting back on the bran muffins, you have persistent gas pain, or the problem becomes such a nuisance that the idea of taking

period facts
Doctors define a menstrual cycle as normal if the time from the start of one period to the beginning of the next **is between 24 and 35 days**, and menstruation lasts from three to eight days.

an elevator with others is enough to send you hoofing it up 18 flights of stairs.

• You have sudden abdominal bloating that's not due to eating more and exercising less, or you have unexplained weight gain or loss in addition to bloating. These could be signs of ovarian cancer.

11 You've got awful cramps and you're not even having a period.

Acetaminophen or ibuprofen should pull the plug on pain.

Relax in a bubble bath if:

• The pain usually appears in the middle of your menstrual cycle, then goes away. This probably means it's triggered by ovulation. Tell your OB-GYN about it at your next appointment.

See your OB-GYN if:

• The pain is generally mild but chronic. Fibroid tumors, ovarian cysts, endometriosis, and pelvic inflammatory disease can all cramp your style.

• You've gone through menopause. It could be something as harmless as a benign cyst, which can be removed. Because the risk of some female cancers increases with age, though, constant cramping could also be a sign of something serious, such as ovarian or uterine cancer.

Call 911 if:

• The pain is severe enough to stop you in your tracks; you also feel feverish, dizzy, or faint; or you have trouble breathing. It could be a heart attack.

• You could be pregnant—you and your baby could be at risk.

12 Your periods are as predictable as the stock market.

Ask your doctor to find out what's been causing your irregular cycles instead of just treating the symptoms with something like birth control pills. You don't want to overlook potentially serious problems.

Relax in a bubble bath if:

• You've traveled across time zones, been stressed out, or changed your diet or exercise routine recently. These factors could all throw your cycle off track, but it should return to normal within three months.

See your OB-GYN if:

• Your period lasts longer than eight days. Stress, ectopic (tubal) pregnancies, miscarriages, endometriosis, ovarian cysts, and oral contraceptives can all cause weird periods. But irregular cycles can also indicate thyroid disease, fibroid tumors, endometrial polyps, or polycystic ovary disease. Depending on the cause, your doctor might suggest medication or surgery.

• You're postmenopausal and bleeding; it could be a sign of a benign problem or cancer.

Call 911 if:

• You're soaking through two pads in an hour or one super tampon in three hours, and you feel dizzy or faint. Bleeding this heavy could mean that an ectopic pregnancy has ruptured a fallopian tube or that an ovarian cyst has burst.

13 Your lower back feels out of whack.

You've got company—80 percent of all adult Americans suffer back pain in their lifetimes.

Relax in a bubble bath if:

• You think you overdid it helping a friend move. Most often, back pain results from overuse, and weak abdominal and trunk muscles can make the problem even worse. (Regular crunches will help strengthen those muscles.) With ice and rest, back pain usually goes away within three or four weeks.

See your internist if:

• You're running a fever, which could indicate that you have an infection.

• You're losing weight for no reason or have a history of cancer. Almost any cancer can spread to the bones and cause pain.

• The pain shoots to your legs; your urinary or bowel habits have changed; it hurts when you cough or sneeze; your leg muscles are weak; or your back is swollen, red, or warm to the touch. You could have a disk problem and may need surgery.

14 It feels like there's a marble digging into your feet.

Tender heels could mean you're suffering from plantar fasciitis.

Relax in a bubble bath if:

• The pain responds to rest, ice, compression, and elevation (RICE, in sports docs' terms). When you walk or run too much, the plantar fascia, a band that runs from your heel to the ball of your foot, becomes inflamed and painful, says Robert Stanton, M.D., clinical instructor of orthopedic surgery at Yale University School of Medicine. Once you've healed, stretch your Achilles tendon, which connects your calf to your heel, to prevent a recurrence.

See your orthopedist if:

• A week passes but you're still hurting—you may have a stress fracture. Your doctor may give you an ankle splint to help you heal faster.

Most people are unable to effectively track **changes in their moles,** so it's best to get your doctor to examine them for you.

15 You look like you're wearing camouflage—only you're naked.

You can usually blame patches of dark skin on hormonal changes caused by pregnancy or birth control pills, and lighter spots on eczema or other skin conditions. Pigmentation problems aren't usually medical red flags, says Lynn McKinley-Grant, M.D., associate clinical professor

Seventy-five percent of Americans will experience **foot problems** in their lives, women about four times as often as men.

of dermatology at George Washington University in Washington, D.C. But see a dermatologist for treatment, which can include bleaching creams, Retin-A, anti-inflammatory drugs, and steroid ointments.

16 Your nails have strange growths no manicure could cover.

Unattractive, yes, but thick, yellow, crumbly nails aren't a health emergency—fungus is likely making them funky. See a dermatologist; new oral medications like Lamisil work well, McKinley-Grant says.

17 You can play connect-the-dots with your moles.

Used to be that moles were a turn-on; now they're skin-cancer hot spots. A recent study published in the *Archives of Dermatology* suggests that most people are unable to effectively track changes in their moles, so it's best to get your doctor to examine them for you.

Relax in a bubble bath if:

• You've lived with the same moles your whole life.

See your doctor if:

• Your moles are new or have these characteristics: 1) asymmetry (one half doesn't match the other half); 2) ragged, blurred, or irregular borders; 3) uneven color throughout; 4) diameter larger than a pencil eraser. These are all signs of melanoma, which surgery can usually cure if you catch it early. ✳

Freelance writer Linda Rao is the co-author of Good Carbs, Bad Carbs: An Indispensable Guide to Eating the Right Carbs for Losing Weight and Optimum Health.

Q+A
What to Do If You're Black and Blue

I seem to bruise really easily. Is there anything I can do to prevent the black-and-blue look?

PART OF YOUR PROBLEM is probably that you're thin-skinned (and we're not talking about an inability to handle criticism). Thinner-than-average skin is more vulnerable to bruising, and it doesn't conceal injuries as well as thick skin. About all you can do is wear long-sleeved shirts and pants to provide a little extra protection against bumps and scrapes. To bolster your skin's camouflaging effects, use sunscreen religiously. Too much exposure to sun decreases skin's elasticity and damages blood vessels. You might also want to limit your use of aspirin and other over-the-counter painkillers, as they can increase the likelihood of bruising.

If you're just generally a bit clumsy, it makes sense that you have bruises, and they are probably nothing to worry about. Check with your doctor, though, if you bruise without good reason, especially in unusual areas—such as the chest, abdomen, or face—or if your bruising is accompanied by frequent nosebleeds, bleeding gums, profound fatigue, or minor cuts that continue to bleed even after several minutes of pressure. These symptoms could be related to an underlying condition, such as hemophilia or a low blood-platelet count.

A More Convenient Way to Check Your Blood Pressure

The next time you make a run for a carton of milk, keep your eye out for medical specials. Grocery stores and drugstores across the country offer Lifeclinic Health Stations, where you can check your pulse and blood pressure for free. Many allow you to zap your results directly to the Lifeclinic Web site, where you can track your readings. Visit www.lifeclinic.com to find a station near you.

SELF-CARE
get a leg up on cramps

Is the nightmare that's waking you in your legs, not your head? Welcome to nighttime muscle cramps, which grip the legs of as many as 95 percent of Americans, the majority of them women. Why do your legs—usually the calves—hurt like the dickens after dark? Your muscles could be seeking revenge for overtaxing them during the day. Dehydration and high heels can also be at the heart of this agony. Here's how to deal with a leg cramp, get back to sleep, and ease the next-day ache.

when the cramp strikes:

Stretch. Sit on the floor, with legs in front of you and knees slightly bent. Grab your toes—or use a towel if you can't reach—and pull them toward you, straightening and stretching your legs.

Massage. Rub or knead the tightened muscle until it relaxes.

Walk it off. A stroll around the bedroom with your weight on your heels should relieve the pain.

Ice it. The cold will help relax the muscle.

the morning after:

Rest a sore calf on a warm towel or heating pad, or relax in the tub.

every day:

To prevent future cramps, be sure to stretch your calves daily, drink plenty of water, and get enough vitamin E and potassium—thought to be cramp-fighters. Some good sources include bananas, oatmeal, nuts, and spinach.

Call a doctor if you continue to get cramps no matter how much you stretch and hydrate. She may want to prescribe a muscle relaxant or antispasm medication to calm your cramping legs.

Lessons from the E.R.

Top emergency-room doctors explain why home is often where the hurt is—and how to avoid the most common accidents and injuries.

BY MICHELLE DALLY

Diane Hinchcliffe, 37, was putting the finishing touches on dinner. It had been a long day, and ending up in the emergency room was the last thing this Palo Alto, California, mother of two had in mind. "I just wanted to light a candle," she says. But the wick was buried in the wax, a problem Hinchcliffe had remedied in the past with a paring knife. So she tried it again. Holding the large candle in one hand, she used her other hand to dig out the wick with the knife. This time, however, the candle suddenly split down the middle and the knife wound up embedded in her palm.

"I hit the exact spot where the radial artery goes into your hand," Hinchcliffe remembers. She spent hours in the emergency room, the doctors barely able to stem the flow of blood. An on-duty doctor stitched the wound, which reopened weeks later due to internal bleeding. It took months before the ordeal was over and Hinchcliffe regained full use of her hand. Now, she says, if she encounters an uncooperative wick, she lights another candle or relies on the dimmer switch for mood lighting.

You'd think people would have mastered basic safety rules by now and that emergency-room trips would be dropping off. But E.R.s across the country clocked 102.8 million visits in 1999, the most recent year for which stats are available. That's more than 280,000 visits a day—a 14 percent increase from 1992.

So what's going on? Are more people taking up extreme sports or driving more dangerously on the highways? Neither. Many of the people who visit the E.R. are like Diane Hinchcliffe: They had no clue that what they were doing was an invitation to disaster. Statistically, one in five people will have made a trip to the E.R. in 2002 and, chances are, they aren't the Evel Knievel type. In fact, many of the accidents occur not in high-risk settings but rather in home sweet home. Accidents in the home killed almost 30,000 Americans in 2000 and sent 7.1 million to the E.R. with disabling injuries.

E.R. docs insist, though, that these household mishaps—as well as many other emergency-room injuries—are eminently preventable. So we asked physicians at trauma centers around the country about the most common injuries they treat and, more importantly, how you can lower your risk of ever seeing the inside of an E.R. (except on television). At the top of the list are things you probably do every day without even thinking about them.

Danger Overhead

Something as simple as changing a lightbulb or dusting a ceiling fan can be an accident waiting to happen. According to Joseph Scott, M.D., of South Miami Hospital, a common injury results from people working on overhead jobs without wearing protective eyewear. As Scott suggests, all it takes is a small foreign object—a speck of dust, a fragment of wood, a paint chip from the ceiling—to fall into your eye and scratch the cornea, or worse. "I see that once a week, if not more often," Scott says.

• **Stay-safe Rx:** Before you become the next corneal abrasion in line in the emergency room, swallow your fashion sense and get a pair of those inexpensive plastic work goggles from your local hardware store. Don them before tackling any job that requires looking up.

Crises in the Kitchen

If home is where the hurt is, the kitchen is the hot spot. "For adults, the most common injury in the kitchen is when people try to open a package with a knife—frozen hamburgers, that sort of thing," says Susan Nedza, M.D., an E.R. doctor at Elmhurst Hospital in Elmhurst, Illinois. "We see lots of hand lacerations." Right behind those injuries are people slicing open their fingers while they are trying to cut a bagel, says Neil Flomenbaum, M.D., chief of emergency medicine at New York Presbyterian Hospital. And, of course, don't forget about those pesky candlewicks.

• **Stay-safe Rx:** Always use the proper tool for the job—a pair of blunt-tipped scissors to open a plastic or cardboard package of frozen food, for instance, or a bagel holder for those slippery discs of dough. In fact, say E.R. docs, you really should never hold something in one hand and a knife in the other; it just invites disaster. Place the object firmly on a cutting board.

Do-It-Yourself Disasters

Kathy Tanner, a 49-year-old human-resources specialist from McLean, Virginia, knew she wasn't any type of expert at home-security systems. But that didn't stop her from climbing up a ladder on New Year's Eve to try to disconnect her home alarm when it wouldn't stop buzzing.

Problem is, she wound up ushering in 2000 at the local doc-in-the-box with severely bruised ribs after a nasty fall from that ladder.

Tanner, as it turns out, has company. In 2000 alone, almost 10,000 Americans ended up in the E.R. after falling off ladders and stepladders. That's just the tip of the iceberg. There were some 365,799 visits to the emergency room because of other home-improvement mishaps. And the accidents are an equal-opportunity phenomenon. "It seems that more women are being injured around the house doing projects such as painting, wallpapering, and other tasks," says Bob Suter, a doctor at Medical City Dallas Hospitals and a member of the board of directors of the American College of Emergency Physicians.

• **Stay-safe Rx:** You don't have to be a do-it-yourself statistic. Slow down and read the directions for all equipment or tools you're using, suggests Andrew Erdman, M.D., of Denver General Hospital. Use the safety guards on power tools, such as blade guards on table saws. Wear the appropriate clothing—long-sleeved shirts, long pants, work boots, and plastic goggles—especially when hammering or using a nail gun. Finally, when fatigue catches up with you, stop working: That's when accidents happen.

In terms of not being the fall guy—or the fall woman, in Kathy Tanner's situation—the basic rule, according to Suter, is never climb a ladder when your balance could be compromised. Pregnant women, for example, should stay on solid ground because their new center of gravity affects their ability to balance. Cold or allergy sufferers should also stay grounded because their condition can affect their middle ear, which regulates balance. What's more, alcohol and over-the-counter and prescription medications can also affect your footing while you're on a ladder.

Grillers Beware

So all you want to do is relax around the barbecue with some friends, right? But along with the burgers, steaks, and roasted vegetables can come an unwelcome dose of food poisoning. In fact, this is so common at summer

> Before you become the next corneal abrasion in line in the emergency room, swallow your fashion sense and get a pair of those inexpensive plastic work goggles.

cookouts that exposure to a certain kind of *E. coli* bacteria has actually been dubbed the "barbecue syndrome." That's because grilling usually requires handling meat at temperatures that encourage bacterial growth. But bugs in your burgers aren't the only danger associated with grilling. Any time you have an open flame, there's the potential for, well, getting burned. And, boy, have E.R. doctors seen their share of burns—most of them are due to squirting lighter fluid on an already lit grill.

• Stay-safe Rx: To protect yourself from barbecue syndrome, marinate your main dish in the refrigerator—not out on the counter—and throw out the meat-soaked marinade (never use it as a sauce unless you boil it first). After your dinner hits the grill, wash your hands, utensils, and any plates touched by the raw stuff. Use a meat thermometer to ensure that meat is adequately cooked. Each type of meat has its own safe temperature: For ground beef, it should be 160 degrees; chicken breast, 170 degrees; pork chops, 160 degrees; and a decent beef steak, 145 degrees for medium rare and up to 170 degrees for well done.

And to keep yourself from being flambéed along with that flank steak, follow the doctors' orders: Never *ever* use charcoal lighter fluid on a fire. When you're using a gas grill, always remember to leave the grill hood open until you get it lit. Also, keep combustibles—pine needles or stacks of leaves, which can be set off with a single spark—a generous distance from the fire. And, finally, just in case, you should always have a fire extinguisher or garden hose at your fingertips in case something unexpected happens.

Bad Chemistry

Cleaning is boring and time-consuming. It can also be harmful to your health. Using several household cleansers to attack a dirty bathroom could result in serious respiratory problems. For instance, if you try a product containing chlorine bleach to remove the soap scum from the tile and then finish up with an all-purpose ammonia cleaner, you have unwittingly created chloramine gas. Breathing it can inflame your lungs or cause you to develop chemical pneumonia, which makes your lungs fill up with fluid. Another chemical cocktail to avoid: chlorine bleach mixed with anything containing acid (like toilet-bowl cleaners). This mixture can create chlorine gas, which can be fatal if inhaled long enough in a confined space.

• Stay-safe Rx: The golden rule from E.R. doctors is pretty simple: Never attempt to concoct your own supercleanser by mixing two (or more) together. Neither should you use one cleanser right after the other. If one product doesn't do the job, rinse the surface thoroughly with water before you decide to try something else.

Always read the product labels for chemical culprits like ammonia or chlorine bleach. And any time you do use these harsh chemicals, be sure to ventilate the area by opening a window or turning on a fan. Better yet, you could shop for products that don't have ammonia or bleach in the ingredient list, such as a natural all-purpose cleanser like castile soap. Instead of using commercial window cleaners, try mixing your own with lemon juice and water, and clean with nonchlorinated bleach.

> You don't have to be a do-it-yourself statistic. Slow down and read the directions for any piece of equipment or tool you're using.

keeping kids safe from common culprits

Adults, of course, aren't the only ones who end up in the E.R. Kids are regular customers, too. And the more active they are, the more likely they are to get hurt: Bike-riding, skateboarding, and jungle-gym accidents are all too common. Proper supervision and protective gear, such as helmets and wrist and knee pads, can keep your little ones safe—even prevent debilitating and deadly head injuries. The American Academy of Pediatrics is so serious about this that they recently issued new guidelines suggesting that all kids who ride skate-boards and scooters (as well as bikes) should wear hel-mets and protective gear.

Accidental poisoning is also a problem, but before you blame household cleaners or insecticides, think again. Mouthwash, children's and adults' vitamins, and prescrip-tion drugs are the main culprits. "Children's vitamins with iron are designed to look cute and taste good, but based on the number of tablets a kid takes, the iron can cause a lot of problems," says Susan Nedza, M.D., of Elmhurst Hospital in Elmhurst, Illinois.

To prevent kids from accidentally poisoning themselves:

Store all vitamins, substances that contain alcohol (like mouthwash), and medicines out of children's reach at all times.

Ask for childproof containers for all pills, even if you don't have kids. A recent study found that 23 percent of the oral prescription drugs ingested by children under the age of 5 belonged to someone who did not live with the child.

And be prepared, just in case the unthinkable hap-pens. Keep the number of your local poison-control cen-ter near the phone; store syrup of ipecac in your medicine cabinet for inducing vomiting of a noncaustic substance; and keep activated charcoal on hand to absorb caustic substances. Oh, yes, and stay two steps ahead of your always-curious child.

Drugs and Herbs: Risky Combos

Some E.R. visits are actually prompted by efforts to *improve* health. For instance, people who take some over-the-counter decongestants for two or three days in a row to relieve a cold or allergy are increasing their blood pressure, says Judy Gorham, director of emer-gency services at Ivinson Memorial Hospital in Laramie, Wyoming. "They might be experiencing pressure in their chest, or they might have a headache, and they'll come to the E.R.," she says. "They could potentially have a stroke."

OK, everyone can understand how medicine might be dangerous, but what about herbal supplements? They're safe, right? Wrong, according to many E.R. doctors. Depending on what you take, the herbal sup-plement in combination with a prescribed medication could be deadly. "Once you're talking about two or three chemicals that you put in your body at once, no one knows what the results will be," Suter cautions.

Sometimes herbs alone are the problem. If you have a heart condition, for instance, and take an herbal remedy with ephedrine in it (mahuang and other diet supplements), you might experience a racing heart at the least and even death, in rare cases, at worst. And what about the people popping ginkgo or ginseng every day for increased energy and sharper mental function? Those herbs can prolong bleeding—not a good idea if you're scheduled for surgery or are about to start your period.

• Stay-safe Rx: Before you take any herbal or other over-the-counter drug, check with your doctor or phar-macist to see if it's going to interfere with the medications you're currently taking or with an underlying medical condition. Be particularly careful if you're at high risk for stroke. Not exactly rocket science—but in the end, keep-ing out of the E.R. means staying in touch with your common sense. ✳

Michelle Dally was on the Pulitzer Prize–winning staff of the **Denver Post** *in 2000. She currently contributes to* **U.S. News & World Report.**

when germ-fighting goes too far

Germ-fighting products have moved beyond the cleaning and medicine aisles, plotting to eradicate bacteria everywhere. But the products may, in fact, be aiding and abetting their intended targets. "Having so many antibacterial products available to us might be promoting resistance," says Kimberly M. Thompson, M.D., of the Harvard School of Public Health and author of the new book *Overkill: How Our Nation's Abuse of Antibiotics and Other Germ Killers Is Hurting Your Health and What You Can Do About It*. "We're not exposing ourselves to enough challenging germs, so our bodies might begin to have trouble fighting them." Virtually every soap and cleaning product you can think of now comes in antibacterial formula—and it doesn't stop there. Some manufacturers have clearly gone overboard.

rating key:

✳ *A little obsessive*

✳✳ *Niles Crane would beam with pride*

✳✳✳ *Why not just don an airtight suit?*

PRODUCT	PURPOSE	OVERREACTION RATING
Virofree Portable Germicidal Spray	Spray on any suspicious surface before you touch it: Think restroom doors, restaurant chairs, or the pen you "borrowed" from your co-worker's desk.	✳✳
Playskool classic favorites Mr. Potato Head, Lincoln Logs, Tinkertoys, Weeble (made with Microban)	Germ and bacteria protection is embedded inside the plastic ... too bad it doesn't protect your tot from picking up germs that land on the toy's surface.	✳
MicroTouch ClearTek 3000 Clean Screen self-service kiosks	A touch-screen that ensures that bank customers won't pick up fellow users' germs .	✳
ToTo Toilets	A protected plastic seat to keep your bacteria from mingling with anyone else's—no ifs, ands, or butts.	✳✳✳

Q+A
Checking up on Hotel Hygiene

I know hotels change the sheets, but what about the bedspreads and blankets in the closet? It grosses me out to think that so many people use them. Can I catch anything from them?

STOP LOSING SLEEP over the blankets—it's very unlikely that you'll get sick from curling up with them. Germs thrive in moist environments, and the dryness of most hotel rooms (thanks to modern ventilation systems) means that even if the last guest had a sneezing fit in bed, it's unlikely that the germs will still be there when you check in. Of course, if the bedspread or anything else in the room looks dirty or smells suspicious, ask for a different room (and, of course, consider crossing that place off your lodging list).

While the bed linens may be safe, watch out for the bathroom. Viruses and bacteria that can cause an upset stomach (including the infamous *E. coli* bacteria, and sometimes even the hepatitis A virus) hang out under the toilet seat and—wish we were kidding here—in the sink. Also, always put down the toilet lid before you flush: The spray can spread germs up to 20 feet, probably within range of your toothbrush. No need to cancel that much-anticipated weekend getaway, though. You can keep these germs from causing problems by always washing your hands after each bathroom visit.

winning the cold war

Here's how to tell whether it's the flu or a cold, why it matters, and what to do about it.

BY CHRISTIE ASCHWANDEN

Last February, I caught the crud. Or rather the crud caught me. On the morning I was to travel across the country for an important ski race, I awoke with a sore throat. I told myself it was nothing, but by the time the plane took off, my brain felt like it was hurling itself against the inside of my skull. When I arrived at my destination hours later, I was coughing, dizzy, and achy all over. My hearty appetite had vanished, and my nose had turned into a prolific ... um ... factory.

What luck. Instead of skiing, I spent the weekend in a musty motel room, sweating and shivering with fever.

I thought a few days of bed rest would clear this up, but six weeks later I found myself sleeping 14 hours a day and waking up exhausted. The five-minute walk to my mailbox felt like a marathon.

What could be making me feel so miserable for so long? I had to have something serious: Ebola, or congestive heart failure, or maybe mononucleosis. I was hoping for mono when I went in for tests. At least that isn't fatal.

It wasn't mono, after all—or any of the other diseases I feared were fueling my fatigue. It was the flu.

The flu? If someone like me—a longtime health writer with access to top-notch medical information—could be confounded by such a common condition, chances are you could be, too. The flu is a master of disguise, and it's particularly difficult to diagnose and treat. The problem is that folks often mistake a cold for the flu, and vice versa.

Can you tell the difference? If you have a fever, chances are it's not a cold. **Body aches** are a tip-off that you've got the **flu.** And if you've got a **scratchy throat,** you can bet it's just a **cold.**

But there are actually clear distinctions between the two, as I found out too late. Here are some tips to help you distinguish between these common maladies. They could help you make a speedy recovery or keep you from getting sick in the first place.

Flu

What it is: The term "flu" is often applied to any bug that makes you feel lousy. But influenza, which attacks 10 to 20 percent of Americans in an average flu season (November to March), is caused by a specific virus. It is a respiratory illness; there is no such thing as stomach flu.

How to tell: "When you have a fever and a cough together, that's a good sign you've got influenza," says Carolyn Bridges, M.D., a medical epidemiologist at the

Centers for Disease Control and Prevention (CDC) in Atlanta. Other true flu symptoms include headache, fatigue, nasal congestion, body aches, and sore throat.

How to treat it: Both colds and the flu will almost always get better on their own with rest and lots of fluids. If it is influenza, taking a prescription flu drug—such as Flumadine, Tamiflu, Relenza, or Symmetrel—might speed the recovery process along.

Just don't expect miracles. These drugs must be taken within 48 hours, and they won't make you feel better overnight. "Particularly in healthy subjects, these drugs decrease the likelihood of complications and reduce the time a person is sick by about a day or a day and a half," explains Robert Couch, M.D., a virus expert at Baylor College of Medicine in Houston.

How to prevent it: If properly matched to the type of flu circulating, prescription drugs can also prevent flu symptoms, if taken before exposure. Couch says the drugs are especially useful in fending off a flu infection in elderly people or those with chronic illnesses. But they're no substitute for the flu vaccine.

"By far, the best strategy for fighting influenza is to prevent it with a flu vaccine," Bridges says. While the vaccine is an inactive form of the virus, Bridges says, it's a myth that it can give you the flu. But it may give you a sore arm and occasionally may cause body aches and low-grade fever.

The influenza virus is constantly changing, so the vaccine is updated each year to respond to the specific viruses that are thought to be the most likely to circulate. If the match of vaccine to viral strain is good, the vaccine is 70 to 90 percent effective. Even when it's not a perfect match, it will lessen the severity of your symptoms and reduce complications. The CDC recommends a yearly flu shot for anyone with a chronic disease, a compromised immune system, or severe anemia. It also advises a vaccine for anyone over age 50, women who will be more than three months

pregnant during flu season, and all health-care workers.

Potential complications: It's important to monitor flu symptoms carefully. If you experience a spike in fever or a sudden worsening of symptoms, see your doctor immediately; this could indicate that a complication has developed. The CDC estimates that influenza kills 20,000 people a year, but when a particularly insidious strain arises, that number skyrockets. Even when it doesn't kill, the flu can cause serious complications, such as pneumonia, bronchitis, and asthma attacks. Clearly, the best treatment for this potentially deadly virus is vaccination before the flu season begins.

Cold

What it is: A respiratory illness that can be caused by one of at least 200 different viruses.

How to tell: Typical symptoms include nasal congestion, sneezing, a runny nose, and a scratchy throat. Less than 10 percent of colds have a fever associated with them.

How to treat it: Though usually milder than the flu, colds are actually more difficult to treat with drugs. "Colds are very brief illnesses. If you want to make a brief illness even briefer, you need something extremely potent," Couch says. A million purported cold cures exist, but since the average cold is gone in a week, you're likely to feel better soon no matter which remedy you try. "I don't know of anything that significantly reduces the severity or duration of the common cold," says Ronald Turner, M.D., a cold expert at the Medical University of South Carolina.

Over-the-counter medications may assuage those symptoms, but they don't stop the virus from reproducing and, thus, won't speed recovery. The problem is that once you notice cold symptoms, the virus has probably already released hundreds of new particles. Symptoms typically begin 10 to 12 hours after the virus is produced in the nose and peak about 36 to 72 hours later. Symptoms such as runny nose, watery eyes, and scratchy throat come from your body's response to the virus—not the virus itself, Turner says. So the notion that a depressed immune system makes you more vulnerable to colds may be wrong.

The CDC advises **flu shots for women** who will be at least three months pregnant during flu season, November to March.

is it the flu or a cold?

Fight the right enemy: Figuring out the cause of your misery can help you feel better faster.

	FLU	COLD
symptoms		
cough	usually	sometimes
runny nose/congestion	yes	yes
sneezing	rarely	yes
sore throat	yes	sometimes
scratchy throat	rarely	yes
fever	yes	rarely
body aches	yes	rarely
headache	yes	sometimes
fatigue	yes (severe)	yes (mild)
treatment		
prescription drugs	yes	no
over-the-counter drugs	yes*	yes*
antibiotics	no	no
rest and fluids	yes	yes
prevention		
vaccine	yes	no
good hygiene	yes	yes

*may ease symptoms, but won't speed recovery

Research suggests an active immune response may give a cold its bite.

Also remember that antibiotics are totally ineffective against both colds and the flu, since antibiotics kill bacteria, not viruses. Taking antibiotics "just in case" is bad medicine; there is growing evidence that indiscriminate use is spawning antibiotic-resistant bacteria, Couch says. **How to prevent it:** There's no vaccine for colds, but it is possible to protect yourself from infection. "Things we know work: Wash your hands a lot and keep them away from your eyes and nose," says Jack Walton, M.D., of the University of Virginia Health System in Charlottesville. But, this information came too late to save me from six weeks of misery and my saint-of-a-husband from my whining. This winter, I'm doing everything I can to keep the crud away and crossing my freshly washed fingers that it works. ✳

Christie Aschwanden is a **Health** *contributing editor.*

Q+A
How to Avoid Picking Up Restroom Germs

What's the best way to keep my washed hands germ-free in a public rest room?

HOW GOOFY are you willing to look? Because to keep your hands really clean, you have to manage to do your bathroom business without touching anything. No door handles or faucets—and towel dispensers might as well be called germ-dispensers. To protect yourself from infectious diseases like cold and flu (the majority of which are transmitted by touch), the Centers for Disease Control (CDC) recommends drying your hands with paper towels and using the towels as a barrier between you and the faucet, the bathroom door, and other surfaces.

How thoroughly you dry your hands is also important. That's why the CDC recommends paper towels over hand blow-dryers—as long as you don't touch the dispenser. Studies have shown that people who use paper towels tend to dry their hands more completely than people using other methods. Most give up on the air dryers too soon and wipe their still-damp hands on their clothing, a surefire way to end up with more germs. If you're really concerned about picking up bugs in bathrooms, grab a couple of paper towels—one to dry your hands with and one to use as a germ shield.

Discover the best way to beat the sniffles—on the Web

To outsmart hay fever and learn to defend yourself, log on to www.weather.com/activities/health to check the local pollen count for more than 100 major U.S. cities. If it's high, you may want to stay indoors in the early morning and late afternoon, the two peak pollen times. With information on colds and allergies, the site can also help you figure out the culprit behind your stuffy nose.

the danger lurking in the air you breathe

Tiny dust particles aren't as harmless as you think.
They're causing surges in heart attacks—and everyone is at risk.
We take an in-depth look at the air around you, and the best
ways you can protect yourself from it.

BY PETER JARET

PHOTOGRAPHY BY JEFF STEPHENS

After working more than a decade with the North Carolina State Highway Patrol, Fred Hargro Jr. knows there are thousands of ways to spell trouble—from drunken drivers and reckless motorists to bona fide bad guys. "With a job like this, you find yourself in all kinds of situations," says the 31-year-old line sergeant, pulling on his bulletproof vest at the start of the evening shift.

For the next few days, though, Hargro will be helping track down an unusual culprit. Electrodes attached to his chest will measure subtle changes in his heart rate. Sophisticated devices installed in the back of his patrol car will continuously monitor the air he breathes, on the lookout for what environmental experts call particulate pollution—a.k.a. dust and soot.

Every breath you take carries tiny particles into your lungs, spewed out by power plants and factories, emitted by cars and trucks, whipped into the air by windstorms,

and, in smaller amounts, created by activities as basic as cooking and cleaning. And now evidence suggests that as many as 50,000 Americans may die each year from inhaling these microscopic specks. Worldwide, that number could be as high as 2.8 million deaths annually, according to the World Health Organization. As experts anticipated, people who have respiratory problems are more likely to die when air quality is bad. But many others are dying in a way researchers would never have predicted: as a result of sudden heart failure, sometimes within hours after a surge in levels of dust and soot in the air. And while the risk is greatest for the elderly living in urban areas, early evidence shows that there is some cause for concern for people of all ages, no matter where they live.

It's not surprising that soot and dust cause so many problems for the lungs, especially in people who have respiratory conditions such as asthma or nasal allergies. Studies show that on days when the air is thick with these tiny specks, people with asthma have to take higher doses of medications to control their symptoms. In a 1999 study, Israeli researchers found that children growing up near industrial sites that spew out particles suffer from coughs and congestion far more than kids raised away from particulate pollution. And, indeed, deaths from respiratory problems do rise on smoggy, sooty days.

But the link between hazy days and heart attacks was unexpected. The first signs of trouble were spotted just over a decade ago. In 1991, Joel Schwartz, Ph.D., at the time an epidemiologist with the U.S. Environmental Protection Agency (EPA), measured daily levels of particles in the air in Detroit and then compared those levels with the total number of deaths recorded each day. When particle levels climbed, so did the number of people dying. One after another, evaluations of other cities showed the same disturbing pattern.

"For a long time, in fact, we assumed that what we were looking at were essentially respiratory problems," says Morton Lippmann, Ph.D., program director for the New York University-EPA Particulate Matter

Vacuuming, dusting, and even cooking can kick up large quantities of microscopic specks. So can just walking through the house.

Health Research Center. And, at first, the researchers thought the particulates might be innocent bystanders: Because all kinds of noxious particles and gases tend to hang out together on polluted days, some other form of air pollution—such as carbon monoxide gas—might be the actual culprit. To find out, Jonathan Samet, M.D., an epidemiology professor and chair of the Johns Hopkins University School of Hygiene and Public Health, compared death rates in 20 cities with levels of five major air pollutants: ozone, carbon monoxide, sulfur dioxide, nitrogen dioxide, and particulates. Of the gases, only

ozone showed any link to mortality, a weak correlation strictly in the summer. But when Samet zeroed in on the particles, bingo: For every increase of just 10 micrograms per cubic meter of air, the number of reported deaths climbed one half of 1 percent—and particulate levels can jump by more than 10 times that on a hazy day.

Further research turned up evidence that not all dust and soot poses an equal threat. "The bigger the particle, in fact, the less dangerous it's likely to be," says James H. Ware, Ph.D., professor of biostatistics at the Harvard School of Public Health. Motes, the specks you see tumbling in a beam of light, are among the biggest. These and the other particles large enough to be seen are usually trapped in your nose and eliminated before they can cause problems. But midsized particles can slip through and reach your lungs, aggravating respiratory problems. And the particles that threaten your heart are too small to see except under a microscope, or as a haze in the air. "The smallest ones can reach the bloodstream, where they may be carried throughout the body," says Robert Devlin, Ph.D., who heads up clinical research at the National Health and Environmental Effects Research Laboratory at the EPA.

If these microscopic bits reach the heart muscle, scientists now think, they may cause subtle abnormalities in the heart's ability to vary its rhythm in response to changing demands, such as the need to beat faster during exercise or more slowly while sleeping. In 1999, researchers at Brigham Young University hooked up seven people to electrodes similar to the ones worn by Hargro and the North Carolina State Highway Patrol volunteers. They then monitored the research subjects' heart rates on low-, medium-, and high-particulate days. When the air was thick with dust and soot, they found, hearts were less able to adapt their rhythms to the bodies' needs than when the air was clear. "Decreases in heart-rate variability are particularly worrisome because the heart's ability to vary its rhythm is a key measure of cardiac health," says cardiologist Tom Griggs, M.D., the medical director of the highway patrol study. Indeed, decreased heart-rate variability has been found to increase the risk of a heart attack.

Several other studies reinforced the connection. In 2001, a team from Harvard found in interviews with Boston-area heart-attack patients that their symptoms often began within a few hours of a recorded surge in particulate levels.

What about people who don't have heart or lung diseases? Ongoing studies like the one Hargro has volunteered for should help answer that question conclusively. But there is already evidence that no one can breathe easily on hazy, polluted days. In research for the EPA, Devlin has discovered that healthy volunteers exposed to particulates generate abnormally high levels of fibrinogen, a substance involved in blood clotting. Even in a seemingly healthy person, an increase can be dangerous because many Americans have some undetected narrowing of their arteries, increasing the likelihood of a clot getting stuck and interrupting blood flow—the very definition of a heart attack.

Also, evidence suggests that polluted air may compromise lung capacity, a standard measure of respiratory health. For instance, Yale University epidemiology professor Brian Leaderer, Ph.D., found that a group of 473 healthy, nonsmoking women experienced a distinct drop-off in how much air they could take in and exhale on days when dust and soot levels were elevated. "We're

Pieces of dust and soot stirred with each passing vehicle can go **straight from your lungs to your heart.**

talking about small changes, to be sure," says Leaderer. "But the striking thing is that they showed up even with low levels of particulates—levels routinely found in many places in the country."

"Over time, exposure could be having chronic effects that are difficult for us to measure," Devlin says. But death rates can be tracked—and that news is daunting: In a 16-year study published in March 2002, researchers followed 500,000 Americans in 116 cities and found that long-term exposure to particulates increased the number of deaths from all causes by 4 percent per 10-microgram particulate increase. Most of the increase came from spikes in heart disease and lung cancer fatalities. Even scarier, deaths from both causes went up more for non-smokers than for former smokers and current smokers—while low-fat diets, low body fat, high fiber consumption, and other healthy habits did not offer protection.

No matter where you live, avoiding dust and soot entirely isn't an option, since the stuff is generated by hundreds of sources. Two of the biggest contributors are diesel engines and coal-burning power plants, both typically concentrated in urban areas. However, even suburban and rural areas can have higher-than-average levels of tiny soot particles, thanks to other dust devils out there. A few years ago, Ann Miguel, Ph.D., a researcher at the California Institute of Technology, vacuumed dust from the surfaces of streets in suburban southern California. When she analyzed it in her lab, she found everything from bits of rubber from tires and latex from brake linings to soil, animal dander, mold spores, and pieces of pollen—much of it whipped up into the air each time a vehicle passed by.

Worse yet, when particles spin up into the air, they have a tendency to pick up all kinds of nasty hitchhikers,

easy steps to cleaner air

While government regulations will continue to decrease air pollution, you can help, too. A few environmentally friendly choices can go a long way toward clearing the air of even more of these potentially harmful particles. Here's what the experts recommend to benefit your lungs and heart—and the environment.

Heed smog alerts. On days when local officials declare a smog alert, people with respiratory or cardiovascular problems should try to stay indoors and keep windows and doors closed. Even if you're healthy, keep an eye on smog if you exercise outside. A vigorous workout can quadruple the amount of air—and particulates—you inhale, all while your heart is pumping hard. Since motor vehicles are prime producers of particles, avoid running or bicycling along busy roads, especially around rush hour. Schedule workouts for early in the morning or in the evening, when smog levels are at their lowest. When air pollution index levels climb above 300—considered the unhealthy zone for most people (over 100 is unhealthy for some sensitive groups)—move indoors.

Get a good filter. Equipping your home with a HEPA (high-efficiency particulate air) filter can lower particulate levels by as much as 76 percent. To find more information on filters, check out the American Lung Association's Web site at www.lungusa.org.

Hit the fan. Cooking, especially broiling and sautéing, can send indoor particle levels soaring. That's no reason to give up your favorite recipes—instead, install a fan that vents to the outside (be sure to get one approved for kitchen use).

Upgrade your vacuum. Vacuums equipped with HEPA filters capture far more small particles than those with less-effective filters. If trading in the whole machine is too pricey, try switching to vacuum bags labeled "microfiltration." They're more expensive, but they can cut particulate levels for much less than the cost of a new vacuum.

Ban smoking. Cigarette smoke contains a slew of noxious particles, one reason secondhand smoke is dangerous. Ask your smoking friends to light up outside (if, that is, you can't get them to quit).

Open up. When the outside air quality is good, open up your windows or doors. Fresh air mixing with indoor air dilutes the concentration of those trapped airborne particles. But shut up the house if you can see haze, if it's very windy, or if there's a smog alert.

Idle less. Don't allow a car to run inside an attached garage; high levels of particulates and noxious fumes can build up. Pull onto the driveway or street if you need to warm up the car. If you're just waiting for a passenger, turn off the engine.

Do your part. When pollution levels rise, officials in many cities declare "spare-the-air" days. You really can make a difference by following their advice to limit driving and refrain from burning fires and using outdoor grills—all of which add particulates and noxious gases to already-polluted air. And the next time you're shopping for a car, consider fuel-efficient models with low emissions, or one of the new hybrid cars that combine gas-powered and electric engines.

Devlin says. "Particulates attract toxic metals, acidic aerosols, and even other particles. And unlike pollutant gases such as carbon monoxide, which dissipate quickly in the air, particulates can remain suspended for weeks, even months."

Local weather conditions can add to the witches' brew of troublemaking particles, too. For example, health experts worry about periodic storms of thick dust that can carry tiny specks blown from the Sahara Desert all the way across the Atlantic Ocean, landing in Texas and other southwestern or central states. In Phoenix, there's concern about what experts call fugitive dust: fine soil blown into the air from roads and farms or when land is cleared for new developments.

Don't think you can banish the problem by simply keeping your windows closed and shutting your doors. A team of Harvard University researchers has found that common household chores such as dusting, vacuuming, and, yes, even cooking can send large amounts of tiny particles spinning into the air you breathe. And even just walking through the house can create a surge in airborne particulates.

The good news is that particulate levels have gradually come down over the past 20 years, thanks to federal regulations already in place. Prodded by tougher EPA guidelines on particle emissions from diesel engines, the automobile industry built advanced emissions-control devices for cars and trucks—devices that have proved to be less expensive and more effective than many experts predicted. Since 1994, the levels of particles spewed out by diesel trucks have been cut by 90 percent.

Today, there is hope that air quality will soon begin to improve more rapidly: Alarmed by the growing evidence of danger, the EPA set tough new Clean Air Act standards in 1997 to reduce particle emissions. For the first time, the agency established limits on the tiniest particles—the specks that now appear to cause the greatest danger. But before the new rules could go into effect, opponents went to court and blocked them,

arguing that the new limits would be exceedingly expensive to meet. No surprise, the loudest opposition came from industries that spew out much of the dust and soot you breathe. In 2002, the Supreme Court ruled in favor of the EPA, agreeing that clean-air standards should be based on public-health considerations, no matter what the cost.

The agency is monitoring particulate levels around the country and expects to begin alerting states where levels exceed the new limits. Since the new guidelines have been debated for years, power companies already have focused on finding solutions. And new filtering technologies have been developed, for example, that can capture more of the smallest particles now being coughed into the air by coal-burning power plants.

Still, clearing the air won't happen overnight, and full compliance with the stricter guidelines isn't required until 2017. But by EPA estimates, the new limits could save 15,000 lives a year and prevent serious respiratory problems in as many as 250,000 children annually.

"The more we learn about the hazards of these particles, the more imperative it is to reduce the amount being emitted into the air," Ware says. "The less of them we breathe in, the healthier we'll be." ✳

> Clearing the air won't happen overnight, but the EPA estimates that stricter guidelines could save 15,000 lives a year.

Peter Jaret is a Health *contributing editor.*

Every Breath You Take

Overall air quality in the United States—including levels of particulates—continues to improve, thanks to tougher regulations and improved emissions-control devices. Still, whether you live in a rural town or a traffic-tangled city, there are plenty of dangers lurking in the air you breathe. Knowing about these airborne hazards can help you avoid them as much as possible. Here's a lineup of some of the worst offenders.

Offender	carbon minoxide	lead	ozone	nitrogen oxides	sulfur dioxide
What it is	A colorless, odorless gas	A toxic metal that can become airborne	A colorless gas made up of three oxygen molecules	Odorless gases made up of nitrogen and oxygen that cause the reddish-brown haze that settles over many U.S. cities	A gas composed of sulfur and oxygen
Where it comes from	Vehicle exhaust accounts for 60 percent nationwide and as much as 95 percent in traffic-snarled urban areas.	The main culprits are lead smelters, waste incinerators, utilities, and lead-acid battery manufacturers. Inside, most comes from flaking lead paint, tracked-in contaminated soil, and the dusty clothes of workers who encounter lead.	Principle sources include industrial emissions, gasoline vapors, and chemical solvents.	Motor vehicles, electric utilities, industries, and businesses that burn fuels are the major sources. Gas stoves and heaters produce nitrogen oxides indoors.	More than 65 percent—13 million tons a year—comes from electric utilities, particularly those that burn coal. Other sources include petroleum refineries and metal-processing plants.
Why worry	This gas interferes with the delivery of oxygen to organs and tissues. It's most dangerous to people with heart disease, but at high levels it can also cause problems for healthy people.	Lead can damage internal organs, the brain, and nerve cells. High levels are linked to memory loss, mood changes, high blood pressure, heart disease, and in kids, brain damage.	Over time, exposure to ozone has been shown to cause lung damage. (Ozone levels are usually highest on hot, dry summer days.)	Nitrogen oxides can cause lung irritation and even damage lung tissue. Studies have shown that exposure can reduce lung function.	Sulfur dioxide aggravates lung and heart conditions. The estimated 16 million Americans with asthma are particularly susceptible.
National trend	Down	Down	Down	Up	Down

Q+A
How Candles Affect Your Health

I've heard that burning candles regularly may be bad for my health. Is this true?

IF YOU'RE LIGHTING candles to unwind, then the stress you're snuffing out is considerably more harmful than fumes. That said, you may want to modify your choice of candles, particularly if you have certain respiratory problems. Smoke from typical petroleum-based paraffin candles does contain some carcinogens, but levels are way below dangerous amounts. More troublesome, though, are the small particles of soot these candles put out, which pollute indoor air. Some research suggests that these particles can be an irritant for people with asthma or bronchitis. You can limit soot by burning unscented candles rather than scented ones, trimming wicks after each use, placing candles away from drafts, and extinguishing the flames with a candle snuffer rather than blowing them out.

You might try also switching to beeswax, the cleanest form of candle wax, or the newer (and cheaper) soy-wax candles. Available at many health-food stores, soy-wax candles reportedly are carcinogen-free and biodegradable, and a study found their flames to be nearly soot-free.

Q+A
How a Gas Stove Can Poison Your Home

How important is it for my gas stove to be vented to the outside?

SINCE GAS RANGES give off carbon monoxide—an odorless and colorless gas that reduces your blood's ability to carry oxygen—the Environmental Protection Agency recommends outside venting to ensure that dangerous levels can't accumulate in your home. This is especially important in winter, when folks in colder climates seal and insulate their homes so well. Even so, it's probably not necessary to call a contractor and start busting out walls. If your range is installed properly and is in good working order—vented to the outside or not—it shouldn't produce risky levels of carbon monoxide. You can make sure by getting it inspected by your local gas company. Plus, you can install a carbon-monoxide detector that will alert you when levels reach the danger zone (you can pick up a good combination smoke alarm and carbon monoxide detector for $30 to $50 at hardware stores).

In any case, if you start to experience the symptoms of carbon-monoxide poisoning—confusion, headaches, nausea, dizziness, and shortness of breath—in your home and the symptoms disappear when you leave, have your appliances and your home checked immediately, and visit your doctor.

Protect Your Family From This Toxic Lumber

A freak thunderstorm or an ant invasion can all but ruin a summer picnic. Then again, so might your picnic table if it's made of pressure-treated lumber. The bright green or brown wood, which has been used for decades to make everything from outdoor furniture to borders for raised gardens, has been banned by the Environmental Protection Agency (EPA).

The reason is because of the protective chemical combination called chromated copper arsenate (known as CCA), which is infused into the wood. Arsenic, an insecticide and a known carcinogen that forms from CCA, is particularly harmful. "CCA can leach from the wood and leave residues of arsenic on its surface and in the soil below," says David Stilwell, Ph.D., a chemist in the department of analytical chemistry at the Connecticut Agricultural Experiment Station. "A major concern is that children get arsenic on their hands and ingest it because of their frequent hand-to-mouth activity."

The EPA ban will eliminate all pressure-treated wood in homes by January 2004, and Home Depot and Lowe's plan to phase out the material well ahead of the deadline. In the meantime, the EPA suggests you always wash your hands and clothes after coming into contact with CCA and look to widely available alternatives such as wood treated with ammonia, copper, and quaternary ammonia (ACQ lumber), or Trex Wood Polymer, made from waste-wood fiber and recycled plastics. For now, the EPA is not recommending that existing structures be removed or replaced, but at your next picnic, break out the checkered tablecloth to keep the table—and yourself—covered.

Hot New Health Trends Can Shape Up Your City

BY DARYN ELLER

Most people who are trying to lose weight don't shout it from the rooftops, but when Barb Maiers set out to drop 10 postpartum pounds, she told almost everybody. And everybody in town—Dyersville, Iowa, population about 4,000—understood: Many of them had also joined Fight the Fat, a community-wide weight-loss program. "When all of us got together at weekly meetings, it was like a big pep rally," says Maiers, 36, the director of a day-care center.

Dyersville is one of several communities where health-care advocates have set up programs geared to combat the rising obesity rate. Most of these efforts provide nutrition education and group exercise activities; they also encourage local restaurants and grocery stores to highlight (and sometimes expand) their low-calorie offerings.

It sounds great—but can a public approach to a personal matter succeed? "Until you have some kind of evaluation of individuals who start with the program and where they wind up after time, it's hard to say what the value of those programs might be," says William Hobson, director of the Office of Special Programs at the U.S. Department of Health and Human Services.

But some experts are already weighing in favorably. "Community efforts are the way to go," says John Foreyt, Ph.D., an obesity researcher and professor of medicine at Baylor College of Medicine in Houston. The buzz these programs generate—the *Today* show even covered a New York City effort called Lighten Up Brooklyn—may help nudge couch potatoes into action. "If the whole city does it, you start to think, 'Maybe this is important,'" says Howard M. Shapiro, an osteopathic physician, author of *Dr. Shapiro's Picture Perfect Weight Loss 30 Day Plan*, and an adviser to Lighten Up Brooklyn and other community weight-loss programs.

The numbers on the scale are impressive. Maiers lost 14 pounds, and she wasn't alone: The original 383 Fight the Fat participants lost a total of 3,998 pounds. The eight-week Lighten Up Brooklyn program kicked off in spring 2002 with borough president Marty Markowitz promising to lay off the cheesecake. He dropped from 194 pounds to 183, and the 5,921 people who stayed with the program (7,457 originally signed up) lost an average of 14 pounds each.

When it's so hard for most people to lose weight by themselves, what accounts for these group success stories? One factor, undoubtedly, is that the organizers make it easy for participants to exercise and to eat healthy food. In Dyersville, for instance, a local recreation center started offering workout classes specifically designed for overweight exercisers. When Markowitz threw down the gauntlet in Brooklyn, some eateries put special light items on their menus to attract dieting New Yorkers.

Then there's civic pride. In 2000, when *Men's Fitness* magazine named Philadelphia the nation's heaviest city, civic leaders created 76 Tons of Fun, a program designed in part to move the city down on the fat list. It worked. By the end of 2001, 26,000 Philadelphians had lost an average of 5.3 pounds each—shy of 76 tons, but a hefty feat even so—and the city dropped to fourth on the *Men's Fitness* list (Houston has held the top spot for the past two years). The program continues to thrive, particularly in underserved areas. "We try to select communities that are least likely to have access to health information," says Philadelphia health czar Gwen Foster. "Then we grow the program by having those people who've been successful become lifestyle coaches and help others lose weight."

Like 76 Tons of Fun, the other groups depend heavily on mutual support. It certainly worked in Barb Maiers' household. Although her husband didn't officially enroll in Fight the Fat, he still lowered his cholesterol and lost about 7 pounds just by hanging out with his wife. "He started walking with me and, because I began cooking healthier, eating less fat and more fruits and vegetables," Maiers says. "That's one of the good things about the program. It has a ripple effect."

In some ways, these health-improvement efforts are akin to underground political movements—they foster a new wave of activism in the community. It's this bottom-up approach—not a gimmicky diet or fitness craze—that may chip away at the obesity rate. "If we all tried to start some grassroots efforts," Foreyt says, "we could make a major difference in the health of our society." ✳

Daryn Eller lives in Los Angeles and has written for O *and* **Parenting.**

Seeking Better Sleep

Are your nights not as restful as they should be? A new discovery could be your key to sound slumber.

BY CHRISTIE ASCHWANDEN

Tina Chavez never had trouble sleeping—until, that is, about three years ago, when the 48-year-old from Los Alamos, New Mexico, began routinely waking up in the middle of the night. After two years of tossing and turning, she finally sought help. Chavez's doctor sent her to Barry Krakow, M.D., director of the Sleep and Human Health Institute in Albuquerque. Krakow immediately suspected that Chavez's insomnia might be a symptom of a more serious medical condition: sleep apnea, a disorder in which people struggle to breathe while sleeping. Once Chavez was diagnosed with apnea, she received treatment—and began sleeping through the night.

While most experts consider daytime sleepiness the hallmark symptom of sleep apnea, few doctors make the link with insomnia. Krakow, author of the book *Insomnia Cures,* has uncovered evidence that suggests this oversight may be hiding a silent epidemic.

Conventional wisdom holds that only middle-aged overweight men develop sleep apnea, but that notion is changing. While it's true that until middle age the condition is more common in men than women, for some reason women begin to catch up after menopause. "The more we learn about sleep apnea, the more prevalent it seems," says Nancy Collop, M.D., a sleep specialist at the University of Mississippi Medical Center in Jackson. The problem strikes an estimated 5 to 10 percent of people, and Collop suspects sleep apnea may be underdiagnosed in women. Making a link between insomnia and sleep apnea could help turn up cases of apnea that might otherwise go undetected, Krakow says.

People with sleep apnea can unknowingly suffer hundreds of minisuffocation episodes each night. "Everybody's throat tissue gets narrower when they're asleep, but in people with sleep apnea this narrowing makes breathing difficult," Collop says. If the throat becomes too narrow, breathing stops entirely. The lack of air triggers the body to wake up and prevents sufferers from falling into a deep sleep. People with apnea may also have trouble staying asleep, Krakow says. Or they may unwittingly realize they're continually struggling for breath and become subconsciously afraid to fall asleep.

More than half of adults regularly suffer from insomnia, according to the National Sleep Foundation.

Sleep apnea boosts the risks of strokes, high blood pressure, and possible heart attacks, making treatment crucial.

what's keeping you awake?

Common reasons why you could be tossing and turning—and how to get the sleep you need.

PROBLEM	CULPRIT	SOLUTION
Anxiety about a big presentation made you toss and turn. You aced the talk but still can't fall asleep.	Conditioned insomnia	Those nervous nights trained you to worry about falling asleep. Rewire yourself to relax: If you're not asleep in 20 minutes, get up and do something until you're drowsy. Just make sure it's something restful (striking a yoga pose or listening to soothing music) and not stressful (like paying the bills).
After a lifetime of blissful snoozing, you suddenly can't fall asleep.	You've started a new prescription medication.	Antidepressants and asthma medications are most often to blame. Talk to your doctor about switching medications or changing doses.
You're feeling down and, despite a lingering fatigue, you can't fall asleep.	Depression	Everyone feels blue once in a while. But if your mood starts to interfere with your sleep and other normal activities, it's time to seek help. Your doctor can help you select the best treatment for you.

Krakow's research shows that even in insomnia cases where stress or trauma seem the obvious culprit, apnea is often the cause. In one study, Krakow examined crime victims who suffered from insomnia and found that 91 percent of them had a form of sleep apnea.

Most sufferers also complain of more than restless nights. A common problem—one Chavez's husband endured for years—is snoring. "About half of habitual snorers have some sort of sleep apnea," Collop says. Other symptoms, including daily headaches, memory lapses, or waking up to go to the bathroom, may also indicate apnea.

The disorder boosts the risk of strokes, high blood pressure, and possibly heart attacks, making treatment crucial. Luckily, the problem is curable. A general practitioner might recommend an over-the-counter nasal strip or a custom-fit dental device that positions the jaw for a wider airway. The most common and effective treatment (and the one that worked best for Chavez) is wearing a Continuous Positive Airway Pressure, or CPAP, machine while you sleep. The small device blows air through the nose to prevent the throat from collapsing. It took Chavez a week or so to get used to the device, but she says it was worth it. "I'm thinking clearer, I'm stronger, and I feel like a productive member of my community again," she says. Her husband is sleeping better, too: She no longer snores. ✳

People with untreated sleep apnea are three times more likely to have traffic accidents.

Colorado-based freelance writer Christie Aschwanden is a contributing editor.

Pillow Talk: Tools for a Better Slumber

The difference between a blissful night's slumber and a morning's struggle to camouflage those bags under your eyes could be right under your head. The perfect pillow can't exactly cure an insomniac, but it could save you from a restless night. To cut through the fluff in pillow picking, we consulted three experts for the lowdown on finding one to match your sleep style: Meir Kryger, M.D., director of the St. Boniface General Hospital Sleep Lab in Winnipeg, Manitoba; Rick Williams, senior buyer for the Company Store; and Eileen McGill, full-time sleep concierge at the Benjamin Hotel in New York City, where guests can choose from a menu of nearly a dozen pillows and even bedside milk and cookies (our favorite sedatives).

Water-Filled Pillow

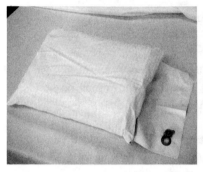

Prime candidates: the every-which-way sleeper; aquatic addicts
Why: The water level can be adjusted to make it firmer or softer, depending on your preference.

Foam Anti-Snore Pillow

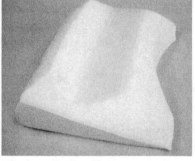

Prime candidates: loud-snoring back sleepers; sleep apnea patients
Why: The contoured foam tilts the back, chin, and forehead slightly, opening the airway to help keep breathing quieter and more rhythmic.

Buckwheat Pillow

Prime candidates: neck-strained earth-firsters
Why: The springy, eco-friendly buckwheat supports your head and neck for proper alignment—and fewer morning kinks.

Extra-Soft Feather or Down Pillow

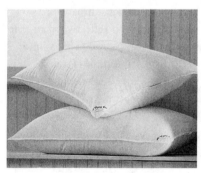

Prime candidates: face-first stomach sleepers
Why: An extra-soft and squishy pillow provides just enough cushion but doesn't get in the way; it also keeps your neck slightly elevated and in line with your spine.

Body Pillow

Prime candidates: side sleepers; pregnant women; people with back problems; lonely singletons
Why: It can be positioned to fit your curves. Ease lower-back pain by placing the pillow between or under your knees, or hug it tight for comfort.

Neck Roll

Prime candidates: frequent flyers; sleepy commuters
Why: The roll cradles your neck and head while you're on the go, cushioning you from jarring motions so you can rest easy.

Photos: (top left and middle) courtesy of Hudson Industries; (top right) courtesy of www.gaiam.com; (bottom row) courtesy of The Company Store

Q+A
How morning-after sunscreen can work for you

Can you undo the damage of all those beach-and-baby-oil days?

AN EXPERIMENTAL LOTION that repairs DNA damage caused by the sun may actually be able to reduce the threat of skin cancer.

Researchers at AGI Dermatics in Long Island, New York, have found that the so-called morning-after sunscreen, a.k.a. Dimericine, cut the risk of basal-cell skin cancer by a third and the incidence of precancerous spots in half when tested in people with a rare genetic disorder that makes them highly prone to non-melanoma skin cancers. This may mean that the lotion will help the rest of us avoid the sun-related cancer, too; more tests are planned to see if it will. Even so, don't think it's OK to tan today without worrying about tomorrow. Daily sunscreen use (always apply a minimum of SPF 15) is still your best defense against cancer, not to mention wrinkles.

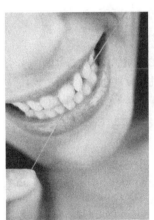

another advantage of flossing

Floss now, and you will smile later—especially if oral surgery's in your future. Researchers have found that people who stick to a regular brushing and floss-ing regimen feel less pain after wisdom-tooth removal than do those with more lax oral-hygiene habits.

Be Good to Your Feet—Hold Off on High Heels

So you know better than to sabotage your feet, knees, and back with stilettos. But here's the problem: Strutting your stuff in wide, chunky heels might do just as much damage to your body.

A recent study published in the British medical journal *The Lancet* found that walking in wide, 2³⁄₄-inch-high heels increased knee-joint pressure slightly more than walking in a narrower high heel. Over time, this additional stress on the knees may damage cartilage and raise the risk of developing arthritis of the knee.

Wide heels are especially worrisome to doctors because they're often more comfortable than their spiky-heeled sisters. As a result, "women tend to wear them routinely and for longer periods of time than stilettos," says D. Casey Kerrigan, M.D., director of the Center for Rehabilitation Science at the Spaulding Rehabilitation Hospital and the lead author of the study.

Other troubles that might result from high heels come in the form of back pain, misaligned posture, and foot problems such as bunions, corns, calluses, and hammertoes. But that doesn't mean you're sentenced to a closetful of flats. "You should treat high heels like dessert: On occasion they are OK, but they shouldn't be everyday fare," says Carol Frey, M.D., director of the Orthopaedic Foot & Ankle Center in Manhattan Beach, California.

myth: Eating and swimming don't mix.
reality check: "When you eat a large meal, the main concern is that blood is going to the gut instead of the large muscles, which may cause muscle cramping," says Christine Rosenbloom, Ph.D., sports-nutrition expert and spokeswoman for the American Dietetic Association. Light, recreational swimming that doesn't demand strenuous effort, like a friendly chicken fight or a saltwater splash in the waves, should not be a problem, she says. If you're swimming for serious exercise, though, follow the same guidelines as for other sports: Eat small amounts of energy-providing food (like a piece of fruit or yogurt) about 20 minutes before taking the plunge.

Good Question
about Women's Health

by Nancy Snyderman

If You Have a Tilted Uterus, Join the Club

My doctor told me that I have a tilted uterus. What does this mean? Should I be worried?

Things in our bodies are rarely straight, and the uterus is no exception. "Tilted uterus" is a generic term doctors use to explain to a woman how her uterus fits in her pelvis. The top of the uterus typically tilts forward slightly, but every woman is a little different. Up to 20 percent of women have what's called a retroverted uterus, which means it tilts backward. Does it matter? No. It's nothing to be concerned about; it's not a sign of disease or a risk factor for irregular menstrual periods. And, except in highly unusual situations, there is no fertility risk associated with a tilted uterus, nor should it affect pregnancy. All it means is that your body is not as symmetrical as you may think.

How to Protect Yourself From the Hazards of Ozone Pollution

Why do I always feel sniffly and slightly sick on ozone-alert days?

All pollution, including ozone, can injure your heart and lungs, and the effects must be taken seriously. Scientists say that even low levels of ozone pollution can be harmful to your health. Exposure to ozone breaks down the elastic fibers that allow your lungs to expand, making breathing more difficult and often painful. Other common side effects include watery eyes and an itchy, runny nose. If you notice any of these symptoms on days with ozone alerts, slow down. Take a day off from your exercise regimen or exercise indoors, where ozone levels are usually lower than they are outside. If you want to exercise outdoors, do it first thing in the morning before the pollutants in the air get stirred up. And, if you can, work from home to avoid breathing the bad air on the way to and from your office.

If you do feel the effects of pollution, there are a lot of prescription medications that can help you breathe more easily. Most likely, your doctor will prescribe an inhaler, which opens up your bronchial tubes.

Get the Best Treatment for Canker Sores

I often get multiple canker sores in my mouth. Sometimes they're so bad that my face swells. Can they be harmful? Is there anything I can do to prevent them?

Annoying as they undoubtedly are, canker sores are typically nothing to be concerned about. Everyone will suffer through one or two of them at some point in their lives. But for people who get these sores frequently, the biggest frustration of all is that there's little you can do to prevent getting them.

Canker sores typically begin with a burning or tingling sensation on the inside of the cheek or on the tongue, followed by a red bump. They are caused by one of a host of viruses that thrive in the mouth. Stress and dehydration

Exposure to ozone breaks down the elastic fibers that allow your lungs to expand, making breathing more difficult and often painful.

can make your mouth more vulnerable to these viruses or kick the ones that are already living there into high gear. Saliva fights bacteria and viral infections, so if you are dehydrated and producing less saliva, you'll miss out on its disease-fighting benefits. For women, hormonal changes, certain medications (especially chemotherapy drugs), or sometimes even shifts in the weather or temperature can also trigger a sore outbreak. And some doctors think that deficiencies in vitamin B-12, zinc, magnesium, and folic acid may play a role. To minimize outbreaks, keep a diary to figure out what triggers the sores and avoid the suspected culprits.

Canker sores usually heal in about a week. If they're particularly painful, you can try an over-the-counter medication such as acetaminophen or ibuprofen, or a topical treatment like Zilactin, which numbs the area and prevents irritation. Another option is to ask your doctor or pharmacist to concoct a commonly used solution known as "magic formula," which is a combination of Maalox (to coat the mouth), Nystatin (to ward off infections), and Xylocaine (to numb the pain). To reduce the swelling, you can ask your doctor to prescribe antibiotics or corticosteroids.

If you frequently get sores that persist for longer than two weeks, you should see a doctor to make sure they're not indicators of a more serious problem, such as mouth cancer.

Protect Your College Student from this Dormitory Threat

I've read that meningitis is on the rise in young adults. How does it spread, and what can I do to keep from getting it?

Bacterial meningococcal meningitis, an infection of the spinal fluid and the fluid surrounding the brain, strikes about 3,000 people in the United States each year, and the number of cases in the ages of 15 to 24 has nearly doubled in the last 10 years. It's particularly lethal among college students because their immune systems are often suppressed from partying too hard and not getting enough sleep.

The infection spreads through coughing, sneezing, and kissing, and the most common symptoms include

headache, high fever, rash, and a stiff neck. Once someone gets it, meningitis can spread like wildfire, especially among kids who live on top of each other in dormitories. Because it spreads so quickly and shuts down the body so fast, most of the time the antibiotics used to treat it don't have a chance to work. Between 10 and 13 percent of patients die from the infection, and another 10 percent suffer severe side effects, including brain damage and hearing loss.

Obviously, this is a serious threat. But for less than the price of a pair of sneakers (about $50) you can get a meningococcus vaccine that's readily available and effective. And most doctors will tell you—as I will—that if your child goes away to boarding school or college, get him or her vaccinated. Many colleges now even require it for incoming freshmen.

How to Treat Sensitive Teeth

My teeth are getting more and more sensitive to hot and cold foods. Can I do anything to stop this?

Any change in sensitivity should be taken seriously; it's a sign that your teeth are wearing abnormally. Since aches could be the result of several things—a crack, a loose filling, decay, or nighttime teeth-grinding—your dentist needs to examine you.

Many dental problems begin when the hard enamel covering the tooth wears down. Without this protection, the sensitive nerves and blood vessels inside the tooth are exposed to the elements. Things like eating hard foods, chewing on ice, and drinking hot or cold liquids (which causes teeth to expand and contract) can also expose smaller nerves running through your teeth, making them more sensitive.

Although there's not much you can do to stop the pain once it's started (short of putting down the ice-cream cone), an American Dental Association-approved toothpaste for sensitive teeth may help protect the exposed nerves and prevent future aches. Be sure to avoid stiff toothbrushes, which only make your teeth wear even more; in fact, everyone should be using a soft or extra-soft brush. Depending on the cause of your problem, your dentist may suggest a protective sealant or a mouth guard to stop teeth-grinding.

The Knee Surgery Risks You Should Know About

I'm having knee surgery soon, and I heard that there's a risk of life-threatening infections. How can I lower my chances of having complications?

Anytime you invade a joint capsule, whether it's open or arthroscopic surgery, you open up a very sterile part of your body to bacteria. In 2001, three previously healthy people died and at least four others developed serious infections after routine knee surgery. One of the victims, a 23-year-old man, died from a bacterial infection, which he seems to have contracted from donated cartilage.

About 50,000 people a year have knee surgery, and most have no serious complications. So the risk of infection is very low, about 0.5 to 1 percent.

One of the popular ways of restoring cartilage is to use donated cartilage from a cadaver. While the U.S. Food and Drug Administration requires that donated tissues and cartilage be tested for diseases like HIV and hepatitis, it doesn't require testing for bacteria. Still, about 50,000 people a year have knee surgery, and most have no serious complications. The risk of infection is very low, about 0.5 to 1 percent.

The first thing you can do to reduce your risk is to ask your doctor if knee surgery is your only treatment option. Should you decide to go ahead with the surgery and are still especially worried, it may be possible to use your own cartilage (taken either from your other knee or from healthy spots in your damaged knee). If you are having a procedure that involves donor cartilage, be sure to ask your doctor about where the tissue will come from. Though it's no guarantee against problems, it might be worth asking your surgeon to use tissue from a member of the American Association of Tissue Banks, which requires its members to complete an accreditation process, open its doors to inspections, and follow certain guidelines.

Weighing the Long-Term Effects of Ritalin

I'm concerned about the long-term effects of Ritalin. Should I take my child off the stimulant?

Recent research has called into question the impact of using Ritalin to treat children with attention deficit hyperactivity disorder (ADHD) over extended periods, but so far there's no definitive proof that it causes problems. Doctors are just now looking at adults in their 20s, 30s, and 40s who took Ritalin for many years as children, and we have to wait for the data to come in before drawing conclusions. The only significant effect of continuous use that researchers know about is a slight decrease in physical growth, but this effect is generally short-lived. If Ritalin were indeed dangerous, I think we would have known it by now.

If your child has ADHD to the point that it interferes with school and social behavior, consider continuing the medication under a doctor's watchful eye. There is no doubt that in the short-term Ritalin helps some ADHD kids improve their behavior. What is less certain is whether taking Ritalin will likewise improve an ADHD child's long-term academic success and behavior.

Ritalin does have some known short-term side effects including insomnia, dry mouth, loss of appetite, and irritability. For some kids those are mild; for others, the side effects outweigh the benefits. In most cases, Ritalin is just one part of a treatment plan; skills-management programs and behavioral therapy are other important components. You should talk with your doctor about formulating a detailed treatment plan that includes the best dose to minimize side effects.

A Medicine Mix You Need to Avoid

Is it dangerous to take ibuprofen and aspirin at the same time?

No, but if you're taking aspirin daily to prevent heart attacks and you routinely take ibuprofen for muscle aches or other problems, you should rethink your painkiller of choice. A study in *The New England Journal of Medicine* showed that ibuprofen seems to prevent aspirin from performing its normal "thinning" effects on blood platelets, which doctors know can reduce the risk of heart attacks and stroke. What's more, the researchers found that when ibuprofen was given in the commonly prescribed three-times-per-day dose, enough ibuprofen remained in the body overnight to undermine aspirin's heart-protecting benefits the next day.

If you take ibuprofen every once in a while, you don't need to worry. But if you're popping it daily, talk to your doctor about substituting another painkiller, such as acetaminophen.

Right and Wrong Positions for Sleep

Is one sleeping position better than another?

If you are healthy (and acrobatically inclined), you could sleep upside down and it wouldn't matter. Most people naturally roll into a position that feels right for them. But for folks with certain health conditions, the best sleep position involves more than just comfort. In particular: People with acid reflux (aka, heartburn) should avoid sleeping flat on their backs, which makes it easier for stomach acids to creep up the esophagus. If you have to sleep on your back, use pillows to prop up your head so that gravity will help keep stomach contents where they belong. Or better yet, sleep on your side.

Snorers and people with sleep apnea should stay off their backs completely. When you're on your back, your tongue and other parts of the throat are more likely to block the airway.

People with heart disease or heart failure should sleep on their sides—in particular, on their right sides. Researchers suspect that this position allows the heart to shift a bit from left to right, giving the heart and lungs more room to work.

Neck- or back-pain sufferers should skip sleeping on their stomachs. This position stresses the neck muscles and increases the curve in your lower back. Try putting a pillow under your stomach to flatten out the curve, or curl into the fetal position with bent knees to reduce the tension on your back and neck.

And, of course, flat-back sleeping is always best for infants. Research has linked stomach sleeping (which used to be the preferred position) to sudden infant death syndrome, and even the American Academy of Pediatrics is now recommending that babies should sleep on their backs.

Your Heart May Be Trying to Tell You Something

After I've stopped exercising, my heart rate doesn't go back down very quickly. What does this mean?

The most likely reason for a prolonged elevated heart rate after exercise is that you're not in the best shape. But if you've been exercising regularly and your pulse does not drop by more than 12 beats during the first minute of cooldown (and you haven't been sick recently), see your doctor. You may need an exercise-stress test, which involves running on a treadmill while hooked up to a heart-rate monitor. This will help your doctor assess your heart's internal nervous system, which tells it to speed up or to stay steady depending on your level of activity. Heart-rate recovery is a simple but powerful measure of how well this system is working. If your heart rate does not drop during cooldown, it could be seriously out of whack. For instance, a recent study found that people who have an abnormal heart-rate recovery and also are in poor physical shape are at high risk for heart attack.

> If your heart rate does not drop during cooldown, it could be seriously out of whack.

Your heart rate shouldn't be considered on its own, though. Your doctor will review it in combination with your overall health and other exercise test findings. If your doctor rules out serious conditions, try sticking to a fitness routine and using a heart-rate monitor to track your progress.

Nancy Snyderman, M.D. is a medical correspondent for ABC News and author of **Girl in the Mirror: Mothers and Daughters in the Years of Adolescence.**

watch out for optical delusions

Many people think they can trash their specs post-LASIK, but it's not always that clear-cut.

BY CAROL KRUCOFF

My fingernails dug into a rubber squeezie ball as I settled back into a reclining chair and watched the surgeon position a laser over my right eye. He'd given me Valium to relax and drops to numb my eyes, but my heart still thumped wildly the day I went in for surgery to correct my vision. I'd sworn back in the 1980s never to undergo such a procedure, after writing an article about the serious problems some people experienced from a pioneering form of the surgery, radial keratotomy. But with friends touting the newer, most common type, laser in-situ keratomileusis (LASIK), the idea of being able to see without glasses or contacts was too enticing to pass up.

So nearsighted I couldn't read the clock on my nightstand from bed—much less watch TV—I'd worn glasses since fourth grade. While I didn't mind wearing my specs around the house, I preferred contacts out in the world since I disliked how frames looked and felt. And at 47, I would soon need bifocals to correct presbyopia, the aging-eye condition that makes it hard to

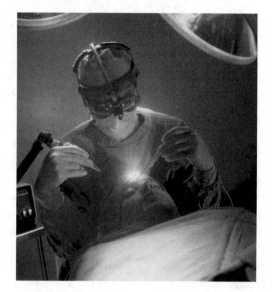

read small print. The goal: reshaping my 20/600 corneas to 20/20 in my right, dominant eye, and 20/40 in my left, a slight undercorrection that would leave me nearsighted enough to read a menu or price tag (but not a novel) without reading glasses. The hope was to live daily life virtually glasses-free. I figured the $4,000 fee (not covered by insurance) would be recouped over time by savings on glasses, contacts, and lens solutions. Despite initial misgivings, I expected perfection, and even plotted to give my glasses to Goodwill. I imagined how roomy my purse would be without my "eye gear"—never dreaming I'd need an even bigger one for eyedrops, glasses, and contacts after the surgery.

The procedure took minutes and was painless. I stared at a red light and was plunged into darkness for a few seconds while the laser vaporized tissue. My strongest memory is of the surgeon exclaiming, "Perfect!" as he completed his work on each eye.

The next morning I awoke to a miraculous sight: the clock on the VCR across the room—in focus. I tested 20/20 in my right eye and 20/40 in my left, just as expected. But my excitement was tempered with concern

> The healing process can be slow and difficult, and **there's no guarantee** of a positive outcome.

LASIK basics

With popular celebrities such as Tiger Woods and Reese Witherspoon correcting their vision with LASIK, it's not surprising that some experts estimate that as many as 20 percent of people who wear glasses or contacts will undergo the procedure by 2015. While serious adverse complications rarely occur, according to a recent report from the American Academy of Ophthalmology, many people will experience dry eyes and nighttime starbursts, at least temporarily. The key is to set your sights on realistic goals—don't expect eagle eyes post-LASIK.

Research suggests that people with mild to moderate nearsightedness or astigmatism experience the best results. Poor candidates include people who have an eye disease, take certain medications (such as steroids) that cause fluctuations in vision, have a disease such as diabetes or rheumatoid arthritis that may affect healing, are pregnant or nursing (they might have "refractive instability," which means their vision may change), or are in their early 20s.

Before you go under the laser, visit these sites:

• To help you determine if LASIK is right for you, check out the new guidelines from the American Society of Cataract and Refractive Surgery at www.eyesurgeryeducation.com.
• The U.S. Food and Drug Administration offers a checklist at www.fda.gov/cdrh/lasik for prospective patients as well as information on risks, expectations, and choosing a surgeon.
• The American Academy of Ophthalmology provides information about LASIK on its site, www.aao.org, and through the Medem Medical Library, www.medem.com.

Over the next few months, however, the scratchiness subsided enough for me to tolerate contacts. At the six-month marker, I could get through a day without needing drops every few hours. And now, after about a year, both eyes have stabilized around 20/70, and contacts are relatively comfortable, although I still see some haloes and glare at night and use drops occasionally. My surgeon recommends a second surgery—free—but there's no way I'd go through again what was, for me, an excruciating healing process, especially with no guarantee of the outcome.

The good news is that my near vision is great. Ironically, this means I don't need glasses or contacts in the house, but rely on them to navigate the outside world. I can read the clock on my nightstand and see individual hairs on my legs when shaving in the shower. And my distance vision is much better, so the world is no longer a big blur—it's a little blur.

Hindsight may be 20/20, but mine is fuzzier. Now that the worst is over (I hope), I'm not sorry I had LASIK. I'm less dependent on glasses—I'm just not living in the glasses-free world I envisioned. ✳

Carol Krucoff is co-author of Healing Moves: How to Cure, Relieve, and Prevent Common Ailments With Exercise.

Long-Wearing Lenses Now Good for 30 Days

Oxygen isn't just for lungs—it also protects your eyes from harmful bacteria, which can build up under extended-wear contacts. But these lenses may deserve another look. The U.S. Food and Drug Administration recently OK'd contacts made with "hyper-oxygen transmissible materials" (translation: They allow lots of cleansing air to reach your peepers) for up to 30 days without a break. Ciba Vision and Bausch & Lomb offer these breathable sight savers.

Why LASIK spells TROUBLE *if you wear contacts*

If you wear contacts, you may want to avoid LASIK surgery to correct your vision problems. Long-term lens use can lead to a loss of eye moisture, and a recent study found that LASIK can make the dry-eye problem worse.

over a lingering blurriness and stickiness of my eyes, which I was told would improve in a week or two.

Instead, the dryness continued and the blurring grew progressively worse as my vision regressed. A month after the surgery, I could no longer read street signs, tested about 20/50 in each eye, and had to order new lenses for my glasses so I could drive. My eyes were so irritated I couldn't wear contact lenses for nearly two months and had to use eye drops constantly. It appeared that the surgery I'd hoped would free me from glasses had instead made me even more dependent on them.

How to be a Health-Savvy Shopper

Retailers use subtle strategies to influence your behavior in their stores. Use these tips to beat them at their own game.

BY KERRI CONAN

After many laps in a Wal-Mart Supercenter—just one of many places now available for my ultimate grocery-shopping convenience—I'm beat. No wonder, I measured it: Heel-toe, heel-toe, the joint's longer than a football field.

Swirling with color and action, Wal-Mart is the epitome of the modern market. Today's stores are designed to distract you, to suck you in, to occupy you for hours as you try to navigate a cart (which sometimes seems to have a mind of its own) through aisles and aisles of choices. Somewhere between the free samples of artichoke-crab dip and a pyramid of colossal strawberries, you're supposed to get swept up in the excitement and toss out the shopping list. Usually the produce department does the trick. Or the florist. Or the deli. Some stores even place the bakery right up front, bathing the entryway with the aromas of fresh-baked honey-wheat bread and cinnamon rolls. Not surprisingly, you come home with bags full of junk food, cases of soda, and enough paper towels to fill a Hyundai.

Two can play the superstore game: All it takes is a quick course on the psychology of retail design *(and a shopping list—don't forget the list)*

Even if you patronize the smaller boutique markets, the variety is at once thrilling and overwhelming. It's never been easier to stock your kitchen, thanks to the proliferation of markets—large and small—brimming with global ingredients (not to mention sushi, organic produce, and cappuccino). So why does shopping feel so complicated?

"This is a powerful time to be a consumer," says Carl Steidtmann, Ph.D., director and chief economist for Deloitte Research, one of the world's leading retail analysts. "But so much choice means that in some ways it's harder. You have to evaluate what's important to you—whether that's price, convenience, selection, service, or organics—then patronize the stores that deliver on those values."

Time to get a grip on that cart and reclaim your power. Two can play the supermarket game: All it takes is a quick course on the psychology of store design (and a shopping list—don't forget the list). Once you're aware of the subtle strategies that influence your shopping behavior, you become the navigator. Use this insider's guide to sift through today's supermarket options, locate the freshest, most healthful foods available, and make the best decisions for you and your family.

Start with "where"

Modern supermarkets fall into four general categories: the stadium-sized superstores, the membership clubs, the chains, and the specialty markets. Each is going after a particular type of shopper, from large, budget-conscious families to selective singles who desire only the best (and usually priciest) the epicurean world has to offer. And the competition is hot.

Such huge outfits as Wal-Mart Supercenters and the more-upscale SuperTargets are giving traditional chain grocery stores—like Publix in the South, Safeway in the West, and Kroger across the country—a run for their money: These hybrids are out to create the ultimate one-stop shopping experience. They let you not only replenish your pantry, but pick up a new desk lamp for your office and get your hair cut and colored besides. This approach has forced the chains to innovate as well. Some have added conveniences such as in-house gyms, child care, and banking services. In some of the larger chains, "smart shelves" automatically alert stockers when a product runs low (so you'll never encounter an empty shelf), and new devices can identify customers' thumbprints (not just their debit cards), thus moving bodies through the checkout lines even faster.

Getting to know you—*every little thing* about you

While the superstores and chains want to hook you in and keep you there by offering you soup-to-nuts services, the specialty markets want to do it by forming a close personal relationship with you. These stores, like national chains Whole Foods and Wild Oats, and regional stores such as Wegmans in the East, Andronico's in the Bay Area, and H-E-B's Central Market in Texas, hope to establish a neighborhood hangout for food-savvy shoppers eager to commune (and who don't balk at a $4 loaf of olive-rosemary focaccia or a $20 bottle of extra-virgin olive oil). They do it in part through posters explaining the origins of foods, recipes, menu boards to describe the endless platters of prepared dishes, and brochures galore.

"We want happy customers, not full carts. We'd just rather they come back," says Danny Wegman, president of Wegmans Foods. Revolutionize the fluorescent-lit experience with warm lighting and hip decor, and suddenly where you shop becomes a lifestyle decision. The brand message: The price is worth it, and so are you.

> You'd better stay away from club stores altogether **if you're tempted** to buy snacks, candy, big-screen TVs, or jumbo packs of men's briefs.

The membership clubs don't expect you to drop in for everyday shopping, but they work hard to occasionally attract serious food fans with high-quality meats, bagged mesclun mixes, sophisticated sauces, and substantial wine and liquor bargains. The catch? Almost everything comes in bulk sizes, so it's easy to ring up a tab of corresponding proportions. You'd better stay away from club stores altogether if you're tempted by snacks, candy, big-screen TVs, or jumbo packs of men's briefs.

In-store psych

What all these stores have in common is the need to keep you and your cart cruising the aisles for as long as possible. So they spend big bucks analyzing how you shop. Company executives hire experts like Paco Underhill, author of *Why We Buy: The Science of Shopping*, to videotape their customers in action. Or they'll bring in a research firm to conduct personal interviews or follow you and your groceries home. Most try to capture data from high-tech cash registers and shopper bonus or discount cards.

One thing stores have learned from all this data is the effectiveness of corralling you. Think about your last visit to a supermarket. Did you have a choice of doors to enter? Once you got inside, was it convenient for you to veer off in any direction, or did the displays herd your cart onto a set path? Do you find yourself shopping that store the same way time after time? The industry refers to this movement as a "traffic pattern." And it's anything but accidental. While supermarket layouts vary, all use similar tricks to control your movement. Most involve

Don't just be a passive mouse in their maze: **Get to know your favorite stores** so you can locate the best products, and make the smartest decisions for you and your family.

distracting you with visuals. Some displays are set up to create a mini traffic jam so that everyone pauses long enough to add more items to their carts.

Here are some details: Nearly all grocery stores arrange the perishable departments—produce, dairy, meat, seafood, deli, bakery, "meal solutions" (prepared meals

The buying game

Today's grocery stores try to monopolize your time while filling your cart in the process. Here's how to play to your advantage.

• **Make time for cooking classes** with new-product demos—just watch out for the hard sell.

• **Perks** such as in-store gyms, day care, and hair salons can be pluses for multitaskers.

• **Fresh-baked aromatherapy:** Many stores place their bakeries and cafes near the entrance to entice you with inviting scents.

• **Grocer gridlock:** Beware of dead ends and "end-cap" displays designed to encourage impulse shopping.

• **Power-shop** the perimeter for the best service and the freshest foods—even fishmongers.

or components that you assemble and finish at home), and cafe—around the outside, in what supermarkets call the "perimeter." These areas offer a bounty of convenient plumbing and wiring for kitchens, coolers, and freezers. There's nothing terribly sinister about that, but this placement creates the need to lure customers back into the center of the store with not-so-subtle—but highly effective—merchandising traps.

There's no reason, though, to feel like a mouse in a maze. Just become an active shopper—being passive virtually guarantees your cart will track through the store like a carnival ride and increases your odds of adding on extras. Here are six shop-smart strategies to help ensure that your next trip to the market will be healthy—for your diet, your stress level, and your bank account.

Stick to the perimeter.
Here, you'll find the freshest, most innovative, most healthful foods. You'll also find the most service, because departments full of perishables require warm bodies and constant attention. This strategy is crucial for anyone who seeks a painless modern-shopping experience, because you'll be exploring the very best a market has to offer while saving time and energy.

Know the traps—and avoid them.
"Endcap" displays—those towers of seasonal treats, soft drinks, or canned goods that round off both ends of an aisle—draw customers away from the perimeter and into the depths of the store. Some stores are even starting to use warm and fuzzy lifestyle photos of attractive, catalog-perfect families to drag you into little cul-de-sacs for dead-end shopping. Only visit the center aisles where you know you'll find necessities.

Pick a store—any store—and get to know it.
Instead of wandering from market to market for all the things on your list, cut down on the frustration factor and only shop the store that best fits your needs. Get to know the terrain—picking up a few items in an unfamiliar spot won't save you time, and you'll probably end up roaming the aisles looking for items and buying what you don't need.

Make a plan.

Think in terms of meals, and organize your shopping list by recipe components. Planning ahead for future meals will save you time later on and prevent inconvenient trips to the store for missing ingredients. This way, when an item that's not on the list catches your eye, impulse won't take over. Weigh the savings—if it's a staple, it may be a good buy, but not if the bargain won't even fit in your pantry.

Get involved.

Participate in your supermarket's special promotions—such as a wellness program or a cooking class. Pick up the store's publications, or log on to its Web site once in a while. Consider signing up for the frequent-shopper program.

Plan your meals ahead and stick to your list so impulse won't take over on your next grocery trip.

Pipe up.

Because supermarkets are more competitive than most businesses, you and your dollars matter to them. The industry has mighty big changes in the works—including occasion-driven stocking arrangements in stores (for example, grouping breakfast foods like cereal, milk, and bananas together in the same aisle); recycling centers where consumers can drop off containers; and a broader variety of bulk items. So now's a good time to chime in. Ask for the products you want (and when you're not happy with a purchase, return it and explain why). Fill out a comment card, or visit the customer-service counter. If you don't get satisfaction at the local level, contact store headquarters by phone or the Internet. ✳

Freelance writer Kerri Conan is the author of numerous articles about food and retailing trends.

Q+A
How to Prevent a "Brain Freeze"

Every time I eat ice cream or sip a shake, I end up with "brain freeze." Is there a cure?

THERE'S NOT MUCH YOU CAN DO to get rid of that stabbing "ice-cream headache" except wait it out. But, fortunately, you can prevent it in the first place—without giving up your Cherry Garcia. The key: Savor slowly. The nerve in the back of your mouth that's sensitive to extreme cold—the one that triggers the headaches—is more likely to be annoyed if you suck down large bites of your mint chocolate-chip ice cream than if you take delicate licks or spoonfuls. Same goes with sipping Slurpees rather than, well, slurping them.

A Painkiller's *Quiet Problem*

The latest Hollywood high could be
in your medicine cabinet. Here's how a common
prescription drug is robbing unsuspecting
women of their health—and hearing.

BY LINDA MARSA

Christina Jaeger's ears seemed clogged. At first, she attributed it to a recent vacation to her native Australia—maybe it was the changes in cabin pressure in the plane or too much swimming at the Great Barrier Reef. But weeks went by and her hearing kept getting worse. The 37-year-old model and fitness trainer, who runs her own studio in Sherman Oaks, California, shuttled from specialist to specialist for months, trying to find the cause.

By July 2001, the intense ringing in her ears sounded like a helicopter whirling in her head, virtually drowning out the sounds of the world. Desperate for a diagnosis, Jaeger went to the House Ear Institute in Los Angeles, one of the country's leading centers for hearing-related research, and divulged everything that might help. When she admitted she was taking high doses of the painkiller Vicodin, the doctor immediately identified it as the culprit.

Jaeger is one of a growing number of women who are misusing prescription painkillers—specifically ones that combine a codeine-like drug called hydrocodone with acetaminophen (the active ingredient in Tylenol). According to the U.S. Department of Justice Drug Enforcement Agency (DEA), hydrocodone, commonly prescribed for short-term relief of mild to moderate pain, is most likely to be abused by white women ages 20 to 40—from soccer moms complaining of migraines to baby boomers with aging backs. The drugs are so prone to abuse, in fact, that the DEA is considering making them substantially harder to get. Unfortunately, many doctors are unaware of the likelihood of addiction and the hearing loss that can accompany it—and women like Jaeger are paying the price.

Dependence on a drug can happen to anybody—even if you take the medication at the doses prescribed by your doctor.

When she was prescribed Vicodin seven years ago for a painful post-op infection, little did Jaeger know that she was heading toward overuse. It's the same route taken by Melanie Griffith and Matthew Perry, both of whom recently went public with their addictions. Hydrocodone has become the current Hollywood high, supplanting cocaine as the new party drug. Its popularity for legitimate medical use makes it easy for addicts to get their hands on it: More than 90 million prescriptions for the 482 types of hydrocodone pills (including those sold under the brand names Vicodin, Lortab, Lorcet, Hydrocet, Norco) were written last year alone, according to the DEA.

The little pills, which provide relief by blocking the nerve signals from the pain pathways in the brain, worked well for Jaeger. But when she stopped taking them, she suffered classic withdrawal symptoms—the shakes, tremors, shivering, chills, hot and cold sweats, and horrific nausea, as well as constipation. Over the next six years, Jaeger weaned herself off the drug five times, only to relapse when her back pain became intolerable.

"Even after four or five months, some people still get body aches—and one little pill can make them go away," a DEA official says (the agency will not allow names to be published). Withdrawal symptoms are common signs of physical dependence. "Dependence can happen to anybody," explains Clifford A. Bernstein, M.D., medical director of the Waismann Institute, an opiate detox center in Beverly Hills, California. "And when it's time for the next dose, you feel crummy, reinforcing in your mind that you need the drug."

Although doctors aren't allowed to prescribe more than eight pills per day, tolerance can lead people to increase the dose on their own to get the same effects. Addicts have been known to take 20 pills a day—perhaps even more.

Both the patient and physician labeling warn that Vicodin is habit-forming, even at the doses prescribed. However, in 2000, the manufacturer at the time, Knoll Labs (now a division of Abbott Laboratories), was so concerned about the propensity for abuse that it sent out specific warnings to 10,000 doctors and pharmacists, according to Jennifer Smoter, a spokeswoman for Abbott. The educational program is still underway because many medical professionals remain unaware of the risk. Part of the problem stems from the drug's classification. "Because it's Schedule III, doctors perceive it as innocuous," a DEA official says. Highly addictive pills such as OxyContin, the headline-grabber for prescription abuse, are classified as Schedule II narcotics. Schedule III indicates a lower likelihood of abuse.

But hydrocodone drugs are as addictive as OxyContin and morphine, the DEA official says. For this reason, the DEA is currently reviewing the classification of all hydrocodone drugs to see if they should be moved to Schedule II. If hydrocodone is reclassified, doctors won't be allowed to call in prescriptions except in emergencies (and then only if followed up by a written prescription), and no refills will be permitted.

These restrictions would reduce abuse but not prevent it. Once Jaeger couldn't get enough Vicodin from her physician, she found another doctor willing to write prescriptions in exchange for exorbitant amounts of money. If the drug was reclassified, she still might find a willing doctor, although it would be more risky and probably costlier. As it was, the prescriptions cost her $1,200 a week. It took another $10,000 for the detox program she hoped would save her hearing.

If physicians and patients are unaware of the addictive nature of hydrocodone, they're even more in the dark about the potential to cause hearing loss. Doctors at the House Ear Institute first noticed a link in 1993, when they encountered a group of puzzling cases with the same constellation of symptoms: ringing in the ears followed by fluctuating hearing loss in alternating ears, and then total hearing loss in both ears. "The common denominator was abuse of Vicodin or chemically comparable drugs," says Rick A. Friedman, M.D., Ph.D., a research scientist at the Institute. The pills damage the delicate hair cells inside the inner ear that detect sound vibrations. When the cells are destroyed, the ability to sense sound is lost.

pain relief—the safe way

There's no reason to skip the relief that hydrocodone can offer for mild to moderate pain, says Clifford A. Bernstein, M.D., medical director of the Waismann Institute, an opiate detox center in Beverly Hills, California. So go ahead and fill a prescription if you have teeth pulled or a flare-up of an old back injury. But if you're still in pain after a couple of weeks, go back to your doctor to discuss options. And if you have ringing in your ears, talk to your doctor immediately about lowering your dose.

For serious chronic pain, your physician may opt to offer relief now and worry about weaning you off the drug later. "For cases such as cancer, you shouldn't worry about addiction," Bernstein says. But long-term users do need to be on the lookout for liver toxicity caused by the acetaminophen in drugs like Vicodin. Your doctor should give you a liver screening twice a year or switch you to a hydrocodone drug with a different analgesic.

Whenever you take controlled substances, make sure you know the proper dose and when to stop taking it before you leave your doctor's office. And be honest with your doctor about any increases in the dose you're taking.

Since Friedman and his colleagues described their 13 patients with opiate-related hearing loss at the American Otological Society's annual meeting in 1999, ear specialists around the country have identified at least 40 more cases. Most were abusers taking 20 or more pills a day, but at least one woman lost her hearing at normal doses. With millions of people taking these painkillers daily, the number of hearing-loss cases is tiny. But experts are convinced that the problem is under-reported due to hidden addictions and doctors who don't see the link.

In 2000, the U.S. Food and Drug Administration worked with Vicodin's manufacturer to add a warning to the label saying that abuse could lead to hearing loss. There was, however, no mandate to inform doctors. "Labeling changes are done all the time, but not everything warrants a 'dear doctor' letter," says FDA spokeswoman Susan Cruzan. Doctors may not always check for new information on a drug they've been prescribing for years. And there's no mention of hearing loss in the handout that comes with a prescription. For someone like Jaeger, knowing the cause early enough to prevent deafness is vital.

Going deaf, Jaeger says, "made me feel totally isolated." She can now drive and go to the movies again, thanks to her cochlear implants, which restored 70 percent of her hearing. However, after the operation, doctors tried to prescribe her Vicodin for the pain. "I went crazy when they did that," she says. "I started screaming at them, 'don't you know why I'm here?'" ✳

Linda Marsa covers health and medicine for the Los Angeles Times.

prescription crib sheet

Ever wonder what the scribbles on your doctor's prescription pad really mean? An encoded love note to the pharmacist? Could be, but more likely the Rx (literally "recipe" in Latin) is a string of Latin abbreviations. Sharpen your prescription knowledge with this quick course in medical shorthand.

abbreviation	Latin words	translation
a.c.	ante cibum	before meals
p.c.	post cibum	after meals
c	cum	with
s	sine	without
d	dies	day
b.i.d.	bis in die	twice a day
t.i.d.	ter in die	three times a day
q.i.d.	quater in die	four times a day
p.r.n.	pro re nata	as needed
h.s.	hora somni	bedtime
O.D.	oculo dextro	right eye
O.S.	oculo sinistro	left eye
O.U.	oculo utro	in each eye
p.o.	per os	by mouth
gtt	gutta	drop

Pain Relief Without a Pill

The millions of women who suffer from the chronic pain of fibromyalgia may be better off investing in sneakers than in pain pills. Researchers in Finland and Canada found that a few hours of weekly cardiovascular exercise, such as walking, was more effective in alleviating fibromyalgia symptoms than medication or alternative treatments. But be patient: Maximum relief came after a full year of working out.

Over-the-Counter Overdose

People supersize it at the movies, so it's no wonder they do it at the drugstore, too. One-third of Americans admit to taking more than the recommended dose of a nonprescription medicine.

—from Harris Interactive's "A Dose of Reality" survey

don't let this supplement trap you

Shop for a pill to help you sleep, build muscle, or lose weight, and you could end up addicted to a dangerous "date-rape" drug.

BY LINDA MARSA

Sleepless nights were only the beginning. When Samantha Lewis (her name has been changed), 45, a fitness-minded mother of three from Toronto, suffered severe, inexplicable insomnia three years ago, her first thought was to take something "natural" instead of a prescription drug. So when a health-club friend told her about GHB (gamma-hydroxy-butyrate), a liquid nutritional supplement that would help her sleep, Lewis immediately decided to try it.

For a few months, it worked better than she could have imagined. "I felt great, and I'd wake up feeling refreshed," she says. Gradually, though, she needed more of it to get the same somnolent effect. And while she slept soundly at night, she began to notice during the day that her hands would shake—and shake. The only way she knew to stop the tremors was to sip a capful of GHB. "I knew I was hooked," Lewis

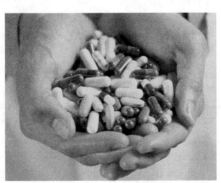

says. "It was horrible—I had gone through my whole life without doing drugs, and now I was an addict."

Hundreds of health-conscious women across the United States and Canada are taking products containing GHB—or GBL (gamma-butyrolactone) or BD (1,4 butane-diol), two of its chemical cousins—that they believe will help them lose weight, sleep better, or build more athletic bodies. Instead, they're unwittingly taking a "date-rape drug"—one so potent that nearly 13,000 overdoses and 71 GHB-related deaths were recorded by federal drug authorities as of December 2000. Although GHB is a compound that naturally occurs in tiny amounts in the brain, the liquid is highly addictive and can damage brain cells, perhaps permanently. It makes detox an ordeal and may wreck sleep patterns for years, breaking apart the lives of people who've innocently started to take it.

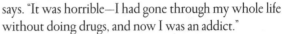

After one woman began taking GHB to help her sleep she said, "I knew I was hooked. It was horrible—I had gone through my whole life without doing drugs, and now I was an addict."

Within 24 hours of going off a "natural fat burner," a 40-year old Dallas mom began to hallucinate, sweat, and shake.

After gaining notoriety as a date-rape drug, it found its way into teenager rave parties for its euphoric effects—relaxation, loss of inhibition and coordination—without alcohol's hangover or calories. But the new addicts aren't club kids: They include executives and IT engineers who need a quick energy boost and salespeople and flight attendants who take GHB to combat jet lag. Hoping it would pump up muscle growth, body-builders latched onto products with names like Blue Nitro, Enliven, and Weight Belt Cleaner when a 1970s study observed that GHB triggered the release of natural growth hormones. That was disproved, yet the drug remained popular in weight rooms nationwide, where it was—and still is—seen as an alternative to steroids.

Despite the fact that GHB was banned by the U.S. Food and Drug Administration (FDA) in 1990—thanks to dozens of reports of the drug's adverse effects (from nausea and vomiting to comas, seizures, and death)—its use is still rampant. To sidestep the restrictions, supplement makers formulated so-called precursors to GHB, a loophole that ensnared scores more women. These compounds at first seemed safe or at least less dangerous than GHB itself. But because they convert to GHB when metabolized by the body, they have the same effect as the real thing. In March 2000, the federal government extended the GHB ban to sales of its like-minded cousins.

Yet products containing GHB still occasionally show up on store shelves, some Internet sites hawk do-it-yourself kits to insomniacs or overweight adults, and people in health clubs continue to sell "home brews," which aren't that hard to make (a main ingredient is gamma-butyrolactone, an industrial solvent used as a paint thinner and engine degreaser). "Unfortunately, the long arm of the law isn't always long enough," says Trinka Porrata, a retired Los Angeles Police Department narcotics detective who runs a Web site about the dangers of GHB and similar drugs.

Today, perhaps to again outpace FDA restrictions, products are being sold as "GHB alternatives," but they may not be any safer than the compounds they're designed to replace. They claim to be GHB-free, but chemical analyses still sometimes detect it or one of its analogs, such as GBL or BD, according to Deborah Zvosec, Ph.D., a researcher at the Hennepin County Medical Center in Minneapolis who has extensively studied GHB. Or they may contain another analog, gamma-valerolactone, which has yet to be banned but is believed to have the same consequences as GHB. "You should definitely avoid any product marketed as a 'replacement' or 'alternative' to GHB, one that has the same claims, or is compared to the older analog products," Zvosec explains. "These manufacturers are skating through legal loopholes like crazy."

Despite the ban, Lenora Blackard, a 40-year-old Dallas mom, encountered a GHB cousin three years ago, when she was stymied trying to lose the 25 pounds she had gained during her third pregnancy. "I was working out really hard and nothing was happening," says Blackard, who, along with her personal-trainer husband, co-owned a gym at the time. She read about and decided to take Renewtrient, a supplement touted on the Internet as a "natural fat burner." She drank it four times a day for six weeks, but "I wasn't losing so I thought, 'forget this,'" she recalls.

Within 24 hours of stopping the supplement, which contained GBL, she started experiencing flu-like symptoms. Then she began to hallucinate, sweat profusely, and have tremors in her hands as her heart rate soared. Her husband rushed her to the hospital, but doctors weren't able to diagnose the cause. Blackard couldn't shake the symptoms for months. She later realized they were signs of dependence on the "natural" supplement.

In the three years since, she hasn't fully recovered. "I still have trouble sleeping," Blackard says. "And my body feels tight and tense. But at least I escaped with my life. Others haven't been so lucky."

Adding to the frustration over continued availability of GHB-type substances is that experts have little information about what GHB does to the brain (the National Institute on Drug Abuse has only recently funded research to track its effects). Yet this much is known: GHB (and likely its analogs) can disturb sleep patterns, maybe permanently, by overriding normal sleep cycles. Doctors also speculate that GHB disrupts key brain chemicals,

Illegal chemicals lurking in some diet and sleep supplements are leaving health-conscious women addicted.

including serotonin, epinephrine, and dopamine, which regulate mood, sleep, motor function, and impulse control.

Those changes to brain chemicals may explain why the drug is so difficult to kick. When Lewis stopped taking GHB, she had such terrible withdrawal effects—including hallucinations, 48-hour bouts of insomnia, and tremors—that she would relapse right away. She checked herself into a local addiction-treatment center, but the doctors there didn't seem to know what GHB was or how to help her detox.

"This is one of the most addictive drugs I've ever seen, and most substance abuse-treatment programs don't screen for GHB," says Karen Miotto, M.D., a psychiatrist at the University of California at Los Angeles Medical School who has treated several addicts. "People are in total denial that they have a problem. Withdrawals are protracted (often taking weeks), and some people never get back to feeling normal." In contrast, withdrawal from other drugs usually takes only a few days.

While withdrawal is a nightmare, continued use can be lethal. The drug is actually legal in some European countries, where it is used as an anesthetic and a narcolepsy treatment. But it is so potent that dosing needs to be exact: While less than 1 gram is considered a "normal" dose for relaxation, taking between 1 and 2 grams suppresses the heart rate and affects balance. This is especially true for women, whose overdose risk is higher because they are generally smaller than men. And because there is no control over the purity or potency of GHB, GBL, or similar supplements (and few labels reveal how much of the chemical is in a product), it's easy to take a potentially lethal overdose.

Higher doses can at times lead quickly to unconsciousness or coma. "The effects of an overdose are severe and life-threatening, and the loss of consciousness happens suddenly," warns Jo Ellen Dyer, an associate professor at the University of California-San Francisco and a toxicologist with the California Poison Control System who has researched GHB. "Some women have passed out behind the wheel and were killed in head-on collisions. Others drowned in a bath or hot tub, or just keeled over and died of a head injury."

In 2001, Lewis herself was almost a statistic: She accidentally overdosed and nearly died. "I woke up in the hospital tethered to life support, with my husband crying next to my bed," she says. Finally, she found the resolve to quit the drug and a doctor who could treat her. She's been "GHB-free" since, but she still hasn't slept through the night.

Like other women, Lewis had her well-being completely devastated by a pill she'd taken with much hope—yet she's

how to avoid GHB

Despite a U.S. Food and Drug Administration ban on sales of GHB, makers of GHB's druglike relatives keep their lucrative businesses alive by selling substances that "convert into GHB" when ingested. Here's what to look for—and steer clear of.

Stay away from these Ingredients, which metabolize into GHB. Be aware that some products may contain these compounds but not list them on the label:

- GBL: gamma-butyrolactone
- 2 (3H)-furanone dihydro
- BD: 1,4-butanediol
- Tetramethylene glycol
- Sucol-B
- "Proprietary polyhydroxyl complex"

Watch out for products with the following brand names. While these products—containing GHB, GBL, and BD—are illegal, they may still pop up on the market.

- Blue Nitro or Blue Nitro Vitality (GBL)
- Dream On (BD or GBL)
- Enliven (BD)
- Revitalize Plus (BD)
- fX, Orange fX Rush, Lemon fX Drops, Cherry fX Bombs (BD)
- Jolt (GBL)
- NRG3 (BD)
- Serenity (BD)
- Thunder Nectar (BD)

Avoid anything that says it's a "GHB alternative. "Some products marketed as "GHB alternatives" contain GHB or its banned analogs, and others may contain another analog (such as gamma-valerolactone) that is still legal but just as harmful and addictive as GHB. Since these products—often sold on the Internet and found on store shelves—haven't been well-researched, it's safest to avoid them altogether.

beginning to see an end to her ordeal. "I sleep maybe three or four hours at a time," she says. "But at least GHB isn't running my life." ✳

Linda Marsa covers health and medicine for the Los Angeles Times.

Q+A
Put a Stop to Pre-Dawn Allergy Attacks

I take prescription allergy drugs, but even so, sometimes sneezing fits wake me up at night. What can I do?

TRY TAKING YOUR MEDS right before bed to ensure that the drugs will be circulating in your bloodstream when you really need them—between 4 and 8 a.m. That's when your body's natural defenses against allergy symptoms are at their lowest. This strategy works best with prescription antihistamine pills (such as Zyrtec or Allegra). The evidence isn't as clear whether it is effective with once-a-day nasal steroids; check with your doctor before changing your schedule.

Taking over-the-counter allergy pills as a nightcap, however, won't ward off pre-dawn sneezing fits: Most wear off after six hours. And if your allergies are bad enough to wake you, you probably shouldn't self-treat anyway—see a doctor.

sweat harder, live longer

The sweat you spend on the treadmill may be a better life-span predictor than health risks like high blood pressure and smoking. Stanford University researchers calculated how hard study participants worked out using metabolic equivalents, or METS. (METS measure the amount of oxygen your body needs for a task. Sitting takes one MET; a brisk walk requires five.) For each additional MET, people in the study increased their chances of living longer by 12 percent. So the key to a longer life could be as simple as adding a little intensity to your workout.

relief on the cheap

Attention, bargain shoppers: We've discovered a helpful tool at wwwrxaminer.com that, for a $10 fee, will list comparable generic or lower-cost alternatives to high-priced medications. Just get your doctor's OK before you switch.

An Extra Benefit of Lowering Your Cholesterol

Next time you're in a funk, forgo the shopping spree and try lowering your cholesterol instead. According to a study published in the *Journal of Behavioral Medicine*, a drop in cholesterol—even a slight one—can improve your mood. Researchers quizzed 212 men and women on a 12-month cholesterol-lowering diet about anxiety, depression, and hostility. They found that most of the people who reduced their level of total cholesterol and LDLs ("bad" cholesterol) also reported feeling less anxious, with women showing the biggest improvement. The link between mood and cholesterol is unclear, though researchers theorize that improving your health has a positive effect on your psyche. For a mood boost, try these cholesterol-reducing tips.

Choose foods low in saturated fat, such as low-fat or nonfat dairy products, nuts, and oatmeal.

Cook with olive oil instead of butter or margarine.

Select lean red meat, broiled or grilled fish, and skinless chicken breasts.

Eat grains, fruits, and vegetables, which are low in saturated fat and cholesterol and loaded with vitamins, minerals, and fiber.

Exercise regularly.

how your favorite TV shows rate on health issues

"People get most of their health information from entertainment TV," says Neal Baer, formerly a producer with *ER,* the series that set the standard for dramatizing health concerns. A recent study he co-authored in the journal *Health Affairs* confirms his point. So we checked out how accurate the medical sagas really are on some key episodes of popular shows. We rated them from 1 (needs treatment) to 10 (safe and sound). See if your favorite show really is good medicine—or just fakes it on TV.

SHOW	ISSUE	PLOT	VIEWERS	REALITY CHECK	RATING
ER, "Good Touch, Bad Touch"	Testicular cancer	A 20-year-old student complains of shortness of breath. Dr. Anna Del Amico makes the diagnosis: testicular cancer, the most common type of cancer for men 15 to 34.	29 million	"I wish there was more of a take-away message, such as 'do self-exams,'" says Doug Bank, president of the Testicular Cancer Resource Center. Still, a touchy subject covered well.	Emergency avoided: 7
Third Watch, "Know Thyself"	Alcoholism	Fred's alcoholism forces his wife, Faith, to flash back to life with her abusive, drunken father. Now it's transference time. Faith has little sympathy for Fred, her new "dad."	13 million	It won the 2001 Best Drama Series Episode Prism Award, which honors an outstanding media depiction of substance abuse. Faith's struggles give the subject more than a touch of truth; not everyone's sympathetic to an alcoholic.	Sober and somber: 8
Friends, "The One with Ross' Sandwich"	Anger management	After experiencing sandwich rage, Ross sees a psychiatrist, who gives him tranquilizers to temper his moods. But when Ross learns that his sister, Monica, is sleeping with his friend Chandler, the tranquilizers wear off pretty fast.	23 million	Nearly one-quarter of American adults are diagnosed with a psychological disorder each year, according to the American Psychiatric Association. But *Friends* didn't specify Ross' condition and just went for the pills. Irresponsible. As Baer says, "It's dangerous to send out this kind of misinformation."	Unhelpful and not even funny: 2
Days of Our Lives, various episodes	Impotence	Kate and Victor try to rectify his impotence. Sadly, he's only dysfunctional around her, not his lover, Nicole.	4.5 million	There's more dimension to impotence than just the physical failings, and the producers were accurate in portraying the psychological aspects.	Frisky and philandering, but at least gets at the heart of the matter: 9
Felicity, "The Last Thanksgiving"	Depression	Noel's unshakable bad mood leads to alienation from his loved ones over the holidays. A heart-to-heart with his brother reveals that their father dealt with depression, too. By show's end, Noel sits alone on a couch, eats strudel, and calls a psychologist.	3.7 million	Noel has all the symptoms of depression: self-pity, trouble facing the world, feelings of hopelessness, and a family history of the disease. Because self-medication by strudel would not work, he took the right step by making an appointment with a doc.	Self-important, but also self-serving: 7

VitalStats

220 Calories in a Slim-Fast bar

34, 5 Grams of carbohydrate, fat in a Slim-Fast bar

204 Calories in a Pop-Tart

37, 5 Grams of carbohydrate, fat in a Pop-Tart

3 Percent of women over age 40 who would buy products with overweight people in ads

21 Percent of women under 40 who would

52 Percent of patients at the Mayo Clinic Sleep Disorders Center who own at least one pet

60 Percent of those patients who allow their pets to sleep in their bedrooms

53 Percent who feel their pets disrupt their sleep

1 Rank of Russell Crowe among men whom women would choose to spend a night with

11 Rank of George W. Bush

25 Percent of Americans with high blood pressure

73 Percent of study participants who reduced dependence on meds by eating a bowl of oatmeal daily

$197.63 Projected annual savings per person

Sources: Slim-Fast, National Center for Health Statistics, National Sleep Foundation, Jericho Communications, USDA

TEST YOURSELF
Your Guy's Biggest Health Risks

Madonna may be able to recite husband Guy Ritchie's measurements or what thoughts keep him up at night, but does she know if he's at risk for prostate cancer or when it's time to get his colon checked? How much do you know about the health risks in your guy's life?

1. Which illness kills the most men in the United States?
   A. heart disease   B. lung cancer   C. prostate cancer

2. Which kind of cancer is most common in men?
   A. prostate   B. lung   C. skin

3. A 50-year-old man should be tested for colon cancer every:
   A. year   B. two years   C. five years

4. How many questions does a man typically ask his doctor during a physical examination?
   A. five   B. two   C. zero

5. Which of the following is not a risk factor for prostate cancer?
   A. number of sexual partners   B. frequency of sex
   C. cigarette smoking

answers:

1. A. We started you off with an easy one: Men are almost twice as likely to die from diseases of the heart as from all types of cancer combined. Give yourself a bonus point if you knew that the same goes for women.

2. C. Skin cancer is by far the most common, accounting for more than 40 percent of all cancers. Although the most common type, basal cell carcinoma, is rarely life-threatening, don't take skin cancer lightly: Melanomas result in 79 percent of skin-cancer deaths.

3. A. He's not gonna like this, but he needs a fecal occult blood test annually and a flexible sigmoidoscopy every five years, beginning at age 50. The sexes are equal on this one.

4. C. None. Zip. Zero. And that's if he goes to the doctor at all. Encourage him to write questions on paper in advance and send them to the doc via e-mail. Or go along and make inquiries yourself.

5. B. The frequency of sex has no effect on cancer risk. But unprotected sex with multiple partners can double his chance of developing the disease; recent studies suggest a sexually transmitted infection might be involved in some cases of prostate cancer.

chapter 4

food and nutrition

savor the health

Building a Better Food Pyramid

The USDA's Food Guide Pyramid is under attack. Here's what you can learn from its critics—and how to use it to devise a healthier diet.

BY DOROTHY FOLTZ-GRAY

RECIPES BY KAREN LEVIN

I heard my first lecture about food as a chubby and ever-hungry fourth grader. My gym teacher, himself well-padded, unrolled a huge chart covered with pictures of fruits, vegetables, meats, and cheeses, and with his wooden pointer stabbed at the foods we should be eating. I can't say any scales fell from my eyes about my eating habits that day, but I was moved to daydream about an afternoon snack.

Since then, I have heard a lot more about what I should ingest, and, like many Americans, I've faced my share of confusion, the most recent being over the Food Guide Pyramid. This icon, the supposed pinnacle of healthy eating advice, is currently under fire. Critics are saying it may not be the healthiest way to eat after all.

Taking aim at the pyramid is prominent American scientist Walter C. Willett, M.D., chairman of the department of nutrition at the Harvard School of Public Health and professor of medicine at Harvard Medical School in Boston. In his book, *Eat, Drink, and Be Healthy,* Willett blasts the U.S. Department of Agriculture (USDA), creators of the 1992-established Food Guide Pyramid, for offering "wishy-washy, scientifically unfounded advice" and a diet heavy on red meat, fuzzy about carbohydrates, and dismissive of healthy oils in nuts and plants. Worse, he says, the pyramid's misinformation contributes to obesity, poor health, and even premature death.

But Willett doesn't just criticize. He offers up his own pyramid, one that focuses on whole grains, plant oils, and vegetables. And his points aren't exactly new: He reiterates what food scientists, nutritionists, and even the USDA have been espousing for years: You can't eat too many fruits and vegetables. He also urges Americans to reconfigure the protein on their plates to include less red meat and more nuts, beans, and fish. More controversial, though, is that he dares to pair "fat" with "good health," and challenges the conventional notions about Americans needing more dairy products than they get.

> The nutrition community is at fault for **oversimplifying its message,** selling the public short with its paternalistic attitude.
>
> —*Walter C. Willett, M.D.*

By toppling the long-standing pyramid and creating his own, Willett has put forth some ideas worth incorporating in your diet, and we've put his principles to work in our easy, tasty recipes. Most of his pyramid is easy to interpret, with a foundation based on daily exercise and weight control. But here's your guide through some of the more questionable aspects.

Doubts about Dairy?

One aspect of Willett's pyramid that has generated heated debate is that it limits dairy products to only one or two low-fat servings per day. The Food Guide Pyramid recommends two to three servings, and it doesn't distinguish between high-fat and low-fat dairy products. That is the crux of Willett's concerns: Whole-milk dairy products (including full-fat milk, ice cream, and cheeses), with their higher levels of saturated fats, raise cholesterol levels, push up the risk of heart disease and pile on the calories in a country whose obesity rate tops 55 percent.

In essence, Willett questions whether what you get from dairy—calcium, primarily—is worth the risks associated with high-fat foods. Calcium is a component in building bone and may even be helpful in weight loss and controlling blood pressure. But when it comes to preventing osteoporosis, it's not clear if dairy products are the only solution. Willett cites one large study that found that people who drank two or more glasses of milk a day were as likely to break a hip or forearm (a typical marker for brittle bones) as women who had only a glass or less a week. There are other long-term studies that show similar results. In addition, some countries, including Japan and Peru, have very low rates of osteoporosis but consume very little dairy.

Willett admits, though, that the definitive word about dairy products and calcium simply isn't in. "There are more questions to answer," he says. "We need calcium, but the question is how much and from where. In the meantime it makes sense to be moderate."

So what does that mean for a dairy-lover like me, who often ends her day with a large glass of milk at bedtime? Not a huge change: Willett's not wiping all dairy completely off the map—just the full-fat dairy. There are plenty of other ways for people to get calcium, he says, such as from broccoli, tofu, calcium supplements, and fortified foods.

how the pyramids stack up

Nutrition guru Walter C. Willett, M.D., of Harvard has reconfigured the USDA Food Guide Pyramid, causing a stir in health circles. But his ideas aren't too radical: Exercise and weight control form the base, with healthy fats and whole grains just behind. He de-emphasizes red meat and high-fat dairy items, and encourages getting protein from nuts and legumes rather than sources like fish and chicken. Willett also allows for alcohol in moderation and vitamin supplements.

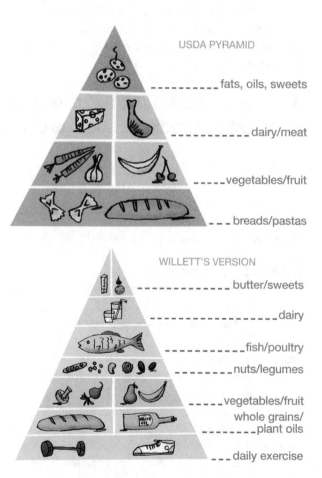

USDA PYRAMID
- fats, oils, sweets
- dairy/meat
- vegetables/fruit
- breads/pastas

WILLETT'S VERSION
- butter/sweets
- dairy
- fish/poultry
- nuts/legumes
- vegetables/fruit
- whole grains/plant oils
- daily exercise

All Carbs are Not Equal

Willett's views on carbohydrates have also raised some dander. Bread, cereal, rice, and pasta form the pedestal of the USDA's pyramid, with no distinction between whole-grain foods, such as whole-wheat breads and pastas, and refined foods, such as white bread and white rice—a melding that Willett feels has contributed to American obesity. The government's version also clumps potatoes, a starchy carbohydrate, with vegetables. Willett, by contrast, lauds whole-grain foods and equates starchy, refined carbohydrates with sweets, placing them at the very top of the pyramid, in the "Use Sparingly" spot.

The reason? Potatoes and such refined carbohydrates as white-flour products are digested almost as fast as sugar, causing a rapid rise in blood sugar and insulin. These rises are associated with increased risk for heart disease and diabetes. Whole-grain foods are digested more slowly, keeping blood sugar even and decreasing those risks. Filling up on whole grains and their Willett-pyramid neighbors, fruits and vegetables, also brings you more fiber, vitamins, and minerals than refined carbs, decreasing the risk of various cancers and gastrointestinal troubles.

The new food pyramid allows more liberal use of flavorful ingredients such as olives and olive oil.

If you're getting bored with whole-grain bread, try more exotic grains, such as bulgur wheat and whole-wheat couscous. Toss prepared bulgur with tomatoes, red onions, parsley, garbanzo beans, and olive oil, and you'll wonder why grains got so refined in the first place.

Fat Makes a Comeback

Even dicier than messing with America's potatoes and biscuits is lauding fat, albeit healthy fats. Since the early 1980s, fat has been the dietary whipping boy, the kid in the corner. Indeed, the USDA pyramid still wields that paddle, exhorting consumers to use all fats sparingly. Willett's happy to denounce saturated fats, such as butter, even putting red meat, typically high in saturated fat, into the "Use Sparingly" category. But he grants plant oils—such as olive, canola, and peanut oils—star billing, asserting that they're as important to health as whole grains. "People are harming themselves by eliminating the good types of fat from their diet," Willett says, citing studies that show that people who eat monounsaturated or polyunsaturated oils have lower LDL (bad cholesterol), lower triglycerides, and a lowered risk of erratic heartbeats and blood clots. Further, he asserts that you don't have to be miserly with fat if it's the right kind.

But Willett isn't suggesting that you pour healthy oils over everything you eat, even though these good fats sit right next to whole-grain foods on one of the most generous platforms of his pyramid. If you eat more calories than you burn—regardless of whether those calories are from fat, protein, or carbs—you'll gain weight. Eat more calories from fat, and you'll have to cut back elsewhere to avoid gaining weight.

The good news is that switching from saturated fats to healthy fats isn't exactly a hardship. Pop a few nuts into the stir-fry, or pour a little olive oil and coarse salt on your ex-butter plate to have with whole-wheat bread.

So What's for Dinner?

Interestingly enough, the 2000 USDA Dietary Guidelines for Americans, on which the government's pyramid is based, are already more closely aligned with Willett's approach than the Food Guide Pyramid, particularly when it comes to whole grains and healthy fats. According to USDA spokesman John Webster, the department is "currently in the early stages of examining the pyramid—although it's too early to predict what, if any, revisions will be recommended." Nonetheless, despite creeping recognition that science has outpaced the 1992 pyramid, Willett's critics still worry that his changes will confuse Americans further about what to eat. Willett's not buying it. "The nutrition community is heavily at fault for oversimplifying its message, for saying that people can't make distinctions. That's a paternalistic attitude and sells the public short."

Willett's criticisms of the USDA pyramid are valid, but his version also has potential pitfalls—if, for example, you see it as a license to guzzle fat or cut back on calcium. It's difficult to put everything about healthy eating into a symbol. But Willett's pyramid raises good points you can use to help improve your diet. With its reliance on savory olive oil, crisp vegetables, and anything-but-bland grains, it's also the building block for some outstanding but easy-to-make meals. And we've created a few recipes that incorporate these ideas. Try our Curried Carrot, Sweet Potato, and Ginger Soup; Pan-Grilled Salmon with Pineapple Salsa; or Spicy Chickpeas. Unlike the pyramids in Egypt, this one takes no heroics.

Dorothy Foltz-Gray is the author of With or Without Her, *a memoir about losing her twin sister.*

Spicy Chickpeas

SERVES 6
PREPARATION: 10 MINUTES
COOKING: 10 MINUTES

Chickpeas rank as a slowly digested, fiber-rich carbohydrate.

1 tablespoon canola oil

1 medium red onion, chopped

1 teaspoon chili powder

1 teaspoon ground cumin

¼ teaspoon salt

4 garlic cloves, minced

1 (15½-ounce) can chickpeas, rinsed and drained

¼ cup spicy chipotle salsa

¼ cup chopped cilantro

1 tablespoon hot pepper vinegar

4 lime wedges (optional)

1. Heat oil in a nonstick skillet over medium-high heat. Add onion; sauté 5 minutes or until onions are tender. Add chili powder, cumin, salt, and garlic; cook 2 minutes or until spices are fragrant. Stir in next 4 ingredients (through vinegar); cook 3 minutes or until thoroughly heated. Garnish with lime wedges. Serving size: ½ cup.

Per Serving: Calories 89 (29% from fat); Fat 3.0g (sat 0.2g, mono 1.5g, poly 1g); Protein 2.8g; Carbohydrate 13.4g; Fiber 2.7g; Cholesterol 0mg; Iron 0.9mg; Sodium 239mg; Calcium 27mg

White Beans, Greens, and Rosemary

SERVES 4
PREPARATION: 5 MINUTES
COOKING: 20 MINUTES

Willett favors pastas made from whole-wheat flour because they contain more fiber than plain pasta.

12 ounces whole-wheat penne pasta

8 cups packed kale leaves (stems discarded)

1 teaspoon olive oil

4 garlic cloves, minced

1½ teaspoons dried rosemary

½ teaspoon crushed red pepper

1 (15-ounce) can cannellini beans, drained and rinsed

1 cup lower sodium low-fat chicken broth

2 tablespoons lemon juice

½ cup grated fresh Parmesan cheese

1. Cook pasta according to package directions. When pasta is almost tender, add kale and cook 1 minute or until pasta and kale are tender; drain.

2. Heat oil in a large skillet over medium-high heat. Add garlic, rosemary, and red pepper; cook 2 minutes or until spices are fragrant. Add beans; cook 2 minutes or until thoroughly heated. Combine pasta mixture, bean mixture, and remaining ingredients; toss well. Serving size: 2 cups.

Per Serving: Calories 271 (17% from fat); Fat 5.4g (sat 2.2g, mono 1.6g, poly 0.7g); Protein 15.5g; Carbohydrate 44.5g; Fiber 4.3g; Cholesterol 8mg; Iron 4.2mg; Sodium 320mg; Calcium 415mg

Curried Carrot, Sweet Potato, and Ginger Soup

SERVES 5
PREPARATION: 10 MINUTES
COOKING: 30 MINUTES

This soup gets its wonderful texture from puréed carrots and sweet potatoes rather than cream, a dairy product Willett discourages due to its high saturated-fat content.

2 teaspoons canola oil

½ cup chopped shallots

3 cups (½-inch) cubed peeled sweet potato

1½ cups (¼-inch) sliced peeled carrots

1 tablespoon grated ginger

2 teaspoons curry powder

3 cups fat-free, less-sodium chicken broth

½ teaspoon salt

1. Heat oil in a large saucepan over medium-high heat. Add shallots; sauté 3 minutes or until tender. Add potato, carrots, ginger, and curry; cook 2 minutes. Add broth; bring to a boil. Cover, reduce heat, and simmer 25 minutes or until vegetables are tender; stir in salt.

2. Pour half of soup in a food processor; pulse until smooth. Repeat procedure with remaining soup. Serving size: 1¼ cups.

Per Serving: Calories 144 (14% from fat); Fat 2.3g (sat 0.2g, mono 1.1g, poly 0.7g); Protein 4.1g; Carbohydrate 27.3g; Fiber 3.9g; Cholesterol 0mg; Iron 1.1mg; Sodium 531mg; Calcium 38mg

Vegetable Soup with Pistou

SERVES 6
PREPARATION: 15 MINUTES
COOKING: 55 MINUTES

This version of the classic French soup is loaded with vegetables, including white beans—a perfect replacement for meat in the Willett plan.

PISTOU:

½ teaspoon salt

2 garlic cloves, peeled

1 cup basil leaves

1½ tablespoons olive oil

1 teaspoon lemon juice

SOUP:

2 cups halved grape tomatoes (about 1 pint)

2 tablespoons garlic, thinly sliced, divided

¼ teaspoon salt, divided

¼ teaspoon black pepper, divided

Cooking spray

2 tablespoons olive oil

3½ cups chopped onions

2 cups chopped peeled sweet potato

1 cup chopped carrots

3 thyme sprigs

1 bay leaf

2 (15-ounce) cans small white beans, drained and rinsed

3 cups fat-free, less-sodium chicken broth

2 cups water

2 cups (½-inch) cut green beans (about 8 ounces)

1. To prepare pistou, combine $1/2$ teaspoon salt and 2 garlic cloves in a food processor; process until minced. Add basil; process until finely chopped. Add $1^1/2$ tablespoons oil and lemon juice, process until blended. Set aside.

2. Preheat oven to 400°.

3. To prepare soup, combine grape tomatoes, 2 teaspoons sliced garlic, $1/8$ teaspoon salt, and $1/8$ teaspoon pepper in a small bowl; toss well. Coat a foil-lined baking sheet with cooking spray. Spoon tomato mixture onto baking sheet. Bake at 400° for 15 minutes. Set aside.

4. Heat oil in a Dutch oven over medium heat; add 4 teaspoons garlic and onions. Sauté 10 minutes, stirring frequently; add remaining $1/8$ teaspoons of salt

and pepper. Add sweet potato, carrots, thyme, and bay leaf; sauté 10 minutes, stirring frequently. Add white beans; cook 5 minutes, stirring occasionally. Add broth, water, and green beans; simmer 15 minutes or until beans are tender. Discard bay leaf and thyme sprigs. Stir in pistou and tomato mixture. Serving size: $1^2/3$ cups.

Per Serving: Calories 301 (30% from fat); Fat 10.5g (sat 1.8g, mono 6.7g, poly 1.1g); Protein 11.5g; Carbohydrate 44g; Fiber 9.7g; Cholesterol 2mg; Iron 3mg; Sodium 786mg; Calcium 116mg

Fresh Tuna Salad

SERVES 4
PREPARATION: 10 MINUTES
COOKING: 7 MINUTES

Fresh or canned, tuna is a great source of protein because it's low in saturated fat, the kind of fat that promotes heart disease. Multigrain bread, which is higher in fiber than white, is used to make some tasty croutons for this easy, main-course salad.

2 (1-ounce) slices multigrain bread

Cooking spray

1 (1-pound) tuna steak (about ¾-inch thick)

½ teaspoon salt

½ teaspoon black pepper

⅓ cup low-fat Italian salad dressing

½ teaspoon dried tarragon

8 cups mesclun salad greens

2 cups cherry tomatoes, halved

¼ cup sliced red onion

1. Coat both sides of bread with cooking spray; toast. Cut into 1-inch pieces.

2. Sprinkle tuna with salt and pepper; coat with cooking spray. Heat a nonstick skillet coated with cooking spray over medium-high heat; cook tuna 2 minutes on each side or until desired degree of doneness. Cool 5 minutes; cut into 1-inch cubes.

3. Combine dressing and tarragon in a small bowl. Combine greens, tomatoes, and onion in a bowl; toss with dressing. Add tuna and bread; toss well. Serving size: $2^1/2$ cups.

Per Serving: Calories 214 (17% from fat); Fat 4.1g (sat 0.7g, mono 0.9g, poly 1.9g); Protein 30.4g; Carbohydrate 14.5g; Fiber 4.3g; Cholesterol 52mg; Iron 3.2mg; Sodium 601mg; Calcium 98mg

Roasted Swordfish with Vegetables Provençal

SERVES 4
PREPARATION: 10 MINUTES
COOKING: 24 MINUTES

A French technique that can easily translate into Willett's philosophy is the practice of roasting vegetables with olive oil—a healthy fat—and herbs. Here, we've paired those vegetables with swordfish. The balsamic glaze that tops the dish is made with a small amount of sugar, an ingredient used sparingly in the Willett pyramid.

4 cups (12 ounces) green beans, cut into 1-inch pieces
2 cups grape or cherry tomatoes, halved
1 tablespoon olive oil
½ teaspoon salt, divided
½ teaspoon pepper, divided
2 garlic cloves, minced
4 (6-ounce) swordfish steaks (about ¾-inch thick)
Cooking spray
1 (15.8-ounce) can of small white beans, rinsed and drained
8 pitted kalamata olives
1½ tablespoons chopped fresh thyme
¼ cup packed light brown sugar
¼ cup balsamic vinegar

1. Preheat oven to 425°.
2. Combine green beans, tomatoes, oil, ¼ teaspoon salt, ¼ teaspoon pepper, and garlic in an 11 x 7-inch baking dish; toss. Bake at 425° for 10 minutes or until green beans are crisp-tender.
3. Season swordfish with remaining ¼ teaspoons salt and pepper; coat each side with cooking spray. Heat a nonstick grill pan coated with cooking spray over medium-high heat. Sear fish 2 minutes on each side; place fish on top of green-bean mixture. Top with white beans, olives, and thyme. Bake 10 minutes or until fish flakes easily when tested with a fork.
4. Combine sugar and vinegar in a small saucepan over medium-high heat; boil 1 minute or until mixture begins to thicken. Drizzle each serving with syrup. Serving size: 1 swordfish steak and about 1½ cups vegetables.

Per Serving: Calories 387 (29% from fat); Fat 12.8g (sat 2.6g, mono 6.7g, poly 2.2g); Protein 39.9g; Carbohydrate 31.9g; Fiber 7.1g; Cholesterol 66mg; Iron 3.9g; Sodium 829mg; Calcium 97mg

Chicken Vindaloo

SERVES 4
PREPARATION: 15 MINUTES
MARINATING: 4 HOURS
COOKING: 26 MINUTES

Full of spice, this traditional Indian dish is a natural for the Willett plan. It's prepared with vegetables and chicken, which Willett considers a healthier alternative to red meat.

1 pound boneless, skinless chicken thighs, cut into 1-inch cubes
2 tablespoons minced fresh ginger
¼ cup rice vinegar
2 teaspoons ground coriander
2 teaspoons ground cumin
1 teaspoon ground cardamom
2 teaspoons chili paste with garlic
¼ teaspoon ground cinnamon
⅛ teaspoon ground cloves
6 garlic cloves, minced
1 tablespoon canola oil
1 cup diced onion
1 diced red bell pepper
1 diced yellow bell pepper
½ cup fat-free, less-sodium chicken broth
¾ teaspoon salt
1 tablespoon cornstarch
2 tablespoons water
¼ cup chopped cilantro
4 cups cooked brown rice

1. Combine first 10 ingredients (through garlic) in a zip-top plastic bag. Marinate in refrigerator at least 4 hours, turning occasionally.
2. Heat oil in a large skillet over medium-high heat. Add onion; sauté 4 minutes. Add chicken mixture and bell peppers; sauté 5 minutes or until chicken is thoroughly browned on all sides. Add broth and salt; simmer, uncovered, 15 minutes or until chicken is done. Combine cornstarch and water in a small bowl; stir well. Add cornstarch mixture to chicken mixture; simmer 2 minutes or until sauce thickens. Stir in cilantro. Serve over rice. Serving size: ¾ cup chicken and 1 cup rice.

Per Serving: Calories 462 (20% from fat); Fat 10.4g (sat 1.8g, mono 4.1g, poly 2.9g); Protein 29.8g; Carbohydrate 61.9g; Fiber 6.9g; Cholesterol 94mg; Iron 3.1mg; Sodium 718mg; Calcium 77mg

Stir-fried Bok Choy, Shiitakes, and Chicken

SERVES 5
PREPARATION: 5 MINUTES
MARINATING: 2 HOURS
COOKING: 15 MINUTES

If you're cutting back on dairy products, a stir-fry that includes calcium-rich bok choy is a good way to get more of this mineral.

1 pound chicken tenders
3 tablespoons fish sauce
2 tablespoons dark sesame oil, divided
2 teaspoons grated fresh ginger
¼ teaspoon crushed red pepper
2 garlic cloves, minced
8 ounces soba noodles
1 pound coarsely chopped bok choy (about 12 cups)
¼ cup cold water
2 teaspoons cornstarch
½ pound thinly sliced shiitake mushrooms (about 6 cups)
½ cup chopped cilantro

1. Combine chicken, fish sauce, 1 tablespoon sesame oil, and next 3 ingredients (through garlic) in a large zip-top plastic bag; seal and marinate in refrigerator 2 hours. Remove chicken from bag; reserve marinade.
2. Cook noodles according to package directions; set aside. Remove center stalks from bok choy and coarsely chop. Repeat procedure with bok choy leaves and set aside separately. Combine water and cornstarch; mix well and set aside.
3. Heat remaining 1 tablespoon oil in a wok or large nonstick skillet over medium-high heat. Add chicken; stir-fry 2 minutes. Transfer to bowl; set aside. Add reserved marinade, bok choy stalks, and mushrooms; stir-fry 3 minutes. Add bok choy leaves, chicken, and cornstarch mixture; stir-fry 2 minutes or until sauce thickens. Serve chicken mixture over noodles. Top with cilantro. Serving size: 1¼ cups stir-fry and ½ cup noodles.

Per Serving: Calories 365 (17% from fat); Fat 7g (sat 1.1g, mono 2.5g, poly 2.7g); Protein 33.2g; Carbohydrate 44.4g; Fiber 3.4g; Cholesterol 53mg; Iron 3mg; Sodium 644mg; Calcium 117mg

Pan-Grilled Salmon with Pineapple Salsa

SERVES 4
PREPARATION: 5 MINUTES
COOKING: 8 MINUTES

Fish is prominent in the Willett plan since it's a lean protein source. Salmon is particularly good because it contains plenty of heart-healthy fats called omega-3s.

1 cup chopped fresh pineapple
2 tablespoons finely chopped red onion
2 tablespoon chopped cilantro
1 tablespoon rice vinegar
⅛ teaspoon ground red pepper
Cooking spray
4 (6-ounce) salmon fillets (about ½-inch thick)
½ teaspoon salt

1. Combine first 5 ingredients (through pepper) in a bowl; set aside.
2. Heat a nonstick grill pan coated with cooking spray over medium-high heat. Sprinkle fish with salt. Cook fish 4 minutes on each side or until it flakes easily when tested with a fork. Top with salsa. Serving size: 1 fillet and ⅓ cup salsa.

Per Serving: Calories 294 (41% from fat); Fat 13.2g (sat 3.1g, mono 5.7g, poly 3.2g); Protein 36.4g; Carbohydrate 5.6g; Fiber 0.6g; Cholesterol 87mg; Iron 0.8mg; Sodium 375mg; Calcium 26mg ✳

Frequent contributor Karen Levin is a Chicago-based cookbook author and recipe developer.

Fruits That Give You More Vitamin C

The National Institutes of Health recently suggested increasing the recommended daily allowance of vitamin C from 75 milligrams to 90 milligrams for women, the same as for men. To meet the new goal, try one of the following:

- 1½ cups orange juice
- 1 large kiwi fruit
- 1 cup cooked, chopped broccoli
- ⅓ cup chopped sweet red peppers
- 9 large strawberries
- half a small cantaloupe

WILL THE USDA WARM UP TO SUPER-SIZE PORTIONS?

THE PYRAMIDS of Egypt have stood unchanged for thousands of years, but the one built by the U.S. Department of Agriculture (USDA) may be less enduring. After 11 years, the USDA is thinking of renovating it—and one adjustment under consideration is increasing recommended serving sizes. Those in favor of the change say current portion sizes don't measure up to the way people eat. But do we really want the government to sanction a mixing-bowl's worth of pasta as a single serving?

The super-sizing might make sense if the number of recommended servings is also cut. That's a possibility, according to John Webster, director of public information and governmental affairs for the USDA. So you could go from the current six to 11 servings ($^1/_2$-cup each) in the carb group to, say, two to four servings ($1^1/_2$-cup each).

Melanie Polk, director of nutrition education at the American Institute for Cancer Research, doesn't think it's a good idea to tamper with serving sizes or numbers. "People need the variety that comes from many servings," she explains. "It's not just about calories. Different foods provide you with essential nutrients." In this age of value-sized combo meals, though, people often get variety and too much food all at once.

Instead of adjusting the serving sizes to match the way people eat, it sounds like some simple, self-imposed portion control is in order.

veggies get the boot

In a move much like recent business trends, home meals are getting downsized. The marketing firm NPD Group reports that meals in American households today have 8 percent fewer dishes than they did 10 years ago. Side dishes—especially veggies and salads—usually get laid off first. If you're too busy to assemble a multi-course meal, hang on to the salad bowl and toss the breadbasket.

sample serving sizes move into the 21st century

Standard food serving guidelines—like figuring a serving of meat for a cassette tape—are so last century. Since debit cards and personal digital assistants (PDAs) have replaced checkbooks and date books in your purse, here's a modern way to spot serving sizes:

FOOD ITEM	MODERN EQUIVALENT
a medium potato	the mini (6 oz.) soda can
3 ounces of meat	floppy disk
one scoop of ice cream	a round iMac mouse
3 ounces of grilled fish	PDA
1 ounce of cheese	pager
1 tablespoon of olive oil (or other cooking oil)	an individual eye-shadow compact
a serving of pretzels or other snack food	a coffee mug's full

the cost of going green

Back-to-the-earth types typically shed luxuries in the pursuit of a simpler life. But going green can mean you'll need a whole new set of kitchen gear—some of which isn't so simple or cheap. Here's what an all-natural day could cost you.

- Glass of carrot juice, using Champion juicer..............................$330
- Dried fruit for granola, made with Excalibur dehydrator................$200
- Wheat grass, grown in Automatic Sprouter................................$260
- Fruit smoothie, whipped up in Vitamix blender..........................$460

A Nutrition Nightmare:
"I Won't Eat That"

The new trend in eating calls for nixing entire food groups.
Is this a dieter's dream or a recipe for disaster?

BY SHARON GOLDMAN EDRY

When Jill Meyer goes to a friend's house for dinner, she usually offers to bring a dish—even when it's not a potluck. That's because she can't eat meat or fish. Or dairy. Or eggs. Or food that's nonorganic, processed, or canned. Or even anything cooked. "People don't know how to accommodate me, so either I just eat salad or bring my own food," she says. She may be a tough dinner guest, but Meyer, a 31-year-old from Buffalo, New York, says her new lifestyle is healthier and more "natural." She also finds it hard to argue with the 24 pounds she's dropped since she started eating this way. "I was shocked beyond belief when I got on the scale," she says happily.

Counting calories may not be cool anymore, but the wholesale removal of food groups—or restricting your diet to foods prepared a certain way—is a trendy, no-brainer way to lose weight. Don't want to eat that cake for dessert? Just say, "I don't do sugar." Need an excuse to get out of a high-calorie restaurant dinner? How about, "I only eat raw"? Of course, there are legitimate health reasons for adopting diet restrictions; diabetics and people with high blood pressure have been doing it for years. And there is a long tradition of ethical and religious justifications for swearing off animal foods, in particular. But for more and more women, an obsession with "good

Counting calories may not be cool anymore, but the wholesale removal of food groups—or restricting your diet to foods prepared a certain way—is a trendy, no-brainer way to lose weight.

health" has a convenient side effect: fitting into a size 2 dress without appearing like a slave to dieting, says Elizabeth Carll, Ph.D., a psychologist and eating-disorder specialist in Long Island, New York. "It would appear rather rigid to not eat so many different things in order to be thin, but it's hard to argue with it if you say you're doing it for health reasons," she says. But she and other nutritional and medical experts say fussy eating may create more health problems than it solves.

Ellen Montague recognized the true motives behind her elimination diet before doing any damage to her body. For the 41-year-old therapist from Fort Collins, Colorado, what began as a vegetarian diet soon turned into a personal embargo on wheat, sugar, cheese, tomatoes, and corn. She convinced herself and others that she was allergic to this mixed bag of foods, but she began to suspect that her limited eating was really just a diet in disguise. "As I got older, I started to worry more about gaining weight," Montague says. "And somehow I made the connection between eliminating foods and not getting fat."

After Montague read *Health Food Junkies: Overcoming the Obsession with Healthy Eating* by Steven Bratman, M.D., she realized that her eating habits were bordering on the extreme. Bratman asserts that for some, fixating on eating "healthy" or "pure" foods can become a dangerous disorder, which he calls orthorexia nervosa. (While anorexics focus on the quantity of food, orthorexics focus on the quality.) Weight loss is a common hidden agenda among female orthorexics, he says. "You can pretend you're above the notion of dieting by saying you're interested only in 'healthy' foods," he says.

And there's no doubt that such diets work, weight loss-wise—at least in the short term. According to Neal Barnard, M.D., an expert on vegetarian and vegan diets and author of *Turn Off the Fat Genes: The Revolutionary Guide to Losing Weight*, studies show that a switch to veganism (which eliminates all animal products, including dairy, eggs, and even gelatin, which comes from the bones, skin, and tendons of animals) can result in a loss of an average of 20 pounds. The few small-scale studies on raw-food devotees indicate that people who shun the stove typically lose a lot of weight as well. Almost any diet, like Sugar Busters, for instance, that excludes entire food categories, will result in pound-shedding if you end up eating fewer total calories, says Edith Hogan, R.D., a spokeswoman for the American Dietetic Association. "If a person was eating a diet high in simple, sugary carbohydrates and all of a sudden they swap them with less caloric foods, they'll automatically lose weight," she says.

Some women are up front about their motives for adopting a restrictive eating plan. "It's almost like an automatic weight-loss mechanism," says 24-year-old Katy Morrison, a public relations coordinator living in Berkeley, California, who has been a vegan for several months and a vegetarian for more than a year. While she says she follows the diet for ethical and health reasons, it also helps her say no to one of her weaknesses: chocolate. Brownies simply are not allowed on her eating plan, which makes it "really easy" to turn them down, Morrison says. "It's great to know that when I finish eating a gluttonous meal, all I can have for dessert is sorbet or fruit," she says. For others, a structured diet can help ease the burden of refusing food when pressure from family and friends runs high.

As for those who pin their food fussiness on allergies, experts point out the truth: Only 2 to 3 percent of the population have true food allergies, typically to foods such as peanuts or shrimp, explains Dean Metcalfe, M.D., chief of the allergic diseases laboratory at the National Institute of Allergy and Infectious Diseases in Bethesda, Maryland.

Most people who think they have an allergy, he says, may have an intolerance to dairy or wheat gluten, or simply (gasp!) gas or other natural responses to hard-to-digest foods. (Food intolerances differ from allergies in that intolerances do not involve the immune system.) "The confusion comes in when the general public sees any adverse reaction to food as an allergy," he says.

No matter why a woman stops eating foods such as meat, fish, dairy, and eggs, dietitians believe that her nutrition can suffer as a result. "It can be hard to get all the right nutrients on these diets, including calcium, magnesium, B_{12}, and folic acid," Hogan says. While you can get some of these valuable vitamins and minerals from fruits and veggies (although B_{12} is found mostly in animal products), you may have to eat more than you're used to—or more than you can stomach. "It's not just a matter of throwing in a few pieces of tofu. You have to pay particular attention every single day," Hogan says.

That's not to say all vegetarians or people on restricted diets for ethical or medical reasons are nutritional train wrecks. It is possible to maintain a healthy balance. But women must be careful that they don't take their diets to extremes. "It crosses the line if you start avoiding social situations because the nature of the diet controls your behavior," Carll says. She also points out that if a woman adheres to a strict diet to maintain an inappropriately low weight, she may have a problem. But these diets don't cause eating disorders any more than any other type of obsessive relationship with food does. While there is a high incidence of veganism and vegetarianism among anorexics, the vast majority of veggies are not and will not become anorexics, Carll says. "The precursor to developing an eating disorder is a diet that goes out of control, no matter what the diet."

For Ellen Montague, who has started to eat meat again, deciding to relax about food was the best diet of all. "I thought I was eating for positive health reasons , but it was really to conform to a thin female ideal without saying I was on a diet," she says. Montague has a new mantra: "I'm shooting for moderation now." ✳

No matter why a woman stops eating foods such as meat, fish, dairy, and eggs, dietitians believe that her **nutrition can suffer** *as a result.*

Sharon Goldman Edry also writes for **Self** *and the* **New York Daily News.**

EIGHT STEPS TO A
Healthy Diet
you can really love

Even die-hard fans of burgers and fries can retrain their taste buds and learn to like more healthful foods.

BY DARYN ELLER

If brussels sprouts inspired as much ardor as french fries or if people were as wild about cauliflower as they are about chocolate cake, the world would undoubtedly be a healthier place. But one big obstacle stands in the way: "Our brains are hardwired to like anything associated with calorie density," explains Linda Bartoshuk, Ph.D., a professor at the Yale School of Medicine and a taste researcher. It's a survival mechanism built in to help people endure during times of famine. "That explains why fat, starches, and sugar are so powerful," Bartoshuk says. "We have evolved to love high-calorie foods." Problem is, despite the fact that famine is rare in the modern world, the brain hasn't yet absorbed the news—so many people continue to operate in survival mode, eating rich foods in abundance and passing over healthier selections.

You can, however, learn to desire fats and sweets a little less and to love other kinds of foods, including ones with disease-preventing qualities. The following eight-step retraining program for your taste buds is designed to help you do just that. Unlike a lot of diet turnaround strategies, this program is based on the simple notion that healthy eating is all about pleasure. After all, the more you like good-for-you foods, the more you'll want to eat them.

1. Sweeten the pot.

A spoonful of sugar works just as well on vegetables as it does in making medicine go down. In a study she conducted with adult college students, psychologist Elizabeth D. Capaldi, Ph.D., found that they liked broccoli and cauliflower more when the vegetables were accented with a 5 percent sugar solution. "It also produced a greater liking for the vegetables later when they were unsweetened," says Capaldi, a professor of psychology at the State University of New York at Buffalo. Go lightly when you sprinkle on sugar; overly sweetened vegetables can be off-putting.

Try this: If sugared broccoli seems too odd, stir-fry veggies with a mix of soy sauce, sugar, garlic, and ginger to create a sweet glaze.

> **A spoonful of sugar** works as well on vegetables as it does in making medicine go down. Research shows that people learned to like broccoli and cauliflower more when the veggies were accented with a little sugar.

2. Banish bitterness.

Do you typically turn up your nose at brussels sprouts, beet greens, and other bitter veggies, many of which happen to have cancer-fighting properties? Many people (women more often than men) are born with taste buds that can't tolerate bitter foods. But bitterness can be blunted with just a shake of the hand. Sprinkle a little salt on the offending edible or toss it with a salty condiment such as anchovies, salad dressing, or an Asian condiment like hoisin or oyster sauce. One caveat: Skip this strategy if you have any health problems that prevent you from eating salt.

Try this: Keep a jar of capers or olives on hand and stir a few of them in with bitter foods. The briny taste of these bite-sized additions will do the trick.

3. Add fire.

Spicy sauces and salsas not only change the flavor of a food, they can change the way you feel. According to Adam Drewnowski, Ph.D., director of the University of Washington Nutritional Sciences program, hot foods are believed to trigger secretion of a neuropeptide called substance P, which is similar to endorphins, those feel-good brain chemicals. If you learn to associate specific foods with pleasant feelings, Bartoshuk says, you'll likely desire them more.

Try this: If such foods as chicken breast and fish seem bland, try spooning a piquant tomatillo salsa on top or mixing them with a pungent curry to make them more interesting—and effective.

4. Choose cooked over raw.

"If your idea of eating vegetables is some celery with dip or a spinach salad, you're never going to consume very many of them," contends Drewnowski. Most people can only eat so many raw vegetables, and some vegetables they'll never eat raw at all. Cooking softens the flavor and texture of vegetables, making them more palatable. Plus, cooking condenses them: One serving of raw spinach leaves is a full cup; steam or stir-fry them, and a serving shrinks to half a cup. Think how much easier it will be to get your five a day!

Try this: Give roasting a shot. When roasted in a hot oven (400°), just about any vegetable—even asparagus and squash—can take on a sweet, caramelized flavor.

our favorite low-fat picks

Here are some of the healthy goodies you'll find in the pantries, freezers, and refrigerators of *Health's* editorial team:

- Hot Italian turkey sausage (great in tomato sauce)
- Eggo Waffles: Special K, Nutrigrain varieties
- Peter Pan's Reduced-fat Peanut Butter
- Lean Cuisine's Pepperoni French Bread Pizza
- Morningstar Farms' Spicy Black Bean Burgers
- Low-fat Cheddar cheeses: Kraft, Cracker Barrel
- Reduced-fat sour cream (terrific for making dips)
- Hellmann's Light Mayonnaise
- Skim Plus Milk
- Land O' Lakes Spread with Sweet Cream (margarine)
- Baked Ruffles: Cheddar & Sour Cream
- Robert's American Gourmet: Veggie Booty, Personality Puffs
- Pringles Right Crisps
- Reduced-fat Oreos
- York Peppermint Patties
- Nilla Wafers
- Low-fat Entenmann's Crumb Cake
- Sorbet: Ben & Jerry's, Sharon's
- Edy's Grand Light: Vanilla, French Silk

5. Don't fear fat.

Sometimes foods are just unacceptable without some fat added to ease the way. "Julia Child was right," Drewnowski says. "If you want to get people to eat vegetables, you have to make them taste good, and often that means adding a little butter or oil." But think drops of olive oil, a trickle of butter; a little fat can go a long way.

Try this: Brush thinly sliced yellow squash or zucchini with olive oil, grill slices on the barbecue or under the broiler, and lightly salt—it's a lot healthier than eating a bag of potato chips.

6. Gradually go for lower fat.

Although adding a little fat here and there to make healthy foods more tantalizing may improve your diet, keeping your overall fat intake low is still important. But what if skim milk doesn't go down quite as easily as whole, and premium ice cream is just too hard to resist? Take heart: Evidence suggests that if you make the change gradually, you probably won't miss the fat—and you may even grow to dislike it. Participants in the Women's Health Trial, a long-term study for the prevention of breast cancer at Fred Hutchinson Cancer Center in Seattle, reported that after reducing fat in their diets they actually felt physically uncomfortable when eating high-fat foods. One explanation may be that the body loses some of its ability to break down fat, making it more difficult to digest. "You develop what's called a 'conditioned aversion' to high-fat foods," Bartoshuk explains.

Try this: Switch from whole milk to 2 percent first, then try 1 percent and, finally, skim. Better yet, try a skim milk enhanced with extra milk protein. It tastes creamier and has more calcium than the regular skim. (See box on page 173 for our list of favorite low-fat foods.)

7. Buy the best.

There can be a big difference between a flavorless supermarket tomato and one that's grown by a local farmer who concentrates on only a few small crops. Foods purchased at specialty markets are often tastier, whether you're getting fruits and veggies from a roadside stand or meat from a butcher. Sure, you can hide the taste of foods you don't like, but you may not have to if you buy the freshest and most flavorful foods you can find. You may spend a bit more to get quality items, but the chances

> You may notice that **your food likings shift on their own** as you get older. Not as many people in their 60s are eating pizza and drinking coke.

are that you'll end up saving both money and calories because you'll eat them—instead of letting them rot in the fridge while you call the pizza delivery guy. Plus, a specialty shop should offer some healthier choices, such as lean cuts of meat.

Try this: Conduct your own search for the best-tasting tomato: Case the farmers' markets and natural-food stores. Compare what you buy at each place until you find the best purveyor.

8. Wait it out.

Unfortunately, your tastes won't change overnight, but if you stick with the program, it'll happen. "Over time, your taste buds will adapt and your preferences will adjust, but it takes two to four months," Capaldi says. "Patience and persistence are the key."

Try this: Introduce one of these strategies every week instead of adopting them all at once. That way, it will be easier to maintain your fortitude.

Interestingly, you may notice your likings are gradually shifting on their own. Drewnowski's studies have found that taste preferences change for the better with age, probably, he thinks, because people don't need as many calories as they get older. "We found that people in their 60s are less likely to be eating pizza and drinking Coke," he says. "They're eating broccoli." ✳

Daryn Eller is a writer in Venice, California, who frequently covers health topics.

clean plate club

Sixty-seven percent of Americans eat everything on their plates, no matter how much is on it.

—*American Institute for Cancer Research*

Global Food Trends Get Quirky

Food manufacturers in the United States have always reinvented old products in the hopes of boosting sales. (Purple ketchup, anyone?) But Americans aren't exactly the only ones with a taste for some pretty funky foods. Here's just a sampling of what kinds of foods are showing up on store shelves worldwide—and a hint of what's to come stateside.

Germany: Turbo Gum—a new energizing gum that contains coffee and guarana. Chewing three pieces of this pick-me-up will give you the kick of half a cup of espresso.

Finland: Functional cheese—a light Edam cheese with a twist: It provides intestinal benefits.

South Africa: Glow-in-the-dark Fanta Orange soft-drink cans—just in case you need to quench your thirst during a blackout.

England: Energy drinks containing red and black Asian ants—thought to enhance the immune system and improve sexual function.

Australia: Popcorn Fish—nuggets of battered fish that not only resemble everyone's favorite movie snack but also are packaged in popcorn-style containers.

Hong Kong: Carrot-flavored milk.

United States: Bottled dill pickle juice—a sports drink for pregnant women? The water is also spiked with vitamins C and E.

no reason to wine?

While studies have shown that wine-drinkers are healthier than beer-drinkers or abstainers, the choice of beverage may not be the distinguishing factor. A recent Danish study showed that the average wine-drinker tends to have more characteristics that correlate with good health than the typical Bud man (or woman)—including more education, increased wealth, and better access to health care.

sizing up the ideal muffin

For bakery-perfect muffins, use a spring-handled ice cream scoop to fill muffin cups to just the right level.

—*from "All About Baking"*
on www.bettycrocker.com

LABEL FABLES:
How to tell if your nutrition bar is for real

TRUTH SEEKERS at consumerlab.com, an independent commercial testing company, investigated 30 nutrition bars and found that more than half fudged the claims on their labels. To see if your favorite bar is telling the truth about its fat, calorie, and carb counts, grab your calculator:

1. Add the protein and carb (minus fiber) grams together and multiply by four.
2. Mulitply the fat grams by nine.
3. Add the two numbers.

If the total is more than a few calories off from the amount listed, your bar could be hiding something. Brands that passed the test include Luna, Balance, met-Rx, and Gatorade Energy bars.

HIS smoking can makeYOU fat

First we found out that secondhand smoke can harm your lungs. Now researchers say your husband's cigarette habit could be clouding your diet sense. A recent study shows that the nonsmoking wives of men who smoke eat more fat and consume less fiber, vitamin A, and folate than women whose husbands eschew the deadly habit. If you can't get him to quit, you should pay extra attention to your diet (and send him outside for his nicotine fix).

no-stress diet

Getting on the health track is simple—and satisfying—with our meal-planning basics and low-maintenance menus.

RECIPES AND TEXT BY MARGE PERRY

Millions of Americans repeatedly resolve to stop overdoing it on food and underdoing it on exercise. So they strip their diets down to the bare minimum in an effort to regain some measure of control over their health. But that's unnecessary. Deprivation and denial are out, and so are promises that can't be kept. What's in is realism: resolving to make healthful changes based on truths about your lifestyle and schedule, your likes and dislikes, your energy level and time commitments. There's no point in telling yourself you'll cook elaborate, healthful meals every night if you're really the TV-dinner type, or that you'll quit entertaining cold-turkey if socializing is in your blood.

With this in mind, we've created two menus to get you back on the road to healthy living—one for quick weeknight meals and another that feeds your need to break bread with family and friends—while keeping your stress level at a minimum. Each abides by the following basic principles, which can make meal planning easier no matter what the occasion.
• Choose main courses and sides you can cook in about the same amount of time or at the same oven temperature.
• Cut back on dishes that require last-minute attention.
• Use ingredients that you can buy already prepared. (Think shredded cheese or bagged chopped vegetables.)
Our easy menus put these strategies into action. You can mix and match any of these entrées and sides, depending on your tastes, for suppers that will keep that take-back-your-health resolution simple and satisfying.

entertaining menu
Rice with Pan-Roasted Corn

Hearts of Palm, Black Bean, and Orange Salad

Chilean Sea Bass • Banana Caramel Pecan Crepes

With dessert: 755 calories (26% from fat); 21.9g fat

Without dessert: 493 calories (24% from fat); 13.4g fat

Rice with Pan-Roasted Corn
SERVES 6
PREPARATION: 5 MINUTES
COOKING: 26 MINUTES

1 cup uncooked jasmine rice
1 tablespoon vegetable oil
1 cup frozen whole-kernel corn, thawed
½ teaspoon salt
½ teaspoon dried oregano
1 cup chopped fresh cilantro

1. Cook rice according to package directions, omitting salt and fat.
2. Heat oil in a large nonstick skillet over medium-high heat. Add corn and salt; sauté 5 minutes or until lightly browned. Stir in oregano; cook 1 minute. Stir in cilantro; remove from heat.
3. Combine rice and corn mixture; toss well. Serving size: $^3/_4$ cup.

Per serving: Calories 160 (14% from fat); Fat 2.5g (sat 0.2g, mono 1.4g, poly 0.8g); Protein 3g; Carbohydrate 31.4g; Fiber 1.6g; Cholesterol 0mg; Iron 0.6mg; Sodium 201mg; Calcium 8mg

Hearts of Palm, Black Bean, and Orange Salad

SERVES 6
PREPARATION: 10 MINUTES

VINAIGRETTE:

1 (11-ounce) can mandarin oranges in light syrup, undrained
2 tablespoons extra-virgin olive oil
2 tablespoons white wine vinegar
½ teaspoon salt
½ teaspoon ground coriander seeds
⅛ teaspoon ground red pepper

SALAD:

10 cups romaine lettuce (about 3 heads), torn
1 (15-ounce) can black beans, rinsed and drained
1 (14-ounce) can hearts of palm, drained

1. To prepare the vinaigrette, drain oranges in a colander over a large bowl, reserving ¼ cup syrup. Discard remaining syrup.
2. Combine 1¼ cup syrup, oil, and next 4 ingredients (white wine vinegar through pepper) in a small bowl; stir with a whisk until blended.
3. To prepare the salad, place oranges, lettuce, beans, and hearts of palm in a large bowl; drizzle with vinaigrette. Toss gently to coat. Serving size: 1½ cups.

Per serving: Calories 143 (30% from fat); Fat 5.2g (sat 0.7g, mono 3.4g, poly 0.6g); Protein 4.9g; Carbohydrate 22.4g; Fiber 5.8g; Cholesterol 0mg; Iron 4.3mg; Sodium 690mg; Calcium 105mg

Chilean Sea Bass

SERVES 6
PREPARATION: 5 MINUTES
COOKING: 15 MINUTES

2 tablespoons fresh lime juice
2 tablespoons fresh orange juice
1 tablespoon olive oil
1½ teaspoons grated lime rind
1 jalapeño pepper, seeded and minced
Cooking spray
6 (6-ounce) sea bass fillets (about 2 inches thick)
Dash of salt

1. Preheat oven to 450°.
2. Combine first 5 ingredients (lime juice through jalapeño) in a small bowl; stir well with a whisk.
3. Place fillets in an 11 x 7-inch baking dish coated with cooking spray. Spoon lime mixture over fillets. Bake for 15 minutes or until fish flakes easily when tested with a fork. Sprinkle with salt. Serving size: 1 fillet.

Per serving: Calories 190 (28% from fat); Fat 5.7g (sat 1.2g, mono 2.4g, poly 1.5g); Protein 31.4g; Carbohydrate 1.2g; Fiber 0.2g; Cholesterol 70mg; Iron 0.5mg; Sodium 116mg; Calcium 19mg

Banana Caramel Pecan Crepes

SERVES 6
PREPARATION: 10 MINUTES
COOKING: 4 MINUTES

2 tablespoons butter
¼ cup chopped pecans
4 medium firm bananas, peeled and sliced (about 2½ pounds)
½ cup fat-free caramel sundae syrup, divided
6 (9-inch) prepared French crepes (such as Melissa's)

1. Melt butter in a large nonstick skillet over medium-high heat. Add pecans; sauté 1 minute. Add bananas; sauté 2 minutes. Drizzle with ⅓ cup syrup; cook 1 minute. Remove from heat.
2. Spoon about ⅓ cup banana mixture into the center of each crepe. Fold sides and ends over. Place on a serving platter, seam sides down; drizzle with remaining syrup. Serving size: 1 filled crepe and 1 teaspoon syrup.

Per serving: Calories 262 (28% from fat); Fat 8.5g (sat 3.4g, mono 3.3g, poly 1.3g); Protein 3.7g; Carbohydrate 45.5g; Fiber 2.3g; Cholesterol 15.9mg; Iron 0.7mg; Sodium 181mg; Calcium 59mg

weeknight menu

Ginger-Honey Chicken or Spice-Rubbed Flank Steak

Roasted Green Beans

Rosemary Potato Wedges

Mixed Salad Greens with Sherry Vinegar
(toss greens with vinegar)

Pineapple-Orange Compote
(Combine cut pineapple with orange sections and garnish with mint leaves)

Chicken menu: 509 calories (20% from fat); 11.1g fat
Steak menu: 583 calories (30% from fat); 19.6g fat

Ginger-Honey Chicken

SERVES 4
PREPARATION: 10 MINUTES
COOKING: 11 MINUTES

½ teaspoon salt
¾ teaspoon ground ginger
4 chicken thighs (about 1 pound), skinned
1 tablespoon minced peeled fresh ginger
3 tablespoons honey
1 tablespoon fresh lemon juice
1 tablespoon low-sodium soy sauce
Cooking spray

1. Preheat broiler.
2. Combine salt and ground ginger in a small bowl; rub chicken with mixture.
3. Combine minced ginger, honey, lemon juice, and soy sauce in a small bowl; stir well with a whisk.
4. Place chicken on a broiler pan coated with cooking spray. Broil 5 minutes; turn. Baste with honey mixture. Broil 3 minutes; turn. Baste with remaining honey mixture. Broil 3 minutes or until done.
5. Brush drippings from bottom of pan onto chicken. Serving size: 1 chicken thigh.

Per Serving: Calories 155 (19% from fat); Fat 3.4g (sat 0.9g, mono 1.0g, poly 0.8g); Protein 17g, Carbohydrate 14.2g; Fiber 0.2g; Cholesterol 71mg; Iron 1.1mg; Sodium 501mg; Calcium 11mg

Spice-Rubbed Flank Steak

SERVES 4
PREPARATION: 10 MINUTES
COOKING: 12 MINUTES

1 tablespoon brown sugar
½ teaspoon ground cumin
½ teaspoon salt
½ teaspoon garlic powder
½ teaspoon ground ginger
½ teaspoon ground cinnamon
¼ teaspoon black pepper
1 (12-ounce) flank steak, trimmed
Cooking spray

1. Preheat broiler.
2. Combine first 7 ingredients (brown sugar through pepper) in a small bowl; rub evenly over steak.
3. Place steak on a broiler pan coated with cooking spray; broil 6 minutes on each side or until desired degree of doneness.
4. Let stand 3 minutes; cut steak diagonally across grain into thin slices. Serving size: 3 ounces.

Per serving: 229 calories (48% from fat); Fat 11.9g (sat 5g, mono 4.9g, poly 0.4g); Protein 25.6g; Carbohydrate 3.3g; Fiber 0.3g; Cholesterol 64mg; Iron 3.4mg; Sodium 302mg; Calcium 13mg

Roasted Green Beans

SERVES 4
PREPARATION: 5 MINUTES
COOKING: 10 MINUTES

1 teaspoon olive oil
1 teaspoon balsamic vinegar
½ teaspoon dried tarragon
½ teaspoon salt
1 pound green beans, trimmed

1. Preheat oven to 500°.
2. Combine first 4 ingredients (olive oil through salt) in a large bowl. Add green beans; toss to coat. Place green bean mixture in a 13 x 9-inch baking dish; bake at 500° for 10 minutes or until crisp-tender. Serving size: 1 cup.

Per serving: Calories 47 (21% from fat); Fat 1.3g (sat 0.2g, mono 0.8g, poly 0.2g); Protein 2.1g; Carbohydrate 8.4g; Fiber 3.9g; Cholesterol 0mg; Iron 1.3mg; Sodium 301mg; Calcium 45mg

Rosemary Potato Wedges

SERVES 4
PREPARATION: 10 MINUTES
COOKING: 15 MINUTES

2 baking potatoes, cut into 12 wedges each
5 teaspoons olive oil
1 teaspoon chopped fresh rosemary
1 teaspoon salt
¼ teaspoon black pepper
Cooking spray

1. Preheat oven to 500°.
2. Combine first 5 ingredients (potatoes through pepper) in a large bowl; toss to coat. Place potatoes in a single layer on a jelly-roll pan coated with cooking spray. Bake for 15 minutes or until tender, stirring once. Serving size: 6 wedges.

Per serving: Calories 204 (25% from fat); Fat 5.8g (sat 0.8g, mono 4.2g, poly 0.5g); Protein 3.3g; Carbohydrate 35.8g; Fiber 3.4g; Cholesterol 0mg; Iron 2mg; Sodium 598mg; Calcium 15mg ✳

Marge Perry writes a syndicated daily newspaper column called "Dinner Tonight," and is a frequent contributor to Health.

www = Web Weight Watch

To find out the best way to reach your goal weight, visit www.foodfit.com. Click on "Tools," then "Weight Calculator," and key in your vital stats after you've registered. The site will tell you how many calories you should eat daily—and how much exercise you need to do—to drop those extra pounds.

Fight Fat with Fat

THE BAD NEWS: Chronic stress—like being under constant deadline pressure—can add pounds to your waistline. The good news: You can thwart this tendency by adding more fat to your diet. While that might seem counter-intuitive, it is actually a sound strategy, explains Carolyn Berdanier, Ph.D., professor emerita of foods and nutrition at the University of Georgia. When you're stressed out, your body creates new fat cells so you'll have stored energy to give you a boost during difficult times. "Increasing your fat intake lets your body know that fat is readily available," Berdanier says, so the body won't produce fat cells to compensate.

"We're not talking about big changes—maybe a 5 percent increase," she says. For the average person, that translates to an extra 3 grams of fat per day. Make sure you keep calories at a steady level, though, or you will gain. To maintain your normal calorie intake, simply swap carbohydrate calories for fat calories. For instance, you can have an open-faced sandwich to save about 90 calories from a slice of whole-wheat bread and add a 2-ounce slice of low-fat Swiss cheese instead. If salads are your style, skip the pita bread on the side (100 calories for half) and top the greens with half a can of white tuna in water. Or for a sweet treat, bag the mini rice cakes (10 at 77 calories) and reach for a handful of Hershey's Reese's Pieces.

Here are some other diet tips to ward off unwanted stress and pounds:

Load up on fruits and veggies. The fiber in these foods will help if you get constipated or have other gastrointestinal problems during times of high stress.

Cut back on caffeine. It mimics the hormones that surge when you're under pressure, adding to your stress level.

Eat more often. Spreading your daily calories among several small meals and snacks helps keep your blood-sugar level even—giving you a steady energy supply to cope with whatever the day throws at you.

A few extra grams of fat a day could save you from weight gain by staving off stress-related hunger pangs.

Diet Foods You'll Love

Waistline watchers rejoice! Some of your forbidden favorites may not be so bad for you after all.

BY MAUREEN CALLAHAN

Eat a cookie, lose an inch. Sounds like Bridget Jones' idea of a diet. But bringing some once-banned foods into your eating plan—within reason, of course—while adding other good stuff to your plate is actually sound weight-loss advice. Research is turning up a host of unlikely foods (cookies and peanuts among them) that may be your best weight-loss allies. That's thanks to their ability to squelch your appetite, make you feel more satisfied for longer, or prevent the downward spiral of a binge. Certainly, you still need to be mindful of portions and make use of your gym membership. But forget surviving on only lettuce or melba toast for days. Add these foods to your plate for the edge you need to get—or stay—slim.

Peanuts

Fat-laden peanuts used to be snack-time pariahs. Now, two studies suggest they can suppress your appetite and help you stick to your diet plan. In one, Harvard researcher Kathy McManus, R.D., asked 51 people in a group of 101 dieters to follow a low-fat eating plan. The rest ate the same number of calories a day (1,200 for women; 1,500 for men), but they snacked on heart-healthy unsaturated fats, including about an ounce of peanuts or mixed nuts, or peanut butter on whole-wheat crackers. A year and a half later, members of the group on

the peanut plan lost weight, kept it off, and continued to stick with their regimens long after the study ended. The group without the moderate-fat snacks had twice as many dropouts and gained an average of 5 pounds.

"No one food made this diet work," explains McManus, a dietitian at Boston's Brigham and Women's Hospital. "It was a balance of foods and paying attention to portion sizes." But including peanuts and peanut butter could contribute to making people feel satisfied, she says. That's the word from a recent study done at Purdue University; researchers there found that munching on peanuts or peanut butter staved off hunger in some folks for two hours. Other snacks they tested curbed appetite for only 30 minutes.

Olive Oil

In addition to its four-star status in heart health, olive oil is assuming a golden position in weight loss. In the Harvard study on unsaturated fats, olive oil was one of the mono-unsaturated fats that helped people feel satisfied longer—a quality that can mean less foraging after meals for you.

Researchers involved in a Penn State study on diets enriched with monounsaturated fats suggest that eating these fats may make it easier to stick with a healthy, fat-restricted diet plan. A study from France gets even more specific: Men who ate a lunch that included mashed potatoes prepared with a monounsaturated-rich fat like olive oil stayed satisfied longer than when they ate the same lunch with potatoes or rice prepared with a polyunsaturated fat like corn oil. "These preliminary data suggest that the type of oil you cook with may affect satiety," says researcher Steve E. Specter, Ph.D. So try roasting veggies in olive oil at dinner if you want to keep from rummaging around the freezer for ice cream at midnight.

Apples

Apples can help put hunger on the skids, thanks to their high fiber content. Be it a Granny Smith, Macintosh, or Golden Delicious, you can expect one large apple to deliver a hefty 5.7 grams of fiber, the bulk of it soluble. Soluble fibers absorb water to form gels that fill up the stomach and delay its emptying. These fibers also cause you to absorb less of the fat and protein calories at a meal, which some researchers say can help contribute to long-term weight loss. A report from the National Institutes of Health confirms that the less fiber in your diet, the more likely you are to gain weight. Still, Americans continue to eat a paltry 15 grams of fiber per day, rather than the recommended 25 to 30 grams.

Cereal

If you can't cut down the fat in your diet, breakfast cereal may help. When a University of California-Berkeley study looked at the eating habits of 19,000 Americans older than 12, researchers noticed that cereal-eaters tend to take in less fat and more fiber than noncereal-eaters. Lead study author Gladys Block, Ph.D., also finds that

Foods like cereal, apples, and olive oil can keep you satisfied longer—staving off extra calories and pounds.

people who eat cereal for breakfast have a lower body mass index (read: less excess body fat) and healthier diets than people who start their days with foods like bagels, French toast, or omelettes.

Eating cereal at other meals might offer even stronger weight-loss benefits. In a recent Purdue University study, researchers found that dieters who ate a serving of cereal, skim milk, and a piece of fruit twice a day—once at breakfast and again as a replacement for lunch or dinner—lost an average of 4 pounds in two weeks. Kellogg's Special K was used in this study, but other cereals should have the same effect, says lead researcher Richard Mattes, Ph.D. The key: By replacing their regular fare with cereal, these folks naturally cut calories. And they didn't make up for those missing calories—roughly 600 of them—at other times of the day.

Kidney Beans

Kidney beans aren't a weight-loss surprise. They're low in calories and high in fiber, as well as filling. But some researchers think there's another reason why these legumes help keep you trim. It's based on a popular but controversial theory called glycemic index (GI) that ranks carbs based on how they affect blood sugar. Speculation is that high-GI foods, such as white rice, white bread, and potatoes—because they are rapidly digested and cause a quick spike in blood sugar—can flood the body with insulin and trigger feelings of hunger. Low-GI foods, such as kidney beans, pintos, and limas, have little impact on blood sugar since they are absorbed slowly.

"Theoretically, low-GI foods can help with weight loss since they help suppress hunger," says researcher Susan Roberts, Ph.D., of Tufts University. In a study of overweight teenage boys, Roberts and her colleagues noticed that those fed high-glycemic meals at breakfast and lunch ate 81 percent more calories in the five hours after lunch than boys fed low-GI meals. Critics contend that most people eat a variety of foods at meals, so pinpointing the GI of single foods may not have much effect on weight loss. Although more long-term studies are needed to prove this theory, dieters can still benefit from including low-GI foods at meals, if only to help temper the impact of high-GI foods.

Weight-loss programs work better when you're **not deprived.** Trying not to eat foods you love, such as cookies, is almost like trying not to breathe.

Chocolate Chip Cookies

For every time you've gotten the aren't-you-on-a-diet look when caught with a cookie, here's sweet revenge. Weight-loss programs simply work better when you're not deprived. Trying not to eat foods you love is almost like trying not to breathe. "When dieting is too restrictive, your body will take over and demand a binge," says John Foreyt, Ph.D., a weight-control expert at Baylor College of Medicine.

If counting the calories in beverages but downing a cookie sounds contradictory, keep in mind that the success rate of diets that severely restrict eating is abysmal—usually around 10 percent. Foreyt, who is also director of Baylor's Nutrition Research Center, says that in studies and in private counseling, "we find that by allowing people to work a bottle of beer or a cookie—or whatever it is they really like—into their diets, they don't feel as deprived." In the real world, that means the occasional or even daily indulgence: one premium chocolate, a bottle of Bud, a glass of Chardonnay, or whatever keeps you satisfied. If the calorie tab is small—about 150 calories or less (that's about two Chips Ahoy cookies)—your weight-loss efforts won't be sabotaged.

Unsweetened Iced Tea

Americans swill huge 32-ounce Big Gulp sodas and grande lattes faster than a Humvee eats up gasoline. That could be part of the reason why 6 out of 10 Americans are overweight, Mattes says. But if you substitute a glass of unsweetened iced tea for a cola every day for a year, you've saved roughly 51,100 calories—that's 15 pounds.

The fix is easy once you realize you have the problem. In a recent study, Mattes and colleagues demonstrated that people make adjustments for extra food calories they eat (in this case, an extra 500 calories' worth of jelly beans) by cutting back at other meals. But when those calories come in a glass, people don't compensate. The point? Beverages count, Mattes says. "If you are going to drink soda or sweetened drinks, you have to consciously offset it by adjusting your intake of other components in your diet." That's not so easy, because fluids aren't satiating. Just switch to no-calorie beverages like unsweetened iced tea, black coffee, diet soft drinks, or good old water, and you won't need to make up the difference. ✳

Contributing editor Maureen Callahan, R.D., received the James Beard Award in 1997 for her diet and nutrition reporting.

why fat-free often equals flavor-free

There's a reason fat-free cookies lack taste: They lack fat. While scientists have long thought people could detect fat only by smell or texture, new research shows that taste buds are the true fat detectors and can tell when your favorite Cheddar has been swapped for skim. With the skinny on fat, manufacturers might finally make guilt-free tastier.

I'll Just Have a Sliver …

Up to 40% of people underestimate how much they eat.

—*from a study presented at the American Diabetes Association's annual meeting*

FOODS THAT FEED MORE THAN JUST AN APPETITE

With the emphasis on Americans' expanding waistlines, it's easy to forget that food can do more than transform your shape from Calista Flockhart to Queen Latifah. Certain foods eaten regularly can do everything from helping your night vision to boosting your brainpower. Check out this guide to head-to-toe nourishment:

hair: wheat A great source of biotin, wheat is an important nutrient for healthy, shiny hair.

stomach: garlic The herb may help ward off stomach cancer.

brain: cookies Research shows that sugar fuels the brain and may boost your memory.

eyes: sweet potatoes Vitamin A in these spuds can help improve night vision.

nails: oysters The zinc in oysters can be good for your skin and nails.

toenails: cashews The biotin in cashews helps strengthen nails.

lungs: tomatoes A British study shows that eating tomatoes more than three times a week may help prevent respiratory disease.

skin: acorn squash Rich in vitamin A, acorn squash may help reduce the risk of the most common type of skin cancer—basal cell carcinoma—by 70 percent.

heart: tofu The magnesium in tofu can help prevent blood clots and high blood pressure.

bones: carrots The potassium and magnesium in carrots may help buttress your bones.

legs: bananas Loaded with potassium, bananas help get your muscles moving and may prevent cramping.

The Virtues of Eating Often

NEW RESEARCH could help you justify a diet of frequent grazing: Your cholesterol level may depend not only on what you eat but also on how often you chow down, say researchers in the United Kingdom. A report in the *British Medical Journal* found that middle-aged men and women who ate six or more times a day had about 5 percent lower total cholesterol levels (including the "bad" kind) than those who sat down for one or two meals a day. The results are particularly striking since the frequent eaters tended to consume more calories, including more fat.

Once-a-day eaters may metabolize food differently than those who munch continuously, say the researchers. This isn't license for a doughnut break at 10:30 a.m. and an afternoon snack of fries: Cholesterol watchers should graze on more fruits and vegetables, divide meals into smaller amounts throughout the day, and cut back on saturated fat.

food facts

Which fruit packs more fiber: strawberries or blackberries?

How many calories, on average, are in a slice of homemade apple pie?

Which has more vitamin C: a Florida orange or a California navel orange?

need help? Check out the U.S. Department of Agriculture's Nutrient Data Laboratory at www.nal.usda.gov/fnic/cgibin/nut_search.pl. It has detailed info on nearly 6,000 fresh and packaged foods.

(Answers: blackberries; 410; a navel has about 12 milligrams more.)

dressing "on the side"—not as helpful as you think

Think you're being virtuous when you order that sauce or dressing "on the side"? According to the *Environmental Nutrition* newsletter, many restaurants are extra generous when they ladle out their accompaniments, serving up to twice as much dressing as they would in a typical tossed salad.

To avoid eating the entire portion, waist-watchers should spoon out a tablespoon or so of sauce and ask the server to remove the vat.

Reap the Benefits
of a
KitchenGarden

*Dig in and plant a patch—it's good
for you, inside and out.*

BY JANET LEMBKE

A kitchen garden, whether it fills up an entire yard or is confined to a porch full of pots, is well worth the effort: the incomparably fresh flavors, the sensuous colors, and the satisfaction of eating vegetables, fruits, and seeds you grew yourself. Plus, gardening can give you a great workout: Wielding a hoe is good for the upper body; squatting to pick your garden treasures firms up the thighs. And you don't even need a green thumb to reap the rewards, if you stick to these tried-and-true favorites. Just put in a half-hour each morning to weed and water—perhaps the best exercise there is for sunshine-starved bodies—and you'll be pleased with the payoff: a bumper crop and some daily soul satisfaction.

Tomatoes: *the biggest reward*
The joy of cradling the year's first red, ripe tomato is surpassed only by each juicy bite. This fruit tops the gardener's list for sheer flavor, plus its versatility in the kitchen. Aside from eating tomatoes fresh off the vine, you can juice them, can them, stew them, and use them to make relish and pickles.

Beginners need not be intimidated: Tomatoes are deceptively easy to grow. Plant them in the sunniest spot, and give them some marigolds for company; the flowers help ward off worms that can attack plants.

For a longer yield, put in two sets of seedlings two weeks apart. As the tomatoes grow, use stakes or cages to give the plants needed support. Clip off the shoots that sprout at the junction of branches and stems, or the plants will put their energy into growing leaves rather than luscious fruit.

Sunflowers: *the most glorious*
Who wants a garden that's all substance—and no flash? Sunflowers provide you with a bit of both. Gorgeous and bearing a bounty of nutritious seeds, sunflowers are easy to grow. And we're not alone in our praise of these majestic flowers: The Aztecs left carvings showing priestesses who were crowned with the flowers or bearing them in their

hands; in the temples, the conquistadors found sunflowers wrought of gold.

The seeds make a perfect healthy snack—but if you're not careful, you might lose them to backyard bluebirds. To save a few morsels for yourself, cover some flower heads with netting or a sack.

For best results, plant them in a spot that gets at least six hours of sunlight a day. Place seeds in cultivated earth as soon as the soil has warmed. If you want to fuss over the low-maintenance plant, reap larger blooms by pinching off shoots as the sunflowers mature. But beware: Large blooms can be heavy, so be ready to prop up the plants with stakes.

a gardener's resource guide:

Avid gardeners are quick to offer advice because they know the value of just the right tool or a prolific variety of plant. Rather than learn the hard way, try these trusted selections.

favorite tools

There's no way to skip the hard work involved in gardening. But to make your efforts a little easier, you can rely on these helpers:

Homi: This Korean hand hoe has a 6-inch, forged-steel, teardrop-shaped blade with a sharp point set at a right angle to the wooden handle. It slices easily through weed roots and carves furrows for seeds. You may want to get two different-sized homis, one short (from the Cook's Garden, 800-457-9703, www.cooksgarden.com) and one long (the E-Z Digger from Stillbrook Horticultural Supplies, 800-414-4468, www.stillbrook.com).

Trowel: A garden trowel, a handheld shovel, is an essential garden tool that's easy to find. Beware, though: Many cheaper versions will bend at the neck all too readily, so splurge a little. Stillbrook offers an excellent selection, as do other catalogs.

Hand Pruner: You can use a pruner to snip everything from tender herbs to tough, prickly eggplant stems. One good choice is a Fiskar (608-643-4389, www.fiskars.com), but others can get the job done as well. You'll find Fiskars at your hardware store or garden center. Order other good ones from Stillbrook or the oh-so-tempting Gardener's Supply Company (800-427-3363, www.gardeners.com).

Stool: A wise option for support when harvesting these long rows of beans is a lightweight tripod stool with aluminum legs. You can purchase one from Campmor (800-226-7667, www.campmor.com). You'll find them listed under camping furniture. Replacement stool tops (they wear out after five or six years) are sold directly by the manufacturer, Camp Time (509-928-3051, www.camptime.net).

Lightweight tiller/cultivator: You can depend on this machine to fight those persistent weeds. The 20-pound Mantis starts with a purr and cultivates a 20- by 50-foot plot in 15 or 20 minutes. The Mantis, with a 0.9-horsepower 2-cycle engine, is $299, plus shipping and handling (800-366-6268, www.mantisgardentools.com). Similar machines are available from Troy-Bilt (800-828-5500, www.troybilt.com) and Honda (800-426-7701, www.hondapowerequipment.com).

seed companies

One of the joys of growing vegetables is leafing through garden catalogs. The eye delights, the mouth waters, and bad weather seems to recede. Here are some trustworthy seed companies, most of which offer organic selections.

W. Atlee Burpee & Co.
800-888-1447
www.burpee.com

The Cook's Garden
800-457-9703
www.cooksgarden.com

Johnny's Selected Seeds
207-437-4301
www.johnnyseeds.com

Park Seed
800-845-3369
www.parkseed.com

Southern Exposure Exchange
540-894-9480
www.southernexposure.com

totally tomatoes
803-663-0016
www.totallytomato.com

Broccoli: *the bar-none healthiest*

Broccoli is one of the most nutritious vegetables around. It's chock-full of antioxidants, vitamin C, folate, fiber, and a wealth of minerals. Even better, when you grow the vegetable yourself, you get tender, green clusters with a flavor that far surpasses what you can find at your local grocery store.

In warmer climates, like the South, the young seedlings should be set in the earth no later than March 1. If you missed the planting deadline this spring, consider a fall crop planted in August or September, once temperatures are consistently cool.

You'll have the best luck with young plants set in a sunny spot. Because cabbage caterpillars are as fond of broccoli as we are, apply a dusting or two of *Bacillus thuringiensis,* a natural insecticide. When the center head is about an inch across, nourish it with a ring of rich compost 2 inches from the base. About six weeks after planting, the dark-green heads should be ready for harvest. And the plants will keep yielding, with new stalks sprouting in the junctions of leaf and stem. Once the weather turns warm on your spring crop, the heads of broccoli burst with tiny yellow flowers like skyrockets, signaling that the year's harvest is over.

Beans: *a sure success for the brown thumb*

Snap beans, so-called because they break with a crisp little ping, are fail-safe. Known scientifically as *Phaseolus vulgaris* or "common bean," they are anything but: Beans come in a wondrous array of varieties, shapes, and colors. Pods may be round or flat, curved or straight, long and slender, or plump and wide. And colors range from yellow mottled with bronze stripes to a royal purple. Bush varieties are particularly easy because they don't require

*Tending broccoli, picking beans, and doing other garden tasks are **good for the body and refreshing for the soul**—with a basketful of nutrient-rich produce as the rich reward.*

a fence for climbing: Try Kentucky Wonder with its large, flat pods; the ever-dependable Blue Lake; and Burpee's yellow Gold Mine.

When the danger of frost is over, put an ounce of seeds in cultivated earth—that's enough for about a 25-foot row—and wait a week or two. (Unfortunately, some insects are fond of bean plants. Try companion planting with marigolds, onions, or garlic to ward off unwanted nibblers.) New leaves lift into the air like green banners. Look for crisp, firm pods about 60 days later. Pick mature pods and go back for more every other day until, in two or three weeks, the yield ceases.

Cucumbers: *the most prolific*

Cucumbers are easy to nurture—perhaps too easy. You just might end up with a garden full of vines and more cucumbers than you care to pick. Be moderate. Plant just four to six seedlings and place the rows a foot or two apart.

But don't shy away. Cucumbers rate high in potassium, as well as providing some vitamin C, folic acid, and fiber. The skin contains vitamin A. Eat them raw or transform them into pickles and soups.

The plants come in a wondrous variety, from climbers that need supports to the little pickling types no bigger than a finger. One variety that doesn't require stakes is a bush type that hugs the ground and spreads out neatly. Despite the expression "cool as a cucumber," these plants thrive in the heat and are quick to express their displeasure by wilting when the temperature dips. Harvest quickly since a neglected cucumber will yellow and become bitter-tasting. ✳

Avid gardener and cook Janet Lembke is the author of several natural-history books, including **Touching Earth** *and* **Despicable Species.**

tips for
farmers' market
buys

For the freshest fruits and vegetables, cut out the middleman: Skip the grocery store and head straight to your local farmers' market. To get the most out of your next trip, consider these tips from Deborah Madison, author of *Local Flavors: Cooking and Eating from America's Farmers' Markets.*

Take it slow: Walk around to check out what's available and compare prices before you buy.

Speak up: If you need a tip on how to cook a particular type of produce, ask. (If the seller can't help you, a nearby customer usually can.)

Carry cash: Few farmers accept checks or have lots of change on hand.

Stock up: If you see something you really like, ask how long it will be available.

Q+A
Watch Out for Carrots
in a Low-Carb Diet

If carrots are good for me, why does my low-carb diet limit how many I can eat?

PASTA AND COOKIES aren't the only carbs in your kitchen. With almost 8 grams of carbohydrates in a single stick, carrots are carb capsules. A snack of four large carrots packs as many carbs as a bagel.

But before you toss your sticks, be aware that the 40-calorie, fat-free carrot can be a healthy alternative to snacking on chips. Consider carrots to be a high-quality carb, rich in disease-fighting beta-carotene and fiber, compared with the relative nutrient wasteland of a slice of white bread. Eaten in moderation, carrots can be a low-carb dieter's friend: With 4 grams of cholesterol-lowering fiber per cup, raw or steamed carrots will help you feel full. But beware of the juiced carrot, which doesn't have any of the beneficial fiber. If you're watching carbs, try substituting a side of carrots for potatoes or peas, and limit yourself to about 3 or 4 ounces (about one large carrot) at a time.

feed your man tomatoes and help him stay cancer-free

Wave a white flag if you two are battling over the last slice of pizza—a hearty helping of tomato sauce is just what your guy needs. A recent report in the *Journal of the National Cancer Institute* showed that eating tomato products (including sauce and ketchup) two or more times a week can reduce a man's risk of prostate cancer by as much as 36 percent. So spoon out the salsa and keep his parts healthy.

Get Your Fruits and Veggies from a Wrap

THE U.S. DEPARTMENT OF AGRICULTURE has developed a way to turn fruits and veggies into paper-thin wraps that may replace the plastic films covering your favorite microwave meals. When heated, these edible packages dissolve to become sauces for the foods they cover. The multipurpose wraps, expected to hit stores by 2003, also come in rolls, so toss the tin foil and instead cover leftover pasta with a tomato-sauce film.

Color Your Diet for Good Health

New research says this nutrition plan is
not only easy, but good for you, too.

BY ANNE UNDERWOOD

RECIPES BY LORI LONGBOTHAM

As an artist, Joy Noel Travalino of Hartsdale, New York, believes that food should be a feast for the eyes as well as the palate. As she navigates the aisles of her local supermarket, she seems to be composing a still life. "I've always been visual, so it's natural for me to choose the most colorful fruits and vegetables," she says. For salad, she heads toward the baby lettuce greens with edible flowers—orange nasturtiums and purple-and-yellow Johnny-jump-ups. Fragrant basil, purple figs, and blood oranges find their way into her basket, along with strawberries, blueberries, organic carrots, and heirloom tomatoes ranging in hue from yellow to almost purple. The cornucopia, she says, "reminds me of the open-air flower markets of Provence."

There's no denying that the meal she creates will be beautiful, but as a former medical writer, she knows there's another, equally powerful reason to eat your colors—health. A diet that's rich in the vast spectrum of colorful fruits and vegetables is the latest (and possibly easiest to accomplish) nutrition advice coming from experts. The concept of color coding sounds ridiculously simple, but it's scientifically valid, says Lorelei DiSogra, R.D., director of the National Cancer Institute (NCI) program called 5 a Day for Better Health. In spring 2002, the organization launched a campaign called "Savor the Spectrum," urging Americans to eat fruits and vegetables from each of the four primary color groups every day—yellow-orange, red, green, and blue-purple—with white onions and garlic rounding out the palette.

What does color have to do with disease prevention? For starters, you have the effects of the pigments themselves—most of them potent antioxidants. "When you see colors on your plate, you know you're doing good things for yourself," DiSogra says. "You're getting the beneficial compounds from fruits and vegetables that you need to help prevent heart attack, cancer, stroke, and diabetes." Take lycopene, the red tint in tomatoes. Powerful scientific evidence has linked high intake with reduced risk of prostate cancer, and more preliminary research suggests it also protects against lung cancer, breast cancer, and even heart disease—still the number-one killer of both women and men.

Pigments are just the first line of defense. Think of them as signposts for even more beneficial compounds. These include vitamins, minerals, and fiber, but also

When you see colors on your plate, you know you're doing good things for yourself. You're getting the compounds you need to help prevent heart attack, cancer, stroke, and diabetes.

—*Lorelei DiSogra, R.D.*

phytochemicals that help detoxify the body, battle tumor growth, and activate protective genes. "Almost across the board, the most intensely colored fruits and vegetables have the highest levels of protective phytonutrients," says endocrinologist Daniel Nadeau, M.D., director of the HealthReach Diabetes, Endocrine, and Nutrition Center in Hampton, New Hampshire.

Spinach is just one example. With its dark green hue, it's practically a one-stop pharmacy, according to Nadeau. It delivers at least three important antioxidants, including the yellow pigment lutein, which helps prevent macular degeneration, the leading cause of blindness in the elderly. A 1-cup serving of raw spinach contains about three-quarters of your daily vitamin A, a quarter of your folic-acid needs, and a whopping 185 percent of your vitamin K—a nutrient correlated with bone strength. Stack those benefits against a head of pale iceberg lettuce, and guess which one barely nudges the nutrition meter. "Iceberg lettuce has little in common with food—no color, no flavor, almost no calories, and virtually no nutrients," Nadeau says.

Horticulturists have heard the rallying cry and are busy breeding more intensely colored produce. "Our motto is 'foods of color for health,'" says Leonard Pike, Ph.D., professor of horticulture at Texas A&M University in College Station, Texas. "They taste good, look good, and are better for you." Pike is the creator of the hybrid BetaSweet carrot, which is orange on the inside and maroon on the outside. (The carrots became available in fall 2002 in some major supermarket chains.) Pike's colleague, professor David Byrne, Ph.D., is hard at work on red-fleshed "blood peaches" and plums with more red-purple pigments throughout. The pigments add powerful anthocyanins (also found in blueberries and cherries), considerably boosting their antioxidant power.

The point is simple. As Byrne and Pike know, you can use food to paint the picture of health. But experts say you need to eat a diet with the most vibrant colors—and the entire palette of them—to do that. And despite the NCI's five-a-day mantra, seven to nine portions from the color wheel are what adults need for optimum health. Says the NCI's DiSogra, "The science just gets stronger every year."

Anne Underwood, a Newsweek *health and medicine writer, is co-author, along with James Joseph, Ph.D., and Daniel Nadeau, M.D., of* The Color Code.

paint your plate

One of the very first color-themed meals dates to 1889. That's when chef Raffaele Esposito of Naples, Italy, created Pizza Margherita in the Italian national colors—red (tomato sauce), white (mozzarella), and green (basil)—to honor Italy's Queen Margherita. Most of us don't have personal chefs to make sure we eat a variety of colors every day, but here are some tips to help.

Savor smoothies.
Making smoothies is only slightly harder than pouring a glass of orange juice. Toss any fruit you fancy into the blender along with OJ, and you have instantly boosted your color intake. Markets offer peeled and sliced melon, kiwis, strawberries, even mangoes and papayas. Check the freezer section for packages of frozen fruits, including blueberries and raspberries.

Challenge yourself.
Try adding more colors to every dish, from salads to stir-fries to your favorite pasta meal. Combine lettuce with bagged multicolored Asian greens, arugula, and watercress. Add reds (onions, radicchio, and bell peppers), oranges (grated carrots or tangerine sections), and purples (shredded cabbage, raisins, grated beets, or blackberries). Make a stir-fry with a member from every color group—red bell pepper, eggplant, summer squash, and broccoli—and serve over rice. Combine sweet potatoes or butternut squash with leafy greens, garlic, and onion, toss with penne, and top with Parmesan.

Be adventurous.
Odessa Piper, chef-proprietor of L'Etoile Restaurant in Madison, Wisconsin, combs her local farmers' market for the most colorful and intriguing foods she can find, from candy-striped beets to Beauty Heart radishes with magenta flesh and lime-green skin. "The radishes are like an acid trip," Piper says. Can't find these in your market? Online sources like Melissa's (www.melissas.com) carry a wide range of exotic and colorful items.

Chicken Sauté with Peaches and Basil

PREP: 10 MINUTES   COOK: 15 MINUTES
SERVES 4

½ teaspoon salt

¼ teaspoon freshly ground black pepper

4 (4-ounce) skinless, boneless chicken breast halves

2 tablespoons butter

2 cups fresh or frozen sliced peaches

¾ cup fat-free, low-sodium chicken broth

¼ cup chopped shallots

¼ teaspoon finely grated lemon zest

3 large fresh basil leaves, torn

1. Combine the salt and pepper in a zip-top plastic bag with the chicken. Seal and shake well. Melt the butter in a large nonstick skillet over medium-high heat until bubbling. Add the chicken and cook 5 minutes per side until cooked through. Transfer to a plate and cover with foil; keep warm.
2. Combine the peaches, broth, shallots, and lemon zest in the skillet with the drippings. Bring to a simmer and cook 3 minutes until heated through.
3. Remove from heat and stir in the basil. Spoon the sauce and peaches over the chicken.
Note: If using fresh peaches, blanch them in boiling water for 1 minute. Peel, pit, and cut into $^1/_2$-inch-thick wedges to measure 2 cups.

Per serving (1 chicken breast half and $^1/_2$ cup peach mixture): Calories 224; Fat 7g (sat 4g, mono 2g, poly 1g); Protein 28g; Fiber 2g; Cholesterol 81mg; Iron 1mg; Sodium 511mg; Calcium 26mg

Orange, Blackberry, and Honey Dessert Sauce

PREP: 7 MINUTES; SERVES 4

1 cup navel orange sections

1 cup blackberries

1 tablespoon honey

1 tablespoon fresh orange juice

½ pint raspberry sorbet

½ pint vanilla low-fat frozen yogurt

4 tablespoons sliced almonds, toasted

1. Combine oranges (and any juices from cutting board), blackberries, honey, and juice in a bowl.
2. Divide the sorbet and yogurt among 4 bowls. Top with the fruit and sprinkle with nuts.

Per serving (1 scoop sorbet, 1 scoop yogurt, $^1/_3$ cup fruit, 1 tablespoon almonds): Calories 202; Fat 4g (sat 1g, mono 2g, poly 1g); Protein 4g; Fiber 5g; Cholesterol 3mg; Iron 0mg; Sodium 30mg; Calcium 123mg

Roasted Squash and Chard Pasta

PREP: 15 MINUTES   COOK: 40 MINUTES; SERVES 6

4 cups (½-inch) peeled cubed butternut squash

2 cups (1-inch) diced red onion

4 tablespoons olive oil, divided

1¼ teaspoons salt, divided

½ teaspoon freshly ground black pepper, divided

1 pound castellane or orecchiette pasta (such as Barilla)

4 cups torn Swiss chard leaves, stems discarded (about 5 ounces)

2 teaspoons finely chopped fresh sage

3 bacon slices, cooked crisp, cut into ½-inch pieces

¼ cup (1 ounce) shaved fresh Parmesan cheese

1. Preheat oven to 450°.
2. Toss the squash and onion in a large bowl with 2 tablespoons oil, $^1/_2$ teaspoon salt, and $^1/_4$ teaspoon pepper. Spread in a single layer on a nonstick baking sheet, and bake 25 minutes, turning until tender and browned.
3. Cook the pasta according to package directions until al dente. Place chard in a large bowl. Drain the pasta in a sieve over the bowl of chard; let stand 1 minute. Drain chard well; squeeze out excess water. Toss with pasta in a large bowl along with roasted squash and onion, remaining 2 tablespoons oil, remaining salt and pepper, sage, and bacon. Top with cheese and serve.

Per serving (2 cups): Calories 304; Fat 14g (sat 3g, mono 8g, poly 1g); Protein 10g; Fiber 5g; Cholesterol 9mg; Iron 2mg; Sodium 747mg; Calcium 187mg

Mango-Ginger-Strawberry Smoothie

PREP: 5 MINUTES; SERVES 2

1 cup chopped peeled mango

1 cup hulled strawberries

¾ cup crushed ice

½ cup vanilla low-fat yogurt

¼ cup cold water

2 teaspoons minced crystallized ginger

2 teaspoons honey

1. Combine all the ingredients in a blender and puree until well-blended. Pour into 2 glasses.

Per serving ($1^1/2$ cups): Calories 133; Fat 1g (sat 1g, mono 0g, poly 0g); Protein 4g; Fiber 3g; Cholesterol 3mg; Iron 1mg; Sodium 49mg; Calcium 139mg

Raspberry Corn Muffins

PREP: 25 MINUTES   COOK: 20 MINUTES
MAKES 12 MUFFINS

1½ cups all-purpose flour

½ cup yellow cornmeal

½ cup packed brown sugar

1 teaspoon baking powder

1 teaspoon baking soda

¼ teaspoon salt

1¼ cups plain low-fat yogurt

3 tablespoons vegetable oil

1 teaspoon grated lemon rind

2 large eggs, lightly beaten

Cooking spray

1 cup fresh raspberries

½ teaspoon granulated sugar

1. Preheat oven to 375°.

2. Whisk flour and next 5 ingredients in a bowl. Whisk yogurt, oil, lemon rind, and eggs. Pour into flour mixture, stirring until just blended. Spoon batter into 12 muffin cups coated with cooking spray. Sprinkle evenly with raspberries and $^1/2$ teaspoon of sugar.

3. Bake 20 minutes or until muffins spring back when touched lightly in the center. Remove from the oven and cool 5 minutes in the pan. Remove muffins from the pan and transfer to a wire rack to cool.

Per serving (1 muffin): Calories 157; Fat 3g (sat 1g, mono 1g, poly 1g); Protein 4g; Fiber 2g; Cholesterol 2mg; Iron 1mg; Sodium 265mg; Calcium 69mg

Orange-Ginger Salmon with Sautéed Greens

PREP: 30 MINUTES   COOK: 14 MINUTES;   SERVES 4

3 tablespoons low-sodium soy sauce

2 teaspoons grated peeled fresh ginger

1½ teaspoons brown sugar

1 teaspoon finely grated fresh orange zest

4 (4-ounce) skinless salmon fillets (about 1 inch thick)

2 teaspoons vegetable oil

3 cups coarsely chopped fresh basil

¼ teaspoon salt

⅛ teaspoon freshly ground black pepper

2 garlic cloves, minced

1 pound fresh spinach, stems trimmed (about 16 cups)

1 teaspoon dark sesame oil

1. Combine the soy sauce, ginger, brown sugar, and orange zest in a zip-top plastic bag. Add the fish and marinate 20 minutes (or longer in refrigerator). Remove the fish; reserve marinade.

2. Heat the vegetable oil in a large nonstick skillet over medium-high heat. Add the fish and cook 3 minutes, without turning. Reduce heat to medium, turn the fish, and cover. Cook 3 minutes or until just cooked through. Transfer to a plate. Cover with foil; keep warm.

3. Return the skillet to the heat. To make glaze, pour the marinade into the skillet and bring to a boil. Simmer 1 minute. Transfer to a bowl and cover with foil. Wipe out skillet with a paper towel.

4. Return the skillet to medium-high heat. Add half the basil, salt, pepper, garlic, spinach, and 3 tablespoons water. Cover and cook 2 minutes, or until the spinach is wilted. Transfer to a bowl and repeat with remaining basil, salt, pepper, garlic, spinach, and water. Combine with other spinach and toss with sesame oil.

5. Divide the greens among 4 plates. Top with the salmon, drizzle with glaze, and serve.

Per serving (1 salmon filet, $^2/3$ cup spinach mixture, and $1^1/2$ teaspoons glaze): Calories 287; Fat 16g (sat 3g, mono 5g, poly 7g); Protein 27g; Fiber 5g; Cholesterol 67mg; Iron 5mg; Sodium 705mg; Calcium 182mg ✳

New York–based food writer Lori Longbotham is the author of **Lemon Zest.**

When Salad Makes a Supper

RECIPES AND TEXT BY LESLIE REVSIN

We admit it. Sometimes, we crave salads. Well, maybe "crave" is too strong a word, better reserved for chocolate and caffeine. Honestly, though, especially when the weather gets warmer, we desire the cool crunch of fresh veggies dressed with the tang of a perfect vinaigrette. But the lettuce-and-tomato version that passes for a side dish just isn't enough to get us through our salad days: We want main-dish versions with some bulk and body to satisfy our not-quite craving. These salads do the trick, incorporating grains and legumes, seafood and poultry. Their textures and components—from chewy whole-wheat berries with grilled chicken and apples to fragrant basmati rice tossed with sun-dried tomatoes, feta cheese, and fresh mint—take taste buds into new territory.

Tabbouleh Cobb Salad

SERVES 4
PREPARATION: 15 MINUTES
SOAKING: 30 MINUTES

TABBOULEH:
½ cup boiling water
½ cup uncooked bulgur
¼ cup chopped fresh parsley
1 tablespoon fresh lemon juice
1 tablespoon olive oil
¼ teaspoon black pepper

SALAD:
8 cups torn romaine lettuce
2 cups cubed smoked turkey breast (about 12 ounces)
2 cups grape or cherry tomatoes, halved
1 cup seeded chopped cucumber
1 cup thinly sliced green onion
1 (15-ounce) can chickpeas (garbanzo beans), drained
¾ cup Roasted Red Pepper Dressing (recipe follows)

1. To prepare tabbouleh, combine water and bulgur; let stand 30 minutes.
2. Combine bulgur mixture, parsley, lemon juice, oil, and pepper.
3. To prepare salad, place 2 cups of lettuce in each of 4 shallow bowls. Divide tabbouleh and remaining ingredients evenly in rows over lettuce, starting with ¹/₄ cup tabbouleh, ¹/₂ cup each turkey and tomatoes, ¹/₄ cup each cucumber and onion, and about ¹/₃ cup chickpeas. Drizzle with 3 tablespoons dressing. Serving size: 1 salad.

Per serving: Calories 336 (26% from fat); Fat 10.5g (sat 2.5g, mono 4.2g, poly 1.5g); Protein 26g; Carbohydrate 42g; Fiber 12g; Cholesterol 46mg; Iron 5mg; Sodium 1,092mg; Calcium 115mg

Roasted Red Pepper Dressing

SERVES 4
PREPARATION: 5 MINUTES

1½ tablespoons vegetable broth
1 tablespoon red wine vinegar
1½ teaspoons olive oil
½ teaspoon salt
½ teaspoon Dijon mustard
¼ teaspoon dried thyme
¼ teaspoon black pepper
2 (7-ounce) bottles roasted red bell peppers, drained

1. Place all ingredients in a blender and process until smooth. Refrigerate dressing in an airtight container for up to 1 week. Serving size: 3 tablespoons.

Per serving: Calories 49 (43% from fat); Fat 2.4g (sat 0.4g, mono 1.3g, poly 0.5g); Protein 1.4g; Carbohydrate 5.6g; Fiber 0.8g; Cholesterol 0mg; Iron 1mg; Sodium 692mg; Calcium 13mg

Grilled Chicken and Wheat-Berry Salad

SERVES 16
PREPARATION: 4 MINUTES
COOKING: 2 HOURS, 15 MINUTES
GRILLING: 10 MINUTES

Although they need little tending, the wheat berries do require a long cooking time. You may want to boil them on the week-end or the night before.

4 cups water
1 cup hard winter wheat berries, rinsed and drained
1 bay leaf
2 cups baby spinach leaves, divided
1 cup green apple, peeled and cut into julienne strips
½ cup diced red bell pepper
3 tablespoons Cucumber Yogurt Dressing (recipe follows)
2 teaspoons Dijon mustard
4 (4-ounce) skinless, boneless chicken breasts
¼ teaspoon salt
¼ teaspoon black pepper
Cooking spray
¼ cup chopped green onion

1. Preheat grill.
2. Combine first 3 ingredients in a saucepan over medium-high heat. Bring mixture to a simmer; cover and cook for 2 hours, 15 minutes or until wheat berries are almost tender. Drain and place in a bowl; discard bay leaf. Coarsely chop 1 cup spinach leaves. Add chopped spinach leaves, apple, bell pepper, dressing, and mustard to the wheat berries, and toss well.
3. Sprinkle chicken with salt and pepper. Place chicken on a grill rack coated with cooking spray; grill 5 minutes on each side or until done. Thinly slice chicken.
4. Divide remaining spinach evenly among 4 plates. Place ½ cup wheat-berry mixture on top of spinach. Arrange chicken evenly over berry mixture; sprinkle with green onions.

Per serving: Calories 332 (31% from fat); Fat 12g (sat 2g, mono 6.7g, poly 1.4g); Protein 29g; Carbohydrate 30.1g; Fiber 3g; Cholesterol 63mg; Iron 4mg; Sodium 792mg; Calcium 113mg

Cucumber Yogurt Dressing

SERVES 16
PREPARATION: 10 MINUTES

1 cup chopped seeded peeled cucumber
3 tablespoons plain low-fat yogurt
2 tablespoons olive oil
1 teaspoon balsamic vinegar
¼ teaspoon salt
¼ teaspoon black pepper
⅛ teaspoon dried dill

1. Place all ingredients in a blender and process until the mixture is smooth. Refrigerate dressing in an airtight container for up to 1 week. Serving size: 1 tablespoon.
Note: Though 86 percent of the calories from this dressing come from fat, it still has less than 2 grams of fat per tablespoon—far less than full-fat dressings, which carry anywhere from 7 to 10 grams of fat per tablespoon.

Per serving: Calories 18 (86% from fat); Fat 1.8g (sat 0.3g, mono 1.3g, poly 0.2g); Protein 0.2g; Carbohydrate 0.5g; Fiber 0.1g; Cholesterol 0mg; Iron 0mg; Sodium 39mg; Calcium 7mg

Grilled-Vegetable Salad with Lentils

SERVES 4
PREPARATION: 25 MINUTES
COOKING: 35 MINUTES

LENTILS:

1⅓ cups dried lentils

4 cups water

1 bay leaf

½ cup finely chopped red onion

2 tablespoons coarsely chopped walnuts

1½ tablespoons extra-virgin olive oil

1½ tablespoons red wine vinegar

1 teaspoon dried herbes de Provence

½ teaspoon salt

¼ teaspoon black pepper

1 small garlic clove, minced

VEGETABLES:

24 asparagus spears, trimmed (about 12 ounces)

2 zucchini, cut diagonally into 1-inch-thick slices

1 small yellow bell pepper, quartered

1 small orange bell pepper, quartered

1 small red bell pepper, quartered

1 (12-ounce) eggplant, cut crosswise into
  ½-inch-thick slices

1½ tablespoons olive oil

2 teaspoons red wine vinegar

1 teaspoon chopped fresh or ¼ teaspoon dried thyme

1 teaspoon dried herbes de Provence

½ teaspoon salt

¼ teaspoon black pepper

1. Prepare grill.
2. To prepare lentils, rinse and drain lentils. Place water, lentils, and bay leaf in a medium saucepan; bring to a boil. Reduce heat and simmer 20 minutes. Drain; discard bay leaf. Combine lentils, red onion, and the next 7 ingredients (through garlic) in a large bowl.
3. To prepare vegetables, combine asparagus and next 6 ingredients (through oil) in a large bowl, and toss well to coat. Grill zucchini, peppers, and eggplant 15 minutes, turning once. Grill asparagus 6 minutes, turning once. Place vegetables in a bowl; drizzle with 2 teaspoons vinegar. Sprinkle with remaining ingredients; toss well to coat. Serve with lentils. Serving size:

1 cup lentils, 3 quarters bell pepper, half a zucchini, and about 3 slices eggplant.

Per serving: Calories 404 (29% from fat); Fat 13.8g (sat 1.8g, mono 8g, poly 3.2g); Protein 20g; Carbohydrate 55g; Fiber 21g; Cholesterol 0mg; Iron 8mg; Sodium 599mg; Calcium 110mg

Mediterranean Basmati Salad

SERVES 4
PREPARATION: 10 MINUTES
SOAKING: 40 MINUTES
COOKING: 25 MINUTES

2 sun-dried tomatoes, packed without oil

¼ cup hot water

1¼ cups uncooked basmati rice

2 cups water

½ teaspoon salt

⅔ cup (2.5 ounces) feta cheese, crumbled

2 tablespoons dried currants

2 tablespoons chopped fresh mint

1 tablespoon olive oil

¼ teaspoon black pepper

2 tablespoons pine nuts, toasted

1. Combine tomatoes and water in a small bowl; let stand 10 minutes. Drain and chop; set aside.
2. Place rice in a large bowl; cover with water to 2 inches above rice. Soak 30 minutes; stirring occasionally. Drain and rinse.
3. Combine rice and 2 cups water in a small saucepan; stir in salt. Bring to a boil over medium-high heat, stirring frequently. Boil 5 minutes or until water level falls just below rice. Cover, reduce heat to low, and cook 10 minutes. Remove from heat; let stand, covered, 10 minutes.
4. Spoon rice into a bowl; cool completely and fluff with a fork. Stir in tomatoes, feta, and next 4 ingredients (through pepper); toss well to combine. Sprinkle with pine nuts. Serving size: 1½ cups.

Per serving: Calories 358 (29% from fat); Fat 11.7g (sat 4.8g, mono 4.7g, poly 1.7g); Protein 10g; Carbohydrate 57g; Fiber 1g; Cholesterol 22mg; Iron 1mg; Sodium 609mg; Calcium 142mg

Panzanella Salad with Shrimp

SERVES 6
PREPARATION: 20 MINUTES
COOKING: 10 MINUTES

6 cups (½-inch) cubed day-old country-style wheat bread
1½ tablespoons fresh lemon juice
3 tablespoons olive oil, divided
1 teaspoon finely chopped fresh rosemary
½ teaspoon salt, divided
¼ teaspoon freshly ground black pepper
2 garlic cloves, minced and divided
8 cups chopped plum tomato (about 16)
6 pitted kalamata olives, chopped
1½ pounds large shrimp, peeled and deveined
1 cup torn fresh basil leaves

1. Preheat oven to 425°.
2. Arrange bread cubes on a baking sheet; bake at 425° for 5 minutes or until lightly toasted and dry. Cool completely; set aside.
3. Combine lemon juice and 2^1/$_2$ tablespoons oil in a large bowl; stir with a whisk. Stir in rosemary, ^{1}/$_4$ teaspoon salt, pepper, and 1 garlic clove. Add tomatoes and olives; mix well.
4. Heat 1^1/$_2$ teaspoons oil in a large nonstick skillet; add shrimp and ^{1}/$_4$ teaspoon salt. Cook 3 minutes, stirring occasionally; add 1 garlic clove. Cook 2 minutes or until shrimp are cooked through. Remove from heat.
5. Add bread cubes and shrimp to tomato mixture; toss. Add basil; toss to combine. Serve immediately. Serving size: 2 cups.

Per serving: Calories 498 (28% from fat); Fat 15.7g (sat 2.3g, mono 7.6g, poly 4.6g); Protein 33g; Carbohydrate 59g; Fiber 8g; Cholesterol 172mg; Iron 7mg; Sodium 767mg; Calcium 125mg ✳

Leslie Revsin is the author of Great Fish, Quick, *a finalist for the Julia Child Award. She is currently working on a book about entertaining.*

Q+A
Frozen Vegetables vs. Fresh

How do canned and frozen vegetables compare with fresh, nutritionwise?

BY THE TIME VEGGIES go from store to stove to table, there's very little difference in nutritional value among fresh, canned, and frozen. So it's best to focus on just getting your veggies...period.

Many nutrients begin to fade as fresh produce is transported to supermarket aisles. Frozen and canned veggies go from harvest to the package within hours, giving them a slight edge over, say, fresh artichokes that take a road trip from California to the East Coast. But the cooking process necessary to package canned and frozen veggies can reduce nutrients, wiping out any significant nutritional advantage.

In some cases, canned and frozen vegetables are actually more nutritious than their fresh counterparts. Canned pumpkin is higher in vitamin A than fresh, and canned tomatoes have an edge over fresh in the benefits derived from lycopene, a nutrient that has been linked to a lower incidence of several different kinds of cancer. The caveat: Some canned veggies contain 10 times more sodium than fresh or frozen. Choose low-sodium versions if you can.

What really drains nutrients is overcooking or boiling veggies in too much water. Steaming or microwaving them until they're just crisp-tender is best.

keep veggies fresh

To avoid limp-lettuce syndrome, wrap unwashed veggies in paper towels and tuck them into unsealed plastic bags in the crisper.

—University of California–Berkeley Wellness Letter

GREAT GRAINS

Expand your whole-grains glossary and experience their delicious diversity with these eight must-make recipes.

TEXT BY LIZ ZACK

RECIPES BY CINDA CHAVICH

Like flossing, getting regular oil changes, and making nice to your brother's whiny wife, eating whole grains is something you probably don't do as often as you should. You know brown rice is better than white and that whole wheat beats Wonder Bread, but how often do you actually act on that information?

Just how good whole grains are for you definitely bears repeating. Packed with serious fiber, protein, and carbohydrates, whole grains can take a merely average diet to the next level. In contrast, processed grains, such as white flour and white rice, are stripped of their nutrients during milling. Alton Brown, the host of the Food Network television show *Good Eats*, explains it this way. "Imagine yourself as wheat," he says. "You're wearing a coat and you're carrying a purse. The coat is the outer bran and the purse is the wheat germ, the actual seed. To make white flour, you get rid of your coat and drop your purse." But the "coat" and the "purse" aren't just your accessories: The bran is where most of the fiber in grains resides, and the germ packs significant quantities of heart-healthy vitamin E.

The catch is, many of us don't know that there are options beyond brown rice and whole-wheat bread. There's a whole world of grains out there—from bulgur to kasha to barley—that have flavors and textures all their own. We've created eight nutrient-packed dishes featuring a variety of grains, some unique and some old standbys, to show you how you can reap their delicious benefits—without ever having to OD on brown rice again.

Four-Grain Flapjacks

SERVES 9
PREPARATION: 30 MINUTES
COOKING: 10 MINUTES

1 cup barley flour
½ cup whole-wheat flour
½ cup regular oats
½ cup stone-ground yellow cornmeal
1½ teaspoons baking soda
1 teaspoon baking powder
Dash of salt
2½ cups nonfat buttermilk
¼ cup maple syrup
¼ cup butter, melted
3 large egg yolks
3 large egg whites
Cooking spray

1. Lightly spoon barley flour and wheat flour into dry measuring cups; level with a knife. Combine barley

whole grains defined

Pearl barley: The same grain that's malted to make beer and whiskey gets steamed and polished into pearls. Pearl barley can be ground to make barley flour; whole, it makes a great addition to soups and stews.

Oats: Oats are the most nutritious of the cereal grasses (with instant oatmeal some of the fiber gets lost in the processing).

Wheat berries: Wheat berries are whole, unprocessed kernels of wheat with a nutty, crunchy texture. Look for them in health-food stores or large supermarkets, and add them to soups, breads, and hot cereals.

Whole-wheat flour: An unmilled version of white flour, whole-wheat flour makes hearty pasta and deeply flavored breads. To convert a regular bread recipe into a whole-wheat recipe, substitute half of the white flour with whole-wheat flour.

Cornmeal: Made by grinding dried corn kernels, cornmeal can be yellow, white, or blue, depending on the type of corn used. Water-ground (rather than the more common steel-ground variety) is healthier because it contains some of the hull and germ. It can last up to four months in the refrigerator.

Wheat germ: Wheat germ is the nutrient-packed center of the wheat berry, the source of all the vitamins, minerals, and proteins. It adds a nutty flavor to hot cereals and yeast breads.

Bulgur: Bulgur is made from wheat kernels that have been steamed, dried, and crushed. Its tender, chewy texture is favored by Middle Eastern cooks.

Flaxseed: Flaxseed has calcium, niacin, vitamin E, and iron. It is a great way to get omega-3 fatty acids.

Millet: One-third of the world's population eats millet as a staple of their diets. Rich in protein, the tiny grains are prepared like rice, or ground and used like flour.

kasha: Kasha—aka, roasted buckwheat groats—have a nutty, toasty flavor that makes them perfect for pilafs.

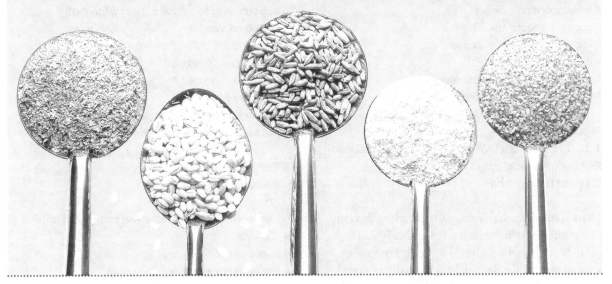

flour, wheat flour, and next 5 ingredients (through salt) in a large bowl; stir with a whisk.

2. Combine buttermilk, maple syrup, butter, and egg yolks in a bowl, and stir with a whisk. Add buttermilk mixture to flour mixture, stirring until combined.

3. Beat egg whites with an electric mixer at high speed until stiff peaks form (do not overbeat). Fold into batter. Spoon about $1/3$ cup batter onto a hot nonstick griddle or nonstick skillet coated with cooking spray. Turn flapjacks when tops are covered with bubbles and edges are cooked. Serving size: 2 flapjacks.

Per serving: 247 Calories (29% from fat); Fat 8.2g (sat 4.2g, mono 2.5g, poly 0.8g); Protein 8.4g; Carbohydrate 35.8g; Fiber 3.5g; Cholesterol 87mg; Iron 1.6mg; Sodium 434mg; Calcium 116mg

Creamy Polenta with Artichoke, Caramelized Onion, and Olive Ragout

SERVES 4
PREPARATION: 30 MINUTES
COOKING: 60 MINUTES
STANDING: 30 MINUTES

POLENTA:

5 cups water

1 tablespoon butter

¼ teaspoon salt

1 cup stone-ground yellow cornmeal

1 cup frozen whole-kernel corn, thawed

½ cup (2 ounces) shredded fresh Parmesan cheese

3 tablespoons fat-free sour cream

1 tablespoon chopped fresh basil

RAGOUT:

1 cup boiling water

½ cup sun-dried tomatoes, packed without oil

2 tablespoons olive oil

3 cups thinly sliced onion

2 cups chopped red bell pepper

4 garlic cloves, minced

1 teaspoon Hungarian sweet paprika

¼ teaspoon crushed red pepper

½ cup dry white wine

½ cup water

1 (14-ounce) can artichoke hearts, drained and chopped

2 tablespoons sliced ripe olives

Chopped basil (optional)

1. To prepare polenta, bring water to a boil in a large saucepan; stir in butter and salt. Gradually add cornmeal, stirring well with a whisk. Cook 5 minutes, stirring constantly. Reduce heat to medium; cook 15 minutes, stirring frequently. Stir in corn; cook 1 minute. Remove from heat; stir in cheese, sour cream, and basil. Cover; set aside.

2. To prepare ragout, combine boiling water and sun-dried tomatoes in a bowl; let stand 30 minutes or until soft. Drain and slice.

3. Heat oil in a large nonstick skillet over medium-high heat. Add onion; cook 15 minutes or until lightly browned, stirring frequently. Add bell pepper and garlic; cook 15 minutes or until golden brown, stirring

frequently. Stir in paprika and crushed red pepper. Add tomatoes, wine, water, and artichokes; stir well. Cover, reduce heat to low; simmer 10 minutes. Stir in olives. Serve over polenta. Garnish with chopped basil, if desired. Serving size: 1 cup polenta and ³/₄ cup ragout.

Per serving: Calories 366 (29% from fat); Fat 12.5g (sat 4.9g, mono 4.8g, poly 1.3g); Protein 13.7g; Carbohydrate 52.2g; Fiber 7.7g; Cholesterol 18mg; Iron 2.4mg; Sodium 983mg; Calcium 216mg

Whole-Wheat Pasta Shells with Spicy Tomato Pesto and Winter Greens

SERVES 5
PREPARATION: 15 MINUTES
COOKING: 13 MINUTES
STANDING: 30 MINUTES

PESTO:

1 cup boiling water

½ cup sun-dried tomatoes, packed without oil

¼ cup sliced almonds

¼ cup (1 ounce) grated Parmesan cheese

¼ cup chopped fresh basil

2 garlic cloves, minced

½ teaspoon salt

¼ teaspoon crushed red pepper

1½ tablespoons extra-virgin olive oil

GREENS:

1 tablespoon olive oil

1 cup chopped onion

3 cups trimmed Swiss chard, sliced into ½-inch strips

¼ cup water

¼ teaspoon salt

¼ teaspoon black pepper

PASTA:

8 cups hot cooked (about 4 cups uncooked) whole-wheat pasta shells

4 teaspoons grated fresh Parmesan cheese

1. To prepare pesto, combine boiling water and sun-dried tomatoes in a bowl; let stand 30 minutes or until soft. Drain tomatoes in a colander over a bowl, reserving ¹/₂ cup liquid.

2. Drop tomatoes, almonds, cheese, basil, and garlic through food chute with food processor on; process until minced. Keeping processor on, add salt and red pepper. Slowly pour $1^1/_2$ tablespoons oil through food chute; process until well-blended, scraping sides. Add reserved soaking liquid 1 tablespoon at a time until mixture appears smooth. Set aside.

3. To prepare greens, heat 1 tablespoon oil in a large nonstick skillet over medium-high heat. Add onion; cook 10 minutes or until lightly browned, stirring frequently. Add Swiss chard; stir-fry 1 minute or until leaves turn bright green. Add water, salt, and pepper; cover and cook 2 minutes.

4. Combine pesto and hot cooked pasta in a large bowl; toss well. Add greens mixture; toss well. Sprinkle with Parmesan. Serving size: 2 cups.

Per serving: 355 Calories (30% from fat); Fat 12.4g (sat 2.6g, mono 7.1g, poly 1.6g); Protein 14.3g; Carbohydrate 51.9g; Fiber 6.6g; Cholesterol 5mg; Iron 2.9mg; Sodium 608mg; Calcium 147mg

Kasha Pilaf

SERVES 4
PREPARATION: 10 MINUTES
COOKING: 21 MINUTES

1 cup uncooked kasha (buckwheat groats)
1 large egg, lightly beaten
1 tablespoon olive oil
1½ teaspoons butter
1½ cups chopped onion
¼ teaspoon salt
1 (15.75-ounce) can fat-free, less-sodium
  chicken broth
1 tablespoon chopped fresh or 1 teaspoon dried dill

1. Combine kasha and egg in a small bowl; stir well.
2. Heat oil and butter in a large saucepan over medium heat. Add onion; cook 5 minutes or until soft. Add kasha mixture; cook 1 minute. Stir in salt and broth; bring to a boil. Cover, reduce heat, and simmer 15 minutes or until kasha is tender.
3. Remove from heat; fluff with a fork. Stir in dill. Serving size: $1^1/_4$ cups.

Per serving: Calories 229 (30% from fat); Fat 8g (sat 2.4g, mono 3.7g, poly 0.9g); Protein 8.2g; Carbohydrate 34g; Fiber 4.7g; Cholesterol 59mg; Iron 1.3mg; Sodium 382mg; Calcium 27mg

Tuscan Wheat-Berry Soup with White Beans

SERVES 6
SOAKING: 3 HOURS
PREPARATION: 10 MINUTES
COOKING: 85 MINUTES

1½ cups uncooked wheat berries or spelt
4 cups water
3 celery stalks, coarsely chopped
3 garlic cloves, minced
1 large onion, quartered
1 carrot, peeled, coarsely chopped
2 tablespoons olive oil
2 teaspoons chopped fresh rosemary
1 (14½-ounce) can plum tomatoes, drained and chopped
1 cup dry white wine
2 (16-ounce) cans cannellini beans or other white beans,
  rinsed and drained, divided
3 (15.75-ounce) cans fat-free, less-sodium chicken broth
½ teaspoon salt
¼ teaspoon black pepper

1. Soak wheat berries in water for 3 hours; drain.
2. Place celery, garlic, onion, and carrot in a food processor; process until vegetables are finely chopped.
3. Heat oil in a large Dutch oven over medium-high heat. Add onion mixture; sauté 15 minutes or until onion is tender. Stir in rosemary and tomatoes. Reduce heat; simmer 10 minutes.
4. Place wine and 1 can beans in a blender or food processor; process until smooth. Add bean mixture to vegetable mixture. Stir in chicken broth; bring to a boil. Stir in wheat berries; cover, reduce heat, and simmer 1 hour or until wheat berries are tender-crunchy. Stir in salt, pepper, and remaining can of beans. Remove from heat; cover and let stand 5 minutes. Serving size: $1^3/_4$ cup.

Per serving: 251 Calories (24% from fat); Fat 7.2g (sat 1.4g, mono 3.3g, poly 0.6g); Protein 9.4g; Carbohydrate 37.4g; Fiber 3.2g; Cholesterol 4mg; Iron 2.5mg; Sodium 501mg; Calcium 66mg

Bulgur with Roasted Eggplant and Peppers

SERVES 4
PREPARATION: 25 MINUTES
COOKING: 60 MINUTES
STANDING: 20 MINUTES

5 cups (1-inch) cubed peeled eggplant (about 1 pound)
¾ teaspoon salt, divided
1½ cups chopped red bell pepper
1½ cups chopped yellow bell pepper
2 cups chopped onion
2 tablespoons and ¼ teaspoon olive oil, divided
Cooking spray
¼ teaspoon freshly ground black pepper
1 whole garlic head
1 teaspoon ground cumin
½ teaspoon ground turmeric
¼ teaspoon ground ginger
1 (15.75-ounce) can fat-free, less-sodium chicken broth
1 cup coarsely ground uncooked bulgur wheat
2 tablespoons chopped fresh parsley
1 tablespoon fresh lemon juice

1. Preheat oven to 450°.
2. Place eggplant in a colander. Sprinkle with ½ teaspoon salt; toss. Let stand 20 minutes. Drain and pat dry with paper towels. Combine eggplant, bell peppers, onion, and 1 tablespoon oil in a large bowl; toss well. Spread eggplant mixture evenly in a jelly-roll pan coated with cooking spray; sprinkle with ¼ teaspoon salt and black pepper.
3. Remove white, papery skin from garlic head (do not peel or separate the cloves). Cut off top ¼ inch of garlic head using a serrated knife; discard top. Rub ¼ teaspoon oil over bottom portion of garlic head. Add garlic head, cut side up, to eggplant mixture. Bake at 450° for 40 minutes or until vegetables are browned, stirring occasionally.
4. Heat 1 tablespoon oil in a large Dutch oven over medium-high heat. Add cumin, turmeric, ginger, and chicken broth. Bring to a boil. Stir in bulgur; cover, reduce heat, and simmer over medium-low heat 20 minutes or until liquid is absorbed.
5. Remove garlic from eggplant mixture. Separate cloves; squeeze to extract garlic pulp. Discard skins. Stir garlic pulp, eggplant mixture, parsley,

and lemon juice into bulgur mixture. Serving size: 1 cup.

Per serving: Calories 300 (25% from fat); Fat 9.1 (sat 1.5g, mono 5.3g, poly 1g); Protein 9.5g; Carbohydrate 50.6g; Fiber 13.1g; Cholesterol 2mg; Iron 2.5mg; Sodium 511mg; Calcium 80mg

Spicy Sausage, Barley, and Mushroom Stew

SERVES 6
PREPARATION: 15 MINUTES
COOKING: 95 MINUTES

2 teaspoons olive oil
2 cups thinly sliced onion
8 ounces spicy turkey Italian sausage
1 cup chopped celery
1 cup sliced carrot
2 garlic cloves, minced
1 bay leaf
5 cups thinly sliced shiitake mushroom caps (about ½ pound mushrooms)
1½ cups chopped portobello mushroom
½ cup uncooked pearl barley
3 (15.75-ounce) cans fat-free, less-sodium chicken broth
2 tablespoons brandy
1 teaspoon salt
¼ teaspoon freshly ground black pepper
⅓ cup coarsely chopped fresh parsley

1. Heat oil in a large Dutch oven over medium heat. Add onion; cook 5 minutes or until slightly soft. Remove casings from sausage. Add sausage to pan; cook 8 minutes or until sausage is browned, stirring to crumble. Add celery, carrot, garlic, and bay leaf; cook 10 minutes or until onions are golden brown, stirring frequently. Stir in mushrooms; cook 10 minutes or until mushrooms release moisture. Stir in barley, chicken broth, brandy, salt, and pepper. Bring to a boil; cover, reduce heat, and simmer 1 hour or until barley is tender. Discard bay leaf. Sprinkle with parsley. Serve immediately. Serving size: about 1 cup.

Per serving: 215 Calories (30% from fat); Fat 7.2g (sat 2g, mono 2.5g, poly 1.8g); Protein 13.3g; Carbohydrates 23.4g; Fiber 4.7g; Cholesterol 27mg; Iron 2.4mg; Sodium 527mg; Calcium 54mg

Hearty Multigrain Bread

SERVES 24
PREPARATION: 30 MINUTES
COOKING: 35 MINUTES
RISING: 2 HOURS

DOUGH:

1⅔ cups fat-free milk

⅔ cup quick-cooking oats

⅓ cup wheat germ

⅓ cup yellow cornmeal

2 cups whole-wheat flour, divided

2 packages active dry yeast

1 cup warm water (100° to 110°)

3 tablespoons canola oil

3 tablespoons dark molasses

1 tablespoon honey

2 teaspoons flaxseed

2 teaspoons poppy seeds

2 teaspoons uncooked millet

1¼ teaspoons salt

3 cups all-purpose flour, divided

Cooking spray

TOPPING:

1 tablespoon fat-free milk

1 large egg

1 teaspoon flaxseed

1 teaspoon poppy seeds

1 teaspoon uncooked millet

1 teaspoon quick-cooking oats

1. To prepare dough, cook 1²/₃ cups milk in a heavy saucepan over medium-high heat to 180° or until tiny bubbles form around edge (do not boil). Remove from heat. Combine ²/₃ cup oats, wheat germ, and cornmeal in a large bowl; stir in scalded milk. Cool until warm (100° to 110°).

2. Lightly spoon whole-wheat flour into dry measuring cups; level with a knife. Combine 1¹/₂ cups wheat flour and yeast in a bowl, stirring with a whisk. Add flour mixture to milk mixture; stir well to combine. Add water and next 7 ingredients (through salt) to milk mixture; stir until well blended.

3. Lightly spoon all-purpose flour into dry measuring cups; level with a knife. Add ¹/₂ cup whole-wheat flour and 2¹/₂ cups all purpose flour to milk mixture;

stir until a soft dough forms. Turn dough out onto a floured surface; let rest 5 minutes. Knead dough until smooth and elastic (about 8 minutes); add enough of remaining flour, 1 tablespoon at a time, to prevent dough from sticking to hands (dough will feel tacky).

4. Place dough in a large bowl coated with cooking spray, turning to coat top. Cover and let rise in a warm place (85°), free from drafts, 1 hour or until doubled in size. (Press two fingers into dough. If indentation remains, dough has risen enough.) Punch dough down; cover and let rest 5 minutes. Divide in half. Working with one portion at a time (cover remaining dough to keep from drying), roll each portion into a 13 x 7-inch rectangle on a floured surface. Roll up each rectangle tightly, starting with a long edge, pressing firmly to eliminate air pockets; pinch seam and ends to seal. Place each roll, seam side down, in an 8 x 4-inch loaf pan coated with cooking spray. Cover and let rise 1 hour or until doubled in size. (Press two fingers into dough. If indentation remains, dough has risen enough.)

5. Preheat oven to 375°.

6. To prepare topping, combine 1 tablespoon milk and egg in a small bowl; brush over loaves. Combine flaxseed, poppy seeds, millet, and 1 teaspoon oats in a bowl; sprinkle seed mixture over loaves.

7. Bake at 375° for 15 minutes. Reduce heat to 350°, bake 20 minutes or until loaves are browned on bottom and sound hollow when tapped. Remove from pan; cool on wire racks. Serving size: 1 slice.

Per serving: 154 Calories (17% from fat); Fat 3g (sat 0.4g, mono 1.3g, poly 0.9g); Protein 5.4g; Carbohydrate 27g; Fiber 2.5g; Cholesterol 9mg; Iron 2mg; Sodium 137mg; Calcium 50mg ✳

Freelance writer Liz Zack is working on a book about gourmet packed lunches. Cinda Chavich's latest book is High Plains: The Joy of Alberta Cuisine.

FIGHT BACTERIA:
Dry your Dishes

Be sure to dry your next batch of clean dishes before you shelve them: Dishes stowed in the cabinet wet are breeding grounds for bacteria.

—*Journal of the American Dietetic Association*

Take a Second Look at Soy

This wonder food has come under attack. Is the backlash warranted?

BY LYNN PROWITT-SMITH

You probably know people like me: I'm the type who gets worked up reading ingredient labels. I pay unfathomable prices for organic blueberries. And I am, of course, fully fluent in soy: I make a great tofu stir-fry, love miso, and can recommend the best soy ice cream—I've tried them all. Soy's a staple in my house, and not just because it tastes good. As you've likely heard, it contains plant chemicals thought to help prevent some of the top killer diseases, including heart disease, osteoporosis, prostate cancer, and breast cancer.

But lately, my miracle food has come under attack. Some research has linked soy to increased risk of kidney stones, thyroid problems, Alzheimer's disease, and even breast cancer. Before I trashed my Tofutti Cuties, though, I went digging for the real story. What I found: lots of research, some of it conflicting and some of it confusing. But the take-home message from health experts is that soy is still good for most women—but we shouldn't overdo it. Here's a look at the studies and the warnings, plus some advice about how relevant they are to you.

Cancer causer?

U.S. researchers started tracking soy when they found that Asian women have a much lower incidence of heart disease and breast cancer than do American women. While there are many possible reasons for these health differences, scientists zeroed in on the higher amounts of soy in the typical Asian diet. Soy contains large concentrations of plant chemicals called isoflavones, which fall into a class of compounds known as phytoestrogens ("phyto" simply means "plant"). Isoflavones have a tiny fraction of the power of estradiol, the estrogen that courses through women's bodies. A few studies have shown that soy consumption or isoflavone intake can

Many of the cautions surrounding soy are unfounded or meant for people with special conditions. But **soy can have powerful effects,** and, as with any food, it should be eaten in moderation.

lower levels of estradiol in women by 20 percent or more. Over years or decades, that could protect women from tumors that feed on estrogen, particularly breast tumors.

Using the same logic, however, other researchers arrived at the opposite conclusion: Because isoflavones behave like estrogen, they could actually stimulate the growth of estrogen-dependent tumors in certain cases. This flip-flop doesn't help when you're in the grocery store trying to decide on dinner.

The problem is that hundreds of studies on isoflavones and breast cancer have turned up dramatically conflicting results. In test-tube and animal studies, isoflavones have been shown both to inhibit and accelerate the growth of breast-cancer cells. However, most—but not all—of the relatively few human studies have concluded that eating soy may decrease breast-cancer risk.

The key may be in the timing. The decision on whether to eat soy—and how much—may depend largely on your life stage. For instance, most researchers now think that soy is most protective before and possibly during puberty, because it may change the structure of the breast tissue to make it more resistant to cancer later in life. During adolescence, breast cells grow rapidly and are more vulnerable to cancer-causing influences. Since the potential for damage is great, the benefits of soy may be the most valuable during this stage.

Soy also gets the green light for women in their child-bearing years. Experts such as Claude Hughes, M.D., Ph.D., a consulting professor in the department of obstetrics and gynecology at Duke University Medical Center, believe that soy will help premenopausal women decrease breast-cancer risk in later years. "Once a woman is through puberty, it's reasonable to suppose that the less estrogen her breast is bathed in, the better," he says.

But he says that women who are pregnant or nursing may want to limit soy intake. In studies, rats exposed to soy in utero were more prone to developing tumors. "We know that, in humans, phytoestrogens get into the amniotic fluid," Hughes says. While he acknowledges that animal studies don't always predict what will happen in humans, Hughes advises pregnant and nursing women to play it safe and eat only a couple of servings of soy each week.

The key may be in the timing. The decision on whether to eat soy—and how much—may depend largely on **your life stage.**

how much soy?

We took a look at a few common soy products to see how isoflavone amounts stacked up. For healthy people, the closest there is to an expert recommendation is to eat like the Japanese—which means about 30 to 40 milligrams per day. Be aware, though, that isoflavone content can vary even within one brand, so use this chart as a guideline only. Check the labels and, if they don't list isoflavone content, estimate 2 milligrams of isoflavones for every gram of soy protein listed.

milligrams of isoflavones per 3.5-ounce serving

soy sauce 2
soy breakfast sausage 4
soy noodles 9
soy milk 10
immature soybeans
   (edamame, green soybeans) 14
soy hot dogs 15
tofu yogurt 16
tofu 28
tempeh burger 29
soy cheese 31
miso 43
tempeh 44
soybean chips 54
mature soybeans, boiled 55
soy protein isolate
   (found in shake mixes and protein bars) 97
soy protein concentrate
   (found in textured vegetable protein) 102
instant soy beverage powder 110

Isoflavone counts are rounded. Table adapted from the U.S. Department of Agriculture-Iowa State University Database on the Isoflavone Content of Foods, 1999.

skip soy?

Talk to your doctor about the safety of eating large amounts of soy if you:

- have or have had breast cancer
- are at very high risk for breast cancer
- have a personal or family history of kidney stones
- are pregnant or nursing

For postmenopausal women, a reasonable amount of soy should be fine. But women who have breast cancer, are breast-cancer survivors, or are at high risk for the disease (such as a strong family history) should be extra cautious about soy intake. Experts suspect that the weak estrogenic effects of soy may be active in women whose levels of natural estrogen are low. Indeed, in mice with estrogen levels similar to that of a postmenopausal woman, soy causes estrogen-dependent tumors to grow. Again, there is no evidence that this happens in humans, but the animal studies indicate reason for caution.

For postmenopausal women who have breast cancer or are at high risk, experts say that a modest amount of soy is OK. But keep tabs on how much you eat, particularly if you take soy supplements for hot flashes, cholesterol control, or osteoporosis prevention. These supplements contain heavy doses of isoflavones, so it's easy to get too much. And talk to your doctor if you're not sure about your risk or how much soy to take.

Thyroid threat?

The concerns about soy and your thyroid have been overblown, unless you never eat salt or already have a thyroid problem. Soy is only one of many foods containing compounds called goitrogens, which in large amounts can hamper thyroid function. (Goitrogens are also found in such cruciferous vegetables as cauliflower.) A deficiency in iodine, which is essential for thyroid hormone synthesis, can make animals and humans especially vulnerable to these goitrogens.

The best source of iodine is table salt, so the vast majority of people in this country get far more iodine than they need. Other sources include shellfish, saltwater fish, and kelp. "For healthy adults who consume sufficient amounts of iodine, I don't think there's a concern at all,"

says Mark Messina, Ph.D., adjunct associate professor of nutrition at Loma Linda University. "If you have a compromised thyroid function or if you consume inadequate amounts of iodine, you may need to be careful." But then, it's important to get treated for a thyroid condition, no matter how much soy you eat. Thyroid function is checked with a simple blood test that all women should have every five years starting at age 35.

Kidney stone scare?

Recent headlines warning that eating soy foods might increase the risk of kidney stones were also misleading. Kidney stones form when oxalate binds to calcium in the urine and creates tiny crystals that stick together. The bad press for soybeans is a result of a study that found that soybeans are high in oxalate. But soy's oxalate content is no higher than that of other legumes, such as peanuts and beans. Linda Massey, Ph.D., R.D., a professor of human nutrition at Washington State University in Spokane, who headed the oxalate study, says other foods measure higher in oxalate: Parsley ranks number one, spinach and rhubarb tie for second, and legumes come in third. People with a personal or family history of kidney stones should limit their soy intake, just as they should be careful about eating too much of these other foods.

Alzheimer's alert?

A study published last year in the *Journal of the American College of Nutrition* caused a stir: It showed a correlation between tofu consumption and cognitive decline in older men and suggested that soy might make them more vulnerable to Alzheimer's. These findings run counter to virtually all of the other research in this area, and several experts have raised some questions about the study's weaknesses. According to Clare Hasler, Ph.D., the founding director of the Functional Foods for Health Program at the University of Illinois at Urbana-Champaign, several studies since have shown that soy may improve cognitive function. Researchers are continuing to study the effects of soy on the brain, but for now it appears not to be a concern.

Toss tofu in—or out?

Clearly, many cautions surrounding soy are unfounded or meant for people with special conditions. But soy can have powerful effects, and, as with any food, it should be eaten in moderation. Expert recommendations vary, with some suggesting very small amounts and others touting the benefits of 80 or more milligrams of isoflavones per day. Consuming between 30 and 40 milligrams each day (about as much as the Japanese get) is probably a good bet, and most likely that's more than you're eating now.

But if you, like me, do eat a lot of soy, count your isoflavones. The amount is generally not listed on food labels and can vary widely. As a conservative rule of thumb, when you're buying whole foods, count 2 milligrams of isoflavones for every gram of soy protein. Scan the chart for rough estimates of the level of isoflavones in one 3-ounce serving of specific soy products.

Keep in mind that soy specialty products like protein drink mixes and meal-replacement bars may be pumped up with some extra isoflavones. "You can buy soy milk that contains a modest amount of isoflavones," says Bill Helferich, Ph.D., associate professor of food science and human nutrition at the University of Illinois. "But you can also buy a product that looks like an instant breakfast drink with soy in it, and it's enhanced with isoflavones from an extract. So it really is no longer a food, it's a supplement with pharmacological doses."

The best advice remains to eat a varied diet—including soy, if it's to your liking. No need to toss your Tofutti Cuties. Just don't eat them all in one day. ✳

Lynn Prowitt–Smith is a health writer who has also contributed to Fitness *and* Newsweek.

Soy Products Face Meaty New Competition

A new meat substitute is poised to compete with tofu for the vegetarian entrée of choice. Mycoprotein, a mushroom-derived substance, is not only high in protein, low in fat, and cholesterol-free, but it also has the density and texture of meat—a boon for those who dislike tofu's spongy "mouth feel." When compared by weight, mycoprotein is said to have nearly as much protein as an egg, more fiber than a baked potato, and two-thirds the fat of a skinless chicken breast.

The ingredient, which has been sold in Europe for nearly 16 years, gained U.S. Food and Drug Administration approval in 2002. The eight-product line, marketed by Quorn Foods, will include frozen foods like "chicken" nuggets, ground "beef," and entrées such as "meat" lasagna. It's about time that tofu got some meaty competition.

Get High (Nutrition) with Hemp

DESPITE its deadhead connotations, hemp isn't just for smoking or rope-making. You can eat it, too—and maybe you should. The plant's seeds and oil—which are used in a variety of foods, including pretzels, waffles, breads, and cereals—contain a cache of nutrients hard to come by in vegetarian sources. Hemp seeds pack protein in amounts that rival chicken or eggs and essential fatty acids like those found in flaxseed oil and cold-water fish like salmon.

But don't expect a high from hemp brownies. The edible form of hemp doesn't typically contain THC, the psychoactive component in marijuana. Even so, the Drug Enforcement Agency (DEA) and pot-legalization activists have been battling loudly over hemp-food regulation. Activists protested the DEA's recent move to ban all foods containing THC. But the regulation just formalizes a previously unspoken rule: Most hemp importers have been selling "zero-THC" hemp-seed products all along, says Richard Rose, director of the Hemp Food Association. Even hemp products with a trace of THC wouldn't make consumers test positive for drug use.

Hemp seeds pack protein in amounts that rival chicken or eggs and essential fatty acids like those found in flaxseed oil and cold–water fish like salmon.

EGGS:
the perfect food

RECIPES AND TEXT BY MARIE SIMMONS

Like hip-huggers and platform shoes, eggs are back in fashion. For almost three decades, these breakfast favorites were thought to increase heart-disease risk because of their high cholesterol content. But researchers have all but exonerated dietary cholesterol as a culprit in heart disease, instead pointing to saturated fat. Saturated fat is one thing eggs are light on (one egg contains less than 2 grams). Even the stodgy American Heart Association has OK'd up to seven eggs per week for people on low-fat diets.

And for good reason: Eggs are near perfect, healthwise. They offer such good-for-you nutrients as protein, essential fatty acids, significant amounts of all vitamins except C, and a wide variety of minerals, including calcium, iron, and magnesium. Plus, research has shown that egg yolks contain lutein and zeaxanthin, two antioxidants that may reduce the risk of cataracts and macular degeneration, a condition that can cause blindness. Best of all, eggs are more versatile in the kitchen than a five-star chef. They can be homey, as in our New American Deviled Eggs, or highfalutin, as in our Cheddar, Chive, and Canadian Bacon Soufflé. If there's an egg in the fridge, you've got a meal—what could be more stylish than that?

New American Deviled Eggs

SERVES 16
PREPARATION: 8 MINUTES
CHILLING: 1 HOUR

8 hard-boiled large eggs, shells removed
¼ cup plain fat-free yogurt
2 tablespoons low-fat mayonnaise
⅔ cup cooked cubed peeled baking potato
1 teaspoon curry powder
½ teaspoon salt
½ teaspoon grated peeled fresh ginger
⅛ teaspoon hot pepper sauce
2 tablespoons chopped green onions (optional)

1. Slice eggs in half lengthwise; remove yolks and reserve 4 whole yolks for another use.
2. Combine yogurt and next 6 ingredients (through hot pepper sauce) in a bowl; mash with a fork. Add remaining yolks; beat with a mixer at high speed until smooth. Spoon 1 tablespoon yolk mixture into each egg-white half. Cover and chill 1 hour. Garnish with green onions, if desired. Serving size: 1 egg half.

Per Serving: Calories 34 (38% from fat); Fat 1.4g (sat 0.4g, mono 0.5g, poly 0.2g); Protein 2.7g; Carbohydrate 2.5g; Fiber 0.2g; Cholesterol 53mg; Iron 0.2g; Sodium 123mg; Calcium 13mg

Vanilla Custard Sauce with Strawberries

SERVES 6
PREPARATION: 10 MINUTES
COOKING: 15 MINUTES

1 large egg

⅓ cup sugar

1 tablespoon cornstarch

2 cups 1% low-fat milk

1 teaspoon vanilla extract

4 cups quartered small strawberries

1. Beat egg in a medium bowl until frothy.

2. Combine sugar and cornstarch in a small, heavy saucepan. Stir in milk; heat over medium-high heat to 180° or until tiny bubbles form around edge (do not boil). Gradually add hot milk to eggs, stirring constantly with a whisk. Return mixture to pan. Cook over medium heat until thick, stirring constantly (do not boil). Remove from heat; stir in vanilla. Cover and chill. Serve over strawberries. Serving size: $^1/_3$ cup sauce and $^2/_3$ cup strawberries.

Per Serving: Calories 132 (14% from fat); Fat 2.1g (sat 0.8g, mono 0.5g, poly 0.3g); Protein 4.7g; Carbohydrate 24.6g; Fiber 2.6g; Cholesterol 40mg; Iron 0.6g; Sodium 55mg; Calcium 110mg

Warm Egg Salad on Toast

SERVES 4
PREPARATION: 5 MINUTES

8 hard-boiled large eggs, shells removed

¼ cup low-fat mayonnaise

¼ cup plain nonfat yogurt

¼ cup minced celery

1 tablespoon grated onion

½ teaspoon Dijon mustard

½ teaspoon salt

¼ teaspoon black pepper

4 teaspoons low-fat mayonnaise

4 (1-ounce) slices multigrain bread, toasted

4 tomato slices

1 tablespoon thinly sliced fresh basil (optional)

1. Cut eggs in half lengthwise; remove yolks and reserve 4 whole yolks for another use. Combine remaining yolks, ¼ cup mayonnaise, and yogurt.

Coarsely chop egg whites; add to yolk mixture. Stir in next 5 ingredients (through pepper).

2. Spread 1 teaspoon mayonnaise over one side of a slice of toast. Top with tomato slice and $^1/_2$ cup egg mixture. Repeat procedure with remaining egg mixture, toast, and tomato. Sprinkle each with basil, if desired. Serving size: 1 sandwich.

Per Serving: Calories 253 (25% from fat); Fat 7.4g (sat 1.6g, mono 4.4g, poly 1.4g); Protein 14.5g; Carbohydrate 36.1g; Fiber 10.2g; Cholesterol 213mg; Iron 2.6g; Sodium 773mg; Calcium 250mg

Southwest Breakfast Wrap

SERVES 4
PREPARATION: 10 MINUTES
COOKING: 2 MINUTES

¾ cup fresh white corn kernels (about 2 ears)

2 tablespoons finely diced green bell pepper

2 tablespoons finely diced seeded plum tomato

1 teaspoon minced seeded jalapeño pepper

1 tablespoon minced fresh cilantro

1 tablespoon fresh lime juice

½ teaspoon salt, divided

4 large eggs, lightly beaten

¼ teaspoon ground cumin

Cooking spray

2 tablespoons finely shredded Monterey Jack cheese

4 (8-inch) flour tortillas

4 lettuce leaves

1. Combine first 6 ingredients (through lime juice) in a small bowl; stir in $^1/_4$ teaspoon salt.

2. Combine remaining $^1/_4$ teaspoon salt with eggs and cumin. Heat a medium nonstick skillet coated with cooking spray over medium heat. Add egg mixture; cook 2 minutes, stirring gently until set. Remove from heat; sprinkle with cheese.

3. Warm tortillas according to package directions. Top each tortilla with a lettuce leaf and $^1/_4$ cup corn mixture. Divide egg mixture evenly among tortillas; roll up. Serve immediately. Serving size: 1 wrap.

Per Serving: Calories 300 (28% from fat); Fat 9.7g (sat 2.8g, mono 3.6g, poly 1.6g); Protein 14.4g; Carbohydrate 41.1g; Fiber 2.4g; Cholesterol 215mg; Iron 2.4g; Sodium 646mg; Calcium 165mg

Cheddar, Chive, and Canadian Bacon Soufflé

SERVES 6
PREPARATION: 30 MINUTES
COOKING: 1 HOUR, 3 MINUTES

This soufflé does not rise over the lip of the dish like a traditional soufflé because the bread crumbs are too heavy to be lifted by the egg whites.

1 (8-ounce) loaf French bread
1 teaspoon butter
2 tablespoons minced shallot
½ teaspoon salt
2 cups 1% low-fat milk
½ cup (2 ounces) reduced-fat shredded Cheddar cheese
⅓ cup chopped Canadian bacon
¼ teaspoon dry mustard
¼ cup chopped fresh chives
3 large egg yolks
Cooking spray
4 large egg whites
¼ teaspoon cream of tartar

1. Preheat oven to 375°.
2. Place bread in a food processor; pulse 10 times or until the coarse crumbs measure 4 cups. Set aside. Melt butter in a small skillet over medium heat; add shallot. Sauté 3 minutes or until soft (do not brown); stir in salt. Combine shallot mixture, milk, and next 5 ingredients (through egg yolks) in a large bowl; stir well. Add 3½ cups bread crumbs; stir until well-blended.
3. Coat a 1½-quart soufflé dish with cooking spray; sprinkle remaining ½ cup bread crumbs over bottom and sides.
4. Place egg whites and cream of tartar in a large bowl; beat with a mixer at high speed until stiff peaks form. Gently stir ¼ egg-white mixture into shallot mixture; gently fold in remaining egg-white mixture. Spoon into soufflé dish. Bake at 375° for 1 hour or until soufflé is set. Serve immediately. Serving size: ⅙ of soufflé.

Per Serving: Calories 238 (29% from fat); Fat 7.6g (sat 3.4g, mono 2.5g, poly 0.7g); Protein 16.3g; Carbohydrate 25g; Fiber 1.2g; Cholesterol 121mg; Iron 1.5g; Sodium 736mg; Calcium 233mg

Florentine Potato Casserole

SERVES 8
PREPARATION: 20 MINUTES
COOKING: 1 HOUR, 38 MINUTES

2 pounds Yukon gold or red potatoes
Cooking spray
2 cups sliced mushrooms
½ cup chopped onion
1 garlic clove, minced
¼ cup fat-free, less-sodium chicken broth
1 (10-ounce) package frozen chopped spinach, thawed, drained, and squeezed dry
1 teaspoon salt, divided
½ teaspoon black pepper, divided
¼ cup chopped reduced-fat ham
2½ cups 1% low-fat milk
2 tablespoons all-purpose flour
4 large eggs, lightly beaten
½ cup (2 ounces) shredded fontina cheese
2 tablespoons grated Parmesan cheese

1. Place potatoes in a stockpot; cover with water (to 2 inches above potatoes); bring to a boil. Cook 40 minutes or until tender. Drain. Cool; peel and cut into ¼-inch-thick slices.
2. Heat a large nonstick skillet coated with cooking spray over medium-high heat. Add mushrooms; sauté 5 minutes. Add onion and garlic, sauté 3 minutes. Add broth; cook until evaporated. Stir in spinach, ½ teaspoon salt, and ¼ teaspoon black pepper.
3. Preheat oven to 350°.
4. Place half the potatoes in a single layer on the bottom of an 11 x 7-inch baking dish. Spoon mushroom mixture over potatoes; sprinkle with ham. Layer remaining potatoes over top.
5. Combine ½ teaspoon salt, ¼ teaspoon black pepper, milk, flour, and eggs. Pour over potatoes (dish will be full). Bake at 350° for 30 minutes. Sprinkle with cheeses; bake an additional 20 minutes. Serving size: ⅛ of casserole.

Per Serving: Calories 221 (26% from fat); Fat 6.4g (sat 3g, mono 1.9g, poly 0.6g); Protein 13g; Carbohydrate 29g; Fiber 3.3g; Cholesterol 121mg; Iron 1.8g; Sodium 523mg; Calcium 205mg ✳

Marie Simmons is the author of The Good Egg, *2001 winner of the James Beard Award for Best Single-Subject Cookbook.*

what you Really Need to Know about milk

While critics question the virtues of milk, others say pour it on for good health. Here's the bottom line.

BY TIMOTHY GOWER

Talk about slaying a sacred cow. In recent years, a band of dietary dissidents has tried to convince American consumers that milk and other dairy products—which you probably thought were healthy and wholesome—cause cancer, heart disease, diabetes, obesity, and a long list of other illnesses. For example, one activist group, the Physicians Committee for Responsible Medicine, blames dairy foods for everything from ovarian cancer to colicky babies. Another organization, People for the Ethical Treatment of Animals (PETA), sends members dressed as cows to schools, hoping to persuade children that drinking the white stuff will make them fat and pimply.

"We've got hundreds of lines of converging evidence that milk

does not 'do a body good,'" quips Robert Cohen, author of *Milk: The Deadly Poison* and one of the shrillest dairy critics in the United States.

Hold on, here. Humans have been drinking cow's milk and eating dairy foods since about 4000 B.C. In recent years, women in particular have been hit with the message that they need to consume more calcium-rich milk as a way to prevent osteoporosis, the bone-weakening condition that afflicts 28 million people in the United States. But is that the wrong message, as the antimilk league would have you believe?

It's tempting to dismiss some of this dairy-dumping talk outright since it comes from groups that are obviously pushing a larger agenda, such as veganism or animal rights. However, some credible research has raised questions about whether

A pint of contention: Milk is maligned as a cancer-causer and bone-breaker. But evidence suggests that it's neither.

dairy is fully deserving of its pure and healthy reputation. For instance, a study published in 2001 in *The American Journal of Clinical Nutrition* reported that diets rich in dairy foods appear to increase the risk for prostate cancer. How, exactly? One theory is that high levels of calcium decrease the production of parathyroid hormone, which, in turn, suppresses levels of vitamin D. This key vitamin controls the growth of tumors.

These findings didn't come as a complete surprise: Researchers have long suspected that there was a link between high cancer risk and diets that include lots of animal foods, including milk and other dairy products. The high fat content of milk, cheese, and meat is usually the reason cited. Switch to low-fat varieties, and you lower your cancer odds, right? Maybe not. Researchers have begun to suspect that even low- and nonfat dairy foods could make certain people sick. For example, epidemiologist and gynecologist Daniel W. Cramer, M.D., of Boston's Brigham and Women's Hospital, believes some women may carry a gene that makes their bodies more susceptible to galactose, a form of sugar in milk, modestly increasing their risk for ovarian cancer.

The spotlight has shined even more brightly on a substance called insulin-like growth factor, or IGF-I, which causes human cells to multiply. Although it's essential to human health, IGF-I has a potential downside: It can encourage the growth of precancerous cells. IGF-I is produced by the liver and found in some foods, dairy products being the richest sources in the human diet. To milk bashers, that spells danger. Any time you drink a cool glass, "you're delivering IGF-I to your body," Cohen warns.

Milk critics' most surprising claim is that dairy foods are anything but bone-savers—bone-breakers is more like it. They point to a 1997 Harvard School of Public Health study of almost 78,000 female nurses. It found that women who drank two or more glasses of milk per day suffered more hip fractures than those who drank milk less than once a week or not at all. PETA official Bruce Friedrich was quick to conclude, "Milk appears to cause osteoporosis."

But before you dash to the fridge and pour that jug of 1-percent milk down the drain, consider the other side of this dairy tale. For instance, while Cramer cautions his patients to limit how much dairy they consume, he concedes that his theory about galactose and ovarian cancer "is still largely theoretical" and notes that certain other measures (such as taking oral contraceptives or increasing antioxidants in your diet) could be much more important for the prevention of ovarian cancer.

Likewise, there is no conclusive evidence that growth factors in dairy products cause any disease. Scientists do know that people with high levels of IGF-I in their blood have an increased risk for breast, colorectal, lung, and prostate cancers. But as one recent study suggests, that doesn't necessarily mean that drinking milk causes cancer.

Harvard University epidemiologist Jing Ma, Ph.D., and her colleagues measured IGF-I levels in blood samples from about 500 men over 40. Then they tallied how many of these men developed colon cancer over a 13-year period, noting how much milk and other dairy products they consumed. And, to be sure, the frequent milk-drinkers and cheese-eaters had high levels of IGF-I in their blood. So you would assume that these guys were probably more likely to develop colon cancer.

"Quite the opposite," Ma explains. "People who drank more milk tended to have a lower risk of colorectal cancer." Ma believes that milk actually protects frequent drinkers against colon cancer, a finding that is supported by other research. A 1999 experiment, for instance, found that calcium supplements appear to prevent the

Women have been told that they need to consume more calcium-rich milk as a way to prevent oseoporosis. But is that the wrong message, as the antimilk league would have you believe?

the new milk:
do you know what you're drinking?

Americans may be sipping less milk these days, but one type of dairy beverage is hot: flavored milk. According to MarketResearch.com, sales of drinks such as Starbucks' popular Frappuccino and Nestle's NesQuik will increase by about 10 percent annually over the next five years. The beverage industry is marketing jazzed-up milk drinks as hip alternatives to soda.

But should you consider swigging flavored milk as a convenient and tasty source of bone-building calcium? A 16-ounce bottle of chocolate-flavored NesQuik contains 800 milligrams of this critical mineral—more than three-quarters of the recommended daily calcium intake for a woman under age 50. But it also contains more calories than a medium order of McDonald's fries (460 compared with 450) and a half-day's worth of saturated fat (10 grams). Frappuccinos are made with low-fat milk and provide 250 milligrams of calcium, but a single 9.5-ounce bottle of the mocha-flavored variety has nearly as much sugar as a Milky Way candy bar.

As long as you don't live on it alone, flavored milk can be a healthy treat, especially when you consider some of the beverage alternatives. "After all, if you drink a soda, you will get zero milligrams of calcium," says nutritionist Jo Ann Hattner, R.D., a spokeswoman for the American Dietetic Association. Just be sure that you read product labels and note the serving sizes, she says. For instance, a bottle of NesQuik contains two servings (although it is hard to resist polishing off the whole thing at one sitting).

also influenced by a person's genes and other factors. Milner thinks that milk could offer some protection against certain malignancies, but, he says, "I don't think it's a magic bullet."

Finally, the claim that milk is bad for bones comes as news to epidemiologist Diane Feskanich, Ph.D., the lead author of the Harvard study that is often cited as evidence that dairy indeed causes osteoporosis. Feskanich points out that the increased number of broken bones among milk-drinkers in her study was modest—too small from which to draw conclusions. "There's no evidence that milk is harmful," Feskanich says. On the other hand, she hasn't found any evidence that consuming large amounts

Before you dash to the fridge to dump your jug of 1 percent, **consider both sides of the story.**

of calcium—whether through dairy foods or other sources—prevents hip fractures, either. Feskanich worries that women are pursuing high calcium intakes at the expense of exercise, which "all studies have shown improves bone density and decreases fracture risk."

Robert Heaney, M.D., an osteoporosis expert at Creighton University in Omaha, Nebraska, says that this study shouldn't discourage anyone from consuming dairy foods. Heaney's own review of the scientific literature found 50 of 52 studies concluding that increasing calcium intake—whether through dairy products, calcium-fortified foods, or supplements—strengthens bones and reduces the risk for fractures.

So is it OK to shop the dairy aisle on your next grocery trip? Although scientists still have a lot to learn about how milk and other dairy products affect your health, most experts agree that dairy foods are neither poison nor panacea—just a good way to get the recommended daily dose of calcium (a cup of skim milk or low-fat yogurt has about 300 milligrams) along with protein and some other key nutrients. Want milk? Pour it on—and let the critics have a cow. ✳

recurrence of colon tumors. In fact, even the men in Ma's study who had high levels of IGF-I in their blood had a lower risk for colon cancer if they frequently drank milk or ate dairy foods.

The bottom line is that no one can say with absolute certainty that consuming dairy foods prevents or causes cancer, says John Milner, Ph.D., chief of nutrition research at the National Cancer Institute. Evidence is conflicting, at best, notes Milner, as scientists are still trying to determine just how diet affects one's risk for cancer, which is

---

Contributing editor Timothy Gower is the co-author of
A Doctor's Guide to Herbs and Supplements.

Q+A
Be Safe with Raw Fish

I love ceviche, but could my marinated-fish fetish harm me?

THE CHANCE of getting food poisoning from ceviche is very small if you're basically healthy and stay away from the dish in dives. In fact, ceviche is probably one step safer than sushi because the lime or lemon juice used to marinate the appetizer thwarts the growth of unfriendly bacteria that could make your tummy throw a tantrum. But there's no such thing as completely safe ceviche.

The only surefire way to kill bacteria and parasites is by turning on the heat (which, of course, misses the whole point of ceviche). That said, certain folks—older adults, children, people with compromised immune systems, and pregnant women—should never partake. If the fish is funky, these people are more likely to get sick and their illnesses will be more severe.

fish found
to be healthy meal for expecting moms

EXPECTING? Order the catch of the day. Researchers in Denmark found that pregnant women who eat fish at least once a week are less likely to deliver prematurely and have low birth-weight babies than those who skip seafood. The researchers suspect that the omega-3 fatty acids in fish help protect against complications. Just keep in mind that some fish contain high levels of mercury, which may be harmful to your unborn child. To be safe, avoid shark, swordfish, king mackerel, and tilefish, and eat an average of no more than 12 ounces (about three or four servings) of cooked fish per week (no sushi—sorry!).

find wine-worthy advice at
winespectator.com

Now that you've perfected your Wiener schnitzel, you need to find a gewürztraminer to complement it. No need to take a wine class—just visit Wine Spectator's site and click on "Dining" for a list of worthy choices. Also check out the Wine Ratings section and search by type, region, vintage, or price (including $10 and under). Up pops an extensive list from about 10,000 reviews, complete with tasting notes.

Take Care of Picnic Perishables

While you're busy playing Frisbee, the potato salad you brought to the family picnic is busy too—growing germs. Perishable foods should not be left out for longer than two hours, so be sure to bring a cooler. For more tips on food safety, visit www.extension.iastate.edu/foodsafety.

BBQ for Bees

At your next barbecue, feed the bees so they won't feed on you: Put out a small plate of what you're serving (the more barbecue sauce the better) before the guests arrive. Once the bees find the feast, carefully move it a safe distance away from your party.

the HIDDEN DANGERS of too much vitamin A

Postmenopausal women who consume too much vitamin A might be putting their bones at risk. While the vitamin is necessary for growth, vision, reproduction, and a healthy immune system, researchers are finding that the upper limit of the recommended dosage (3,000 micrograms a day) could be too high.

A study published in The Journal of the American Medical Association found that women who consumed over 2,000 micrograms of retinol—the active form of vitamin A—a day were twice as likely to experience a hip fracture than women who got 500 micrograms a day. The researchers caution that since most multivitamins contain 1,500 micrograms of retinol and you can readily consume 500 micrograms in fortified milk and breakfast cereals, it can be easy to reach high levels without knowing it.

This Fatty Acid Can Actually Help Manage Diabetes

THE GOOD PRESS keeps coming for conjugated linoleic acid, or CLA. Researchers at Purdue University recently discovered that this fatty acid, found in meats and dairy products, can lower blood-sugar levels in people with Type 2 diabetes. "Along with diet and exercise, CLA could help manage the disease," says the study's lead researcher Martha Belury, Ph.D., now at Northwest Hospital in Seattle.

Type 2 diabetics who took 6 grams of a CLA supplement daily for eight weeks saw their blood-sugar levels drop by 3 percent. However, until further research determines the long-term effects of regular CLA consumption in large amounts, Belury recommends sticking with natural sources (a glass of 2 percent milk contains about 25 milligrams of CLA) instead of supplements.

we all *do* scream

Americans love their ice cream: They indulge in a bowl or cone an average of 2.2 times per week.

—*Mintel Consumer Intelligence*

cheese: the latest "in" thing for dessert

Many diners are waving away the dessert tray in favor of the latest cheese plate. This après-dinner phenomenon is popping up on menus from Manhattan's über-trendy Artisanal (with its own cheese cave) to the most casual French bistros on San Francisco's Left Bank—and plenty of other places in between. Originating in Europe, the cheese course usually consists of four to six varieties that range in texture from soft to hard and in taste from mild to sharp.

Just because cheese is high in fat and cholesterol doesn't mean you

have to sit this course out. "Cheese is a great source of protein in a calcium package, which is especially important for women," says Leslie Bonci, R.D., a spokeswoman for the American Dietetic Association. "The important thing is that you're not eating a pound of cheese as an afternoon snack. It's better to sample cheeses with fruits after a meal so you're less likely to overindulge."

A healthy indulgence is a slice or two of each of the cheeses, not exceeding 4 ounces—about the size of a glasses case—per sitting. Pregnant women should avoid blue cheese and softer varieties, because these often contain more bacteria (which could potentially harm the baby) than harder, aged cheeses.

"Good" Bacteria Pills May Soothe Stomach Woes

The probiotics found naturally in yogurt are showing up in dairy products and in supplements. Is this good news for digestion?

BY AMY PATUREL

Crippled by what felt like an Olympic gymnastics meet in her stomach—complete with flip-flops, somersaults, and the inevitable spill—28-year-old Rebecca Stow needed more than a bottle of Pepto-Bismol to wipe out the competition. The cramps, nausea, and diarrhea erupted after she began a three-month course of antibiotics for acne. So when even prescription drugs failed to calm her stormy stomach, Stow began swallowing billions of bacteria every day. "I took two acidophilus pills in the morning and two at night for six months," Stow says. "The intense pain gradually got better, and I got my life back."

Stow joins a growing number of Americans who are consuming probiotics—"friendly" bacteria such as acidophilus—in search of gastrointestinal relief. The idea is simple enough: More than 500 kinds of bacteria, some good and some bad, duke it out for control over your digestive system. The number of good micro-organisms, such as probiotics, in your system can determine whether your stomach is Lake Placid or tidal wave. Acidophilus and other probiotics are starting to show up in foods and supplements claiming not only to help ease digestive problems but to boost your ability to absorb nutrients and even help prevent illness. Are these bugs too good to be true?

The idea of probiotics is nothing new. Yogurts that naturally contain live cultures like acidophilus have been on the market for years. For more than a decade, companies in Europe and Asia have been fortifying other dairy products and even nondairy foods like sports drinks with specific strains of probiotics that promise additional health benefits. "In Finland, as much as 90 percent of people regularly consume probiotics in foods and in supplements every day, compared with around 10 percent in

*Fans claim that **consuming more probiotics** can help keep the peace in your GI tract and buffer the effects of antibiotic-induced stomach woes.*

the States," explains Barry Goldin, Ph.D., professor of family medicine and community health at Tufts University School of Medicine. What is new, though, is a growing push by U.S. food companies to give dairy products sold stateside a bacteria boost and to market probiotics in the form of pills, powders, and capsules. While Americans aren't exactly gobbling up more probiotic-fortified dairy, the supplement business is booming, bringing in around $68 million annually.

It's hard to resist the appeal of a pill that claims to keep the peace in your gastrointestinal (GI) tract. The premise is that when healthy cells are under bacterial attack, probiotics stick to your intestinal lining and produce antibodies that are toxic to the disease-causing bacteria. Probiotics restore the depleted intestine with new, healthful bacteria that crowd out the bad bugs by keeping them from attaching to the intestinal wall.

Like Stow, people commonly turn to probiotics to thwart antibiotic-induced ills. Research shows that antibiotics like tetracycline kill both good and bad bacteria, leaving your body open to the risk of an invasion of bad bacteria—and stomach troubles. A study published in 2001 in the medical journal *Digestion* found that adults taking lactobacillus GG (LGG), one of the most widely used probiotics, while on antibiotics experienced significantly less bloating and diarrhea than those who went bug-free. "If someone is put on a high course of antibiotics, probiotics can provide additional protection," says Goldin, who helped isolate LGG. And with increased reliance on antibiotics, some experts like C. Gregory Albers, M.D., director of diagnostic GI services at the University of California, Irvine, suspect that the need for probiotics could become all the more important.

The supposed intestinal benefits of good bacteria go beyond buffering the effects of antibiotics. Other preliminary studies suggest that the LGG strain shows promise in treating more serious intestinal conditions, including Crohn's disease and irritable bowel syndrome (IBS), a mysterious condition that results in cramps, diarrhea,

probiotic foods and supplements

A healthy person looking for a boost of good bacteria should focus on foods fortified with probiotics, says researcher Barry Goldin, Ph.D. Dairy products like yogurt, sour cream, and cheese contain the good stuff: Look for the words "live and active cultures" on the label. Some yogurts that boast beneficial bacteria include Colombo, Dannon, Horizon Organic Dairy, and Stonyfield Farm, which are available in supermarkets as well as health-food stores. Aim for two to three servings a day to reach the suggested dose of 10 billion live micro-organisms.

If you decide to try higher amounts of probiotics or specific strains like LGG to target antibiotic-associated stomach troubles, Goldin suggests taking supplements throughout the course of your treatment and for two weeks following. Health-food stores feature a shelf full of options, such as pills, powders, or capsules; look for products containing acidophilus, bifidobacterium, *L. casei, L. reuteri, L. bulgaricus,* and *S. thermophilus* (Probiotica and Bifa-15 are two good bets).

If you're taking a trip to a foreign country, Goldin recommends eating yogurt with live cultures daily or taking an LGG supplement two weeks prior to the trip and throughout your vacation. In the United States, Culturelle is the only product with LGG (and it must be refrigerated), so when you arrive at your destination, shop around for an LGG supplement you can take.

constipation, gas, and bloating. "I often recommend my Crohn's and IBS patients take probiotics regularly in addition to their other medications," Albers says.

There is even some evidence that probiotics may help stave off the dreaded "traveler's diarrhea" that can quickly cramp a good vacation; probiotics may also offer some relief for people suffering from lactose intolerance. According to researchers from the Harvard University

*Probiotics may be able to help people with **serious stomach problems** who have not found much relief from conventional treatment options.*

Medical School, most probiotics in foods like yogurt feed on lactose, the sugar molecule found in dairy that many people are unable to digest. Still, some experts warn that probiotics may not wipe out enough lactose to make a significant difference, so people might be better off taking pills containing lactase, the enzyme that breaks down lactose.

In addition to easing stomach ailments, probiotics seem to provide a natural alternative to medications that combat common female dilemmas. "Family doctors and OB-GYNs have been using probiotics for years to treat urinary tract and vaginal infections," Albers says. The good bacteria take up residence in the vagina and release hydrogen peroxide, which produces an environment hostile to yeast and other bacteria.

But not everyone is pushing probiotics as the next big thing. Researchers at the Mayo Clinic in Rochester, Minnesota, studied a group of adult patients taking antibiotics; half of them were supplemented with LGG. "We found no significant difference in the rate of diarrhea between those who took LGG and those who didn't," explains Scott C. Litin, M.D., professor of medicine at the Mayo Clinic and co-author of the study. "There is a well-established association between LGG and decreased incidence of diarrhea for children taking antibiotics, but there are few studies in adults that confirm this."

And although studies report no side effects for probiotics, there are some risks that are associated with their use, particularly in supplement form, says Christina Surawicz, M.D., professor of medicine at the University of Washington and chief of gastroenterology at Harborview Medical Center. "The industry is totally unregulated, and supplements may contain foreign substances," says Surawicz, who has researched the effects of probiotics on antibiotic-induced diarrhea. And no one knows what type of probiotic or which combination works best for specific indications. "It's probably OK to treat some illnesses like mild antibiotic-associated diarrhea and traveler's diarrhea with probiotics, but if I were leaving on an overseas vacation, I might be just as happy with Pepto-Bismol," she says.

If you have a more serious affliction, such as Crohn's or IBS, ask your doctor about taking probiotics as part of your treatment plan. It might help, particularly if you have found little relief through conventional means. If your digestive ups and downs are of the typical variety, though, you should probably wait for more solid research before shelling out the bucks for probiotic powders and pills—and cultivate your taste for yogurt. ✳

Los Angeles–based writer Amy Paturel also contributes to **Cooking Light.**

Honey: the All-Natural Hangover Cure

At your next evening soiree, serve some toast and honey:
The fructose in this sweet treat can help your body metabolize alcohol and prevent the I-just-can't-face-the-world feeling the morning after.

—*National Headache Foundation*

The Latest in Healthy Foods—Edible Vaccines

Eating for your health may soon take on greater significance. Australian scientists are genetically modifying plants—including lettuce, tomato, and soybean varieties—to carry vaccines for measles and malaria. Biologists in the United States are developing a herpes vaccine in wheat seed, and the National Institutes of Health has funded research for vaccines you can eat. Even baby food may one day be available in a disease-fighting variety.

Scientists hope vaccine-packed foods will be cheaper, stay fresh longer, and be easier to distribute than the injectable varieties. They expect edible vaccines to reach the market in the next decade.

the medicines and foods you should never mix

Coffee and Danish go together just fine, but coffee and asthma meds don't. In fact, that's only one of the potentially dangerous medicine-food combinations that could dupe your body into absorbing too much or too little of your prescription medicine. Watch out for these pairings.

DRUG/DRUG TYPE	USED TO TREAT	EXAMPLES	FOODS TO AVOID
bronchodilators	asthma	Theo-Dur 24, Uniphyl	high-fat and high-carbohydrate meals products containing caffeine
diuretics and ACE inhibitors	heart problems	Accupril Capoten Dyazide Maxzide Prinivil Univasc Vasotec Zestril	bananas oranges green, leafy vegetables other potassium-rich foods (Note: Medications such as HydroDiuril and Dyrenium actually work better when taken with potassium-rich foods.)
anticoagulants	blood clots	Coumadin	broccoli spinach kale turnip greens other vitamin K–rich foods
MAO inhibitors	depression, anxiety	Nardil Parnate	cheese yogurt raisins bananas soy sauce cured meats other foods containing tyramine
quinolones	bacterial infections	Cipro Floxin Levaquin Trovan	milk yogurt other calcium-rich foods products containing caffeine
antifungals	fungal infections	Diflucan Grifulvin Nizoral Sporanox	dairy products

Sources: National Consumers League and the U.S. Food and Drug Administration

Jerky Goes Gourmet

Jerky is not just convenience-store fare anymore. Jerky producers are trying to appeal to gourmands with elk, buffalo, salmon, and ostrich versions, which may leave hardcore enthusiasts asking, "Where's the beef?"

Good Question
about Food and Nutrition

by Nancy Snyderman

Eat the Right Foods to Get the Most From Your Cholesterol Medication

I've heard that taking high doses of antioxidants cancels out the benefits of cholesterol-lowering medications. Should I give up my multivitamin?

If you're taking drugs to lower your cholesterol, the best way to get antioxidants is to eat a balanced diet rich in fruits and vegetables and not rely on supplements. Here's why: University of Washington researchers recently found that megadoses of antioxidants blunted the ability of the common cholesterol-lowing treatment—niacin plus a statin—to raise HDL levels (good cholesterol). After one year, a group that was taking the niacin/statin combo alone increased HDL levels by an average of 25 percent, while people who took antioxidants in addition increased HDL levels by only 19 percent. Keep in mind that the antioxidant doses given in this study were quite high—in some cases, 10 times more than what is typically found in multivitamins. You should play it safe and just take the standard minimum dosage of antioxidants.

> You're better off trying to lower cholesterol with **diet and lifestyle changes** before resorting to prescription drugs.

Still, any time your cholesterol level is out of whack, you're better off trying to lower it with diet and lifestyle changes before resorting to prescription drugs (unless your doctor advises otherwise). That means adding more fruits and vegetables, lowering dietary fat, kicking the nicotine habit, and exercising.

Prevent Heart Disease with a Healthy Diet—Not this Supplement

I've heard the supplement L-arginine can help prevent heart disease and cancer. Would you recommend taking it?

No. L-arginine fans claim it does miracles—that in addition to preventing heart disease and cancer, it can enhance anything from your sex life to athletic performance. But such over-the-top claims make me skeptical. And there's no scientific proof that L-arginine protects the heart or offers any other health benefits.

L-arginine is a naturally occurring amino acid that helps supply your body with energy. There are some preliminary studies looking into whether it could be used to treat or prevent heart disease. The theory is that L-arginine increases nitric oxide, which acts as a powerful antioxidant, preventing the oxidation in your blood vessels (think rust in pipes) that leads to heart disease. But that's just a theory; no one knows enough about L-arginine to recommend it, even to people who are at high risk for heart disease.

If you eat a balanced diet, you probably get enough L-arginine from poultry, beef, fish, and eggs. While taking small doses of the supplement is probably not dangerous, why do it when you don't know if it will help? You're better off sticking with strategies proven to help avert heart disease and cancer, such as maintaining a healthy diet, exercising regularly, and quitting smoking.

The Hidden Danger Lurking in Your Salad

I've been trying to eat more salads, but I'm worried about getting sick from bacteria in contaminated leaves. Should I be concerned?

The chance of getting ill from salad is small, especially compared with the health risks of eliminating greens from your diet. Still, it's smart to give lettuce a good soaking and be careful when you eat out—I pass up salad bars unless I know a restaurant well, and I never eat raw greens in foreign countries.

Lettuce and other veggies and fruits are exposed to all kinds of pesticides and animal and human waste unless they're organic or grown in a controlled environment.

Lettuce and other veggies and fruits are exposed to all kinds of pesticides and animal and human waste unless they're organic or grown in a controlled environment.

So you should thoroughly clean produce before eating it. With a head of lettuce, remove the outer leaves, rinse and soak the greens in water, and then hold the leaves upside down so they'll drip-dry. Even the bagged, pre-washed salad mixes need a soaking. Finish with a salad spinner to keep leaves crisp.

Unfortunately, contaminated leaves aren't the only potential threat lurking in your salad bowl. A recent report issued by the Centers for Disease Control and Prevention (CDC) detailed salmonella poisonings in four states that were traced back to contaminated alfalfa sprouts. Both the CDC and the U.S. Food and Drug Administration (FDA) recommend that young children, elderly people, and any other person with a compromised immune system steer clear of uncooked sprouts. The FDA even recommends that you cook your sprouts before eating them.

When Carrots Go Skin Deep

My weight-loss efforts have paid off big time, but now my palms have turned a funky yellow color. Should I be concerned?

Probably not. But palm reading can tell you a lot about your diet (if not about your love life). In your case, the yellowish tinge indicates that, in your quest to lose weight, you've probably started eating more fruits and vegetables—specifically, yellow-orange veggies like carrots. Loading up on yellow-orange foods (Cheetos not included) can cause a common condition called carotenemia, a scary-sounding word for a harmless phenomenon: Carotenes, nutrients that give yellow and orange fruits and veggies their color, are easily stored in the body, showing up on your skin. Balance your diet with some green vegetables, and your palms should return to their normal shade.

Now, if you start seeing yellow not just in your palms but in your eyes, you might have a more serious problem. When the whites of your eyes turn yellow, it could be a sign that your liver is not working properly, and you need to see a doctor. Jaundice is the likely culprit.

Nancy Snyderman, M.D. is a medical correspondent for ABC News and author of Girl in the Mirror: Mothers and Daughters in the Years of Adolescence.

food for the Heart, from the Heart

To help his ailing father reclaim his health, a chef uncovers the light side of his native Mexican cuisine—and shares his culinary secrets.

BY MAUREEN CALLAHAN

PHOTOGRAPHY BY VICTORIA PEARSON

After 25 years working as a chef at Harry's Plaza Café in Santa Barbara, California, Joe Vazquez was ready to retire. He sold his furniture, packed his bags, and was all set to move back to his native Mexico. But one thing stood in the way: a silly little stress test. His doctor had suggested it many times before, but Joe, then 67, kept putting it off. "He thought it was old age that was making him tired and out of breath," says his son Alberto. The family finally convinced Joe to take the test in late April 2001. It was scheduled for his first full day of retirement.

The results changed everything. "My younger brother Michael called and said, 'Dude, Dad's in the hospital. They're doing more tests. I think you should be here,'" says Alberto, 34, who had also taken up the toque, working as executive

sous-chef at Pedals Café, a Mediterranean-style restaurant at the Santa Monica resort Shutters on the Beach.

Alberto hopped in his car and drove an hour up the coast to Santa Barbara, where he found out that his father had five clogged arteries, several total blockages among them.

"My dad, he speaks with his eyes a lot," Alberto says. "It hurt me to see such a strong man look so vulnerable."

Joe's strength pulled him through heart surgery, though, and as he recuperated, Alberto and his brothers got busy. Their father's return to Mexico was out of the question, so they set out to re-create his life in California. "We furnished my dad's house in the matter of a day. I went to Macy's and racked up my credit card just buying him stuff—pajamas, robes, you name it."

But Joe would need more than a new La-Z-Boy and loungewear. He had to change his lifestyle—specifically, his

stocking the pantry, Mexican style

To prepare for his dad's homecoming from the hospital, Alberto filled the kitchen with healthy Mexican ingredients, everything from chiles to tomatillos to reduced-fat tortillas. "I wanted to spoil him," says Alberto. "But my goal was also to show him that healthy foods didn't have to taste boring." Here's a quick recap of these Mexican specialities. You should be able to find these in the produce department of large supermarkets or Mexican-foods stores.

Chiles del arbol: About 2 to 3 inches in length, these slender, bright red "tree" chiles are typically sold dried. Drying concentrates their flavor and their heat. Take care adding them to dishes, as they are very hot.

Nopales: The light green oval leaves of the prickly pear cactus, this popular Mexican vegetable tastes like a cross between asparagus and broccoli. Thorns must be removed (easily done with a vegetable peeler) before the flesh can be cut into strips and steamed or boiled.

Cilantro: Sold in bunches like parsley, this leafy green herb adds a pungent, almost "soapy" flavor to spicy foods.

Poblanos: Best known as the chile of choice for the Mexican specialty chiles rellenos, the dark *poblano* chile has a savory, mildly hot flavor. During their peak season (summer to early fall) you can find roasted versions of poblanos, with a wonderful smoky flavor, in many Mexican markets.

Serrano chiles: A small, slim, green chile (about 2 inches long), *serranos* are typically used to add a touch of heat to fresh salsas and guacamole. The seeds, which pack far more heat than the flesh, are typically removed.

Tomatillos: Often called the Mexican green tomato, this tart fruit can be eaten raw or cooked. Its flavor is part herbaceous, part tart apple. If left in its thin parchment covering, a *tomatillo* can be stored in a paper bag in the refrigerator for up to one month.

Queso Oaxaca: Just as with American cheeses, Mexican cheese (*queso*) comes in many varieties, ranging from hard to soft to creamy. Reduced-fat versions are scarce, except for this one, which is made with skim milk.

diet. "I took it upon myself to figure out his meals," Alberto says. The goal was to not let his dad miss the foods he loves. "I just went with my gut instincts," he says. Alberto stocked up on chiles—fresh, roasted, dried—since Joe loves spicy foods, the hotter the better. Roasted *poblanos,* which are about as common in Mexican markets as white bread is in American grocery stores, went in his shopping cart. So, too, did the fiery little green peppers called *serranos* and the dried red *chiles del arbol.* "I bought salmon. I bought all kinds of fish. I bought tons of vegetables. I just went crazy," Alberto says. Then he went to his dad's newly furnished digs and started cooking.

Lard was out, so Alberto flavored olive oil with fresh herbs, chiles, and garlic. He used salsas to add flavor and spice to foods. Sometimes his training and love for Italian cuisine showed through. "I would use olive oil, basil leaves, capers, olives, and even balsamic vinegar," he says. "I learned from Italian chefs basically the same thing I learned from my dad and mom about Mexican cooking. Start a dish with the best ingredients you can possibly find. You're not going to make a bad tomato taste good." Bad tomatoes make for bad *pico de gallo.*

Alberto admits he was skeptical at first. "I thought this low-fat stuff was going to be boring. But it isn't."

And after more than a year on his new diet, the only reminder of Joe's bypass is his scar. "You wouldn't recognize him," Alberto says. "It used to be that he would walk a short distance and be out of breath. Now he doesn't sit still. He goes walking every day, sometimes for half an hour or more." And he's moved to his home state Jalisco, in central Mexico,

"I learned from Italian chefs basically the same thing I learned from my dad and mom about Mexican cooking. Start a dish with the best ingredients you can possibly find. You're not going to make a bad tomato taste good."

—*Alberto Vázquez*

to be near his eight siblings. But he visits California frequently. "My first stop is Alberto's house," Joe says. "I stay there for three to four days and he cooks for me. I love it."

We asked Alberto to share a sampling of his father's favorites with us. These dishes are more reminiscent of authentic Mexican cuisine (and much more delicious) than the Tex-Mex tacos and burritos you're probably more familiar with.

Breakfast Burrito with Eggs and *Nopales*
SERVES 4
PREPARATION: 15 MINUTES
COOKING: 7 MINUTES

Nopales—*fresh cactus paddles—taste like a cross between asparagus and broccoli.*

2 cactus pads, spines removed and trimmed
¾ cup egg substitute
¾ teaspoon salt
1 teaspoon vegetable oil
⅓ cup chopped onion
1 teaspoon chopped, seeded *serrano* chile
4 (6-inch) corn tortillas
½ cup (2 ounces) part-skim *queso* Oaxaca, grated (or light Monterey Jack)
¼ cup chopped seeded plum tomato
4 teaspoons Salsa de Tomatillo (recipe follows)
4 teaspoons chopped fresh cilantro

1. Steam cactus, covered, 5 minutes; cool. Chop to measure ¹/₂ cup; set aside.
2. Combine egg substitute and salt in a small bowl, stir with a fork.
3. Heat oil in a large nonstick pan over medium heat; add onion and *serrano*, stirring frequently. Sauté 2 minutes; stir in egg mixture, stirring constantly to prevent egg from sticking to pan. Remove from pan when eggs are thoroughly cooked; keep warm.
4. Stack tortillas; wrap in damp paper towels and microwave on high for 25 seconds.
5. Place one tortilla on each of 4 plates. Spoon ¹/₄ cup egg mixture over half of tortilla; top with 2 tablespoons cactus, 2 tablespoons cheese, 1 tablespoon tomato, 1 teaspoon Salsa de Tomatillo, and 1 teaspoon cilantro. Fold remaining tortilla half over filling;

repeat with remaining tortillas and ingredients.
Note: Look for cactus paddles in the produce section of most supermarkets.
Per serving: Calories 163 (32% from fat); Fat 6g (sat 2g, mono 2g, poly 1.6g); Protein 11g; Carbohydrate 17g; Fiber 3g; Cholesterol 9mg; Iron 2mg; Sodium 687mg; Calcium 198mg

Salsa de Tomatillo
SERVES 16
PREPARATION: 5 MINUTES

The chiles del arbol add fire to this salsa.

15 tomatillos, peeled and halved
2-3 *chiles del arbol*
4 garlic cloves
1 tablespoon water
½ teaspoon salt
¼ teaspoon pepper

1. Place all ingredients in a food processor; pulse until coarsely chopped. Serving size: 2 tablespoons.
Per serving: Calories 12 (23% from fat); Fat 0g; Protein 0g; Carbohydrate 2g; Fiber 1g; Cholesterol 0mg; Iron 0mg; Sodium 74mg; Calcium 4mg

Chili-Oregano-Garlic Oil
PREPARATION: 5 MINUTES
COOKING: 10 MINUTES
STANDING: 15 MINUTES

To replace lard, Alberto steeps a variety of herbs and seasonings in lightly flavored olive oil.

1 cup light olive oil
3 garlic cloves
1-2 *chiles del arbol* (see box on page 221)
¼ bunch fresh oregano

1. Combine all ingredients in a saucepan over low heat; cook 10 minutes. Remove from heat; cool 15 minutes. Strain oil through a cheesecloth-lined colander into a bowl; discard solids. Serving size: 1 teaspoon (yields 1 cup).
Note: To play it safe, refrigerate homemade flavored oil immediately after it's prepared and use it within one week. The reason: Ingredients such as garlic and herbs may carry spores that could cause food

poisoning. Oil provides a perfect environment for spores to grow, particularly if it stands at room temperature.

Per serving: Calories 40 (100% from fat); Fat 5g (sat 0.6g, mono 3.3g, poly 0.4g); Protein 0g; Carbohydrate 0g; Fiber 0g; Cholesterol 0mg; Iron 0mg; Sodium 0mg; Calcium 0mg

Grilled Swordfish with Grilled Green Onions and Zucchini

SERVES 4
PREPARATION: 5 MINUTES
COOKING: 8 MINUTES

Alberto quickly learned great ways to lighten fish.

2 teaspoons Chili-Oregano-Garlic Oil (recipe above) or prepared chili-garlic oil, divided
4 (6-ounce) swordfish steaks (about 1½ inches thick)
6 green onions
2 medium zucchini, halved lengthwise
½ teaspoon salt, divided
¼ teaspoon black pepper
Cooking spray
2 teaspoons fresh lime juice
¾ teaspoon crushed red pepper
¼ cup Pico de Gallo (recipe follows)
Cilantro sprigs (optional)

1. Prepare grill.
2. Brush 1 teaspoon oil over fish; sprinkle fish, green onions, and zucchini with $^1/_4$ teaspoon salt and black pepper.
3. Place fish and zucchini on grill rack coated with cooking spray; grill 4 minutes. Add green onions; turn fish and zucchini. Grill 4 minutes or until fish and vegetables are cooked through. Remove from grill; chop vegetables. Combine vegetables, 1 teaspoon oil, $^1/_4$ teaspoon salt, lime juice, and crushed red pepper; toss to combine. Serve with Pico de Gallo; garnish with cilantro sprigs, if desired. Serving size: 1 swordfish fillet, $^1/_2$ cup zucchini mixture, and 1 tablespoon Pico de Gallo.

Per serving: Calories 194 (33% from fat); Fat 7g (sat 1.6g, mono 3.5g, poly 1.4g); Protein 25g; Carbohydrate 7.5g; Fiber 2.7g; Cholesterol 45mg; Iron 2mg; Sodium 434mg; Calcium 57mg

Pico de Gallo

SERVES 12
PREPARATION: 15 MINUTES

1½ cups diced plum tomatoes (about 3)
⅓ cup minced red onion
2 tablespoons minced fresh cilantro
2 tablespoons fresh lime juice
½ teaspoon seeded, minced *serrano* chile
¼ teaspoon salt

1. Combine all ingredients in a small bowl; stir well. Serving size: 2 tablespoons.

Per serving: Calories 6 (8% from fat); Fat 0g; Protein 0g; Carbohydrate 1g; Fiber 0g; Cholesterol 0mg; Iron 0mg; Sodium 51mg; Calcium 2mg

Grouper Fillets with Fire-Roasted Peppers

SERVES 4
PREPARATION: 10 MINUTES
COOKING: 32 MINUTES

Alberto's training in Italian cuisine is extensive. The salsa paired with this fish has distinct Italian influences, including balsamic vinegar and roasted peppers.

1 large yellow bell pepper (about ¾ pound)
1 large red bell pepper (about ¾ pound)
2 tablespoons minced fresh basil
2 tablespoons minced fresh cilantro
4 teaspoons olive oil, divided
1 tablespoons balsamic vinegar
½ teaspoon salt, divided
¼ teaspoon freshly ground black pepper, divided
2 garlic cloves, thinly sliced
4 (6-ounce) grouper fillets (1-inch thick) or any other firm, white fish

1. Preheat broiler.
2. Cut bell peppers in half lengthwise; discard seeds and membranes. Place bell pepper halves, skin sides up, on a foil-lined baking sheet; flatten with hand. Broil 12 minutes or until peppers are blackened. Place bell peppers in a zip-top plastic bag; seal. Let stand 10 minutes; peel and cut into $^1/_2$-inch strips. Combine bell peppers, basil, cilantro, 3 teaspoons oil, vinegar, $^1/_4$ teaspoon salt, $^1/_8$ teaspoon black pepper, and garlic in a medium bowl.

3. Sprinkle fish with $^1/_4$ teaspoon salt and $^1/_8$ teaspoon pepper. Heat 1 teaspoon oil in a large nonstick skillet over medium heat. Add fish; cook 5 minutes on each side or until fish flakes easily when tested with a fork. Serve with roasted peppers. Serving size: 1 fillet and $^1/_2$ cup roasted peppers.

Per serving: Calories 248 (24% from fat); Fat 7g (sat 1.1g, mono 3.7g, poly 1.1g); Protein 35g; Carbohydrate 12g; Fiber 4g; Cholesterol 63mg; Iron 2mg; Sodium 389mg; Calcium 69mg

Grilled Chicken Breast with Charred Corn Salsa

SERVES 4
PREPARATION: 10 MINUTES
COOKING: 15 MINUTES
MARINATING: 30 MINUTES

Grilling is a perfect way to add a smoky flavor to foods without extra fat.

3 tablespoons fresh lime juice, divided
1½ tablespoons olive oil, divided
½ teaspoon salt, divided
¼ teaspoon lemon pepper
4 (5-ounce) skinless, boneless chicken breast halves
1 cup fresh corn kernels (about 2 ears)
½ cup chopped red onion
1 (7-ounce) bottle roasted red bell peppers, chopped
1 tablespoon chopped fresh cilantro
¼ teaspoon freshly ground black pepper
Cooking spray
4 lime slices
4 cilantro sprigs (optional)

1. Prepare grill.
2. Combine 2 tablespoons lime juice, $^1/_2$ tablespoon oil, $^1/_4$ teaspoon salt, lemon pepper, and chicken in a large zip-top plastic bag. Seal and marinate in refrigerator 30 minutes.
3. While chicken marinates, heat $^1/_2$ tablespoon oil in a cast-iron skillet over high heat. Add corn, onion, and bell peppers; sauté 4 to 5 minutes or until slightly blackened. Transfer corn mixture to a bowl; stir in 1 tablespoon lime juice, $^1/_2$ tablespoon oil, $^1/_4$ teaspoon salt, cilantro, and black pepper.
4. Remove chicken from bag; discard marinade. Place chicken on grill rack coated with cooking spray; grill 4 to 5 minutes on each side or until done. Serve chicken with salsa and lime slices. Garnish with cilantro sprigs, if desired. Serving size: 1 chicken breast, $^1/_3$ cup salsa, and 1 lime slice.

Per serving: Calories 270 (25% from fat); Fat 8g (sat 1.2g, mono 4.2g, poly 1.0g); Protein 35g; Carbohydrate 15g; Fiber 2g; Cholesterol 82mg; Iron 2mg; Sodium 596mg; Calcium 28mg

Drunken Beans

SERVES 12
SOAKING: OVERNIGHT
PREPARATION: 10 MINUTES
COOKING: 82 MINUTES

Alberto likes to cook up a big pot of frijoles—beans—in plenty of water, store them in the refrigerator in their liquids to keep them moist, and then use them for stews, burritos, and refried beans.

1 pound dried pinto beans
1 gallon water (16 cups)
2 tablespoons Chili-Oregano-Garlic Oil (recipe on page 222) or prepared chili-garlic oil
1 cup chopped onion
1 garlic clove, minced
1 *serrano* chili pepper, seeded and chopped
2 roasted *poblano* peppers, seeded and chopped
1 teaspoon salt
½ teaspoon pepper
½ cup chopped green onion

1. Soak beans overnight; drain. Wash beans; place in a large Dutch oven. Cover with 1 gallon water; bring to a boil. Reduce heat and simmer 1 hour or until beans are almost tender. Remove from heat; drain beans, reserving 2 cups cooking liquid.
2. Heat oil in a saucepan over medium-high heat. Add onion, garlic, and *serrano;* sauté 2 minutes or until onions are soft. Add beans, reserved liquid, *poblano,* salt, and pepper; cook 20 minutes or until beans are tender. Sprinkle with green onion. Serving size: $^1/_2$ cup.

Per serving: Calories 151 (16% from fat); Fat 3g (sat 0.4g, mono 1.8g, poly 0.4g); Protein 8g; Carbohydrate 25g; Fiber 8g; Cholesterol 0mg; Iron 2mg; Sodium 198mg; Calcium 47mg ✳

Contributing Editor Maureen Callahan, R.D., is a freelance food and nutrition writer based in Arvada, Colorado.

10 easy ways to shave calories and shed pounds

1 Skinny dip
Dunk six boiled shrimp into 2 tablespoons of cocktail sauce instead of dipping six fried shrimp into 2 tablespoons of tartar sauce.
calories saved: 133

2 Steamy options
Savor your greens steamed with a dash of lemon, balsamic vinegar, or minced herbs instead of butter or oil.
calories saved: 100 per tablespoon of fat

3 Wrap it
Bag the rice. Wrap your chicken-and-veggie stir-fry (or tuna or egg salad) in fresh lettuce, Vietnamese-style.
calories saved: 159

4 A big buzz
Chocoholics can get a buzz—plus fiber, iron, and calcium—from a hefty handful of chocolate-covered raisins instead of a Snickers bar.
calories saved: 160

5 Breakfast bests
For a great home-style breakfast, swap fried eggs for poached and trade four strips of regular bacon for one slice of Canadian bacon.
calories saved: 216

6 Downsize
Taking the kids to McDonald's? Order medium fries instead of large and hold the cheese on that Quarter Pounder.
calories saved: 190

7 Snack in a crunch
Keep the crunch and add the fiber: Pair a domino-sized chunk of cheddar cheese with apple slices instead of three Ritz crackers.
calories saved: 155

8 Cheers
Celebrate the weekend with a Bloody Mary instead of a piña colada. Or pass on alcohol and sip sparkling water with lime instead of light beer.
calories saved: 108

9 Chew on this
Gum addict? Replace 10 sticks of regular chewing gum with sugar-free.
calories saved: 150

10 Walk this way
Skip the snack altogether and take a walk around the block instead.
calories saved: Countless

Add a Little Flavor and Help Fight Cancer

Season your next Italian supper with a pinch of antioxidants. Researchers have found that herbs such as oregano, dill, thyme, and rosemary serve up more cancer protection than fruits and vegetables. And you don't have to choke down a bowlful, either—a single tablespoon of fresh oregano equals the antioxidant protection of an entire apple.

No Need to Worry—Your Child Can Still Be a Healthy Eater

FRETTING THAT YOUR child eats too much may turn her from a regular to a plus size. Researchers recently found that moms who try to regulate their kids' weight by keeping certain foods (like sweets) off-limits may be paving the road to weight gain. Controlling moms "interfere with their kids' ability to self-regulate," explains lead study author Donna Spruijt-Metz, Ph.D., of the University of Southern California in Alhambra. Instead of paying attention to body signals and eating when they're truly hungry, she says, "they learn to eat when food is available."

What's a mother to do? "Never use food as a reward or punishment," Spruijt-Metz advises. "Continue to offer healthy foods, and your child will eventually try them, get used to them, and learn to eat healthier."

VitalStats

8 | Number of ginseng supplements out of 22 tested that contained pesticide

1 | Number of iron supplements out of 19 tested that contained lead

4 | Number of valerian supplements out of 17 tested that contained no detectable amount of valerian

$14 billion | Amount Americans spend each year on dietary supplements

81 | Percent of women in 1991 who said they need to improve their physical appearance

68 | Percent of women in 2001 who said the same

247 | Percent increase in cosmetic surgery for women from 1992 to 2000

112 | Percent increase for men

22 | Percent of West Coast residents who've had a massage in the last 12 months

13 | Percent of Southerners who have

Sources: consumerlab.com, *Yankelvich Monitor,* American Society of Plastic Surgeons, American Massage Therapy Association

Free Yourself from Time Constraints for an Enjoyable Dining Experience

Can't get reservations at the tony new bistro in town? The path to getting ahead of the hipsters could be switching to the slow lane. "For Americans who are always multitasking, measuring time in minutes, and juggling demands, slowing down is an indulgence," says Sylvia Tawse, member of the Boulder, Colorado, chapter of Slow Food, an international organization fighting against fast-food blandness and favoring locally grown pleasures. Tawse recently threw a slow (five-and-a-half-hour) birthday party for herself and 13 friends (along with two dogs and 18 farm cats).

"I didn't want to be the perfect Martha Stewart hostess with the table set and ready to go once the guests arrived," Tawse says. "We all put on aprons and cooked together. There was no agenda, except to share time." Recent research lauds the benefits of savoring the moment: A study published in the *Journal of Experimental Psychology* showed that trying to do two things at once may be less efficient because switching your attention drains mental energy.

Freedom from time constraints is key to entertaining slowly—no rushing through a meal to catch *ER.* Here are some other ways to decelerate: Prepare a time-consuming—but not overly labor-intensive—dish, such as a stew, soup, or pot roast. Serve several courses, even if some simply consist of sampling fruit or farmstead cheese, and take breaks in between each. Finally, put on a classic Ella Fitzgerald tune and cap the evening with a slow dance.

chapter 5

fitness

fun ways to firm up

find the right workout for any age

The key to staying fit for the long haul? Working out smarter—not harder.

BY SHEREE CRUTE

Just about every woman has weight fluctuations: They come with hormones. Starting in your early to mid-30s, though, the extra pounds that used to come and go start behaving like ill-mannered dinner guests—they arrive and they stay, despite hard time on the treadmill and a couple of days of light eating. The logical response? Work out even harder and eat even lighter, until you get that needle to move, right?

Not exactly. Health and fitness experts are beginning to see that the way to manage your weight as you age is to work out smarter (not harder) and ensure that you're eating enough (not necessarily less). The goal: to keep your hormones, which not only diminish with age but can be thrown off kilter by crushing workouts and low-calorie diets, in balance.

What do hormones, those vexing harbingers of pimples, PMS, and perimenopause, have to do with the way your body responds to running, kickboxing, or dieting? Plenty, researchers say. Substances like estrogen and progesterone are part of the chemical relay system that tells the brain, among other things, when the body should store fat and

Too much exercise and not enough food disturbs the body's natural hormone balance, making it tougher to lose weight.

when to burn it. The combination of too much exercise and not enough food disturbs the body's natural hormone balance, which experts say might make it tougher to lose weight. Research on mice suggests that estrogen, one of the many hormones in this complex balancing act, helps the body burn fat.

Exercise- and diet-related hormonal shifts have long been recognized in competitive female athletes, but recently, some physicians say they've noticed similar changes in women in their 30s and 40s who are struggling to hold the line on their dress sizes. Not only can this sabotage your weight-loss efforts, but it may also set you up for fertility problems, osteoporosis, and heart disease.

"If you exercise a moderate amount, it's good for everything, but if you overexercise, it's bad for everything," says Lisa Callahan, M.D., medical director of the Women's Sports Medicine Center at the Hospital for Special Surgery in New York City.

Callahan, author of the recent book *The Fitness Factor,* says that the phenomenon known as the female-athlete triad—disordered eating, loss of your period (which scientists call amenorrhea), and a drop in bone density—isn't

It's a good idea to **start weight training in your 20s or 30s—** it will serve your bones well in the future.

just an affliction of Olympic runners, gymnasts, and ballerinas, or anorexics and bulimics who diet and exercise to extremes. Many active women, she says, don't eat enough for their activity level and metabolism—that is, their eating is disordered—and they get caught in the triad.

The resulting low levels of estrogen and other hormones can be serious. Even if a woman doesn't stop menstruating, she may cease ovulating or ovulate less frequently, both of which affect fertility.

Now estrogen also puts a woman's heart at risk, according to Anne Zeni Hoch, D.O., a doctor of osteopathic medicine and director of the women's sports program at the Medical College of Wisconsin in Milwaukee. Hoch's recent studies have found that the arteries of some female athletes in their 20s with amenorrhea were as inflexible as a 50-year-old woman's. Estrogen is thought to keep arteries supple, reducing the risks of high blood pressure and cardiovascular disease. While Hoch studied competitive athletes whose periods had stopped, research shows that any active woman's arteries can be adversely affected when estrogen runs very low.

The antidote hinges on making sure you meet your nutritional needs, factoring in your activity level and changes in your body as you age. The details are often surprising: For instance, you may find out you can actually go a little easier on working out and eat a little more, says Leslie Bonci, R.D., director of sports nutrition at the University of Pittsburgh Medical Center. "I'm always telling my patients, 'You're allowed to eat!'"

That is, in fact, just what she said recently to 40-year-old Tracy Linza of Pittsburgh. Linza, who runs three times a week, weight-trains, and hikes and bikes for fun, decided to get serious about shedding the extra 55 pounds she'd been carrying for 12 years.

Bonci put Linza on a healthy, 2,100-calorie-a-day plan. After one year, Linza had lost 30 pounds. "I was a little surprised by the calorie level, but Dr. Bonci was basing it on my level of activity," she says.

Here are some general guidelines for exercising and eating to stay strong, healthy, and in perfect balance at any age.

The 20s:

You're young—you can handle anything (within reason) fitnesswise. A typical healthy 20-something woman can do higher-impact workouts, such as jumping rope and running, so try a variety of activities. And start strength-training—it will serve your bones well in the future. You're also able to burn calories pretty efficiently, so you need more to sustain you than you will in your 30s.

The 30s:

For many women, the 30s is the childbearing decade. This is also the time when they begin to lose muscle mass, so "there's a setup for weight fluctuations," Callahan says. Women with more muscle are better at burning calories, she says, so those who didn't begin lifting weights in their 20s should start now. Shift toward medium-impact weight-bearing workouts that put the large muscles of the legs, butt, and back to work with less joint-jarring force. For example, try low-impact aerobics, moderate jogging, and power walking. Regardless of your activity level, your caloric needs are likely to drop slightly.

The 40s:

To maximize benefits for your heart and bones, choose a variety of low- to medium-impact activities to prevent overuse injuries, boredom, and burnout. Tai Chi, yoga, or Pilates can reduce stress, increase flexibility, develop balance, and keep joints moving smoothly. And because muscles may take longer to rebuild and recover after exercise, be sure to rest at least two days a week.

The 50s:

Women can continue many of the fitness habits they developed throughout their 40s, but if joint trouble is an issue, non-weight-bearing activities such as water aerobics can help challenge muscles without taxing joints. Mind/body workouts like yoga and Pilates can help post-menopausal women maintain mobility, flexibility, and balance—which can become more limited over time. ✳

Sheree Crute is editor–at–large for **Heart & Soul** *magazine.*

Move Your Body, Free Your Mind

If you've got work to do but you're feeling uninspired, a little exercise could help flex those creative muscles.

BY DARYN ELLER

This is a true story: I was sitting at my desk, facing the challenge of how to begin a piece about the power of exercise to enhance creative thinking. Naturally, I wanted this beginning to engage you, but nothing was coming to mind. Zilch. So I did what I often do: I went to the pool and swam for an hour. Now here I am, typing away, my writer's block well behind me.

Exercise can do that for you. "It helps me get a fresh perspective on things," says Katlin Kirker, a 45-year-old painter who takes work-break walks on the beach near her home in Venice, California, whenever she needs to clear her mind. One writer I know generates so many ideas when running that he tucks a pad of paper and pen into his pocket before leaving the house.

It's all too easy to shrug off exercise, especially when you've got a lot of work to do. Why spend the time sweating when you could be pushing some of that paper off your desk? But research suggests that exercise can get your creative juices flowing and may even make you more productive. And it doesn't just apply to "creative types" like writers, musicians, and artists. Anyone who needs to solve problems and generate ideas can get a mental boost from a good workout.

> Why should you spend time sweating when there's work on your desk? Because research suggests that exercise can get your creative juices flowing.

The best measure so far of the exercise-creativity connection is a 1997 study conducted at Middlesex University in Middlesex, England, involving two groups of men and women ages 19 to 59. On the first day of the study, the researchers had the group do aerobic exercise for 25 minutes and then they asked them to think of as many uses for empty cardboard boxes and tin cans as they possibly could. On the second day, the group watched an "emotionally neutral" video on rock formations. They were then given the same creativity test. After working out, the volunteers came up with more solutions to the cardboard box/tin can dilemma than they did after watching the video.

What is it about exercise that can make people better thinkers? Robert E. Thayer, Ph.D., a professor of psychology at California State University-Long Beach and author of *Calm Energy: How People Regulate Mood with Food and Exercise,* believes it may have to do with the ability of physical activity to alter some factors that inhibit creativity. One is a lack of energy. "When you exercise, you experience a host of physiological changes, such as an increase in metabolism, more cardiac activity, and the release of neurotransmitters that affect alertness," Thayer says. "These all add to a state of general bodily arousal, and that increases energy."

Another factor could be mood, says Eric Maisel, Ph.D., a California psychotherapist and author of *Write Mind: 299 Things Writers Should Never Say to Themselves (and What They Should Say Instead).* "What often stops people from creating is that they're depressed, so it's perfectly logical that if exercise reduces your experience of depression, you're more likely to create," he says. "Same with anxiety. Creative blocks can be a form of performance anxiety, so anything that reduces anxiety can help."

Another theory of Maisel's—and the one I relate to the most—is that exercise produces a state Zen Buddhists call the "empty mind." When the mind empties, preoccupations slip away and that nagging little voice inside your head that says "Maybe I'm just not smart enough to figure this out" or "I used to be a good writer but not anymore" shuts up. During those moments of silence, creative thoughts have a chance to develop. "If we're always worried about something or concerned about our to-do list, there is no way for ideas to enter our brain," Maisel says. "But with the emptying of the mind, worries fade away, and when that happens, ideas come."

While you can't exactly prescribe a workout to build creativity like you would to build biceps, the 25 minutes of aerobic exercise employed in the Middlesex study is a good place to start. (By the way, in the study, volunteers did instructor-led aerobic exercise, but the researchers speculate that running and walking may be equally—and possibly even more—beneficial.) And a longer, harder session may make you even more creative, depending on the reason for your imaginative angst. For instance, if stress is hindering your thought process, an hour of vigorous aerobic exercise could spark a breakthrough. "Heavy exercise, like working out hard at the gym for an hour, has been shown to significantly decrease tension," Thayer says. "But it can also make you very tired afterward, and you may not get a resurgence of energy for a while." Sometimes, though, less is better: If you need more energy, Thayer's studies have shown that a fast-paced walk as brief as 10 minutes can help. "We've found that

a workout for your brain

Brain Gym movements were created in the 1970s by educator Paul E. Dennison, Ph.D. These short, easy exercises are designed to enhance neural connections and reduce stress. "We often have ideas in our heads, but they don't always come out of our hands or our mouths quite the way we envision them," explains Susan Berg, Ph.D., a certified Brain Gym instructor in the Philadelphia area. "When you move, a part of your brain called the reticular activating system—the area responsible for arousing the brain—wakes up, helping your mind focus and your thoughts flow."

Most of the Brain Gym movements are designed to help shuttle information between the left and right sides of your brain. When you don't have time to squeeze in a longer workout, try this: Stand with your arms at your sides. Simultaneously bend your right knee and left elbow at a 90-degree angle, and move them toward each other. (Don't crouch to make them meet. It's not necessary that they touch.) Return to the starting position, then repeat with your left knee and right elbow. Continue at a moderate pace for about 1 minute. You'll find this move and others at www.braingym.org.

short, brisk walks can raise energy for up to two hours afterward," he reports.

You may have to experiment a little to find out what works for you. For me, a moderate workout is best—that is, one long enough to help me get an "empty mind" but not so hard that it tires me out. Once I get to that quiet state, so many ideas start percolating in my head that when I get home, I often go straight to my desk to capitalize on the momentum. Need proof that it works? I finished this article, didn't I? ✳

Daryn Eller lives in Venice, California, and has written for O, Self, *and* Parenting.

exercise your right to brag

If you spread the word that you're working out, you'll be more likely to stick with your fitness routine.

—*International Health, Racquet & Sportsclub Association*

Get on the Ball

Body rolling, a new fitness fad, promises to stretch, massage, and strengthen—all with the help of a little ball. Does it deliver?

BY CATHERINE GUTHRIE

PHOTOGRAPHY BY ERICKA McCONNELL

I am squatting on a patch of nubby, brown carpet, my left butt cheek planted firmly on top of a bright red ball the size of a cantaloupe. "Feel all your weight dropping into the ball," coos the woman kneeling next to me. I squeeze my eyes shut as I try to picture my gluteus moving away from my maximus. No dice. My butt doesn't budge. Oh dear, I'm only five minutes into this hour-long body-rolling session. It's going to be a long morning.

Ordinarily, I avoid exercise that involves cute accoutrements. Nothing makes me hightail it out of a gym class faster than spotting a plastic step or a mile-long rubber band. I'd trade a gym full of equipment for a pair of sturdy shoes and a hiking trail any day.

But hiking doesn't soothe the tension burrowed deep inside the muscles of my lower back. Neither do the rare massages or chiropractic visits that my tight purse strings allow. So, on the recommendation of a friend, I've shelved my skepticism and decided to try body rolling.

A new type of exercise, body rolling blends the stretching of yoga with the release of massage. It works by squeezing the kinks out of muscles, literally rolling them out, one by one, with balls that range from 3 to 9 inches in diameter. The balls also differ in density so you can adjust the amount of pressure being applied to your muscles, much like a massage therapist uses varying pressure on different areas of the body.

The idea behind body rolling is that tension starts where the muscle originates—in the dense fibrous tendons that anchor them to bone. It's this precise attention to stretching muscles from tendon to tendon that makes the exercise unique. "Starting at the origin and working your way down allows for a complete release," says Yamuna Zake, a mind-body entrepreneur who has also been a yoga instructor and massage therapist. The practice, which Zake developed 10 years ago, is similar to yoga in that as you stretch, you also strengthen muscles and improve balance and posture.

Zake says body rolling grew out of her own hands-on massage technique, in which she combines pressure and traction to coax muscles into releasing their grip. Her goal was to develop a self-massage and stretching tool that clients could use at home when they were pressed for time, money, or both. "In the beginning, I raided toy stores looking for the perfect ball, but they were all either too hard or too big," she says. "So I designed my own."

Zake has traveled the country nearly nonstop the past two years, certifying more than 250 body-rolling instructors in her wake. Deborah Powers, a massage therapist in Port Huron, Michigan, is one of them. Within minutes of meeting her, I'm flat on her living-room floor, a ball wedged between my back and the carpet. My first impulse is to zip up and down on the balls, ironing out the muscles along my spine. Powers is quick to put on the brakes. There are routines designed specifically for releasing different muscle groups in the back, side, and chest, as well as more focused workouts for specific conditions, such as scoliosis, herniated disks, and sciatica, she explains. Each uses one or a combination of five different balls of various sizes. Working the long muscles of the back and the hamstrings calls for the cantaloupe ball, while the smaller muscles of the feet wrap easily around a lemon-sized ball. The muscles in the body naturally follow a set of lines. "By using those lines as a road map, you can set off a chain reaction of muscle release," Powers says.

As I inhale, the ball presses deep into the tangle of knots that sprout alongside my spine. "Sink into the ball," she tells me. "That's it. Now breathe." The sensation is similar to being kneaded by a strong-armed Swedish masseuse. The snarls open and loosen ever so slightly. I may not do back flips out the door, but it's definitely a start.

Although body rolling's claims haven't been put to the test by sports science, the practice has won over a number of supporters. Elizabeth Larkam, a lecturer in the department of exercise and sport science at the University of San Francisco, describes it as "an ingenious form of sensory stimulation." The nervous system is wired to respond best to movement that is generated from within, as opposed to when a massage therapist initiates a move. "In body rolling, the combination of the ball's pressure along with creating your own movement has a tremendous calming effect," she explains.

Richard Cotton, an exercise physiologist and spokesman for the American Council on Exercise, an organization that sets certification standards for fitness instructors, sees body rolling as a natural offshoot of the growing popularity of balls as fitness equipment. "The stimulation from balls not only stretches muscle, but also increases the range of motion of joints," he says.

how to get your body rollin'

One of the best things about the body-rolling workout is that you don't have to spend very much to get started. The strong, rubbery balls cost between $1.75 and $22, depending on size and density. For beginners, one ball is enough: At $16, the 9-inch orb is a good starter, since it works most major muscle groups. Yamuna Zake, the former yoga instructor and massage therapist who created the workout, also offers an instructional video and CD. They're available, along with the balls, at Zake's Web site, www.bodylogic.com.

Still, it helps to have a certified instructor roll you through your first few workouts. You can expect to pay $45 to $60 for a private session or $10 to $15 for a class offered through a gym or yoga studio. There are more than 250 instructors worldwide. To locate one in your area, call BodyLogic at 888-226-9616. Once you've learned the basic moves, you may want to see a more technical explanation of different body-rolling routines. For that, check out Zake's detailed book, *Body Rolling: An Experiential Approach to Complete Muscle Release.*

But don't confuse the workout balls created by Zake with the overgrown beach balls so common in gyms today. Some gym balls puff up to 60 inches in diameter, dwarfing the spheres used in body rolling. "Those big balls offer a big stretch, but the results are only temporary," Zake says. "They don't get at the spot where tension originates."

I'm dubious at first, but after rolling out my left hamstring inch by inch, from pelvis to shinbone, Powers has me stand up in a before-and-after comparison. Sure enough, my left leg is loosey-goosey. My right is like a banjo string that's been tuned a bit too tightly. After 15 minutes of doing the body-rolling exercises on both legs, I can bend over and place my palms flat against the floor, a move I can usually only execute at the end of a two-hour yoga class.

There is, however, one drawback to body rolling: It's not quick. A full-body rollout can easily take an hour. By the time I'd breathed and sunk into every vertebra, I'd spent nearly 15 minutes on my back alone. Powers assures me that I can cut my session in half by focusing on my trouble spots. That's good: Since body rolling isn't a cardio workout, most people use it in addition to their regular fitness routine. If you've barely got time to squeeze a 20-minute jog into your day, it may be tough to scrounge up another 15 to 30 minutes for a basic body-rolling routine, much less a full-body one.

> One needs to bring to body rolling **a willingness to revel** in sensation.
>
> —*Elizabeth Larkam*

Larkam says the fact that the exercise takes so much time is both one of its biggest benefits and one reason it turns some people off. "One needs to bring to body rolling a willingness to revel in sensation," she says. "That's not a comfortable thing for many people."

At the end of 60 minutes, I'd managed to steamroll most of my neck, torso, and legs. I stood taller and considerably more relaxed than when I'd started. Best of all, the angry muscles in my lower back were assuaged.

The routine I learned is easy enough to do on the hardwood floor in my living room. And even though I'm usually a skeptic when it comes to exercise gear, I now have my own red ball. It lives in my closet, right next to my hiking boots. ✳

Catherine Guthrie is a freelance health and medical writer whose work has appeared in Self, Yoga Journal, *and on* WebMD.com.

happy trails

If you think outdoor workouts and the Web have nothing in common, check out www.traillink.com. Type in your location to find a rail trail—an abandoned railroad corridor that has been turned into a public fitness path—good for walking, running, biking, or inline skating.

does that come in a size
XXXX-Small?

You may be trying to lose inches, but your workout clothes might be gaining them. Companies like Nike and Hind have begun to "vanity size" their fitness apparel—meaning that today's "medium" may be yesterday's "large." We say the size on the label might give your self-image a sizable boost, but remember: The scale still measures pounds the old-fashioned way.

Q+A
Don't Depend on Exercise Machines' Calorie Counters

Are those "calories burned" counters on exercise machines accurate?

SOME CALORIE COUNTERS are fairly accurate, and some need a serious reality check. The challenge is figuring out which machines to trust. The first clue to a machine's effectiveness is whether or not you're required to punch in your weight, says exercise physiologist Richard Cotton, a spokesman for the American Council on Exercise. "The number of calories you burn depends on how much you weigh," he explains. If the counter doesn't plug this information into its formula, chances are that the results will be way off. Even if weight is factored in, you shouldn't assume that the machine is on target. The formula could be based on a superfit triathlete or a couch spud who hasn't worked out since Reagan was president—neither of which probably applies to you.

Still, even if it won't tell you exactly how many Oreos you've burned off, a calorie counter can help you track your workout progress. If a machine says you burned 5 percent more calories this week than last, for instance, that means that your workout was 5 percent more intense. Challenge yourself to push the calories-burned number a bit higher (no more than 10 percent a week to avoid injury) to maximize results.

get more from your fitness tapes

Whether you want to sculpt "8-minute buns" or sweat to the "firefighter's workout," the instructor is key to a good fitness video. In her book, *The Fitness Factor: Every Woman's Key to a Lifetime of Health and Well-Being*, Lisa Callahan, M.D., offers a buyers' guide to workout tapes. She suggests looking for these features on the label before buying: a wide variety of exercises, beginner alternatives for more advanced moves, and alignment tips to prevent injury.

Q+A
Are jogging strollers safe for moms and babies?

I'm a new mom, and I like to run while pushing my baby in a jogging stroller. Could this be harmful to my little one—or to me?

BE SENSIBLE while you're piloting the stroller, and both you and baby should be safe. That means no running while wearing a headset or chatting on a cell phone. And follow the guidelines for use: Don't strap your baby in until the child's at least six weeks old and has good neck control. Give little heads extra stability by placing a rolled towel or a pillow beneath the neck. Also remember that while you're sweating away, your baby may not be, so dress your child accordingly.

Just paying attention to your baby's safety needs, though, won't protect you from getting a few aches. Keeping a two-handed "death grip" on the stroller's handlebar can strain your upper back and may limit the motion of your lower back, causing soreness. Try using a one-handed push, switching hands frequently. If you find yourself tensing up, stop and stretch (a good idea even if you're not pushing a stroller).

A more likely source of strain is from trying to do too much too soon. It's better to add two minutes to your workout every other day than it is to add one minute every day. And be careful on the downhills: That's where you're more likely to hurt a knee or twist an ankle—and let the stroller get away from you.

body work

3 Steps to Strong, Sexy Legs

WORKOUT CREATED BY PETRA KOLBER

PHOTOGRAPHY BY DAVID MARTINEZ

We know all too well how tough it can be to stay motivated to exercise. When your workout screams "boring," you need a power play.

This workout combines muscle-toning squats with cardio-intense jumps. Besides adding a burst of levity to a ho-hum fitness regimen, it will target the large muscles in your butt and thighs, boosting your heart rate. Zoom past a fitness or weight-loss plateau—and prepare for invigorating winter sports, such as skiing, skating, and snowshoeing.

This workout can't replace your normal exercise routine, but it can offer a quick alternative. Each set should take approximately 10 minutes. When time permits, try challenging yourself with two or three sets. During the power plays, be sure to land softly with your knees slightly bent. Do 8 to 12 repetitions of the strength move, then the companion power play for 30 to 45 seconds. That's one set—and one jump closer to a stronger, healthier you.

pop-up

1A | Stand with your feet hip-distance apart.

1B | Bend your knees and lower your hips toward the floor. Push your hips back as if to sit in a chair. Be sure your knees don't jut past your toes. Raise your arms in front of you for balance. Rise and repeat 8 to 12 times.

1C | Power play: Lower yourself into squat position. Swing your arms down and back for momentum. Then, using your glutes and thighs, jump up as if shooting a basketball, lifting your arms overhead for maximum height. Land softly in the squat position, lowering your arms.

dancer's leap

2A | Stand with your feet a little wider than shoulder-distance apart and your feet turned out about 45 degrees.

2B | Bend your knees until your thighs are almost parallel to the floor. Make sure that your knees are in line with your toes. Rise and repeat 8 to 12 times.

2C | Power play: From the plié position, use your inner thighs and glutes to push yourself into a high jump. Land with your feet together and your knees slightly bent. Then push off again, using your outer thighs and glutes to separate your feet and land in a plié.

turbo jump

3A | Stand on your right leg with your left knee lifted.

3B | Keeping your left foot off the ground, bend your right knee and lower your hips. Keep your abs tight and your right knee over your toes. Reach forward with your elbows bent. Return to starting position. Do 8 to 12 repetitions with each leg.

3C | Power play: Using your thighs and glutes, push off with your right leg and leap up and forward as far as you can, landing softly on your left leg. Quickly leap from your left leg, then continue to alternate legs for 30 to 45 seconds. ✳

Petra Kolber is a contributing editor and Reebok University master trainer. She can be reached via our Web site (www.health.com) or hers (www.petrakolber.com).

body work

Make Your Hips More Flexible

WORKOUT CREATED BY PETRA KOLBER　　**PHOTOGRAPHY BY DAVID MARTINEZ**

If you've tried sitting on the floor "Indian-style" and your knees won't go anywhere near the ground, welcome to the world of tight hip and groin muscles. It might not sound like much of a problem, but stiff hips can lead to lower-back pain, turn your stride into a shuffle, and limit your agility on the basketball or tennis court.

Heaping yourself into a chair for hours without a break allows muscles in the back of your legs and the front of your hips to shorten. But after a few weeks of doing these simple stretches, you should notice improvements in your posture and the way you move. They're inspired by

Active-Isolated Stretching, a concept developed by exercise physiologist Jim Wharton and his son, Phil, co-authors of *The Whartons' Stretch Book*. All you need is a rope or towel to gently coax muscles into a deeper stretch.

Tips for success: Get your blood pumping with at least five minutes of brisk walking or calisthenics before stretching, since warm muscles are more pliable. Breathe deeply and exhale as you ease into your stretch (make sure you don't bounce). And give hips a break from sitting at your desk: Walk around now and then during the day.

seated hamstring stretch

1A | Sit upright on the ground with your legs extended in front of you. Place a rope or towel under the arches of your feet, holding one end in each hand.

1B | Gently pull on the rope, drawing your chest toward your knees and contracting both thighs. Keep your back straight and allow your body to hinge forward at the hips, not the lower back. Lower your chest toward your knees until you feel a slight stretch through the back of your legs. Hold the stretch for 2 breaths and return to the starting position. Repeat 12 times.

single hamstring stretch

2A | Lie faceup on the ground. Bend your right knee, placing your right foot flat on the ground. Put a rope or towel under the arch of your left foot, then extend your straightened left leg on the ground, holding one end of the rope or towel in each hand.

2B | As you raise your straightened leg, contract the muscles in the front of your left thigh as if to lock your knee. Lift your left leg and pull it toward you as far as you can. Hold this stretch for 2 breaths, then return your left leg to the starting position. You will probably feel the stretch in your hamstrings as you tighten the front of your thigh. Repeat 12 times, then switch legs.

diagonal hip stretch

3A | Lie on your back, then place a rope or towel under the arch of your left foot (keep foot relaxed but slightly flexed to hold the rope in place). Extend your left leg out to the side as shown.

3B | Holding the ends of the rope or towel in your left hand, contract your inner thigh and carry your leg across your body until you can feel the stretch through your left hip. Avoid allowing your left hip to roll over your right hip. Hold this stretch for 2 breaths, then return to the starting position. Repeat 12 times, then switch legs.

standing hip stretch

4A | Stand next to something sturdy, holding on with your left hand for balance. Bend your knees slightly and keep your back straight. Bend your right leg back at the knee and place a towel or rope just above your right ankle. Bring both knees together and keep your hip-bones parallel to the ground.

4B | With your ab muscles tight and your standing leg slightly bent, use the rope or towel to pull your leg as you contract your butt and hamstrings. Hold for 2 breaths, then return to the starting position. Repeat 12 times, then switch legs. ✳

Petra Kolber is a contributing editor and Reebok University master trainer. She can be reached via our Web site (www.health.com) or hers (www.petrakolber.com).

241

THE LAST
Ab Workout
You'll Ever Need

Still churning out crunch after crunch with no results? Update your ab routine with our three-point plan.

WORKOUT BY TRISH MUSE

PHOTOGRAPHY BY DAVID ROTH

Next to walking, the stomach crunch is probably the most popular exercise around (breathing, swallowing, and sex don't count). And for good reason. The basic crunch has long been the gold standard of abdominal exercises. But if you've ever done it, you've probably experienced the crunch conundrum: that, despite triple-digit crunch-a-thons, your abs don't feel any stronger or look any trimmer.

It's not because the crunch is worthless. But even a good exercise, done with impeccable form, will lose its punch after a while. That's because, when challenged, your muscles adapt relatively quickly, so what was tough at first will become easy. And—sorry to say—easy won't get you the abs you want. To keep your muscles interested, you have to switch exercises every three to four weeks.

We've asked physical therapist and personal trainer Trish Muse, creator and star of several fitness videos, including the aptly named *Ab Attack*, to devise three balanced, super-efficient ab workouts. This way, you don't have to reinvent the wheel every month or so—just switch from one workout to another. Adopt this smarter strategy, and chances are you'll see more progress with less work.

the ab rotation

Start by doing Routine 1 three or four days a week (do the routine every other day to avoid working the same body part two days in a row). After about a month, go on to Routine 2, then Routine 3. Do one to three sets of 8 to 12 reps of each exercise in the routine. If an exercise is so easy you feel you could do reps for days, double-check your form. To adjust the difficulty level, follow our modification tips. You should come close to fatigue in your last 2 or 3 reps of each set.

During each exercise, **draw your navel in toward your spine.** Think of your abdominal muscles as a corset that you're cinching tighter and tighter.

routine one

single leg pelvic tilt

1 | Stand with your feet hip-width apart, knees slightly bent. Shift your weight to your right foot and lift your left, placing the tip of your toe a few inches forward on the ground for balance.

Contract your abdominal muscles by drawing them in toward your spine. Tilt your pelvis backward as if it's a bucket and you're pouring water out the back. Using your abs and maintaining the pelvic tilt, allow your left leg to lift an inch or two from the ground. Lift with your abs, not your hip and leg. Complete the set; switch legs.

Less difficult: Hold on to a chair for support, or just barely lift your leg in the tilt.
More difficult: Loop elastic tubing or a band around both ankles for resistance, or use an ankle weight.

superman lift

2A | Lie facedown with your arms extended forward and legs extended behind you.

2B | Contract your lower-back muscles and lift your upper torso and arms off the ground. Return to the starting position, then complete the set.

side crunch and rotation

3 | Lie on your left side, your left hipbone directly below your right. Bend your knees and hips at 90-degree angles. Place your right hand on your right ear and your left hand behind your left ear, right elbow pointing upward. Contract your abdominals and lift your torso from the ground, bringing your left arm up and over toward the inside of your right knee. Complete the set, then switch sides.

Less difficult: Eliminate the rotation.
More difficult: Straighten your legs slightly.

routine two

backward lean

1A | Sit with your knees bent, feet flat on the ground, and arms extended.

1B | Contract your ab muscles, pulling your navel toward your spine. With your back straight, slowly lean backward at about a 45-degree angle. Keep your chest up, shoulders down. Hold 3 to 5 seconds; return to starting position.
Less difficult: Don't lean back as far; place hands behind knees for support.
More difficult: Don't use your arms, or extend them above your head.

Breathe naturally. It helps to exhale during the contraction and inhale on the return.

the swim

2A | Lying facedown, extend your arms forward, keeping them close to your head. Extend your legs behind you. Contract your back muscles and simultaneously lift your right arm and left leg a few inches off the ground, keeping your trunk as still as possible.

2B | Lower your arm and leg, then lift your left arm and right leg. Do 8 to 12 alternate repetitions on each side.

side crunch

3 | Lie on your left side with your left hipbone directly below your right. Place your fists at your temples. Contract the muscles of your right side (the obliques) as you lift both your torso and your legs from the ground slightly. Using your abdominal muscles for control, slowly lower your torso and legs. Complete the set, then switch sides.
Less difficult: Move only your upper body.
More difficult: Lift slightly higher and hold slightly longer.

routine three

the plank

1A | Get on your knees, supporting yourself with your forearms.

1B | Straighten your legs, stepping back one foot at a time. Hover in that position for 10 to 15 seconds, shoulders squared and spine straight from your neck to your butt.

Less difficult: When straightening your legs, rest on your knees with your back straight; keep your toes on the ground.

More difficult: Do this with straight arms as if doing a push-up.

knee circles

2A | Sit with your arms at your sides, knees bent. Contract your abs and lift your feet off the ground slightly.

2B | Slowly draw an imaginary circle with your knees. Keep your torso stable. One circle equals one repetition.

Less difficult: Lift one foot off the ground.

Least difficult: Keep feet on the ground.

If you need **more of a challenge,** lean back
and reach slightly farther.

backward lean and reach

3 | Sit with your knees bent, feet flat on the ground. Contracting your abs, recline to about a 45-degree angle with your back straight. At the same time, rotate your torso slightly, moving your left arm behind you and your right arm in front. As you rotate, turn your head and look behind you.

Less difficult: Lean back or rotate less, or use a hand behind your knees.

More difficult: Lean and reach slightly farther. ✳

Personal trainer Trish Muse's Web site is www.bodyproductions.com.

body work

Sculpt a Better Back for Power and Great Posture

WORKOUT CREATED BY PETRA KOLBER   PHOTOGRAPHY BY DAVID MARTINEZ

Out of sight and out of mind, your upper back too often gets ignored. But with just a few minutes and the right types of exercises, you can stop the neglect.

The upper-back muscles aren't just key to looking great in spaghetti straps. Your largest—the latissimus dorsi, a fan-shaped muscle that runs from the top of your pelvis to your shoulders, and the trapezius, which forms a T down your spine and between your shoulder blades—are the prime movers when you swim, row, cross-country ski, or do pull-ups. And with these muscles strong and toned, you'll maintain good posture by taking some stress off your lower back and stabilizing your shoulders.

Our workout uses rubber exercise tubing to target these multipurpose muscles. Rubber tubing is available for less than $10 by mail order and in sporting-goods stores. (Ours is from SPRI Products, 800-222-7774 or www.spriproducts.com.)

Concentrate on initiating each move by contracting your upper-back muscles, not pulling with your arms. Keep the focus on your back. These moves are subtle, but the results aren't.

shoulder blade shrug

1A | Lie facedown on the floor. Prop yourself up on your elbows, keeping them directly underneath your shoulders. Hold your abs tight and shrug your shoulders slightly, raising them toward your ears.

1B | With your forearms firmly planted on the floor, move your shoulders in a diagonal line away from your ears toward your hips, as though you were trying to put your shoulder blades into your back pockets. This will lift your abdomen slightly. Keep your neck relaxed and your spine long. Hold this position for 3 breaths and then return to the starting position. Repeat 8 to 12 times. Build to three sets.

2A

2B

single arm pull-down

2A | Stand with your feet hip-width apart, knees slightly bent. Hold the tubing in front of you, with your right arm straight and your left arm bent. Adjust the tension of the band as needed.

2B | With your right arm stable, use a slow and controlled motion to draw your left arm down and behind you in an arc. Your left hand will be just outside of your peripheral vision. You should feel tension throughout this move. Hold for 3 breaths and then release. Repeat 8 to 12 times per side. Build to three sets on each arm.

seated row

3A | Sit on the floor with your legs extended in front of you, resting your feet against the legs of a sturdy chair. Wrap the tubing around the back legs of the chair at a level even with your waist. Grasp one handle of the tubing in each hand and extend your arms in front of you. Your knees and elbows should be slightly bent and your back should be straight.

3B | Holding your torso stable, gently squeeze your shoulder blades together. Once you can go no farther, draw your hands in toward your lower ribs. Hold this position for 3 breaths and then return to the starting position. Repeat 8 to 12 times. Build to three sets.

upper-back squeeze

4A | Grasp one handle of the tubing in each hand and lie facedown on the floor. Position the tubing against your upper back and extend your arms out at the shoulders to form a T with your body. Make sure the tubing is taut across your back (adjust the tension by wrapping the tubing around your wrists). Gently rest your fingertips on the floor and keep your elbows slightly bent.

4B | Visualize someone holding a tennis ball between your shoulder blades. Without bending your elbows any farther, draw your shoulder blades together, imagining that they are squeezing the ball. Hold for 3 breaths and then return to the starting position. Repeat 8 to 12 times. Build to three sets. ✳

Petra Kolber is a contributing editor as well as Reebok University master trainer. She can be reached via our Web site (www.health.com) or hers (www.petrakolber.com).

body work Shoulder the Load

WORKOUT CREATED BY PETRA KOLBER   **PHOTOGRAPHY BY DAVID MARTINEZ**

A sly glance over a strong and graceful shoulder can be a surefire way to intimidate an opponent just before you deliver a killer tennis serve. But over time, repetitive moves—like pitching a softball, painting, or hanging wallpaper—can pinch and irritate tendons in your shoulder as they rub against bone. And then, there you are: a card-carrying member of the impingement party.

No fewer than nine muscles crisscross your shoulder, forming your body's most mobile—and unstable—joint. These exercises will help you keep those muscles in shape. You won't need to lift much weight; use 2 to 5 pounds for these exercises, unless we say otherwise. Trust us: More isn't better here—unless you're talking more compliments on your tennis game.

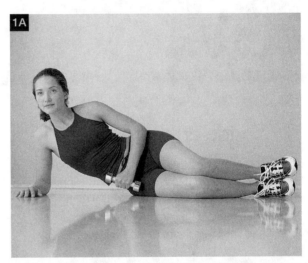

external rotation

1A | Lie on your right side, holding a weight no heavier than 3 pounds in your left hand. Bend your left elbow at a 90-degree angle.

1B | Keeping your left elbow tucked near your hip, rotate your arm at your shoulder until your left hand points to the ceiling. (Keep your palm facing forward.) Pause and return to the starting position. Do 8 to 12 repetitions, then switch arms.

Try these five moves to **power up and protect** your body's most unstable joint.

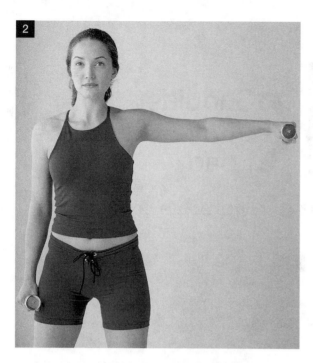

side-arm side raise

2 | Stand with both arms at your sides, holding a weight in each hand. Bend your left elbow slightly, and then extend your left arm until it's parallel to the floor. Pause, then return to the starting position. Do 8 to 12 repetitions, then switch arms.

single-arm front raise

3 | Stand with your feet hip-distance apart, arms by your sides, holding a weight in each hand. With your palms facing in, lift your right hand until your arm is parallel to the floor. Pause; return to starting position. Do 12 to 15 repetitions, then switch arms.

bent-over fly

4A | Stand with a weight in your left hand. Keeping your abs tight, bend your knees and hinge forward from your hips. Brace yourself by placing your right hand on your thigh.

4B | Keeping your right hand on your thigh and your upper body steady, raise your left hand to the side so that your arm is parallel to the floor. Pause, then return to the starting position. Do 8 to 12 repetitions, then switch arms.

No fewer than nine muscles crisscross your shoulder, forming your body's most mobile joint. These exercises will help you keep those muscles in shape.

overhead press

5A | Stand with your feet hip-distance apart and your knees slightly bent, holding weights at your shoulders with your palms facing each other.

5B | Keeping your abdominal muscles tight and your back straight, press the weights over your head. Be sure to avoid arching your back and locking your elbows at the top of the movement. Return to the starting position. Do 12 to 15 repetitions. ✳

Contributing Editor Petra Kolber is a Reebok University master trainer. She can be reached via our Web site (www.health.com) or hers (www.petrakolber.com).

Pump Up Your Confidence

One woman learns that the benefits of weight-lifting go much deeper than muscle.

BY DOROTHY FOLTZ-GRAY

For years, I thought of weight rooms as a male province, a world of big machines and even bigger men. I ventured in once or twice, but boredom and intimidation sent me scurrying back to running and swimming, exercise realms many women feel more comfortable in. Then, as research touting all the good things strength training can do for women—like halting bone loss, improving balance, boosting metabolism and mood, and toning the body—continued to emerge, I began to reconsider.

So, last spring, I signed up for a strength-training class at the local YMCA. And as the music started—a kind of African percussive meets Britney Spears—I knew I'd found the class that I was after. I loved the sight of my arms flexing, my thighs squatting, and my shoulders pressing in unison with 10 other women (and a few men). Within weeks, I felt much stronger.

But the real surprise came more slowly. By June, I felt a new comfort emerging about my body. My class was forcing me to stand in front of full-length mirrors on a regular basis—an experience I'd never had before. As I watched my body work, the legs I'd condemned as big reintroduced themselves to me as the power behind my squats and lunges.

In truth, my physique hadn't changed that much. Sure, I was more toned, and my clothes hung better. But more importantly, I had begun to experience my body in a new way—as powerful and functional, the very body I needed to do the work I was doing. Strength training was sculpting the way I viewed my body. But how?

Most of the research on the psychological effects of fitness has focused on aerobic exercise, not weight training. And those studies only observed changes in mood and self-confidence, not body image—the picture we hold of ourselves in our minds. But in the early '90s, Larry Tucker, Ph.D., a professor at Brigham Young University in Provo, Utah, speculated that strength training could do more for body image than aerobic exercise could.

To test his thesis, he gathered 60 inactive women of average weight (ages 35 to 49), divided them into two groups, and asked them to rate how they felt about different parts of their bodies in terms of strength, flexibility, and appearance. Then, one group walked while the other group lifted weights three days a week for 12 weeks. The results were striking: The second time the groups took the survey, the body-image scores of the weight-lifting women had improved more than twice as much as the walkers' had.

The power of strength training to transform body image lies in its ability to show measurable, visible progress, Tucker says. "The main effect of aerobic exercise is that the heart gets stronger, and you can't see that change," he says. But when you strength train, you can see your body getting firmer and stronger as you increase the amount of weight and the number of reps. "So you have more opportunity to see that what you do is making a difference—one of the main ingredients for changing emotional well-being and body image," he says.

Another factor is the power of the burn. Weight training stresses muscles, creating small tears in the muscle fibers. Your muscles respond by laying down new layers. That little reconstruction project burns calories as it makes your muscles larger and stronger. These changes happen so fast that a typical woman who trains consistently could double the amount of weight she lifts within two months.

But physiology is only part of the equation. Strength training also triggers a psychological process that begins to undo the negative thoughts many women have harbored about their bodies since toddlerhood. "Women have always looked at their bodies from a cosmetic perspective," says Lisa Callahan, M.D., co-founder and medical director of the Women's Sports Medicine Center in New York City and author of *The Fitness Factor.* "But when you do a biceps curl, there's a new feeling of power. You see a muscle move and grow, and you begin to challenge yourself. It's a new way of looking at your body. You can admire it as a finely tuned machine."

And it doesn't vanish when the workout ends. "You have a different level of confidence, and that makes life so much easier," Callahan says. "You get used to taking better

five ways to boost your body image

If you need to pump up more than your muscles, these weight-room tricks can strengthen your confidence.

1. Arm yourself. Seeing the fruits of your labor may be the encouragement you need. Women who lift weights tend to see results fastest in their upper bodies. So keep your biceps, triceps, pectorals, and deltoids challenged by adding some push-ups, pull-ups, or bench presses.

2. Push the limits. Don't sell yourself short. Pound for pound, women's legs are just as strong as men's. Instead of leg extensions and hamstring curls, get on the leg-press machine where you can really push some pounds. Add weight a little at a time. Press, without locking your knees, until your eighth rep becomes difficult to finish. Your power just might surprise you.

3. Chart your progress. Keeping a workout record can be a pain, but it's a great way to track how far you've come.

4. Check your attitude. A workout can boost your spirits, but sometimes it seems to make things worse. Know the difference and don't hesitate to take a break for as long as you need to get your mind right.

5. Dress the part. OK, it might sound a little shallow, but if flattering, colorful workout togs give you a lift, wear them.

care of yourself—like asking for a raise, talking to your child's teacher, confronting problems in a relationship."

Still, not all women confront a mirror easily, nor do they have to. If it's really hard for you, consider working with a therapist to help you learn to appreciate your body for the way it looks and all it can do.

With each class, I get a new lesson in what I should have already known: My body—its form, strength, balance, energy, and calm—is a tool I'm lucky to have. I like my class and its mirror of messages. The most important is that this is the body I'm supposed to have—big legs and all. ✳

Dorothy Foltz–Gray is a Contributing Editor.

SWEAT FOR A CAUSE

Can't stick with exercise? Helping others may be just the incentive you need.

BY MICHELLE DALLY

Just six months. That's how long the average American sticks with an exercise program. No wonder: The pursuit of a smaller jeans size gets boring, and the gratification of working up a good sweat can be fleeting. Bribing yourself with new workout clothes or hiring a personal trainer can keep you psyched for a while. Some people, though, are finding that fitness seems almost effortless if their sweat has a purpose.

Active volunteering—i.e., doing physical work for a meaningful cause—is helping a growing number of people satisfy their needs to stay fit and connected to their communities. The concept goes beyond Race for the Cure and other fund-raising fitness events. Whether it's training with a group of inner-city kids to run a footrace or giving abandoned dogs a much-needed opportunity to stretch their legs, these volunteers sweat with those they serve. In the process, they're developing good habits that are tough to break.

Helen Clark, 47, a volunteer with the Colorado Therapeutic Riding Center in Longmont, gives riding lessons to those with physical, mental, and emotional disabilities. During each hour-long session, Clark walks or trots alongside a horse while the student rides. In an indoor arena covered with 3 inches of sand, she and her fellow volunteers get quite a workout.

"We keep joking that we're going to have buns of steel," says Clark, who was named National Volunteer of the Year by the North American Riding for the Handicapped Association last year. The workout is a great fringe benefit, she says, but watching the horses and riders relate is the real reward.

"There's a bond there," Clark says. "I've actually seen a student have a seizure while on the horse, and the horse will stand perfectly still; they seem to know when something's not right."

Sarah Levin, Ph.D., a consultant for the Division of Nutrition and Physical Activity at the Centers for Disease Control and Prevention in Atlanta, thinks volunteering is a wonderful way for people—especially busy ones—to stick with an exercise program. "I think in general that humans like giving, and it's not something they'd want to stop doing," Levin says. "They'd be more committedbecause someone's relying on them."

Gretchen Mavrovouniotis, 40, takes inmates at the City of Irvine (California) Animal Shelter along with her on her daily walk. "When you're working on a computer all day, it's nice to get out in the fresh air and get some exercise," says the self-employed business consultant. "The fact that you know you're helping out the dog, doing something to make them more adoptable—that's why I like it."

Kym Davis Rogers, a trial attorney for the U.S. Department of Justice in Washington, D.C., is just as loyal to Kids Enjoy Exercise Now (K.E.E.N.), a program for children with such disabilities as autism and Down's syndrome.

"We do basketball and soccer drills and play kickball, and we're running around with the kids; that's the best way to encourage them," Rogers says.

They encourage her, too. Helping the K.E.E.N. kids makes working up a sweat more than just a means to an end. Of course, a personal perk here and there also helps keep volunteers interested. Rogers got a big one on her second day as a K.E.E.N. volunteer: "It was the day I met my husband." ✳

Michelle Dally also contributes to U.S. News & World Report.

Q+A
What to Do About Knee Pain

I find that after I run, the back of my knee often hurts. What could be the cause, and how can I ease the pain?

PLENTY CAN GO WRONG with the knees, so if your pain doesn't improve in a week or if it's severe, see a doctor. It sounds like you could have a case of tendinitis. The normal wear and tear of running—its repetitive motions and pounding—can strain calf or hamstring muscles, causing swelling in the tendons that connect the muscles to your knee. Overuse is the primary cause, but other contributing factors are insufficient warm-up and stretching, less-than-perfect form, hilly routes, and poor-fitting shoes.

If you treat it right, tendinitis will go away. Sneak back into your workouts too soon, though, and it may plague you for life. Mild tendinitis means one to two weeks of rest. Ice the injury for the first two or three days (20 minutes, three to four times a day), then use a hot pack or heating pad with the same frequency after that. Take an anti-inflammatory pain reliever—such as ibuprofen, naproxen sodium, or aspirin—according to label directions. When you're ready to restart your workouts, add 10 to 15 minutes of warm-up to your routine and stretch while cooling down. If the pain persists, see your doctor to rule out more serious problems, such as torn cartilage.

WALK AWAY FROM CANCER RISKS

Researchers have discovered that walking or hiking at least four hours a week cuts the risk of pancreatic cancer in half. Inactivity and obesity may significantly increase your chances of developing this difficult-to-treat disease that kills nearly 29,000 Americans each year.

dog lovers: *get moving!*

Shaggy and Scooby may keep fit by running from villains, but most dogs and their owners apparently need a bit of motivation to get moving. Australian researchers found that dog owners were even less likely than folks without four-legged playmates to get the recommended 150 minutes of exercise per week. No need to wait for a crime caper to get going: Try a game of fetch or a walk around the block.

healthBUZZ
thumbs UP

High tea: Forget the crumpets and add chocolate. Penn State researchers found that consuming moderate amounts of tea and chocolate, both high in antioxidant flavonoids, can reduce the risk of cardiovascular disease.

Killer mouthwash: A swish of genetically engineered bacteria might fend off cavity-causing germs, say researchers at the University of Florida College of Dentistry. But keep brushing: The lead researcher has been working on the magic wash for more than 25 years, although human trials are planned for some time in 2003.

thumbs DOWN

Mouthing off: The United States received a lackluster "C" on a report card released by the advocacy group Oral Health America. Flossing regularly may be a pain, but it could help boost the country's dental grade-point average.

Stress pains: Twenty-somethings who feel stuck in a rut are twice as likely to suffer lower-back pain in their 30s compared with carefree types, according to a report in the *American Journal of Public Health*. More reason for a spontaneous outing—even if just for a day.

Can You be Fat and Fit?

These exercise instructors scoff at the idea that fitness comes in only one size.

BY LINDA VILLAROSA

PHOTOGRAPHY BY BOB COSCARELLI

There is absolutely no arguing that Dee Hakala is fit. She teaches eight one-hour exercise classes weekly and still manages to squeeze in two 45-minute weight-training sessions, throwing in a few sprints to keep it interesting. But that's not all: Hakala, who lives in the southwest suburbs of Chicago, averages 50 miles a week on her bike. She even dreams of training for a century—a 100-mile bike race—something only a tiny fraction of the population is fit enough to do.

One other thing is absolutely certain about Hakala. She is a big woman. At 5 feet, 220 pounds, her body mass index (or BMI, the weight-to-height ratio that correlates closely with body-fat percentage) comes to 43, which is defined as "extremely obese." The National Institutes of Health (NIH) notes that for her height, a healthy weight is between 97 and 128. And the NIH is crystal clear on the serious health consequences of being overweight: An adult with a BMI of 25 or higher—145 pounds or more for a person who is 5 feet, 4 inches tall—is considered at greater risk for premature death and disability.

Although the numbers make it sound as though she has one foot in the grave, 44-year-old Hakala scoffs at these dire predictions. She's quite happy with her weight. In fact, she considers herself practically svelte compared with her size over a decade ago, when she weighed 360 pounds. And she's firmly uninterested in losing any more weight. "My cholesterol is under 200, my blood pressure is 120/70, and I feel great," says Hakala, author of *Thin Is Just a Four-Letter Word: Living Fit for All Shapes and Sizes.* "I eat healthy foods, I'm happy, and I'm moving my body every day—who cares if I don't fit into those height- and weight-chart averages?"

Hakala is fit and fat, a seeming oxymoron to anyone who thinks that overweight people do nothing but sit on the couch and stuff their faces. But an outspoken group of respected health and fitness experts contends that too much emphasis has been put on weight, and that fitness is more important to good health and longevity. They stress that not only is it OK to be overweight as long as

> I eat healthy foods, I'm happy, and I'm moving my body every day—who cares if I don't fit into those height- and weight-chart averages?
>
> —*Dee Hakala*

you exercise, but that it's better to be fit and fat than it is to be thin and sedentary. And, like Hakala, a growing number of exercise instructors is creating a new kind of fitness role model who is in tip-top shape without being reed-thin.

"The vast majority of research on obesity and health has either ignored physical activity or measured it so poorly that it was worthless," says Steven Blair, director of research at the Cooper Institute, a wellness and fitness research center in Dallas. "Our research has shown that the mortality rate is twice as high in individuals who are not overweight but are sedentary, compared to those who are obese but moderately fit."

Blair is the main cheerleader for the fit-and-fat camp. His research followed 25,000 middle-aged men for a decade and found that those who were physically fit, regardless of size, were healthier and lived longer than their unfit counterparts (the results from a yet-unpublished study show that the effects are the same for women). Blair is passionate about the fit-and-fat connection and vehement about his findings, perhaps because he fits the profile, too. Though he runs four to five miles every day, at 5 feet, 4 inches and 185 pounds, his BMI of 32 defines him as obese. "I'm short, fat, and bald, and I'm never going to be tall, thin, and have hair," he says. "But I'm doing a lot for myself and for my health by keeping in shape."

Not everyone in the field of health and fitness agrees with the fit-and-fat premise, though. The anti-obesity camp firmly believes that being overweight is the problem. Physical activity is very good for you, they say, but in order to lower the risk of heart disease, diabetes, and other life-threatening illness, it is more important for overweight people to lose weight. "We know from a range of studies that an overweight person who exercises a great deal reduces the risk of serious illness and death. But for moderate exercise, we really don't have an answer," says

OFF THE CHARTS: Dee Hakala's body mass index may be high, but so was her score on our fitness test.

Barry M. Popkin, Ph.D., professor of nutrition at the University of North Carolina at Chapel Hill. "However, it is clear that losing weight, even just a few pounds, helps immensely."

Popkin and others can argue all they want, but Lynne Drake, who is 4 feet, 10 inches and weighs 190, won't try to lose weight. Been there, done that. A registered practical nurse and certified fitness instructor, Drake got off the weight-loss bandwagon several years ago and instead jumped on the treadmill. She teaches 12 exercise classes each week and does brisk, 30- to 60-minute walks on weekends. "In the past I did ridiculous things to lose weight, including every kind of crazy diet and even illegal drugs," says Drake, 39, who lives in Georgetown, Ontario, a suburb of Toronto. "I was fixated on pounds, inches, clothing size. But now I'm more focused on feeling good and being healthy. I am fat and fit, and I'm in better shape than many of those skinny women in the fashion industry."

Looking at Hakala, Drake, and even Blair, an obvious question comes to mind: If these folks exercise so much, especially compared with the majority of Americans who exercise only very little or not at all, why don't they lose weight? Glenn A. Gaesser, Ph.D., an associate professor of exercise physiology and associate director of the adult fitness program at the University of Virginia in Charlottesville, explains that it's all in the genes. "We can only control our weight to a limited degree, so the chances of someone with a BMI of 40 ever slimming way down are almost nonexistent," says Gaesser, co-author of *The SPARK: The Revolutionary 3-Week Fitness Plan That Changes Everything You Know About Exercise, Weight Control, and Health.* "The chances of a fat person—who probably has all the genes for fat going against her—ever being thin are probably not very different from someone who is really short and wants to be tall."

Research shows that the mortality rate is twice as high in people who are not overweight but sedentary, compared to those who are obese but moderately fit.

Even as the experts continue to bicker over the scientific ins and outs of the fit-and-fat theory, people like Hakala and Drake are living proof that you can not only be both but also be an effective fitness instructor for anyone, regardless of size. Hakala, whose New Face of Fitness classes are packed with students of all weights, ages, and medical conditions, puts it this way: "If you're a good instructor, you're just a good instructor, no matter who you are or what you look like."

Still, some people will be uncomfortable with an exercise instructor who falls outside the thin, muscular fitness ideal. Becky Singleton not only teaches kickboxing, step aerobics, Spinning, and boot-camp classes in the Boston area, she also gets in her own four- to six-mile run or Spinning workout when she can find time. Still, at 5 feet, 7 inches and 182 pounds, she is classified as overweight. And although her classes are wildly popular, she finds that she has to deal with the occasional comment from a disgruntled student. "I am in fabulous cardiovascular shape. If you said go run 10 miles, I could," says Singleton, 37. "But still, every time I get a student who's new to my class, that person looks really surprised when they see my size."

LOOKS CAN DECEIVE: Some students learn the hard way that Becky Singleton teaches a mean Spinning class.

That misperception ends when the workout begins, Singleton says. About a year ago, she recalls walking into her Spinning class on a cold day and noticing a new student, a small-framed slip of a woman. As Singleton took off her coat, the new woman turned to the guy on the bike next to her, asking in a loud whisper, "Is that the instructor? She's awfully big, isn't she?"

Singleton chuckles about the incident. "Ten minutes into the class, she was barely hanging in there and wanted to stop. An hour later, she was completely exhausted. After the class I said to her, 'You know, you can never judge a book by its cover. I'm going to go run six miles now. Buh-bye.'"

Now the woman is one of Singleton's personal-training clients. "I taught her a lesson," she says. "I think a lightbulb went off in her head that you don't have to be thin in order to be fit." ✳

Linda Villarosa, a New York Times *contributing health and fitness writer, is the author of* Body & Soul: The Black Women's Guide to Physical Health and Emotional Well-Being.

beautiful body tops beautiful beau
Sixty-one percent of women would trade a date with Brad Pitt for a better body.

—*Russell Athletic's For the Long Run survey*

How Do You Measure Up?

No matter what your size, this simple test should give you an idea of how fit you really are. All you need is a timer and a 12-inch platform, such as stair step, a sturdy box, or a bench used for step aerobics. Set your timer for three minutes and start stepping on and off the platform, maintaining a steady rhythm—one foot up, then the other, one foot down, then the other. Feel free to change the foot you lead with during the test. At the end of the three minutes, immediately take your pulse for one minute, then check your results against the chart below. Just in case you're wondering, Dee Hakala took the test three times for accuracy. Her stats: 89-91, good to excellent for her age category.

women

age	18-25	26-35	36-45	46-55	56-65	65+
excellent	<85	<88	<90	<94	<95	<90
good	85-98	88-99	90-102	94-104	95-104	90-102
above average	99-108	100-111	103-110	105-115	105-112	103-115
average	109-117	112-119	111-118	116-120	113-118	116-122
below average	118-126	120-126	119-128	121-126	119-128	123-128
poor	127-140	127-138	129-140	127-135	129-139	129-134
very poor	>140	>138	>140	>135	>139	>134

men

age	18-25	26-35	36-45	46-55	56-65	65+
excellent	<79	<81	<83	<87	<86	<88
good	79-89	81-89	83-96	87-97	86-97	88-96
above average	90-99	90-99	97-103	98-105	98-103	97-103
average	100-105	100-107	104-112	106-116	104-112	104-113
below average	106-116	108-117	113-119	117-122	113-120	114-120
poor	117-128	118-128	120-130	123-132	121-129	121-130
very poor	>128	>128	>130	>132	>129	>130

Source: Personal Trainer Manual, American Council on Exercise

Burn Extra Calories Outside the Gym

By taking a do-it-yourself approach to everyday tasks—that means saying no to drive-through car washes, remote controls, even interoffice e-mail—the average person stands to considerably increase her monthly energy expenditure, up from 1,700 calories the automated way to as much as 10,500 the active way, according to a commentary in the *Mayo Clinic Proceedings*. "I think inactivity is the major public-health problem of this century," says study author Steven N. Blair, a researcher at the Cooper Institute in Dallas. "Physical activity has been engineered out of daily life." Now's a perfect time to engineer it back into yours. For some little moves that could help you ignite a monthly calorie bonfire, take cues from the chart below.

AUTOMATED: CALORIES BURNED		DO-IT-YOURSELF: CALORIES BURNED	
Using a drive-through car wash	18	Washing and waxing the car by hand	300
Paying for gas at the pump	0.6	Walking into the station to pay	5
Hiring someone to clean and iron	0	Ironing and vacuuming for an hour	152
Buying presliced vegetables	0	Washing and chopping vegetables for 15 minutes	10 to 13
Waiting for pizza delivery	15	Making your own pizza	25
Using a lawn service	0	Gardening and mowing for an hour	360
Shopping online for an hour	30	Shopping at the mall for an hour	145 to 240
Letting the dog out the back door	2	Walking the dog for 30 minutes	125
Driving 40 minutes and walking 5 minutes from the parking lot	22	Walking 15 minutes to and from the bus stop twice a day	60
Sending an e-mail to a colleague	2 to 3	Walking to a colleague's office, standing, and talking (three minutes)	6
Taking the elevator up three flights of stairs	0.3	Walking up three flights	15
Letting the cashier unload the shopping cart	2	Unloading a full shopping cart	6
Using the remote control	less than 1	Changing the channel manually	3
Reclining while talking on the phone for 30 minutes	4	Standing and chatting on the phone for 30 minutes	20
Using the garage-door opener	less than 1	Raising and lowering the garage door manually twice a day	2 to 3

myth: Stretch before you sweat.
reality check: Stretching before

you've warmed up can actually strain your muscles, according to the American Council on Exercise. Wait until after your workout to reach for your toes.

How to Rate Your Fitness Routine

Have you logged hours at the gym but find your jeans are still just-out-of-the-dryer tight? It could be because what you consider a power walk is really a leisurely stroll. According to a study in the journal *Preventive Medicine*, people often overestimate the intensity of their workouts. In the study, 66 men and women recorded how long and hard they thought they exercised for two weeks, and then they checked their estimates against a heart-rate monitor. The participants didn't fudge on the lengths of their workouts, but almost half said they exercised moderately for at least 10 minutes, while, according to the monitors, only 15 percent actually did.

"It's a lot easier to determine that you walked for 10 minutes or for two miles than it is to figure out how vigorously you walked," says lead study author Glen E. Duncan, Ph.D., research fellow at the University of Florida Health Science Center in Gainesville. And miscalculating your intensity level can have repercussions. "Underestimating the intensity of your workouts could lead to overeating and weight gain if you think you've burned more calories than you have. Still, any amount of exercise is better for your heart and overall health than no exercise at all."

So how can you tell if you're exercising at that moderate level? The best way: Use a heart-rate monitor for a few days. But if you don't want to invest the $60 or so it would cost you to get a decent model (such as Polar's A1 monitor), you can try this convenient—but less accurate—test: Talk aloud while you're working out. During moderate exercise, you should be able to rattle off a quick grocery list, but if you can give a blow-by-blow account of your most recent relationship drama, step up the pace. To give your workout a boost, try walking or running to a fast-paced Latin tune, hitting some hills or stairs, or exercising with a friend who's in a bit better shape than you are (and striving to stay ahead).

Q+A
Why You Should Warm Up Your Work Out

Do I burn more calories running outside in the cold than inside on the treadmill?

YES—but the payoff is small. In cold temperatures, your body must work harder to maintain its 98.6-degree setting, whether you are exercising or not. One way the body tries to stay warm is through shivering, which can increase its heat production—and its calorie-burning capacity—up to five times.

But before you go on a deep-freeze diet, consider this: If you're shivering while running, you may not be exerting yourself enough. The energy you spend running should warm you up and put a quick end to the calorie-consuming quakes. So the difference between braving the cold instead of staying toasty on the treadmill isn't enough to burn off your midafternoon Snickers™ snack. Also, very cold temperatures can stiffen your muscles, making it difficult to keep up your pace and causing your aerobic workout to suffer. On bone-chilling days, you're probably better off inside than out—but do whatever keeps you moving.

Title IX: *One Step Forward, One Step Back*

Although the average number of women's college-sports teams has risen from two to eight per school since Title IX was enacted in 1972, the percentage of women's teams coached by women has dropped from 90 to 46.

—*American Association of University Women*

The Future of Phys. Ed.

Gym classes are changing across the country. Today's P.E. is more like a health club than your old high school gym.

BY SHARLENE K. JOHNSON

In the interest of full disclosure, I must tell you that I despised P.E. when I was in school. I detested softballs flying at my face, loathed struggling up the climbing rope in front of 30 other kids, and cringed at being one of the last ones picked for the dodge-ball team. So I perfected the art of hovering in the background.

Fast-forward 18 years: I'm in a school gym to find out if it's true what they say, that P.E. has changed. I watch as a couple dozen 15- and 16-year-olds file into the "fitness center" at Rocky Mountain High School in Fort Collins, Colorado. It's at least four times the size of the weight room I remember from my high school, and everyone uses it—not just the jocks.

I try to spot the athletes and think I have them pegged, although I can't be sure as I watch the students work out on treadmills, bikes, and weight machines.

After 20 minutes, the class heads out for softball. Students pair off to practice catching and throwing. Then I spot her, my wallflower twin. Like me at 15, she doesn't seem to have an athletic bone in her body. Her throw is awkward and she can't catch, but when the ball manages to find her mitt, her partner is quick with praise.

Why hadn't I spotted this girl when I was in the gym? How had I missed the downward gaze and hunched posture that spotlights her lack of athletic confidence? Then I remember: She was one of the students on the Spinning bikes, pedaling just as smoothly and confidently as anyone else.

This is part of what the new P.E. hopes to accomplish: to engage all students, not just the athletic elite, in fun activities that will instill a lifelong commitment to fitness. Teachers, P.E. experts, and advocates all have their say.

> ## Variety is the key to getting teens hooked on lifelong fitness.
> —*Jo Laccrichio, Rocky Mountain High School P.E.*

But the innovative programs evolving from the gym class I knew are raising new questions, especially when it comes to one of the hottest trends—modeling P.E. facilities after health clubs. Are these new approaches effective? It's too early to tell if they'll have a long-term effect on kids' fitness habits, but the early results seem promising.

A successful P.E. program, according to some teachers, is one that helps get kids moving during school hours and afterward. "You should see this gym after school gets out;

it's packed," says Jo Laccrichio, a Rocky Mountain High School P.E. teacher. "After they graduate, these kids are not going to be intimidated by the equipment at health clubs."

But it's not just about getting kids hooked on health-club fitness gadgets. On most days, the students in Laccrichio's first-period dance and aerobics class practice everything from the fox-trot to choreographed hip-hop routines. Once or twice a week, she teaches her students how to circuit-train. In the gym, they move from machine to machine every three minutes, at the sound of the coach's whistle.

Students at Rocky Mountain need just two P.E. classes to graduate, but many choose to take more. "If we had only traditional classes, we wouldn't see nearly as many kids taking P.E.," predicts Laccrichio, who also teaches an adventure-P.E. class that includes hiking, climbing, and scuba diving. "Variety is the key to getting them hooked on lifelong fitness." And after all, getting kids off the sidelines and planting the seeds of active living are the primary goals of these new programs. Challenging old ideas about P.E. is one way to go about it.

There's definitely a pressing need to turn kids on to fitness. Within the last 20 years, the percentage of overweight children between the ages of 6 and 11 almost doubled. For children aged 12 to 19, the number nearly tripled, from 5 to 14 percent. And Type 2 diabetes, often associated with obesity, can no longer be called "adult-onset diabetes" because diagnoses in kids are on the rise.

Despite the need, there's a good chance that your child may not be getting physical education at all. The Centers for Disease Control and Prevention (CDC) estimates that in the past 10 years, the number of students involved in daily physical-education classes has fallen by more than a third. Illinois is now the only state that requires daily P.E. classes in kindergarten through 12th grade.

Playing it Forward

Rocky Mountain High School is one of a small but growing number of schools across the country where P.E. programs are being modeled more after fitness clubs. In Naperville, Illinois, kids at Madison Middle School wear black and gold T-shirts emblazoned with "Getting Fit for Life at the Madison Health Club," which is the school's fitness center, located next to the gymnasium. Students work out there once a week, but on other days you might

P.E. lessons for a grown-up's workout

To give your own workouts a boost, borrow a page from the new P.E. lesson plan. If these strategies can capture a child's short attention span, imagine what they can do for your exercise routine. Here's your homework assignment.

take it outside
Vary your routine with activities like hiking, cycling, and inline skating. Even bowling and fly-fishing are better than sitting in front of the TV.

cross-train
Don't do the same thing day after day. Try yoga on Monday, weight training on Tuesday, kickboxing on Wednesday, Spinning on Friday, and step aerobics on Saturday. Cross training not only prevents plateaus and boredom, but also gives your muscles a better workout.

move it, move it, move it
Instead of a grinding 50-minute cardio workout on a single machine, alternate three to four minutes each on the treadmill, stationary bicycle, rowing machine, stair climber, elliptical machine, or whatever is available. Move quickly from station to station—you'll be surprised how time will fly.

use a heart-rate monitor
Strap one on to take the guesswork out of gauging workout intensity.

hire a teacher
Some personal trainers will allow you to split the cost of their time with one or two other students. If you can't swing regular sessions, splurge now and then on a refresher course.

keep a fitness log
Tracking your progress is a great motivator. Use a journal—or your PDA—to note your successes.

Many classes strive to cover a wider variety of topics, ranging from muscle groups and fitness-program design to the benefits of inline skating, ultimate Frisbee, aerobics, and dance.

find them on the rock-climbing wall, in the gym, or out on the field playing individual or team sports.

Naperville's P.E. program has been heralded as a model one by the CDC and by P.E.4Life, a nonprofit physical-education advocacy group in Washington, D.C. Those groups cite the program for its emphasis on quality physical education every day and because it has the active backing of the community and local government.

Yet the health-club approach is only one of the changes going on with school gyms. P.E.'s modern grading system is also markedly different. "Our kids have their own goals, and they are assessed on whether or not they do their personal best," says Melanie Champion, a P.E. teacher at South Brunswick Middle School in Brunswick County, North Carolina. If a student feels she's accomplished something on the field or in the gym, the more likely she is to stick to an active lifestyle.

But how do teachers know if a child really is doing her best? Some use heart-rate monitors, which beep whenever someone is either working below her target heart-rate zone or pushing herself beyond her limits. Students can monitor their pulses the old-fashioned way, too.

Some P.E. programs have also branched out beyond teaching such skills as shooting hoops, hitting home runs, and spiking volleyballs. These days, many classes strive to cover a wider variety of topics, ranging from muscle groups and fitness-program design to the benefits of inline skating, ultimate Frisbee, aerobics, and dance. "Dance is something kids can do for the rest of their lives," says Brandy Cruthird, who owns a health club and teaches P.E. at Josiah Quincy Upper School, both in Boston. "It's fun, noncompetitive, and kids love it. Plus, it's a great cardiovascular workout, which is the whole point."

That's not to say team sports and skill building are extinct. They've just evolved from the days when students played the same way professional athletes do. "When we played flag football, we played 11 on 11," says Phil Lawler, a Madison Middle School teacher and coordinator for the Naperville school district's P.E.

program. "But that usually meant the best athlete was quarterback, his best friend was a receiver, and everyone else was just standing around. Now, we play football four-on-four, soccer five-on-five, basketball three-on-three—smaller games, with a lot more movement." And a better chance that all children will play a more active role in the game.

The Obstacle Course

Money is one of the main barriers between kids and more innovative P.E. classes. Some claim that physical-education classes squander the money needed for academics. But teachers like Champion argue persuasively that cutting back on physical education to boost children's test scores is counterproductive. "Active and healthy children learn better," she says.

Some changes cost nothing to implement, but often money for facilities or equipment such as heart-rate monitors is scarce. To fill the need, many schools are seeking state and federal grants, establishing partnerships with local hospitals and health-care agencies, and raising their own cash. At Rocky Mountain, student athletes have sold candy to buy fitness equipment. In Boston, Cruthird gets around the lack of gym space at her 3-year-old pilot school by taking her students to a nearby YMCA for aerobics classes.

Relief is on the horizon. The Physical Education for Progress Act, which Congress passed in December 2000, authorized $400 million in grants over five years to help start, expand, and improve P.E. in all grades. In 2001, schools received about $5 million of the grants.

But are the changes really worth the money? Have they fully engaged students and sparked interest in active lifestyles? "I'm not saying that P.E. is every child's favorite class," Lawler says. "But I can say that every child is comfortable being here, and no one is left on the sidelines." ✳

Sharlene K. Johnson is a freelance writer based in Fort Collins, Colorado.

rating combat fitness programs

Some martial arts are designed to help you protect yourself; others are more health club than fight club. How to tell.

Class	Best for	What to expect	Whup-ass factor	Details
Aikido Training to balance body, mind, and spirit.	Zen-seekers looking for a workout and a spiritual connection.	To hit the ground a lot at first; to immobilize someone with a joint lock (think Vulcan nerve pinch).	In six weeks, you'll be more aware of your surroundings and know how to get out of your attacker's way.	Aikido Association of America: www.aaa-aikido.com or 773-525-3141
Chinese Martial Arts or Kung Fu The basis of many martial arts (includes Tai Chi).	Can't-make-up-my-mind types. There are as many as 1,000 styles to choose from.	A mix of kicking, punching, grappling, and ground fighting.	Sharpen your self-defense smarts with kung fu styles in the Koshu category.	www.kungfuonline.com or check the phone book
Karate Shotokan is the most popular form of this Japanese art.	Bruce Lee fans and anyone who wants overall muscle power.	Minimal contact, at least in Shotokan; low stances, super-powerful kicks, and major hip action.	"You hit them once, and they're on the floor," says fifth-degree black belt Nina Chenault.	Shotokan Karate of America: www.ska.org or 213-437-0988
Krav Maga Developed in Israel in 1948. It's not pretty; it's all about survival.	Self-defense students looking for the next new thing.	To practice defending yourself while being choked or pinned.	Israeli police use it. Need we say more?	Krav Maga Association of America: www.kravmaga.com or 310-966-1300
Muay Thai Off-the-ropes Thai boxing; fitness kick-boxing got its start here.	Competitive, athletic types who want a tough lower-body workout.	To get in shape fast with jump-rope and push-up drills.	"You'll know the basics in six months," says Dawn DelVecchio, co-owner of Alive 'N Kickin' gym in Santa Fe, New Mexico.	United States Muay Thai Association: www.usmta.com
Self-Defense Courses Lessons on avoiding—or escaping—attacks.	Women who want to be prepared for a nightmare scenario.	Plenty of role-playing to learn how to escape an attacker.	The mantra says it all: "Do anything that's necessary to get to safety," Chenault says.	Check community centers. Also, visit safetyforwomen.com/Self_Defense.
Tae Kwon Do Korean martial art known for dynamic kicks.	Olympic wannabes and people who want a good lower-body workout.	A sore butt by the end of your first week.	After six months of training, you'll be able to use simple techniques to defend yourself.	The United States Tae Kwon Do Union: www.ustu.org or 719-866-4632

1 can of whup-ass: A good start, and a good workout, but don't depend on it if you need to deliver a smackdown.

2 cans: Sound self-defense basics, but not designed to beat off real-life thugs.

3 cans: You've got the skills and the smarts to bring pain to anyone who crosses you.

4 cans: When you enter the bar, sailors close their tabs and flee.

VitalStats

4.3 | Average number of miles each American walks per day

35 | Average number of miles each American drives per day

27 | Percent of driving trips that are less than one mile

75,000 | Number of miles walked by age 50

34 | The equivalent distance in treks along the entire Appalachian Trail

23 | Percent of Americans who exercised more than 100 days in 1990

20.7 | Percent who exercised more than 100 days in 2001

1 | Rank of spring among seasons in which men reportedly fall in love

1 | Rank of height among qualities women most desire in a man

80 | Percent of females whose most common sexual fantasies involve someone they know

1 | Rank of a day spa as the place where women are most likely to get a massage

1 | Rank of home as the place for men

Sources: American Podiatric Medical Association, Cambridge Energy Research Associates, Clallam Transit System, *International Journal of Wilderness*, SGMA, *Sexy Origins and Intimate Things*, American Massage Therapy Association

Look to the Animal Kingdom for True Fitness

AS BUSY as your day is, chances are it still doesn't compare with the typical on-the-go wild animal. Columbia University researchers compared the calories burned by hundreds of mammals (everything from mice to orangutans) with domesticated creatures (humans as well as pets). The scientists found that wild animals are so active that they burn twice as many calories as the modern city-dwelling Tarzan and Jane.

People are much more sedentary now than in their hunter-and-gatherer days, says study director Steven Heymsfield, M.D., professor of medicine at Columbia. "The decrease in activity is far greater than we appreciate," he explains. According to the study, certain populations, such as elite athletes, army recruits, or subsistence farmers, come close to matching animals when it comes to calorie burning. But on average, most people would have to add a four- to five-hour run to their daily routines to burn as many calories as your typical wolf or wildcat.

Since you probably don't have time to squeeze marathon training into your day's schedule, here are some suggestions for aping the actions of our animal friends—and boosting your calorie burn.

Animals can ...	You can ...
Climb trees to escape predators	Use the stairs to escape an elevator full of bad cologne
Chase down their prey and deliver it a bite to the neck	Ride your bike down to the deli and grab a bite
Dig burrows in the dirt to bed down for the night	Dig out a section of your lawn and put in a flower bed
Attract would-be mates with courtship dances	Invite your partner to go out for a night of dancing

chapter 6

healthy
looks

**a busy woman's guide
to beauty and style**

the face of health

BY LYNNE CUSACK

PHOTOGRAPHY BY JENNY ACHESON

Whether a woman is the face of health—or not—isn't about how much broccoli and tofu she eats a day, how often she flosses and exfoliates, or how fast she runs a 5K. It has nothing to do with height, weight, or age. The winners of our second annual Face of Health contest have something much more significant in common: an unabashed spirit, irrepressible confidence, and an openness that instantly makes you want to get to know them better. Profiled over the next few pages, these four women share a joyfulness you just can't miss.

Jenny's smart beauty

• **Practice safe sunning:** Sunblock (specifically Neutrogena's Healthy Defense Daily Moisturizer SPF 30) and a big straw hat are necessities for fair-skinned Werner, who has her freckles and moles checked by a dermatologist every six months.

• **For a fast hair fix:** "As a busy mom, I don't have time to wash my hair every day. Instead, I use baby powder between washings. It absorbs the oils on my scalp and around my hairline."

• **Stay shine-free:** "I don't like wearing a lot of makeup. Instead of applying powder throughout the day, I use Clinique's Stay-Matte Oil-Blotting Sheets."

JENNY

Jenny MacKinnon Werner
31, married, one child
Full-time student
Reston, Virginia

"There's nothing wrong with acting like a kid sometimes."

Living the Fitness Legacy

You might say Jenny Werner was destined to live a fit life. A full-time student of public relations at Virginia's George Mason University and a first-time mom, Werner grew up in a small coastal community south of Santa Barbara, California, where the glorious weather practically demanded you get out and go. For good measure, she had a powerful role model: her dad. "He was kind of a health fanatic when I was growing up," Werner says. As a child, she would ride her bike alongside him as he ran—until she was able to keep up on foot, that is. "My dad is still a huge motivator for me," she says. "He lives on a boat in Seattle and caravans up to Alaska with friends every year."

So it's no surprise that Werner is passing on the family fitness tradition to her daughter, Cameryn.

The 14-month-old is already a runner (via jogging stroller) and seasoned outdoor adventurer. "We took her to the woods with us for the first time when she was about 3 or 4 months old," Werner says. Though it's a bit early for Cameryn to shoot the white-water rapids with Mom and Dad, she often accompanies them in their kayaks (Christmas gifts to each other) around peaceful lake waters.

When we first told Werner that her husband, David, had nominated her for this contest, she was flabbergasted. But to David, the choice was obvious: "She's a fantastic woman inside and out," he wrote. Equally devoted to her husband, Werner says sharing goals is a big factor in their happiness as a couple: "We have so many ideas for our life."

Alisa's smart beauty

- **Drink lots of water:** Placas says hydrating is her most important beauty ritual.

- **Tame your mane:** Fighting a headful of natural curls screams "time waster!" to Placas. Her 15-second alternative: she uses Redken's Hardwear Super Strong Gel, Styling No. 16 to tame the frizzies and control curls.

- **Go light on the makeup:** "I don't like using traditional foundation—it feels too heavy," Placas says. "My makeup secret is a product that doubles as a foundation and a powder—Clinique's Superpowder Double Face Makeup."

ALISA

Alisa Placas
27, single
Computer animator
Cambridge, Massachusetts

"I tend to be serious, but I have a large capacity for silliness."

True to Herself

"The cornerstone of health and beauty lies in a person's self-worth," Alisa Placas wrote in her entry. "I do not let other people make me feel that my value is based solely on my appearance. By determining my own self-worth and setting that standard high, I possess great confidence. This is what people see when they look in my face."

Wise words from one so young, but in Placas' case, the seeds were planted early in life.

"As a child, my extreme shyness kept me from being the 'cool' or 'funny' kid, but knowing my self-worth saved me," she says. "I never felt pressure to do things in order to seek approval or acceptance." Placas credits her parents, who

didn't so much counsel her about self-esteem as reinforce her strengths—in particular, her tendencies to be independent and to meet challenges head-on. Placas says these qualities have fueled her career as a freelance computer animator. "Early on, my boss would assume I could do certain things I'd never done before," she says. "Inside I'd be sweating, thinking 'Now what?' But I'd simply approach whatever it was logically and work it out."

Placas takes a refreshingly realistic view of herself that will serve her as well in the future as it does now. "I may not have the most talent or experience, but my strong work ethic makes me a great asset to anyone, anywhere," she says.

Gail's smart beauty

● **It's all in the eyebrows:** "Brows frame the eyes," Gatling says. "I'm a big believer in making sure mine are well-defined. Nicely groomed eyebrows can really open up your face."

● **Take it all off:** She swears by Ultima II's Going, Going, Gone, a one-step makeup remover that keeps pace with her busy life. "I'm always on the lookout for products that cut out extra steps," she says.

● **Pamper yourself:** "I like to treat myself to relaxing spa treatments. My advice: Try something new with each visit."

GAIL

Gail Gray Gatling
46, married, two children
Student
Germantown, Maryland

"Learning something new every day is incredibly energizing."

Strength in Knowledge

Some people take pleasure in the treasure; Gail Gatling delights in the hunt. "I love to discover new information," she says. "If I'm interested in something, I'll talk to everyone about it. People enjoy sharing what they know. I can learn new things from an 8-year-old!" From the latest art or restaurant opening to the ultimate destressor to the newest best-kept secret, Gatling's gotta know it. But the mother of two and liberal-studies master's student at Excelsior College doesn't keep all that data to herself. What use would it be if she didn't share it? For instance, recently, an employee of Gatling's husband, Jeff, was dying of cancer. Touched by the woman's physical and

mental suffering, Gatling set out to help. She found a spiritualist who specializes in cranial massages for people with terminal disease. The massages, the woman said, brought moments of peace and comfort during her final days.

Gatling is reaching out beyond her circle of friends to share what she has learned. She recently completed a manuscript for a book, called *Explore*, intended to empower women to overcome sexism, racism, and, as Gatling puts it, "any other '-ism' that inhibits women's growth." Ambitious, yes—but it's easy to have faith in Gatling's enthusiasm and resolve. "I like to challenge myself," she says. "It makes me want to wake up in the morning and start a new day."

Denise's smart beauty

• **Listen to grandma:** Vibal uses skincare products from Pond's. "I can remember my grandmother using their products—and she still has incredible skin today, at 92!"

• **Make time for hair repairs:** A zealous surfer, Vibal spends lots of time in the ocean, which can wreak havoc on hair. Still, Vibal's is strong and healthy: She conditions it several times a week with Hair Repair Intensive Conditioner from St. Ives.

• **Bust bad habits:** "I'm an avid nail biter," Vibal says. "When I have the urge, I coat my nails with a sour-tasting polish to prevent me from biting."

DENISE

Denise Vibal
28, married
Zookeeper
Long Island, New York

"Helping others has a positive effect on how you look and feel."

The Art of Giving

Denise Vibal has one of those faces—friendly, open, maybe a little familiar. You can just tell she's someone you could count on to care.

That's no fleeting first impression. Vibal goes out of her way to distribute kindnesses—small and large—to family (it was her mother who nominated her for this contest), friends, and even strangers. For instance, this native of the New York City area was especially devastated by the September 11 terrorist attacks, and she knew she had to do something even though she was living in San Diego at the time. "The World Trade Center is close to where I grew up. I know several people who work in that area," she says.

One day, soon after the September 11 attacks, Vibal visited a local surfers' hangout and struck up a conversation with the owner. She mentioned she was a budding artist, and the two hatched a plan on the spot to hold a sale of Vibal's acrylic paintings for charity. "The event provided a much-needed way for people to contribute," she says. The proceeds—$425 in all—benefited the children of 9/11 victims.

Vibal and her husband, Derek, also a displaced New Yorker, had been considering moving home to be closer to their families. September 11 strengthened their decision, and they returned in April 2002. "It's so important to surround yourself with strong supporters," Vibal says. ✳

Q+A
How to Fix Your Face at the Drugstore Counter

I'd love to try some concealers and foundations at my drugstore. But how can I pick the right colors without testing them on my skin first?

WHILE YOU CAN'T PLAY before you pay, you will increase the odds of getting makeup you love with these tips from Collier Strong, consulting makeup artist for L'Oréal:

Opt for foundation in a see-through bottle. Bring several shades to the best-lit area of the store—typically near a window or the front door, where there's natural light. Then try to match the color to the skin on the back of your hand.

Take the foundation you're currently using, dab a bit on your skin, and try to match that to the shade in the drugstore bottle.

If you don't see an exact match for your current concealer, go a little lighter, not darker. Concealers are generally easier to pick than foundations because your options are usually narrowed to a few shades, such as fair, light, medium, and dark.

Shop at a retailer that offers a money-back guarantee, such as Rite Aid or CVS.

Q+A
The Best Way to Remove Eye Makeup

For years, I've removed my eye makeup with baby oil or petroleum jelly, but I was recently told that this isn't a good idea. What gives?

THESE OLD STANDBYS might indeed cause trouble for you in the future. "Heavy products could leave behind clogged pores and acne in your eye or upper-cheek area," explains Andrew Kaufman, M.D., assistant clinical professor of dermatology at the University of California at Los Angeles School of Medicine. That's particularly true if you're under age 40, when skin tends to be oilier, or if your skin is already acne-prone.

These products may also cause sties or inflamed hair follicles. Try safer choices, such as Earth Therapeutics' Natural Milk Nutrient Wash, Aveda's Pure Gel Eye Makeup Remover, and Talika's Lash Conditioning Cleanser.

Q+A
Making Your Look Last

I don't have a lot of time to reapply makeup. How can I make it last through my evening commute?

IF YOU WANT your look to stay put without a lot of primping, long-lasting cosmetics really do the trick. Here are a few products and how they work:

For foundation, try Ultima II's Wonderwear Cream Makeup or Estée Lauder's Double Wear Foundation. Both contain polymers that keep makeup from wearing off and provide a barrier to water, oil, and sweat.

If your blush usually fades to pale, switch to a stay-put formula like Almay's Stay Smooth Beyond Powder Blush. The powder is wrapped in liquid to prevent slipping and streaking.

For extra durability, set your look with a dusting of powder, such as Revlon's ColorStay Powder, which uses what's called "transfer-resistant technology" to stay in place.

For lipstick longevity, try L'Oréal's Endless 8-Hour Comfortable Lipcolour, which is made with silicone to protect the color and contains ingredients that evaporate more slowly than components in regular lipsticks. If your favorite shade lacks staying power, put on Shu Uemura Lip Fix first; it's a prelipstick primer that prevents feathering and smearing.

You can make the color on your lids last by prepping them with foundation or Le Mirador's Firming Eye Shadow Base: Its vitamin-enriched, oil-free formula keeps eye shadow from slipping away. Then apply a won't-budge product, such as Clinique's High Impact Eye Shadow. It's made with treated pigments that hug your lids for hours.

To keep mascara from disappearing, skip the waterproof formulations, since they tend to flake, advises Nancy Sprague, a New York-based makeup artist. Instead, try Max Factor's Lashfinity, which will last up to 12 hours thanks to a color-bond system that keeps lashes smudge- and smear-proof.

Q+A
Avoid Headband Headaches

I love headbands, but I could do without their pinching and headaches. Are there any pain-free—and fashionable—options?

SWEEPING YOUR HAIR BACK doesn't have to be a major headache. "For the most comfort, seek out headbands without teeth—they can cause pinching—and those that have cloth or rubber on the tips to eliminate behind-the-ear aches," suggests Betsy Cantalino, owner of Classic Look Salon in Ridgewood, New Jersey. Hard plastic also tends to be painful since it doesn't conform to the shape of your head.

Look for some of the newer, softer styles in springy silks, chiffons, and pale microsuedes. Wrap Star, for instance, is a long piece of fabric—available in many styles, including microsuede, shantung, and Oriental brocade—attached to a hair comb. Simply secure the comb and tie the fabric comfortably under your hair in back. Other options include Frédéric Fekkai's Beauty Wrap, a silk gauze bandeau, or the Cutout Headband Tie, a full-circle band of leather with soft, leather-covered elastic in back. Both slip on your head—and stay put. ·

Q+A
Does Your Hair Salon Practice Good Hygiene?

At my salon, I noticed that the brushes and combs weren't being washed and combed out between clients. Is there any risk of spreading something?

RELAX—you're not likely to leave the salon with anything other than a fresh new 'do. "The two main things you could get are head lice and a fungal infection of the scalp, though chances are small," says Jerome L. Shupack, M.D., professor of clinical dermatology at New York University. Still, your salon should be practicing good hair hygiene. To make sure yours does, Alex Casalino, co-owner of Cristophe Salon in Newport Beach, California, suggests checking to see if each beauty station has a bottle of comb and scissor disinfectant, which kills fungi and drowns lice, and that brushes and combs are cleaned between clients. "If they're washed and hair-free, then lice shouldn't be an issue since they tend to cling to hair, not brush bristles," Shupack says. And don't be afraid to ask how and when the tools are cleaned. Of course, you could bring along a brush from home—but if your concern is that great, it might be best to find a new salon.

Q+A
Hard Water Hard on Hair

My new house has hard water, and it's starting to take a toll on my hair. What can I do to get my dull, brittle locks back into shape?

FIRST, GET TO THE ROOT of the problem by seeing what you can do about the water. A water softener can reduce the concentration of hard minerals in your water system—ones like calcium and magnesium, which make it difficult for soaps to lather up and rinse off your hair and skin. The resulting residue can leave your locks lifeless and brittle and your skin dry and irritated, says D'Anne Kleinsmith, M.D., a dermatologist in West Bloomfield, Michigan. If you don't want to invest in a whole-house system, you can install a water-softening kit under your sink or attach one to your shower head (available at hardware stores for about $75).

Second, remove residue with a deep cleanser. We like Pantene's Pro-V Purity Clarifying Shampoo, Clinique's Exceptionally Clean Clarifying Shampoo, and Clairol's Herbal Essences Clarifying Shampoo. With hard water, conditioning is especially important. It can help soften hair and restore its luster, according to Myles Haddad, a Pantene hairstylist. You may even want to use a deep conditioner designed for weekly use.

DRESS TO IMPRESS
while you're pregnant

Leaving the slinky "look, I'm pregnant" dresses to the Hollywood celebs? That doesn't mean you're stuck with tent-like outfits with bows, big collars, and bright prints, or your husband's old button-downs. New maternity lines give moms-to-be fashionable options without breaking the bank.

"The biggest change in maternity clothes is that they look like your regular clothes—they're just roomier where your belly is and are cut slimmer in places where you don't gain weight, like your shoulders," says Kim DeYoung, who created her line of classic pieces, Metromom Maternity, after being frustrated by the limited clothing options while she was pregnant. Other innovations:

- **Better fabrics.** More stretch fabrics and sophisticated silhouettes up the style factor while flattering your figure.

- **Realistic proportions.** In years past, pants, skirts, and shorts were made to accommodate your growing middle with a large, stretchy panel at the waist—forcing you into a long top that covered it. "Especially if you're short or petite, having to wear a long shirt or sweater can throw off your proportions and make you look dumpy," DeYoung says. Today's styles from Gap, Old Navy, Metromom, Babystyle, and Mimi Maternity offer no-panel pants with drawstrings, elastic waists that grow with you, low-cut styles, or smaller side panels.

- **Active style.** The right gear makes it easier to stay fit all nine months. Companies like Liz Lange for Nike and Power of Two by Adidas have pants, shorts, swimsuits, and bras with what you need: built-in stomach and breast supports.

medical myth: tainted thongs
Rumor has it the sexy skivvies cause yeast and bladder infections—and even hemorrhoids.

reality check: thong absolution
"There is no correlation between thongs and infections or hemorrhoids. Not only could nobody prove it, no one would even research it," says Ernst G. Bartsich, M.D., clinical professor of obstetrics and gynecology at Cornell University-Weill Medical College.

Q+A
Find a Bra that Really Fits

After years of discomfort, my New Year's resolution is to finally find a bra that feels great. Any suggestions?

HERE'S YET ANOTHER resolution that starts with a look in the mirror. The first step is to size yourself up. "The reason most bras are uncomfortable is that they're the wrong size," says Joanne Kaye, director of merchandising for Bali Brands. "Your bra size can change over the years due to childbirth, weight changes, and how and if you work out." The ideal way to figure out your size is to get a professional bra fitting; these days, most department stores and lingerie shops have on-staff fitters or regularly sponsor free fitting clinics.

Once you've got the right size, go for the latest performance material: microfiber. This fabric is softer than silk, breathable, and supportive; plus it wicks away moisture—all of which adds to your comfort. Opt for seamless styles, such as Barely There's Body Revolution, for a smooth silhouette. If you hate the dig of underwire, you can get the same support with wire-free bras; try Bali's Soft Embrace.

a quick fit check

- *If your bra cups wrinkle, the cup size is too big.*
- *The center seam should lie against your breast bone without gaps between the cups.*
- *The lower edge of the bra band should anchor below your shoulder blades in the back.*
- *If the back of your bra rides up, either the cups are too small or the straps are adjusted incorrectly.*
- *If your skin overlaps the bra band in back or under your arms, the bra is too small.*

our 17-Point plan for a more beautiful body

Pamper yourself with these techniques—they're guaranteed to get you looking and feeling better than ever.

BY MICHELE BENDER

1 **Get your skin in shape.** Cornelia Zicu of New York's Peninsula Spa suggests regenerating and hydrating skin with her Romanian grandmother's remedy. Mix together (in order): 1 cup oatmeal, 2 teaspoons clover honey, 2 teaspoons olive oil, 2 teaspoons powdered milk, $1/2$ cup water, and 3 tablespoons Epsom salts. Apply to your damp body and face, and then rinse. Finish with a thick lotion, such as Palmer's Cocoa Butter Formula.

2 **Start glowing.** Two advantages to self-tanners: They're a healthy way to get a sun-kissed glow, and you can add the blush of spring even when it's still winter outside. Mix 2 parts self-tanner with 1 part moisturizer, then apply it to your face. "This prevents your skin from getting too dark so you can make a realistic transition from the winter pales to a warm-weather glow," says Judy Naake of St. Tropez Tanning Essentials.

3 **Steam-clean your face.** Why go to the gym for a sauna experience when you can get the same effect at home? Boil 4 to 5 cups of water, pour it into a heat-resistant bowl, and add 3 to 5 drops of a calming essential oil, such as rose or ylang-ylang. Cover your head with a towel and let the steam envelop your face for 10 minutes. Follow up by applying an exfoliator containing an alpha hydroxy acid.

I give my lifeless skin a dose of healthy color by using a hint of tinted moisturizer with SPF—and it does double duty by protecting my skin against the sun.

—*Caroline Pieper Vogt, director of marketing, Clarins*

4 **Take a salt bath with a hint of scent.** An occasional long bath in Epsom salts, with a little bath oil mixed into the water, can help your skin feel smoother, suggests dermatologist David Leffell, M.D. While your tub is filling, add 2 to 4 cups of salts; then mix in 4 to 6 drops of essential oils. Choose the right fragrance for your mood: Lavender has a calming effect, while lemon will awaken your senses.

5 **Reacquaint yourself with nature.** Take a hike this weekend. A brisk walk exhilarates your senses with the sights, scents, and sounds of the natural world. "You breathe more deeply when you're out in the fresh air, which increases oxygenation and improves both your skin color and circulation," explains Laurie Polis, M.D., director of Soho Skin and Laser Dermatology in New York City.

6 **Add a splash of color to your makeup.** "The look this season is sheer makeup accented with lots of vibrant hues," notes Collier Strong, consulting makeup artist for L'Oréal. Swap muted earth tones and neutrals for soft citrus shades. Use lip and cheek stains to add color, while letting your natural skin tones come through. Try lining brown eyes with navy, green eyes with purple, and blue eyes with pale green hues.

7 **Give your nails a break.** Take a two-week hiatus from dark polish, which can leave nails yellow and discolored. After your nails have taken a breather, they'll be ready for one of spring's fruity new shades, from light peach to Caribbean pink. Give some of our favorites a try: Avon's Nailwear in Wink, Lancôme's Lollipop, or L'Oréal's Shock Proof Nail Color in Mango Monarch.

8 **Give your H$_2$O a kick.** As the weather warms up, it's even more important to get your eight glasses of water a day. Try this spa trick: Pop some sliced cucumber in a pitcher of water and refrigerate for a few hours. The water will be infused with cucumber extract, a good thing since studies at the Smell and Taste Treatment and Research Foundation in Chicago found that cucumber's fresh scent and taste reduce anxiety.

9 **Add a touch of romance to your wardrobe.** Sizzling hot this year are fanciful, feminine clothes, according to fashion expert Kimberly Bonnell, author of *What to Wear: A Style Handbook.* Sounds like a perfect excuse to go shopping! Go ahead and treat yourself to a lacy or peasant-style blouse, a skirt flounced with exotic embroidery, or a top of flirty, flowing chiffon.

I switch from a thick face cream to a lighter lotion with SPF 15 in more humid weather because **my skin doesn't need the extra moisturizing** of a heavy cream.

—*Roberta Weiss, vice president of marketing, Origins*

10 Cool your heels. And keep them odor- and sweat-free with products that use a blend of marine and botanical extracts to help hydrate and soften tired, achy feet. Two of our favorites: Heel to Toe Moisturizing Marine Foot Masque and Creative Nail Design's Spa Pedicure Marine Masque. And they're easy to use. Simply massage the mask into your feet, wait 10 minutes or so, and then rinse with warm water.

11 Rinse in some shine. Yves Durif of New York City's Yves Durif Salon suggests this pick-me-up for listless locks: After shampooing, rinse with a solution of 1 cup warm water and $1/2$ cup apple-cider vinegar, followed by a douse of cold water. It reduces frizz and removes dirt, mineral deposits, and soapy residue. Not a do-it-yourselfer? Try a ready-made cider rinse, such as Rene Furterer Fioravanti Beautifying Rinse.

12 Pamper parched lips. This quick lip fix from Marcia Kilgore of New York's BlissSpa will revitalize your kisser: Put a thin coat of facial moisturizer on your lips, then blot lightly with a tissue. Next, press a piece of Scotch tape over your lips and gently pull off dead skin cells. Follow with a rich emollient lip balm containing beeswax, such as Burt's Beeswax Lip Balm, or aloe, such as Clinique's Superbalm Lip Treatment.

13 Plan a yoga get-together. Push back the furniture and ask a few friends over for a private yoga class. Use a video or DVD like *Crunch Total Yoga* or *Basic Yoga Workout for Dummies,* or hire a teacher from a local studio. Not only will this help you reconnect with your friends, but yoga—by reducing stress hormones in the body—also improves circulation, giving skin a healthy glow.

14 Spring-clean your cosmetic bag. Toss liquid makeup that has dried up or gotten pasty. "Never add water to bring a product back to its original consistency," cautions Barney Kenet, M.D., author of *How to Wash Your Face.* "This can introduce bacteria." You can keep powder products, such as eye shadows and blushes, for many years—not an ideal option if keeping up with trends is your thing.

I have my brows professionally shaped. **A lighter brow is a great look** and really opens up your face.

—*Lisa Mataro, vice president of marketing, Elizabeth Arden*

15 Try this recipe for winter-rough hands. Jennifer Jaqua of Jaqua Girls swears by this hand mask: Mix $1/4$ cup honey, 1 tablespoon kaolin clay, and $1/2$ teaspoon apricot kernel oil (all available at health-food stores). Keep the mixture on hands for five minutes. Rinse and then apply a glycerin- or shea butter–based cream, such as Neutrogena's Norwegian Formula Hand Cream or Earth Therapeutics' Gardener's Hand Cream.

16 Treat thirsty tresses. Frosty outside air and dry indoor heat can leave hair frizzy and split. "Get it back into shape with an intense conditioning treatment," says stylist Philippe Barr of Frédéric Fekkai. Comb in a conditioner from roots to ends. Slick hair into a ponytail or pile it under a cap, then head out for a walk or run. The conditioner will penetrate your hair as your body heats up.

17 Unkink with a partner. Have your partner trace soft, gentle circles and S-shaped waves along your back, neck, and arms. Massaging in an irregular circular motion really stimulates nerves. "With a straight line, the nerves anticipate the touch," says Lou Paget, author of *How to Be a Great Lover.* "An irregular touch pattern catches them off guard." ✳

Michele Bender is a contributing editor.

how we rate at-home bikini line care

We're all for low-maintenance summer looks. But there's no compromise when it comes to the bikini line: You've got to keep it clean (or undercover, but for beach-lovers like us, that's not an option). To get smooth with a minimum of fuss, we tried the newest do-it-yourself hair-removal products on the market. Here, we bare all.

Product	Claims	Tester's Take	Caveat
Marzena Petite Natural Wax Strips	Natural pine wax, not paraffin, forms the base of this product. The natural wax supposedly ensures a better grip on each strand of hair.	"This was easier than a lot of products I've tried, including other wax kits. It hurt less as it went along, and it worked pretty well."	"The strips were hard to separate from the protective packaging. Also, residual stickiness didn't clean up with soap and water. I had to use rubbing alcohol."
VEET Bikini Kit	To prevent irritation, this cream covers the surface of the skin with a protective layer of oil. Its special spatula is designed to make hair removal super-speedy.	"I've used a few depilatories in my day, all of which were a pain to remove, but this spatula makes it much easier."	"I had to wait 10 minutes for the formula to work. I don't have patience for things like this. Plus, not all of the hair was removed the first time, so I had to do it again."
Nair Vanilla Smoothie Bikini Crème	This fast-acting depilatory is formulated to avoid irritation.	"This didn't irritate my sensitive skin at all. After using it, the hair grew in more slowly than when I shave."	"It was messy—there's lots of product and hair to wipe off when you're done."
Noxzema Bikini Size Disposable Razors for Women	This mini razor (half the size of a standard one) is shaped to negotiate curves and crevices.	"The less-than-inch-long blade and the way it was angled made it easy to shave this tricky area. It removed hair better than my regular razor."	"Shaving took a little longer than usual, but it was worth it—I wasn't worried about nicking a very sensitive spot."
Nair Cool Fruit Wax Strips	The thin strips are shaped to conform to the topography of this area, and are scented with apple, berry, or peach/melon.	"It was easy to use—you warm the strips by rubbing them with your hands, so no appliances are involved."	"The results were only OK. Not all of the hairs were pulled out, so I needed to use the strip more than once."

Q+A
Trust the Pros for the Best Eyebrow Grooming

I recently had my eyebrows shaped at the salon. After tweezing, the stylist trimmed them with scissors! Should I sue?

DON'T CALL your lawyer (unless you're unhappy with the result). Scissors are actually a great eyebrow-styling tool. "Trimming the brows lightens them by taking off some of the excess length and bulk and getting rid of flyaway hairs," says Ramy, an eyebrow expert and creator of Ramy Beauty Therapy Cosmetics. Concerned that your trimmed brows will grow back thicker or fuller? Don't worry, Ramy says—that's a myth. But brows can't get beautiful with trimming alone. Tweezing is still necessary to remove stray hairs that interfere with the shape. And heed this warning: You might want to leave this to a professional, or you could risk going too short.

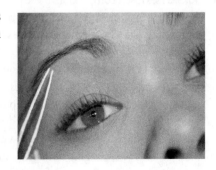

Is Stress Damaging Your Looks?

Inner turmoil can take a toll on your outer appearance. Here are some ways you can fight back.

BY CHRISTINE COBURN

You can barely look at a newspaper without being overwhelmed by the latest health threat, be it viruses, secondhand smoke, or food poisoning. But you're more likely to succumb to stress than to bacteria in your burger.

"Stress has become the epidemic of the 21st century," says Mark Hyman, M.D., medical director for the Canyon Ranch Spas. Not only does it make you snap at the kids and do stupid things in traffic, it raises the risk of heart disease, stroke, and osteoporosis. Under its grip, "our adrenaline spikes, stress hormones surge, blood pressure rises, breathing speeds up, blood sugar increases, and digestive functions slow," he says. And it can take a toll on your looks: a lackluster complexion, more breakouts than a 15-year-old, or an alarming amount of hair in the drain.

How can stress be the culprit? "Stress produces a 'fight or flight' response that was designed to save us from predators," Hyman explains. And although we're no longer racing from saber-toothed tigers, today's stresses can make us feel as if we are: trying to pull together a professional look while attempting to dress several not-so-cooperative kids, shoveling down breakfast in a matter of minutes, dodging similarly frantic folks on the freeway—all before 8:30 a.m. Stress hormones and their effects can aggravate skin problems from excess oil to eczema, can mess with your tresses, and often have whole-body beauty consequences.

Of course, the best solution is to attack the very source of your tension and anxiety. But your looks don't have to suffer while you're working on that. Here are the best fast-fixes for the not-so-pretty symptoms of stress.

• Your Skin •

While it might take years for stress to produce noticeable symptoms in other organs, it can surface immediately in your skin," says Katie Rodan, M.D., assistant professor of dermatology at Stanford University. In fact, a study published in 2001 in the *Archives of Dermatology* found that stress triggered just about every skin condition you can think of—sometimes in as little as seconds (hives) or days (psoriasis). "While we don't understand the direct connection between stress and specific skin conditions, we know that it exists," Rodan says. Fortunately, your daily stresses don't have to show up on your face. Get your complexion back in bloom with these strategies.

Acne

You've gotten flare-ups on your face at the most trying of times, right? Researchers are confirming what you already suspect: that stress and acne are connected. "The most common theory is that breakouts are hormonally induced and caused specifically by surges in the male hormone testosterone," says Jerome Z. Litt, M.D., professor of dermatology at Case Western University in Cleveland and author of *Your Skin from A to Z.* This hormone, along with cortisol, spikes even in women.
Solution: No need to dip into your teen's acne-treatment stash and suffer flaky skin later: There are effective grown-up options for the common adolescent affliction. "Adult creams tend to have a more moisturizing base, so you don't get the dryness and flaking you see with traditional teen-acne fighters," says Richard Maksimoski, director of product development for the Andrew Jergens company. "They also contain extra anti-inflammatory ingredients because adults tend to get more redness and swelling." Try remedies such as Neutrogena's Healthy Skin Anti-Wrinkle

The effects of a stressed life can be written all over your face and body: thinning hair, dark eye circles, dry skin patches.

5 ways to boost your well-being

Of course, beauty treatments are only part of the stress antidote. To restore yourself to radiance, you should conquer what's causing you anxiety or tension to begin with. "Research shows that a positive or relaxed frame of mind can help you overcome even the most serious physical conditions," says Mark Hyman, M.D., medical director for the Canyon Ranch Spas. "When you're relaxed, your blood pressure decreases, your food is absorbed more efficiently, your respiratory rate slows, your heartbeat regulates, and your cortisol levels drop." Fortunately, there are dozens of opportunities every day to make a dent in your stress level. Our experts on the art of calming down suggest a few good ways to start.

1. Schedule stress sessions: You schedule everything else—why not manage anxiety this way, too? "Set aside a specific time every day when you'll give yourself permission to worry," says Anita Barbee, Ph.D., a professor of social work at the University of Louisville who specializes in women's health. "During that time, make a list of everything that's troubling you; then make an adjacent list of possible solutions." Whenever your free-floating anxiety returns, remind yourself to save it for your next stress session.
2. Breathe: The shallow gulps you take when you're tense make you even edgier. "If you're feeling frantic, stop, close your eyes, and refocus your breathing," suggests Allen Elkin, Ph.D., director of the New York City Stress Management and Counseling Center and author of

Stress Management for Dummies. "Inhale slowly through your nose, directing the air deep into your belly. Exhale slowly through your mouth." Repeat 5 to 10 times.
3. Use scents: A scent can become your personal Pavlovian stimulus. "If you connect a certain fragrance with an emotionally uplifting situation, you can use it to trigger a relaxation response," Barbee says. For example, sniffing a perfume that you wore on a wonderful weekend getaway can make you recall that warm and fuzzy frame of mind in a high-stakes meeting or standstill traffic.
4. Flex: "You can achieve deep relaxation by tensing and releasing individual muscle groups," Elkin notes. "Practice by clenching your fist. Feel the strain in your hand and forearm, hold it for seven seconds, and then release. Let the feeling of relaxation deepen for 30 seconds. Repeat three times. Then move on to another muscle group." In only a few minutes, you can relax your entire body—from neck to toes.
5. Get moving: If there's a magical cure for general anxiety and the moodiness it can cause, our experts agree that moderate exercise is it. "There are volumes of research about the mood benefits of exercise," Hyman notes. "It causes physiological changes that counteract the effects of stress. We know now that it reduces cortisol levels, increases your serotonin (the 'happiness hormone'), and helps you recover more rapidly from the stress response." So skip rope with your children, walk the dog, bound up the stairs—simply get going.

Anti-Blemish, Bioré's Double Agent, and Clinique's Acne Solutions Emergency Gel Lotion (or, if necessary, prescription creams Differin, Azelex, or Klaron).

Dryness and Flaking

"We know for sure that stress decreases the skin's barrier function, or its ability to retain moisture," Rodan says. "We just don't know precisely why." The result: dry, flaky skin, redness, and a less-than-radiant look.

Solution: If you've been using a basic moisturizer, it's time for an upgrade. Dead skin cells don't rest on the skin smoothly, and moisture can easily escape from the uneven surface. Exfoliating exposes healthy cells that retain moisture better. Moisturizers with treatment benefits often contain heavy exfoliators like retinols (such as L'Oréal's Plenitude RevitaLift Complete or Avon's Anew Advanced All-in-One Self Adjusting Perfecting Creme) or hydroxy acids (like Lubriderm's Skin Renewal Age Defying Moisturizer).

To add extra luster to your skin, look for products that combine exfoliators with light-reflecting particles that minimize fine lines and wrinkles (try Olay's Total Effects or Estée Lauder's Idealis). If in a month or so you notice that over-the-counter brands aren't working, see a dermatologist for prescription-strength versions.

Psoriasis and Eczema

Psoriasis, which is caused by a sudden overproduction of skin cells, appears more often as red, itchy bumps covered in white scales. Eczema, an inflammation of the upper layers of the skin, usually begins as redness and itching that develops into scaly, cracked areas, thanks to repeated scratching. Both conditions can be aggravated by a stress-related loss of moisture.

Solution: Over-the-counter hydrocortisone creams may ease both psoriasis and eczema. One remedy is new on the market: Eucerin's Itch-Relief Moisturizing Spray is the first lotion in spray form developed for such pestering itches. If you use over-the-counter medications for seven days and find no improvement, see a dermatologist. Psoriasis is often soothed with prescription vitamin D or vitamin A creams (like Dovonex or Tazorac) or UV light. Eczema may respond well to prescription-strength cortisone creams or Protopic, a new steroid-free salve that prevents the autoimmune short-circuit that causes the problem. With both conditions, help yourself out by using gentle, soap-free cleansers (like Aveeno or Basis).

Rosacea

Often appearing as tender patches of redness, dilated blood vessels, and swelling on the cheeks, chin, and forehead, rosacea is a chronic skin condition not fully understood by doctors. While its cause is uncertain, stress is cited as a trigger that could worsen the condition.

Solution: Stop swelling with prescription sulfa lotions (like Novacet and Sulfacet-R), metronidazole creams (like Metrocream and Metrogel), or antibiotics. Avoid harsh soaps and alcohol-based cleansers and astringents, which irritate rosacea. Bypassing alcoholic beverages, reducing caffeine intake, and avoiding spicy foods—also suspected rosacea triggers—can help calm your complexion, too.

Undereye Bags

This all-too-common problem needs little description: puffy, discolored rings often linked to a sleepless night. "When we're tired, fluids pool underneath the eyes," Litt says.

Solution: Lessen the swelling with an anti-inflammatory eye gel containing cucumber, witch hazel, or chamomile (such as Clarins' Eye Contour Gel). Speed up effects by chilling them in the fridge. Sleep, of course, can help toss bags. While you're getting shut-eye, elevate your head with an extra pillow to let gravity help drain the pooling fluids.

• Your Hair •

Complexion problems are bad enough, but say "thinning hair," and stress will soar higher than a post-holiday credit-card bill. Squelch the stress by looking at two facts: First, you're not going to go bald. "No one loses all of his or her hair strictly due to stress—no one," assures Amy McMichael, M.D., a hair-loss expert and associate professor of dermatology at Wake Forest University. And second: Stress won't make you go gray. "Hair goes gray over a period of years due to declining pigment production, which you may notice more when you're stressed," Litt says. Nevertheless, stress can create some bad hair days, if you let it. Here's how to tame them.

Shedding or Thinning

Stress can jump-start your hair's natural shedding phase, causing you to lose clumps instead of a strand here and there, as you would normally. This condition, known as telogen effluvium, is temporary and in all but the rarest cases is noticeable only to you. "You have a hundred

5 high-anxiety beauty habits to break

Some stress-related beauty disasters are self-inflicted. We're not chiding you; we're just pointing out that they're avoidable and the habits that cause them are changeable. "In many cases, just making someone aware of a habit is enough to cure it," notes Katie Rodan, M.D., assistant professor of dermatology at Stanford University. If that's not enough, try these techniques for preventing your own beauty-sabotaging tendencies.

1. Splitting or twisting hair: Many people pluck out hairs, divide split ends, or pull at brows or lashes. "It's a diversion for an overactive mind," says Jerome Litt, M.D., professor of dermatology at Case Western University in Cleveland. Most of the time, this nervous habit results in severe split ends and a permanent case of the frizzies. To beat it, tie your hair back or wear a little extra mascara or brow gel—anything to create an obstacle to plucking. Also try giving yourself something else to play with: squeezable stress balls, a bowl of marbles on your desk, or even Play-Doh.

2. Nail biting: "This is by far the most common habit," Rodan says. "It can cause bleeding and even permanent damage to your nail plate." Dark polish or an expensive manicure can stop biters in the act—as will a paint-on, bitter-tasting deterrent (such as Orly's No Bite) or a Band-Aid on "favorite" fingers. "Some people find that substituting another oral activity, like sucking a lollipop or chewing gum, can also help conquer the urge," says stress expert Allen Elkin, Ph.D. Of course, you still need to deal with what's causing the stress: You don't want to just substitute gum snapping for nail biting.

3. Lip biting: This chronic habit can lead to cracking, chapping, and peeling. In some instances, infections can be transferred from the fingers to the lips or vice versa. A dramatic shade of lipstick can be a deterrent—do you really want to walk around with smudges on your teeth? You're also less likely to bite if you keep lips well-moisturized with a basic, flavorless lip balm, such as Carmex, Blistex, or Chapstick. And keeping your mouth occupied with other activities—like sucking on sugar-free hard candies—can get you through moments of weakness.

4. Picking or scratching your skin: In extreme cases, people scratch until they scar the skin. In general, though, scratching just makes skin more susceptible to rashes, blisters, and sores or even to serious infections like staph. Keeping nails very short (just don't bite them!) will make it more difficult to actually damage the skin. Covering the areas you tend to scratch with extra layers of clothing or a Band-Aid can also be a reminder to stop yourself in the act. Better yet, substitute the helpful act of self-massage for the destructive act of scratching. Of course, if you actually are itchy, try a heavier body lotion or see your dermatologist.

5. Stress eating: Running to the fridge or the office vending machine is a classic coping mechanism. To get a handle on your appetite, "begin by figuring out why you crave what you crave," Elkin suggests. Do you eat candy bars for the chocolate taste? Maybe sipping on a sugar-free hot chocolate will do the trick. Even better, substitute a nonfood treat that makes you happy or zaps stress. Put on a little mood music or check out your favorite joke site on the Web.

---

thousand hairs on your head," Rodan says. "Even the loss of half of that would not be noticeable to anyone else."

In rarer cases, sudden hair loss is caused by a genetic autoimmune condition known as alopecia areata. "This type of hair loss runs in families and tends to be concentrated in the crown, rather than distributed evenly all over the head," Rodan explains. The condition can even cause the loss of lashes, brows, and body hair. Solution: Time. Regular hair loss will slow in a month or so, and the follicles will begin the growing phase in the following month. Some doctors will prescribe minoxidil (known as Rogaine) to regrow hair, although by the time the product is thought to start working, hair is naturally growing back anyway. Another option is treating the scalp with steroid creams or injections, which reduce stress-induced inflammation and allow the follicle to return to its normal function, Rodan says. In the case of alopecia, some doctors have begun prescribing a combination treatment of minoxidil and Retin-A, which may produce faster regrowth.

Dry, Itchy Scalp and Dandruff

"Your scalp is an extension of your complexion," Rodan says, "therefore, it can have the same stress-induced reactions as the rest of your skin." That can spell dryness and irritation, and a buildup of flakes that typically end up on the shoulders of your favorite jacket. How do you tell the difference between the two conditions? Small, dry flakes are symptomatic of dry scalp; larger, sticky flakes are more likely to be dandruff.

Solution: If your problem is dry scalp, try switching to a moisturizing shampoo; look for one containing hylauronic acid, panthenol, glycerin, or hydrolyzed wheat protein. If this doesn't work, a medicated shampoo containing zinc, tar, or salicylic acid might do the trick. For dandruff, first try an over-the-counter dandruff shampoo; those containing selenium sulfide, coal tar, or salicylic acid tend to be the most effective. In either case, if you're still seeing flakes after two weeks or so, see a dermatologist, who can prescribe more potent shampoos or steroid treatments.

Oily Scalp

Stress can shift sebaceous glands located at the base of the hair follicles into secreting oils on overdrive—resulting in an oily scalp, which then leads to oily hair.

Solution: Switch to a shampoo for oily hair and, if you must use conditioner, apply it only to the ends of your hair. If that doesn't help, ask your dermatologist for a prescription-strength shampoo that contains salicylic acid, which will dry the scalp—and consequently your hair—of excess oils.

• Your Body •

Even if your face and hair are OK, stress can break out as perspiration rings, fingernail ridges, or even extra fat. Here's how to heal what's happening below the neck.

Warts

Your stressed-out immune system can create just the right environment for the viruses that cause warts to grow, particularly on your hands and feet.

Solution: If over-the-counter wart remedies with salicylic acid (like Mediplast's Plaster Patches) don't work, a dermatologist can remove the growth with a scalpel, using local anesthesia, or by spraying it with liquid nitrogen (a process that may have to be repeated more than once).

Perspiration

When the heat is on—figuratively—the increase in adrenaline can affect your sweat glands, adding "sweat rings" to your daily list of what to worry about.

Solution: Assuming over-the-counter antiperspirants (rather than deodorants, which merely masks odors) have failed, a more powerful sweat-fighter is available only from a dermatologist. She may prescribe a stronger aluminum chloride antiperspirant than you can get on the shelves (such as Drysol's Dab-O-Matic) to reduce the activity of your sweat glands. Doctors might rely on probanthine—a drug that blocks the nerve impulses to glands—to control dampness, or antibiotics such as erythromycin to control odor. Your physician will ease you off the meds when the problem gets under control.

Fingernail Ridges

"A serious physical or mental trauma can stop the blood supply to places the body thinks are expendable—like the nails," Litt explains. "In this case, the nail temporarily stops growing, and when it begins growing again, it forms a ridge." That white streak in the midsection of your thumbnail is a direct product of stress, too, Litt says. "It's the result of absentmindedly rubbing your finger on your thumbnail."

Solution: The only real cure is time. It takes about six months to grow the ridge out. In the meantime, camouflage the problem with paint-on ridge fillers, such as Sally Hansen's Get Even Hydrating Ridge Filler or Orly's Ridgefiller Primer Basecoat. White spots can be covered with polish.

Weight Gain

"It isn't just our imagination—stress can make us fat," Hyman says. According to research at Stanford University, stress not only increases insulin and blood-sugar levels (which boosts your cravings for carbohydrates), but also it can change your metabolism in a way that causes you to store more fat around the organs in the center of the body.

Solution: While you can't do much to fix your metabolism, you can avoid the reach-for-a-carb reflex. Try substituting a healthy alternative for sugary or starchy snacks: Stash a bag full of veggie sticks and fruit in the company fridge. And don't forget that a little physical activity—like going for a walk around the block—is a great way to combat both the appetite surges and their results. ✳

Christine Coburn is a freelance beauty writer.

Q+A
No Tan is a Good Tan

A friend told me that tanning beds are safer than outdoor sunbathing, but I'm not convinced. Is she right?

IT'S A GOOD THING that you don't believe everything you hear. Indoor tanning has been touted as a safe alternative to soaking up real rays because tanning beds are said to emit mostly UVA radiation, not the UVB rays that are known to cause a host of skin problems.

The real story: "Any form of ultraviolet light—be it from the sun or a tanning bed—is hazardous to your health," says Seth Matarasso, M.D., associate clinical professor of dermatology at University of California at San Francisco School of Medicine. And tanning beds do emit some UVB radiation. In fact, a recent study found that tanning beds may be just as bad as baking in your backyard, causing the same damage that can lead to skin cancer, not to mention the premature aging and wrinkles also linked to UV exposure. In addition, only 27 states have any regulations concerning tanning beds, and the rules vary greatly from state to state. That means that tanning beds aren't always monitored for cleanliness and safety, potentially setting you up for other problems—a bacterial or fungal infection, for instance.

"The bottom line," Matarasso says, "is that no tan is a good tan unless it comes out of a bottle."

Q+A
Protect Your Face from the Sun Without Causing Acne

Sunscreens tend to clog my pores and cause breakouts. How can I keep my skin clear and stay protected?

THE SOLUTION may be as simple as switching products. "It's mainly the oil in sunscreens that causes acne and breakouts," says Peter L. Kopelson, M.D., a Beverly Hills, California-based dermatologist. Your best option is an oil-free, noncomedogenic (anti-pore-clogging) sunscreen designed specifically for the face, such as Clinique's City Block SPF 15, Aveeno's Radiant Skin Daily Moisturizer with SPF 15, or Nivea's Alpha-Flavon Perfect Protection Creme SPF 15. The gentler ingredients in these face-only formulas help prevent breakouts as well.

If you still have problems after switching, add an over-the-counter cleanser or acne product to your skin regimen. Look for products that have glycolic acid, salicylic acid, or benzoyl peroxide. "These break up dirt and oil in the pores," Kopelson explains. A few favorites: DDF's Glycolic Daily Cleansing Pads, Murad's Clarifying Skin Cleanser, and BeneFit's Boo Boo Zap.

SUNSCREEN THAT SUITS YOU

Maybe the reason you don't like sunscreen is that you haven't found the one product that suits your lifestyle. Maybe slathering it on makes your tennis-racket grip slip or your skin break out. We get that. But don't write the stuff off. Manufacturers have answered the call for pet peeve–proof formulations. Here's how to find your sunscreen match.

For the multi-tasker: Select a tinted moisturizer or foundation that doubles as sunscreen. Opt for one that's SPF 15 or higher, like Neutrogena's Healthy Defense SPF 30 Daily Moisturizer.

Touch-ups are necessary, though: It can settle into facial lines and wear off during the day, leaving you less protected.

For the natural woman: Aubrey Organics' Titania Full Spectrum Sunblock SPF 25 is chock-full of natural ingredients, including moisturizing shea butter and Canadian willow herb extract to protect the skin from irritation.

For the sporty sister: You need a greaseless, water-resistant sunscreen that won't leave your hands so slippery you can't keep hold of the bike handlebars. Ombrelle's Sport Spray SPF 15 by

L'Oréal fits the bill and comes in an easy-to-use spray bottle.

For the sensitive type: If your skin is prone to breakouts, opt for a product that is oil-free and labeled "noncomedogenic" (won't clog pores). Try Clinique's Sun Care SPF 30 or Banana Boat's VitaSkin Facial Care Lotion, which is enriched with vitamins A, C, and E.

For the girl on the go: If you gotta travel light, check out SPF to Go, sunscreen that comes in a single-use foil packet with a built-in spout. It's cheap (about $1 per packet) and easy to stash.

EIGHT GREAT
Hygiene Tips You Should Know

Keeping brushes and applicators clean is crucial to save your face from harmful bacteria. The clean routine doesn't have to be a chore—just follow these simple housekeeping how–tos.

BY ANNA ROUFOS

My approach to makeup maintenance used to be, in a word, minimal. I'd keep products around until I used them up, which could sometimes take years. I mean, some of the stuff in the bottom of my bag dated back to when Boy George was big. After all, I figured, this stuff costs money, so why not make it last? Besides, only purists and clean freaks pay attention to details like expiration dates and washing out brushes and sponges.

Then I began to notice that my skin didn't look as good as it used to. It seemed like I was breaking out more often for no good reason. I hadn't made any major dietary shifts, and as far as I could tell, my hormones were ebbing and flowing as usual. I had no choice but to consider that my laid-back attitude about hygiene was to blame. Maybe those purists were actually on to something.

But when I started digging up the dirt on beauty and cleanliness (or lack thereof), I found out that you don't have to be obsessive to protect yourself from breakouts, infections,

and other potential problems. A germ-free existence is as unnecessary as it is impractical. Plus, it takes a pretty hefty dose of germs to cause real trouble. But, the fact is, even a little diligence can pay off. "It definitely makes a difference when you use fresh products and applicators," says beauty expert Bobbi Brown. "Brushes and old makeup get filled with lots of bacteria, which isn't good for your skin." And products that haven't been gathering dust for years—or that are kept clean with minor upkeep—yield better results.

So I've cleaned up my act, and you can too, without a lot of fuss. Here's a look at what's worth doing—and why.

Easy Steps with Big Dividends
Adopting a few good habits will keep products fresher and minimize the chances of spreading germs that could lead to skin problems, cold sores, and eye infections.

1. Wash up. It may seem like common sense, but how often do you wash your hands right before you apply your makeup (the shower you took 20 minutes prior doesn't count)? Not only are you spreading whatever's on your hands to your face, but you're also probably contaminating the entire container with bacteria by sticking a dirty finger in it, says Audrey Kunin, M.D., associate clinical instructor at the University of Kansas Medical School Department of Dermatology. This slashes the product's shelf life and increases the risk that you'll spread germs every time you apply it.

2. Don't share—or borrow.

This is especially important if you or the person you share with already has an infection. For example, if your friend has a cold sore and you use her lip balm, you could get one, too. If someone ends up borrowing your balm, though, you don't have to throw it out—just dip it in some

rubbing alcohol and wipe it dry. Avoid using communal tester products at the cosmetics counter, too. Ask the salesperson to shave off the surface of a lipstick, for instance, or provide you with samples that haven't come into contact with anyone else's skin.

3. Clean your applicators.

"If you keep using your tools without washing them, oil and bacteria build up, which can cause clogged pores, acne, or skin irritation," says Vicki Albert Chavin, M.D., a dermatologist in Framingham, Massachusetts. No need to pull out the pressure washer, though. Rinse brushes, sponges, and makeup pads about once a week with a gentle cleanser (the same one you use to clean your face is fine). "Once you wash it, let the applicator

when extra care is called for

In certain circumstances, you do have to go out of your way to keep clean. For instance:

If you're prone to infections. Some people spend the entire spring season nursing cold sores. If this sounds like you, pay special attention to keeping products and applicators clean. If you have a cold sore, eye infection, or a cold or virus, immediately toss any product or applicator that has come in contact with your skin: You could make the problem worse or cause a second infection. Use disposable cotton swabs or a clean finger for application during the course of the infection (and once you touch the infected area, don't touch the product again).

If you use three-in-one cosmetics. Multi-use sticks and creams for eyes, lips, and cheeks are great for streamlining your makeup routine. But because they contact several areas of your face—particularly the vulnerable eyes—it pays to wipe the surface of the product with a cotton swab or tissue to remove bacteria before applying it to each area, says dermatologist Audrey Kunin, M.D. When you use them, start with eyes, then cheeks—saving the mouth, a bacteria hangout, for last.

If you frequent nail salons. Nail instruments that aren't properly sanitized can easily cause bacterial, yeast, or fungal infections, says Suzanne Levine, a podiatrist in New York City. "Unfortunately, many salons are not sterilizing their instruments properly." She goes so far as to recommend bringing your own tools to a salon for a pedicure or manicure. For convenience, bring along OPI's Swiss Clean Nail Healthcare Pack—a kit that holds most of your nail necessities.

But using your own tools won't help much if you don't keep them clean. Spray them with a disinfectant like Lysol before each use. Bacteria on nail surfaces usually don't cause a problem, but don't cut into the sides of your nails with cuticle cutters: This can give germs a portal into the nail, where they can cause infection and set you up for a fungus. Symptoms of an infection include pain, redness, itching, and pus in or around the nail area, or greenish discoloration. If you notice any of these signs, see your doctor (a dermatologist for fingernails and a podiatrist for toenails).

dry completely before returning it to the container," adds Arlette Palo, vice president of product development at Clinique. "A damp applicator in a closed compact would be an ideal environment for bacteria." If this sounds like too much trouble, try disposable cotton pads or swabs instead of reusable applicators.

4. Treat blemishes right. Pimple-popping is best left to a professional, but if you just can't resist, at least make sure you're doing it the safe way. Start with clean hands and face. Then steam your face over a basin of hot water to encourage pores to dilate. Use a tissue to cover your fingers as you gently squeeze the blemish, says Debra Jaliman, M.D., clinical instructor of dermatology at the Mount Sinai School of Medicine in New York City. This extra-careful technique will release the offending clog while minimizing skin irritation and your chances of infection.

5. Take care of your toothbrush. Although dentists advise replacing your toothbrush every four to six months (or whenever it begins to show signs of wear), it's not because they're concerned about germs. "If the bristles

antibacterials: necessary—or not?

Everyone's getting into the antibacterial act: Body washes, body sponges, makeup pads, and even specially treated skin towels are now on the market. But do you need them? According to Stuart Levy, M.D., director of the Center for Adaptation Genetics and Drug Resistance at Tufts University in Boston, there is no advantage to using antibacterial products in everyday circumstances. And if you do make them part of your routine, they might let you down when you really need them—like when you or someone in your home is sick, Levy says, and you want to contain the spread of illness. Why? The powerful antibacterial agents in these products may kill off normal bacteria, creating an ideal environment for "superbugs" that are impervious to antibiotics. You're better off using clean linens each time you wash your face, frequently washing your hands with soap and water, keeping your makeup applicators clean, and washing loofahs and sponges with a disinfectant at least once a month.

sizing up your salon

If sharing lip balm with a friend is a no-no, getting your hair and nails done at a salon with tools used on hundreds of strangers has got to be a prelude to a dirty disaster, right? Not necessarily. We secretly swabbed objects in a typical hair and nail salon in Warren, Michigan, to see what germs were lurking. The good news: Most of the objects we tested were relatively clean. What we did find—bacteria on a hairbrush, a cuticle pusher, and a haircut cape—wasn't life-threatening (it probably means they weren't cleaned properly between clients), but it could cause minor infections and breakouts.

While our results were tame, be wary on your next salon visit. "Your risk of contracting a contagious disease is low, but real," says Shelley A. Sekula-Rodriguez, M.D., past president of the Texas Dermatological Society. Hepatitis B and C are the most dangerous diseases that can linger on surfaces. Hepatitis B can be infectious for at least a week on headrests and instruments. And razors, nail files, and scissors can transmit hepatitis C.

"Disposable instruments are ideal, but performing proper sterilization should eliminate most bacteria and yeast," Sekula-Rodriguez says. Check the label on the cleaning solution your stylist uses: If you see "tuberculocidal disinfectant" or "sterilant," it's the right stuff. Ask how long the tools have been soaking (30 minutes is best). Steam sterilization, a.k.a. autoclaving, destroys some bacteria, but not enough to keep you safe.

are frayed, they're less effective. They'll also scrape against tissue, possibly injuring your gums," says Matthew Messina, D.D.S., a consumer adviser for the American Dental Association. According to Messina, it would take a lot of bacteria to cause an oral infection; still, it makes good sense to keep your toothbrush clean. You don't have go so far as to disinfect your brush in the microwave or the dishwasher, though. While they're effective, these methods are a hassle to do every day, and they're tough on bristles, besides. A better practice: Rinse your brush well with warm water and soak it in a disinfectant mouthwash, such as Listerine, for five to 10 minutes. Try working it into your daily routine. For instance, after you brush your teeth in the morning, soak your toothbrush while you take your shower. When you get out, store it in an upright position to allow it to dry completely. This procedure kills off much of the bacteria that need water to live, Messina says. One exception to the four-to-six month replacement rule: Make sure you buy a new toothbrush after a cold or infection has run its course so you don't reinfect yourself.

6. Lather up, then floss. There's one simple step in oral hygiene that you probably never even considered: Wash your hands before you floss your teeth. "During flossing, your hands come into contact with the oral tissues more than at any other time," says Robert Hepps, D.D.S., founder of the California Academy of Aesthetic Dentistry in San Francisco. "So you are basically wiping whatever debris is on your fingers onto the tissues of your mouth, which could cause an infection."

when to trash it

After three months: lip glosses, liquid foundations, tinted moisturizers, and concealers that you use fingers to apply; mascara, eyeliner, and eye shadow

After six months: 3-in-1 products for eyes, cheeks, and lips; lip glosses that you apply with a wand

After one year: creams, moisturizers, sunscreens, prescription topicals, such as Retin-A; foundations, powders, and concealers that you apply with sponges, pads, or applicators; and lipsticks

7. Pitch it promptly. You know that tube of elderberry lipstick you bought four years ago in a fit of makeup boredom? Toss it out, dermatologists say—even if you never opened it. Although the government doesn't regulate the shelf life of beauty products, most of them are developed to last only a year or two unopened. But once the product is exposed to the air (or to your skin), it might deteriorate even more quickly, losing color and intensity, and maybe even spoiling. Over time, some products, such as sunscreens and skin creams, can also lose their effectiveness.

Of course, if the cosmetics you use have expiration dates on the labels, trust them. And throw away a product if its color or texture has changed or if it has an unusual odor. Otherwise, check out the box on this page for guidelines from dermatologists on when you should pitch past-their-prime products.

8. Stow it safely. Cosmetics stored in the bathroom may deteriorate even more quickly since humidity causes bacteria, yeast, and fungus to grow. So it's a good idea to stash your makeup and skin-care items in a cool, dry place outside the bathroom, such as in a basket in your hall closet for easy access and transport. If you're the type who likes to stock up on a favorite product, Palo suggests that you store the unopened surplus cosmetics in the refrigerator until you're ready to use them. ✳

Freelance writer Anna Roufos contributes to Self *and* More.

Q+A
What those little red lines on your skin really mean
I just noticed a tiny red line on my nose. What is it, and what can I do about it?

WE HATE TO BE the bearers of bad news, but it sounds like you have what's commonly known as a broken capillary. "Broken" is misleading; these red lines are enlarged, dilated, intact capillaries that become visible when they're too close to the skin's surface. The lines can be caused by a number of factors, including heredity and sun exposure, says Harold Lancer, M.D., a Beverly Hills, California-based dermatologist. "Unfortunately, if you see one, chances are you're going to get more."

But the news is not all glum: Most enlarged capillaries can be reduced or removed with lasers. And mild ones may be treatable with prescription medications like medronidazole, a topical cream that reduces yeast and bacteria—both of which make lines more visible. Ask your dermatologist which solution is right for you. Until then, use a concealer with a greenish tinge to counter the redness.

healthBUZZ

thumbs UP

Smoke shield: University of Arizona Health Sciences Center research suggests that antioxidant supplements may block some of the damaging effects of second-hand smoke.

Bone—and brain—boost: A preliminary study in Nutrition Research found that the memory-enhancing herb ginkgo biloba contains compounds that enhance bone formation. But don't ditch the dairy until further research confirms the findings.

thumbs DOWN

Fast music: Israeli researchers have found that the faster the music on car stereos, the more risks drivers take—making them up to twice as likely to have accidents as people with subtler music tastes.

Pay cut: In the 10 industries that employed the most women from 1995 to 2000, the U.S. General Accounting Office found that the salary gap for managers had widened in 7 of the 10 trades.

Q + A
Save Your Gums with the Right Toothbrush Techniques

Will those new supercharged, battery-operated toothbrushes hurt my gums?

EVEN THOUGH THEY SPIN like those high-speed buffers at the car wash, electric and battery-operated toothbrushes shouldn't be harmful. The spinning brushes have bristles that are soft and rounded on the ends so they don't irritate your gums. And, as dentists say, toothbrushes don't make gums recede; people do. How you use your toothbrush is more important than whether it's battery operated or not. Make sure your technique is up to snuff: Hold the toothbrush (you should use only soft bristles) at a 45-degree angle to your teeth so the bristles don't rub flat against your teeth or gums. Then gently move the bristles back and forth over your teeth; use an up-and-down motion on the back of your front teeth. Extra-fancy brushes that cost nearly $100 may win an advantage on one point, though: Some shut off when you press too hard. If you're doing all the right moves but your gums are bleeding, then it's time for a dental checkup.

myth: Popping mints and swirling mouthwash will kill germs and leave your mouth minty fresh.

reality check: Sugar feeds all sorts of bacteria, says Bryan Edgar, D.D.S., a member of the Academy of General Dentistry. So mints that contain the sweet stuff can actually make your breath worse. For a quick fix, switch to sugar-free mints or mouthwash. For a longer lasting solution, brush your tongue (in addition to your teeth) and drink plenty of water to boost saliva production and freshen breath.

Fix Body Odor with a Pill ...*or just stick with your roll-on*

In the ongoing battle against body odors, the latest weapon works from within: Body Mint is a deodorant that comes in an over-the-counter pill containing 100 milligrams of chlorophyllin, a derivative of chlorophyll (the natural compound that makes plants green). The manufacturer claims that two pills daily keep your whole body odor-free. The theory: Because chlorophyll is a binding agent, it may absorb odor molecules. But can you really swallow a sweeter smell? Beyond preliminary tests conducted by the company, there is no scientific proof that the pills work. And 99 percent of body odor is caused by bacteria on the skin's surface, so it's unclear how an oral pill could kill them, says Robert Brodell, M.D., head of dermatology at Northeastern Ohio Universities College of Medicine. "That doesn't mean it can't work, but I'm skeptical." And at $20 for 60 pills (available at www.bodymint.com), it could be an expensive gamble—unless you have a serious problem and have exhausted your options.

SOAP STAR: THE BAR IS BACK

Over the last few years, soap dishes have been standing empty while body washes and liquid cleansers edged their way into everyone's showers. One reason for solid soap's decline: its harsh reputation. "The old way of making bar soap was to mix fats with alkaline chemicals to strip dirty oils from the skin," says David J. Leffell, M.D., author of *Total Skin* and professor of dermatology and surgery at the Yale University School of Medicine. "However, this also stripped off the lipid layer that coats the skin and keeps moisture in." Another factor: Germophobes thought liquids were more hygienic than solid soaps, which Leffell says isn't true (it's difficult for bacteria or other germs to grow on solid soap, so bars are just as safe as liquids).

Now solid cleansers are making a comeback, and this time they're raising the bar. The new soaps are not only gentler—many have glycerin, a moisturizing cleanser—but they're stocked with other beneficial ingredients.

• Aveeno's cleansing bars contain natural oatmeal, which has an anti-itch and moisturizing effect.
• Archipeligo's Milk Soap is infused with milk to help heal dry skin.
• Avon's Wellness VitaTonics and Earth Therapeutics' Green Tea Herbal Soap are chock-full of antioxidants.
• Others, like Bliss' Enorma-Lyptus Soap, have essential oils to soothe your senses.

This doesn't mean old faves are washed up, though. Some of the classics are just as solid as the new soaps.
• Basis' Sensitive Skin Bar wards off irritation.
• Neutrogena's Cleansing Bar for Acne-Prone Skin fights breakouts.

The new soaps are not only gentler; many have such benefits as essential oils and antioxidants.

Q+A
Why You Should Wash Your Face Before Your Workout

I see a lot of women at the gym working out with their makeup on. Isn't it better to exercise with a clean face?

SPORT A FACEFUL of makeup at the gym, and you'll do more than break a sweat—you'll break out. "Sweating increases your skin's production of oil. Combining that with certain types of makeup can cause or worsen blackheads, whiteheads, and acne," says Amy B. Lewis, M.D., assistant clinical professor of dermatology at the State University of New York Downstate Medical Center. "Even oil-free products contain other ingredients that can clog pores." For preworkout makeup removal without water, try face wipes, such as Stila's Sport H2off, or Cetaphil's Gentle Skin Cleanser on a cotton ball. If you must wear makeup to buff up, stick with powder products, which are less likely to lead to blemishes. And lipstick is OK: The lips are among the few body parts that don't sweat.

Q+A
Tips for a Whiter Smile

I'd like to use a do-it-yourself kit to bleach my teeth, but I don't want my smile to look fake. Any tips for getting a natural shade?

IF YOU BLEACH teeth continually, you won't get a sense of the real color—and you risk going too white. Prevent a faux-looking grin by taking a break after beginning an at-home treatment. "Take a weeklong hiatus from your treatments after four weeks, or as soon as you notice a major change," says Michel Mouravieff, D.M.D., a dentist based in Ridgewood, New Jersey. "Teeth get dehydrated as you're whitening them, so you can't see the actual color until the teeth rehydrate."

Once your teeth are three or four shades lighter, you should stop the treatments: Anything more can be too much (check an old photo of yourself to help judge the change in shade). If you're not satisfied with your at-home results, consider enlisting the help of your dentist.

simple changes, Big Beauty payoffs

Try these 5 surgery-free solutions for your hardest beauty problems.

BY JENNIFER LAING

When you consider the stats on cosmetic surgery, you might think a standing appointment with a skin doctor is an inevitable part of your future. Between 2000 and 2001 (the most recent years for which statistics are available), the number of Botox injections increased 25 percent, chemical peels were up 23 percent, and microdermabrasion jumped 47 percent, according to the American Academy of Cosmetic Surgery. But as the medical world continues to perfect such anti-aging procedures (and debut new ones), beauty-product developers have kept pace. Now you can get smoother skin, brighter eyes, and fuller-looking lips just by knowing which products to use and how to use them. We've talked to the experts, tested the products, and tried the tips—and here, we share with you the best look-great-fast fixes for your biggest beauty concerns.

1
• *Make Wrinkles Retreat* •

Switch to a heavy-duty moisturizer.

Creams and lotions usually reserved for very dry skin plump up skin cells with moisture, which temporarily softens the appearance of lines. A heavy cream will contain a combination of rich ingredients (look for petrolatum, sweet almond oil, shea butter, and the like) and will keep the skin moisturized longer than a lighter-weight version.

Get primed.

Makeup primers like Smashbox's Photo Finish and Prescriptives' Magic Invisible Line Smoother are the cosmetic equivalent of Spackle. Dab them directly onto your fine lines and wrinkles, or blend them all over your skin to fill in grooves and creases. Because they're transparent and silicone-based, primers (also known as line-smoothing gels) are virtually undetectable and create a smooth, even surface on which to apply foundation and other makeup. The effect lasts until you wash it off.

Go the retinoid route.

Prescription retinoids like Retin A and Renova have been clinically proven to reduce fine lines and wrinkles in about six weeks with nightly use. These mild acids work like alpha hydroxy acids (AHAs), speeding up the skin's ability to exfoliate, increasing cell turnover, and revealing fresher skin faster than the body normally does on its own, says New York City dermatologist Bradford Katchen, M.D. Retinol, the over-the-counter version in products like L'Oréal's Plénitude Line Eraser and ROC's Retinol Actif Pur Daily SPF 15, is not as powerful but will still generate some noticeable improvement in 12 weeks. Using sunscreen during treatment with over-the-counter creams or prescription retinoids is essential: The products make the skin more susceptible to sun damage.

· Get an Instant Eye Boost ·

Play up top lashes.

Droopy top lashes can make your whole eye look like it's sagging. Give the lid a lift by first blending a dark eyeliner along the top lashes (start at the inner corner of your eye and follow the lash line to the outer corner, concentrating the color on the outer third of the lid) and then curling and coating lashes with mascara. Leave your lower lashes bare: Lining them only draws attention to dark circles and makes the eye look smaller.

Use concealer strategically.

If puffy eyes or dark circles make you look like you pulled an all-nighter—even when you've had eight hours of sleep—cover them up with a swipe of concealer in just the right place. Some people are naturally more prone to puffiness (which is caused by fluid retention in the tissue around the eyes) than others, and as the skin ages and loses elasticity the problem can seem more pronounced. The best tactic: Blend a liquid concealer only on the line created by the bag—the swollen area itself doesn't need coverage, says Alison Raffaele, a makeup artist who specializes in cover-up (Skin Alison Raffaele). If dark circles are your nemesis, erase them by blending concealer over the entire eye area—including circles and from lashes to brows—to even out your skin tone and give you a well-rested look. Always use your fingers to apply concealer around the eye; this allows you to achieve a flawless finish.

Brighten up with an eye pencil.

Line the inner rim of your lower lashes with an eye pencil (in white or flesh tones for light skin; in golden tones for dark skin) to erase any redness around your eyes and make whites look brighter and larger. We like Chanel's Line Perfector Face Pencil and Three Custom Color Specialists' Clarifier Pencil. Be sure to blend well so that people will notice your eyes, not the liner.

Pick the right eye cream—and put it on ice.

Creams containing anti-inflammatory ingredients can help reduce eye puffiness, says Dennis Gross, M.D., a New York City–based dermatologist. Cucumber extract, caffeine, and vitamin K have been shown to constrict blood vessels and cut down on fluid retention. Refrigerating your eye cream can also help, since the chilled cream works like a cold compress, reducing swelling.

· Fake a Face Lift ·

Treat yourself to a mask.

Most masks labeled "firming" or "deep-cleansing" contain alcohol, clay, minerals, and seaweed—ingredients that tighten pores and provide a subtle but noticeable lift. (We like Clarins' Extra-Firming Facial Mask.) The effects won't last more than a day, though, so plan to use the mask the night before an important event. Do a trial run first; you don't want to risk irritated skin if the mask's ingredients don't agree with you.

Play down your shadows.

The natural shadows around your nose and mouth can drag down your face. New York City–based makeup artist Morgen Schick DeMann recommends looking straight into a mirror to identify where your features cast shadows (typically under your nose, in the grooves that run from your nose to your mouth, and in the lower corners of your lips). Prep your skin with foundation primer, then use a

> *A swipe of concealer in just the right place can disguise the puffy eyes and dark circles that make you look like you pulled an all-nighter.*

small nylon brush to blend a rich concealer (the type that comes in a pot or compact), one or two shades lighter than your skin tone, on the shadowed areas. Dust with powder to set.

Shape up your brows.

Well-groomed brows can give your entire face an instant lift. If you're starting from scratch, see a professional aesthetician for a proper plucking or waxing. Then you can follow the line of the new brow, tweezing stray hairs as necessary. "Your brows are like your hair—after a while you need to have them professionally shaped to maintain the style," says eyebrow designer Eliza Petrescu of Avon Salon & Spa in New York City. She suggests a maintenance shaping every two months or so.

• Smooth Out Skin Flaws •

Try a do-it-yourself peel.

Usually in your early 30s you'll start to see the first signs of aging skin: fine lines, a lackluster appearance, and hyperpigmentation (dark, freckle-like spots that appear on the skin and can be caused by sun exposure, birth-control pills, and age). One way to maintain a smoother, more even complexion is with a retexturizing treatment, an ultramild, do-it-yourself version of a dermatologist's peel.

"A home peel is a quick fix," Gross says. "It can instantly exfoliate, firm, tone, and improve the radiancy of the skin." The process is simple: You apply a solution of exfoliating ingredients (usually alpha and/or beta hydroxy acids) to slough off a superficial layer of skin. Because skin sensitivity varies from person to person, it's important to test these products (apply a little to a patch on your inner arm) to make sure they work for your skin type before using them on your face.

Home peels, such as M.D. Skincare's Alpha Beta Peel and Ellen Lange's Retexturizing Peel Kit, generally contain no more than 20 percent AHA compared with about twice that amount used in the doctor's office. Some peels can be used daily; others weekly or monthly. Even if you choose a product for daily use, try it a couple of times and wait a couple of days to see how your skin reacts; then adjust the frequency accordingly. You should expect some slight tingling but no harsh burning. (If you're already using a prescription retinoid treatment, check with your derm before trying a do-it-yourself peel.)

Switch to a light-reflecting lotion.

A face lotion containing light-reflective particles, such as Estée Lauder's LightSource SPF 15 or Revlon's Skinlights Face Illuminator Lotion, works much like the proverbial Vaseline on the camera lens: It puts your face in soft-focus, so imperfections and flaws are less noticeable. Wear it alone or under foundation.

Well-groomed brows can give your entire face a lift. But you may want to seek help from a professional before you start plucking.

Use foundation to your advantage.

If your skin is fairly smooth and free of dry patches, a little foundation may be all that's needed to even things out, according to makeup artist Raffaele. She suggests using a damp sponge—which gives a more sheer effect than fingers or a dry sponge—to dab and blend liquid foundation over areas that need coverage. If you have light skin, match the foundation to your skin tone and apply it to the inner corners of your eyes, around your nostrils, and on your chin. Darker-skinned women, who are prone to skin-tone variations, should match foundation to their dominant tone, and blend as necessary. Finish with a dusting of translucent powder to set.

• Make Lips Fuller •

Get addicted to balm.

Lip balms contain ingredients like petrolatum and beeswax, which trap moisture in your lips, keeping them smoother, softer, and slightly fuller. If your lips are very dry and prone to flaking, a balm with a built-in exfoliant, like Clinique's All About Lips, will help shed the dry skin as it moisturizes.

Pencil in some pout.

As the collagen in your lips begins to break down with age, your lip line can become less defined. A nude-toned liner, used sparingly to emphasize the center of the lower lip, will add fullness and shape. Apply it after lip color so you can be sure exactly which areas need emphasis.

Switch lip shades.

As you age, pastels and candy colors can look dated, while deep, dark shades actually make lips appear thinner. The best choice for making the most of what you've got: light, neutral tones. They look the most natural, Raffaele says. A glossy or shimmery finish will add extra depth and give lips the illusion of plumpness. ✳

Freelance writer Jennifer Laing also contributes to In Style, Food & Wine, *and the* New York Times' *Style section.*

FIX TIRED-LOOKING EYES

You've finally caught up on your sleep. So why, when you look in the mirror, do you see tired eyes peering back at you? It could be because you're not giving the delicate skin around your eyes the special care it needs.

"The skin here is thinner and more sensitive than that on the rest of the face, which can cause several common problems," says Lenore Kakita, M.D., a dermatologist and associate clinical professor at the University of California-Los Angeles. It absorbs chemicals in lotions, makeup, and cleansers more rapidly than skin on other parts of your face and body, making it susceptible to irritation.

Start by using eye-specific products, which are made with gentler ingredients than those formulated for other uses. Then choose the right eyes-only aids for your particular needs. For fine lines and wrinkles, try creams with retinol, such as L'Oréal's Plenitude Revitalift Eye Anti-Wrinkle & Firming Cream. Remedy dry patches with hydrating products: Try Estée Lauder's Advanced Night Repair Eye Recovery Complex, Sundári's Chamomile Eye Oil, or Neutrogena's Visibly Firm Eye Cream. If dryness persists, see your dermatologist; it may be a sign of eczema, which frequently makes an appearance on the upper eyelids.

Be extra diligent about protecting against sun damage. The area around your peepers has less collagen, so it tends to break down faster and be more susceptible to sun damage and wrinkles. Shield it by wearing sunglasses and using sunscreens created for the eye area, such as Shiseido's Sun Protection Eye Cream SPF 15.

Before applying lotions, creams, or makeup around your eyes, be sure to wash your hands. This reduces the chances of getting superficial skin infections in the eye area. And, of course, don't forget about keeping up with nature's best refresher: that much-needed sleep.

Cosmetic Supplements

Should you trust them to improve your appearance?

COSMETICS COMPANIES are offering supplements that claim to bring you healthier hair, skin, and nails. Should you start popping the pills?

It's true that certain nutrients—or lack thereof—can affect your looks, says Marsha Gordon, M.D., associate clinical professor at Mount Sinai School of Medicine. But she cautions, "You're better off getting your vitamins from fresh fruits and vegetables than from a pill." And food contains other nutrients that your body needs. If you're not getting the recommended five to nine servings of fruits and vegetables per day, supplements are OK. But a basic multivitamin should do—no need for something labeled specifically for hair, skin, or nails.

winter-fresh skin strategies

Even if you love the crisp, brisk days of winter, you probably don't love what they do to your complexion. "Skin gets dry because the wind and cold weather irritate it, and the lack of humidity in the air causes it to lose moisture rapidly," says Elizabeth McBurney, M.D., clinical professor of dermatology at Tulane University. "This causes flakes and scaly patches, which in turn give you a sallow, dull appearance."

To breathe life into your looks, here's what the experts suggest.

Fight back with steam. Soften dry patches by steaming your face over a bowl of boiling water (cover your head with a towel) for several minutes. Follow up with an exfoliating mask or scrub and then slick on a rich moisturizer, such as Clinique's Moisture Surge Extra.

Take tougher measures. For stubborn flaky areas on your face, McBurney suggests using a 1 percent hydrocortisone cream (available over the counter) followed by a moisturizer. When dry flakes begin to disappear, use a lotion with glycolic acid, such as Neutrogena's Healthy Skin Face Lotion.

Choose double-duty products. Avoid caking with products that provide both color and moisture. Try cream blushes, such as L'Oréal's Translucide Gel Blush, and check out tinted moisturizers.

Warm up your face with color. Peachy or rosy blushes can give you that "I just ran three miles" look. For a richer lip color, use a tinted lip stain, such as Benefit's Benetint, rather than a lipstick. Top it off with a balm to lock in moisture.

Pay close attention to your eyes. Give eyes a wake-up call by placing a bit of satin white or ivory eye shadow under your brow bone and another small dab just above your lash line in the middle of your lid. "This will catch the light and give the illusion of brightness," says Brigitte Reiss-Andersen, a New York–based makeup artist. Also, camouflage dark circles with such products as Christian Dior's Smoothing Anti-Fatigue Concealer.

new life, new look

There are those defining moments when, either by fate or by choice, your world changes in ways you didn't anticipate. These four readers seized the opportunity to take their lives in new directions—and we gave them new looks to match.

BY BARBARA STEPKO

PHOTOGRAPHY BY MARILI FORASTIERI

Often, especially during turbulent times, people take comfort in familiarity, in reassuring day-to-day routines. But sometimes life has a few surprises in store. Maybe you decide to take a detour or fate throws you an unexpected curve. Scary? Of course. But once you get beyond the initial flash of fear, you often figure out that change can be good—not a road-block to run from, but a challenge to rise to.

A few months ago, we asked readers to share with us their tales of transformation. The letters poured in, but there were four women whose stories were particularly inspiring. Their circumstances are different, but a similar thread runs through their tales: Each woman discovered that she had the power to redefine herself. For Kelly Pope and Teresa Vaz, these turning points were born of loss; for Lori Flammer and Terry Chandler, the realization that their old lives just weren't satisfying sent them seeking new directions.

Because these women reshaped themselves on the inside, we decided they deserved an outer transformation as well. So, with the help of top makeup artists and hair pros, we arranged makeovers—new looks to go with their new takes on life. The makeover experience validated

their collective belief that wonderful things can emerge even from the most trying of circumstances.

choosing simplicity over stress

Lori Flammer
**25; yoga instructor;
Moretown, Vermont**

She had the life she'd always dreamed of: Lori Flammer was living in New York City and pursuing a career in documentary film-making. But something was missing. "The pressure I was putting on myself to succeed was wearing me down," she says. "There was an emptiness to the work I was doing. In my heart, I knew I wasn't ful-filled." So she decided it was time for a change.

Despite the concerns of family and friends, Flammer quit her job and then enrolled in a weeklong program at

Kripalu, a spiritual retreat and yoga center in Lenox, Massachusetts. She did volunteer work in exchange for room and board and her own place in the community.

The slower pace—along with the relaxation and spiritual dimension of yoga—agreed with Flammer. She returned to New York only to pack her possessions and move to Vermont, where she now teaches yoga classes. "Yoga puts you in touch with your body," she explains. "It's a way to release tension and clear your mind so you can deal with the issues in your life calmly and serenely." Now Flammer has more time for herself. She and her boyfriend, Jonathan, take advantage of the countryside around them—kayaking in a river near their home and mountain-biking a few times a week in the surrounding hills. "Nature brings you in touch with the spirit of who you are and the core of your being," she says.

To others who are dissatisfied without knowing quite why, Flammer offers this advice: "There's a little voice in each of us. Listen to it. It just might be your key to inner peace."

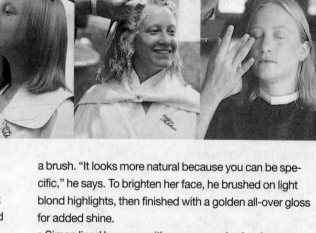

Lori's new look

"With her pale eyes and fair complexion, Lori's face is the perfect canvas for makeup," says makeup artist Joe Simon. Her straight, one-length hair, though, weighed down her face and made her look tired.

• To give her hair a polished look, hairstylist Jean-Patrick Basset cut off 6 inches, then added angled layers around her face. After applying texturizing balm, he used a blow-dryer and his hands to flip out the ends.
• Her strawberry-blond shade didn't need a drastic change. So colorist Frances Mousseron used baliage, a method of highlighting in which color is painted on with a brush. "It looks more natural because you can be specific," he says. To brighten her face, he brushed on light blond highlights, then finished with a golden all-over gloss for added shine.
• Simon lined her eyes with cream eye shadow in warm tones of brown and gold. Then he applied black mascara. "The trick is in the application," he says. "Bring your chin up, look down, and hold skin around the brows taut. Then stroke on color."

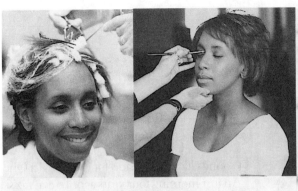

Kelly's new look

A beautiful complexion like Pope's is made for rich, dramatic makeup. Her hair, though, needed help. Relaxing had taken its toll—leaving strands dry and damaged.

• Even a small trim can make a big impact. Hairstylist Jean-Patrick Basset didn't take any length off, but instead cut layers along the front and sides to even out Pope's style. "It's a softer look—not as blunt as before," he says.

• A kinder way to color fragile hair: Colorist Frances Mousseron applied chestnut-brown highlights, concentrating on the hair around Pope's face. "It's the perfect shade to complement her complexion," he explains. Finally, he added a clear gloss all over to bring back a healthy-looking shine.

• Pope's large, pretty eyes can take on lots of color. Makeup artist Jenn Streicher layered on a trio of tones: a charcoal shadow over the lid, a lighter shadow in the crease, and a pale shade across the brow bone. Her eyes were then lined with a brown shadow, followed by two coats of black mascara.

a legacy of learning

Kelly Richmond Pope

27; Assistant Professor of Accounting, University of North Carolina at Greensboro; Durham, North Carolina

The human heart is resilient, and Kelly Richmond Pope is living proof. In the span of just four years, she lost the three most important people in her life.

Right before Pope was to begin her master's program in 1996, her mother died of breast cancer. Kelly then had second thoughts about pursuing her degree, but she challenged herself: If she could get through school at that time of her life, she could get through anything. And she did. But two years into her Ph.D. program, her father died of non-Hodgkin's lymphoma, a disease he was diagnosed with right before Pope's mother died. A few months later, her grandmother passed away as well. Yet, somehow, Pope carried on: While grieving the deaths of those closest to her, she planned her wedding, settled her father's estate, and earned her Ph.D.

A former gymnast and dancer, Pope has always been active. As she dealt with her losses, she learned to redirect her grief into energy, using stress to fuel her workouts. Pope also draws emotional strength from the people around her: her husband, Lorence, and a close-knit group of friends. "Who you are as a person is loosely defined by who you surround yourself with," Pope says. "I believe if they are hardworking and spiritual, you'll be that way, too."

What really keeps her going, though, are the words of her father. "When my mother died, he said, 'You know your mother wouldn't want us to sit around and feel sad,'" Pope recalls. "I've kept that with me. If I'm down, knowing that my parents would be proud keeps me going."

finding strength to begin anew

Teresa Vaz
**38; teacher;
Castro Valley, California**

It sounds like a bad made-for-TV movie: One August morning four years ago, Teresa Vaz's husband of 12 years said, "I don't want to be married anymore." She remembers the exact moment as if it were yesterday. "I felt like I had been kicked in the stomach," she says. "Life as I knew it crumbled. I never thought I would recover."

A stay-at-home mom with three young children (then ages 5, 6, and 7), Vaz was terrified she wouldn't be able to support her family. "For months, I'd wait until the kids were asleep and then break down and cry," she says. "In the morning, I'd put on this fake smile, but inside it was complete turmoil."

Ultimately, though, it was the power of family that pulled Vaz together. "My kids are my source of strength," she says. "One look at them and I knew what I had to do." About four months later, with the help of her parents, she began to attend California State at Hayward to obtain her degree in teaching. It wasn't easy, she says, but "it's amazing how much energy fear can give you."

She graduated in December 2001, and was offered a long-term substitute position at her children's school, starting in 2002. The graduation ceremony stirred up all kinds of emotions. "You know, your sense of self-worth goes down the drain when you're going through a divorce," Vaz says. "But when I held that diploma, I thought, 'I did it.' For the first time, I felt something that went deeper than the pain. It was empowering."

Vaz admits her life hasn't exactly turned out the way she planned, but she no longer sees that as a bad thing. "I've crossed paths with some amazing people—those who have supported and cared about me, teachers who have touched me forever," she says. "I would have never met any of them if it weren't for my situation."

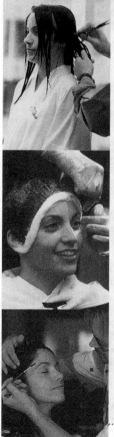

Teresa's new look

Half Irish and half Portuguese, Vaz is blessed with an exotic look that begged to be played up with color. Her long, thick hair was another plus, but it overpowered her face—and much of it had turned gray.

• To bring out Teresa's lovely face, hairstylist Jean-Patrick Basset trimmed 2½ inches off her hair, then added long layers along the sides and the back. This low-maintenance cut is perfect for her single-mom lifestyle.
• Her hair color was warmed up to flatter her skin tone. Colorist Frances Mousseron used a semipermanent, single-process formula in chestnut brown on the roots (which gradually rinses out after three weeks of shampoos) and a matching gloss on the ends to soften uneven color from a previous dye job.
• For well-groomed eyebrows, makeup artist Joe Simon taught Vaz a foolproof trick: First, draw a line along the bottom of your brow with a white eye pencil. Then carefully pluck only the hairs that fall below that line.

building a slimmer existence

Terry Chandler
41; homemaker;
Athens, Alabama

A few years ago, Terry Chandler would never have dreamed of entering a contest related to women's health and beauty. She had been overweight most of her life, topping out just before her 20th birthday at 295 pounds. Finally, at the age of 36, she made a promise to herself. "I decided I wasn't going to be fat and 40," she says. "After decades of merely existing, I was ready to live."

Her husband and three children, who were all overweight, signed on, too. "It was a partnership of self-love, wise food choices, and physical activity," Chandler says. Armed with low-fat cookbooks, she learned to enjoy a lot of the same foods she had eaten before, but in a healthier way. "Everyone who eats at our house says the same thing: 'This can't be low-fat!'"

Chandler has also discovered a love for exercise. "I never worked out before because I'd get too winded," she says. But now she bicycles daily and walks every other day down country roads around her home. She lifts weights and stretches to a yoga videotape twice a week. The results are apparent: In two years, Chandler has shed 113 pounds and is still losing.

The benefits of her new healthy lifestyle have been amazing for Chandler—and her entire family. Her husband, who has lost 35 pounds, no longer has to take cholesterol-lowering medication, and her oldest daughter pared down to a size 8 from a size 20. To top it all off, Chandler may start teaching an aerobics class at a new fitness center being built in her town. And she's found an exciting new hobby: shopping for clothes. "When I was heavy, I couldn't find anything that didn't look matronly," she says. "But now, shopping is actually becoming a lot of fun!" ✴

Barbara Stepko is a New York–based freelancer.

Terry's New Look

The essence of modern beauty: Find your best feature and work it. Chandler's sparkling blue eyes are the focus of her face, so makeup artist Jenn Streicher wanted to show them off with color. And her hairstyle got a much-needed lift with some subtle reproportioning.

• To bring out blue or green eyes, Streicher suggests using warm earth tones. For Chandler, she chose a dark brown powder shadow for the lid, then swept a golden tone across the crease.
• Hairstylist Jean-Patrick Basset decided to "connect" Chandler's choppy layers by trimming them with a razor—rather than with scissors—for a lighter, wispier look. Bonus: The fullness of her new style actually slims her face and makes her hair appear longer than it did before.
• Even blond hair can get dull sometimes, so colorist Frances Mousseron added highlights to brighten up Chandler's face. He used crescendo tone highlights: They start out dark at the bottom, gradually becoming lighter at the roots.

VitalStats

32 | Percent of women who wear fragrance six to seven days a week

26 | Percent of men who do

10 | Percent of the population allergic to a cosmetic item

1 | Rank of fragrance among cosmetic products that cause allergic reactions

2 in 3 | Number of teenage boys who believe they will make $1 million by age 40

1 in 3 | Number of teenage girls who believe the same thing

4 | Percent of all U.S. households that are worth $1 million or more

$41,560 | Median income of males ages 35 to 44

$30,471 | Median income of females ages 35 to 44

228/9 | Calories/fat grams in two pieces of roasted chicken breasts with skin

358/21 | Calories/fat grams in 1 cup of potato salad

92/1 | Calories/fat grams in a slice of watermelon

78 | Percent of families that eat fried foods at least four times a week

3 million | Number of public-library items checked out daily in the United States

6 million | Number of videos rented daily

1 in 4 | Chance that an American falls asleep with the TV on at least three nights a week

Sources: National Center for Policy Analysis, Census Bureau, USDA, Kaiser Family Foundation, West Soy, American Academy of Dermatology

How Cancer Patients Can Boost Their Self-Image

When I lost my hair, eyelashes, and eyebrows, I felt as if I were being erased," says Vickie Girard, a two-time breast-cancer survivor who was recently diagnosed for the third time. In addition to losing her hair, Girard's skin got extremely dry and her nails became brittle—side effects that cancer patients deal with all the time. While doctors are working on better treatments for breast cancer, programs across the country are springing up to help women overcome the just-as-devastating effects on their self-image. Here's who's reaching out with good—and often free—advice:

The Image Enhancement Program at Cancer Treatment Centers of America (www.cancercenter.com or 800-273-1255) has shown Girard and many others how to work with their looks while battling this disease.

Look Good ... Feel Better (www.lookgoodfeelbetter.org or 800-395-5665) caters to teens and women, offering free group workshops on hair and makeup and a self-help video. The program is available in cancer centers, hospitals, and American Cancer Society offices nationwide.

The Avon Salon & Spa Breast Cancer Support Program (888-577-2866) in New York City offers complimentary consultations with stylists, who show patients how to style their changing hair or work with their wigs.

Hope Aesthetics (www.hopeskincare.com or 800-266-4799) is a line of skin-care products originally developed for cancer patients by Vincene Parinello, a former nurse and cancer survivor. Products are especially hydrating and vitamin-rich. Ten percent of proceeds go to the Hope for Others Foundation, a nonprofit organization that provides financial assistance to cancer patients and their families.

chapter 7

mind and spirit

relax, revitalize, renew

it's time to get happy

We all want to feel good about ourselves. But sometimes that's easier said than done. Our 5-step guide is designed to help you attain the happiness you deserve.

BY ALICE LESCH KELLY

A few people are as happy as they'd ever want to be. The rest of us keep self-help authors on the best-seller list. We soak up their advice, hoping to find the secret to a blissful (or at least satisfying) life. And that is no easy task. But even if you've tried and failed—repeatedly—it truly is possible to up your smile quotient. And this five-step program, based on information from top authors and expert researchers, really works, if you stick with it.

If you're not quite as happy as you'd like to be, there's more than likely a good reason. "Happiness has a genetic component—some people are more prone to being happy than others," says Howard C. Cutler, M.D., a psychiatrist who co-authored the Dalai Lama's book *The Art of Happiness: A Handbook for Living.* The majority of

scientists now believe that being happy is just like being a good singer, a fast runner, or a great cook: To some people, it comes naturally, but the rest of us have to sweat for it. Everyone has what researchers call a "happiness set point," or a baseline level of happiness at which your psyche is most comfortable. It's similar to your weight set point, the one that your body naturally returns to in spite of salad suppers and skipped desserts. But just like your weight, your happiness set point can be bumped out of its comfort zone—if you really work at it.

A number of experts, from psychologists to motivational speakers and, yes, even the Dalai Lama, offer a range of suggestions on just how to ratchet your set point and increase your level of day-to-day happiness. We've researched their techniques and asked the tough questions to develop our concrete real-life plan.

6 tips to ease your way to happiness

1. Don't go it alone. Like most other skills, happiness is easier to learn about if you have good teachers. Spend time with happy people, and keep reading those best-selling books.

2. Do focus on feeling great. When you are tempted to give in to your inner grouch, just remember how terrific it feels to be happy.

3. Don't try consumer therapy. You know you can't buy happiness, but you still head to the mall to beat a bad mood. Maybe a BMW convertible or yet another new pair of boots seems like a quick cure, but research shows that even lottery winners are only happier for a short time before they return to their previous levels of life satisfaction (their set points). And the credit card bill won't help.

4. Do plan happiness. Each morning, think of little ways you can squeeze in some extra joy: Bring a vase of fragrant flowers to work, try a new hairstyle, pin up a picture of a vacation spot, find five minutes to go for a walk.

5. Don't rush it. Learning to be happy may require changing some deeply held habits, and that takes time. Be patient.

6. Do get help. If you're suffering from something worse than garden-variety blues, you may need medication or therapy for clinical depression. See your doctor if you're not sure.

One warning: Don't overwhelm yourself by taking on all five steps at once. Instead, incorporate one each week, or try two at a time. Keep in mind, though, that happiness doesn't come easy. "It takes consistent effort over a period of time," Cutler says. "It requires reshaping your outlook and attitudes, and that obviously doesn't happen overnight." But the end result is truly worth the effort.

step 1
admit you deserve it

Without even realizing it, you may believe that you shouldn't be happy. The first task on your quest is to take a hard look at your decisions: Have you made poor choices? Are you mired in unhappiness because of missed opportunities? Do you put yourself in destructive situations because you believe subconsciously that you don't deserve to be treated with respect? Before you can find happiness, you must believe you are worthy of it.

But isn't that selfish? Won't family and friends be mad if you stop caring for them and go off in search of happiness? The answer is no, according to the Dalai Lama. "I believe that the very purpose of our life is to seek happiness," he writes in *The Art of Happiness.* In fact, studies confirm that happy people are more generous and less self-focused, so they enrich—rather than detract from—the lives of the people around them. "People who are chronically unhappy are kind of socially crippled," says David C. Rowe, Ph.D., professor of family studies and

the quiz
the satisfaction scale

Researchers use the following quiz, known as the Satisfaction with Life Scale, to measure subjects' happiness levels. Although the questions may sound similar (and deceptively simple), they actually are an accurate measure of the slightly different ways people evaluate their own happiness, says the scale's designer, Ed Diener, Ph.D., professor of psychology at the University of Illinois. Be honest as you rate each statement. Then tally up the numbers corresponding to your answers to get your total score, and compare it to the key below. Repeat the quiz every few weeks to measure changes over time.

1. In most ways, my life is close to my ideal.
2. The conditions of my life are excellent.
3. I am satisfied with my life.
4. So far, I have gotten the important things I want in life.
5. If I could live my life over, I would change almost nothing.

strongly disagree	disagree	slightly disagree	on the fence	slightly agree	agree	strongly agree
1	2	3	4	5	6	7

key

31-35	= Extremely satisfied
26-30	= Satisfied
21-25	= Slightly satisfied
20	= Neutral
15-19	= Slightly dissatisfied
10-14	= Dissatisfied
5-9	= Extremely dissatisfied

human development at the University of Arizona. "Chronically unhappy people spread unhappiness."

To teach yourself that you deserve happiness, try self-affirmation. These simple positive messages may seem silly, but it turns out that they are powerful aids to rewriting the messages in your head. If you suspect you're having trouble accomplishing this first step, think about seeking help. Enlist friends and family to tell you about little things they appreciate. Or consider asking a therapist to help you put your experiences into perspective.

step 2
make it a goal

The second step to happiness is to actively decide that you want it, just the way you decide to lose 5 pounds or save up for a vacation. Sure, that sounds goofy—after all, who doesn't want to be happy? But in reality, many people are trapped in patterns that don't allow it. They're chained to negative habits and emotions, such as fear, shyness, hatred, or resentment, that keep them in unpleasant jobs or destructive relationships.

It takes serious soul-searching to identify the negative emotions that trap you. Then you must commit to making the choices, both large and small, that will reduce them. For example, if rage interferes with your happiness, consider an anger-management class. If jealousy is an issue, ask friends how they cope with situations that would turn you green. Identifying the problem and deciding to make a change are great starts.

step 3
control your responses

Bad things happen—your mom gets cancer, your husband walks out on you—and you can't deny that they hurt. But when life throws curveballs, the happiest people are determined to recover as soon as they can, says

Bad things happen. It's how you handle it that's important. Happy people are determined to recover as soon as they can when life throws them curveballs.

Barry Neil Kaufman, the author of *Happiness Is a Choice* and founder of the Option Institute, a personal-growth center in Sheffield, Massachusetts. It's not that happy people don't suffer. Actually, most of them feel their emotions—including sadness—deeply. But they know that the black days will end and happiness will return.

No need to wait for the completion of the first two steps to start working on this task. It's a crucial ability for living a happy life, so start as soon as you're ready. The goal is to reclaim the power over your happiness from outside sources—your boss, your spouse, or even the luck of the draw—and give it firmly to an internal, controllable source: you. Try to look for the benefit in even the worst events, even if you have to really dig to find it, Kaufman says. For example, maybe your mom's illness will allow you to show your love by caring for her or provide a chance to talk about things that were once taboo. Eventually, you'll find at least one small advantage.

If you think silver linings are for wimps, and your typical response is to get angry and agitated, you're wrapping yourself in negativity. Put your reactions to the test of logic: Was that guy who cut you off in traffic really out to get you, or was he just late for work? Don't you feel silly for letting him ruin your day? All your negative reactions add up. And they're not just bad for your happiness quotient; the stress hormones they pump into your system are bad for your health. When you analyze the negative effect that the tension has on your emotions and behavior, it becomes obvious that you're better off brushing aside the anger. Even if you think the other driver is a self-important jerk, you can be the better person and back off.

step 4
rediscover your dreams

Sometimes, people's ideas of what will bring them happiness—a new car, perhaps, or more money—get so distorted that they actually move away from happiness, Cutler says. And getting back on track is a step that you can take at any time.

You probably know people who are hardworking and successful but who are still unfulfilled. And you're way too smart to be like that—blindly striving for society's prefabricated expectations. But it's still easy to get swept up in your to-do list and other people's demands, temporarily losing sight of your own day-to-day desires. Sometimes, even your long-term goals can get sidelined for a while. When that happens, you know what you have to do. "There is no need to look outside of yourself for answers," Kaufman says. You know best the things that will make you happy. But rediscovering your own heart requires conscious self-examination and effort.

This exercise from corporate consultants Rick Foster and Greg Hicks, co-authors of *How We Choose to Be Happy*, can help: Set a timer for four minutes, and write a "dream list" of everything that makes you happy. Write as fast as you can without stopping, include small things and big things, and don't judge them. When you're finished, check out your list, and think about the feelings that bubbled up. For example, do you plop down in front of the tube most nights even though television never made it onto the list? This exercise acts as a sort of crystal ball—it may show that you're subconsciously postponing happiness by wasting time on activities that aren't your true priorities.

"Living in the moment" may sound cliché, but it's popular because it works. Take time out to simply enjoy where you are.

why be happy?

If future happiness isn't sufficient motivation for the hard work it takes to change your life, consider these benefits. According to Ed Diener, Ph.D., a professor of psychology at the University of Illinois, compared with unhappy people, those who are happy:

- have stronger immune systems and may live longer
- earn more money
- have more friends
- have better marriages
- cope better in difficult situations
- have higher self-esteem
- are more altruistic

step 5
take a time-out to say thanks

Just about every self-help guru encourages us to "live in the moment." Like most clichés, it's popular because it works. It's also perhaps the easiest step to accomplish—one that you can start right away and benefit from immediately (although the full power comes with practice).

The key is to push aside thoughts of past mistakes and future worries, and prevent your mind from racing off in a million directions at once. Start small: Several times a day, give thanks—for your children, the flame of fall leaves outside your window, your best friend. During their research, Hicks and Foster noted that happy people often stop a conversation to comment on something good—the delicious taste of their lunch, the prettiness of the restaurant, the gorgeous weather. "These people actually do appreciation time-outs, when they literally stop to acknowledge what's happening," Foster says. "When you are in the moment, you are experiencing life at its richest."

Spend a few minutes over your morning coffee writing in a gratitude journal. Train yourself to appreciate the good rather than dwelling on the bad. Cutler recommends a daily meditation program, starting with just five

Train yourself to appreciate the good rather than dwelling on the bad.

minutes once or twice a day, to quiet your mind and practice staying in the present. Meditation doesn't have to involve special techniques (although some people do find them useful). Just take a few deep breaths to calm yourself, and gently push away distracting thoughts as they crop up. After you become adept at these short meditations, you will find it easier to summon that in-the-moment feeling throughout the day. ✳

When you are in the moment, you are experiencing life at its richest.

Alice Lesch Kelly, a health and psychology writer in Newton, Massachusetts, also writes for O *and* Glamour.

WEB WATCH:
quash ugly rumors with online facts

If the outrageous horror-story e-mail hoaxes—bananas with flesh-eating disease, roving bands of kidney thieves, and the like—aren't bad enough, what about the ones that sound nearly credible? Before you abandon fruit or fear for your organs, check one of these hoax- and rumor-exposing Web sites: www.cdc.gov/hoax_rumors.htm, www.urbanlegends.about.com, or www.quackwatch.com.

Found:
An Antidote to Low Self-Esteem

CALL IT the flounder factor. Down-and-out people who lack confidence tend to put off even those activities that they know would boost their spirits. In one recent Canadian-U.S. study, self-confident people more often chose to watch a comedy video than folks with low self-esteem, even though both groups believed the video would make them happy. (The researchers got their two test groups into a funk by having them listen to Prokofiev's dolorous *Russia Under the Mongolian Yoke* played at half-speed.) "Rather than actively trying to improve their mood, people with low self-esteem are more apt to wallow in their sadness and hope it passes by itself," says Jonathon D. Brown, Ph.D., an associate professor of psychology at the University of Washington and co-author of the study.

Arduous as it may seem, action is the only antidote. Everyone should have a dozen or so techniques on hand to combat wallowing, explains Steve Wilson, a psychologist and regional vice president of the nonprofit organization National Association for Self-Esteem. "These should be things you are good at and enjoy and that give you a sense of completion, whether it's painting the fence or taking a bath," he says. The key is to practice those techniques before you need them—in other words, do them when you're still feeling good. "If you know something will make you feel better, don't ask yourself if you feel like doing it," Wilson says. Just do it. While everyone experiences the occasional funk, if you're constantly low and self-critical, seek professional help. You may be suffering from treatable depression.

SELF-QUIZ
are you blirtatious?

No, that's not a typo—it's a newly discovered personality trait. To find out how blirtatious you are, answer these questions:

1 You're in the express line at the supermarket, and the guy in front of you has a whole cart full of groceries. Your reaction is to:
A: Immediately demand that he move to another line in the name of fairness and justice.
B: Close your eyes and use deep, rhythmic breathing to keep your blood pressure from making your head explode.

2 Your boss asks if you can meet with her at 8 a.m. on Monday instead of over lunch on Friday. How do you say no?
A: "No," about .00139 seconds after she asks.
B: You hem and haw, then e-mail a credible excuse a few hours later.

3 Your sister's new dog turns out to be the ugliest animal this side of Godzilla. You're most likely to:
A: Warn her right away not to let the creature see its own reflection.
B: Hold your tongue, hoping the animal will one day shed its skin and become a golden retriever.

personal prognosis:

If you answered A to two or more questions—and didn't even pause to consider—you probably have blirtatious tendencies. "Blirtatious-ness refers to the extent to which people respond to each other quickly and effusively. If you're blirtatious, no sooner do thoughts come to your mind than they fly out of your mouth," explains William B. Swann, Ph.D., professor of psychology at the University of Texas at Austin, who coined the term.

In his study, people who scored high for blurting tended to be regarded as likable and competent by those who just met them. But this effect can last about as long as it takes to get out the next blurt, as blurting tends to magnify personality traits, for better or worse. (A brazen blurt could reveal shallowness or intelligence.) "You'd want a blurter on your debate team, but not as a confidant," he notes. For a more scientific assessment, take his test at www.outofservice.com/blirt.

9 Easy Ways to Shake the Blahs

Try these ideas to slump-proof your life and feel better about yourself, your job, and your body.

BY LINDA RAO

Another day looms: The alarm rings, but you barely have the energy to crawl out of bed. You go to work, but it's as exciting as a root canal. When the day ends, you know you should exercise, but the couch is calling your name.

What's going on? Well, if you were suffering from depression, you'd have some of the classic symptoms: changes in your weight, appetite, or sleep patterns; feelings of guilt, worthlessness, or profound sadness. But this isn't that bad: You're not suicidal, but you're not yourself, either.

The good news is that you're just in a slump. But you do need a boost more than ever. First you've got to decide what kind of slump you're in—emotional, physical, or work-related—and our simple quiz will help you figure that out. Then you can break out of your rut—and begin feeling good again.

You've got to figure out what kind of slump you're in before you break out of the rut and start feeling good again.

The Emotional Slump

You know your slump is emotional when nothing really excites you—not even sex. "Thirty to 40 percent of us walk around in an emotional limbo at some point," says life coach Maryann Troiani, co-author of *Spontaneous Optimism: Proven Strategies for Health, Prosperity & Happiness.* Troiani recommends three simple changes for getting out of an emotional slump.

1 **Flip your thought switch.** Improve your mood by replacing negative thoughts ("Why do these things always happen to me?") with positive ones ("What can I do to improve this situation?").

2 **Hang out with an optimist.** Happiness is contagious, so make plans with positive-minded people rather than the-glass-is-half-empty types.

3 **Choose your words.** Take the negative edge out of your vocabulary: Instead of saying you feel "nervous," say you feel "concerned."

Happiness is contagious—so **hang out with positive-minded people** when your spirit needs a lift.

The Physical Slump

This might be the easiest slump to spot. "You tend to feel tired, tense, and irritable, and crave carbs or sweets," says Marie-Annette Brown, Ph.D., R.N., co-author of *When Your Body Gets the Blues*. Here's how to beat the blahs.

1 Eat lunch outside. Light improves your concentration and energizes you, so make lunch a picnic.

2 Start moving. Boost your mood with exercise. Try 20 minutes of brisk walking five days a week.

3 Get your vitamins. Be sure you're getting vitamins B_1, B_2, B_6, and D, as well as the minerals folate and selenium. All these improve the effectiveness of mood-enhancing brain chemicals.

The Work Slump

Career counselor Richard J. Leider asked people ages 65 and older what they would do differently if they could live their lives over: "They wished they had been more reflective, more courageous, and had more purpose in their lives," Leider says. "These three elements weave through most work slumps." Most recently the co-author of *Whistle While You Work: Heeding Your Life's Calling* Leider recommends these tips for getting out of a rut at work.

1 Seek out mentors. Find someone to listen, someone who will encourage you to act, and someone who's living the life you want to live.

2 Define your purpose. To remind you why work matters, complete this sentence: "The reason I get up in the morning is to _____."

3 Create a master dream list. List your professional dreams and choose one to work on now. ✳

Freelance writer Linda Rao is co-author of Good Carbs, Bad Carbs.

are you in a slump?

Choose the answer that best describes your feelings.

1. I focus on problems, not solutions.
A. rarely   B. occasionally   C. often   D. most of the time

2. On Mondays, I dread going to the office.
A. rarely   B. occasionally   C. often   D. most of the time

3. I feel like I need a nap in the afternoon.
A. rarely   B. occasionally   C. often   D. most of the time

4. I tend to slouch.
A. rarely   B. occasionally   C. often   D. most of the time

5. I don't feel enthusiastic about my work.
A. rarely   B. occasionally   C. often   D. most of the time

6. When emotions run high, I crave junk food or carbs.
A. rarely   B. occasionally   C. often   D. most of the time

7. When someone asks how I'm feeling, I say "tired" or "overwhelmed."
A. rarely   B. occasionally   C. often   D. most of the time

8. I don't know how to measure my success as a person.
A. rarely   B. occasionally   C. often   D. most of the time

9. I eat more than I would like, especially late in the day.
A. rarely   B. occasionally   C. often   D. most of the time

If you answered …

• C or D to questions 1, 4, and 7, you're in an emotional slump.

• C or D to questions 2, 5, and 8, you're in a work slump.

• C or D to questions 3, 6, and 9, you're in a physical slump.

• mostly C or D, some of these suggestions may lift your spirits.

• mostly A or B, congrats! You're probably slump-free.

how to *really* reach your goals

BY MARGIT FEURY

Whatever causes the itch for a change, now is the time to reassess your strategy. And we've got a plan that will work for you—because it's based on who you are, not just what you hope to achieve.

"People need to decide what is most important to them personally. I call these our 'governing goals,'" says Hyrum Smith, co-chairman of Franklin Covey, a performance coaching firm. "Just as our country's forefathers wrote down what mattered to them—freedom of speech, freedom of religion, etc.—you need to write your own constitution. Then mold your goals from that." Focus on your most-desired and realistic targets, so you don't fritter away time on less-important matters.

But before you start, there's one more thing you need to do: Make sure your goals match your personality. It turns out that most people fall into one of four categories when it comes to getting things done. Find your type with the following quiz, then try our program. You'll be amazed at how easily the customized strategies will turn your goals into successes.

• find your style •

You've taken tests like these before, so you know you probably won't fit neatly into any one of our four personality categories. But no worries: You can still learn valuable tips and tricks by identifying your predominant M.O.—and then check the description of the other personality types to pick up some additional pointers. So choose the answer that best matches your most common reaction, and—for best results—be honest.

1. On a group hike, your priority is to:
A. reach the summit
B. break a sweat
C. walk with someone interesting
D. see the scenic overlook, even if it means veering off alone and catching up with the group later

2. An old friend calls Friday night to say she'll be in town Saturday and wants to take you to a cool art opening—but you've planned to spend the day cleaning. You:
A. say you're busy, but invite her to visit after the opening
B. stay up late making sure your place looks presentable, then head off to the gallery in the morning
C. blow off the cleaning and spend the day with your friend; she'll understand the mess
D. go to the gallery, but make an excuse to keep her from coming over to see the dust and dirt

3. With two free hours at home, you:
A. clean out a closet
B. flip through magazines looking for tasty recipes, career tips, or redecorating ideas
C. call friends to chat and make plans
D. light an aromatherapy candle and stretch out in a hot bath

4. You and a few friends are trying to decide where to go for dinner. You:
A. have a hankering for Chinese, so you convince them to go to your favorite Asian place
B. look online for the latest reviews of hot new places and push for one of those
C. offer options but happily go wherever the others choose
D. suggest a place with a cozy atmosphere where it's quiet enough to talk

5. You were planning a workout, but your friend calls with a last-minute invitation to a potluck dinner. You:
A. work out, then throw together a quick tried-and-true dish
B. skip the exercise and create a healthy dish that looks and tastes great; then you primp for the party
C. dig out the cookbook, dash to the store, and make a fabulous dish; bring your sneakers to the party so you can organize an after-dinner stroll
D. try a new recipe that sounds easy and leave time to walk to the party

answer key:

Mostly As: You are a Doer. You focus on results.

Mostly Bs: You are a Reflector. You focus on rewards.

Mostly Cs: You are a Joiner. You focus on the company you keep.

Mostly Ds: You are an Experiencer. You focus on the journey.

No clear pattern? Match each of your goals to the personality that fits how you handle that type of situation.

• the doer •

You are a self-starter. You excel at getting things done when you have a due date and are motivated by a list of goals. But beware: Sometimes you become too focused on checking things off your list, says Steven Ungerleider, Ph.D., a psychologist in Eugene, Oregon, and author of *Mental Training for Peak Performance*. "This can lead to sloppy results." Also, if you are totally focused on one specific target, you can get completely thrown off track by even one minor setback.

classic pitfalls

• **Unrealistic time frames.** You won't get thinner thighs in 30 days. Don't give up if results aren't immediate. Instead, adjust your expectations and start with renewed energy.

• **Striving solo.** Doers tend to go it alone. Instead, realize that no one has all the tools for every task. Hard as it is, learn to ask for help.

to-do list

• **Start a contest.** If getting in shape is your target, for example, organize your co-workers to see who can accumulate 50 hours of exercise first.

• **Split it up.** For large goals, such as changing careers, set up interim goals. Little successes, such as completing one course in a new field each semester, will keep you from getting frustrated at the elusive target.

• **Make it public.** Develop a "contract" by telling a friend about your specific goal, the deadline, and a reward. This usually works best if the friend shares a contract with you, too.

• **Plan a break.** Chances are you're overdoing it. Try to schedule in some extra sleep.

• the reflector •

Your drive to succeed is guided by the desire for pats on the back, Ungerleider says. For instance, if you lose 20 pounds, you are probably more thrilled by hearing people say how terrific you look than you are about dropping a couple of sizes (well, almost). But approval-seeking can become excessive: "I work with women who say they want to lose weight because their husbands want them to be thinner," says San Francisco-based sports psychologist Jim Taylor, Ph.D., author of *Prime Sport: Triumph of the Athlete Mind*. But remember: Real commitment can't be motivated by someone else. It may sound trite, but it has to come from you.

anatomy of a goal

Why do some goals seem effortless while others die in a heap of good intentions? Just saying "I want to lose weight" or "I want to earn more money" won't work, says Gary Ryan Blair, a consultant who assists executives at IBM, General Electric, and FedEx with goal setting. If you aren't making progress, evaluate your goals with these three questions:

1. Is your goal specific? When you give someone driving directions, you don't just say "I live near the high school." That person needs specific details or she will wander aimlessly. By the same logic, think of your goal as a specific destination, then decide the best route to get there. That way you'll easily see when you've taken a wrong turn.

2. Is your goal measurable? Whenever you flip on an NBA game, you check who's ahead. Without the score, it wouldn't be fun. The same is true of goals: You need to know if you're winning, losing, or holding steady. Running out of steam? Take a lesson from the coach: Change strategies, give a pep talk, or bench your star player (that's you) so she can recharge.

3. Do you have a deadline? Your phone bill is due by a certain day—if you're late, you're penalized. Your goals need consequences too, or they will always be less urgent than the phone bill. Keep your motivation high by dangling a reward or penalty based on your deadline performance.

classic pitfalls

• Action without planning. Carefully plan your final goal and your strategy for getting there. Then you won't be easily blown off track.

• Spreading yourself thin. Success demands focus. Zero in on your most important goals and put the rest aside. Say no to requests that pull you in different directions.

to-do list

• Make it personal. Look at your goals and decide which are imposed by others and which are yours. For best results, ditch as many of the external ones as you can.

• Pick your passion. Create new goals that are entirely yours. Need help? Think about what you have been passionate about since childhood.

• Bribe some company. Encourage a friend to join in so you can pat each other on the back.

• Show off. Plan to display your accomplishments. Take before-and-after photos, get a new skirt to show off your sleek new legs, or pick a nice frame for your diploma.

• the joiner •

A social animal, you'd rather skip a new movie if it means going solo. A Joiner's goal-setting strategy works best when it includes others. Everyone's a Joiner, to some extent. "Most people are more committed to others than to themselves," says Gary Ryan Blair, founder of the Goals Guy, a Florida-based personal coaching company.

But Joiners may focus too much on socializing—and a group is apt to get sidetracked, or faster folks may be held back by slower ones. On the other hand, groups can become overly competitive, Taylor says. A Joiner learning about finances may sign up for an investment club even though she can't cover her bills.

classic pitfalls

• Goals without purpose. Ask a kid why she drew on the wall and she'll say "just 'cause." Are you adopting goals just 'cause everyone is doing it?

• Fear of the unknown. Do some research and replace intimidation with knowledge.

to-do list

• Buddy up. Find a partner to keep you honest. And do the same for someone else for extra motivation.

• Build groups. If you can't find a club for your interest, start one. Trying to get ahead at work? Invite colleagues out for "career cocktails."

• Set up a group reward. Plan a fun vacation with a few of your friends, then have each person declare one goal that must be accomplished before you officially book the trip.

• Work the Web. Start an e-mail group so your friends can report on their progress.

• the experiencer •

Nobody has to tell you to stop and smell the flowers. You aim for goals that are spiritual, stress-relieving, or self-exploratory. Stumbling blocks don't hurt so much—you know that they are just a part of the ride. "This is very healthy and can lead to wonderful outcomes, both physically and emotionally," Ungerleider says. But Experiencers may shy away from setting firm goals and instead get lost in enjoying the tasks—and never achieve results. That doesn't mean you should stop enjoying the journey, but be sure to target some specifics so you don't miss your true potential.

classic pitfalls

• Taking on too much. Take stock of your time and energy, planning only as much as you can realistically do. Then cut back a little more to leave extra time to enjoy the ride.

• Over-researching. If you endlessly prepare, you may never move forward. You can't anticipate everything, so just pick a plan and go for it.

to-do list

• Define limits. Set some goals that you can accomplish in a short time frame so you get a few things finished. Make sure you don't take on too much.

• Prioritize. Keep a notebook with all your great ideas; divide into sections for immediate and long-term goals. Flip through it for inspiration.

• Take lessons. Sign up for a class that will help you reach your goals, even indirectly. To save money, for example, study car or bike repair.

• Make appointments. If, like Klein, you have books stacking up, find a new place to read—and plan a weekly date to go there. ✳

Use Color to Pick Up Your Mood

When your spirits need a boost and a Caribbean vacation just isn't in the cards, try putting the colors of the rainbow to work. "Research shows that you can change your mood just by the colors you surround yourself with," says Leatrice Eiseman, executive director of the Pantone Color Institute and author of *Colors for Your Every Mood*. "Even a small colored object, like a bracelet or a handbag, can give you benefits," she says.

Here's how hues can work magic on you—and some new products that can brighten your day.

Yellow: This is the choice when you need mental clarity. "The ancients believed yellow was the color of insight," Eiseman says. Fill a yellow sachet with AromaFloria's Inhalation Beads and take a whiff (www.aromafloria.com).

Blue: Shades of blue have a calming effect and can create serenity. Drop a soothing Space NK tablet in your bath and mellow out—or just display some in a container for a quick relaxation hit (www.spacenk.com).

Orange: It can make you feel more optimistic and wake you up when you're sluggish. But you don't have to go Burger King–bright to reap the benefits. Shades from pale apricot to the sun-kissed orange of Aromapharmacy's Mind & Body Cleanser will do (www.aromapharmacy.com).

Green: Brings balance to your mind and your hectic day-to-day routine. "With this color around, you feel in control and more in sync," Eiseman explains. Try this stylish way to go green: Lands' End driving shoes (www.landsend.com).

Red: It can boost your energy level since it is said to stimulate the heart rate. "Red is like a shot of adrenaline," Eiseman says. Wear it to avoid that afternoon work slump; slip on a White & Warren's sweater to power you through (www.whiteandwarren.com).

Purple: Tones of lilac and violet can spark creativity. Pick a pair of purple Maurice Malone shades when you need some inspiration (www.mojadesign.com).

Negative Thinking Linked to Medication Side Effects

You've probably heard of the placebo effect, when people taking a dummy pill boast of improvements. Researchers at Brigham and Women's Hospital in Boston have coined a new phrase, the "nocebo effect," which hinges on the power of negative thinking. If people have had bad experiences with a medication in the past, they're more likely to feel side effects when taking a new drug, the researchers say.

turn to good art for a good mood

As if you needed a reason to surround yourself with beauty: A recent study found that viewing works of art can decrease stress. If you can't get to the Met, visit www.print-art.com and take a peek at these mood-enhancers:

• Gustav Klimt's *The Kiss*

• Henri Matisse's *Blue Nude*

• Vincent Van Gogh's *Sunflowers*

Choose wisely, however; the study found that some paintings had the opposite effect. Both Pablo Picasso's *Guernica* and Edvard Munch's *The Scream* increased stress levels.

Shed Your Stress with these Easy Moves

WORKOUT CREATED BY PETRA KOLBER   **PHOTOGRAPHY BY DAVID MARTINEZ**

After a day spent hunched over your desk, it's tempting to plop down on a comfy couch with the remote in your hand and recharge. But inertia can be a wicked, wicked thing—and not just because it can play itself out on the scale. It saps your energy and leads to tight muscles that make you more prone to injury when you do get yourself moving.

What's the antidote? A quick afternoon stretch. These six moves concentrate on the places most people tend to store tension—pretty much everywhere from the waist up. Do them at your desk or workstation to loosen up, ward off the aches and pains stress can cause, and correct Quasimodo-like posture.

> Instead of reaching for coffee, try **these moves.** They'll help **de-stress** your body and **calm** your mind.
>
> —*trainer Petra Kolber*

The whole routine can take about 20 minutes, but if you can't spare the time, do a single rep of each move or pick the stretch your body needs the most. They can help you look taller and more confident—which could work in your favor at the afternoon meeting.

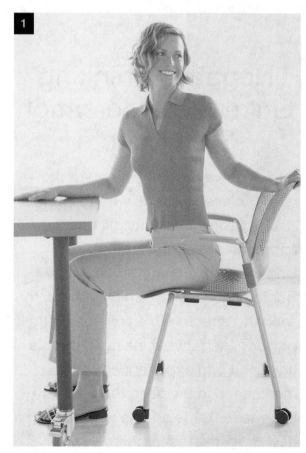

torso rotation

1 | Sit with your feet hip-distance apart. Rotate your torso to the left, placing your left hand on your chair for support. Turn until you feel gentle rotation along your spine. Hold for 3 to 5 breaths. Slowly return to the starting position. Repeat 4 times in each direction.

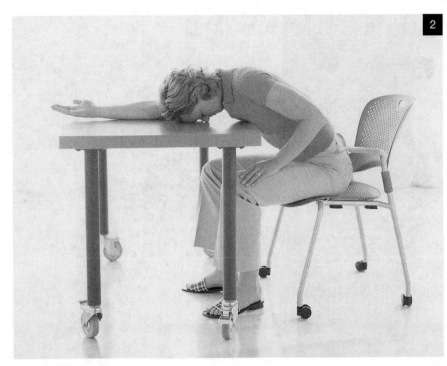

reach, roll and lift

2 | Sit with your abs lifted. Hinge forward from your hips, resting your head on your desk. Reach forward with your right arm until you feel a gentle stretch. Turn your palm upward, then lift your right arm. Return to the starting position. Repeat 4 times with each arm.

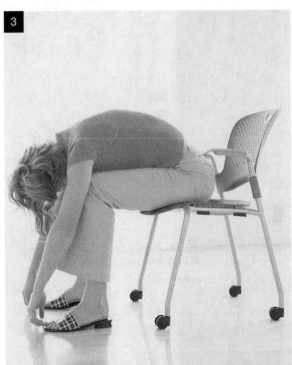

spinal roll down

3 | Sit upright at your desk with your hands resting on your thighs. Keep your abs tight as you slowly roll down, one vertebra at a time, until your torso rests on or near your lap. Take 3 to 5 deep breaths. Slowly roll up to the starting position. Repeat 4 times.

chest stretch

4 | Stand with your chest lifted. Extend your arms out to your sides. Keeping your back straight, move your arms behind you until you feel a gentle stretch through your chest. Hold for 3 to 5 breaths and return to the starting position. Repeat 4 times.

breath combo

5A | Stand with your feet hip-distance apart and your arms relaxed at your sides. Exhale, and as you inhale, reach overhead.

5B | Exhale again and draw your hands downward and together in front of your chest.

5C | Inhale, then as you exhale, press your arms out forward, allowing your neck to relax and your back to round slightly. Return to the starting position. Repeat 4 times. ✳

Contributing Editor Petra Kolber is a Reebok University master trainer. Find more of her exercises at www.health.com *or* www.petrakolber.com.

The Right Kind of Stress Keeps You Healthy

Will your next spa weekend kick off with a 10-page-long multiple-choice examination? It might not be a bad idea: New research shows that short bouts of the right kind of stress may keep you healthy. A research team from the Netherlands and Ohio State University found that the saliva of people exposed to an active stressor (taking a difficult test) contained increased levels of a protein that protects against infection. But exposure to a more passive stress (watching a surgical video—so gross that some participants fainted) yielded lower levels of the protein.

The difference between active and passive stress is mostly just a matter of a person's perception, explains lead study author Jos A. Bosch, Ph.D., a postdoctoral fellow in oral biology at Ohio State. "Active stress is perceived as challenging," Bosch says. "Passive stresses are not perceived as challenging; they are situations that you have to endure."

What makes active stress healthy, Bosch says, is that "in challenging situations, the body prepares for fight or flight." Adrenaline goes up, the heart rate goes up, and your immune system becomes prepared for action as well.

Are you still not sure if your stress is good? Here are some situations where stress is on your side—and others to avoid.

IT'S ACTIVE STRESS IF...

• You finish your tax return with only an hour to spare.
• You disguise yourself as the UPS delivery person in order to sneak past the boss's office and avoid a staff meeting.
• You come to work early and respond to 73 e-mails so you'll have time for a massage in the middle of the day.
• You're pitching in the softball team's play-off game.
• You impress your dinner guests by painstakingly re-creating a recipe you saw on *Iron Chef*.

BUT IT'S PASSIVE STRESS IF...

•You get a ride to the post office from your sister, only to have the car stuck in traffic and the radio locked on "adult contemporary."
•Your boss finds out and retaliates by moving your desk next to that guy who eats three bean burritos for lunch every day.
•The massage therapist keeps quoting lines from *The Sopranos*.
•Your car breaks down on the way to the game.
•You end up in the emergency room for two hours getting the sea-urchin spines removed from your lips and fingers.

Q+A
Kick Bad Habits NOW

IN 1995, CHARLES S. PLATKIN weighed 210 pounds—a burdensome load for his 5-foot-9-inch frame—and was on the relationship merry-go-round. Since then, the 39-year-old has gotten married, shed 50 pounds, and authored *Breaking the Pattern: The 5 Principles You Need to Remodel Your Life.* We asked Platkin for his secrets to breaking out of cycles that can keep you from making life changes.

Q: What are some of the common patterns that trip people up?
A: Dieting déjà vu (losing and regaining weight) is a big one for women. Toxic relationships—with co-workers, friends, mates, or family members—that always end the same way make up another bad cycle. Other patterns are career dissatisfaction and financial discontent.

Q: How long does it take for someone to slip into a bad pattern?
A: Since something negative usually has many short-term benefits, it takes less time to set a pattern than to break one. For instance, a toxic relationship can be exciting in the beginning but then fizzle and fall into a negative pattern.

Q: How can you break the patterns?
A: First, be a detective and identify the bad patterns in your life. If you think about your failures instead of running away from them, you'll be less likely to repeat mistakes. Next, accept that you're responsible for your choices. Finally, set goals so that you'll know where you're going, and think about achievement as the result of your choices.

Q: How long does it take to break a pattern?
A: It takes about six to 10 weeks to get used to being in a different place, but then it takes at least a year to make it a part of your life.

Q: How much can you change?
A: A lot more than you might think. People generally feel they've been given what they've got and that's it. But you can make significant behavior changes. Still, there are limits. It's unlikely that at this stage in my life I could become an astronaut or president. Be realistic.

Q: Can you break patterns in other people?
A: Possible, but unlikely. If your objective is to change another person, think about why you're in that kind of relationship anyway.

knitting:
the new yoga

Women—from hip urbanites to cancer survivors—are discovering the calming benefits of needlework.

BY EVA MARER

Every Friday, a group of women who work at Oxford University Press in New York City slip away from their computers, blow off their lunch breaks, and take over an empty office. Lissy Blomster, a 25-year-old art buyer and the motivating spirit behind this group, pushes aside an abandoned stack of papers to perch on a desk, swinging her black-stockinged feet. The others fan around her in a circle of hastily assembled chairs, spilling soft balls of yarn around their ankles: loopy mauve, canary yellow, forest green, blood red.

The clamor of knitting needles sets in, and slowly, the knots of the week unravel. The women lean over to gossip about 24-year-old Phebe Szatmari's boyfriend, swap stitching suggestions, or fondle works-in-progress: scarves, sweaters, socks. "I can tell when I'm feeling stressed because my stitches are always tighter," says photo researcher Donatella Accardi, 34. "But by the time I get back to my desk, I'm totally relaxed."

Once considered an activity for seniors or back-to-the-earth types, knitting has become what some folks are calling "the new yoga": the latest way to relax. Professional women say it burns off anxiety and makes them more clearheaded at work; cancer patients and others grappling with serious illnesses find that it helps them to cope with their situations. Even such Hollywood stars as Julia Roberts and Cameron Diaz are getting into the stitch, picking up needles to pass downtime on movie sets. And perhaps most importantly, according to those who are caught up in the craze, knitting threads together women of all backgrounds and generations in groups that provide the support they just can't get on their daily social rounds.

Like the Oxford gals, the new generation of knitters is young, urban, and sophisticated. According to Research Incorporated, a marketing research firm in Atlanta, the number of knitters younger than 35 doubled between 1998 and 2000 (the most recent data available) to an estimated 4 million. Approximately 38 million American women—one in four—know how to knit or crochet.

For many, knitting is the comfort food of crafts. The art's calming effects come from the repetitive rhythms of needles, yarn, and hands, explains Bernadette Murphy, a California-based author of *Zen and the Art of Knitting.* She says it induces the classic "relaxation response," marked by a lowered heart rate and blood pressure. This response was identified in the mid-1980s by Herbert Benson, M.D., president of the Harvard Mind/Body Medical Institute.

> The **repetitive rhythms** of needles, yarn, and hands **lower heart rate** and blood pressure.

While Benson has not studied knitting specifically, he agrees that it could evoke a powerful physical effect. "Any kind of repetitive activity, whether it's reciting the rosary or knitting, can induce a meditative state in the brain," Benson says. Unlike ordinary rest, meditation increases mental alertness and relaxation, increasing mental well-being.

"When I knit, I lose all track of time," says Accardi, echoing the sentiments of many other women who report a kind of knitter's high. The same kind of mental buzz might happen when you're reading a good book, Szatmari adds. "But when you're knitting, your thoughts are your book," she says. "Your mind meanders along and brings you to whatever you need to be thinking about." Blomster agrees: "Knitting helps me shift gears, clear my head, and start fresh."

This ability to lose oneself—as well as to find oneself—in the knit-one-purl-two rhythm helps explain why this craft has such appeal for people with serious illnesses.

"I have always been a passionate knitter, but the more my life unraveled, the more I knitted," says Tanya Parieaux, 55, a breast-cancer survivor. "I felt like I was dying inside, but every time I picked up my knitting needles, I was moving forward and creating life. It brought me hope." Parieaux's belief in the healing power of knitting inspired her to form Threads of Life, a volunteer group that teaches knitting to patients in several Seattle-area hospitals.

"It's pretty wonderful to see people who are so very ill suddenly forget themselves and just break out laughing," Parieaux says. For cancer patients in particular, knitting can be a healing art. The repetitive action of knitting helps to relieve emotional stress, which can actually reduce the body's ability to tolerate chemotherapy and magnify unpleasant side effects, such as nausea, says Julie Gralow, M.D., a breast-cancer specialist at the University of Washington Medical Center in Seattle and sponsor of Parieaux's knitting program.

Knitting as a social activity confers benefits that go beyond mental and physical relaxation. Traditionally, knitters stitched alone, but the new trend is knitting in groups, according to the Knitting Guild of America, an Ohio-based outfit that organizes knitting circles across the United States. These circles have become kind of casual group-therapy sessions, replacing the typical tangle of modern communication—unwieldy masses of telephone, fax, and personal-computer cords—with skeins of yarn. Therefore, knitters are looping into the proven power of support groups to relieve anxiety and depression and create positive medical outcomes, Gralow says.

Crafting in groups allows people reluctant to spill their guts in a traditional therapeutic setting a safe circle to share their woes and listen to advice. "It's easier to be revealing when you have something to do with your hands," Murphy says.

For the Oxford circle, knitting together is equal parts stitch-and-bitch and back-to-the-future, enabling them to connect not just to each other, but to generations of knitters past. "In the '70s, a lot of people considered the domestic arts antifeminist, and you wouldn't be caught dead knitting," says

knitting 101

Here's how you can get into the stitch.

• Visit your local yarn shop. Employees are usually crack knitters and can guide you to what you need. Staffers at the New York City yarn shop Wool Gathering recommend wool or acrylic yarns and size-8 needles for beginners.

• Start with the basics. Anyone who knows how to knit can teach you the basic knit-and-purl technique, or you can visit the Craft Yarn Council of America's Learn to Knit site at www.learntoknit.com for a quick lesson. Hone your skills on the easiest project: a scarf.

• Join a knitting circle. Many yarn shops offer beginners' classes or can point you to a local group. If none exists in your area, the Knitting Guild of America (800-274-6034; www.tkga.com) will help you set one up.

• Get inspired. For intermediate knitters, books with lush illustrations can inspire ideas. One of our personal favorites is *Knitter's Stash: Favorite Patterns from America's Yarn Shops* by Barbara Albright.

• Go public with your passion. The Craft Yarn Council of America (www.craftyarncouncil.com) sponsors its annual Knit-Out & Crochet—complete with teaching demonstrations, charity auctions, celebrity appearances, and fashion shows—in dozens of cities across the country. Click on the Knit-Out logo on their Web site or call 800-662-9999 to receive a free brochure.

43-year-old art buyer Andrea Suffredini, a mother of four and one of the oldest members of the Oxford circle. "But as my mother gets older, I'm feeling sentimental about passing along these family traditions to my kids, including the boys," she says.

These days, she finds herself knitting quietly with her mother during family gatherings. "Even when we're not getting along, knitting in silence helps us bridge that generation gap," Suffredini says. Finding comfort in stressful times, renewing ties with friends and family, creating handmade treasures to pass on to loved ones—these are the threads that weave together knitting's past, present, and future. ✳

Eva Marer is a freelance health and fitness writer based in New York City.

Seven Simple Steps that Will Help You Sleep

If you can't turn off your mind at night, these tips may help quiet your thoughts—and let you get some rest.

BY LYDIA DENWORTH

My husband runs a business that's tied to the stock market. As prices fall, so does his sleep. I'll roll over to find him wide awake on his side of the bed. "I'm whirring," he'll say. That's our expression for those long nighttime hours when the brain shifts into overdrive and you can't slow it down. The more we have to worry about, the more we whirr.

Of course, we aren't the only ones staring at the ceiling. In an April 2002 poll by the National Sleep Foundation (NSF), 63 percent of women reported that they experience insomnia at least a few nights a week.

But it doesn't always take a crisis to get you whirring. In fact, those everyday concerns—an upcoming exam, problems in a marriage, job stress—can keep you awake as much as larger-scale troubles. "Thoughts seem more dramatic at night because we don't have any distraction," explains NSF president James Walsh, Ph.D. "When we turn out the lights at night, it's just us and our thoughts. They can get the best of us." And it's all too easy to let one restless night turn into another: Then add to your worries that you're not getting enough sleep, and the cycle continues.

There are ways to kick your worries out of bed. But first you have to be sure you're practicing the fundamentals of getting a good night's sleep: Avoid exercise, caffeine, and alcohol close to bedtime; keep consistent wake times; keep the bedroom dark and quiet; and try relaxing rituals like a hot bath or a book that's not too gripping. "Watch what you do in the couple hours before bed," Walsh says. "Don't balance your checkbook or try to solve marital problems."

These basics are more important in times of stress. "Coffee may not bother you on a typical day," Walsh says, "but when there are multiple stressors, it may keep you awake."

Still, even these healthy sleep habits don't always stop your thoughts from spinning. That conversation with your boss or the unpaid bill on the hallway table can loom larger than it should. On these nights, you need specific techniques for hitting the "off" button. Try these suggestions.

1. Distract your mind. Try to think of a mental task—somewhere between easy and engrossing—that requires just a little concentration. If counting sheep doesn't work for you (one of Walsh's patients complained that his kept getting caught on the fence), experiment. Count backwards or in another language, or replay a pleasant activity in your mind.

Thoughts seem more dramatic

at night because we don't have any distraction. When we turn out the lights, it's just us and our thoughts. They can get the best of us.

—James Walsh, Ph.D.

2. Start a worry book. "For half an hour every afternoon, well before bedtime, at a set time and place, write down the things that you worry about," says Joyce Walsleben, Ph.D., co-author of the book *A Woman's Guide to Sleep* and director of the New York University School of Medicine Sleep

how do you get to sleep?

Sixty-three percent of women experience insomnia each week. We asked these four hard-charging women how they turn their minds off at night. Here's what they had to say.

Patricia Braun, assistant district attorney, Manhattan D.A.'s office, and mother of an 8-month-old son: "Catholics are lucky because we can pray the rosary. There are five decades in a rosary, and I almost never finish the second decade."

Judith Curr, executive vice president and publisher of Atria Books: "I try to imagine my last game of golf. I remember all the shots and by the time I get to the fourth hole, I'm asleep."

Joyce Walsleben, Ph.D., co-author of *A Woman's Guide to Sleep:* "If I'm starting to think about work or anything else, I talk to myself. I say, 'Don't even go there.' You have to practice, but the process of saying it is enough."

Alice Domar, Ph.D., director of the Mind/Body Center for Women's Health at the Mind/Body Medical Institute in Boston: "I've been worried about work a lot at night, so I say to myself over and over, almost like a mantra, 'My life is not my job.'"

Disorders Center. She suggests recording your worries on one side of the page and on the opposite side writing down at least one active step you can take to ease those worries. Then put the book away.

3. Challenge the thoughts that keep you up.
If the same thought continues going round and round in your head—"I'm going to blow this project at work," for example—stop and ask yourself if it's true. (Probably not.) Then replace the negative thought with a positive one: "I'm making progress on this project every day."

4. Take a deep breath, literally.
Deep breathing, in which you use your diaphragm and count one breath to one number, is an effective relaxation exercise. Try simply counting down from 10, or up to four and back again. Physiologically, such breathing helps lower your heart rate, breathing rate, and blood pressure. Psychologically, it helps distract your mind.

5. Get up after 20 minutes or so.
Sometimes, the idea of not sleeping is itself the problem. You can get so caught up in the fact that what you're doing to fall asleep isn't working that you start to associate it with not sleeping. That's when it's time to take a break. "Go ahead and watch television or read—something that will keep your attention but isn't terribly exciting," Walsh says.

6. Keep track of when in the month you are lying awake.
Women 35 or over might be undergoing hormone shifts, which can keep sleep at bay. If you let your doctor know which nights you're awake—and she sees a pattern—she may prescribe low-dose estrogen pills.

7. Turn the clock away from the bed.
This way, you won't be as susceptible to obsessing over how long you've been awake. Waking up periodically is a natural part of the sleep cycle, and monitoring the length of your wakefulness won't change anything. "The last thing you want to do is wake up and say, 'Oh my god, what a bad night. I hope I do better tonight,'" says Walsleben. "You have just done yourself in." ✳

New York–based journalist Lydia Denworth also writes for Redbook, Ladies' Home Journal, *and* House & Garden.

when all else fails …

Sometimes it seems as if nothing you try will help you get to sleep. If you're going through a divorce, have had a death in the family, or are otherwise experiencing upheaval, your sleep will suffer. That's when it's OK to take a sleeping pill. "A lot of people go without sleep needlessly," says James Walsh, Ph.D., president of the National Sleep Foundation. "And these days there are sleeping pills on the market that are short-acting and don't affect you during the daytime—the chance of getting hooked is very small." Sleep experts tend to prefer prescription medicines to over-the-counter drugs, which tend to pack more of a wallop. Ask your doctor which one she recommends.

dear diary,
what do my dreams mean?

Eveland Fairfield, inventor of the Personal Method of Interpreting Dreams, says dreams are like the game show *Jeopardy*—they provide the answers but not the questions. To create your dream diary, follow this shortened version of the six-step method. Remember to jot down your dream as completely as you can before tackling these questions:

1 What did you do yesterday that set the stage for this dream?

2 What were you thinking about that may have prompted this dream?

3 What people, places, or objects appear in this dream, and what further associations do these bring to mind?

4 What emotions did you have toward these people or objects in the dream, and how do they differ from your waking emotions?

5 What is your dream telling you about how you might change your thoughts, attitudes, or behavior in regard to this person or object?

6 What relationships or issues need to be explored further or in other dreams?

Dreams could be a window to your real emotions

YOU MIGHT WANT TO lie down for this: New research suggests that women who make an effort to recall and interpret their dreams can gain insights into their relationships. In a recent University of Maryland study, researchers found that dream interpretation as part of couples therapy greatly improved relations. And a study currently under way at Rush-Presbyterian-St. Luke's Medical Center in Chicago suggests that "dream work" can help women suffering from clinical depression after a divorce or separation.

"Dreaming is a natural healing system," says Montague Ullman, M.D., clinical professor emeritus of psychiatry at Albert Einstein College of Medicine in New York City. "Dreams reveal your truest emotions and allow you to be honest with yourself in a way you seldom are in waking life." That kind of emotional honesty helps you resolve unfinished business from the past that can get in the way of your current relationships, he says.

For example, recently divorced women in the Chicago study often dreamed of their ex-spouses as rejecting or punishing. Typical visions: exes dragging dirt onto new white carpet or not showing up for a labor-intensive meal. "Just talking through these dreams helped women get in touch with their feelings of abandonment and failure, their sense of being devalued, and also their fear of being alone and unloved in the future," says lead study author Rosalind W. Cartwright, Ph.D., chairwoman of the psychology department at Rush University. "We also helped them short-circuit negative dream images by developing more positive associations." For example, instead of assuming that dreams of solo dining are symbolic of a life destined for loneliness, she says, think about them as a sign of independence.

Simply remembering dreams can be a challenge, but Cartwright says that anyone can master the art of recall. "The key is to avoid orienting to the outside world abruptly when you awake," she says. "Don't open your eyes and don't move while you rehearse the last image you can remember." Then give your dream a tag such as "My date with Guy Pearce."

When decoding your dreams, don't assume every pencil is a phallus, as Freud once believed. "Everyone has her own dream language," says Eveland Fairfield, the founder of YourGuidingDreams.com and inventor of the Personal Method of Interpreting Dreams. For instance, dreaming that you encounter your lover naked in a public place might mean that there's nothing artificial between you two—or it could mean that you're afraid of being exposed. By jotting down your dreams, you can begin to link your life events with your personal dream symbols, and even influence the content of your dreams. You may catch a glimpse of your true self, and make your deepest dreams come true.

Q+A
What it Means When Dreams Won't Let You Rest

I have very vivid dreams that sometimes wake me in the middle of the night. Is there anything I can do to get a more restful night's sleep?

AN ACTIVE DREAM LIFE is actually a sign of good health, so don't worry about this happening—unless what's waking you are recurring nightmares. Dreams show that you're a deep sleeper: You dream in all stages of sleep, but you recall the most dreams from REM sleep, the deepest, most restful and restorative kind of sleep. People with sleep apnea, for instance, often have less awareness of dreams. They are constantly awakened during REM sleep because they can't catch their breath.

But if nightmares are repeatedly jolting you awake, they could indicate that you have an underlying problem that needs to be treated. Between 4 and 8 percent of Americans experience nightmares on a regular basis. While researchers and doctors aren't exactly sure what causes them, bad dreams are often associated with depression, anxiety, schizophrenia, and post-traumatic stress disorder. Once you've figured out what's causing your nightmares, then you and your doctor can find an appropriate treatment plan for you. In some cases, prescription antidepressants may help; in others, the solution might be psychotherapy.

If you don't think your dreams are linked to psychiatric problems, certain habits could be causing a hyperactive dream life. Smoking, drinking alcohol or caffeine, eating after 9 p.m., and using recreational drugs can influence your sleep cycle and shift your dreams into overdrive. Keep a diary of your daily habits and dreams to help you identify and eliminate the triggers.

How Hope and Humor Help Your Health

A new study finds that planning your summer vacation or weekend leisure is essential to your health. Looking forward to pleasurable events triggers healthy changes in your mood and maybe in your body, say researchers at the University of California, Irvine, College of Medicine. Psychological tests indicated that anticipating laughter—in this study, preparing to watch a funny video—reduced levels of tension, fatigue, anger, and depression. Unpublished data by the same research team show that these mood changes are accompanied by favorable physical changes, such as reduced levels of stress hormones. "The body prepares itself for pleasure," says study author Lee S. Berk, Ph.D. "Expectation is a synonym for hope. If doctors can learn to elicit hope in their patients, it could be a powerful tool for battling chronic disease." So schedule some fun in your weekly planner and reap the benefits of looking forward to it.

healthBUZZ
thumbs UP

Prickly Weight-Loss Plant: A cactus used by South African bushmen to kill their appetites during long treks could find its way to the United States. The drug manufacturer Pfizer is set to research the hoodia plant, which may cause people to feel more full after eating.

Suds Up, Dad: Children who are regularly bathed by their fathers in their first year are less likely to encounter behavioral problems later in life, according to a British study. It goes to show that the father-child relationship can be a key to healthy—and clean—living.

thumbs DOWN

Supermarket Salmonella: Doctors from the University of Maryland and the U.S. Food and Drug Administration went shopping and bought chicken, beef, turkey, pork—and salmonella. One in five meats purchased at Washington, D.C.-area grocery stores carried the bacteria. Protect yourself: Make sure meat is thoroughly cooked, and be vigilant about washing up after handling raw meat.

Superbugs, Part 2: A new study finds that an estimated 2 million patients a year acquire infections in U.S. hospitals. The culprit: bacteria that can live up to three months on fabrics and plastics. Request clean linens daily.

five secrets to a stress-free getaway

Sometimes bad vacations happen to good people.
But don't give up. Read these tips and learn how
you can pack it all in and still have a ball.

BY NICHOLE BERNIER AHERN

It was supposed to have been the ultimate mother-daughter vacation: a road trip through central Spain to meet up with my sister, who was studying abroad. There were to be 10 days of castles and olive groves, luxury resorts and pottery shopping, and nights of sangria-drenched bonding. We bonded all right—over our adversity: First, our outbound flight reservation was lost. Our rental car got impounded and couldn't be sprung loose because it was an obscure national holiday. When we returned the car, we were charged a rate well above what we'd reserved, and my sister's best student-Spanish couldn't convince the rental agent otherwise. Just when we thought we were home-free, my passport was stolen and couldn't be replaced because it was—you guessed it—an obscure national holiday.

As a veteran travel writer, I should have known better. Most of our quandaries probably could have been avoided with more careful planning. But in my enthusiasm to be on vacation, I'd decided not to sweat the small stuff. Unfortunately, once I did begin sweating, I couldn't stop. So in the end, I carried my stress from Madrid to Cordoba, Seville, and Grenada. *Mea* major *culpa*.

Of all the lessons I learned on that trip, perhaps the biggest was that jagged emotions and dashed expectations can be a far worse travel disaster than stolen passports or overpriced transport. Truth is, many people short-circuit their chances of having a great vacation because they fail to prepare adequately—both logistically and psychologically. Great vacations don't just happen on their own; they require careful consideration in advance. And the more complicated the trip—carefully orchestrated connections, activities scheduled to the minute—the more likely it is that some small piece will fall out of sync. The kids will throw tantrums, medication will run out, budgets will be exceeded. It takes the best of attitudes to have a good time.

That is not to say you're helpless—far from it. The best insurance policy is to start out as an empowered traveler—to be savvy enough to take defensive maneuvers before you pack the first suitcase or board the first flight. The second step is to select a destination that's in line with your inner vacation desires. To help, we've provided two fabulous trip ideas (one luxury, one budget-minded) in these four travel categories: family-oriented, romantic, educational, and active. Plus—even more important—we'll guide you through five ways to ensure that no matter where you're going, you'll get there with a healthy attitude intact.

1 Consider the brag factor.

Everyone has conscious—or subconscious—vacation desires. It's your job to figure out yours (and your traveling companions') and plan accordingly. Sometimes

Jagged emotions and dashed expectations can be a far worse travel disaster than stolen passports or overpriced transport.

that's easier said than done. So think of it this way: What would you want to brag to your friends about when you return? That you pedaled the canyons in Moab, maybe, or sampled every spa service at Canyon Ranch? Deciding whether your trip is supposed to be an escape, an exploration, or something in between affects everything you plan, down to the accommodations. If you're going the escape route, for instance, be wary of bunking down at the home of dear relatives (it may be less stressful to stay in a hotel than to try to meld with the flow of your hosts—even if that means a shorter trip). Adventure-seekers risk being bored to tears at a lounge-on-the-

beach resort, no matter how exotic the island. Choosing a kitchen-equipped condo may seem like a boon—especially for budget-minded families and big groups—but it means someone has to do the cooking. And if it's the same someone who does it all the time at home, she might find her vacation reality bears more resemblance to her daily life than the getaway of her dreams.

It's all too common to go back to work with the feeling that you need a "vacation from your vacation." Think about how you'd like to feel when you return and trust those messages.

Great vacations don't just happen. They take careful planning and the ability to roll with the punches.

2 Plan your departure—and your return.

Taking off on a haphazard and rushed note sets you up to carry on stress along with your tote bag—which may take several days to dissipate, says Alice D. Domar, Ph.D., a health psychologist with Harvard Medical School and author of *Self-Nurture*. Ease your way there and back by packing days in advance, working off a detailed checklist complete with all the minutiae, down to canceling the newspaper and setting the timers on your lamps. Give yourself a day to get organized before you leave—and rather than returning at the eleventh hour, try coming home a full day early to simply do laundry and get a decent night's sleep. Chances are, you'll carry that

vacation glow back into the office (for the first few minutes anyway).

3 Go incognito.

Many working folks feel guilty about leaving the office and overcompensate by bringing along their cell phones and laptops—defeating the purpose of a getaway. "We all think we're indispensable. But even President Bush goes on vacation," Domar says. "The question is: How much anxiety do you have about leaving work? That's your issue to resolve before you go." Domar recommends thinking twice about distributing contact information to colleagues. It sends the message that you are willing to chat about work. Instead, entrust your hotel phone number to one colleague who will use it only when it's necessary.

4 Expect the unexpected and roll with it.

While it's good to know what you want out of a vacation and plan with that goal in mind, know you won't always hit the target dead-on. Rigid expectations can turn a sudden snowfall, for instance, into frustration, when it could be a chance to frolic. And your reaction isn't going to stop the heavens from dumping the white stuff, anyway. Give yourself some leeway with emotional expectations, too: Not every trip has to be a second honeymoon. Many vacations have been dubbed disasters when the actual events don't live up to overly specific images, even if the reality is wonderful—perhaps better than planned, but just different. When travel brings you surprises, take lots of snapshots (otherwise, they might not believe you back home).

5 Give each other room to get along.

Another source of trip stress for many people comes from an unexpected place: their travel partners. Spending time with someone intermittently during the week is quite different from being inseparable for 24 hours a day, seven days a week. Understandably, it can lead some travelers to worry about how their relationship will bear up under the intensity of nonstop togetherness.

"We have fantasies that as soon as we're on vacation with a partner it's going to be perfect," Domar says. But you are still the same people, albeit in completely new surroundings, with different schedules, different time zones, different sightseeing interests, different environments, weather, and eating habits. "It can be stressful, especially since some people don't adapt well to change," she says.

The vacation may well become the blissful, relaxing time that you envisioned when you planned it, but it probably won't happen immediately. Permit yourselves some downtime before you plan to hit a fast-paced touring itinerary. If you have different ideas of what constitutes a great afternoon of sightseeing, consider building in some independent time: For an afternoon in Florence, one

Eight Fun Trips for You to Try

Family Fun

Luxury: *Four Seasons Hualalai, Hawaii* A vacation can be great for parents and kids. This Big Island resort mixes plush bungalows, a world-class golf course, and snorkeling and scuba for "big kids" with a sand-bottom kiddie pool, in-room video games, and gecko-hunting excursions for little vacationers. And nearby attractions appeal to all ages: orchards of Kona coffee and macadamia-nut trees, ancient fishing villages, archaeological parks, and Hawaiian royal mansions. Room-and-car packages start at $485 per night. Details: 800-819-5053, www.fourseasons.com/vacations/hualalai

Budget: *Discovery Cove, Orlando, Florida* Cross a water park with a petting zoo and add a dash of "Flipper"—that's Discovery Cove. The highlight is swimming alongside dolphins, but kids also can snorkel around a coral reef, wade with stingrays, and feed more than 200 tropical birds in a free-flight aviary. The $199 admission includes a seven-day pass to Sea World. Cap the fantasy element with a themed jungle, space, or train suite at the Holiday Inn Family Suites Resort starting at $125 a night. Details: 877-434-7268, www.discoverycove.com; 877-387-5437, or you can visit www.hifamilysuites.com

Romantic Retreats

Luxury: *The Boulders, Carefree, Arizona* Be seduced by the drama of the red-rock Sonoran Desert and the sensual pleasures of this resort. Revel in fine cuisine and exotic activities such as moonlight cycling. At the Golden Door Spa, experience a wrap that uses real gem bits crushed into ionized clay. Evening temps are just cool enough to justify lounging by the wood-burning hearth. Summer rates run from $169 per night, but during the winter, you'll pay $520. Details: 800-553-1717, www.wyndham.com/boulders

Budget: *PlumpJack Squaw Valley Inn, Lake Tahoe* This virtually unknown 60-room inn has recently been transformed from ski-cabin simple to sophisticated, with chic decor worthy of its Shakespearean namesake. The cellar and frequently changing menu are inspired by the PlumpJack Company's winery and San Francisco restaurant. With the glittering lake and wildflowers as a backdrop, summer activities include horseback riding, boating, hiking, and biking (the inn loans them)—or guests can ride the cable car to the mountaintop Olympic complex with its swimming pool, hot tub, and ice-skating rink. Rooms start at $130 per night. Details: 800-323-7666, www.plumpjack.com

Educational Escapes

Luxury: *Smithsonian Study Tours Cruise* China's legendary Yangtze River, where work is under way on the decades-long Three Gorges project to build the world's largest dam—turning the waterway into a power source while flooding the architecture and artifacts of centuries-old villages. With Smithsonian Study Tours, a travel division of the Institute, you ply the river on a luxury cruise vessel as a series of informal lectures and slide shows provide rich historical context—a living IMAX experience. Itineraries blanket the world via land, rail, or sea—Arizona to Antarctica—all led by specialists in local culture, geography, politics, environment, and language. Tours range from three days to three weeks; from $840 to $36,000. Details: 877-338-8687, www.smithsonianstudytours.com

Budget: *Earthwatch Institute* It's noon in Nevis, and although the Caribbean Sea beckons, swimming can wait. At the Coconut Walk Estate, a historic sugar plantation, you're part of a research team cataloguing artifacts of the

person might climb the Duomo while the other visits a handmade leather and paper store. You might find out that some time apart actually gives you extra things to talk about over dinner. You'll toast your good judgment on your next adventure. ✳

Nichole Bernier Ahern writes—and travels—for Condé Nast Traveler, Self, *and* Sports Illustrated Women.

island's days of slavery. Then you'll dine on conch fritters and goat-milk soup before retiring to the Pond Hill Guesthouse. Earthwatch Institute's trips are vacations with a mission: Unpaid volunteers connect with working scientists. One- to four-week trips cost $1,000 to $2,000 and typically include meals and lodging. Details: 800-776-0188, www.earthwatch.org

Active Adventures

Luxury: *Topnotch at Stowe, Vermont* This 120-acre resort may look cushy, but it's also an athletic getaway. Topnotch has golf, canoeing, fly-fishing, inline skating, and more. The equestrian center offers guided trail rides and riding lessons; and the 13-court tennis academy features seminars on sports psychology. After all the activity, hit the hot tub with a cascading hydromassage waterfall. Then refuel on sesame-crusted tuna with orange-soy glaze and udon noodles. Rates range from $170 per night to $1,700 for a three-night fitness package for two. Details: 800-451-8686, www.topnotch-resort.com

Budget: *Strathcona Park Lodge, Vancouver Island, Canada* This Canadian outpost is an adventure camp with the breathtaking vistas of a top resort, minus the hefty price tag. Perched on Upper Campbell Lake next to the 626,000-acre Strathcona Provincial Park, the lodge is a magnet for hikers, kayakers, sailors, and rock climbers. Choose a stress-reducing Wellness Week or a Family Adventure Week (both from $500 to $1,000) that includes outdoor problem-solving activities emphasizing accomplishment and discovery. Details: 250-286-3122, www.strathcona.bc.ca

Unwind in Style Between Flights

With longer security lines and more time spent in terminals, airport spas defrazzle travelers' nerves while providing a much more revitalizing way to spend a long layover than browsing the paperbacks at the newsstand. Walk-ins are welcomed and prices are competitive, with real-world rates at around $35 for a haircut and style, about $15 for a 10-minute massage, and $17 and up for a basic manicure. Here's a sampling of the spas offering on-the-fly services.

Newark Airport
D_parture Spa: Touch up before takeoff with a facial, manicure, pedicure, or massage.

Pittsburgh International Airport
Touch N Go: Stop here for rubs that soothe travel-weary necks, backs, shoulders, and feet.

Chicago O'Hare
Backrub Hub: Sit back, relax, and enjoy a revitalizing chair massage.

Logan Airport, Boston
Nailport: For the traveler with a connecting flight, manicures and pedicures done in 20 minutes, drying time not included.
Classique Nail and Hair Salon: Freshen up with some quick beauty fixes.
Polished: Restock your toiletry bag with high-end beauty products; polish your look with a manicure or pedicure.

Denver International Airport
A Massage Inc.: Try a 10-minute "Fly By" chair massage or a 30-minute "Layover" chair massage.

Orlando International Airport
Profiles Express: Primp before hitting Disney World with a massage, hair-styling, or manicure.

Calgary International Airport
Massage Garage: Treat yourself to a 10-minute spot massage for coach-cramped shoulders and feet.
O$_2$raOxygen Lounge: Airplane cabin fever? Breathe in oxygen-enriched air ($1 per minute) or treat skin to a pre-flight lift with a facial.

finding the bright side of being laid off

Losing a job might feel like the end of the world, but it could be the start of something good.

BY KIMBERLY GOAD

I was a widow who had agreed to go on a blind date before I'd officially buried my dearly departed. At least that was the way it felt to me.

Let me explain. In fall 2001, only five days after the magazine I worked for announced it would be suspending publication, I ventured out on my first job interview. Even though I had been a freelancer for years and knew I could get enough work to pay the bills, I was anxious to start again, full-time, at a new magazine.

So there I was, sitting across from an editor who offered her condolences and then listened politely as I gave a lengthy account of why the magazine had folded, when the staff had been told, how much I'd loved the job. I was, in short, entertaining another suitor—a handsome suitor with great benefits and windowed offices, at that—with stories of my ex.

Big mistake. "A blind date doesn't want to hear about how great your ex was. The date wants to hear about how great he is," says Richmond Fourmy, vice president of consulting for Right Management Consultants, an Atlanta-based firm that counsels people who have been fired or laid off. Needless to say, I didn't get the job.

Post-pink-slip panic, I would soon discover, has the power to sink any job search. Yet with unemployment climbing, it's natural to panic. What else are you supposed to do?

For starters, you should be aware that the reality isn't nearly as grim as the numbers suggest. While sudden unemployment is nothing to celebrate, it can offer benefits. When the shock wears off, the experience of losing a job can shake you out of complacency and into healthy emotional growth and even into a life that you love.

Robert K. Otterbourg, author of *Switching Careers*, knows that losing a job is traumatic. "You're going to have a period of real anguish," he says. Still, Otterbourg believes the experience can be liberating, such as how going through a divorce can help you discover what you really want out of a marriage. You can change careers without worrying about the practical implications of giving up a six-figure salary in the name of "starting over."

When the shock wears off, the experience of losing a job can shake you out of complacency and into healthy emotional growth and even into a life that you love.

You can finally redefine your notion of success and strike that elusive balance between work and play. And the soul-searching process of figuring out what you want from a career and from the rest of your life means you're far more likely to get it—and be happy.

That's what happened to Tonya Dietsch, who lives in San Jose, California. She devoted five years of her life to two failed Internet startups. When the second company let go of her and her staff, "my stomach dropped," she says. "That night, I went home and drank a bottle of wine. And for two or three weeks, I couldn't function. I didn't leave the house, and I watched TV all day."

Slowly, though, Dietsch began to realize something big: She didn't want to pursue another grueling dot-com dream. And at age 36, she was looking for more than financial rewards. "I realized I needed to figure out how to be human again." Dietsch had been saving, and she had a little money to work with, so she spent a few months doing some of the things she had always wanted to do: She completed a triathlon and took a trip to Italy—her first vacation in five years.

But it wasn't until she was taking a walk with a friend and their dogs in summer 2001 that things really crystallized. Dietsch had always loved animals, but she didn't know exactly how to parlay that interest into a career.

"You should become a dog trainer," her friend said. "This is your calling." Dietsch realized her friend was right, and after talking with several trainers, she came up with a plan: Work a 9-to-5 job to pay the bills and take a second job as an assistant to two dog trainers. Dietsch now spends her days as the director of operations for a software company and her nights preparing for the future. In two years, she hopes to strike out on her own.

Dietsch could have fallen into the common trap of thinking "this is the worst thing in my life," Fourmy says. Instead, she found new direction and happiness in the midst of her career upheaval. She took the approach Fourmy recommends: "You tell yourself, 'this is tough, it hurts; however, there's a big world out there, and I can take these skills and create my ideal job.'"

As for the layoff, Dietsch says, "it needed to happen. I never would have left my last job to go off and do what I love. I may not make as much money, but for me, it's not about getting rich. It's about living a good life."

M. Catherine LaTorre, a New York City attorney, wouldn't have left her job either. But the work in her

after-shock survival kit

Right after your job evaporates and before you determine your next big step, you'll need some practical tools. Here are four expert tips.

• **Realize that downsizing is not a personal affront.** It's natural to be upset and angry, but being laid off probably has nothing to do with your work or personality. "More often than not, the decision was made by people who don't even know who you are," says Robert K. Otterbourg, author of *Switching Careers.*

• **Downsize your budget.** Even if you received a generous severance package, now is not the time to live extravagantly. By preparing to live on a smaller budget, you'll have an easier time if the salary of your new job doesn't equal that of your old one.

• **Think about your real interests.** Rediscover what you truly love, so you can refocus your career in that direction. But how do you uncover your genuine interests? Nick A. Corcodilos, headhunter and author of *Ask the Headhunter,* recommends spending a few days at your local library, seeing which books naturally draw your attention. You should begin to notice some trends in how your interests develop.

• **Use your contacts.** The best way to learn about a new field of work is from the people in it, Otterbourg says. Talk to your friends and acquaintances about prospects in their industry; they may know about an opportunity you don't. The bottom line is that you won't know until you ask.

division slowed to a crawl in 2001, and she was laid off in early September of that year. The fact that she'd seen it coming didn't make it less painful. "Ninety percent of my identity was tied in to being a lawyer," says LaTorre, who's 34. "No matter what happened in life—loneliness, spiritual restlessness, financial woes—I always had my job. It was my life preserver."

Without it, LaTorre didn't know who she was. "Losing a job is a loss of part of ourselves," Otterbourg says. "It's very intense, depending on how invested that person is in the job."

> You tell yourself, "this is tough, it hurts; however, there's a big world out there, and **I can take these skills and create my ideal job**."
> —*Tonya Dietsch*

To reclaim your identity, Fourmy says, "you have to look at your self-worth as being separate from your achievements. The best way to do that is to talk about how the experience makes you feel. Talk to your colleagues, friends, family, and people you trust and ask them: 'What do I mean to you?' You'll find them remarking about who you are as a person, not what you do for work." Seeing a therapist might also help you find your self-esteem outside of your job—it has for LaTorre.

She says that she is only now beginning to experience the freedom to define herself in new ways. LaTorre has revived a translation service that she started to help her pay the bills while she was in law school. "I'm always happy when I'm translating, and I love being at home,"

LaTorre says. "It can be as financially rewarding as law." And she's thriving on it while she considers whether—or how—she really wants to pursue a career in law again.

"Legal work is consuming," LaTorre says. "With a liberated mind, you open up to all these new ideas you never had time for." That's the kind of clean slate that Otterbourg says is the hidden potential in being laid off. "You can do what you want to do," he says.

As for me, the clean slate means more freelance work until I find the right job. And the next time a suitor calls, I'll be over my dearly departed—and ready to move on. ✳

Kimberly Goad's work has appeared in numerous publications, including **Marie Claire, Self,** *and* **New York.**

what does your office say about you?

A messy desk or coffee-mug collection can reveal the real you, a new study suggests. Researchers at the University of Texas at Austin had people look at the offices of folks they had never met, and asked them to make guesses about the personalities of the workers. The researchers found that after 15 minutes of casual observation, it was possible to size up the subjects' character traits accurately.

In some cases, specific environmental cues seemed to play a key role, says study director Samuel Gosling, Ph.D., assistant professor of psychology. A tidy office, for example, was a clear tip-off to conscientiousness. But it was harder to identify cues for other traits. According to the study, here are some traits that might reveal more than your decorating taste.

People may judge you as …	If your office space is...
Open to new experiences	Distinctive, stylish, unconventional, full of a variety of books
Extroverted	Warm (temperature-wise), decorated
Conscientious	Clean, neat, full of similar-genre books and CDs, uncluttered
Emotionally stable	Undecorated, undistinctive, formal

how superstitions can affect your health

Breaking a mirror could result in more than bad luck. New research suggests that the stress associated with deeply held superstitious beliefs can trigger fatal heart attacks, especially in people with heart disease. Researchers from the University of California at San Diego studied more than 47 million death certificates from over 15 years and discovered that fatal heart attacks among Chinese- and Japanese-Americans peaked significantly on the fourth day of the month, the equivalent of Friday the 13th in Chinese and Japanese cultures. No similar pattern in heart fatalities was found among Anglo subjects. The researchers suppose this could be because beliefs about unlucky numbers are taken more seriously in Chinese and Japanese cultures. The team has dubbed this scared-to-death phenomenon the "Baskerville Effect"—for Sir Arthur Conan Doyle's famous Sherlock Holmes novel *The Hound of the Baskervilles,* in which the character Sir Charles dies of a heart attack induced by fright.

But superstition doesn't always spell trouble. The ones shown may predict good health in your future.

superstition	health prediction
Lucky penny	See a penny, pick it up. Taking an active role in determining your fate is healthy. Studies show that chronically ill patients have better outcomes when they're actively involved in treatment.
Four-leaf clover	Keep one as a good-luck charm. The optimism you'll feel is good for your heart and your overall health.
Black cat	Don't panic, but if you see one crossing your path, run the other way—and keep jogging. The benefits of exercise range from improving cardiovascular health to boosting your mood.
Spilled salt	Throw it over your left shoulder—and while you're at it, think about tossing the whole shaker. Anything that lowers your sodium intake is good for you, especially if you have high blood pressure.
An apple a day keeps the doctor away	Besides being low in fat and high in fiber, apples contain a natural chemical that works even better than vitamin C in warding off cancer, according to a recent study.

VIRTUAL REALITY
Can Help You Face Your Fears

The classic phobia treatment—facing your fear over and over—may not be the best path to bravery. A recent report in *Behaviour Research and Therapy* suggests an even better trick. Psychologists at the University of California in Los Angeles exposed two groups of spider-phobes to a daily dose of virtual arachnids. One group saw the same spider every day, while the other group saw a different one each time. After three weeks, both groups returned to the lab for a blind date with a spider they'd never encountered. Those who had seen a variety of spiders took the newcomer in stride. But people who were used to just one spider were terrified of the eight-legged stranger.

Facing your fears in a variety of forms may give you confidence in new situations, explains Hunter Hoffman, Ph.D., a research scientist at the University of Washington Human Interface Technology Laboratory in Seattle. Hoffman's treatment plan: virtual reality. He says about 80 percent of patients get better in just four one-hour sessions with the glove and goggle. Participants start by touching a virtual spider with their cyber-hand (no tactile feedback) and work their way up to simultaneously touching a furry toy spider in the real world.

Virtual reality can also be used to treat fear of heights, flying, and enclosed spaces. Visit the Anxiety Disorders Association of America's Web site, www.adaa.org, for referrals to qualified therapists.

When Accidents are More Than Just Accidents

Seemingly innocent, clumsy behavior may not really be chance. It could be a sign that your life isn't working the way it should.

BY VICTORIA CLAYTON

The alarm clock buzzes. You reach for it and bump it off the bedside table, then hobble to the shower because you wrenched your ankle in last night's tennis match. As you drive to work, you dribble coffee down your new cream-colored blouse. By 10 a.m., it's certain: You're having one of those classic Bad Days. But what about that bicycle spill last week, not to mention those two fender benders and the bruised tailbone you've already had this year? Is someone trying to tell you something?

Maybe. And it's not just that you're clumsy, explains Samantha Dunn, author of *Not by Accident: Reconstructing a Careless Life*. In fact, if you don't take a look at these minor mishaps now, they might get worse later. "Accidents can work like fevers, as symptoms," Dunn says. "If they happen too often, they usually mean you're not paying attention to something in your life that you should be."

Dunn should know. In 1997, she suffered a near-fatal horseback-riding accident that dislocated her shoulder and nearly severed her leg. It forced her to look at how accident-prone she'd been her whole life—especially during the months before the accident: a sprained back, a fall down some stairs, a cracked tailbone, a foot injury. Over the 18 months she spent recovering from the riding accident, she came to the conclusion that she'd been ignoring signs of trouble in her life (in particular an unhealthy marriage) and that they were the root of her mishaps. "The riding accident was explicable," Dunn says. "It wasn't that I was intentionally getting hurt, but I was certainly contributing to my problems."

Experts can lend extra credence to Dunn's theory. Clyde Flanagan, M.D., director of psychoanalysis at the University of South Carolina School of Medicine, says accident-proneness may stem from a complex combination of physical and psychological factors. "I would not say that all accidents have a psychological basis," Flanagan says, but he does believe that strong feelings of guilt, depression, anger, or stress can make a healthy person more likely to have an accident. Whatever unaddressed problem or worry a person has "is like an emotional abscess that's been walled off," Flanagan explains. "The only way for healing to occur is to open it and drain it."

Strong feelings of guilt, depression, anger, or stress can make healthy people more likely to have accidents.

That's what Dunn did. And while her story may be an extreme example, the dynamics at work are the same whether you're dealing with minor accidents or serious ones. How do you know if you're contributing to your own recent spills? Here are three common scenarios in which your clumsiness might be trying to tell you something—and what you can do about it.

troubled mind

Everybody's got problems at home or work: the passive-aggressive boss or the fight you and your sister always seem to have. If you don't deal with them, they can play like background noise, distracting you from what you're doing. And that can be a dangerous thing—several studies have shown that drivers with marital problems suffer more traffic accidents around the time they file for divorce. Dunn's near-fatal accident falls into this category.

Your worries won't necessarily cause something serious; they may just manifest themselves as minor stumbles. San Francisco psychotherapist Robert H. Hopcke, author of *There Are No Accidents*, says, "If I'm having a day when I'm dropping everything, it's probably feelings—anger, anxiety, grief—that are distracting me."

Bottom line: To avoid the bumps and scrapes that are caused by distracted thoughts, Hopcke says, "It's time to back off and start reflecting." You don't have to resolve your problem to resolve your accident-proneness—you just have to get the feelings out so you're not walking around in a fog. Talking or writing about them is the first step.

the "Poor Me" syndrome

The on-and-off numbness in your wrist is now permanent, you broke your foot when the loose step on your porch gave way, and you got a cold right after you were caught in a downpour—just as you thought you would. You might believe you're jinxed, but you may just be waiting to be the victim. "People who are somewhat passive have accidents because they're not taking care of themselves and their situations," Hopcke explains. They find it easier to complain about the problem than to do something about it.

Bottom line: Search for ways to take control: Fix the step, attend to your medical problems, watch the TV weather reports. If you get proactive about the things that are tripping you up, you'll find that your "luck" will improve—and your injury rate will decrease.

the aggressive klutz

The opposite of the victim, you're the most aggressive, goal-oriented person you know. That 5K fund-raiser sponsored by your office? For most of your co-workers, it's a social event, but you want to win. While no one's going to deny that being competitive can be a good thing, it can translate to accidents, especially where sports and exercise are concerned.

Researchers Jodie Plumert, Ph.D., and David Schwebel, Ph.D., have studied aggressive risk-taking behavior in children, and they say that highly competitive people of all ages tend to overestimate their abilities. Their advice: Don't stop skiing or skydiving, but refine your judgment. "The message isn't that you should avoid doing anything fun and challenging," Plumert says. "But you need to be realistic. And some training never hurts."

Bottom line: If you're really competitive, you probably couldn't give that trait up if you tried. Which is fine. But if you keep showing up at work with a new injury, or you always manage to sprain that ankle that just won't heal, give yourself a break. Try activities, like yoga, that encourage you to check your competitive urge at the door. It's good to surrender sometimes—and it's good to do it on the floor. ✳

> You don't have to resolve your problem to resolve your accident-proneness—you just have to get the feelings out so **you're not walking around in a fog.**

Victoria Clayton is a freelance writer whose work has also appeared in Child *and the* Los Angeles Times.

When innocent habit becomes obsession

Everyone has rituals, habits, and worries. But for some people, they're more than idiosyncrasies. Compulsive behavior could be a prelude to illness.

BY ELIZABETH WRAY

On a winter morning, my 17-year-old daughter boards a flight from San Francisco to New York for a visit with her best friend. After watching the plane take off, I make my way back through the terminal, averting my eyes from newsstand displays with their bold headlines of disaster. Terminal. I wish I hadn't thought of that word. Now I can't get it out of my mind. I must defuse it, think of its opposite ... initial, initiate, awaken. I like awaken. I repeat it five times, punctuating each "awaken" with a deep breath. Back home, I return my daughter's forgotten sweater, sprawled ominously on the bedroom floor, to the safety of a drawer.

Wash, rinse, repeat:
A thorough hand-scrubbing is a good thing—but not 50 times a day.

thoughts in bed at night to address her worries. But I'm not inclined to prayer or simple superstitions. I'm obsessed with my fears and I perform rituals to calm them—the classic symptoms of obsessive-compulsive disorder (OCD).

According to the Obsessive-Compulsive Foundation, about 1 in 50 Americans—as many as 5 million—has OCD, a lifelong anxiety disorder in which a person has intrusive thoughts, or obsessions, that must be responded to with rituals, or compulsions, in an attempt to relieve the discomfort they cause. Even if you know little about this condition, you could probably recognize someone who has OCD: the woman who checks the oven 39 times before she feels safe leaving her house; the man who collects stacks of newspapers for fear of losing information; or Jack Nicholson's character in the film *As Good As It Gets*, so obsessed with hygiene that he carries plastic-wrapped utensils to restaurants—and won't eat with anything else.

Clearly, I'm anxious about flying, like many people in the country these days. But I have a hard time shaking my fearful thoughts, and I wish I could respond to them in a more reasonable way, like my friend Wendy. She steps into a plane leading with her "lucky" right foot, says a good-luck expression in Yiddish, and hopes that's enough. My mother "lifts up" good

But these are only the most extreme cases. Although 1 in 50 Americans has the full-blown condition, many more

Everyone has quirks that can border on OCD. It's one thing to need to have your house clean before you leave it, if that means 20 minutes of straightening; it's quite another if the kitchen counter alone takes two hours, and you cancel appointments to get it done.

people (estimates suggest as many as one in five) are like me. They suffer from OC-type behaviors, but not to the degree that the actions are life consuming. And they may not even know it. After all, doesn't everybody have some personal rituals and habits? What about Wendy? Or the woman who always uses the same gym locker or the same restroom stall at work? Or the man who feels compelled to alphabetize his pantry? Are these simply personality quirks, or are they something more?

"Just about everyone has habits that can be considered OCD habits," says Lee Baer, Ph.D., director of research at Massachusetts General Hospital's OCD Clinic and associate professor of psychology at Harvard Medical School. "The question is, where do you draw the line?"

The answer is far from simple. Baer and most other OCD experts use the Yale Brown Obsessive-Compulsive scale—the standard diagnostic tool in America—to determine this condition, which is defined by degree. "The best predictor," Baer says, "is just how much your obsessions and compulsions interfere with your life." It's one thing to need to have your house clean before you leave it, if that means 20 minutes of straightening; it's quite another if the kitchen counter alone takes two hours and you have to cancel appointments to get it done.

It sounds straightforward, but for people like me, it can be a hard call. My obsessions aren't as crippling as those of the woman who never leaves her house for fear of seeing a hearse or the man who makes a U-turn every time his car hits a bump to make sure he hasn't run somebody down. On the other hand, my numerous, embarrassing, secretive rituals seem like more than idiosyncrasies.

My own experience with borderline OCD dates back to my childhood, which is in itself unique since most people first notice OC-type symptoms in late adolescence or early adulthood. Whenever my parents and brother traveled by car on Oklahoma's infamously dangerous two-lane highways, I performed elaborate prayer rituals to ensure their safe arrival. As a teenager, whenever I had a "bad" thought concerning the death of someone I loved, I'd have to bolt from the room out of guilt. Since having children, parental responsibility has fueled my obsessions. Sometimes I can't wear black or red for fear it would affect the safety of my children. If I read something about death or danger in a

OCD: just the facts

Learn more about the disorder with these stats from the Obsessive-Compulsive Foundation.

• One in 50 adults currently has OCD. Twice as many have had it at some point in their lives.

• OCD can start at any time in life, but one-third to one-half of adults with the disorder report that it started during childhood.

• On average, people with OCD spend more than nine years seeking treatment before receiving a correct diagnosis.

• Approximately two-thirds of OCD patients have also suffered at least one bout of major depression at some point in their lives.

• There are a number of disorders that are possibly related to OCD, such as compulsive gambling, eating, nail-biting, and spending, as well as certain sexual behaviors.

• Some experts believe that there may be different types of OCD and that some types are inherited while others are not. The research is not definitive, but there is evidence that OCD that begins in childhood may be different from OCD that begins in adulthood: Individuals with childhood-onset OCD appear more likely to have relatives with the disorder than those whose OCD first appears in adulthood.

newspaper or book, I must find a complete sentence that's either benevolent or neutral before I can turn the page. I don't really believe that reading about death will cause someone I love to die. It's that I don't disbelieve it enough to keep me from my attempts to disarm the thought.

This thought process can grow into what Baer calls an "OCD loop" of ever-increasing obsessions and compulsions that can last for hours. Luckily, mine last only seconds or minutes—but I still feel trapped by them. A therapist friend told me that I don't need to seek help until my compulsions take up more than an hour a day. But some days, I barely slide in under the wire.

According to the Yale Brown scale, my symptoms are possibly self-treatable, but seeing a behavior therapist might help. That sounds better than years of psychoanalysis, which was the primary treatment until the 1970s, even though it proved largely ineffective. The reason: New research suggests OCD is not the result of life experience. Brain-imaging studies, such as those done by Jeffrey Schwartz, M.D., at the University of California-Los Angeles Neuropsychiatric Institute, have shown that the caudate nucleus, which works like an automatic transmission for the brain, gets stuck in gear in OCD patients. The brain is unable to shift between thoughts, which may explain the fixations.

Many people diagnosed with full-blown OCD can find relief through anticompulsive drugs, such as Anafranil, Prozac, or Zoloft, in combination with a form of behavior therapy called exposure and response prevention. In this method, a psychologist or psychiatrist guides a patient as she confronts the things she fears and helps her resist acting on any compulsions that arise. In my case, I would force myself to read the newspaper like a normal person. If I saw a frightening headline and was flooded with fears of those closest to me dying, I would resist performing a neutralizing ritual to feel better. "If you repeat this process often enough," Baer says, "you teach your body that you can feel better without the ritual. You're able to get your behavior under control, and eventually your urges and thoughts will diminish."

My symptoms don't seriously interfere with my work, home, or social life, so I'm inclined to self-treatment. That's how I discovered mindful awareness, which Schwartz recommends in his book, *Brain Lock*. With this technique, you become your own "impartial spectator" who serves as your reality check, calling intrusive thoughts what they are—obsessions and compulsions—and reminding yourself that you're having these thoughts because you have a medical condition. Then, rather than giving in to an impulsive behavior, you respond in a constructive manner. You divert your attention to therapeutic tasks, such as gardening, baking bread, or reading a book. "Mindfulness is a powerful tool for people with OC-type symptoms, as well as for those with OCD," Schwartz says. "It puts you back in control."

Most days, it works for me. When I notice my son has left for school without turning off the light in his room, I reach for the switch against the drone of my usual fears: If I turn off his light, he could die on his way home. But instead

where do you draw the line?

Diagnosing OCD involves determining how much a behavior interferes with your life. In a case of full-blown OCD, a compulsion might affect work, marriage, or friendships. For others it might be simply a personality quirk.

If you think you or someone you know might have OCD, review the list of common symptoms below, or take one of the screening tests in *Getting Control: Overcoming Your Obsessions and Compulsions* by Lee Baer, Ph.D., or *Brain Lock* by Jeffrey Schwartz, M.D. Results should be analyzed with the help of a medical professional.

Obsessions: hygiene, need for order or symmetry, superstition, fear of aggression

Compulsions: washing; checking (such as repeatedly making sure doors are locked); maintaining total order; hoarding or saving; mental rituals to make bad thoughts go away; touching, tapping, or rubbing objects

who can help
Here's where to turn if you need treatment for OCD:
- Obsessive-Compulsive Foundation
  203-315-2190, www.ocfoundation.org
- National Mental Health Association
  800-969-6642, www.nmha.org
- Obsessive-Compulsive Disorder Resource Center
  www.ocdresource.com

of leaving the light on, I tell myself, "That's your OCD talking; it's not real." I remind myself that we live in a world where it's not unusual to feel out of control. Baer says most people with OCD—borderline or full-blown—feel a heightened sense of responsibility, a need to protect the lives of others. That's not such a bad thing, if it finds a constructive outlet in the real world.

So I switch off the light and stand in the darkened room. I notice two gray sneakers, lying on their sides where they were kicked off. Don't pick them up, I say to myself. It's his job to do that. My job is to pay attention, to name my fears, and to not turn away from them. ✳

San Francisco freelancer Elizabeth Wray has also written for House Beautiful *and* Sierra.

movies to fit your mood

Movies are the newest chicken soup for the soul. Everywhere you turn, from Lifetime's "Television for Women" to WE's "Cinematherapy" series, flicks are being sold as a cheap kind of counseling. So which movies fit life's biggest moments? Here's a guide to what to watch—and what to avoid—when you need your own Hollywood ending.

Event	What flicks you should see	Why	What not to see
Getting married	*Four Weddings and a Funeral,* starring Hugh Grant and Andie MacDowell	Laughter is the best medicine for prenuptial anxiety, especially when you're laughing at Grant's romantic angst.	*Gaslight,* starring Ingrid Bergman and Charles Boyer, in which a man tries to drive his new wife crazy. No one needs more jitters at the altar.
Visiting your in-laws	*It's a Wonderful Life,* starring James Stewart and Donna Reed	This sentimental tale of a suicidal man who learns what life would be like without him reminds you that time with relatives is better than at least one alternative: death.	*Home for the Holidays,* starring Holly Hunter, delivers familial anxiety but no laughs. As if you needed more stress.
Breaking up	*Thelma and Louise,* starring Susan Sarandon and Geena Davis	This buddy film about two women escaping bad relationships (and the law) proves you don't need a man. A good road map may be another story.	*What Happened Was. . .,* starring Tom Noonan and Karen Sillas, chronicles the worst first date in history. You'll need a positive attitude when you finally start dating again, and this film won't help.
You're pregnant	*Babyfever,* starring Victoria Foyt and Frances Fisher	This low-budget flick captures a Malibu, California, baby shower where everyone is obsessed with everything about pregnancy. Forget about group therapy for expectant moms—this is it.	*Rosemary's Baby,* starring Mia Farrow and John Cassavetes. Of course, it's a safe assumption you're not carrying Satan's baby, but why even go there?
Attending your high-school reunion	*Grosse Pointe Blank,* starring John Cusack and Minnie Driver	After watching a hit man take care of business at his reunion, you probably won't take yours so seriously. You'll also learn important pitfalls to avoid, such as murder.	*Carrie,* starring Sissy Spacek and Piper Laurie, features an outcast settling the score at her prom. A particularly bad film if you're working through anger.

341

HOW REAL
Soccer Moms
do it all

These pro athletes are shining examples of the skills that make good mothers: flexibility, speed, and agility.

BY ELIZABETH KRIEGER

PHOTOGRAPHY BY MICHAEL JOHNSON

After seeing the high tension, the fast footwork, and Brandi Chastain's chiseled abs during that glorious World Cup win in 1999, it may be hard to imagine the life of a women's pro soccer player as anything similar to life in the rest of the world. Yet four of the 160-plus players in the Women's United Soccer Association (WUSA) have children. (Chastain, stepmom to 13-year-old Cameron, makes five.)

That means that, in addition to playing a world-class sport, these athletes have a round-the-clock schedule to manage, a maxed-out body to contend with, and priorities to rearrange. And as any mom knows, after feedings, burpings, homework sessions, and deciphering the 15-page car-seat manual, there's scarcely time for anything else.

Yet these women have high-visibility, high-stakes jobs, as well. They earn their livings relying on the very skills that also make for good moms: flexibility, speed, and agility. The balancing act is just what they've been practicing for as long as they've been kicking around a black-and-white ball. They put a whole new spin on the term "soccer mom" (and for the record, none of them owns a minivan). And the way these women manage their high-energy lives can be an inspiration to other women—mothers or not—who struggle each and every day to find the time and energy for the demands of life.

Help is not a four-letter word

At their core, these athletes are about getting the job done, whatever that job might be—teaching a 4-year-old to tie his shoes, maybe, or stealing a pass from an opponent. Key to their success, though, is a strong support network of husbands, family, teammates, and unusually supportive employers.

A couple of the women—Joy Fawcett, 34, and Carla Overbeck, 33—rely on their husbands, whose flexible work schedules allow them to share in caring for the

These women put a whole new spin on the term "soccer mom." And the way they **manage high-energy** lives **can be an inspiration** to other women, mothers or not, who struggle to find time and energy for the demands of everyday life.

that just happens to be a pro sport," says Lauren Gregg, WUSA's vice president of player personnel and technical director.

For two of the soccer moms, distance is a complicating factor. Fotopoulos, 26, and Keri Raygor, 29, mother of 2-year-old Bryce, both live miles away from their husbands. While Raygor suits up for the Boston Breakers, her husband, Brian, works for an oil company in Eugene, Oregon. (In off-months, she's the assistant women's soccer coach at the University of Oregon in Eugene.) Fotopoulos spends the season in North Carolina playing for the Carolina Courage, while her husband, George, holds down the fort in Baton Rouge, Louisiana, as the women's soccer coach at Louisiana State University. Being away from each other can be hard. "Sometimes we do feel like single parents, yes," Raygor admits, "but I have a ton of help, especially from my mom."

kids. Fawcett's husband, Walter, is able to tailor his computer job to meet the needs of the couples' three kids: Madilyn Rae, 8 months; Carli, 4; and Katelyn Rose, 7.

Overbeck credits husband, Greg, in part for her return to the field with the U.S. National team a mere two months after the birth of their son, Jackson, who's now 4. "My husband is an incredible support in every way. In fact, he does all of the family cooking!" says Overbeck. (Greg is a restaurateur in the Raleigh, North Carolina, area.)

Teammates are equally ready to lend a hand. "They are always offering themselves up," says Overbeck, who likens her fellow Carolina Courage players to a group of loving "aunties." "If we are going to the movies and I have Jackson with me, one of them will take him to a G-rated movie so we can see the grown-up one."

Danielle Fotopoulos, whose daughter, Alexia, is 16 months old, says her teammates treat her baby as if she were their own. "Except they get to sleep through the night," she jokes.

Help also takes the form of traditional child care, paid for by the WUSA during practice and while teams are traveling to games. "It's all part of helping these women have a family and a career

In the 1996 Olympics Carla Overback helped her team win a gold medal. Today, the mom to 4-year-old Jackson is a Carolina Courage defender.

The kids take cues, too, from their moms' healthy attitudes about food. In the Overbeck household, for instance, pasta, lean meats, and lots of fresh vegetables are on the menu—and little Jackson eats it all. "He even likes asparagus," she says. Fawcett jokes that her three kids know that she doesn't tolerate special meal requests. "They eat whatever I serve them," she says. "They learn that pretty fast!"

Fotopoulos makes sure to keep an eye on her daughter's sugar intake, but fortunately some of her mom's nutritious choices have already rubbed off on the 16-month-old: Two of Alexia's favorite foods are carrots and peas. "If I can teach Alexia good eating habits early, my hope is that it will affect our entire family's nutritional goals," she says.

A fit pregnancy, a quick comeback

The majority of women don't have jobs that require them to worry about 50-yard dashes while pregnant. But watching these athletes take the field so quickly after they have their babies is a real-life testimony to the power of staying active and fit throughout the entire nine months.

"You have to listen to your body," Fawcett says. It's important to know your limits, she says, but to realize that you can stay in shape while you're pregnant—which will make it all the easier to get back to your prepregnancy fitness level. With her doctor's OK, Fawcett worked out with weights until the end of her pregnancy, and it was only in her seventh month that she stopped running sprints. She did miss the camaraderie of team workouts, though. "After a certain point in my pregnancy I couldn't scrimmage anymore, and I had to work out by myself," she says.

Fawcett admits that after her third baby it was harder to find time to exercise, but she remained committed to her goals. A day after she gave birth, she was already on the floor working on her abs; five days later she started kicking the ball around again. Just over a month later she was back in the game, scoring a goal in her second match out.

The Goal: healthy kids, healthy families

The flexible policies of the WUSA encourage keeping the kids close, which offers benefits beyond parent-child bonding. The soccer kids are always welcome to go on the road with their moms or to just hang out on the sidelines during practice. Fotopoulos says that having Alexia on the sidelines is energizing. "I am playing for her, for my whole family," she says. "Without them, I wouldn't be playing."

Soccer has given Overbeck's son a truly global education. "Jackson has been everywhere—to Portugal, Scandinavia, and all over Europe and America," she says. "Sometimes we joke around that the poor kid goes to sleep in one place and wakes up miles and miles away. But he loves it, and it's great for both of us to be together. I think the experience has made him a mellow, adaptable, low-maintenance kid."

His exposure to Overbeck's work life has also provided Jackson with many positive female role models. "Oh, I think my son will be in touch with his feminine side, for sure," she jokes. "And that's a good thing."

Watching these athletes take the field so quickly after they give birth is **a real-life testimony to the power of staying active and fit** throughout the entire nine months.

The women also say their families' active lifestyles help keep them in top form. "I'm lucky. Sports and my family are totally intertwined," says Fawcett, who often kicks the ball around with her kids and husband. Raygor and her husband encourage their son's budding athleticism as well, but say they won't press him to follow in Mommy's cleats.

On most days, the players attend a two-hour practice in the morning, often followed by a weight-lifting session and perhaps a yoga class to help build flexibility. Off-season or on their own, they're experts at squeezing in exercise whenever they can. With the help of well-worn jogging strollers, babysitters, and even some backyard creativity, Fawcett makes whatever free time she has count. "I have to be flexible. If I've planned to go work out in the morning but somehow it just isn't going to happen, I'll fall back on a plan B," she says. "Maybe I'll take the baby with me or maybe I will just do a little skills workout at home. It's simply a real

LONG-DISTANCE CHALLENGE: During the season, Boston Breakers defender Keri Raygor lives in Boston with her son, 2-year-old Bryce, while her husband, Brian, works in Oregon. In off-months, she returns home to coach at the University of Oregon.

priority." While her children nap, Fawcett gets in a few strengthening exercises. To build up speed, she sprints from driveway to driveway in her neighborhood.

Although workouts are a way of life for these women, the players say the "exercise" they do off the field is also a way to decompress. "I use the time to think things through," Raygor says. Practice sessions are usually over by 2 p.m., which gives the moms most of the afternoon to play outside with the kids, run errands, and do other "mom stuff," Overbeck says. She uses the afternoon free time to take Jackson to swimming lessons and play dates with other kids.

Making "me" time

"You have to take time for yourself so you will feel like playing," says Raygor, who uses Bryce's nap time to squeeze in phone calls, answer e-mail, or catch up on her reading.

"After Jackson goes to sleep is my time," Overbeck says. "That's when I can curl up in bed and read a good book." Fotopoulos indulges in massages a few days a week and, if she's got a whole afternoon, goes to a baseball game.

The women also make sure to carve out adults-only time with their husbands to keep their marriages healthy. Raygor and Fotopoulos, who live in separate cities from their husbands, realize it's even more important that they schedule couple time, in addition to e-mailing and calling each other regularly. Some of the players make work-related travel a family affair by having kids and husbands join them on the road.

A new look at the game of life

The athletes have found that their kids put their careers in perspective. "Say I lose a game or have a bad practice and I'm in a terrible mood," Overbeck says. "Jackson will still come running up to me all excited, wanting a big hug. It will instantly make me realize that there are larger things in life. Being a mom is one of those."

Despite the demands motherhood and work place on her time, Fotopoulos says she wouldn't have it any other way: "As long as I keep my priorities in line, there's no downside."

And while it can get harder to manage the logistics with three kids, Fawcett firmly believes that she can have it all. Raygor agrees. The key, she says, is to stay calm and be flexible. "Try not to get so caught up in the details," she advises. "Don't forget to simply take the time to just play." ✳

Elizabeth Krieger is a freelance writer in San Francisco.

Learning from Lockerbie

*While the United States recovers from 9/11,
a Scottish town offers a comforting portrait of how
communities heal. Its past is our future.*

BY MELISSA CHESSHER

As the five students from Lockerbie, Scotland, filed into the office of New Jersey high-school principal Bert Ammerman, their eyes moved from one familiar framed photograph to another: a long view of their hometown's high street, a shot of Queen Elizabeth's comforting visit, the infamous image of a jumbo jet's nose lying, shattered, in a field. Ammerman, who lost his brother when a bomb obliterated Pan Am flight 103 over Lockerbie on December 21, 1988, started to speak softly of how kind their Scottish town was after the disaster, how quiet and respectful the residents were when he walked up the main street the first time he traveled there. "We were all crying. It was so upsetting," says Fiona Pringle, one of the Lockerbie students. "He just kept saying how important it was that something good would come out of something so evil."

Pringle and the other teenagers, part of a student-exchange program started by Ammerman, were at the Northern Valley Regional High School in Demarest because of a connection they share to two of history's most horrific terrorist attacks. After visiting in Ammerman's office, the students and the principal made their way across the East River to Ground Zero, the emotional touchstone for the events of September 11, 2001, when planes flown by terrorists crashed into the World Trade Center towers, the Pentagon, and a field outside Pittsburgh, killing more than 3,000. The five Scots carried laminated cards that read "from Lockerbie to New York" and juxtaposed the Pan Am flight wreckage with New York's twin towers. When they arrived at Ground Zero, though, the discovery of a policeman's body halted their tour, making it impossible to place a memorial plaque on the site. Instead, they presented a book of condolence to city officials in a formal ceremony.

The students' presence at Ground Zero that day points to their town's unique strength: Lockardians wrote the book on wringing every ounce of good from the devastation a terrorist act wreaks. Similarities between Lockerbie's experience and 9/11 are striking: a mass murder committed with planes, emergency workers who found few to save, an extraordinary display of human kindness born out of loss and disaster. The majority of the victims of Pan Am 103 were Americans; it remains the worst mass murder in British history and until September 2001 the deadliest terror attack ever on U.S. civilians. After 9/11, the world press focused on the families who lost one or both parents; after the Pan Am disaster, it was the children—400 parents lost a child, and 46 parents lost their only child.

But before 1988, Lockerbie was as striking in its obscurity as New York is in its international celebrity. One headline from a British paper on the day after the disaster screamed, "Nothing ever happens here." This is a place where women chat about how much ironing they need to do, doctors make house calls, and there's still a milkman who delivers glass bottles before sunrise. Despite the town's

> *Lockerbie's townspeople wrote the book on how to wring every ounce of good out of the devastation that a terrorist act brings.*

size and stoic Scottish disposition, they did—and continue to do—miraculous things to heal themselves and those touched by the air disaster. In fact, Lockerbie offers a comforting template for how a place can heal, providing ideas on how individuals can change a community—any community. The people of Lockerbie have had nearly 14 years to recover, while those affected by 9/11 still have a long way to go. In a very real sense, then, this Scottish town's past is America's future.

The first year:
Do Something

Many in the small village are thankful that darkness cloaked the events of that December night. After exploding, the fuselage and wings loaded with fuel slammed into a residential area, creating a huge crater, destroying houses, and killing 11 people on the ground in addition to all 259 passengers. Witnesses say the neighborhood looked like a war zone as jet fuel rained from the sky in fat globs, spreading fire from tree to tree, car to car, home to home. The flames' orange-red glow soon was tinged with blue from flashing emergency lights as the town's 3,500 population swelled to 10,000 with the arrival of medical crews, police, and the media. About 2,500 search-and-rescue workers scoured 845 square miles of wreckage area, gleaning debris, plane parts, and personal items like Christmas presents, wine bottles, children's toys.

"The Christmas trees disappeared across town overnight," recalls Drew Young, a retired Lockerbie police officer and Boy Scout leader who was walking home from a Scout meeting when he heard the scream of the jet. The disaster shut down Christmas and stole the joy of that season for years to come. Scouts who were delivering Christmas cards as part of an annual fund-raiser switched to delivering messages for emergency workers.

"In a town of 3,500, there were 1,400 volunteers," says Marjory McQueen, a Lockerbie town councillor who says September 11 brought back the emotions of that time in Lockerbie's history. Eight members of her family were in America last year during the attacks, two of them in New York. "When I finally reached my daughter, we talked about how similar it was—the helicopters flying over, the sirens, the chaos," she says. After the air disaster in Lockerbie, McQueen volunteered for the local district attorney, helping with documentation of all the victims. "At that time you needed something to do, and everybody wanted something to do," she says.

In the immediate aftermath, Lockerbie residents—like those in New York—did whatever they could. Young's wife, Annette, cooked for the police officers who were guarding bodies, plane parts, destroyed houses; she took in their laundry, always managing to sneak some chocolates or treats into their finished bags. Elsewhere, farmers' wives made daily trips to town, their trunks filled with cakes, biscuits, and scones. Others organized recreational outings for kids in the most devastated areas. "In the case of Lockerbie and New York City, people's minds were shattered. There was no way to understand or resolve the situation with thought," says John E. Welshons, counselor and author of *Awakening From Grief: Finding the Road Back to Joy.* "So people just naturally fell back on their instincts to love, to help, to serve, to reach out and make a connection with other grieving hearts. When the pain is shared with the community, immediately we feel connected, and that is the beginning of the path to healing."

For Moira Shearer, volunteering to wash victims' clothes was her way to express her gratitude that her family survived. (Shearer's sister-in-law barely escaped with her tiny dog in her arms when a fireman yanked her out of the kitchen door as her house fell down around her.) "The children's clothes—that was the hard part. I can still cry," Shearer says. "Every day we were given a box, and we never knew what would be inside. There was aviation fuel and quite a lot of things on the clothes. Some things would be all torn up and some things would be perfect." Shearer and other women worked in groups of two in shifts; she began work on the first day of March and continued until the last day of June.

Out of that first impulse—the desire to get busy doing something to help—came a metaphor for Lockerbie's big heart: The cleaned-and-pressed clothes were boxed with tissue paper, and a sprig of Scottish heather was placed on top. Police officers from Lockerbie then hand-delivered every box to relatives in America.

After the first year:
Make Connections

Lockerbie continues suffering aftereffects. Like many residents, Shearer is still unnerved by aircraft; last year at an air show, the sonic boom of jets breaking the sound barrier scared her so badly she screamed. Others say they need to watch planes until they pass from view to ensure they're safely beyond Lockerbie. Every anniversary, every trial date, every related news item brings reporters back to question residents and force them to relive the terrible events. James Hill, M.D., one of Lockerbie's four full-time physicians, says the Pan Am crash had a significant effect on the community's overall health for some time afterward. "There are probably a handful of people whose health has never really gotten back to normal as a direct result of what was experienced in the aftermath," he says.

Still, the pain has been dissipated by deep connections Lockardians have found with victims' relatives. When they began arriving, locals could tell who they were and closed ranks around them to shield them from probing reporters. They created the Friendship Group to greet and assist the families, most of whom were American, making endless cups of tea and opening their homes for a chat or a few nights' stay. "They didn't have cars and they didn't know how to drive on the wrong side of the road and they didn't know about the town, so we all volunteered to pick them up and house them and take them somewhere else just to give them a break," Shearer says. Remembering the first American relative she met, she says, "The first thing I said was 'sorry' and I just burst into tears. Then I had to take her to where her husband was."

The friendship group no longer officially exists; there's no need for it. True friendship replaced the organization, and those who return to Lockerbie for annual pilgrimages just call their friends and know they'll be taken in to share a cup of tea. Other organizations, such as Ammerman's student exchange, continue to link Lockerbie and those who suffered losses in America. In 2003, students from several high schools in New Jersey will visit Scotland for two weeks. Syracuse University, which lost 35 students in the Pan Am disaster, also established a student exchange, which brings two of Lockerbie's graduating seniors to the upstate New York school each year. Syracuse also offers 35 scholarships annually, each named for a lost student. Recipients wear a ribbon to commemorate the loss and speak in their classes about their awards' namesakes to remind others of the lives that were lost. According to Thomas Lynch, a funeral director and author of *Bodies in Motion and at Rest* and *The Undertaking* it is this active remembering—bonding through tragedy—that is critical to healing. "When we share grief," he says, "it seems to diminish the burden of it."

June Wilson understands that sharing process as well as anyone. From the moment the nose cone landed across from her home and 119 bodies fell on her family farm, she began to tend to emergency workers and welcome those who showed up on her doorstep looking for the last resting place of their loved ones. "If it was a cold day, we would invite them in for coffee," she says. "We learned quickly that if grieving relatives came and had a talk, then they went away happier." Her involvement went beyond just short-term help. Beside Lockerbie's tiny Presbyterian church at Tundergarth, the gravedigger's cottage was transformed into the Remembrance Room. Almost like a small chapel, the building houses a visitors' book, a collection of profiles of all of those lost, a few chairs, and a commemorative plaque. At the dedication in 1990, guests walked the half-mile from the church to the Wilson farm, where everyone gathered for coffee. One woman asked for a daffodil bulb from the dozens of yellow flowers lining the stone fences, garden, and footpaths around the Wilsons' home. The farmer's wife ended up sending all the guests bulbs via diplomatic bags (she couldn't send vegetation through customs).

Wilson keeps a book of photos from all the families who came to her farm in search of victims' resting places and left as friends. The pages are filled, so she's had to start stuffing the back with the latest, including a photo of an entire family in American-flag sweaters in a post–September 11 tribute. Her "American friends" invite her to weddings and holiday celebrations, send photos of new babies, and remember her with flowers and fruit baskets on special occasions. With the Wilson family's permission, a woman who lost a son built a cairn—a Scottish memorial made of stone—to commemorate him on a hill on her farm. Wilson respects that cairn and the grief it represents; although trespassing is a foreign concept to the Scottish, who allow walkers right-of-passage on private property, she would never divulge that cairn's whereabouts to a curious walker without asking the mother's permission first.

Lockerbie has greeted each anniversary with the solemnity typical of its reserved manner. At the first, after a quiet church service, the townspeople simply gathered in front of the town hall, observing two minutes of silence as the clock struck the moment of the crash. For the 10th, the town maintained its plea for peace and quiet and a chance to mark the occasion as each individual saw fit. Town councillor McQueen says the anniversary was a communal one. "What I had to tell those people is it's not just our 10th anniversary. We share it with people all over the world who see this as the place where they lost their loved ones. And we did not have the opportunity to retreat within ourselves and put up the barriers and say nothing's happening." They organized a wreath-laying ceremony, a church service, and a two-minute moment of silence. Afterward, there was tea at the town hall so people could talk, something a small town is adept at doing. The town also reclaimed a small dose of Christmas cheer: For the first time, they put up Christmas lights, a subtle symbol of Lockerbie's willingness to put away the gloom and celebrate again.

Into the future:
Remember Always

Many who come to Lockerbie wrongly assume the statue of an angel at the main roundabout in town honors those lost in the air disaster (it commemorates World War II dead). But if visitors gaze just above the angel, they can see a huge window in the front of the town hall that weaves stained-glass re-creations of flags from countries that lost citizens in the terrorist attack. There are other memorials to victims, too: a bench on a hill of the golf course, a garden where the wings and fuselage landed, another plaque in another residential area, the Remembrance Room at the church across from where the nose cone landed, and the principal site at the main cemetery—a memorial garden with a large piece of stone listing all those who were lost. "Names and dates proclaim not only that we are mortal, but that we are vital," Lynch says. "I was at Ground Zero yesterday and found more compelling than the sight of the wreckage, the long list of the names of the dead. It restores humanity to this horrible event and in doing so makes it more real and more memorable."

In New York, the city marked its first anniversary with the same dignity and solemnity that it did during the six-month anniversary and at the service that marked the end of the recovery effort at Ground Zero. For those occasions the city sought to limit any political overtures and directed attention to the victims, their families, and the resurgence and recovery of New York City itself. When the last tower beam was removed at Ground Zero, workers carried an empty stretcher off the sight, houses of worship across the city rang bells, and the forlorn wail of bagpipes served as a backdrop to the ceremony.

In Lockerbie, McQueen occasionally provides a tour of the town to groups of American college students studying abroad for the program that lost 35 Syracuse University students. She includes a stop at the remembrance garden where all the names are listed. "I don't believe anyone could approach that stone without feeling something. I have been hundreds of times, but every time I see it, it just

comes back. It's covered in black writing," she says. "These lives should be continuing now."

Similar to "Portraits of Grief," the *New York Times'* series of obituaries of the September 11 victims, a book in the Tundergarth memorial room offers profiles of those who died in the air disaster. An American mother who lost a son on the flight created the book by interviewing victims' families and writing passages about each person. A visitors' book also sits on a pedestal in a corner. An entry from December of 2001 reads: "December 21st changed the world for us. September 11, 2001, changed the world for everyone else."

Like the high-school exchange students who visited Bert Ammerman's New Jersey office, Lockerbie resident Ted Hills' journey took him to Ground Zero. A high-school teacher and bagpipes-band member, he came to New York City in spring 2002 to play with other pipe bands in a march for a cancer-relief charity. "I may not have gone if I didn't have the link because it wouldn't seem right," he says. "But you could see Lockerbie multiplied by a hundred times." He also made another pilgrimage—to the memorial cairn in Arlington National Cemetery that commemorates the victims of Pam Am 103. His mission was simple: He wanted to go there in full dress and play his bagpipe.

But, as often happens with road trips of the heart, the unexpected transpired: He and his wife arrived at the moment the Scottish Parliament had scheduled a wreath-laying service there. No piper was planned, so Hills was invited to play for the ceremony, which was attended by two sets of parents who'd lost children in the disaster. When the dignitaries departed, Hills spoke with one of the couples whose daughter is buried at the Dryfesdale Cemetery in Lockerbie. He then played a series of songs for them: "Highland Cathedral," "Scotland the Brave," "My Home," "Amazing Grace," "Flower of Scotland." Like many in Lockerbie who have offered to do something for a grieving stranger, Hills promised that when he returned home, he would play at the cemetery for their daughter. His wife said she would take flowers, and the mother had one request: "Take just one daisy," she said. "Our daughter loved daisies."

In June 2002, during the gala celebrating Lockerbie's history, Hills played his bagpipe in a Scottish cemetery on the hill where an American daughter is buried, a single wild daisy lying on her grave. ✳

Melissa Chessher, an associate professor at Syracuse University, is writing a book about Lockerbie.

Vital**Stats**

65 | Percent of prescription antihistamine users in a study who didn't even have allergies

85 | Percent who feel that their abilities to drive and care for children are not affected by taking these medications

70 | Percent who report that they experience side effects, such as fatigue and drowsiness, from taking these medications

3 | Percent of female TV network characters who are obese

25 | Percent of American women who are obese

32 | Percent of female TV network characters who are underweight

5 | Percent of American women who are underweight

137 | Average weight most American women think they should be

153 | Actual weight of the average American woman

177 | Average weight most American men think they should be

189 | Actual weight of the average American man

3.2 | Number of drinks it takes for the average American to wake up the next morning with a hangover

7 | Percent of American workers who have reported calling in sick because of a hangover

Sources: NAASO; Alka-Seltzer; The Gallup Organization; Newsstream

Women Approach Leadership with Their Own Style

THINK WOMEN are less assertive than men when it comes to getting ahead at work? Think again. Women are born to lead just like men—they just go about it differently. Understanding those differences could earn you a higher spot on the corporate ladder.

"Men tend to dominate, whereas women gather their power slowly and carefully," says Marianne Schmid Mast, Ph.D., a psychologist and researcher at Northeastern University in Boston. In videotapes comparing the way men and women interacted with their same-sex peers, men were all too eager to jump in and hog the conversation. Women held off for eight minutes before some cut in and spoke up. "Women may feel more comfortable forming hierarchies after getting to know new people," Mast explains.

Compared with their male counterparts, women leaders gather power more slowly and carefully.

Women's wait-and-see approach to throwing their weight around can be a powerful business tool, says Marian Baker, an executive coach and owner of True Spirit Coaching in Chicago (www.marianbaker.com). "Women may have an easier time creating personal relationships, and that helps them tune in to others' goals and values," she says. For example, knowing what keeps your boss awake at night is the first step to solving problems—and getting promoted. And by getting to know her subordinates, a female exec can keep her employees happy by assigning them tasks that match their talents and interests.

Still, sometimes a powerful opening move is your best bet in business, and women who play too nice in the first round may find their opportunities usurped by others. Women are often slower to ask for what they want—whether it's a deal or a raise—and that can create internal frustration at work. Baker offers this tip for getting in touch with your innate confidence: Assign power to a color or a piece of jewelry and wear it on days you need to assert yourself. But no talisman will take the place of eagle eyes. Seeing clearly how people wield power will help you pick out your own path to success.

chapter 8

relationships
and sex

secrets of happiness

Is There a Right Age for Marriage?

Older is better, experts claim. But these five pairs prove that a good marriage can happen at any age.

BY MELISSA SPERL

PHOTOGRAPHY BY NEAL BROWN

Every couple looks for signs that their marriage will work, that they will be among the 50 percent who stay together—or better yet, that they will actually be happy. A major predictor of whether a couple reaches their golden anniversary or divorce court is the age of the bride and groom—and with good reason. Statistically, the older a woman is when she says "I do," the longer that marriage is likely to last. That's probably due—no surprise—to the relative immaturity and inexperience of younger newlyweds, says family therapist Terrence Real, author of the self-help guide *How Can I Get Through to You?*

But that's what the numbers say—and then there's real life. The truth is, marriage at any age has its challenges. Sure, couples who marry straight out of college (or younger) may be sacrificing exploration and experimentation for a measure of stability. The mid-20s might be a more idyllic time to marry, Real says, with careers on track and big dreams to realize—but these couples could be pushing themselves into marriage because "it's just time." And a 30s-or-older bride, while presumably more mature and self-aware, may feel immediate pressure from her biological clock and miss out on getting to know her partner—or be so set in her ways that adding a spouse to her already-established life makes for a tough transition.

"Every age has its pluses and minuses," Real says. "Success is about how a couple manages their assets and liabilities." And, we might add, how hard a couple works at their marriage.

We talked to five couples who prove our point—that any age can be the right age for marriage. Each of them is celebrating their recent triumph over the seven-year itch (which, by the way, is real—studies show that a natural decline in marital happiness happens after seven years). They've lived through some of the classic pressures and problems that come with getting married at the ages they did. And they all sing the praises of their unions while sharing a realistic view of the pitfalls—and insight into the secrets of their success.

The Kids
Kristi & Louis Tallone

Kristi, 26, financial adviser
Louis, 33, landscape manager
Burlington, New Jersey

Kristi was 18 when she married Louis in 1994, after four years of dating. "I was young, but we knew we wanted to get married," she says. "We thought, if we're going to live together, we might as well just do it."

On having kids: The Tallones planned on waiting five years but changed their minds two and a half years into their marriage, when Louis saw 30 approaching. "My dad had me when he was 29," he says. "I wanted to be a young dad, too." So, while her friends were out at clubs, 21-year-old Kristi was home child-rearing (son Louis William is now 4 and daughter Macee is 1). "At the time, I did miss going out and having fun," she says. "But that's just the way it was."

On major hurdles: "Money is the biggest issue," Kristi says. "We were young and we had a lot to learn. A lot of the improvements we made in the communication area came from gaining maturity. The rest came from getting to know each other and respecting each other."

On no regrets: "A lot of my friends are just getting started now, trying so hard to get what I already have," Kristi says. "When I'm in my 30s, Louis and I will have time to enjoy each other."

The Negotiating Artists
Kristen & Andrew Zohn

Kristen, 31, museum curator
Andrew, 32, classical guitarist
Columbus, Georgia

"My parents knew from our first date that this was going to work out," Kristen says. Not everyone was as supportive when the pair started dating, though. "I went to a women's college and was a blazing feminist. Some of my professors wanted me to be a scholar, not get an 'MRS. degree,' " she says. But four years later, at age 24, Kristen got married *and* got her graduate degree in art history, Andrew received his doctorate in music, and both began to pursue the careers that they love.

On having kids (or not): Kristen's mom playfully prods that it's time, but the Zohns are in no rush. "We're having too much fun traveling," she says. Andrew gives 35 to 50 concerts a year in the United States, Canada, and Italy—all hot spots for art, so Kristen tags along.

On major hurdles: Despite their shared love of the arts, Kristen says, "It's amazing how much we don't have in common." But they resolved never to argue, only to discuss—and since neither is a "screamer," they have succeeded. Their biggest difference? Andrew is a saver, his wife a spender. "I don't generally spend more than we have," she says. "But I don't think about saving."

Wise words: Andrew's favorite advice came from one of the two ministers who married them. "There are three people in the relationship," the minister said. "The man, the woman, and the marriage—and couples should put in equal amounts of work on all three." That, for the Zohns, means compromise.

"There are three people in the relationship," a minister told the Zohns. *"The man, the woman, and the marriage—and couples should put in equal amounts of work on all three."*

The Partners-in-Life
Eva & Greg Sandifer

Eva, 32, and Greg, 33,
co-owners of a trucking company
and real-estate properties
Snellville, Georgia

This couple has some history. "We were friends in high school and lost touch for a while but then we met up again. It all started happening from there," Eva says. Both were 25 when they tied the knot, they felt their timing was perfect. "We knew we wanted to be with each other, and we were settled," Greg says.

On building a family—and a business: Their son, Justin, now 6 years old, was born almost exactly a year after their wedding, and at about the same time, the Sandifers started a small trucking company. Both ventures have expanded: They now have a daughter, 1-year-old Trinity; their trucking company has taken off; and they've added a burgeoning real-estate business to their projects. "We both always had a passion for trying something new," Eva says. "And it's ended up really contributing to our marriage."

On major hurdles: They are busy—very busy. Greg is on the road three to four nights a week making deliveries, and Eva works from home, which allows her to be with the kids. And for them, it works. But when problems crop up, the couple relies on their shared Christian faith. "We try to agree on it, ponder on it," Eva says. "We want to come through it together." When their trucking business hit hard times, for example, they depended on prayer to see them through.

On balance: Since the week is all business, weekends are for family activities, such as taking the kids to the park or going to the movies. "That provides a balance that we love," Greg says.

The Team Players
Mary & Bob Kuzmeski

Mary, 38, physician's assistant
Bob, 37, athletic trainer
Hadley, Massachusetts

Bob spent his 20s building his career while Mary was busy doing her own thing—traveling, going out, having fun. But when they met at ages 27 and 28, "we were at a point when our interests were alike," Bob says. They were engaged after dating for a year and a half.

On having kids: Mary and Bob wanted to start a family fairly quickly, but gave themselves two years of one-on-one before one-two-three: Kathleen is now 4 years old, John is 3, and Kevin is 2. "We knew it wouldn't be easy, but it was what we wanted, so we made it fun," Mary says.

On major hurdles: "Communication was a challenge," Mary says. "We worked very hard in the beginning." But ironing out the kinks was a priority—and still is. "We're still getting to know each other's limits and personalities," Mary says. If Bob has a bad day, Mary has learned to step in and take up the slack for him without Bob having to say anything—and he does the same for her.

On partnership: Because of their commitment to teamwork, they say, their marriage gets better every year. "We just don't let issues become issues, and we always make sure to touch base," Mary says. "It took a long time to figure that out, but it was well worth it."

"We just don't let issues become issues, and we always make sure to touch base," Mary Kuzmeski says. "It took a long time to figure that out, but it was well worth it."

success at any age
tips to make your marriage work

One of the keys to marital bliss is separating fantasy from reality. "We're taught that a good marriage is a relatively perfect one," says family therapist Terrence Real. "But in fact, a good marriage is one that has difficulties in it, and the couple manages it." Here are some of his real-life tips for marriage management.

Don't rush parenthood. If you have any time to spare, it's best to be just the two of you for a while before starting a family. No matter how mature and in tune with each other you are, moving directly from early romance to family life leaves out an important developmental stage of bonding as a couple.

Focus on flexibility. Being set in your ways makes marriage harder at first for couples of any age, but especially if you're older when you tie the knot. Rather than hoping rough edges will smooth out on their own, take on the task of blending your separate lives into a new communal life together.

Expect him—and your relationship—to change. As people age and grow, their relationship has to transform along with them. Some lucky couples grow at the same rate and in the same direction. But if that's not your situation, try to accommodate or at least accept the differences in your partner.

The Late Bloomers
Robbin & Eddie Terault

Robbin, 44, newspaper advertising woman
Eddie, 37, cleaning-business owner
Greenfield, Massachusetts

When they took their vows at ages 37 and 30, Robbin and Eddie had dated for seven years and lived together for three. "We met through a mutual friend, one of his roommates," Robbin says. "I would go over to their place and chat, and he asked his roommate about me. It sort of blossomed from there."

On having kids–or wanting to: Robbin gave Eddie a push because her "biological clock was about ready to blow up," as she puts it. "I said, 'Ed, do you want children?' He said yes. I said, 'Do you want them with me?' He said yes. I said, 'Well, we better get married!'" A few months later, Eddie proposed.

On hurry-up-and-wait: Despite the time ticking by, the Teraults took things slowly: They were engaged for a year and a half, with a big wedding in the works, but decided to skip the formality and eloped to Nantucket. Then they let their marriage settle in for a year, making sure they were financially comfortable before having their son, Evan, now 5 years old. Both say they would love to have had more children, if they'd been ready when Robbin was younger.

On major hurdles: Despite the fact that Eddie is seven years younger than Robbin, age has never been an issue. What has caused friction is meshing their parenting decisions. They're learning to check in with each other about what they allow Evan to do or how to punish him. "We have to agree with each other's decisions and back each other up," Robbin says.

On picking your battles: The Teraults may disagree, but they rarely fight. "We let little things go, love each other for the way we are, and accept what we can't change," Robbin says. "When you have a match, you have a match." ✳

Freelancer Melissa Sperl has written for Travel Holiday *and* WeightWatchers.

GETTING MARRIED?
Go online for premarital legal advice

Get expert advice from Auntie Nolo, the Ann Landers of marital law, at www.nolo.com. Click on "Marriage & Living Together" for state-specific marriage requirements, advice on prenups, and details about changing your name (if you so choose). The site also outlines in plain English what the law says about parenting and property rights for unmarried couples.

alcohol-free DATING:
it's all about image

The waiter approaches your table. You and your date are about to order pizza. Dare you ask for a beer? Probably not, according to a study in the journal *Addictive Behavior*. The Southern Illinois University researchers found that given the choice of pineapple juice, tonic water, beer, and diet cola, women avoided beer, not because of taste or alcohol concerns, but because they thought it might make a bad impression. We say if you want a drink, have it (and let him drive).

pick a guy who likes your flavor

Forget schmoozing at the bar. The ice-cream counter may be the best place for you to scout out dates. Wondering if the guy ahead of you in line would make a good match? His flavor preference could be a sign of your compatibility. If only all of life's questions lay in a scoop.

You Like	Your Personality	Your Match Likes
strawberry	thoughtful, logical, loyal, shy	vanilla, rocky road, mint chocolate chip
mint chocolate chip	ambitious, confident, skeptical	mint chocolate chip
coffee	lively, dramatic, flirtatious	strawberry
rocky road	charming, aggressive, enjoy being catered to	rocky road
vanilla	colorful, risk-taker, idealistic	rocky road
butter pecan	devoted, conscientious, respectful	mint chocolate chip

—from research conducted for Dreyer's by the Smell & Taste Treatment and Research Foundation

Debunking Marriage Myths

Getting hitched doesn't mean you have to trade in your slinky lingerie for flannel pajamas. To help you get a clearer picture of wedded life, the National Marriage Project at Rutgers University, a clearinghouse for information on marriage, offers a reality check to counter the following commonly held marriage myths.

myth: Once you exchange vows, you rarely exchange bodily fluids.
reality: Married couples make love more often than singles—and they say the sex is better (and it doesn't matter what you look like in the morning).

myth: No one wants to marry the class brain.
reality: Today's college grads are more likely to say "I do" than their non-collegiate peers.

myth: A good marriage depends on romance and destiny.
reality: The happiest couples credit commitment and companionship—not hot romance—as keys to success.

myth: A baby is a bundle of joy that brings couples closer together.
reality: Despite slightly lower divorce rates, couples with kids don't rate higher on the happiness scale than spouses without. And the added stress sometimes pushes couples apart.

myth: Living together is the same as "getting married minus the piece of paper."
reality: Married mates live longer and healthier lives than folks who just shack up. Studies show that couples who cohabitate without rings are more focused on themselves than on the well-being of their partners.

READY, SET, DATE!

HAVEN'T FLEXED your romance muscles lately? Relationship coach and therapist Nina Atwood takes us through the moves to get the most out of dating. "You know you're ready to date when you're confident that you can handle whatever happens," says Atwood, author of *Be Your Own Dating Service* and *Date Lines.* Visit her online at www.singlescoach.com for more tips on how to leap over your love hurdles.

Q: Is there a best way to flirt?

A: Flirting is letting a man know that you welcome his attention and you find him attractive. If that's your intention, the best way is to be natural. Happy, healthy people attract other happy, healthy people. Don't contrive to be someone you're not.

Q: Should women set out with a relationship goal in mind?

A: I always encourage women to be very honest with men right up front about what they want—whether it's dating, marriage, or children. For instance, you might say: "We're in this to see if we have what it takes to have a lifelong relationship. If you feel at any point that that's no longer a possibility, don't spare my feelings—tell me right away." A woman has more leverage in the beginning, so that's the time to create those agreements.

Q: How can you tell if a man is interested?

A: In a nutshell, if he showers you with attention. Someone who wants to be with you shows it by creating opportunities to connect. That doesn't necessarily mean he's emotionally available or wants a commitment, though.

Q: How do you tell the difference between interest and a real desire to commit?

A: The truth is, a man can behave very romantically with a woman and still not give her his heart. You'd be surprised how many women miss the basics: He's married, has a current addiction, or holds on to bitterness, anger, regrets, or longing for a past relationship. A man who truly wants to commit makes himself available. He doesn't put arbitrary rules on things like when you may call him. He lets you into his home and his life, for example, by introducing you to his friends and family.

Q: How do you know if the relationship has a chance?

A: A good relationship involves two people who want to be together and do the right things to make that happen. Finally—and this is the most important—you really feel connected to him and he to you. That's an emotional wisdom that comes more from your heart and intuition than from your mind.

WHY PEOPLE LIE TO FIND LOVE

You heard that the oh-so-flexible new bachelor in your yoga class is looking to settle down with a smart thrill-seeker who can whip up a lasagna that would make any Italian grandmother proud. With your Ph.D. and lifelong subscription to *Gourmet,* you're the perfect match—almost. Your idea of adventure is watching an episode of *Fear Factor.* Would you dare to stretch the truth for the sake of a date?

"Most of the deceptive tactics people use to attract a date are relatively harmless attempts to make a good first impression," says Wade Rowatt, Ph.D., assistant professor in the department of psychology and neuroscience at Baylor University. And you wouldn't be alone.

In a study of 77 college undergraduate students, Rowatt found that it's not uncommon for people to figure out what a potential mate is looking for and then strategize tactics to attract. "Most of the time, it's just a subtle exaggeration of personality qualities that already exist," Rowatt says. Men often tend to embellish their level of commitment and income, while women are likely to play up their looks when pining for a date, especially when using the Internet. Slight embellishments could serve as goals: Exaggerating aspects of your personality—your desire for adventure, for instance—may spark you to try more new things. Rowatt says, "Sometimes it can be a self-fulfilling prophecy and people could end up more like the person they present themselves as."

Sweat Together, Stay Together?

A physical challenge can reveal the true nature of your relationship. See if yours could survive the test.

BY LAURIE DRAKE

Susan West, a 34-year-old publicist from Washington, D.C., discovered her boyfriend's true character while peering down an impossibly steep ski run. The couple had been dating for about a year when West (we've changed her name for this story) accepted her boyfriend's offer to go on a weeklong vacation in Alta, Utah. For West, the invitation was a testament to their love. But atop the slippery slope, the relationship started to melt.

"He urged me to go down it, saying, 'I know you can do it; you should be more confident,'" West recalls. "So I did—and wiped out. I free-fell 50 feet, landing bruised and shaken in a huge snow pile." Her boyfriend watched her tumble and, not wanting to risk the same fate, took his skis off and walked down the mountain. Over beers at the lodge, West tried to calm down, but her boyfriend never apologized for setting her up for the spill. "I thought, 'How could he have put me in such a dangerous situation? If I can't trust him on the ski slope, I can't trust him with my heart,'" she says. That was the beginning of the end of their relationship. Two months later, West and her boyfriend broke up.

West was lucky. Had it not been for her ill-fated run, she may never have seen her boyfriend's selfish side until they were deeper into their relationship—or even married. If she had her way, she'd use a ski trip as the litmus test for all potential partners. And relationship experts might agree. Because physical challenges of all kinds—from high-altitude hiking to riding a tandem bicycle—force couples to reveal sides of themselves not seen in everyday life.

Sticky situations can whittle away at people's polished and composed exteriors, stripping personalities down to the core—with unexpected results. "In high-stress situations, people become uninhibited and 'act out,' making apparent an aspect of themselves that isn't on the surface," says Keith Johnsgard, Ph.D., professor emeritus of psychology at San Jose State University and author of *The Exercise Prescription for Depression and Anxiety.*

"This can be good. A person who doesn't seem strong might, in an emergency, turn out to be very courageous," Johnsgard says. "And it can be bad. A person who seems really macho might, when the chips are down, become unglued and start crying for his mama."

This concept is the very basis of the CBS reality show *The Amazing Race.* Each week, viewers get a peek at the exchanges between teams of two on shoestring budgets.

> **Sticky situations** can whittle away at people's polished and composed exteriors, stripping personalities down to the core—with unexpected results.

The teams complete such challenges as bungee jumping and navigating unfamiliar streets on a race around the world. The real intrigue, however, is not who snags the million-dollar first-place prize, but watching which couples crumble and which thrive as they negotiate the unknown.

"Over the months of filming the series, all of the contestants' relationships changed significantly, mostly for the better, but some for the worse," says show host Phil Keoghan. "The teams that prevailed were good at collaborating—trusting each other's strengths and knowing their weaknesses. Aggression is needed, but at other times, so is a calm, cool head." Especially when map-reading is required, as first-season contestants Matt and Ana Robar discovered while driving toward Victoria Falls. "Turn right, you moron, turn right!" was a sign of the stress that landed the couple in last place—and their relationship on the brink of a total breakdown.

But that was TV. Dan McClurg, who lives in Lake Tahoe, California, experienced such transgressions of couples communication in real life. He and his girlfriend of two years, Toni Neubauer, were looking forward to trekking in Nepal, where their goal was to summit 18,000-foot Kalapatar. "It's known as the viewing place, because from there you're surrounded by five of the tallest mountains in the world, with Mount Everest towering two miles up vertically," McClurg says. In their mid-50s, both McClurg and Neubauer were physically fit, ready to scramble over the rock-covered glaciers, eager to hike along the narrow trails and switchbacks. Although he welcomed the physical challenge, McClurg wasn't at all prepared for the emotional journey he and his girlfriend were about to embark upon. Neubauer's attempts to school first-time trekker McClurg grated on his frazzled nerves. "As an adventure-tour operator, Toni knows the names of every trail crossing in that part of the world, and she kept trying to educate me," McClurg says. "It was more than I wanted to know, to the point of irritation. I said, 'Enough already!'"

test the bounds of your relationship

Could your relationship survive an *Amazing Race*-type challenge with amazing grace? The payoff is learning a new skill together and gaining a sense of "couple competence," the feeling that if you can make it through this, you can make it through anything. Here are some ways to take the test.

Team-building: The Challenge Ropes Course at the Alisal Guest Ranch near Santa Barbara, California, is a series of team-building exercises that includes walking across a tightrope and zooming down a zip line. Phone 800-425-4725 or visit www.alisal.com for more info. Visit www.upwardenterprises.com to find other ropes courses.

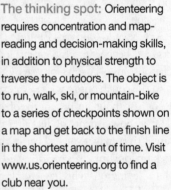

The thinking spot: Orienteering requires concentration and map-reading and decision-making skills, in addition to physical strength to traverse the outdoors. The object is to run, walk, ski, or mountain-bike to a series of checkpoints shown on a map and get back to the finish line in the shortest amount of time. Visit www.us.orienteering.org to find a club near you.

Outdoor expeditions: Yampa River Rafting is a six-day trip that teaches you how to read the currents, scout the rapids, and follow or give commands as you and your crew paddle the Yampa River. It's just one of the Colorado Outward Bound School's wilderness expeditions. Call 866-746-9777 or visit www.cobs.org for more information.

Global adventure: Pass Everest Base Camp on your way to Kalapatar in Nepal, with Sherpas to guide you; explore the rainforest of Ecuador; or meet the shamans of the Amazon. These are just three of the trips offered at Myths and Mountains, an educational adventure-travel company. For more information, call 800-670-6984, visit www.mythsandmountains.com, or send an e-mail to travel@mythsandmountains.com.

Neubauer's need to show off her expertise may have been her way of diffusing her own nervousness. "When people are at the edge of their physical skill level, they have a tendency to revert to the kinds of behaviors where they will most be protecting their own egos," says Kate F. Hays, Ph.D., a sports psychologist in Toronto and author of *Move Your Body, Tone Your Mood.* To temper the urge to snap back when nerves are rattled, Hays suggests that couples think about how each responds to stress before the adventure begins and strategize ways to cool off—even if it means taking some time alone.

At Colorado Outward Bound School, adventure outfitters have been using physical challenges to strengthen relationships of all sorts for years. Couples therapy moves from the couch onto a white-water raft, a rappelling rig, or just about any other type of outdoor apparatus. "The empowerment you feel after conquering a mountain or river makes you feel better about yourself—you stick up for yourself," says Outward Bound instructor Mary Bevington. "This has a ripple effect because when you feel good about yourself, you also feel good about what you bring to the relationship."

Surviving a seven-day-long Outward Bound whitewater rafting trip together in the Grand Canyon brought childhood friends Michiko Lindsey, a 35-year-old lawyer from San Diego, and Molly McDermott, a 35-year-old engineer, wife, and mom from Chicago, closer together.

On the first day of their trip, McDermott was afraid to leave dry land, even to splash around in still water. But by the end of the trip, having successfully paddled the rapids (even blindfolded), she had gained faith in her abilities. Watching her once-timid friend conquer her fears, Lindsey felt a new closeness and respect for her. "Seeing one another in adverse circumstances helped us to open up and pare down to the relationship's deeper issues, like self-esteem and confidence," Lindsey says.

As for the duo on the Nepal climb, after three failed previous solo tries, Neubauer summitted Kalapatar with first-timer McClurg. Though the ascent was a struggle, their relationship grew with the physical triumph. "It helped solidify us because we shared things you can't really explain to anyone else who wasn't there," McClurg says.

Hays calls it "couple competence"—the sense of connection and accomplishment that comes from weathering a challenge. Neubauer ventures to say that "couples who don't sweat together don't stay together. If you've survived a physically rigorous experience, it alters your life, making you question who you are. At those times, you need to talk to someone who can understand." Ideally, someone who's been there. ✳

> When people are at the edge of their physical skill level, they have a tendency to revert to the kinds of behaviors where they will most be protecting their own egos.
>
> —*Kate F. Hays, Ph.D.*

Laurie Drake is a Santa Monica, California–based writer who has contributed to **The New York Times, Allure, Self,** *and* **Westways.**

WHAT MAKES A WOMAN DITCH HER MAN

WHEN it comes to dishing out rejection, men and women can be equally harsh—with one important exception. "Women are less likely to dump someone based solely on looks," says William F. Chaplin, Ph.D., a professor of psychology at the University of Alabama.

In a recent study involving nearly 500 adults, Chaplin found that for women, qualities such as social status ("He doesn't have a car") and financial potential ("He works at Dairy Queen") rated high on their dump-o-meter scale. Both chicks and guys used lies as the most frequent way to give someone the brush-off.

How Emotional Infidelity Damages Your Relationship

THE UNAWARE ADULTERESS spends more time baring her soul than her skin. "Many people commit adultery even though they never become physically involved," says M. Gary Neuman, a Miami marital therapist and author of *Emotional Infidelity.* Seemingly innocent acts such as forwarding a funny e-mail to your friends but not to your husband count as emotional infidelities, and they can be as damaging as a one-night stand, Neuman says. "Any time you divert energy away from your relationship into the hands of a potential lover, you damage its foundation and weaken its bond," he says. Here's how to stay emotionally loyal when sticky situations test your faith.

You accepted a new position hoping it would make you feel more professionally fulfilled, but you end up hating it even more than your former job.
Emotional Infidelity: You share your angst with everyone except your partner because you feel bad about unloading your negative feelings on him.
Faithful Response: Let your partner in on your troubles. It's when couples withhold information from one another that they start living separate lives.
Added Bonus: Sharing your trials with your partner will help you develop a tighter bond. "Everyone needs to be needed, so confide in your partner and work at solving your problem as a team," Neuman says.

The George Clooney look-alike who started working in your office is making it hard to concentrate.
Emotional Infidelity: Whenever you see him standing at the water cooler, you suddenly develop an extreme thirst and slink over to refill your glass.
Faithful Response: Invest in a water pitcher for your desk and admire his great looks from afar. When you speak to him, introduce your partner into the conversation. "Referring to your boyfriend or husband, or using the pronoun 'we,' instead of 'I,' will let him know you're unavailable," Neuman says.
Added Bonus: Being attracted to another man—and wanting to do something about it—offers a chance to figure out what's missing in your own relationship. "Figure out a way with your partner that you can have more fun. That may mean taking a vacation, experimenting with a new sexual technique, or simply hiring a babysitter for a night," Neuman says.

You win a big account at work and your male co-worker wants to take you out to celebrate.
Emotional Infidelity: You accept the invitation and have a blowout night of wining and dining.
Faithful Response: Ask your partner or spouse to come along, or suggest partying at the office.
Added Bonus: Celebrating good moments with your loved one is a great way to share and grow together. It also helps make up for all the complaining you do about your professional woes.

The Sexy Way Your Partner Can Massage Away Your Pain

Forget Midol. The next time you're laid low by period pains, try this partner massage technique from the new book *Women and Pain: Why It Hurts and What You Can Do* by Mark Allen Young, M.D., with Karen Baar: Lie flat on your back on the floor. Have your partner kneel by your head, slide his hands under your back so that they meet at your spine, and then pull them out toward your hips. Next, he should bring his hands over your hips and onto your belly, meeting at the waist. Then he reverses the motion until his hands are at the starting position. Repeat these moves until your cramps are completely gone—or until he starts whining (whichever comes first).

Recharge Your Sex Life with a Doctor Visit

This isn't your average OB-GYN appointment. It's the newest thing in medical checkups, and it could be a new path to pleasure. Here's a behind-the-scenes look.

BY LORI SETO

Use this vibrator to stimulate yourself, and I'll check back in 15 minutes." Should we synchronize our watches? Are the blinds closed? Am I on *Candid Camera*? I'm lying in a doctor's office holding what looks like a finger puppet. The lights are dimmed, and 3-D video glasses with surround sound are slipped onto my head. Images of a woman being ravished by cowboys flash before my eyes; the vibrator's purr fills my ears.

What am I doing here?

I'm 34, happily married, and about to pleasure myself at the Female Sexual Medicine (FSM) Center at the University of California, Los Angeles. I booked their "sexual checkup" because, like an estimated 38 percent of women, I don't reach orgasm during intercourse. Once upon a time, I couldn't get enough. Now? I never crave sex; I merely go through the motions. My ambivalence leaves me—and my husband—frustrated and resentful. This is not the way I want to live my life.

Thanks to a new era of medical research into female sexual dysfunction (FSD) and a culture that increasingly celebrates women's sexual satisfaction, I don't have to. Ever since a 1999 American Medical Association report said that 43 percent of women experience FSD—defined as lack of interest in sex, lack of genital lubrication or sensitivity, inability to have an orgasm, or pain during intercourse—female sexuality has gone prime time. The big O (Oprah) is discussing the big O, explicit sex-education videos are selling like Springsteen tickets, and the Broadway phenomenon *The Vagina Monologues* has turned into a national chorus.

Today, thanks in large part to the co-directors of the UCLA center—urologist Jennifer R. Berman, M.D., and her sister, psychotherapist Laura A. Berman, Ph.D.—exploring the physical causes of FSD and tackling it from a medical standpoint are finally gaining momentum. The best part of the research trend is this: It's about the pleasure, not the plumbing.

With last year's publication of their book *For Women Only: A Revolutionary Guide to Overcoming Sexual Dysfunction and Reclaiming Your Sex Life*, the bold and brainiac Bermans promoted a mind/body approach to diagnosing and treating FSD. Their message? Women have a right to good sex; to get it, you have to look at a combination of physical, emotional, and relationship factors. That's where the sex checkup at UCLA comes in. With its $2,100 price tag, it is the Cadillac of sex treatments.

My exam began on the flight to Los Angeles, as I puzzled over questionnaires mailed to me by the FSM Center. The questions were blush-inducing: Do I think my genitals are attractive? (Hmmm ... I've never really thought about it.) How often do I feel stressed about my sex life? (Come to think of it, pretty often.) Times may have changed on the glossy surface of sex, but as I shielded answers from my husband, who had traveled with me for the weekend, I was starting to realize that I hadn't.

Once at the center, I met with Laura for the psych part of the exam. She explained that the purposes of our conversation were to identify emotional red flags and to devise a game plan for therapy, if needed. "We look at your problem as a big puzzle," she said. "We try to identify all the pieces potentially contributing to the picture." Wearing a sleek wrap dress, leather boots, and a lab coat, Laura reminded me of a savvy, no-nonsense, empathetic girlfriend or sister who wouldn't squeal to Mom about my sexual adventures.

Our conversation covered the basics: "When was your first sexual encounter? Was it a positive experience? How did you learn about sex?" When she hit a red flag, we dove deeper. I was not depressed, acutely stressed, or self-critical; had not experienced sexual or emotional abuse; was not addicted to drugs, alcohol, or cybersex. She suspected that a sense of guilt over a sexually transmitted disease I contracted in my first adult relationship (before I met my husband) was contributing to my lack of desire and physical shutdown. She felt that therapy would help and provided the names of two specialists in my hometown. So far, so good.

Feeling emotionally lighter and encouraged, I moved on to Jennifer for the physical part of the checkup. We discussed my medical history, and she examined my genital area for abnormalities (none were visible). Then she ruled out a long list of common physical triggers for FSD: nerve damage from a hysterectomy or birth; side effects from antidepressants, birth control pills, and the like; and a host of conditions from high blood pressure to vaginal infection.

We're on the front line of the second sexual revolution.
Intimate acts are coming out of the bedroom and into the doctor's office, sans the champagne, silk sheets, and massage oil.

But what followed this routine process reminded me that I wasn't in Kansas anymore: the surreal experience of being handed the means to masturbate and asked to do it right there. Unorthodox? Yes. Uncomfortable? Absolutely. Let's face it; many women wouldn't consider doing this alone in the privacy of their own homes, much less on an examination table in a university clinic. But this is the front line of the second sexual revolution. Intimate acts are coming out of the bedroom and into the doctor's office, sans the champagne, silk sheets, and massage oil. At the Bermans' center, the vibrator is not a toy but a surefire tool to attract blood to the genital area. Vive la révolution!

After quietly stimulating myself while watching the Western-themed erotic video (and checking in the mirror to make sure that my cheeks weren't too flushed), I waited for Jennifer. She knocked, strolled in without showing a hint of self-consciousness, and proceeded to measure blood-flow levels in my clitoris, labia, and vagina using an ultrasound probe. I hoped nothing embarrassing was going on down there, but if it was, Jennifer had seen it a thousand times.

The grand finale was a biothesiometer, another probe used to test the sensitivity of nerves in my vagina and clitoris to subtle heat, cold, and vibration. The nurse handed me a sensor attached to a wire and told me to push the button as soon as I felt something. Acting as if I were a *Jeopardy!* contestant, at first I rushed to press the button before really sensing anything. It was a totally new kind of performance anxiety—what if I don't feel things as quickly as I should?—but after a minute, I relaxed. And just like that, the exam was over.

The verdict? Though results from my blood work would take two weeks, my sensory responses were within a normal range. Jennifer said that my ability to achieve orgasm with a vibrator meant that I was probably OK physically. She prescribed some sexual positions and suggested strengthening my pelvic muscles "to help squeeze his penis upward" against my G-spot. I left with a goody bag of samples (creams, oils, and Viagra tablets) to increase arousal, plus information about Fria, a $129 handheld machine that measures pelvic-floor strength and guides you through exercises. A couple of weeks later, after my blood test showed some slightly low testosterone levels, Jennifer prescribed a hormone supplement for me.

And so the treatment was complete. I had been armed with my own personal arsenal of bedside-table tools for satisfaction, been referred to a sex therapist, and had discovered a device that acts like a personal trainer for my pelvis. I was $2,100 poorer—and it was worth every penny. Now my husband and I talk about sex in a way that we didn't know how to 10 years ago, when we first started dating. Sure, the price tag for getting there was a bit extravagant, and we're still trying to make the big O (orgasm, not Oprah) a part of our regular sex routine. But we don't mind working at it. ✳

New York City–based writer Lori Seto has contributed to **Playboy, Bridal Guide, USA Today,** *and other publications.*

WHY SAME SEX ISN'T SAFE SEX

WOMEN WHO HAVE SEX with women have a dangerous fantasy—that lesbian sex is safe sex. "Some women believe that a lesbian identity is like wearing a giant condom," says Greta R. Bauer, a researcher at the University of Minnesota School of Public Health who published a study on lesbian sexual health in the *American Journal of Public Health.* Yet it appears to be the total number of sexual encounters, rather than the gender of the partners, that most increases women's risk of a sexually transmitted disease (STD).

Pregnancy aside, women who sleep with women expose themselves to the same risks—HIV, chlamydia, herpes, genital warts—as women who only have sex with men. Some studies suggest that women may be more likely to share pesky infections, such as yeast and bacterial vaginosis. In a recent survey of 286 lesbian and bisexual women, Bauer found that 21 percent of respondents reported having had an STD. Despite the evidence that lesbian sex carries risks, women who identified themselves as lesbians were 73 percent less likely than bisexual or heterosexual women to be receiving regular testing for STDs.

"Many women get lulled into a false sense of security," says Caren Stalburg, M.D., an OB-GYN and clinical assistant professor at the University of Michigan. "If they can't get pregnant, they figure the behavior is risk free." It's what you're doing—not whom you're doing it with—that puts you at risk. All women should get an annual pelvic exam, Pap smear, and STD testing—no matter how they define their sexuality.

THE PROS AND CONS OF LUBRICANTS

Reaching for a tube of lube before sex could be a slippery proposition, especially if you're trying to get pregnant.

Most lubricants contain perfumes and chemicals that change the acid balance in the vagina, which will affect the way sperm act. "I would not recommend using lubricants if you're trying to conceive, because we don't know to what degree lubricants damage sperm," says Alan Altman, M.D., professor of gynecology at Harvard Medical School and author of *Making Love the Way We Used to—or Better*. "I find more women are reaching for lubricants because they are easier to use than the gloppy stuff of the past, and they are seen as helpful, not embarrassing." Women certainly have more options to choose from: In 1997, the San Francisco–based sexual resource center Good Vibrations offered 14 lubricants. Today, it carries more than 25.

For women in their 20s and early 30s, the question is not whether you use lubricants, Altman says, but why do you need to? Beyond the issues of desire and arousal, recurring vaginal dryness among women in their reproductive prime could be a sign of a more serious problem with ovulation, which should give moisture levels a natural boost. Reaching for the slippery stuff before consulting your doctor could delay treatment of underlying causes of dryness.

For women over 35 who are not looking to get pregnant and who find a little lube eases the way, leave the Wesson oil in the kitchen and petroleum-based Vaseline to lips: These solutions are breeding grounds for bacteria. Instead, look for products that are water-based and as close in composition to your body's natural lubricants as possible. Altman recommends condom-safe Astroglide and KY Silk-e, which share the same acidic pH as the inside of the vagina. "Anything that changes the environment in the vagina opens the way for yeast infections," Altman says. "And if you really want natural, oral sex is a great lubricant."

sexual ethics

Forty-eight percent of women and 58 percent of men think sex between an unmarried man and woman is morally acceptable.

—GALLUP POLL NEWS SERVICE

a woman's guide to when to have sex

When you and your sweetheart are feeling frisky, it's no fun to kill the mood wondering whether you can have sex or not. Certain situations—a pesky yeast infection, tomorrow's gyno appointment—should influence your decision, says Maida Taylor, M.D., associate clinical professor of obstetrics and gynecology at the University of California at San Francisco. Check out this chart to find out Taylor's take on when sex is safe for both you and your partner, and when you might be better off rediscovering the joys of foreplay.

Can I Still Have Sex When I Have...	Yes/No	Risks	How Long to Abstain	The Last Word
a urinary tract infection (UTI)?	YES	Urinary tract infections aren't contagious. But you should enlist the help of your doctor to find out the cause of your UTI so it doesn't happen again. (In many cases these infections are caused by bacteria from the vaginal or anal area that has traveled up the urethra during sex.) Sex won't delay the cure once you've started taking antibiotics, but friction on already inflamed tissues may worsen symptoms like pressure, pain, and urgency to urinate.	Having sex will not pose any health risks, but it might be uncomfortable. Let your body be your guide.	Make sure to urinate immediately following sex to prevent another infection. Drink at least eight glasses of water a day to help dilute urine, which will make it less caustic and irritating.
a yeast infection?	YES	A woman probably won't transmit a yeast infection to her partner during sex. He may experience some itching, but the organism that causes yeast infections doesn't grow on dry skin (like the shaft of the penis); it's limited to warm, moist environments. Sex may aggravate the woman's symptoms (redness, burning, and itching), but it won't worsen the underlying condition.	No need to say no unless you're uncomfortable.	Use a condom to avoid giving your guy the itch.
a gynecologist's appointment?	NO	Sex can irritate vaginal tissue, increasing your chance of getting a false positive Pap Smear (meaning the test may detect a problem when there's not one).	No intercourse for two days before a Pap test.	Also avoid receiving oral sex 48 hours before your appointment to ensure accurate test results.
a cold or the flu?	YES	Cold and flu germs are spread from the nose and mouth, not through sexual fluids. Sex is technically OK, as long as you don't breathe too deeply on your lover.	You're usually infectious for a few days. When your sniffles or cough start to clear up, you probably won't spread germs.	Kissing is a no-no. Consider sexual positions in which you're not directly face-to-face with your partner.
a cold sore?	NO	The oral type of herpes (herpes simplex I) prefers the mouth, but it will take up residence anywhere it can, including the genitals, if conditions are right. Herpes infections are extremely contagious when a sore is present.	Steer clear of oral sex and kissing until sores completely disappear.	Also be careful about self-stimulation. "I've seen patients who had oral lesions, used spit to masturbate, and infected their own genitals," Taylor says.

Turn Up the Heat in Your Bedroom

Feel like you don't have enough sex in your relationship? Don't worry, you're not alone. Here are the top causes of a sexual slump—and some simple solutions.

BY VICTORIA CLAYTON

So there you are in your 500-thread-count sheets and strappy nightie, curled up with the remote, watching Sarah Jessica Parker's character jump from bed to bed on HBO. And there your spouse is, lying next to you. Which gets you to wondering why you're watching *Sex and the City* instead of having it.

Join the club. The fact is that while innuendo is everywhere—J.Lo baring her belly, Jennifer Love Hewitt baring it all, and sex selling everything from soda to CNN—most of the women out there aren't having sex very often. According to Edward O. Laumann, Ph.D., a sociology professor at the University of Chicago and co-editor of *Sex, Love, and Health in America,* a full half of Americans ages 18 to 59 have sex less than once a week. And roughly 30 percent of women each year report a lack of interest in sex for several months or more.

So is something wrong if you don't want it as often as everyone else seems to? Not necessarily. In fact, what's defined as sexual dysfunction—lacking interest or not being able to have sex—may not be dysfunction at all, Laumann says. "My argument about sexual dysfunction is that it is often a normal, natural control mechanism," he says. In other words, sometimes it's a blip that has more to do with what's going on in your life than it does with what kind of lover, wife, or partner you are.

Scheduling intimacy sounds about as sexy as folding laundry, but it's actually a key way to put sex back into a relationship.

But how do you know whether your sex life has just a little chill or it's in permanent deep-freeze? Here's when no sex tends to be temporary—and reversible.

Vacations are hot; reality's not

That Jamaica trip was steamy—and not just the weather. If vacation sex is satisfying, chances are you've still got the sizzle that helps keep a relationship fulfilling. It's daily life that's getting in the way. You might think that lack of time due to work, kids, and thousands of other daily challenges would be a simple problem, but it's actually one of the hardest to overcome.

Researchers call the situation DINS—Double Income No Sex—and they say it's perfectly natural for libidos to cool off during the career- and family-building years. That doesn't mean you have to settle into a sexual Sahara that lasts until the kids are in college. When sexual frequency starts to slip, it's essential to talk with your spouse and pinpoint each of your low-sex thresholds. At what point (no sex for a week, no sex for a month, etc.) does each partner start to feel rejected or alienated? "That doesn't mean you're going to agree," explains Hilda Hutcherson, M.D., author of *What Your Mother Never Told You About S-e-x.* "If he wants to have intercourse three times a week and you only want it once a week, maybe there's something else you can do one of those other times that falls short of intercourse."

Scheduling intimacy, while it sounds about as sexy as folding laundry, is actually a key way to put it back into a relationship. "Spontaneity is kind of overrated," Hutcherson says. "You can have really great sex by anticipating it. The anticipation adds a little energy and excitement to the encounter."

New mom has a new identity
Of course, the hormone flux after giving birth can put a damper on sex. But what few new moms expect is the psychological cold shower they give themselves. "When you put motherhood and sex in the same thought, many people become uncomfortable," says Laura Berman, Ph.D., founder of the Female Sexual Medicine Center at the University of California-Los Angeles Medical Center. That's because a lot of women have been brought up to believe that a mother has to be proper and saintly, not sexy.

"The first step is to take a look at the message you've bought into," says Berman. "Sometimes you just have to give yourself permission to be a mother and to also be a sexual being." It can even affect your kids' behavior. "Children really do pick up on whether their parents are experiencing a connection, romance, and love in their relationship," Berman explains.

Your problem's in a bottle
Many doctors forget to mention that common medications can put you into a sexual slump. Everything from antidepressants to contraceptives to blood-pressure medicine can decrease libido or lower your ability to reach orgasm. Fortunately, alternatives to many sex-sapping drugs are available.

Sometimes, however, a medical problem may put sex on the not-to-do list. Erratic hormones, for instance, account for about a third of the cases of people who either lack desire or find sex painful. While trickier to get to the bottom of, hormonal problems in men and women are treatable, says endocrinologist Geoffrey Redmond, M.D., director of the Hormone Center of New York. In addition to correcting the underlying physical problem, endocrinologists may prescribe Viagra, testosterone, or even certain antidepressants to reclaim libido.

Your mind is in the way
Sex is the epitome of the mind-body connection, which is why intense psychotherapy can put a wet blanket over

improving sex communication

It's the 21st century, and you'd think Americans would be comfortable talking about sex by now. Far from it. To open communication lines, Hilda Hutcherson, M.D., author of *What Your Mother Never Told You About S-e-x,* offers five starter solutions:

1 | Read a sex book together. Linger on the chapters that describe the techniques that you particularly enjoy. Say something like, "I just love it when you do that to me."

2 | Rent an erotic video and discuss the film's activities that entice you or pique your interest. Tell him, "I'd love to try that."

3 | Share your fantasies with each other. This is no time to be shy: Describe in intimate detail activities that you find pleasurable or would like to try.

4 | If he did something in bed that you particularly liked, let him know immediately after sex: "When you touched me that way, it really drove me wild."

5 | Don't talk about sex in bed. Pick a time that's totally away from the sexual arena. And don't do it when you're tired or angry. Find words that are helpful and at the same time not complaining or accusing.

sexual flames. When you're in therapy or dealing with a serious personal problem, you're likely to be very self-focused. That can be a difficult time to let someone into your physical space.

In other cases, sexual relationships suffer when people are on a spiritual quest or in search of deeper meaning in their lives, contends Elizabeth Abbott, Ph.D., author of *A History of Celibacy*. These spiritual seekers, as she calls them, "find that sex is a distraction that, at this stage of their lives, simply hinders the pursuit. But that's not to say that they're wanting to dump their partner."

According to Hutcherson, "You have to talk and stay in touch about what you're going through—and that will take the emphasis off intercourse." Work something out with your partner where he can touch you or you can touch him without feeling emotionally drained or invaded. Offer a massage, maybe, or go to the back of a movie theater and kiss like teenagers.

So if you're suddenly sexless, don't assume the next step is singledom. Sex isn't a litmus test for a relationship's health. And when you are in a temporary lull, you can

Sex sells everything
from soda to CNN, yet most women aren't having sex very often.

stop feeling inadequate about the frequency and connect with your partner in other ways. "We need to get the idea out of our minds that the only appropriate way to express love and intimacy is through intercourse," says Howard Ruppel, Ph.D., dean of faculty at the Institute for the Advanced Study of Human Sexuality in San Francisco. Ruppel recommends the "smorgasbord approach": daily helpings of kissing, hugging, and heart-to-heart conversation. "When you're at a smorgasbord, you never walk away feeling like you didn't have a whole meal," he says. And that kind of satisfaction—in the bedroom and in life—just requires a little variety. ✴

Freelance writer Victoria Clayton's work has appeared in Cooking Light *and* Yoga Journal.

test your sex life

Do you often joke or argue about your lack of sex? Do you avoid kissing or cuddling your partner because it may lead to sex? If so, it's time to explore why. Answer the questions below for a better clue:

1 | Do you usually have satisfying sex while on vacation or when pressures are off?
2 | Do you have depression, diabetes, high blood pressure, or another medical condition or illness for which you're taking prescription drugs? Does your partner?
3 | Do you experience consistent vaginal dryness or pelvic/breast discomfort?
4 | Have you given birth within the last four years?
5 | Do you or your partner feel lackluster or generally without energy?

answers:

1 | If you answered yes to this question, you've still "got it," but your life is getting in the way of sexual and relationship health. Make sure you talk plainly with your partner, implement the "smorgasbord approach" to intimacy and—of course—go on more vacations.

2-5 | If you answered yes to any of these questions, a physical problem linked either to health conditions or hormonal imbalances is the likely culprit. Consult your family physician or a center that specializes in sexual health.

If you answered no to all or most of the questions, your lack of sex is likely rooted in relationship or psychological conflicts. Consult a psychotherapist, family therapist, or sex therapist. Log on to www.intimacyinstitute.com for more information.

Stimulate Your Senses— and Your Sexuality

IN ANCIENT JERUSALEM, young women put myrrh and balsam in their shoes and clicked their heels when they passed by an attractive man in the marketplace. Cleopatra was said to drench the sails of her boat in perfume and bathe in milk before meeting Mark Antony. And in Shakespeare's day, women tucked peeled apples into their armpits and proffered them to paramours. "Since ancient times, scent has been a signature that men and women have left behind, a lingering reminder that acts as an emotional bond," says Avery Gilbert, Ph.D., president of the Sense of Smell Institute (www.senseofsmell.org) in New York City.

Scents are unequaled in their power to arouse, Gilbert says. And losing your sense of smell could send your sexual yearnings into a nosedive. People who have suffered head injuries or infections that damage nasal nerves often become depressed and report a lack of desire. And recent research shows that birth-control pills can block a woman's sensitivity to smell, which may mean a lowered libido.

To use your sense of smell to heighten your sexual desires, expose your nose to a range of scents. Crush thyme in your fingers before adding it to a sauce or take a whiff of an orange in a fruit bowl, says Mandy Aftel, a psychotherapist, custom perfumer, and the author of *Essence and Alchemy: A Book of Perfume.* "Being alive to fragrance puts you powerfully into the present and in touch with the sensual world," Aftel says. For more on the power of smells, and to create your own signature scent, visit Aftel's Web site at www.aftelier.com.

Need to spice up your love life?
Try redecorating your bedroom

So you want a relationship—or at least a date—but something about you screams "single" so loud you might as well be shouting into a bullhorn. According to feng shui, the ancient art of design, the secret to attracting a lover could be in a makeover, and we're not talking about your looks. Use these ideas to redecorate your bedroom:

- **Act as if** you already have a partner by investing in matching nightstands. The scenario that you create in your mind will eventually come to pass.

- **Ditch** the stuffed animals and dolls on your bed. They send the message that you're already taken.

- **Make room** for your lover-to-be by removing clutter, such as frilly pillows and magazines, from your bed.

- **Store** stuff in your closet, not under your bed, unless you're looking for clutter and baggage in a relationship.

- **Don't** make your bedroom a multipurpose room. Move the television and computer elsewhere (or at least cover them up when not in use) if you don't want these types of distraction to come between you and your would-be lover.

- **Move** photos of family members to another part of the house. Your romantic life will improve if your parents aren't staring at you in bed.

- **Think pink**—or red. Bright red objects, such as hearts and roses, can work wonders to fire up your love life, especially when they're placed in pairs.

- **Above all,** use your intuition. Whatever gets you in the mood for love—soft lighting, scented candles, romantic music—will also attract your ideal lover.

women prove to be better arousal detectors

Princeton University researchers have confirmed what women have long suspected: Men, particularly those who have hit a sexual dry spell, often think a smile means a woman is interested in sex. Women, on the other hand, are more accurate at reading body cues. The researchers found that if a woman thinks a man is aroused, he probably is.

Real Life, Real Answers

Ali Domar, Ph.D., our relationships guru, weighs in on the issues that affect women most in their personal and professional lives.

Bad Move? Make It Better

I recently moved with my husband to his hometown, but I'm beginning to think it was a mistake. He landed a dream job here, near his parents and old friends. I love them, but they're a domineering bunch, and I feel like our identity as a couple is changing. What can I do about this feeling of resentment?

My grad-school mentor, mind/body expert Joan Borysenko, used to say that being resentful is like carrying a hot coal in your hand, waiting to throw it at someone. Who's getting burned? At this point, you are. But you have the power to fix this situation.

First, stop living his life and start living your own. One of the best ways to do that is to get a job. You'll meet people outside of your husband's circle and rediscover your professional self. You also need to make your own friends. Think about what you would have done if you had moved to a new place by yourself: You might have found a biking or hiking club, asked a coworker over for dinner, or joined a church. Remember your single days? You've got to make a conscious effort to meet new people now, like you did then.

Second, you and your husband need to set some ground rules about the amount of time you spend with "his" people. For instance, if there are family events twice a week, you might agree to go to only half of them. The important thing is that you make a plan that both of you agree on.

Finally, remember that your husband's excitement of being back in his hometown may wear off. His family baggage is sure to resurface, and he might find he has less in common with old friends than he thought. Give it some time. When my husband and I got married, we lived near where I grew up, and he felt overwhelmed at

times. But now, he's friends with a lot of my high-school pals. And we've made new friends together, so we've got a whole new group of people to hang out with.

Balancing Salary Differences

I recently became a partner at my law firm, and now I make twice as much money as my husband does. I'm proud of what I've accomplished, but I'm worried that he feels inadequate. How can I enjoy this without hurting him?

Isn't it ironic that more money—which can mean more vacations, more conveniences, more fun—can feel like an issue? You've got a lot to be proud of, but this kind of situation can put a strain on a marriage if you don't deal with it. Many men link financial success to masculinity, and they feel threatened if they're making less than their wives. We've got to figure out a way to help the guys deal with this, though, because about a quarter of wives in the United States earn more than their husbands, and that number will probably continue to grow.

How you proceed depends on a few things. For example, if he is also a lawyer and didn't make partner, that's a far trickier situation than if he is in a profession that is known to be really important but ridiculously underpaid, such as teaching or firefighting. In any case, communication and consideration are vital. There may be certain things about the unequal salaries that bother him, such as your spending money on things he considers unnecessary or pushing to buy things, such as a bigger house, that you wouldn't be able to afford if your salary were equal to his. Brainstorm with him on the best way to make this comfortable for both of you. Some couples agree that the husband will take on more of the domestic responsibilities so he feels he's doing his share. Others put a chunk of her salary in a special account, live on the remaining money, and use the special fund for splurges they both enjoy. Some couples choose to donate some of her salary to a charity they both support. There are solutions that will work for you both; it's just a matter of being creative and loving in the process of figuring out what they are.

Mum's the Word On Sexy-Dressing Coworkers

We just hired a new intern. She's 22 and bright, but she wears skimpy blouses or short skirts that are better suited for the dance floor than the office. Guys at work comment on it, and I'd like to clue her in about how to dress at work. How should I approach her?

Unless she specifically asks for your advice, stay out of it. With all the recent workplace lawsuits and corporate attempts to be politically correct, your good intentions might land you and your company in legal trouble. If you feel things are getting out of hand, alert your company's human-resources department and let them figure out how to handle it. Believe me, you don't want to touch this one.

How to Share Your Past with Your New Man

I'm falling for a great guy, but there are things from my past I'm not anxious to tell him. I've had several sexual partners, one of whom was married, and another who gave me genital herpes. I know I have to tell him about the STD, but how much else should I share?

It sounds like you two are in the first phase of your relationship—the period of unconditional love. He is perfect, you are perfect, both of you are adorable. While you're in this state, there's a huge temptation to tell him all your deep, dark secrets. Resist. Revealing too much too soon might freak him out. Wait until you're seeing him more like a man—and less like a god—and you've decided to move forward with him. Pick a time when you're feeling

especially close. Or just follow his lead: If he opens up about his past, it may be easier for you to do the same.

I disagree with other advice columnists who say that some things are better kept secret. In my opinion, if something has happened in your life that makes you feel guilty, at some point you need to share it with your man. It would be far better for him to hear it from you than from someone else.

Stay-at-Home Mom's Dilemma: Should I Get a Job?

I'm a stay-at-home mom. The more the economy slows, the more stressed-out my husband gets—and the guiltier I feel about not working. Should I go back to work for his sake?

First, ask yourself this: How happy are you at home? If you feel strongly about staying home, at least until your youngest is in school, there are several things you can do. Start by finding out for sure whether you're really in financial trouble or if your husband is just "awfulizing." Ask specific questions about the money situation. If his worries are valid, try to think of different ways to decrease his stress: Can he talk to a headhunter about other jobs? Could you dip into your savings or temporarily cut back on some expenses, just until the kids are in school? If you are willing to go back to work now and the money you bring in will more than offset the cost of child care, it might make you both feel better. He'll be relieved that he is not the only breadwinner, and you may enjoy the fact that you're making money and taking the pressure off him at the same time.

In either case, your husband needs to learn or practice some stress-reducing techniques. Brainstorm together on how he can find time for things that give him a release: an afternoon on the golf course, a hard workout at the gym, and of course, there's always sex.

Alice D. Domar, Ph.D., is a psychologist who focuses on women's issues, stress management, and couples counseling. She's also a Harvard Medical School assistant professor, director of the Mind/Body Center for Women's Health at Boston IVF, Department of Obstetrics and Gynecology at Beth Israel Deaconess Medical Center, and the best-selling author of Self Nurture; Healing Mind, Healthy Woman; *and* Conquering Infertility.

Tribal Friendships:
the popular lifestyle for young urban singles

BY EVA MARER

When 29-year-old Ruth Geyer's father died suddenly, her five best friends—three women and two men—called in sick to work, piled into a rented car, and drove two hours from New York City to Lawnside, New Jersey. During the day, they cooked for out-of-town guests; at night, they camped out on the living room floor. As Geyer made arrangements for the funeral, her friends took care of everything else. "They answered the phone, did laundry, and even cleaned the gutters," she says.

Like Geyer's web of support, tribes of single urban professionals are popping up nationwide and filling roles that were once reserved for families, says Judith Sills, Ph.D., a Philadelphia psychologist who has observed an increase in the phenomenon among her 30-something female patients. Television shows like *Sex and the City* and *Friends* made it cool and funny to be anxious and single. But comrades in cliques do a whole lot more than just stress over sex. "Your tribe has an intense, intimate familiarity with your life that makes you feel grounded," Sills explains. "Whether that's remembering your birthday or driving you to get your car fixed, the network of friends greases the wheels of your life and eases stress." As fewer young adults move straight from the shelter of home to wedded life, the tribe is becoming the new rite of passage for single women.

As fewer single women move straight from their parents' homes to marriage, the tribe is becoming a new rite of passage.

Today's social groups borrow many traits from past packs. Every generation has had its in-crowds with their sense of unique destiny, from the Bloomsbury Group (composed of such early 20th-century intellectuals as Virginia Woolf and John Maynard Keynes) to the hippie communes that were popular during the 1960s. Current coteries, however, are less motivated by a shared political agenda than by the mantra of personal freedom. Urban singles are among the fastest-growing demographic groups in America, according to the most recent U.S. Census figures, and the median age of marriage has reached an all-time high: 25 for women and 27 for men.

"Young people are simply unwilling to settle for anything less than their ideal soul mate," says Howard Devore, Ph.D., a San Francisco psychologist who tracks tribes in singles-studded Silicon Valley. "In the meantime, they rely on the tribe for day-to-day intimacy and emotional support."

Whether they're stretching out in a group yoga class together or dishing over a brew at their favorite local pub, Geyer's tribe moves through space like stars in a constellation. They hold council about every major life decision they encounter, from switching jobs to ditching a mate. "I wouldn't dream of going to a job interview without asking my friends to edit my résumé—and my outfit," says 30-year-old Judy Williams, a fashion consultant who is part of Geyer's group. She credits her clique of friends with coaching

Just as with siblings, your role within the group—the pretty one, the smart one, the funny one—can be comforting, but it can also be stultifying and rigid.

—Diana Adile Kirschner, Ph.D.

her out of a nowheresville relationship and cheering her recent engagement.

Cities, with their transient and impersonal undertones, are perfect breeding grounds for tight-knit crews. "Tribes provide a sense of belonging and empowerment," Devore says. Friendship factions can also school women in the skills—flexibility, forgiveness, and patience—that will help make them better mates later on in life. "The tribe functions like training wheels for emotional development," Devore says.

This sort of reliance on a tribe can have a downside, however. "There's often a pressure to remain single, to be faithful to the tribe," says Ethan Watters, a San Francisco author who is writing a book on the tribal phenomenon to be published in the fall of 2003. Such arrested development is more common among males than females, Devore says. But women also pressure each other to nix the date for a weekend at the beach instead. Lucile Lampton, a 26-year-old art historian who lives in Charleston, South Carolina, felt a constant tug-of-war between her friends and boyfriends. "If I really wanted to get to know somebody, I had to take a break from the group," she says.

Like real families, tribes can also get stuck in negative patterns and turn toxic. "Just as with siblings, your role within the group—the pretty one, the smart one, the funny one—can be comforting, but it can also be stultifying and rigid," explains Diana Adile Kirschner, Ph.D., a psychologist who specializes in relationship counseling for women.

The key to maintaining a healthy tribe is balance. "The walls should not be so high that you can't get in or out," Sills says. And tribes that stand the test of time evolve to fit the changing needs of members. "In our 20s, we hung out every night, going to parties, sharing problems, or just lying around reading magazines," Geyer says. "Now we spend more time at our jobs or with our men. But that core sense of family is there—always." ✳

Eva Marer is a freelance writer who regularly contributes to Health.

in my tribe

For many people, tribal culture is much more than a social life, it's a way of being. For his upcoming book about these bands of urban singles, writer Ethan Watters asked men and women across the nation what the big deal is. Here's what some of them had to say. You can add your voice to the mix at www.urbantribes.net.

"Thanks to my tribe I am far less relationship-hungry. If I want to do something—go hiking, cry on a shoulder, eat wings at a dive bar, or discuss Paul's letter to the Corinthians—I know that I can find a companion."
—Mary Cvetan, 37, Pittsburgh, Pa.

"We talk about buying a house together when we're 70 and hiring a full-time cook and nurse."
—Beau Valtz, 38, Arlington, Mass.

"My parents were hurt and very vocal about how they thought my tribe was more important than they were. I hate to admit this, but I do spend more time with the tribe than with my own family."
—Jennifer Morgan, 31, Columbus, Ohio

"My tribe has provided me with a genuinely stable environment—a safe spot where I can go and talk out professional and personal concerns with people who are experiencing the same thing."
—Ralph Zecca, 26, Washington, D.C.

"My tribe is the best family I ever had: It raised my confidence, helped me to get through tough times, and gave me a sense of belonging."
—Roseanne Ware, 28, Huntington Beach, Calif.

the challenge of forming friendships in your 30s

It seems like it should be so easy. But the truth is that most of us have busy lives—and too little time for our friends.

BY LYDIA DENWORTH

If I had another life, and she had another life, my neighbor Jane could be my best friend. A writer who's always up on the latest media gossip, she wears the funkiest shoes (we should all look so good pushing a stroller) and knows that sometimes maniacal laughter is the only appropriate answer to your preschooler's latest fit. Each time we bump into each other, we say we'll get together soon. But in my vocabulary, "soon" has come to mean "never," and the "I'll call you" promises are starting to sound as empty as a box of Teddy Grahams in a house full of kids.

The last time I saw her, I wanted to say something like, "I'm sorry—I've been too busy to call. And I probably will be like, forever. " I didn't (for fear of sounding lame or psychotic). But I think she would have understood. Jane and I are both living "real-world drift": that stage in life when big changes—marriages, children, career moves—loosen the ties that anchor us to our friends and leave us struggling to keep up with ourselves, much less our pals. Sandy Sheehy, who coined the term, interviewed more than 200 women for her book, *Connecting: The Enduring Power of Female Friendship*, and found that 30-somethings are particularly susceptible. "Even among single women who don't have the demands of a husband or kids, there's a decline in friendship in your 30s," Sheehy says. In other words, 30-something friends are a far cry from *Thirtysomething* and *Friends*.

Sheehy says that a woman's social life tends to pick up again in her 40s—not exactly comforting news. Does this mean you'll be adrift for a decade or so before you get some quality girlfriend time? Maybe not—if you abandon the idea that "quality time" means hanging out for hours, the way they do in TV land. By adopting a new definition of friendship that reflects your life as it really is, you can still get what you need from your friends (and give back). The challenge is to make the most of the time you've got and quit feeling guilty about not living up to old expectations about what friends should do or should be.

That means taking a glass-is-half-full perspective on your relationships with your closest friends. Rather than concentrate on the fact that in-depth conversations are as infrequent as daylong spa treatments, focus on the conversation itself. "Forget about what you're not getting from a friendship," Sheehy says. "The key is when you are together, be totally there. If you have 20 minutes, don't review your shopping list in your head. Focus."

And, Sheehy says, leave the baggage at the door. Lots of women have perfected the art of feeling guilty, and it's easy to beat up on yourself for not having called your closest friend. But if you haven't talked to her since last summer, remember that she hasn't called you, either.

But what about people like my would-be best friend Jane—women you don't have a shraed history with but would like to get to know better? That's the second part of this new definition of friendship for drifters: accepting that not all friendships will be created equal and knowing that

friends in the real world

Keeping up with friends isn't always easy. In fact, it's pretty difficult. Here's how three different women keep bonds strong (or not).

New way of thinking: "I used to feel I had to build a deep friendship with anyone with whom I had anything in common. Now I know it's not possible. If it happens, great. But the people who have staying power in my life are the ones I need to invest the time in."
Sarah; 33; Santa Ana, California; mother of three

Staying in touch: "My friend Melissa is now a working mom, and she wants to spend most of her free time with her kids. So every other Sunday evening, I come over for a *Sex and the City* viewing, with takeout Chinese food. Her husband watches the kids while we gab."
Beth, 38, New York City, editor

Casual Connections: "Especially before I got married, I spent a lot of time with other single friends. However, as people switched jobs or moved to new cities, I found that there wasn't always enough glue to keep the friendships going. But it was great while it lasted."
Sara, 36, New York City, investment banker

they don't have to be. Even coffee-break encounters that never go any further than the office are valuable. Both these types of friendships—close and casual—fill our need for social connection. They just do it in different ways. From our deepest friendships, we draw emotional support; more casual contacts provide us with information and affirmation.

That's important, because in your 30s, you're more likely to have these casual relationships with women whose lives mirror yours: She is exactly as pregnant as you are, or she joined the company at the same time. Sheehy calls friends like these "lifemates" as opposed to "soulmates"—but they're no less important. "You need another mom who says, 'I've got a pediatrician who really listens,' or a single friend who knows the dating rules," she says.

That explains my attraction to Jane. She has kids the same age as mine, the same career, and the same fondness for footwear. Sure, our friendship may never get past small talk and mommy talk. But it somehow works right here, right now. So I'll try not to feel guilty that we don't hang out more. And I'll make a note to call her to schedule lunch—when we both hit 40. ✳

New York–based journalist Lydia Denworth also writes for Redbook *and* House & Garden.

FEMALE FRIENDS: the Best Relationship Predictors

Call it female intuition: The best predictor of your relationship's success may be your best friend—if she's a woman. In a study of 74 couples published in the *Journal of Personality and Social Psychology,* Purdue University researchers found that a woman's pals had the best track record for predicting whether a couple would still be a pair six months later. They proved to be better judges than the man's buddies, mutual friends, or even the woman herself.

Women's gift of gab may be the key to revelation. "It makes sense that a woman's friends would be more

insightful because women tend to disclose more intimate information about their relationships than men do," says Christopher R. Agnew, Ph.D., the lead author of the study. And chances are, even if you see your relationship through rose-tinted glasses, he says, your friends' eyes are wide open to reality.

After just one postdate phone call, your best friend can probably tell whether your new mate is a hunk or a dud—and that may be the best time to ask. "Get your friend's feedback early before you're so entrenched in the relationship that you're unwilling to hear it," says Dru Sherrod, Ph.D.,

a Los Angeles–based psychologist who has researched gender differences in friendships.

While gal pals seem to be the most perceptive when it comes to divining a relationship's fate, they're certainly not the only predictors. The Purdue study revealed that couples who had the highest number of mutual friends were the most lucky in love. Not only did they report more satisfaction with one another but they were also most likely to be together in six months. Sharing friends may mean you are less likely to look outside your circle of intimates and flirt with the unknown.

the truth about lying

The language you use can signal a fib almost as clearly as Pinocchio's nose—to a trained listener. In a recent study by University of Texas at Austin researchers, people were asked their views on such topics as abortion or whether they liked or disliked certain people. To test the truthfulness of their answers, researchers ran the responses through a computer program called a Linguistic Inquiry and Word Count (LIWC). The LIWC spotted liars two-thirds of the time by three main tip-offs. Since it's unlikely you have the program on your laptop, we asked study author Matthew Newman to help us tell fact from fiction in the following scenarios.

1 | Your office mate calls to say she can't make it to work on the day of your joint presentation, so you're on your own.
Explanation: "Something's wrong with the car. The engine won't turn over."
Lie? Likely. "In an attempt to distance themselves from their fibs, liars tend to avoid using the pronouns 'I' or 'me' when recounting their stories," Newman says.
A more believable reply: "I tried to get my car started, but it's dead. I called AAA, so I'll be in as soon as they get it going."

2 | Your boyfriend was out until 4 a.m. after he said he'd be home in time to watch Saturday Night Live with you.
Explanation: "I got smashed at Jim's house and then I passed out."
Lie? Probably. "Liars' stories avoid detail in favor of a few bold facts," Newman says. "If you're lying, not only do you have to construct a story out of nothing but you've also got to make it sound convincing, while worrying, 'Am I getting away with this?' "
A more believable reply: "Jim's uncle gave him a bottle of top-shelf bourbon for his birthday. I'd planned to have just one drink, but then Jim plied me with another and another. When I stood up to leave I couldn't even walk straight, so I sat back down on his couch and passed out."

3 | Your friend never showed up for dinner.
Explanation: "The night was just horrendous. My car got a flat, and then I found out that I had to take my neighbor to the hospital, which was really frustrating."

How to avoid interoffice hostility—*play nice*

NEW RESEARCH suggests that simply leaving a co-worker out of water cooler conversations could spark a hostile response.

In a study published in the December 2001 issue of the *Journal of Personality and Social Psychology*, researchers asked a group of 35 strangers to mingle for about 15 minutes and then told them to choose two people they would like to work with. The researchers discreetly selected "rejects" at random, telling them that no one had picked them. Each of the 35 participants then played computer games under the assumption that their competitor was a stranger in another room. The winner was allowed to blast the loser with an unpleasant noise. Winners who were pegged as rejects punished opponents with higher intensity and longer lasting noises than those who thought they were among the chosen.

"Logically, people who get rejected should become nicer to make friends," says Jean Twenge, Ph.D., an assistant professor of psychology at San Diego State University. "But our research showed that they stopped thinking clearly and became more aggressive instead." So invite the office oddball to your next get-together—it could keep you from getting stabbed in the back later.

Lie? Chances are that this is a lie. "Because liars probably feel some guilt about lying and they're usually worried about getting caught, they tend to express negative emotions such as anger or anxiety when telling fibs," Newman explains.
A more believable reply: "I had some car trouble on I-25, and when I finally got home, I found out that my mother's friend needed a lift to the hospital."

how to spot the hidden message in telephone body language

If you're wondering about that new co-worker of yours, just watch how she talks on the phone. A recent British study revealed five personality types based on the body language of 1,000 callers. "It may seem wacky, but there is some truth to it," says psychologist Lillian Glass, Ph.D., a communication expert and author of *I Know What You're Thinking*. "People tell quite a bit about themselves on the phone." Consistency is key, Glass says. Here's our guide to caller ID.

personality	How she talks	message
Chatty Cathy	Holds phone in dominant hand to matching ear.	"In my other life, I was a telemarketer."
The C.E.O.	Stands while speaking.	"Get to the point, will you?"
The Multitasker	Cradles phone on shoulder.	"Of course I'm listening. I'm also answering my e-mail, making my grocery list, and booking a flight to Cancun. Keep talking."
The Wallflower	Holds receiver to ear opposite dominant hand.	"As soon as I work up the nerve, I'm taking an assertiveness class."
Smooth Operator	Drapes arm over head.	"What do you mean, you have to go? I could talk like this forever!"

socializing
can boost your brain power

Plan a potluck for the Fourth of July and it could save your memory, suggests a Rockefeller University study. Researchers found that songbirds living in large groups have more new brain neurons—which could mean better memory—than those flying solo. People also produce new neurons, so the findings indicate that flocking to social activities might be just the boost your brain needs.

lend an ear
when a friend's in need

In prickly situations, you should use your ears before your mouth, advises Nance Guilmartin, author of the new book *Healing Conversations: What to Say When You Don't Know What to Say.* For instance, imagine that your best friend just lost her job. Instead of asking her what she wants to do now or if she has a résumé you can pass around, she probably needs time to consider her options and accept her loss. "Be a sounding board and a resource," Guilmartin advises. "In the beginning, don't try to talk her in to or out of anything." In other words, give her the license to dream.

The Professional Flirt at Work

Can flirting at the office be good business?

BY SUZANNE TROUP

Flirting is an art form. The coquette who charms a cocktail party is not only accepted but often admired by men and women alike. But flirting at the office, particularly for women, is typically considered quite artless, no matter how gifted the flirt. An office flirt runs the risk of compromising her professional integrity or, even worse, receiving unwanted advances from her superiors. After all, flaunting your sexuality in front of your co-workers is as good as implying that you're so talentless you have to sleep your way to the top, right?

Not according to Peta Heskell, who teaches workshops on the subject at her somewhat scholarly named Flirting Academy in London. For professional women, flirting may be to the new millennium what the power suit was to the '80s—the must-have get-ahead accessory. "Flirting is about making yourself and the people around you feel good," says Heskell, author of *Flirt Coach.* "It's about showing your inner beauty, about allowing others to bask in your glow, and about being vulnerable and open."

Today's office environment has come a long way from the buttoned-up dress-for-success days, when women were instructed to behave like men. That doesn't mean that the world is ready for the other extreme—the sexually charged atmosphere portrayed in (the recently canceled) *Ally McBeal,* in which women sporting midthigh hemlines treat a law firm with all the puerile glee of a summer-camp mixer. Even in Heskell's tamer terms, few women are willing to admit they flirt at work (we've even changed their names for this story). "I'm myself," says

36-year-old graphic designer Donna Ward. "I have a warm personality. It's not the same as flirting." Eileen Bowen, a 38-year-old movie critic, says, "I don't want anyone thinking I would flirt to get ahead. That would be disrespectful of my own abilities." And Lisa Williams, M.D., a 33-year-old former medical consultant, claims, "I'm always kind and I smile. I think some men mistake that for flirtation when, in truth, I am like that with most people."

Heskell blames the PC movement for flirting's bad rap. "Political correctness was one of the most damaging things to happen to male-female relationships," she says. Many people want to—and should—have more fun in the workplace, she says. No argument with that. But what most people think of as flirting—overtly suggestive comments and gestures—is inappropriate, infantile, and may land you in court, contends Nan DeMars, ethics trainer and author of *You Want Me to Do What? When, Where, and How to Draw the Line at Work.* She is much more cautious in her approach to workplace flirting. "Don't flirt," she says. "You could be leaving yourself wide open to legal trouble."

But women should feel free to act more like, well, women, while still being considered tough-as-nails professionals. "We are sexual creatures, after all," Heskell says. And in the real world, a little playful banter could help loosen up the office vibe. Who wouldn't welcome some diversion at a marathon board meeting, for instance? Flirting can be a way for co-workers to relate to each other in a more natural manner that puts everyone at ease—and can even create a more productive office culture.

Although the workplace environment has certainly gotten more casual, even Heskell isn't giving women permission to unbutton their crepe de Chine blouses and lean into the conference table when the negotiations get tough or tensions run high. You have to know where to draw the line or you risk crossing over into tart territory. People take comments differently, and this could lead to problems. "It's all perception," DeMars says. What's considered good, clean fun to one person could constitute harassment for another: Context and delivery are everything. Sexual innuendos, when improperly packaged or undemocratically distributed, can create office rifts.

Barbara Keller, a 32-year-old photo stylist, has this complaint about a makeup artist she works with: "She flirts with the photographer and those people who can help her career. She ignores everybody else. It's transparent." Heskell says the smart flirt will be nice to everyone—the doorman, the elevator guy, the janitors—to offset any potential resentments. "The key is to make everyone feel good and to show people that you're both vulnerable and human," she says. "Your co-workers will notice if you're only nice to the bigwig." In her flirting workshops, Heskell recommends her clients go out of their way to cozy up to the people who might resent them for being attractive or well-liked, to defuse any potential office fires.

"You have to become skilled at reading people," Heskell explains. Among other things, she advises sizing up the men at your office—watching the way they behave, what they wear, how they smile. "Does he dress like a geek?" Heskell asks. "Is he shy?" This man, she suggests, might be more mortified than enchanted by your friendly attempts at office warmth. Then again, maybe not. The key is to be open to the signals people consciously or subconsciously send.

While flirting may be mostly about perception, there's also another very important facet to the flirtatious woman at work: self-perception. The consummately successful career woman may be the same person who uses her talents—professionally and personally—to get the job, the promotion, the best vacation days, but perhaps, as both Heskell and DeMars indicate, there needs to be a new measure of behavioral success. Maybe the new office flirt can be simply a woman who wears skirts of any length, is playful and professional, and who behaves—confidently and knowingly—like herself. ✳

New York–based writer Suzanne Troup also covers topics such as beauty and literature.

body talk

Flirting is all about perception, and words aren't the only office exchanges potentially loaded with suggestive meanings. Whether you intend to or not, you could be flashing your co-worker a smile across the conference table that he might interpret as more than "I liked your presentation." Monica M. Moore, Ph.D., a psychologist and professor at Webster University in St. Louis who specializes in nonverbal courtship, helps us figure out what your body language could be saying to others—and what others might be telling you.

Mouthing Off
The mouth is a very sensual feature that has the potential to attract attention. A seemingly innocent roll of a pen between your lips or a nibble on your pencil could be sending sexual signals. A hopeful suitor could even interpret moistening dry lips as a prelude to a kiss.

Mona Lisa Smile
The coy grin—a half-smile with your teeth just barely showing—could be saying "I'm a woman of mystery and intrigue . . . want to solve my puzzle?"

The Eyes Have It
An eyebrow flash—a quick raise of one or both brows—is a way to comment without words and attract attention without actually asking for it.

Hair Play
What to do about that stray lock of hair that's fallen across your face in the middle of a meeting? Hair twirling or flipping are both playful gestures that could do more than simply clear your vision.

The Office Gait
Walking past co-workers with your shoulders thrown back exhibits an inner confidence that could invite stares.

Primping
A clothes adjustment, such as shifting your skirt or buttoning your sweater, will distract focus from the third-quarter figures to your figure.

RUB OUT REGRET

REMEMBER THAT GUY you dumped in college who's now happily married and successful (while you're still looking for your dream man and the perfect job)? Or the social gaffe you committed at your sister's wedding that offended the groom? Whatever your regrets are, the fact is you can't change the past. But you can change how you feel about it. We asked the experts for their tips.

1. **Allow yourself to mourn.** Turning down that cushy job offer a month before you got laid off was a bad move—so "let yourself feel bad for a while," says Monica Ramirez Basco, Ph.D., author of *Never Good Enough.* Feeling the disappointment is the first step to moving forward.

2. **Check in with reality.** You might think, "If only I had bought into that neighborhood, everything would be better." But Philip Goldberg, Ph.D., co-author of *Making Peace With Your Past,* says that's nonsense. "You have no way of knowing what could have been." To get a little perspective, write down your biggest regrets. Then look at how your life measures up now. Chances are you're better off than you may have thought.

3. **Learn from your mistakes.** Let's say you've decided that dating your coworker really was a screw-up. What then? Mom's advice was true—you can learn from your mistakes. "Think realistically about what you did wrong and how you can prevent it in the future," Goldberg says. (Hint: Say no to after-work drinks next time.)

4. **Remember your reasons.** There's a tendency to ask yourself, "How could I have been so stupid?" But if you take an honest look back at the situation, Goldberg says you'll likely see that what you did made sense at the time. He may seem like he'd be the perfect husband now, but that guy you broke up with in school was a jerk back then, and you got rid of him for a reason.

5. **Don't get paralyzed.** If you regret that comment you made to a friend, you might find yourself avoiding her rather than apologizing and moving on. But that's exactly when you have to make yourself get involved again. Otherwise, you'll "pile regret upon regret," Goldberg says. "You'll regret not only what you said but also that you stayed away from her for so long."

Is your guy mr. right, or mr. right now?

Sure, he makes you laugh, has great dimples, and can whip up a mean fettuccine Alfredo, but how do you know if he's right for you? Laurie Seale, dating guru for Match.com, has the answer. Her forthcoming book, *500 Questions to Ask Before You Ask Them to Bed,* offers a primer on how to find out what kind of guy he really is. The key, she says, is in asking revealing questions that go beyond mere small talk. But 500 of them? You're better off starting with just a few. Here are some to get you going.

Ask your date these **revealing questions** to go beyond the small talk.

Q: What's your biggest dream for yourself, and what are you doing to make it a reality?
The take-away: If he's confronting life's big challenges, he's probably pretty confident (read: mature).

Q: Who is responsible for birth control—the man or the woman?
The take-away: Hope he says "both"—that way, you'll know you're in this together.

Q: What kinds of problems are you likely to confront head-on, and what kinds do you avoid?
The take-away: You'll know whether he'll initiate the tough conversations—or whether you'll have to be the heavy.

Q: When it comes to the news, do you want the "sound bite" version or the whole story?
The take-away: How much he wants to know probably depends on the subject, but this will help you find out if his interests match yours.

Q: What's the difference between sex and making love?
The take-away: This tells you at what point (if ever) he becomes emotionally attached.

Find out if you're more than
JUST A GAL PAL

HE'S YOUR OFFICE BUDDY: You meet for coffee breaks, hang out by the water cooler, chat about your favorite flicks. But is he more interested in being your beau than your buddy? Here are some telltale signs from Pepper Schwartz, Ph.D., author of *The Lifetime Love and Sex Quiz Book*.

- He tells you all about his dates but doesn't want to hear about yours.
- He touches you a lot.
- He often criticizes your present lover.
- He jokes about the two of you getting together someday.

TOP 10 things
men wish you knew

Men may be more sweet and vulnerable than you think—it's just that they don't always show it. We quizzed some real-life good guys about what they wish women knew but are afraid to tell them. Here are our 10 faves:

1 My best friend may be better-looking, but I'm better in bed.

2 We only cry when athletes retire. (We also cry at movies, but it doesn't count in the dark.)

3 Of course we want to grant your every desire, but we wish you'd be a little clearer about what you want.
(translation: Tell me what you want and I'll do it/get it for you. Otherwise, be quiet and let me watch the game in peace.)

4 We know size matters; just don't tell us that.

5 Sometimes we're not in the mood either.

6 It may not be fair, but it's up to you to set boundaries in the relationship.

7 Women should learn to read maps—or at least not be proud of the fact that they don't know how.

8 We hate beer commercials, too.

9 How your ex saved orphans from the church fire is not our favorite story.

10 And yes, we were looking at you. We're always looking at you ... whoever you are.

healthBUZZ

thumbs UP

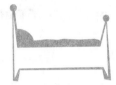

Snooze control: A study of Minneapolis high schools found that starting class nearly 90 minutes later boosted attendance and gave teens much-needed extra sleep time. Maybe more rest will mean less adolescent unrest.

Good-mood food: Studies indicate that fish-eaters are less likely to be depressed. Scientists think the omega-3 fatty acids in fish might help the brain fight psychiatric illness.

thumbs DOWN

Smoke screens: Research published in the *Journal of Health Communication* shows that tobacco companies pump up magazine advertising in the first two months of the year—just when many smokers resolve to quit.

FDA skips females: The U.S. Food and Drug Administration has been lax when it comes to scrutinizing new drugs for gender-specific benefits and risks; women accounted for only about one in five patients in early-stage studies.

a different kind of family

A 71-year-old man, a sixth-grade boy, and me. Somehow, it works.

BY LINDSEY CRITTENDEN

One June morning in New York City, on the way to my nephew's awards day at school, it hits me: I am a parent. A 40-year-old single woman with no children of my own, I didn't take the standard route to get here. But I play many roles to my nephew, whose daddy (my brother) died eight years ago and whose mother sees him only on birthdays, holidays, and occasional weekends. I'm his surrogate mom, his big sister and confidant. I'm the one who sings the *Gilligan's Island* theme song off-key while he grimaces gleefully in the passenger seat. I'm the one who reminds him to put his clothes in the hamper and says "no" to cookies before dinner; who, on long drives, brings M&M's and explains how chemotherapy works and where sperm comes from. And, ever since October 2000, when my mother died, my role has gained a whole new significance. Now, I'm part of a tighter family unit, one point on a triangle made up of my 71-year-old father, my 12-year-old nephew, and me.

On the best of days, co-parenting with my father is surreal. When I meet the puzzled gazes of other parents who assume I'm my nephew's mom—and my dad's much-younger trophy wife—I quickly find a way to work the word "Dad" into the conversation (such as "Pass the bread, Dad" or "Look, Dad, a midsize car"). To the parents of my nephew's classmates, I briefly explain the events that have brought us to this place where we're doing, as my father says, the best we can. I watch as they grapple with what to say. Some acknowledge the loss with "I'm sorry." Others offer up "How nice of you," as though helping raise my nephew were a social favor. I usually end up changing the subject, diverting awkwardness back to a common topic—which teacher is best for math, say, or whether the new restaurant nearby is worth trying.

Sometimes, at one of these restaurants, my father's "best" involves allowing my nephew a second Shirley Temple before dinner—and that's when I chafe at finding myself having to fill the gaping hole left by my mother's death, playing the Enforcer to my dad's Rewarder. The week after my mother died, dirty socks lay on my parents' kitchen floor for four days while I waited for someone other than me to notice. Finally, as I snatched them up and stormed toward the washing machine, I yelled at my father and nephew that I wasn't going to let them turn me into the nag, the shrew. They stared at me as though I had just dropped from another planet. After all, they'd seen the dirty socks too—they just weren't ready to admit what picking them up would have meant: that our lives had to go on, that my mother was gone, and that it was up to all of us to stumble our way into new roles.

I've learned to step back, to let my dad be the one who says (and sticks to) "No means no." He is, after all, my nephew's legal guardian. Stepping back, though, doesn't mean throwing in the towel. I may have no legal claim on my nephew, but I'm invested in how he turns out. And because of my brother, who always struggled with responsibility, I have a pretty low threshold for "I'll do it later" and "You can take it out of my allowance." When my nephew asks "Why do you have to bug me?" after I remind him that my father and I expect him to put effort into his schoolwork, I tell him, "It's my job." And, hearing in my voice the echo of my own parents' lectures, "It's because we love you."

At 4, he asked me, "What's a mother?"; at 8, "Why can't I live with Mommy?"; at 9, "Can DNA be injected into people?" I'm hip to subtext, good at sniffing out the question behind the question, the doubts and worries of a boy who experienced more loss at 10 than most of us have by 40. Family, I tell him, is not all about genetics. Family are the people who love and care for you, who tell you to brush your teeth and tuck you into bed and kiss you good-night.

I'm not a parent because I fit the standard definition or because I feel that I should be. This boy, with his eager enthusiasms and infectious laugh, his love of "Ode to Joy" and model rockets, has brought intimacy, happiness, and clarity into my life. I'm here in New York City this sunny morning because I want to be. And later, at the awards ceremony, when my nephew tugs my hand, saying, "You have to come with me now. Parents are supposed to be there," I follow.

The rest of the world may look at us and wonder, but we know who we are. ✳

Lindsey Crittenden is the author of The View From Below, *a short-story collection. Her writing has appeared in* Reader's Digest, Real Simple, *and other publications.*

Q+A
Why the Stress of Marital Storms is Worse for Women

When it comes to bearing the burdens of marriage, women and men shoulder different weights. "Wives tend to take on the long-term stress of an unhappy marriage more than husbands," says Robert Levenson, Ph.D., a professor of psychology and the director of the Institute of Personality and Social Research at the University of California at Berkeley. And that can lead to a variety of chronic stress ailments, from depression to high blood pressure to heart attacks. By poking, prodding, measuring, and observing 15 couples in long-term first marriages, Levenson has come up with some insights that may help your health, if not your entire marriage.

Q: How do men and women respond differently to the stress and anger that can wreak havoc on marriage?

A Robert Levenson: Men withdraw. They reduce their level of engagement and go away to cool down. Women, on the other hand, tend to stay engaged much longer. If the husband is angry, the wife takes on his state of arousal. She wants to work on the problem and get to the heart of what's creating it.

Q: How does that style of response affect women's health?

A: Women are like the "physicians" of marriage—doing the surgery, fixing the tears in the marital fabric. Yet women really pay a price for what seems to be "the right thing to do." By staying engaged longer, women experience much more stress over time, which can lead to cardiovascular and gastrointestinal problems, wear out the body's organs, and compromise the immune system, making it harder to stave off disease. The male strategy of withdrawal may not be good for the marriage, but it seems to confer a long-term benefit for men's health.

Q: What about the emotional toll it takes on the relationship?

A: In a troubled marriage, women have the frustration of dealing with the underlying problems multiplied by the frustration of working on their own issues. In a happy marriage, wives don't have to do all that repair and rehab work. A good marriage also provides resources and support—for coping, calming, comforting, problem-solving—when confronted with stress from the outside world. When a marriage is in trouble, those supportive qualities are not working properly, which makes life in general more difficult.

Q: What advice do you have for women on coping with marital minefields?

A: Just being aware of the enemy is key. Our bodies did not evolve to deal with chronic stress. If your husband continues to withdraw, it might be wise to borrow his strategy for a while and wait to fight with him again another day. It takes two to work out a marital conflict. You do not have to take all the responsibility for being the repair person. On the other hand, it would be really helpful if husbands realized what a nice gift it would be to their wives to stay with it a bit longer in order to help resolve problems.

Q: Do you have any advice on choosing a mate who can weather the storms?

A: In drawing up your wish list of the ideal life mate, consider whether this is the kind of person who will be a partner to you in dealing with conflict. Does he tackle problems as they arise? Does he really listen to what you have to say? Does he show concern for your opinions and your health? In this instance, nice guys probably finish first.

HOW YOU CAN BE A MAN MAGNET

WANT TO BECOME a man magnet? Turn off the negative buzz in your head and tune in to your natural sensuality. We talked to Jaqueline Lapa Sussman, a psychologist and author of *Images of Desire: Finding Your Natural Sensual Self in Today's Image-Filled Society* about how to do just that.

Q: Do you think women know what men are looking for in a mate?

A: Women are obsessed with weight, skin, breast size, and cellulite. But I interviewed hundreds of men for my book, and they never mentioned weight or breast size as a compelling sensual draw. Instead, they talked about "her smile," "her kindness," "her smell," or "her nonjudgment of me."

Q: What does a poor body image do to your sex life?

A: It can put a real damper on romance, because when you approach your lover, you're actually feeling self-conscious. If you approach your lover feeling, "I'm not good enough," then that is what you bring to the experience of making love to him. Insecurity is a real turnoff.

Q: What makes a woman sensual?

A: Sensuality is an inner emanation, an energy that says, "I know I have it and I know you desire it." Women who have that kind of inner confidence don't have to look perfect. Think of Sophia Loren or Tina Turner. These women are aging, but they still sense their own lusciousness, the fullness of nature in themselves. When you feel that inner fullness, men can't help but be drawn to it.

Q: How can a woman connect with her sensual side?

A: Focus on what makes you feel powerful and sexy and then just let the other stuff go. A man would not be in bed with you if he did not already find you attractive.

THE BODY LANGUAGE OF LOVE

Instead of waiting to hear those three words—I love you—scope out your lover's body for signs of his true emotions. Couples who say they're in love pass body signals back and forth to each other like love notes, according to a study published in the *Journal of Personality and Social Psychology.* Researchers at the University of California at Berkeley interviewed a group of romantically involved couples and then videotaped the partners during directed discussions. They discovered a language of love that is communicated through moves, not words.

"Body language has been looked at in relation to courtship or flirtation, but we're the first to link these cues to the experience of love," says study author Gian Gonzaga, Ph.D., now at the University of California at Los Angeles. And a little can go a long way. "We found that these behaviors predict more satisfaction with the relationship and more willingness to self-sacrifice," Gonzaga says. "It really seems to be part of the process that holds people together." Looking for love? Find it in the following nonverbal cues.

• **Smiling:** People in love often flash each other the "Duchenne smile," a type of smile in which the corners of the eyes crease into crow's feet. This could be the most telling signal of all, because it's nearly impossible to fake.

• **Head Nodding:** Lovers frequently nod to each other, as if in agreement, during a conversation.

• **Gesturing:** The gestures vary widely, but loving couples often "talk with their hands" while speaking to one another.

• **Leaning:** Love is associated with moving closer to or leaning toward the other partner.

So what if you don't get these signals from your Sweetie? "It isn't the best sign, but it doesn't necessarily predict a lack of love," Gonzaga says. Absence of these cues doesn't seem related to relationship problems, such as hostility or conflict. And remember that the signs can have other meanings. "You can lean toward someone because you want to be near him or because you want to hit him," Gonzaga says. Hopefully, it's just a love tap.

Women Could Save Men from Extinction

In Darwin's day, no one questioned that men had social and physical advantages over women. It's no wonder that men formulated the theory of evolution in which only the fittest survive. Times have changed: New research published in the *British Medical Journal* shows that men are facing a health crisis, and unless they start admitting their own vulnerabilities, they may be in danger of extinction themselves.

"Men eat fattier diets, exercise less, drink more excessively, drive more injuriously, and delay seeking medical attention longer than women," says Ronald Nathan, Ph.D., a psychologist who specializes in men's issues. Men also have higher mortality rates for all 15 leading causes of death and a shorter life expectancy than women.

With the introduction of sperm banks and same-sex marriages, an all-female world is not out of the question. But most women would prefer to have men around (you can't play footsie with a test tube). The most influential characters in men's health could be—surprise!—women. Take some time to learn about your man's body beyond the bedroom and show your support by accompanying him to the doctor. Your mate may be your hero, but he probably has an Achilles' heel, too. Acknowledging weaknesses may be essential to the survival of the he-kind.

love is child's play

MARITAL BLISS may have more to do with your childhood play dates than whether you and your mate share a love for art flicks, two-stepping, or spicy foods. Researchers found that how you learned emotional attachment as a kid has a greater influence on marital intimacy than compatibility with your spouse.

VitalStats

24 Percent of women who work in administrative-support jobs

6 Percent of men

18 Percent of women who work in professional specialties

13 Percent of men

71 Percent of condoms used by unmarried men

12 Percent by married couples

16 Percent by married men having affairs

60 Percent of Americans who have forgiven themselves for past mistakes

52 Percent who say they've forgiven others

100 Percent of study participants who lowered stress by forgiving others versus harboring grudges

57 Percent of parents for whom the best part of going on business trips is "not having to clean anything"

70 Percent of Americans who say their favorite way to spend an evening is to stay home

1 in 3 Chance that an American skips exercise because there's no one to watch the kids

1 in 4 Chance neighborhood safety is cited as a reason a woman doesn't exercise more

1 in 4 Chance that a low-income American cites cost as a reason for not eating more healthfully

5 Maximum g-force experienced on Disney's Rock 'n' Roller Coaster

3 Maximum g-force felt by astronauts during a space shuttle launch

Sources: U.S. Census Bureau, Johns Hopkins School of Public Health, Gallup, *Parenting, Psychology Science,* Shape Up America!, www.themeparks.com

INDEX

EDITORIAL CONTRIBUTORS

Sheryl Altman

Maureen Callahan

Celia Carey

Michael Castleman

Cinda Chavich

Melissa Chessher

Rick Chillot

Victoria Clayton

Christine Colburn

Kerri Conan

Lindsey Crittenden

Sheree Crute

Lynne Cusack

Michelle Dally

Lydia Denworth

Emily Delzell

Laurie Drake

Mary Duffy

Daryn Eller

Marget Feury

Laura Flynn McCarthy

Kimberly Goad

Sharon Goldman Edry

Catherine Guthrie

Laurie Herr

Beth Howard

Devon Jersild

Sharlene R. Johnson

Alice Lesch Kelly

Liz Krieger

Carol Krucoff

Jennifer Laing

Michele Lee

Janet Lembke

Karen Levin

Lori Longbotham

Eva Marer

Linda Marsa

Ellen Mazo

Trish Muse

Melba Newsome

Amy Paturel

Kathryn Perrotti-Leavitt

Marge Perry

Jennifer Pirtle

Lynn Prowitt-Smith

Linda Rao

Leslie Revsin

Anna Roufos

Lori Seto

Marie Simmons

Melissa Sperl

Nancy Stedman

Barbara Stepko

Suzanne Troup

Anne Underwood

Linda Villarosa

John F. Wasik

Elizabeth Wray

Liz Zack